TRAGEDY, RITUAL AND MONEY IN ANCIENT GREECE

Richard Seaford is one of the most original and provocative classicists of his age. This volume brings together a wide range of papers written with a single focus. Several are pioneering explorations of the tragic evocation and representation of *rites of passage*: mystic initiation, the wedding, and death ritual. Two papers focus on the shaping power of mystic initiation in two famous passages in the New Testament. The other key factor in the historical context of tragedy is the recent *monetisation* of Athens. One paper explores the presence of money in Greek tragedy, another the shaping influence of money on Wagner's *Ring* and on his Aeschylean model. Other papers reveal the influence of ritual and money on representations of the inner self and on Greek and Indian philosophy. A final piece finds in Greek tragedy horror at the destructive *unlimitedness* of money that is still central to our postmodern world.

RICHARD SEAFORD is Emeritus Professor of Ancient Greek at the University of Exeter. He is the author of numerous papers and books on ancient Greek texts from Homer to the New Testament, among which *Money and the Early Greek Mind: Homer, Philosophy, Tragedy* (2004) and *Cosmology and the Polis: The Social Construction of Space and Time in the Tragedies of Aeschylus* (2012) are also published by Cambridge University Press. He has a particular interest in uncovering the relationship between the economy, ritual, philosophy and drama. He is currently completing a historical comparison of early Greek with early Indian thought. He has been a Fellow of the National Humanities Center (USA), a Distinguished Visiting Professor at the University of Texas at Austin and Honorary President of the British Classical Association. His research has been funded by the Leverhulme Foundation and the Arts and Humanities Research Council.

ROBERT BOSTOCK was awarded a PhD in Classics from the University of Exeter in 2007. He is an Adjunct Associate Lecturer at the University of New England, Australia.

TRAGEDY, RITUAL AND MONEY IN ANCIENT GREECE

Selected Essays

RICHARD SEAFORD

University of Exeter

EDITED WITH A FOREWORD BY

ROBERT BOSTOCK

University of New England, Australia

CAMBRIDGE
UNIVERSITY PRESS

CAMBRIDGE
UNIVERSITY PRESS

University Printing House, Cambridge CB2 8BS, United Kingdom

One Liberty Plaza, 20th Floor, New York, NY 10006, USA

477 Williamstown Road, Port Melbourne, VIC 3207, Australia

314–321, 3rd Floor, Plot 3, Splendor Forum, Jasola District Centre, New Delhi – 110025, India

79 Anson Road, #06-04/06, Singapore 079906

Cambridge University Press is part of the University of Cambridge.

It furthers the University's mission by disseminating knowledge in the pursuit of education, learning and research at the highest international levels of excellence.

www.cambridge.org
Information on this title: www.cambridge.org/9781107171718
DOI: 10.1017/9781316761588

First published 2018

Printed and bound in Great Britain by Clays Ltd, Elcograf S.p.A

A catalogue record for this publication is available from the British Library.

ISBN 978-1-107-17171-8 Hardback

Contents

Foreword

The work of Richard Seaford is distinctive for the way in which it combines the approaches of several disciplines – philology, anthropology, philosophy, and political and economic history – in order to present a diachronic account of the form and central preoccupations of Greek texts of the archaic and classical periods, most notably tragedy. Many of the ideas contained in his three major monographs were developed from observations made in academic papers.[1] The present volume is designed to make readily available certain papers appearing in relatively inaccessible journals, to make other papers more accessible to those without Greek by providing translations, and to illustrate the breadth of Seaford's work by the inclusion of papers on such diverse topics as the New Testament, a Marxist account of the genesis of the inner self, early Indian thought, and the influence of Aeschylus on Wagner.

Seaford's academic career began with a doctoral thesis on Euripides' *Cyclops*, which can be seen as the seed of much subsequent work. As a commentary, that most traditional of genres, it remains grounded in the close reading of primary texts and in textual criticism, and, despite the increasing breadth and abstraction of much of his later studies, the evidence adduced is frequently evaluated in terms of the manuscript tradition of the author under discussion. At the same time, Seaford's choice of readings tends to draw on extra-textual realities beyond what is normal in editorial practice. By concentrating upon ritual structures and religious conceptions alien to the modern reader, he laid the foundation for a series of papers in the 1980s devoted to elucidating the meaning and emotional effect of various tragedies by detecting and describing the evocation of rituals – in particular, certain highly emotional rituals such as mystic initiation, death ritual and wedding ritual – that were central to the lives of

[1] Seaford 1994b, 2004c, 2012a.

the audience.[2] The dramatist could rely upon this centrality in order to evoke emotions and ideas, but did so especially through portraying the perversion of those rituals. Finally, Dionysos looms in the background of the *Cyclops*, and the place of this god in the religion and thought of ancient Greece would come to assume a central role in Seaford's work.[3]

From the analysis of ritual in Greek tragedy there emerged a diachronic dimension. In real life, ritual must end well, as it generally does in Homer; in tragedy, by contrast, it is generally perverted, and often accompanied by intrafamilial killing, which does not occur in Homer. This led to consideration of the socially integrative role of ritual, and so to consideration also of other forms of social integration, such as reciprocity and money.

For Seaford the key difference lies in the type of society in which each genre was produced. The Homeric poems reflect, broadly speaking, a pre-state society in which the most important social group was the family, and in which social integration is achieved to a large extent through reciprocity between households (although even here reciprocity is already in crisis in both epics). Tragedy, on the other hand, was the creation of the democratic polis, which emerged from the limitation of the autonomy of individual households, as well as from the deposition of the ruling household of 'tyrants'. Accordingly, tragedy frequently (though not always) moves from the self-destruction of the ruling household, often accompanied by the perversion of household ritual, to the final creation of benefit for the polis (often in the founding of polis cult). These ideas form the core of *Reciprocity and Ritual* (1994b), a *tour de force* in which the central themes of epic and tragedy are analysed from the perspective of their historical contexts and related to each other diachronically through reference to the structural differences between the societies in which the works were created. The recourse to a historical explanation of the subject matter of Greek tragedy is what perhaps most distinguishes Seaford's work from his contemporaries, given the generally ahistorical approach characteristic of scholarship over the past sixty years.[4]

[2] E.g. in this volume 'The last bath of Agamemnon' (1984b = Chapter 11), 'The destruction of limits in Sophocles' *Electra*' (1985 = Chapter 12), 'The tragic wedding' (1987c = Chapter 13), 'The structural problems of marriage in Euripides' (1990b = Chapter 14). For mystic initiation, see n. 6 below.

[3] See in particular the commentary on Euripides' *Bacchae* (1996a) and the monograph on Dionysos (2006a); also n. 5 below.

[4] This ahistoricism partly represents a reaction to the excesses of the Cambridge school, of which Seaford's work may be viewed as a refined continuation, especially of the work of George Thomson, with its emphasis on socio-economic as well as ritual factors (See Seaford 1997a and 2004a: xxix–xxx). But Seaford's interest is not so much in 'origins' as in the meaning and emotional power of the rituals evoked or described in the texts, not so much in 'survivals of the primitive' as in the historical changes from the eighth to fifth centuries BCE, in particular the development of the polis.

It is also in relation to this diachronic dimension of tragedy that Dionysos assumes a central role. This is an exhilarating aspect of Seaford's work, as time and again we are swept along by the centrality of this paradoxical god in articulating the tension between the two fundamental social units in the developing city-state of the polis: family and citizen body. The historical process is one of transfer – of economic resources, military allegiance, religious practice – from the family to the state, in which problematic tendencies within the family – reciprocal violence, endogamy, excessive accumulation of wealth – are controlled by the supra-familial, impersonal institutions of the state. The mythical catalyst for this transfer is Dionysos. On the basis that tragedy originated and continued to be performed in the cult of Dionysos, and that its earliest themes were about Dionysos, the hypothesis is that the self-destruction or near-self-destruction of the ruling household leading to the establishment of communal cult was a mythical paradigm that derived from the power of Dionysiac myth and cult, where it is most at home (for instance in Euripides' *Bacchae*), and helped to shape tragic myth in general. In Homer, by contrast, the paradigm is absent and accordingly so is Dionysos (almost entirely), although maenadism is twice evoked, along with the destruction of Hektor's household.[5]

Within the analysis of the literary representation of ritual motifs, mystery cult plays an important role. This was given early expression in 'Dionysiac drama and the Dionysiac mysteries' (1981a), and has figured prominently in various manifestations since then. Two aspects may be emphasised: first, the simple identification of references to the mysteries in literary texts, and the explanation of how they contribute to the structure of a work or its articulation of ideas. Given the scarcity of evidence for mystery cult as such, there is always an element of speculation in this area, and different readers will find some identifications more convincing than others. But, as with the identification of other ritual elements, the key is to explain a phrase or scene otherwise misinterpreted owing to neglect of this ritual background.[6] Secondly, a crucial aspect of mystery cult for Seaford is the communality of individuals brought about through mystic initiation. This is viewed in contrast to the isolating effects of a monetised economy, especially as represented by the literary representation of historical and tragic tyrants, and for Seaford this communality also represents an illuminating

[5] See in this volume 'Homeric and tragic sacrifice' (1989b = Chapter 1) and 'Dionysos as destroyer of the household' (1993 = Chapter 2). Note also Henrichs 2013: 570–7, esp. 576–7.

[6] E.g. '1 Corinthians 13.12' (1984a = Chapter 15), 'Sophocles and the mysteries' (1994c = Chapter 10), 'Thunder, lightning and earthquake in the *Bacchae* and Acts of the Apostles' (1997a = Chapter 16), 'The fluttering soul' (2009c = Chapter 18).

contrast with the social atomisation characteristic of contemporary capitalist economies.[7]

Reciprocity was a central element in Seaford's analysis of the relationship between new mechanisms of social integration and the distinctive cultural creations of the polis. From reciprocity he expanded his focus to a contrasting and revolutionary form of economic interaction: coined money. The emergence of this phenomenon in Ionia in the sixth century BCE, and specifically in Miletos, coincided with the beginnings of philosophy, and in Athens (where monetisation came later) with the emergence of tragedy. Seaford's interest in Presocratic philosophy is already evident in the article 'Immortality, salvation and the elements' (1986a = Chapter 9 below), which detects the influence of mystery cult on Presocratic philosophy and on the *Prometheia* trilogy, in addition to making an important early contribution to the interpretation of the Derveni papyrus.[8] The new focus on monetisation elaborated on these ideas by giving a historical account of the unprecedented form that specific concepts assume in Presocratic thought (in particular the cosmos as a single, increasingly abstract substance transformed from and into everything else), while at the same time the analysis of the conflict found in tragedy was deepened by a sharper focus on the dichotomy between reciprocal forms of exchange and a monetised economy (represented by the frequent *isolation* of the individual at the heart of tragedy).[9] This work culminated in the publication of *Money and the Early Greek Mind* (2004c).

Although Seaford is particularly well known for his studies on Dionysos, especially as he appears in Euripides' *Bacchae*, his contribution to the interpretation of Aeschylus is equally important. 'The last bath of Agamemnon' (1984b = Chapter 11) is an early example, focusing on the perversion of death ritual in *Agamemnon*. 'Aeschylus and the unity of opposites' (2003a = Chapter 6) is a wide-ranging analysis of the *Oresteia* as a whole, which goes beyond the traditional but unsatisfactory categories of character analysis and moral responsibility, above all by concentrating on the structural and ultimately moral dichotomy between 'limit' and 'unlimited'. Mention may also be made of the important section on the *Supplices* in 'Tragic wedding' (1987c = Chapter 13). Over the course of his career Seaford has touched upon numerous individual passages within the *Oresteia*, and

7 See 'The politics of the mystic chorus' (2013c = Chapter 8).

8 Cf. Obbink 1997: 40.

9 E.g. 'Dionysos, money, and drama' (2003c = Chapter 3), 'Tragic money' (1998c = Chapter 4), 'Tragic tyranny' (2003b = Chapter 5).

a relatively full *index locorum* has been provided, which will hopefully be of use to future commentators on the trilogy. With *Cosmology and the Polis* (2012a) he concentrated the results of his larger analysis in *Money and the Early Greek Mind* (2004c) on a single author, revealing in Aeschylean tragedy the fundamental but opposed forces of money and communal ritual. Inasmuch as Presocratic philosophy was shaped by the same forces (especially – given its different context – by money), the enquiry explores the extensive and relatively neglected affinities between Aeschylus and Presocratic philosophy (especially Heraclitus and Pythagoreanism).

A general characteristic of Seaford's work is its widening in scope from ideas developed in earlier studies, from an initial basis in editing and interpreting a text, through the ever expanding spheres of ritual, religion, the polis and economics. It is fitting therefore that his current project has widened this scope still further, to ancient India. There are striking similarities in metaphysical thought, particularly in the development of abstract ontology, between Greece and India in the three centuries before Alexander crossed the Indus in 326 BCE. Previous attempts to detect 'influence' range narrowly between the improbable and the imaginary. Building on his work on monetisation in ancient Greece, Seaford instead concentrates on the fact that, outside Greece, the most monetised society in this period was northern India (perhaps also China), in order to seek out the relationship (important in all societies) between metaphysics and socio-economic formation. While a monograph on the subject will appear shortly, the present volume includes a previously unpublished essay (Chapter 19) on why the idea of karma, unknown to ancient Greece, has been so important in religions of Indian origin. In addition to the originality of the argument, not the least remarkable aspect of this chapter is Seaford's ability to navigate through the formidable labyrinth of ancient Indian texts.

The broadly political implications of Seaford's work are illustrated here by two chapters. In 'Historical materialism and the genesis of the Western subject' (2012b = Chapter 17) he engages with the Marxist philosopher Alfred Sohn-Rethel's emphasis on the influence of commodity exchange on early Greek ideas of the unitary self, thus prefiguring the Kantian transcendental self. Seaford incorporates into the argument the differences between the economies of ancient Greece and modern Europe, which are glossed over in Sohn-Rethel's account, and adduces a variety of texts with which the philosopher was unfamiliar, in order to qualify but ultimately support his conclusions. In 'World without limits' (2009e = Chapter 21), which appeared in the *Times Literary Supplement* in the wake of the global financial crisis of 2007–8, Seaford describes for a general audience central elements of his work in relation to the contemporary world, by setting the ancient Greek privileging of *limit* over the unlimited against the adherence of capitalism to the *unlimited* – not only in the accumulation and global flow of capital and the growing disparity between rich and poor but also in cultural practices and intellectual trends.

A note on editorial procedure. The papers have not been revised, but printed as they first appeared (with occasional small corrections, and additions in square brackets). References have been standardised and at times updated. Bibliographical notes, prepared by Seaford, have been appended to each chapter as a postscript to illustrate developments in scholarship since the original publication. In several papers, translations of Greek passages have been added by the editor. Occasionally the Greek itself has been omitted, where linguistic points are not concerned.

Names of authors are given in their Latin form, whereas names of literary characters, mythological figures and historical persons are transliterated (though inconsistencies inevitably remain – e.g. Ajax). Abbreviations of ancient authors and texts, and of standard modern works, follow those of the *Oxford Classical Dictionary* (4th edn, 2012). Note that **GJ** for references to the gold leaves indicate that they are numbered as in Graf and Johnston (2013). No dates are CE unless otherwise indicated.

References to papers of Seaford which appear elsewhere within the present volume are denoted by superscript reference to the chapter number: e.g. 'Seaford 1987c[13]' denotes that the paper appears as Chapter 13. Page numbers of the original publications (e.g. [*[88]*]) have been added for further ease of reference. The editor is solely responsible for any typographical errors.

Thanks are due to Paul Curtis for producing the initial transcript of 'The tragic wedding' (Chapter 13), and to the copy-editor, Hester Higton, for her careful assistance in the preparation of the text.

PART I

Tragedy: General

CHAPTER I

Homeric and Tragic Sacrifice

This chapter is far too brief to attempt a systematic comparison of sacrifice in Homer with sacrifice in tragedy. I will rather, after some preliminary generalisations, discuss the specific case of the famous portent which appeared to the Greeks at Aulis in the epic version on the one hand and the Aeschylean on the other, together with the sacrifice of Iphigeneia which in Aeschylus resulted from the portent. This will lead to a general statement of the positive role which ritual tends to play in Homer as opposed to the negative role it tends to play in tragedy. Many further examples might be given to support this generalisation. But I will confine myself, in the final section, to a single one: Herakles' killing of Lykos and of his own children in Euripides' *Heracles*, which will also illuminate further the puzzling relationship in Aeschylus between portent and sacrifice.

The *Iliad* and the *Odyssey* tend to exclude homicide within the family.[1] They also exclude imagery drawn from animal sacrifice.[2] These two exclusions go together, for Greek sacrifice is, in contrast to the hunt, of domestic animals.[3] Of the numerous and various similes which embellish military killing in the *Iliad*, not one is drawn from the everyday familiarity of blood flowing from the sacrificial weapon. Animal sacrifices that occur

[1] This has been noted in passing by Griffin 1977: 44 (silence on the killings of Iphigeneia and of Klytaimestra), but never, so far as I know, investigated. Kin-killing is mentioned briefly at *Il.* 2.662, 15.335–6, 16.573; *Od.* 19.522–3, but excluded from certain stories where we expect to find it (*Il.* 4.376–9, 6.130–40, 9.458–61 (cf. Plut. *Quomodo adul.* 26f); *Od.* 11.326–7, 15.247–55), or almost excluded (*Il.* 9.529–99; *Od.* 11.271–80, and the various references to the killing of Agamemnon, in most of which it is performed by Aigisthos, whose kinship with Agamemnon is post-Homeric). It is worth adding that Proclus' account of the (attempted) sacrifice of Iphigeneia in the *Cypria* mentions a plural subject rather than Agamemnon (p. 41.47B = 104.18A). So too Hes. fr. 23a.17 ('the Greeks').

[2] There are, however, three similes of the killing of a domestic animal, of which it is apt that two refer to the killing of Agamemnon and his followers as unsuspecting guests by Aigisthos (*Od.* 4.535, 11.411, 413–15). For battle as sacrifice elsewhere see e.g. Pind. fr. 78.

[3] See e.g. Burkert 1985: 55, 58; Stengel 1920: 123. Homeric accounts of animal sacrifice even omit those elements of the ritual which seem to unite the victim with the participants, as I shall show elsewhere. For recent discussion of Homeric animal sacrifice see Kirk 1981; Petropoulou 1987.

in the narrative do in fact contrast with killing in battle: the predictable, peacefully ordered process of killing and cooking the animal ends in the joyful concord of the feast, whereas on the battlefield all is uncontrolled violence. This Homeric tendency to exclude kin-killing and sacrificial imagery is reversed by tragedy: tragic killing is within [88] the family, and is almost always described as (perverted) sacrifice. This distinction is worth making, particularly in view of the current fashion for stressing what is tragic in Homer and Homeric in tragedy.[4]

With this in mind, let us look at the portent, the 'sign', which encouraged the Greek expedition gathered at Aulis. This was related in the lost *Cypria*, but also by Odysseus at *Il.* 2.303–30: the Greeks were offering sacrifice at an altar by a spring under a plane tree, on which were the twittering young of a sparrow. A snake emerged from under the altar and went to the tree, where it ate first the young and then the mother, before being turned into stone by Zeus. Kalkhas interprets this to mean that after nine years' fighting the Greeks will capture Troy, for there were altogether nine sparrows. But what interests me is the contrast between the uncontained brutality between the species (snake and bird), and the absolute solidarity within the family of sparrows. The mother sparrow is caught by the snake only because, unwilling to abandon her children, she hovers desperately over them. The references to her wailing for her children (315 ὀδυρομένη φίλα τέκνα) and to her children as νήπια τέκνα (311) have a human connotation. This suggests another way, not mentioned by Kalkhas, in which the 'sign' resembles what it signifies: the *Iliad* (as well as the *Odyssey*) constantly exhibits the same contrast between touching solidarity within the family and uncontained brutality outside it, as for example in the brutality of Akhilleus and the bravery of Priam after the death of Hektor. Against the brutal moral of the fable of the nightingale caught by the hawk, Hesiod offers the reflection that the violent and cruel are punished by Zeus (*Op.* 238–9). But the violence required to sack Troy must be sanctioned by Zeus.[5] The brutality of the snake he sends occurs during a sacrifice, i.e. in a context in which violence is contained as well as divine good will obtained. The portent 'entered' the sacrifice (321 εἰσῆλθε).[6]

The Aeschylean version of the portent at Aulis, in which two eagles devour a pregnant hare (*Ag.* 114–20), is both different and similar to the

4 E.g. Redfield 1975: chapter 2; Macleod 1982: 7–8; Rutherford 1982; Easterling 1984 (on Sophocles); Herington 1985.

5 Note how at *Il.* 1.5 'And the plan of Zeus was being accomplished' follows immediately the uncontained violence which denies burial to the enemy; cf. *Il.* 24.209–11.

6 Cf. the portent of *Il.* 8, where an eagle lets a fawn drop by the sacrificial altar of Zeus (249).

epic version. Most of the differences are obvious. Different creatures are involved. The devoured young are still unborn. And the narrative context is in two significant respects different. First, the portent does not take place during a sacrifice, as it does in the epic. And second, in the *Cypria* the Greeks embark, after the portent, from Aulis, sack Teuthrania, are scattered by a storm and reassemble at Aulis; Agamemnon then shoots a stag and boasts that he is a better hunter than Artemis, and it is this that angers the goddess and leads to the sacrifice of Iphigeneia as the price for favourable winds. In Aeschylus, on the other hand, there is only one gathering at Aulis, and what angers the goddess is the eagles' feast. This condensation produces a well-known implausibility. Why should Artemis turn against Agamemnon as a result of a portent sent by Zeus? Much of the discussion of this passage has concentrated – without, it seems to me, [89] much success – on finding a motive for Artemis' anger, whether in the brutality of what is symbolised by the portent (the sack of Troy)[7] or in some other unstated motive (e.g. Thyestes' eating of his own children)[8] or, on a more literal reading, in the portent itself.[9] Comparison with the epic version has been relatively neglected, but does I think help to reveal a logic in which the apparent inexplicability of Artemis' angry demand seems unimportant or even appropriate.

In the epic portent, brutality between species contrasts with family solidarity, but is sanctioned, in part by the sacrificial context. The Aeschylean version develops and reverses this idea. The choice of a hare facilitates the link with Artemis,[10] but also allows the young to be devoured while still in the womb: family solidarity takes here an even more extreme, a physical form. The hare is also a characteristic victim of the hunt. She runs, but is caught by the birds of prey, the winged hounds of Zeus (135 πτανοῖσι κυσὶ πατρός).[11] The uncontained violence of the portent is associated by Aeschylus with the uncontained violence of the hunt. There is, unlike in the epic, no sacrificial context. But the eagles do, surprisingly, 'sacrifice' the hare (137 θυομένοισιν). This is significant. For the uncontained violence of the hunt is, like the warfare it here symbolises, antithetical to the sacrifice, in which killing is contained in ritual order[12] and the domestic victim is in

7 E.g. Peradotto 1969; Neitzel 1979; Bergson 1982.
8 Whallon 1961 and (more effectively) Furley 1986; or the offence related in the *Cypria* (see Fraenkel 1950: II.97–8).
9 Lawrence 1976; Sommerstein 1980.
10 See e.g. Peradotto 1969: 244.
11 Mazon (in the Budé edition) compares Xen. *Cyn.* 5.14, 9.10 and Arr. *Cyn.* 17, from which it appears that λοισθίων δρόμων (120) may be a technical term from the hunt.
12 See e.g. Burkert 1983b: 12, 38, 40; Burkert 1985: 58.

a sense a member of the sacrificing group and consents to its own death.[13] If the eagles' feast is a 'sacrifice' it is a grotesque one, in which the norms of civilised, sacrificial killing have been overthrown by absolute violence. Whereas the violence of the epic portent is contained and sanctioned by its sacrificial context, the eagles' feast, because it is itself a grotesque sacrifice, a sacrifice which has turned into its opposite, reverses this containment. The 'sacrifice' of the hare is itself uncontained savagery. So too the violence at Troy is both a sacrifice and a hunt;[14] and the Greek army is in its capture of Troy like a lion 'that eats raw meat'.[15] [*90*]

Here some clarification is needed of what is meant by the 'uncontained violence' of the hunt and of warfare. Both hunting and warfare may in fact of course be culturally structured, so that their violence is in a sense contained, both in (and by) literature and even in actual practice. But the lethal struggle of warfare or of the hunt may also, in actual practice at least, fall entirely outside the control of culture. Hence the tension in some literary representations of warfare, notably in Homer, between cultural control and the (at least potential) uncontrollability of military hostility. An obvious example is Akhilleus, before fighting with Hektor, rejecting his proposal of a burial pact by saying that there can be no pacts between lions and men or between wolves and lambs, and then speaking, as Hektor dies, of eating him raw; but in the end this threat of the absolute violence that obtains between different species is contained by Hektor's funeral. In tragedy too the uncontrolled violence characteristic of hunting and warfare is in tension with (ritual) cultural control (sacrifice, burial, etc.), but the tension tends to result in the failure or subversion of the rituals.

This perverted or anti-sacrificial quality of the 'sacrifice' of the hare helps to explain why it gives rise specifically to the sacrifice of Iphigeneia.

[13] Burkert 1983b: 3–4; Burkert 1985: 55–8; Burkert 1966: 107 n. 43; Stengel 1920: 108–9. [The idea is questioned by Naiden 2007.]

[14] *Ag.* 65, 357–60, 694–5, 735, and in general Vidal-Naquet 1988. It is from this perspective that we may be able to solve the puzzle of 126–30. Why does Kalkhas, having explained that the Greeks will seize Troy, then immediately single out the destruction of herds 'before the walls'? Herds, as domesticated animals, are normally killed by sacrifice. In the *Iliad* the Trojans sacrifice them outside the walls (8.545–9), a practice to which Kassandra refers at *Ag.* 1168–9, a passage compared by Zeitlin 1965: 470 n. 17 with *Ag.* 126–30, where she suggests that Kalkhas means Trojan sacrifices. But πάντα is against this and so is πρὸς τὸ βίαιον, which implies the struggle and violence characteristic of the hunt. What interests Kalkhas, in view of the portent, is the violent death in war of animals that are normally sacrificed.

[15] *Ag.* 827–8; cf. 735: the lion as a member of the household is an ambiguity, apparently transcending the normal division between the household (men and domestic animals) and the savagery of nature. But the ambiguity is resolved by a sacrifice (735) which brings to the household uncontained violence (730–4).

Kalkhas fears that Artemis may create adverse winds (151) 'in her eagerness for another sacrifice, one without music' (or just possibly 'without law', depending on how you take ἄνομον[16]) 'and without a feast': σπευδομένα θυσίαν ἑτέραν ἄνομόν τιν' ἄδαιτον. I have given the usual translation of ἑτέραν as 'another'. But Aeschylus did not write ἄλλην, as he did for example a little later, in the beacon speech, where one beacon gives rise to another (299 ἄλλην ἐκδοχὴν πομποῦ πυρός). ἕτερος refers to one of a pair or to difference, two closely related senses which may occur together,[17] as they do here: the two grotesque sacrifices form a complementary pair. One difference is made explicit in ἄδαιτος ('without a feast'): Iphigeneia, unlike the hare, will not be eaten.[18] The second sacrifice both differs and arises from the first. The implication is that they form a pair because they are different. In fact they do represent opposite extremes of transgression. In the portent one species of wild creature catches and devours another; there is no community between killer and victim, whereas in the sacrifice of Iphigeneia there is far too much community, for they are not only both humans but even of the same family. Between these two extremes there is the normal animal sacrifice, in which man kills a domesticated animal which on the one hand is in a sense a member of the domestic human group (a [91] membership expressed in the ritual) and on the other hand is in fact an outsider, a member of another species (the ritual also expresses separation of the victim from the human group[19]). The two extremes, paradoxically, take on features of each other. Iphigeneia, unlike the tame victim of a normal sacrifice, has to be bridled (238 βίᾳ χαλινῶν) like an untamed member of another species.[20] And the royal birds are described (137) as αὐτότοκον πρὸ λόχου μογέραν πτάκα θυομένοισιν, words which, it has been pointed out, could by a magnificent ambiguity mean either 'sacrificing the poor trembling hare with her young before birth' or 'sacrificing a poor trembling female, his own child, on behalf of the army'. [21] The ambiguity of αὐτότοκον, one may add, assimilates the closeness of the parent–child relationship in the two horrible sacrifices, between the hare and her

[16] Lloyd-Jones 1953.

[17] Cf. e.g. Aesch. *Ag.* 344.

[18] Whereas Thyestes did eat his children – an event to which the following lines (especially τεκνόποινος) allude, according to Furley 1986.

[19] Notably, the pelting of the victim with barley grains: Burkert 1983b: 4–5.

[20] Cf. 133 στόμιον, of what, according to Kalkhas, the Greeks will impose on Troy. The animal substituted for Iphigeneia in the *Cypria* is (unusually for sacrifice) a wild one (ἔλαφον). A comparable horror is the representation of Klytaimestra's murder of her husband as a viper killing an eagle (Aesch. *Cho.* 247–9) – animals similar to those in the epic portent.

[21] Stanford 1939: 143–4.

young and between Agamemnon and his daughter,[22] thereby enhancing the fundamental opposition between the two that consists in the fact that, whereas the portent contrasts brutality and family solidarity, Agamemnon brutally kills his own daughter. Compare the *Iliad*, in which Agamemnon says he will kill Trojan children in their mothers' wombs (6.57–8) but there is no mention anywhere of the sacrifice of Iphigeneia.

The elimination of Agamemnon's hunting offence from the narrative leaves Artemis' demand without an obvious motive, but it also puts the sacrifice of Iphigeneia into a more direct relationship with the war. Sacrifice of a maiden as a preliminary to war is a familiar Greek idea,[23] associated by Walter Burkert with an ethnographically widespread phenomenon: male renunciation of sexuality so as to arouse the aggression necessary to hunting and warfare.[24] On this view the fundamental mechanism involved in the sacrifice is not one of exchange: it is not simply that the maiden is given up to the deity in exchange for success. Rather, the aggression required for the group to kill outsiders (the enemy, other prey) is created, sustained or coordinated by the killing of an insider, a female member of the group. The sacrifice serves a state of mind. Whatever the general truth of this, it is worth noting that the Aeschylean Agamemnon does not sacrifice his daughter unwillingly. The pathos of such an act is exploited in other versions,[25] but not by Aeschylus. It is true that the Aeschylean Agamemnon has doubts about what to do. But they are removed by [92] psychological change before the sacrifice. This change is heralded by his words in the textually problematic lines 215–17, where he speaks of a right (θέμις) to desire strongly (ὀργᾶν) or with passionate emotion (ὀργᾷ περιοργῶς or περιόργῳ) the maiden's blood.[26] It seems that the sacrifice is here envisaged as desirable in itself, not as a means to an end. And I believe that the desire which Agamemnon calls justified is his own desire, not the desire of the army.[27] Having reported these words of Agamemnon, the chorus then refer to his internal change (μετέγνω), a kind of madness (παρακοπά).

[22] This implicitly assimilates Iphigeneia to the unborn hare. Artemis presides over both the physical (birth) and the social (premarital) separation of the girl from her parent, the former as Λοξία. Iphigeneia is πρὸ λόχου also in the sense of 'before giving birth': she is of marriageable age, and her sacrifice is associated here and elsewhere with marriage (Foley 1985: 65–105; Seaford 1987c[13]: 108–9).

[23] See most recently, in relation to Iphigeneia and Artemis, Lloyd-Jones 1983.

[24] Burkert 1983b: 58–72.

[25] E.g. Eur. *IA* 1547–50, and the painting in the House of the Tragic Poet at Pompeii.

[26] παρθενίου θ' αἵματος ὀργᾷ περιόργως ἐπιθυμεῖν θέμις mss., Fraenkel; better is ὀργᾶν, ἅπερ αὐδᾷ περιόργως, θέμις (see Thomson 1966: *ad loc.*).

[27] Dover 1973: 64 argues that this refers to the desire of the army. But (a) we have had no mention of such a desire: at issue is what Agamemnon is to do; (b) a reference to Agamemnon's (mad) desire goes well with the description that follows of his madness; (c) γάρ in 214 might easily introduce

The ordered violence of sacrifice is possible because the victim is, as a domesticated animal, both an insider and an outsider. The order is possible because the victim belongs in a sense to the human group, and consents to its own death. The violence is possible because the victim is after all also an outsider, an animal, and it is this that makes the killing legitimate. Violence may be directed against one's own or another species, and one's own or another group (e.g. household). At one extreme, hunting is violence directed against a different species and a different group. At the other extreme, the sacrifice of Iphigeneia is the killing of a member of the same species and the same (narrowly defined) group. In between these two extremes is the normal sacrifice (different species, same group). To the remaining category (same species, different group) belong human sacrifice of (powerless) outsiders and warfare, which shares the uncontained violence of hunting and even (as with Akhilleus) resembles violence between species. The middle way of normal animal sacrifice, in which the potentially dangerous aggression of the group is channelled onto a convenient, intermediate victim,[28] is specifically human, and may operate as a symbol of social order.[29] Hence the peculiar horror of its dual inversion in Aeschylus: it is precisely by virtue of the close link between the portent and the sacrifice of Iphigeneia that the civilised practice of sacrifice seems to collapse into both the two opposed extremes it must normally exclude.

The logic by which the sacrificial feast of the royal birds of prey produces the king's sacrifice of his own daughter seems then to be composed of various interrelated elements. (1) The frenzied aggression of warfare expressed in the portent may require a renunciation of sexuality marked by the desire for a girl *[93]* victim. (2) It may also produce a loss of discrimination which is dangerously comprehensive: in becoming the hunter of his own kind a man may also become the killer of his own child. (3) Inversion of the sacrificial sign of civilisation is complete only if it manifests both the extremes between and against which sacrifice is defined. (4) The manifestation of one of the two opposed extremes may seem to require, as if to right an upset balance, the manifestation of the other. (5) The sense

explanation of the implied negative answer to the question in 212–13; (d) Lesky 1966: 84 compares the surprising, passionate desire of Eteokles for fratricide in Aesch. *Sept.* Dover objects that Eteokles (unlike Agamemnon) has good reasons for hating his victim and a real need to kill him. But that is not how Eteokles (or the chorus) envisage the matter: it is an external agency (the curse of Oidipous) that instils a passion, very like Agamemnon's (note especially 678 ὀργή, 692 ἵμερος ἐξοτρύνει … αἵματος), to kill his own kin. Fraenkel 1950: II.126 (on 215ff.) may perhaps be right to say that Agamemnon is deliberately vague, meaning himself and his companions.

28 For the idea of sacrifice as controlling dangerous violence see in particular Girard 1977.

29 For sacrifice operating as a 'sign of civilisation' in tragedy see Foley 1985.

that unlimited aggression somehow endangers its successful agent occurs throughout the trilogy, as for instance when Agamemnon will boast, outside the house where he will soon be caught by his own wife in a net, of the Greek army entering Troy like a lion that eats raw meat (827–8). These then are the factors constituting the internal relationship between portent and sacrifice. The obscure necessity of this relationship is expressed, at the narrative level, by the will of a deity. This is not to say that the attempts to explain Artemis' anger merely at the narrative level are worthless; but they cannot entirely dissolve an opacity that derives from the deeper level of structure.

In the epic *Cypria* there was no such opacity: the sacrifice of Iphigeneia was an act of compensation – for Agamemnon's hunting offence. It seems nevertheless to have been performed not specifically by Agamemnon but by the Greeks as a whole. And it turns out to be an animal sacrifice: Artemis substitutes a deer, and makes Iphigeneia immortal. Here, and generally in surviving epic narrative, ritual is, as in life, positive, an expression of order and solidarity in a world of sometimes uncontrollable conflict; and it may also establish narrative closure: the body of Hektor, to take an obvious example, is maltreated by Akhilleus, but finally ransomed by his father and given due funeral ritual by his own people.

In tragedy, on the other hand, ritual very often plays the opposite role. Tragedy tends to convert ritual from an expression of order and group solidarity into an instrument and expression of uncontrollable violence (often within the family).[30] The case of the portent exemplifies a basic opposition between Homer and tragedy. I want now, by way of another example, to compare the Aeschylean passage with the shape that Euripides gives in his *Heracles* to Herakles' revenge killing of Lykos and his subsequent killing of his own children.

On his return to Thebes, Herakles (567–73) says that he will cut off the usurper Lykos' head and give it to the dogs, and that he will also tear apart Lykos' followers and fill the local streams with their blood.[31] As Lykos enters the house 'he will', says Amphitryon, 'be trapped in the sword-carrying meshes of nets' (729–30). The killing of Lykos is followed by the appearance above the house of Iris and Lyssa, sent by Hera to drive Herakles mad. Eventually a messenger emerges to describe Herakles' frenzied slaughter of his own wife and children. Now, despite being imposed by Hera, Herakles' frenzy is also clearly associated by Euripides with the

[30] See e.g. Zeitlin 1965 on corrupted sacrifice in the *Oresteia*, Foley 1985 and Seaford 1985[12].

[31] The water of the Ismenos normally purified (Eur. *Phoen*. 347–8).

state of mind in which Herakles killed Lykos.[32] [94] After killing Lykos, he begins a purificatory sacrifice (922),[33] but then decides to postpone it so as first to kill Eurystheus and then purify himself of both killings in one ritual. It is as if the aggression aroused in the killing of Lykos needs another victim; and in fact the decision to postpone the sacrifice is an early symptom of Herakles' frenzy. Moreover, a little later (966) Herakles is asked by his father whether it is the killing (of Lykos and his followers) that has put him in a Bacchic frenzy.[34]

But what interests us in particular is the part played in this process by ritual. The messenger begins his account of the purificatory sacrifice by telling us that Herakles has killed Lykos and thrown him out of the house. This juxtaposition of funeral ritual unperformed and impending sacrifice enhances the impression that the violence of Lykos' death, uncontained by one ritual (burial), now bursts through into another (the sacrifice). 'Pour away the water,' says Herakles, 'throw away the (sacrificial) basket. Who will give me my bow?' (941–2).[35] In the Homeric portent at Aulis, sacrifice seems to sanction the violence by which it is interrupted. But the violence of Herakles is neither sanctioned nor purified by the sacrifice it interrupts. Rather, it turns the sacrifice into its opposite, the uncontained violence of the hunt (896 κυναγετεῖ τέκνων διωγμόν), a hunt which occurs by the altar and is called a sacrifice. This grotesque combination of sacrifice and hunt is in the eagles' feast a mere metaphor; Euripides, by the device of Herakles' purificatory sacrifice, makes it into a reality.[36] Moreover, the brutality with which snake and eagles destroy offspring together with their parents, a brutality associated by Aeschylus with a man sacrificing his own offspring, is here in Euripides embodied in the very same act as Herakles'

[32] Bond 1981 in his commentary (on 562–82) protests that 'Heracles' plans are reasonable by fifth-century, let alone heroic, standards', and cites Odysseus in the *Odyssey* hanging his faithless maids, and the revenge massacres in Thucydides. This is to miss entirely the significance of Herakles' substitution of savagery for funeral ritual.

[33] An animal sacrifice: Foley 1985: 153 n. 11.

[34] This suggestion by Amphitryon is surely not included as a mere misconception. In fact, ἐβάκχευσεν is more apt than Amphitryon realises (see below). Moreover, at 571 Herakles says he will tear apart (διαφορῶν) his enemies with his arrows. Bond 1981: *ad loc.* notices the oddity of this ('the word is not elsewhere used of missiles'), and pertinently cites the usages of the verb: of the tearing apart of bodies by maenads (Eur. *Bacch.* 739, 746, 1210; cf. 754), or by dogs and birds (Hdt. 7.10; Ar. *Av.* 338). But his explanation, 'the gruesome sense is characteristic of Euripides' style', is quite inadequate. As so often in tragedy, the oddity is the price paid for a powerful association: the word combines assimilation of Herakles to the dogs who will pull Lykos apart (568) with announcement of the theme of savage Dionysiac madness. And cf. 751–2 with 889–90.

[35] The interruption of the sacrifice is stressed again at 1144–5.

[36] Euripides often makes more explicit the Aeschylean ironic use of ritual: Seaford 1984c[II]: 248.

sacrificial hunt of his own family, for in doing so Herakles believes he is killing Eurystheus' children as well as Eurystheus himself (936, 982–3).

Despite these and other differences, we can say that in both plays uncontrolled violence between men, as if they were different species, is expressed in the imagery of the hunt, and accordingly involves (despite seeming justified as revenge) the perversion of the specifically human practice of ordered killing contained in ritual. Moreover, this violence is in both plays also associated with a state of madness in which the avenger sacrifices his own children.[37] *[95]* In this association of uncontrolled violence against enemies, perverted ritual and the frenzied sacrifice of one's own offspring, we have revealed an implicit logic: one of the two opposite extremes which sacrifice must normally exclude gives rise to the other. But at the more superficial level of narrative the child sacrifice is difficult to motivate. Rather, the horror, necessity and inexplicability of the implicit logic is expressed by the intervention of a deity, Artemis in the *Agamemnon*, Hera in the *Heracles*, who have no good and clear motives for their hostility; and even if they had, it might still be impossible to explain, at the level of narrative, why they should have imposed the particular penalty of child sacrifice.

Herakles is asked by his father whether the killing of his enemies has put him in a Bacchic frenzy (966). This is an electrifying dramatic irony, unnoticed by the commentators. Herakles has not yet threatened his children, who are still unaware of the danger they are in. But in myth Bacchic frenzy characteristically makes parents sacrifice their children:[38] the killing of Pentheus by his mother, to take the best-known example, is both a hunt and a sacrifice.[39] The chorus, responding earlier to the noise from within, has already made this very connection: 'he is hunting, pursuing his children. Frenzy will bring her Bacchic revels to completion in [or for] the house' (896–7 οὔποτ' ἄκραντα δόμοισι Λύσσα βακχεύσει).[40] It is above all in Dionysiac myth that we find, among other reversals of the norms

[37] Cf. also Soph. *Aj.* 534, where Ajax, having in his murderous revenge confused animals with humans in a grotesque hunt (297, etc.) which is also a sacrifice (219), says it would have been appropriate (πρέπον ... δαίμονος τοὐμοῦ) to have killed his own son, whom his mother in fact preserved from the danger.

[38] For the ease with which kin-killing in tragedy is associated with Dionysiac frenzy see e.g. Aesch. *Ag.* 1235 (read surely Weil's μαινάδ': see Seaford 1989a: 304–5), *Cho.* 698 (spoken by Elektra); Eur. *Or.* 338.

[39] Eur. *Bacch.* 1108, 1114, 1146, etc. Aeschylus had Pentheus killed like a hare at *Eum.* 26, perhaps also in his *Pentheus* (like the Aulis portent, a sacrifice?).

[40] Cf. 1142, which is corrupt, but in which clearly Herakles, realising what he has done, associates destruction of his own house (ἐμόν in emphatic position) with Bacchic frenzy.

of the polis, precisely our grotesque combination of the uncontained violence of the hunt with the frenzied sacrifice of one's own offspring. At the City Dionysia, in a performance of Dionysiac origin, the polis continued to represent to itself intrafamilial violence expressed in perverted ritual. Whereas the same citizens at the Panathenaia heard, in the recitations of the *Iliad* and the *Odyssey*,[41] heroic poetry from which intrafamilial violence and Dionysiac myth are almost entirely excluded, and in which even in the one example of a Dionysiac narrative, the story of Lykourgos' pursuit of Dionysos and his followers at *Il.* 6.130–140, there is no mention of Lykourgos' frenzied sacrifice of his own family. This generic polarity is worthy, it seems to me, of further investigation.[42]

POSTSCRIPT

On the Homeric background to the Aeschylean sacrifice of Iphigeneia, see J. Heath, 'The serpent and the sparrows: Homer and the parodos of Aeschylus' *Agamemnon*', *CQ* 49 (1999), 396–407. On sacrifice in Attic tragedy, see R. Scodel, 'Δόμων ἄγαλμα: Virgin sacrifice and aesthetic object', *TAPA* 126 (1996), 111–28; A. Henrichs, 'Drama and dromena: bloodshed, violence, and sacrificial metaphor in Euripides', *HSCP* 100 (2000), 173–88; J. Gibert, 'Apollo's sacrifice: the limits of a metaphor in Greek tragedy', *HSCP* 101 (2003), 159–206; D. Roselli, 'Gender, class and ideology: the social function of virgin sacrifice in Euripides' *Children of Herakles*', *ClAnt* 26 (2007), 81–169; A. Henrichs, 'Animal sacrifice in Greek tragedy: ritual, metaphor, problematizations', in C. A. Faraone, and F. S. Naiden (eds.), *Greek and Roman Animal Sacrifice: Ancient Victims, Modern Observers* (Cambridge: Cambridge University Press, 2012), pp. 180–94.

Another study of sacrifice across genres is by C. Segal, 'Sacrifice and violence in the myth of Meleager and Heracles: Homer, Bacchylides, Sophocles', *Helios* 17 (1990), 7–24. On sacrifice in the *Iliad*, see S. Hitch, *King of Sacrifice: Ritual and Royal Authority in the Iliad* (Cambridge, MA: Harvard University Press, 2009).

For the representation of ritual in tragedy, see H. Lloyd-Jones, 'Ritual and tragedy', in F. Graf (ed.), *Ansichten Griechischer Rituale* (Stuttgart: Teubner,

[41] Recitations of epic at the Panathenaia seem even as early as the sixth century to have been confined largely or entirely to the *Iliad* and the *Odyssey*: Lycurg. *Leocr.* 102; Pl. *Ion* (*passim*); Xen. *Symp.* 3.5–6; Davison 1955: 13; Friis Johansen 1967: 235–6; Pfeiffer 1968: 44–5, 73; Herington 1985: 14; etc.

[42] I would like to thank the editor and anonymous referees of *TAPA* for their improvement of this paper, as well as those who contributed to the discussion after its delivery at the APA Convention of 1987.

1998), pp. 271–95 (= H. Lloyd-Jones, *The Further Academic Papers of Hugh Lloyd-Jones* (Oxford: Oxford University Press, 2005), pp. 141–62); S. Gödde, *Das Drama der Hikesie: Ritual und Rhetorik in Aischylos' Hiketiden* (Münster: Aschendorff, 2000); Christiane Sourvinou-Inwood, *Tragedy and Athenian Religion* (Lanham, MD: Lexington Books, 2003).

CHAPTER 2

Dionysos as Destroyer of the Household: Homer, Tragedy and the Polis

I will use the term 'Dionysiac metaphor' to mean any explicit or implicit comparison of behaviour to the frenzy inspired by Dionysos. My main concern is to show what it is about Dionysiac frenzy, and in particular maenadism, that underlies the rare appearance of the Dionysiac metaphor in Homer and its frequent appearance in Greek tragedy. This will lead to the basis for a new, historical approach to the question of why Dionysos is almost entirely absent from Homer.[1]

1. Maenadic Andromakhe in the *Iliad*

In the only Homeric narration of a Dionysiac myth, Lykourgos is said to have pursued the nurses of frenzied Dionysos (*Il.* 6.132 μαινομένοιο Διωνύσοιο τιθήνας). About 250 lines later Andromakhe, anxious about Hektor, rushes to the wall 'like a frenzied woman' (i.e. a maenad: 389 μαινομένῃ εἰκυῖα).[2] Much later in the poem Andromakhe, [*116*] again in fear for Hektor, rushes through the house 'like a maenad' (22.460 μαινάδι ἴση) to the wall, where she sees Hektor dead. There is, apart from these passages, no other mention of maenadism in Homer. It seems that the author of the Lykourgos narrative of *Iliad* 6.130–40 continued to be influenced by the Dionysiac narrative in his description, a little later, of Andromakhe leaving home, and that the result influenced the parallel action of Andromakhe in Book 22.[3]

1 My thanks go to Jon Mikalson, Renate Schlesier, John Wilkins and especially to Helene Foley for their comments. It will be clear from the footnotes that this essay takes one stage further an argument spread among several of my earlier articles.

2 Cf. Hom. *Il.* 22.460 and *Hymn. Hom. Dem.* 386. On the rarity of non-Dionysiac, non-military μαίνεσθαι in Homer see the final section of this chapter. Cf. Segal 1971: 47 n. 31.

3 So Privitera 1970. He argues (61 n. 18) that the word τιθήνη, which occurs four times in these passages (*Il.* 6.132, 389, 467, 22.503) but nowhere else in Homer, was associated with maenadism. Elsewhere in Homer 'nurse' is designated by the more common term τρόφος.

Why does Andromakhe attract the Dionysiac metaphor? It is not only because she rushes twice in a frenzy from the house, as maenads do.[4] In Book 6 Hektor fails to find Andromakhe at home and asks the maids whether she has gone to see her sisters-in-law or to the temple of Athena, where the other Trojan women are propitiating the goddess. The reply comes that she has gone neither to see her sisters-in-law nor to the temple of Athena, but that she has rushed to the city wall, and it is at this point that the Dionysiac metaphor occurs. The careful and repeated specification of the normal reasons for the wife leaving the household increases the sense of anomaly in Andromakhe rushing to the city wall. Characteristic of the maenadic exit is to confuse not only the spatial differentiation of male and female but also their activities: Dionysiac frenzy typically causes women to abandon their weaving and go out to become warriors and hunters.[5] Andromakhe rushes to the very border of the town (393) to plead with Hektor and give military advice (433–9). Hektor then tells her to return home to her weaving: 'War will be the concern of men' (492). But this firm differentiation of the activities of the sexes prefigures (as does much else in the scene) Book 22, in which Andromakhe [117] will abandon her weaving to return, again like a maenad, to the wall.[6]

But there is yet more to the Dionysiac metaphor than this. It is associated, in an interesting manner, with the ritual of marriage. In brief, the exit of Andromakhe seems to re-enact so as to negate the ritual of her wedding. The same combination of Dionysiac metaphor and the negation of wedding ritual can be seen in the movement of Antigone in Euripides' *Phoenician Women*. That this combination is not merely coincidental is suggested by the subversive relationship of maenadism to the process of marriage and is confirmed by its presence in various other tragedies. There is in fact, as I will show, a broad historical context for the functioning of the Dionysiac metaphor and for the near absence of Dionysos from Homer.

[4] If it was this that attracted the image, then the image has itself influenced the narrative to contain further points of correspondence. It is impossible, and for my purposes unimportant, to decide between these two alternatives.

[5] Weaving: Eur. *Bacch.* 117–19, 1236; Ael. *VH* 3.42; Ant. Lib. *Met.* 10; Ov. *Met.* 4.33–6, 390, 394–8; cf. *fr. trag. adesp.* 645.9; also surely Aesch. *Xantriae*. Warriors: Eur. *Bacch.* 52, 752, 761–4; Aesch. *Eum.* 25; for vase paintings of maenads with swords see March 1989: 36; Paus. 2.20.4 (cf. 4.27.6; Lonnoy 1985: 65–71). Hunting: e.g. Eur. *Bacch.* 1236–7 τὰς παρ' ἱστοις ἐκλιποῦσα κερκίδας ἐς μείζον' ἥκω, θῆρας ἀγρεύειν χεροῖν.

[6] Hom. *Il.* 22.440–1, 448 τῆς δ' ἐλελίχθη γυῖα, χαμαὶ δέ οἱ ἔκπεσε κερκίς; cf. Eur. *Bacch.* 118–19 ἀφ' ἱστων παρὰ κερκίδων τ' οἰστρηθεὶς Διονύσῳ.

2. Maenadic Andromakhe and Wedding Ritual

In Book 22 of the *Iliad* Andromakhe rushes through the house like a maenad to the wall, from which she sees her husband dead. She swoons and throws from her head its covering, including the headdress or veil (κρήδεμνον) 'that golden Aphrodite gave her on the day when Hektor of the flashing helm led her [as bride] from the house of Eëtion'.[7] The undoing of Andromakhe's marriage here finds symbolic expression in the reversal of an element in the ritual process. Recovered from her swoon, she begins (477–84):

> Hektor, I am wretched. It was, then, for a single destiny that we two were born, you in Troy in the house of Priam, but I in Thebes under wooded Plakos in the house of Eëtion, who brought me up when little, ill-fated he, and me with a wretched fate. He should never have begotten me. But now you go to the house of Hades under the earth, and leave me in bitter grief, a widow in the house. [*118*]

This picture of the future bride and groom each still in the parental home complements the mention just made of the wedding procession, in which Hektor led Andromakhe from her parental home. A feature of the wedding procession was the praise or *makarismos* of bride and groom. Sappho writes of this very wedding procession (fr. 44.34): 'They hymned Hektor and Andromakhe as like the gods.' And Admetos, returning home from his wife's burial, remembers an earlier processional arrival, with his bride, in which the company, rather than lamenting as now, called them happy (ὀλβίζων) as being 'of good parentage and yoked together from aristocrats on both sides'.[8] The praise of the pair's fitness for each other, as both of high origin,[9] comes appropriately during the processional transfer, in which the bride is publicly united with her husband. Hence the irony here of Andromakhe's 'it was for *one* fate that we were born, both of us' (each in our own house) – ἰῇ ἄρα γιγνόμεθ' αἴσῃ ἀμφότεροι. Despite what was promised by the *makarismos*, the oneness of Hektor and Andromakhe has turned out to be a oneness in disaster, with the journey undertaken now not (as in the wedding) by the bride but by the husband – 'to the house of Hades'.[10]

7 *Il.* 22.468–72. The κρήδεμνον is discussed at length by Nagler 1974: 44–68.

8 Eur. *Alc.* 918–21; see also Eur. *Supp.* 990–9 (see §5 below), *Tro.* 311–13, *Hel.* 640, 1433–5.

9 Cf. Men. Rhet. 2.402.26–403.25; [Dion. Hal.] *Rhet.* 2.265.

10 The irony was suggested in part no doubt by the conception of the bridal journey as a journey to Hades: Seaford 1987c[13]: 106–7.

Another commonplace of the wedding ceremony was the wish that the marriage produce fine children similar to their parents.[11] This idea may be combined with that wish for prosperity (ὄλβος) that is also characteristic of the wedding *makarismos*. In the Theocritean wedding song Zeus is asked to give 'undying ὄλβος to pass down from the well-born to the well-born' (18.52–3). And the same combination is implicit in the following Homeric observation (*Od.* 4.207–8): 'Easily recognisable is the offspring of a man to whom Zeus destines prosperity (ὄλβος) as he marries.' During Andromakhe's first exit Hektor asks Zeus and the other gods to make his son Astyanax like him (or *[119]* even better), pre-eminent among the Trojans as a soldier and a ruler over Troy (*Il.* 6.476–81). But in her second exit Andromakhe dwells at length (22.484–506) on the miserable, dishonoured life that Astyanax will now lead if he survives the war with the Greeks (487; cf. 24.726–35). Here another commonplace of the wedding ceremony has turned into its opposite. Further, not only has the wedding process been symbolically reversed, the whole household has been destroyed.

This account of the Homeric passage is confirmed by the fact that the ironic reversal of elements of wedding ritual, including the *makarismos* and the prayer for fine children like their parents, occurs frequently in tragedy. For example, in Euripides' *Andromache* Andromakhe herself hints at the failed *makarismos* of her wedding, and her abduction from Troy is presented as a cruel wedding procession in reverse.[12] Another example from Euripides is provided by Antigone in the *Phoenician Women*.

3. Maenadic Antigone and Wedding Ritual

In Euripides' *Phoenician Women* Antigone appears with the bodies of her slaughtered mother and brothers and sings a monody that begins (1485–92):

> Not covering (προκαλυπτομένα) the delicacy (ἁβρά) of my grapelike cheek, nor because of my maidenhood feeling shame (αἰδομένα) at the crimson (ἐρύθημα) under my eyes, the redness of my face, I am carried on, a maenad of the dead, throwing off the covering from my hair, relinquishing the saffron luxury of the garment, led,[13] sighing much, by the dead.

[11] Men. Rhet. 2.404.27 τέξετε παῖδας ὑμῖν ὁμοίους καὶ ἐν ἀρετῇ λαμπρούς; 407.9, 23; [Dion. Hal.] *Rhet* 2.266; Catull. 61.209–13 (cf. Hom. *Il.* 6.466–74), 214–18; 64.323–81 (hymeneal: cf. Ar. *Av.* 1734; Eur. *IA* 1063), with 64.343–60; cf. Hom. *Il.* 6.480–1; Theoc. *Id.* 18.21; Sid. Apoll. *Carm.* 15.191; cf. Hes. *Op.* 235 (with West 1978: *ad loc.*); Seaford 1987c[13]: 126 n. 204.

[12] Seaford 1987c[13] (for Andromakhe see especially 129–30).

[13] See n. 17 below.

Antigone shares much with Andromakhe. Told earlier to return from the city wall to her house (193–4), she emerges again and laments her nearest and dearest killed outside the wall and the complete destruction of her household (1504, etc.). She is in her grief-struck movement like a maenad and sheds her headdress in violent grief. The word κρήδεμνον, which occurs in both passages, is rare after the sixth century.[14] *[120]* No doubt Euripides was influenced by the Homeric passage.

One difference between the two cases is that Antigone is unmarried. Her place in the maidens' quarters is stressed throughout the play (89, 194, 1275, 1636). This allows what I believe to be an evocation, in Antigone's discarding of the veil, of the ceremony of the *anakalypteria*, the unveiling of the bride at the wedding,[15] which seems to have occurred just before the bride's processional departure to her new home: hence the conjunction 'I am carried on ... throwing the covering' (φέρομαι ... κράδεμνα δικοῦσα) here.[16]

Furthermore, the movement referred to by φέρομαι is qualified by ἁγεμόνευμα νεκροῖσι πολύστονον, 'led,[17] sighing much, by the dead'. This evokes the widespread association of bridal and funereal procession, of which the most famous example is provided by Antigone herself, in Sophocles.[18] And so the arrival of Antigone with her dead at the house to which she has been confined as a maiden is implicitly compared with three kinds of exit from the house: the exit of the maenad, the exit of the bride (after the *anakalypteria*) for the procession to her new home and the exit of the funereal procession for the tomb.[19]

14 There is, for instance, only one other example in tragedy (Eur. *Tro.* 508).

15 Standard in the descriptions of the bride, sometimes in the wedding song, are delicacy (ἁβρός): cf. e.g. Sapph. fr. 44.7 (of Andromakhe as bride); Soph. *Trach.* 523 – hymeneal, see Seaford 1986b: 53; red colouring (ἐρύθημα): Sapph. fr. 105.1; Theoc. *Id.* 18.31; cf. Eur. *Cyc.* 515 (ῥοδόχρως cj. Seaford 1984b: *ad loc.*); and the association of αἰδώς with the bridal veil: Paus. 3.20.11; *ARV*[2] 1017.44 – the moment after unveiling, it seems (Oakley 1982: 113–18); other vase paintings: Sutton 1981: 185, 186. The veil shed in the *anakalypteria* seems to have been saffron in colour (Cunningham 1984: 9–12; Seaford 1987c[13]: 124–5), like the one shed by Antigone here. And of the three other occurrences of προκαλύπτειν / προκάλυμμα in tragedy, two are of the bridal veil (Eur. *Med.* 1147; Aesch. *Ag.* 691; see Seaford 1987c[13]: 124).

16 The same conjunction occurs in other ironic evocations in tragedy of the *anakalypteria*: Aesch. *Ag.* 690–2, 1178–81, cf. 239; Soph. *Trach.* 1078–9; Seaford 1987c[13]: 124–5.

17 The usual translation is 'leading'. But in fact it seems to me that ἁγεμόνευμα is passive (like φρόνημα, for instance). Antigone is led (φέρομαι) by her dead kin (to the underworld), just as the bride is led by the groom to her new home (itself sometimes imagined as a journey to Hades: see n. 10 above).

18 Soph. *Ant.* 804–5, 810–11, 816, 886, 891, 947, etc.; Seaford 1987c[13]: 107–8.

19 It may be that in all three exits the headdress was imagined as shed (maenads in vase painting are not veiled; mourning: Eur. *Andr.* 830; *Hymn. Hom. Dem.* 41; Hom. *Il.* 22.468) and that all three exits may have been independently associated with the dead (maenadic: see Seaford 1989a: 304; bridal: see n. 10 above), but this is very speculative.

Antigone is a virgin, and so her wedding is not (like Andromakhe's) *recalled* but symbolically *enacted*. However, as Antigone herself has *[121]* stressed and will continue to stress,[20] the death of her kin means that she will not marry. Like Andromakhe's, her wedding is evoked (by the shedding of the veil) so as to be negated – in her case by the power of those funereal connotations that in actual life attached even to the exit of the normal bride and acquired reality in the funeral of an unmarried girl, who would normally be buried with connotations of a wedding (as is Antigone herself in Sophocles). It is as if here too, as in Sophocles, Antigone rejects marriage for a bridal-funereal journey to her dead kin.[21]

4. Maenadism and Marriage Ritual

Both Andromakhe and Antigone are compared to maenads. The comparison is, I believe, in both cases based not only on the frenzied departure from the house but also on the destruction of the household expressed in the negation of the wedding ritual. The aptness of the comparison will now emerge from a brief account of the relationship between maenadism and marriage.[22] (I mean here maenadism as *imagined* by the Greeks, in particular in myth.[23])

Maenadism is antithetical in obvious ways to the *state* of marriage. Less obviously, it is antithetical also to the whole *process* by which girls become wives of citizens. Included in this process, at least in the classical period, was a type of premarital ritual, associated in particular with Artemis, by which the city-state prepared its girls for marriage. The girls leave their homes for a temporary stay in the wild periphery, in which they are imagined as animals to be 'tamed' or 'yoked' in marriage, and the performance of animal sacrifice is imagined as substituting for the sacrifice of the girl. The implied female resistance to the yoke of marriage continues into the wedding ceremony itself.[24] Myths reflecting this process exhibit the tension between *[122]* Artemis' fierce demand for virginity and the mortal necessity of sex and marriage; a period, in the wild, of resistance to men

20 *Phoen.* 1436–7, 1489–92, 1520, 1659, 1671–81; cf. Soph. *Ant.* 891–904.

21 Seaford 1990a: 76–8.

22 Brief, because I have described it in more detail (concentrating on Attica and Argos) in Seaford 1988.

23 I am not concerned here with the problem of the relationship between imagined and actually practised maenadism.

24 Seaford 1987c[13]: 106–7.

ends in marriage (Atalanta, the Proetids) or sexual union (Kallisto), which may be punished by death or metamorphosis into an animal.[25]

Maenads, too, leave home collectively for a rite of passage in the wild periphery, where they resist men, become like animals and perform sacrifice. Hence the frequent association of Artemis with Dionysos.[26] But the two kinds of cult are also opposites. Maenads go to the mountainside not to reject all sexuality, for they give suck there (to animals), and Dionysos is called by Aeschylus a 'yoker of maenads' and has a retinue of lascivious satyrs and so on.[27] They go rather to reject the males of their own household and polis. Accordingly, the Dionysiac thiasos contains married as well as unmarried women, whose departure disrupts the household in different ways.[28] In married women maenadism renews the centrifugal opposition to marriage that had supposedly been overcome in their marital transition,[29] so that, for example, in the *Bacchae* the Theban maenads are compared (in a reversal of the image of yoking the girl in marriage) to fillies that have *left* the yoke.[30] This disruption may in myth take the irreversible form of killing offspring. In unmarried women permanent disruption is of the natal household and results from their sexual union with outsiders (Antiope, Erigone, Karya, the Proetids).[31] Accordingly, men try to confine maenads to the house.[32]

In the collective premarital cult of the polis, the as-yet-untamed virgins in the wild are in a male-controlled, unrepeated liminal phase *[123]* that precedes and consolidates incorporation into the civilised state of marriage. Antithetically, initiation into the maenadic thiasos converts this transitional phase into a destination, to which unmarried and married women may constantly return. In actually practised maenadism, although there may have been less male control than in the premarital cult, the maenad would of course always return to her own household. And precisely because of the

[25] Even Iphigeneia, who presides over the Brauronian preparation of girls for marriage, was in one version married (to Akhilleus).

[26] Seaford 1988: 125; Kolb 1981: 83 n. 20. The earliest example is Hom. *Od.* 11.324–5.

[27] Aesch. fr. 382 μαινάδων ζευκτήριε; Eur. *Bacch.* 699–702, with Dodds 1960: *ad loc.*; Seaford 1988: 125–6.

[28] Note especially Eur. *Bacch.* 35 and 694; Seaford 1988: 126 n. 70.

[29] This means that the ultimate triumph of the negative tendencies of marriage ritual, which is characteristic of tragedy (Seaford 1987c[13]), may be called 'Dionysiac' in a sense.

[30] Eur. *Bacch.* 1056; cf. *Hel.* 543.

[31] Seaford 1988. The Proetids myth exhibits the contradiction between Dionysos and Artemis within itself, for in the Dionysiac version their eventual marriage destroys their father's realm, whereas in the version presided over by Hera and Artemis the royal household and city are saved.

[32] Eur. *Bacch.* 514 (to weave), 226–7, 231, 443. Note also Antiope, Ino (Hyg. *Fab.* 4), Karya and the Proetids (Seaford 1990a).

threat he poses to the marital process, Dionysos may be incorporated into it,[33] so that even such a threatening feature of maenadism as female military autonomy, for example,[34] was at Chios a prelude to peace and marriage.[35] In imagined maenadism, on the other hand, the departure (or return) of the women to the periphery produces a disruption that is permanent. Whereas the premarital sacrifice to Artemis of an animal in place of the girl may be projected in myth as the sacrifice of the girl herself (e.g. Iphigenia), for whom even in the myth an animal victim may be substituted, in maenadic myth this sacrifice is reversed into one in which the youthful victim is human, mistaken for the (young) animal. The youthful[36] Pentheus is sacrificed[37] by his maenadic mother, who mistakes him for a young animal, and is even imagined as a babe in her arms.[38] And similar Dionysiac killing of offspring occurs in other myths, most of them to *[124]* be found in what we know of fifth-century tragedy: the myths of the Minyads, the women of Argos, Ino, Prokne and Lykourgos.[39]

Whereas the sacrifice to Artemis allows the girl (in reality, as well as sometimes in myth) to be incorporated as wife into a household, the maenad's sacrifice of her offspring renders the disruption of her household irreversible. It expresses and confirms the permanence of her departure

33 See, for instance, Seaford 1988: 127 n. 71.

34 See n. 5 above.

35 Seleucus *ap.* Harp. s.v. 'Homeridai': 'At the Chian Dionysia the women once went mad and did battle with men, and they stopped fighting by exchanging bridegrooms and brides as hostages.' This was no doubt enacted in some way in the festival.

36 Eur. *Bacch.* 274, 330, 973–6, 985–6, 1226, 1254, 1308, 1319.

37 Eur. *Bacch.* 1114; Seaford 1988: 124; Seidensticker 1979.

38 Eur. *Bacch.* 1185–7, 969; Seaford 1981a: 268 (cf. maenads attending to the adult head of Dionysos in its λίκνον, 'cradle'). March 1989 has recently suggested that the killing of Pentheus by his mother was an innovation by Euripides. But this is most unlikely, given that (a) it is a general practice of Dionysos to inspire resisting women to kill their children; (b) Aristophanes' hypothesis to Eur. *Bacch.* says ἡ μυθοποιία κεῖται παρ' Αἰσχύλῳ ἐν Πένθει (with this formula one expects Aristophanes to note differences by πλήν, as in the hypothesis to Eur. *Phoen.*); (c) Eur. *Med.* 1282–4 (μίαν δὴ κλύω μίαν τῶν πάρος | γυναῖκ' ἐν φίλοις χέρα βαλεῖν τέκνοις,| Ἰνὼ ...) does not mean (*pace* March) that Agaue killing her son was as yet unknown (the aim of the chorus here is not precision, and apart from Agaue they do not mention the well-known cases of Prokne and Aidon (Hom. *Od.* 19.518–23), for example); (d) we cannot affirm that in the *Medea* Euripides 'innovated child-murder by a mother' (March 1989: 51), because we do not know all the versions of the myth (oral and written) before Euripides (and in fact in an early version that we do know something of – that of Eumelos – Medea *did* kill her children, albeit unintentionally); and (e) similarly, we hardly know anything of the versions (oral and written) of the Agaue myth before Euripides.

39 Minyads: Ant. Lib. *Met.* 10 (they leave their homes and the polis); 'like a fawn': Ael. *VH* 3.42 (cf. Plut. *Quaest. Graec.* 299e); perhaps also in Aesch. *Xantriae*. Argos: Apollod. *Bibl.* 2.2.2 (= Hes. fr. 131), 3.5.2. Ino: Ov. *Met.* 4.523, a detail that may derive from Euripides' *Ino* (cf. Hyg. *Fab.* 4, 'Ino Euripidis' and also, among others, Lucian, *Dial. Meret.* 9); schol. Hom. *Od.* 5.334b; Hyg. *Fab.* 2 (Ino apotheosised by Dionysos). Prokne: Ov. *Met.* 6.587–674; Soph. *Tereus* (esp. fr. 586; Kiso 1984: 67–8, 79–80). Lykourgos: Sutton 1975a: 356–60 (Aesch. *Lycurgia*).

from it. Towards the end of the *Bacchae* Kadmos imagines the possibility of Agaue remaining in her maenadic state, and so being spared the pain of realising what she has done, but then proceeds to bring her out of this state by a series of questions, one of which, at a crucial stage of her emergence, reminds her of her identity by evoking her wedding procession (1273): 'To what house did you come with your hymeneals?' And the very next question is about the son of her marriage. But, pathetically, she cannot of course resume this identity. She must now leave the household. Restored to her sense, she takes her leave of household, of polis and of her father. She calls herself φυγὰς ἐκ θαλάμων, 'a fugitive from the chambers' (1370), a phrase that connotes a reversal of the wedding process, a *departure* from the bridal chamber.[40]

But killing her son excludes her also, once brought to her senses, from the thiasos. She emphasises, at the very end of the play, that she will leave maenadism to others (1386–7). But she does not know, as she leaves Thebes, where she is to go (1366–7, 1383). Between the conflicting collectivities of thiasos on the one hand and Thebes on the other, she is finally isolated.

The daughters of Minyas, after their frenzied sacrifice of their offspring to Dionysos, are turned into birds,[41] like the maenadic infanticide Prokne. This tragic metamorphosis assigns them permanently, disqualified as they are from civilisation, to the realm of nature, but as lonely creatures of darkness – bat, owl and the lamenting *[125]* nightingale. Even Agaue, in embracing the father from whom she must part, is compared to a swan.[42]

Thus we can see that the resemblances between Andromakhe and Antigone are shared also by the maenads with whom they are compared. All are confined by men in the house, from which they depart in a frenzy. Important in the case of each is the destruction of the household,[43] and each laments the death of her nearest and dearest. And because a household is constituted by marriage, in each case its destruction, and the consequent isolation of the female, is associated with the evocation and negation of the transition from maiden to wife. This conclusion must now be tested on further cases of the Dionysiac metaphor.

[40] Cf. Eur. *Andr.* 103–9 (and Seaford 1987c[13]: 129–30).
[41] See especially Ant. Lib. *Met.* 10.
[42] Eur. *Bacch.* 1363–5; Seaford 1988: 127 n. 75.
[43] Antigone: Eur. *Phoen.* 1496, 1504, etc. (also, Antigone will not now marry and continue the line with children). Maenad: e.g. Eur. *Bacch.* 1250, 1304, 1308, 1313, 1374–6, etc.

5. Euadne

In Euripides' *Suppliants* Euadne reacts to her husband's death in battle by rushing from the house, in which she has been confined (even guarded),[44] in a 'maenadic' frenzy: πρὸς δ' ἔβαν δρομὰς ἐξ ἐμῶν οἴκων ἐκβακχευσαμένα (1000–1).[45] Her wedding, like Andromakhe's, is recalled (990–4), but it is also, like Antigone's, enacted (or rather re-enacted) – she is, for example, dressed as a bride and sings a wedding song (1025 ἴτω φῶς γάμοι τε etc.) before triumphantly throwing herself onto the pyre for a union, described in erotic terms, with her dead husband. There is in fact the same subtle combination that we find in the *Phoenician Women* of bridal, funereal and maenadic exit. But there is also a remarkable parallel to the combination of recalled wedding procession and reversed wedding *makarismos* that we found in the maenadic exit of Andromakhe. The first half of Euadne's opening strophe, which recalls her wedding procession and wedding *makarismos*, is mirrored by the second, which describes her maenadic departure [*126*] for her husband's tomb to end her 'painful life and the sufferings of her αἰών' (1004–5). The word αἰών means a *whole* life. The phrase makes sense when applied to Euadne only as a negation of the wedding *makarismos*.[46] The ὄλβος desiderated by the *makarismos* is permanent: it depends on a successfully completed αἰών.[47] But the death of her husband has, as in Andromakhe's case, revealed the true nature of Euadne's αἰών: it can now be seen as one of suffering (αἰῶνος πόνους). Despite the element of triumph in this re-enactment of her wedding, Euadne was after all not blessed (ὀλβία), and the wedding *makarismos* failed. Similarly, the speed of her maenadic exit (1000–1 δρομὰς ἐξ ἐμῶν οἴκων)[48] re-enacts but reverses the speed of her bridal departure (993 ὠκυθόα νύμφα). Here again the maenadic departure from home is associated with the evocation and negation of the bridal transition and the destruction of her (marital and natal) households.[49]

[44] 1038–42. Though she is married, the house is her *father's*. This oddity allows a greater similarity with the bridal departure, and male (paternal) despair at her escape.

[45] Cf. *fr. trag. adesp.* 645.9. At 1062 weaving is mentioned as a preoccupation to be expected of her.

[46] Collard's comment (Collard 1975: II.367: 'Ev's whole life has not been full of πόνοι, but only since the recent death of Cap.; her statement is exaggerated to suit the *sententia* 1006–8') misses this point. See Seaford 1987c[13]: 121–2.

[47] Cf. e.g. Aesch. *Ag.* 928–9; Hdt. 1.32; Soph. *Trach.* 1–3.

[48] Cf. 1038–9 δόμων ἐξώπιος βέβηκε πηδήσασα.

[49] 1095; cf. 1133. Euadne also offends against the spirit of the classical polis as expressed in the funerary legislation (attributed, in Athens, to Solon).

6. Iole

The triumphant but pathetic speed of Euadne's maenadic progress re-enacts and contrasts with the joyful speed of her bridal progress.[50] A similar irony reappears in the Sophoclean description, in a clearly hymeneal context,[51] of Herakles' violent leading of Iole, a swift bride (θοὰν νύμφαν) from Oikhalia:[52] the joyful urgency of the wedding procession here becomes the ruthless urgency of the conqueror.[53] This same combination of the wedding with the brutal abduction of Iole *[127]* from the conquered city reappears, in the same hymeneal context,[54] in Euripides' *Hippolytus* (545–54):

> Aphrodite yoked the Oikhalian filly, the previously unyoked virgin, from her father's house running like a naiad and a maenad (βάκχαν), and gave her, with blood and with smoke, in a murderous wedding, to Herakles. O excessive (τλάμων) in his/her wedding.[55]

The maenadic image here is apt obviously because the girl runs, and so do maenads, but also for two other reasons. First, because it is specifically to avoid the male yoke that she runs, like Helen in Euripides' *Helen* running from the 'wild man' (in fact her husband) 'like a running filly or a maenad of the god'.[56] Second, because her 'wedding' is violently destructive. It is significant that the word βάκχαν ('maenad') introduces the theme of the wedding celebrated with blood and smoke. Maenads cause violent destruction, and the smoke of their torches is well known.[57]

Returning to the Sophoclean passage, we find the irony that Herakles' 'wedding' with Iole means the destruction of her new household as well as of her old one.[58] And so it is, too, in the strikingly similar passage in the

[50] Other examples of the speed of the bridal procession are Sappho frr. 44.11 and 23 (?); Eur. *Hel.* 724.

[51] Seaford 1987c[13]: 128–9; note especially the agency of Aphrodite, which was important at a normal wedding.

[52] Soph. *Trach.* 857–61; cf. also 841–3, where we should probably retain ἄοκνον: Seaford 1987c[13]: 129.

[53] There may have been, for the bride, an element of this ruthless urgency even in the normal wedding procession: Seaford 1987c[13]: 106–7.

[54] Here too (cf. n. 51) the agent of the disastrous transition is Aphrodite.

[55] τὰν μὲν Οἰχαλίᾳ | πῶλον ἄζυγα λέκτρων, | ἄνανδρον τὸ πρὶν καὶ ἄνυμφον, οἴκων | ζεύξασ' ἀπ' Εὐρυτίων (Buttmann: ἀπειρεσίαν mss.) | δρομάδα ναΐδ' ὅπως τε βάκ- | χαν σὺν αἵματι, σὺν καπνῷ, | φονίοισι νυμφείοις (Barrett: φονίοις θ' ὑμεναίοις mss.) | Ἀλκμήνας τόκῳ Κύπρις ἐξέδωκεν· ὦ | τλάμων ὑμεναίων.

[56] Eur. *Hel.* 543–5 ὡς δρομαία πῶλος ἢ βάκχη θεοῦ. Cf. *Bacch.* 1056. Conceivably the Dionysiac metaphor is inspired also by the 'tomb' (*Hel.* 544); cf. n. 19 above. But this is merely speculative.

[57] E.g. Soph. *Ant.* 1126–8; cf. Eur. *Bacch.* 144–6; *Ion* 550; Aesch. *Xantriae* fr. 171; and see §7 below. Vase painting: Arias, Hirmer and Shefton 1962: 372–3.

[58] Soph. *Trach.* 842–3 and 893–5; Seaford 1987c[13]: 128–9. The death of Herakles is described in terms of erotic union: 662, 767–8, 833; Seaford 1986b: 56.

Hippolytus,[59] where the word order gives the [128] impression that resistance of the 'maenad' has brought death, that the violence used by Herakles to master his maenadic bride has somehow destroyed *him*, so that he and his bride are each τλάμων[60] in the wedding. The yoking of the girl, which is a feature of normal marriage, has disastrously failed. And so the maenadic image is here again associated with the destruction of the household through the reversal or negation of the marital transition (here the taming process in that transition).

7. Kassandra

Comparable to Iole is Kassandra in Euripides' *Trojan Women*. In her brief appearance before being taken off to the ships as Agamemnon's 'bride' she is constantly compared to a maenad.[61] In maenadic fashion, she appears from within at a frenzied run: μαινὰς θοάζει δεῦρο Κασσάνδρα δρόμῳ (307). But there is, once again, more to the Dionysiac metaphor than that.

First, like a maenad (see n. 57), she carries torches. Whereas the destructive power of the maenadic torch was merely implicit in the *Hippolytus* passage, here it creates an alarm.[62] Hekabe, when asked to catch the Bacchic girl (342), removes her torches from her with a bitter reflection on the distinction between wedding torches and maenadic torches, which Kassandra has in her maenadic enactment of a wedding confused.[63]

Second, not only does the 'wedding' of Kassandra occur along with the destruction of her natal family, but it will also, Kassandra stresses three times (359, 364, 461), completely destroy the household (δόμους, οἴκους) of her husband. In this dual destruction she resembles Iole and (more remotely) Euadne. Similarly, in the *Iliad* Andromakhe stresses, before losing her husband as well, that all her natal family has been killed.[64] [129]

Third, she utters a wedding *makarismos* more bitter even than Andromakhe's and Euadne's. Like Euadne's it is both pathetic and seriously

[59] This ambiguity (missed entirely by Barrett 1964: *ad loc.*) strengthens the allusion to the destruction of Theseus' household: the same irony of the arrival of the bride bringing catastrophe (also in a triangular situation) occurs in the very next song, with Phaidra herself as bride (755–6): ἐπόρευσας ἐμὰν ἄνασσαν ὀλβίων ἀπ' οἴκων | κακονυμφοτάταν ὄνασιν. And if Renate Schlesier 1993: 108–10 is right to regard 315–22 as maenadic, then Phaidra is another *maenadic* bride destroying the household. Another catastrophic bridal arrival is Helen's: Eur. *Andr.* 103–4.

[60] The adjective τλάμων means both 'suffering' and 'going too far'.

[61] 307, 342–3, 349, 367, 408, 415 and 500. Also at Eur. *Hec.* 121, 676; *Alexandros* fr. 62e.

[62] 298–9 and 342–3 (cf. 344–51).

[63] 348–9 οὐ γὰρ ὀρθὰ πυρφορεῖς μαινὰς θοάζουσ' κτλ.

[64] *Il.* 6.429–30: 'Hektor, you are my father and honoured mother and brother, and you are my sturdy husband.'

meant, even triumphant.[65] The pathos is that both bride and groom will be killed. But the triumph is the ghastly joy of revenge on the groom.[66]

Here again, the maenadic image is associated with a marital transition that brings not life but death and destruction to the bride, the groom and the whole household.[67] And we also find the same combination of bridal, funereal and maenadic exit that we found with the Euripidean Antigone and Euadne.[68]

8. Three Generalisations

On the basis of these and other examples, which we are about to survey, it is possible to make some general observations about the fluidity in tragedy between the Dionysiac metaphor and actual Dionysiac frenzy, and the range of the metaphor's application in tragedy. Of course exceptions to these generalisations exist, and we will consider these, too, briefly.

First, the metaphor and actual frenzy. The Dionysiac metaphor may easily pass into the frenzy actually inspired by Dionysos.[69] For example, Klytaimestra, who in at least one and probably two places in the *Oresteia* attracts the Dionysiac metaphor (basically because she kills kin),[70] is in vase painting (probably inspired by tragedy) actually dressed as a maenad.[71] The story of Prokne killing her own children, *[130]* serving them to her husband and being turned into a nightingale (he into a hoopoe) was the theme of Sophocles' lost play *Tereus*. Prokne seems a prime candidate for the Dionysiac metaphor. But it seems that in the play, as in Ovid, she was actually dressed as a maenad for a Dionysiac festival (see §4 above). It seems that in Euripides' lost *Ino* Agaue's sister Ino was an actual maenad and also (although perhaps not simultaneously) the killer of her own child (see §4 above).

An interesting case of this fluidity between metaphor and reality is provided by Antigone. At the end of the *Phoenician Women* the Dionysiac

[65] 311–13, 327 and 336.

[66] 340, 353–5, 359–60, 404–5 and 460–1.

[67] It is in fact not only wedding ritual that will be subverted: Kassandra knows well that she will also be denied death ritual, thrown out to be a lonely prey for the wild animals (448–50).

[68] 445 (ἐν Ἅιδου νυμφίῳ γημώμεθα), 344, 351–2, 449 and 455–7. The ironic wedding of Kassandra and Agamemnon (in death) is a constant theme of Aeschylus' *Agamemnon*: Seaford 1987c[13]: 127–8.

[69] Just as it often combines with frenzy inspired by another deity (Kassandra by Apollo, Herakles by Lyssa, Orestes by the Furies).

[70] Aesch. *Ag.* 1235 (quoted at n. 76 below), reading Weil's emendation, Ἅιδου μαινάδ'; the phrase βακχείας κακῆς at Aesch. *Cho.* 698 refers to Klytaimestra; see Seaford 1989a.

[71] Seaford 1989a: 305.

metaphor (discussed above) is followed by a passage in which Oidipous tells Antigone to go where Dionysos and the maenads' precinct are in the mountains (Eur. *Phoen.* 1751–3). Antigone rejects this, saying that her previous maenadism in the mountains won no favour from the gods.[72] This sudden mention of maenadism may perplex. But one function of the passage, whether or not it is interpolated (or misplaced), seems to be to assimilate the extreme desolation of Antigone to that of, say, Agaue, who at the end of the *Bacchae* (1383–7), faced like Antigone with exile from Thebes after the destruction of her household, emphatically puts maenadism behind her as well. We will see in due course (in §10 below) that the passage has another function, and that, as it seems in Euripides' lost *Antigone*, Antigone actually appeared as a maenad. There is a difference, however, between the *Bacchae* and the *Phoenician Women*. In the former the maenadic frenzy of Agaue destroyed her household, whereas the (metaphorical) maenadic frenzy of Antigone in the latter was a *response* to the destruction of her household.

This distinction brings me to my second general point. The Euripidean Herakles is said several times, when killing his children, to be in a Bacchic frenzy,[73] and when he comes to his senses he asks whether in his Bacchic frenzy he destroyed the home (οἶκος).[74] But at the onset of his madness he is asked whether his Bacchic frenzy resulted from the killing of his enemies (Lykos et al.): 966–7 οὔ τί που [131] φόνος σ' ἐβάκχευσεν νεκρῶν οὓς ἄρτι καίνεις. This means that Bacchic frenzy may be imagined either as a cause or as a result of slaughter. It is as a *result* of killing his mother that Orestes suffers the 'Bacchic frenzy' inflicted on him by the Furies.[75] But in one of the three passages in which the metaphor occurs something more is implied: line 411, αὗταί σε βακχεύουσι συγγενῆ φόνον, suggests an intimate, internal connection between kin-killing and Dionysiac frenzy. Willink (1986: 153) comments that 'the polluting 'blood' is not simply the *cause* of the punitive 'madness' but also its *essence*'.

And so our metaphor may cover the states of mind that precede, accompany and follow the killing of kin and destruction of the household.

[72] Or reading γε after χάριν in 1757 and ending the question with ἀνεχόρευσα, Antigone says that for her to resume her maenadism would be to give thankless service to the gods.

[73] Eur. *HF* 966, 1086, 1119, 1122; note also 896–7. A model for a *father* inspired by Dionysos to kill his children is the myth of Lykourgos, dramatised by Aeschylus.

[74] The text is corrupt, but the sense is clear: ἦ γὰρ συνήραξ' οἶκον †ἦ βάκχευσ' ἐμόν†; (1142).

[75] Eur. *Or.* 338, 411, 835. This is one element in the application of the maenadic metaphor to the Furies themselves (Aesch. *Eum.* 500). Pursued by the Furies to Athens, Orestes participates in the Dionysiac Anthesteria (Eur. *IT.* 941–60 etc.).

Klytaimestra is a 'maenad of Hades, and breathing truceless Ares on her kin. And how, all-daring, she raised the cry of triumph, as if at the turning point of battle!'[76] It is as 'a maenad of Hades' that she kills Agamemnon. And the cry of triumph in battle is typical of a maenad,[77] as is the idea of breathing violence against kin.[78] This latter is one element, along with the illicit sexual relationship (with Aigisthos) and the destruction of the household, in Klytaimestra's *continuing* 'wicked Bacchic revel in the house', which is denounced in the *Choephori* (698; see n. 70), a state that involves hostility to her own children, a kind of frenzy that can be 'cured'[79] only by the matricide. Here the wicked maenadism threatens to be permanent.

The maenadic exit of Antigone in the *Phoenician Women* is a reaction to the death of kin and the destruction of the household, as is the 'Bacchic' song (νόμον βακχεῖον) sung by Hekabe over the dead body of her only surviving son, Polydoros (Eur. *Hec.* 685–97). The flight from reality characteristic of Dionysiac frenzy may also be found in the immediate reaction to bereavement.[80] Polydoros has, his mother complains, been cut up (διεμοιράσω) – a rare verb certainly [132] associated later in the play (and elsewhere) with Dionysiac ritual dismemberment (σπαραγμός).[81] Hekabe's frenzied lament turns into the fierce desire for revenge on the Thracian Polymnestor, who (like Dionysos' Thracian enemy Lykourgos) is blinded, as his children are torn apart by the 'maenads of Hades' (1076–7 βάκχαις Ἅιδου διαμοιρᾶσαι), the mothers (1157 τοκάδες),[82] who at first behave like nurses and then draw swords – a contradiction typical of maenads.[83]

In the *Hecuba*, then, the Dionysiac metaphor applies both to the reaction to the dismemberment of offspring and to the dismemberment of children in revenge. Similarly, the maenadism of Kassandra is both a frenzied

76 Aesch. *Ag.* 1235–7: Ἅιδου μαινάδ' (Weil: μητέρ' mss.) ἄσπονδόν τ' Ἄρη (Franz: ἀρὰν mss.) | φίλοις πνέουσαν. ὡς δ' ἐπωλολύξατο | ἡ παντότολμος, ὥσπερ ἐν μάχης τροπῇ. See Seaford 1989a.

77 See nn. 5 and 85.

78 Cf. Soph. *Ant.* 136–7; Eur. *Bacch.* 1094, *Phoen.* 789, 794 (and n. 87 below).

79 ἰατρός. Maenadism may be 'cured': see, for example, Apollod. *Bibl.* 2.2.2.

80 Note, for instance, Eur. *Hec.* 689 ἄπιστ' ἄπιστα, etc.; de Martino 1958: 151–6.

81 Eur. *Hec.* 1076–7; *Orph. fr.* 210K. I am indebted in the analysis of this passage to Schlesier 1988: 129. The theme is prefigured a little earlier (656) in the picture of a Spartan mother lamenting for her son and tearing her cheeks (σπαραγμός). σπαραγμός occurs elsewhere in Euripides (outside the *Bacchae*) only of the frenzied actions of the 'maenadic' Antigone (*Phoen.* 1525) and the 'maenadic' Kassandra (*Tro.* 453).

82 The term τοκάς usually refers to mothers of animals and occurs elsewhere of humans only with regard to 'the mother of Bakchos' (Eur. *Hipp.* 560). This suggests the animal nature of the maenads (see §4 above). With the phrase ὅσαι δὲ τοκάδες ἦσαν (1157) compare Eur. *Bacch.* 35–6 ὅσαι γυναῖκες ἦσαν (of maenads).

83 E.g. Eur. *Bacch.* 699–701, 733, 752 etc.; Apollod. *Bibl.* 3.5.2; n. 5 above. Maenads are imagined as nurses of Dionysos.

reaction to the destruction of her natal family and a frenzied prophecy of the destruction she will wreak in revenge on her new household as a maenadic bride. Much the same is true of Iole. And the maenadism of Euadne is also both a frenzied reaction to loss and the frenzy that accompanies further destruction – the suicide that leaves her father lamenting the desolation (ἐρημία) of his household (see n. 49).

I have to this point referred, with four exceptions, to every person who in Homer or Greek tragedy attracts the Dionysiac metaphor: Andromakhe, Antigone, Euadne, Hekabe and her women, Helen, Herakles, Ino, Iole, Kassandra, Klytaimestra, Orestes and Prokne. In every case (except that of Helen) there is destruction of the household,[84] just as there is when the frenzy is actually inspired by Dionysos [133] (Agaue, Lykourgos, etc.). And in five instances the destruction of the household is expressed in the evocation and negation of wedding ritual: Andromakhe, Antigone, Euadne, Iole, Kassandra.

As for the four exceptions, even they confirm that the metaphor is almost always more complex than it seems. First, Aeschylus calls Io a maenad of Hera (*Supp.* 564 θυιὰς Ἥρας). Given the well-known opposition between the goddess of marriage and Dionysos, the actual or potential enemy of marriage (see n. 94), the phrase 'maenad of Hera' is an oxymoron. Io is maenadic because she wanders, apparently unceasingly, as an animal, in a god-sent frenzy far from home, avoiding contact with the male. She is a 'maenad of Hera' because in this case it is paradoxically Hera who, although goddess of marriage, is trying to preserve Io's virginity by sending her off in a frenzy.

Second, in Aeschylus' *Seven against Thebes* a warrior attacking Thebes 'raves like a Bacchant' (498 βακχᾷ … θυιὰς ὥς). Here the point of comparison is not just the frenzy of war (497 ἔνθεος δ' Ἄρει) but also the snakes (around his shield) and the triumphant war cry – both characteristic of maenadism,[85] as well as the 'military' defeat of the self-same city of Thebes by Dionysos and his maenads.[86] This last point also underlies

[84] This is not to say that, conversely, kin-killing and the destruction of the household always attract the Dionysiac metaphor. A notable exception is the Euripidean Medea – although Seneca's repeated comparison of Medea to a maenad (*Med.* 383, 806, 849) presumably derives from a Greek tragedy. Medea is an exception perhaps because she, horrifically, *means* to kill her own children. The metaphor occurs of Demeter *reunited* with her daughter at line 386 of the Homeric *Hymn to Demeter*. As well as 'rushing', Demeter is a female without a male, recalcitrant, isolated and wandering, her veil torn. The metaphor may also subtly qualify the joy of the reunion: Persephone will in fact have to leave her mother to return to Hades.

[85] Eur. *Bacch.* 1133; Seaford 1988: 134, 1989a: 303; cf. my discussion at the beginning of §8 above.

[86] Aesch. *Eum.* 25–6; Eur. *Bacch.* 52; and the other references given above in n. 5.

our third case, from Sophocles' *Antigone*: Kapaneus is 'in a Bacchic frenzy' (βακχεύων) as he rushes against Thebes with the maenadic attributes of war cry and destructive torch (133–7).[87] Finally, in Aeschylus' *Seven against Thebes* (836) the chorus applies to itself the word θυιάς when lamenting the fratricidal slaughter of the royal Theban brothers. Although it is uncertain here that θυιάς by itself is Dionysiac, this is a passage to which I will return.

9. Dionysos, Household and Polis

The connection between Dionysos as destroyer of the household and Dionysos as a god of the whole polis, I suggest, provides a basis *[134]* for understanding historically the place of the Dionysiac metaphor in Homer on the one hand and in Greek tragedy on the other. Whereas in Homer Hektor explicitly reserves war for men as he instructs Andromakhe to return to house and weaving, in tragedy the Thebans are militarily defeated by the maenads, who have left house and weaving. The threat of frenzied female confusion of the gender division basic to the polis must be contained. It must therefore be embodied so as to be propitiated, and the god employed to embody it is Dionysos.[88] Just as Apollo both sends and heals illnesses,[89] so Dionysos both threatens the gender division of the polis and is consequently propitiated and honoured by the whole polis: 'He wishes to have collective honours from all'.[90]

[87] Eur. *Phoen.* 784–800 exploits the similarities and differences between marital and Dionysiac frenzy, again in the attack of the Seven against Thebes.

[88] Dionysos is older than the polis. What qualifies him for his role in the polis is, at least in part, his earlier association with the thiasos, a body that seems to represent a survival, in a modified form, of an ancient cultic and *social* unit distinct from the household on the one hand and the emergent polis on the other: see, among others, Gernet and Boulanger 1970: 123; Seaford 1981a. (This view is, I believe, confirmed by the range of application of the word θίασος in the classical period.) As well as being outside household and polis, the ancient thiasos contains features that were later used to express its symbolic function in the polis: initiation into it involved the ritual disorientation and the ritual death needed as rites of separation before entry into the new group, and these came to acquire a new significance as the frenzy required to destroy the household by killing offspring. The secret ritual of the thiasos remains at the heart of the democratic festival of Dionysos, a combination that underlies the contrast expressed at Eur. *Bacch.* 860–1 ἐν τέλει θεὸς δεινότατος, ἀνθρώποισι δ' ἠπιώτατος (τέλος here means 'initiation ritual'; Seaford 1981a: 261).

[89] Burkert 1985: 146–7 and 267. The ambiguity of Dionysos is well known (see, for example, Eur. *Bacch.* 860–1, quoted in n. 88). An example not cited is Paus. 2.23.7 (having warred against Perseus, Dionysos laid aside his hostility and was greatly honoured by the Argives). Henrichs 1990 has recently driven too firm a wedge between the benign and the dangerous Dionysos.

[90] Eur. *Bacch.* 208–9 ἐξ ἁπάντων βούλεται τιμὰς ἔχειν κοινάς. Cf. e.g. Ov. *Met.* 3.529–30, 'the crowd rushed on – men and women and young brides, the common people and the nobles, all mixed up

All festivals of the polis draw the worshippers from their homes, thereby transcending the division into the households of which the polis is composed. But with Dionysos this function is especially prominent. He is to be worshipped by the citizens 'in the streets ... all mixed up together' – ἄμμιγα πάντας, as the Delphic oracle quoted by Demosthenes has it (21.52). Moreover, the tendency of the household [135] to self-sufficiency is opposed by Dionysos not only on the streets but within the household itself. I am thinking here not just of the well-known stories of the god driving from out of their homes the women who resist him, but also (for example) of the annual sexual union of Dionysos with the wife of the *archon basileus* ('king archon') in what was believed to be the ancient royal palace ([Arist.] *Ath. Pol.* 3.5). The invasion of the royal household by a publicly escorted stranger[91] who symbolically destroys its potential autonomy by having sex with the 'king archon's' wife is of benefit, it is clear from a source dating to the fourth century,[92] to the whole polis.

Three weeks before this event, the sacred marriage of Zeus and Hera, king and queen, celebrated at the Theogamia, benefited Athens in an antithetical way, by marking (it seems) the season for the marriages of citizens.[93] Dionysos and Hera are of course natural enemies.[94] Plutarch associates the careful separation of their rituals with Hera's roles as goddess of marriage and leader of the bride in the wedding.[95] When we do find Zeus, Hera and Dionysos together, in Lesbos in the seventh century, it is in a sanctuary (τέμενος) that, Alcaeus tells us, the Lesbians founded as 'conspicuous, great and common (ξυνόν)'.[96] Dionysos is honoured there as Omestes, 'raw-eater'. The eating of raw food that puts him outside civilisation is here combined with the divine embodiment (in Zeus and Hera) of the civilised idea of marriage, so as to create a sanctuary for the whole community. The frequently noted role of Dionysos as 'the Other' badly needs a *historical* explanation. By a familiar mechanism, the power of Dionysos

together, were borne along to the unknown rites'. Dionysos in general creates concord in place of civil strife: Diod. Sic. 3.66. He is at home in the *agora*: Kolb 1981. He is, in various cities, entitled Polites, Arkhegetes, Demoteles, Demosios, Kathegemon, Saotes, Aisumnetes, For/Before the City (ὁ πρὸ πόλεως): Farnell 1909: 135–8; Privitera 1970: 36.

91 See Jameson 1993: 54–6.

92 [Dem.] 59.73.

93 Seaford 1988: 128.

94 Seaford 1988: 126 n. 66.

95 Plut. fr. 157.

96 Alc. fr. 129.2–3; cf. Sapph. fr. 17. The adjective ξυνόν presumably means 'common to all the people' (cf. e.g. *SIG*[3] 1044.29: τὸ δὲ τέμενος εἶναι [κοι]νόν) but could conceivably mean 'common to the three gods'.

to unite the community derives in part from his coming from outside it, as he does for his sacred marriage.[97]

At Patrai this mechanism is unusually explicit. There Dionysos was [136] honoured as Aisumnetes, a term implying impartial power over all.[98] During his festival images of the god were brought to his sanctuary, each image being named after one of the three ancient cities from which Patrai was composed. His attendants were an equal number of men and women elected by and from the whole people (Paus. 7.20.1 ἐκ πάντων ὁ δῆμος etc.). The aetiological myth of his cult is as follows. Prevented from marrying by their parents, a young couple have sex in the sanctuary of Artemis, with the result that they are sacrificed, as is thereafter the fairest couple of every year. This practice of sacrificing the marriageable young was to cease only when an outside (ξένος) king came bearing an outsider (ξενικός) deity. This turns out to be king Eurypylos, who had been frenzied by an image of Dionysos Aisumnetes but was to find a new home where the people offered a strange (ξένος) sacrifice. And so when he arrives at Patrai (by sea, like Dionysos for his sacred marriage) his frenzy and the human sacrifice are ended, and the cult of Dionysos Aisumnetes is installed. The whole polis makes Dionysos, the impartial outsider, its own, and thereby may reproduce itself through the civilised institution of marriage without sacrificing the young.[99]

There is a similar relationship between Dionysos coming from outside and the sacrifice of the young at Megara.[100] Here a founder of the city is Alkathoos, who after killing a lion builds a temple to Artemis and Apollo and with the help of Apollo builds the city wall. This pattern of killing followed by the incorporation of deity is then repeated, but with the violence this time of an opposite kind, directed not outwards, at a wild animal, but inwards, at Alkathoos' own son, whom he kills in anger because the young man was disrupting a sacrifice (i.e. he kills him at an altar). To purify Alkathoos of the murder there comes to Megara an outsider, Polyidos, great-grandson of the Dionysiac priest Melampous, who

97 See Burkert 1985: 260: 'Once again the community creates its solidarity through the veneration of one who does not belong to it.'

98 The cult was an ancient one: Privitera 1970: 32–3. Information on myth and cult is from Paus. 7.19–21.

99 The people of Patrai had also introduced an image of Dionysos from Kalydon, where the god had imposed frenzy on the Kalydonians after his priest had been resisted by a girl he loved, and demanded the girl be sacrificed to him. The priest sacrificed himself instead, and the girl committed suicide (Paus. 7.21.1–5). This represents the reverse side of Dionysos' power (frenzy and death replace marriage), safely located in another city.

100 Paus. 1.41–3. Cf. Bohringer 1980.

came from outside to purify the Argive Proetids. Polyidos also builds at Megara a temple of Dionysos [137] Patroios. The crisis produced by a parent killing a child is here resolved in the introduction from outside of the cult of the god who so often inspires that very act, and who becomes as Patroios a deity of the whole polis. To take another example, in the myth preserved in detail in the *Bacchae* parental killing of offspring in the royal family is, again, followed by the installation of the outsider god to be honoured by the whole polis (39–40, 208–9, etc.).

In embodying the communal principle of the polis, Dionysos is a potential destroyer of the household, presenting a latent threat to the tendency of the household to autonomy. Whereas in *ritual* the threat is heeded, in the controlled temporary disruption of the royal marriage to the benefit of the whole polis, in *myth* the threat is generally imagined as realised, in the permanent disruption of the household by the horror of intrafamilial killing, a horror that warns that the god must be honoured.

This communality of the polis is established at the expense of women, who, without power in the public sphere, were easily imagined as adhering excessively to the household and as resisting their public powerlessness. These two female threats to the polis may seem antithetical to each other, the one a rejection of the public sphere, the other an attempt to control it. But the Homeric Andromakhe, for example, combines them: it is out of exclusive concern for her household, which contrasts and conflicts with Hektor's sense of public duty, that Andromakhe threatens to confuse, spatially and functionally, the gender division of the polis. And so the threat she presents attracts the Dionysiac metaphor: it is as if inspired by Dionysos.

Normally, in ritual, Dionysos as a god of communality draws women out of the household, inspiring them with a temporary, controlled resistance to public gender division. In this way he counters the two antithetical threats to the polis – offsetting excessive adherence to the household by bringing women out from their homes, and gender confusion by bringing them out for only a temporary, controlled period. Because he is honoured by the whole polis, Dionysos both presents a latent threat to the household and, if deprived of that honour, will destroy the gender division on which the polis is based. Indeed, if Dionysos is resisted, both threats are activated. Female adherence to the household is violently reversed by a frenzy in which women leave their homes and even destroy their families. And this frenzy also endangers [138] male control of the public sphere. In the Theban myth these two reversals of female adherence to the household culminate together in the killing of Pentheus, which, because Pentheus is ruler as well as offspring, means both the destruction of the household and the final victory of the maenads over men.[101]

At the end of the *Bacchae* the royal household has, with help from the god, destroyed itself, with its surviving members to be exiled. But the polis is to benefit (it is now to be endowed with the salutary cult of Dionysos). This pattern, which may be called Dionysiac, reappears in tragedy (again in Thebes) in the three successive disasters of the family of Oidipous, each of which, as we are about to see, involves Dionysos in his role as the enemy of familial introversion, a role he performs through his sexuality, his liberation of women or his imposition of frenzied self-destruction.

10. Tragedy: A Dionysiac Pattern

First, and very briefly, in Sophocles' *Oedipus Tyrannus*, as in the *Bacchae*, the salvation of the polis is linked to the self-destruction of the royal household. As so often, in reality and particularly in myth, the tendency of the household or clan to autonomy takes the form of endogamy.[102] Dionysos is accordingly the enemy of endogamy.[103] And so the chorus' fantasy, just before the catastrophe, that (apparently) Oidipous might turn out to be the son of Dionysos, is the direct opposite of the truth. Dionysos has the same significance in the same *[139]* position (in an optimistic choral song just before the catastrophe) in Sophocles' *Antigone*, as we shall soon see.

Then there are Oidipous' children. In Aeschylus' *Seven against Thebes* King Eteokles, with the enemy at the gates, tries to stop the female chorus running around in flight (191). It is as if the Thebans are being destroyed (194 πορθούμεθα) from within by their own women, he says, and he insists on the spatial and functional division between men and women (200–1), unsuccessfully ordering them inside (201). But in the end he will be lamented by the same chorus, 'maenadic' in their frenzy over the bodies of

[101] The Argive myth contains all these elements, but not in the same combination. In the surviving versions of the Minyads myth the maenadic Minyads are opposed by other maenads, but male opposition does not occur in the associated ritual (Plut. *Quaest. Graec.* 299e–f).

[102] Seaford 1990a. A famous example from Greek history is the Korinthian Bakchiads (Hdt. 5.92). Endogamy and its extreme manifestation as incest (and even endocannibalism) are practices both of tragic kings (τύραννοι) and of the τύραννος in political thought: Pl. *Resp.* 9.571c and 10.619b; Diog. Laert. 1.96 (Periander sleeps with his mother, significantly named Krateia). Incest and endocannibalism: Klymenos and Harpalyke (Hyg. *Fab.* 206; Euphorion fr. 24 Lightfoot); Thyestes and Pelopia (Hyg. *Fab.* 88); Ouranos and Gaia; the sons of Aigyptos (Aesch. *Supp.* 223–6); Pl. *Resp.* 9.571c; cf. Tereus and Philomela and others. See also Lévi-Strauss 1972: 105. In Euripides' *Bacchae* Agaue intends to eat what is in fact Pentheus (1184 and 1242), and an incestuous link between the two is suggested by 812 (cf. 223), taken together with 966–70. See Zeitlin 1990.

[103] Seaford 1988, 1990a.

the 'self-slaughtering' brothers.[104] The city, however, has been saved. The contrast between the salvation of the city and the mutual killing of the royal brothers is stressed twice.[105] The family, it is emphasised several times, has been destroyed.[106] Laios would have saved the polis by having no offspring.[107] Accordingly, the polis is now saved only through the destruction of his line,[108] and this ends the trilogy. The myth, in other versions of which the family in fact lives on, has been reshaped to the Dionysiac pattern.[109] Moreover, the crisis of the play, the point at which Eteokles goes out to fight his brother, is marked by a Dionysiac metaphor that, once again, has not been understood.

'The Erinys of the black goatskin will go out from the house when *[140]* the gods receive sacrifice from hands' (699–700 μελάναιγις ἔξεισι δόμων Ἐρινὺς ὅταν ἐκ χερῶν θεοὶ θυσίαν δέχωνται). These words of the chorus fail to affect Eteokles. In the *Eumenides* (500) Aeschylus bestows the maenadic metaphor on the Furies persecuting Orestes. Similarly, in Euripides' *Orestes* the Erinyes impose a 'Bacchic' frenzy on the matricidal Orestes.[110] The points of correspondence between the Erinyes and maenads are aggressive movement, the frenzy associated with kin-killing and a similarity of appearance and accoutrements such that in vase painting they may be hard to distinguish: they both have snakes, wands or torches and are often similarly dressed.[111]

Now *melanaigis* is, we shall soon see, a Dionysiac term. As with Orestes, the Erinys driving Eteokles is associated with the kin-killing frenzy of a maenad, and that gives ἔξεισι δόμων part of its point: Eteokles, like a maenad, goes out to destroy in a frenzy his household by killing his

104 836 (but cf. §8 above. αὐτοκτόνος (681, 734, 805) refers to the *reflexive* aspect of kin-killing.

105 811–17, 820–1; perhaps at 804 as well (see below). Hutchinson 1985 deletes 820–1. But his only objections are the inept ones that πόλις σέσωται is 'intolerably abrupt and bare' (here stylistic insensitivity combines with the failure to understand the issue of the city's salvation) and that βασιλεύς is 'reserved in fifth-century tragedy for actual monarchs' (this fails to take account of the way in which the brothers are in this part of the play associated with each other – note the dual in 820 – almost to the point of identity; consider 681, for example, as well as the importance of the contrast here between the *royal* household and the polis). Lines 820–1 may originally have been between 803 and 805. Certainly, to delete 804 (with Hutchinson) leaves 803 oddly unanswered until 815. Finally, even were the lines interpolated, this would hardly affect my argument, which is not specifically about Aeschylus.

106 689–91, 801–2, 813, 828 (ἀτέκνους should not of course be changed), 877, 880, 953–60.

107 748–9 θνᾴσκοντα γέννας ἄτερ σῴζειν πόλιν.

108 Note especially 801–2. This logic (somewhat perverse, it is true) escapes those who see in it a reference to saving Thebes from the Epigoni (see Hutchinson 1985: *ad loc.*).

109 Although the old myth may reappear in interpolations: see, for instance, Hutchinson 1985 on 903. Cf. Antigone claiming to be the last of the royal clan (Soph. *Ant.* 941) and so ignoring Ismene.

110 Eur. *Or.* 338, 411, 835.

111 Whallon 1964: 321.

kin. But here, unlike the case of Orestes, the Erinys is actually inspiring the destruction. (The frenzy inspired by the Erinys may, like 'Dionysiac' frenzy, be either a cause or an effect of kin-killing.) And so the Erinys is also associated here, by the term *melanaigis*, with the god who will (unless honoured with sacrifice) inspire kin-killing, namely Dionysos. For *melanaigis*, 'of the black goatskin', occurs elsewhere only as a title of Dionysos. Dionysos Melanaigis had an important cult in Attica.[112] In the briefly recorded aetiological myth, in which he maddens the daughters of Eleuther, there is a clear implication that he enters the house with his black goatskin and drives them out in frenzy.[113] They are restored to sanity by the institution of the cult. Analogously, in the *Seven against Thebes*, the *melanaigis* Erinys will leave the house if the gods are given sacrifices, and so the kin-killing frenzy so often inspired by Dionysos (and here inspired by this Dionysiac Erinys) will be avoided. This gives the phrase ἔξεισι δόμων the other part of its point.

This double association of the Erinys with both maenad and god is *[141]* facilitated by the degree to which Dionysos and his maenads share each other's qualities and attributes (frenzy, animal skins, etc.). The Erinyes also do occasionally wear animal skins,[114] albeit far less frequently than maenads do. The designation of the Erinys as *melanaigis* is facilitated by the Erinyes' black appearance and black clothes, which Aeschylus refers to several times in the *Oresteia*.[115] I have elaborated this point because the latest commentator on the play (Hutchinson 1985) not only fails to notice all this but prefers to take *melanaigis* as a *hapax legomenon* meaning 'like a black storm wind'. This implies the odd idea of a black storm wind *leaving* the house.

In Antigone's case the tendency of the household to autonomy is represented not only by her flouting of the public edict by performing death ritual for her dead kin but also (cf. n. 102) by various suggestions that the family of Oidipous remains doomed to catastrophic endogamy: in particular, Antigone's explicit prioritisation of natal kin over marriage, and her being left to die in confinement, such confinement being in Greek myth generally a symbol of familial introversion.[116] As in the *Oedipus Tyrannus*,

112 Schol. Ar. *Ach*. 146; Nonnus, *Dion*. 27.302; [Parker 2005: 460].

113 *Suda*, s.v. 'Melan': (1) they see a φάσμα of Dionysos with his black goatskin – no doubt in their house (as in other myths of this type); (2) ἐξέμηνεν cf. Eur. *Bacch*. 36 ἐξέμηνα δωμάτων; (3) the name Eleutherai seems to derive from the thiasos of females driven 'free' from their homes, who in the aetiological myth become the daughters of Eleuther.

114 *LIMC*, s.v. 'Erinys' nos. 11 and 109.

115 Aesch. *Ag*. 462, *Cho*. 1049, *Eum*. 52, 352, 370; cf. Eur. *El*. 1345, *Or*. 321, 408.

116 Seaford 1990a.

just before the catastrophe the chorus sings to Dionysos (1140–5): 'As the polis with its whole people is in the grip of a violent disease, come with purifying foot over the Parnassian slope or the sounding channel.' As so often, Dionysos is to come from outside to liberate the female, in the interest of the whole city (πάνδαμος πόλις), from a confinement that expresses the introversion of the household.[117]

Euripides' version of the myth reproduces essentially the same complex of ideas. The suggestions of a quasi-erotic relationship between Antigone and her brother are stronger than in Sophocles. The destruction of the household is expressed, as we have seen, in the maenadic metaphor for Antigone. And the ending of the *Phoenician Women*, whether genuine or not, expresses the victory of the tendency of the household to introversion: Antigone fiercely rejects marriage, expressing the desire to 'lie next to' her brother and to stay with, and [142] die with, her father. It is highly appropriate that along with all this she should reject the invitation to become (once more) a maenad.[118] Accordingly, when in Euripides' lost *Antigone* Antigone does marry and have offspring she also appears as a maenad.[119] In these three versions of the story of Antigone the Dionysiac has, in its various forms (invocation of the god, Dionysiac metaphor, rejection of maenadism, maenadism), the same essential significance.

11. Homeric Exclusions

I return finally to my initial question: Why is Dionysos almost entirely absent from Homer? The old answers – that Homer predates the arrival of Dionysos in Greece and that as a god of the common people Dionysos was of little interest to the aristocratic Homeric milieu – have been shown by others to be untenable: Dionysos was neither newly arrived nor a god merely of the common people.[120] In fact the near absence of Dionysos from Homer is, we shall see, part of the near absence from Homer of a whole complex of ideas that is frequent in tragedy.

The case of Andromakhe, which shares so much with our tragic passages, is in fact unique in Homer. It combines (as we saw at the beginning of

[117] There is also a suggestion here of his role in the polis festival of the Eleusinian mysteries, in which Persephone was liberated from below the earth: Seaford 1990a: 88.

[118] For the detail of this argument see Seaford 1990a; cf. my discussion at the beginning of §8 above.

[119] Seaford 1990a: 89.

[120] See especially Privitera 1970. His own explanation is in terms of genre: Dionysos, for the aristocratic tradition, has his own kind of poetry and is unsuitable as a theme for other kinds. This may be true as far as it goes.

this chapter) detailed attention to the irreversible destruction of a household with the permanent subversion of ritual, and the maenadic metaphor. The first two of these are in Homer most unusual, and the third unique, whereas in tragedy they are frequent and belong together. The exits of Andromakhe represent a pattern that is both tragic and Dionysiac and as such unique in Homer.[121] They are [143] also, let it be mentioned in passing, among those passages argued (on quite different grounds) to be relatively late in the *Iliad*.[122]

This tragic complex of ideas (the destruction of the household, the permanent subversion of ritual, the Dionysiac) includes two further phenomena, which are accordingly also excluded from Homer, namely, violence between members of the same household, and frenzy (outside battle). I shall take these two in turn.

First, the central narratives of the *Iliad* and the *Odyssey* are entirely without violence between members of the same kinship group. And stories in which it occurs are on the whole either not mentioned or mentioned in versions in which it is almost or entirely excluded – for example, the punishment of Lykourgos for opposing Dionysos is to be blinded by Zeus, not the frenzied killing of his wife and son that we find imposed on him by Dionysos in classical vase painting, which probably reflects Aeschylus' version of the story.[123]

Second, not only the frenzy of Lykourgos but frenzy in general (outside battle) is largely excluded from Homer. In particular, the noun λύσσα ('frenzy') and the verb μαίνεσθαι ('to be maddened') and their cognates are, when used of human beings, almost entirely confined to frenzy directed against the alien group, the frenzy of battle. There are six exceptions, and they all prove the rule.

The first exception, and the only hint of the word λύσσα (outside battle), is the verb ἀλύσσω, a form of ἀλύω thought to have been influenced by λύσσα.[124] The verb is used by Priam (*Il.* 22.70) of the dogs who will drink his blood and disfigure his corpse, dogs whom he has raised, he says, at his own table. The same idea is found in the *Bacchae*: the example of Aktaion,

[121] It may be no coincidence that they contain another example of pathetically dislocated ritual, so rare in Homer but frequent in tragedy: sent back to the house by her husband, Andromakhe laments him (with the maids), even though he still lives (*Il.* 6.500 αἱ μὲν ἔτι ζῶον γόον Ἕκτορα ᾧ ἐνὶ οἴκῳ). Cf., among other examples, Aesch. *Ag.* 1322–3; Soph. *Ant.* 801–22.

[122] Shipp 1972: 256 and 311.

[123] Sutton 1975a; Apollod. *Bibl.* 3.5.1 Further examples: Seaford 1989a[13]: 87. See also Carpenter 1993: 198–9.

[124] Chantraine 1968–80: s.v. ἀλύω. Cf. Hom. *Il.* 8.299 κύνα λυσσητῆρα (military). Even the verb ἀλύω in Homer is used (of human beings) only of Akhilleus (*Il.* 24.12); see further on Akhilleus below.

'whom the raw-eating dogs he reared tore apart' (338–9), prefigures the tearing apart of Pentheus by the 'dogs of frenzy' (977). The frenzy of Priam's dogs accompanies both the violence inflicted on a member of the same household *and* the negation of ritual (death ritual).

The remaining exceptions are as follows. The participle μαινόμενος [*144*] ('raving mad') is used of the entirely passive Dionysos in the Lykourgos narrative. And Andromakhe is twice compared to a maenad. In the fifth exception, Zeus disapproves of Akhilleus retaining the corpse of Hektor 'with his heart in a mad rage' (*Il.* 24.114 φρεσὶ μαινομένῃσιν). Here again, frenzy threatens the performance of death ritual, disfigurement of the corpse this time not by dogs but by a human being. But this threat occupies, significantly, a central role in the structure of the *Iliad*, an importance expressed in its unique status in the poem as attracting something like merely moral disapproval from the gods: the narrative closure of the *Iliad* is achieved by the resolution of the anomaly caused precisely by this frenzy of Akhilleus. Both Akhilleus' frenzied, isolating, excessive revenge and the consequent negation of death ritual are ended in his surrender of the corpse to Priam for the public funeral that concludes the poem.

There was a comparable kind of closure in the version of the *Odyssey* that ended at 23.296 with the arrival of Odysseus and Penelope at the bed where they celebrated their first nuptials; for it can be shown that the disorderly, prolonged feasting of the suitors represents a subversion of the due ritual process of the wedding, and that ritual normality is restored by the reunion of Odysseus with Penelope, which is described in a series of parallels to the wedding ritual that culminates in 23.296.[125] The culmination of *subversion* of the marriage process, in the suitors' disorderly feasting, is marked by Telemakhos' accusation that they are 'raving mad' (*Od.* 18.406 μαίνεσθε).[126] This is the sixth and final exception. And so each of the exceptions is associated with one or more of the elements of our tragic complex of ideas: violence within the household, the negation of ritual, and the Dionysiac.

The restoration of ritual normality in the *Odyssey* is also the restoration of the threatened household.[127] The *Iliad* also concludes in ritual restored, but

[125] For this whole argument see Seaford 1994b: 30–73.

[126] This occurs just after the suitors' own admission that 'worse behaviour was prevailing' (404 τὰ χερείονα νικᾷ) at the house. It is significant that one of the (rare) applications of μαίνεσθαι to non-humans is to the centaurs' drunken disruption of Peirithous' wedding (*Od.* 21.298).

[127] The inadequacy of the household ritual to restore *public* order to Ithaca required at a certain point the addition to the narrative of that part of the 'continuation' in which the inevitable dispute between Odysseus and the kin of the dead suitors is resolved.

one that is public, performed by the whole community *[145]* of Trojans and recognised in the truce agreed by the Greeks; whereas the wedding ritual of Andromakhe remains, in contrast to Penelope's, irreversibly negated. Her household is, despite restoration of ritual normality in the public sphere, irreversibly destroyed. And so Andromakhe's frenzied negation of ritual remains, in contrast to Akhilleus', in the end uncontained.[128]

This implicit distinction between household and community is prefigured in the scene between Hektor and Andromakhe in Book 6, a scene perhaps unique in Homer for its stark presentation of the contradiction between a man's feelings for his family and his feeling for his community.[129] Andromakhe tries to move Hektor by describing what will happen to his family if he continues to take the fight to the Greeks and is killed. But Hektor then sends her back home to weave. With the strongest statement that exists in Homer of a man's sense of duty to the community (441–6) he contains the threat that her 'maenadic frenzy' poses to the spatial and functional differentiation of male and female in the city (see §2 above).

Hektor's duty to the community threatens to destroy his household. Hence Andromakhe's maenadic frenzy. And so the contradiction between household and community is here at the heart of our tragic complex of ideas. That is why the contradiction, like the complex, is frequent in tragedy but in Homer unique to the case of Andromakhe. This suggests, moreover, a historical explanation for the near absence of the complex in Homer. Also nearly absent from Homer is the functioning polis. This is, at least partly, because Homeric epic is the product of an earlier stage in the development of the polis than is tragedy. Whatever the prehistory of Dionysos, there was something in it that qualified him for an important role in the development of the polis.[130] Homeric epic partly pre-dates and partly excludes this role and this development. The near absence of the functioning polis from Homer entails the near absence of the contradiction between polis *[146]* and household, of non-military frenzy, of violence within the household, of the permanent subversion of ritual and of the expression of these anomalies in the Dionysiac.

The statement that the polis barely functions in Homer may, I am aware, be controversial, but it cannot be demonstrated at length here.

128 Despite Hektor's containment of it in Book 6 and despite the (no doubt traditional) expression of her feelings about the destruction of her household in the due process of lamentation in Book 24.

129 See, among others, Arthur 1981.

130 See n. 88 above. This is to say that Dionysos' new role (e.g. he seems to have taken over ancient cults of Artemis at Patrai – see §9 – and Argos: the various versions of the Proetids myth) is no doubt an adaptation of his earlier one.

Let it be said merely that all the main features of the polis (an assembly conducting public business, a judicial authority, state organisation in general, an urban centre with public buildings, communal ritual, citizenship, a sense of belonging to a polis, and so on) are either entirely absent from the Homeric narrative or, if present, marginal or ineffective. For example, all that can be found in Homer to compare with the religious festival of the polis is contained in three passages, of which by far the most substantial is the account of the offering made to Athena in her temple on behalf of the city by some noblewomen of Troy led by Hekabe.[131] This exception actually provides another link in our argument, for it is in fact in the sixth book of the *Iliad*. Hekabe is instructed by Hektor to perform the offering. And it is shortly thereafter, when Hektor returns to his own home and finds Andromakhe absent, that he asks the question that produces in reply the Dionysiac metaphor: 'No, she has gone neither to see her sisters-in-law nor to the temple of Athena with the other Trojan women to propitiate the goddess. She has gone rather to the city wall like a maenad.' The women's offering to Athena represents a role for women in the public sphere, a role instigated by the man who is himself uniquely associated with the public sphere, Hektor. It is not coincidental that the full significance of this ritual, by far the closest in Homer to a polis cult, emerges in the contrast it provides to the maenadic action of Andromakhe. In this action, circumscribed in Book 6 but reactivated in Book 22, we approach the world of tragedy. But tragedy, it is I hope no longer unfashionable to say, actually originates in polis cult, a cult celebrating the potentially catastrophic triumph of Dionysos Eleuthereus, or Liberator, originally perhaps the liberator of women from their homes.[132]

POSTSCRIPT

The Dionysiac content of Athenian tragedy was the theme of two other papers in the same volume: R. Schlesier, 'Mixtures of masks: maenads as tragic models' (chapter 4), and Froma Zeitlin, 'Staging Dionysus between Thebes and Athens' (chapter 6). See also D. Pozzi, 'Deianira

[131] Hom. *Il.* 6.297–311 (note line 300, the priestess appointed by the 'Trojans'). Cf. *Od.* 3.57–9 and 20.276–8 (cf. 21.258–9).

[132] The epithet Eleuthereus may mean just 'of Eleutherai', but Eleutherai itself may derive from the women running 'free' from their homes (cf. e.g. the place names Aphetai and Klazomenai), i.e. liberated by Dionysos: see n. 113 above and Thomson 1946: 172. Dionysos as liberator: see e.g. n. 117 above; Eur. *Bacch.* 445, 498, 613, 649; Connor (1989). Plutarch (*Mor.* 716b) takes Dionysos Eleuthereus to be (psychic) 'Liberator'.

vere Oenei filia', *Hermes* 124 (1996), 104–8; A. Henrichs, '"Why should I dance?": choral self-referentiality in Greek tragedy', *Arion* 3 (1994–5) 56–111; F. Zeitlin, 'Intimate relations: children, childbearing, and parentage on the Euripidean stage', in M. Revermann and P. Wilson (eds.), *Performance, Iconography, Reception: Studies in Honour of Oliver Taplin* (Oxford: Oxford University Press, 2008), pp. 318–32; and 'Re-reading Dionysos in the theater', in R. Schlesier (ed.), *A Different God? Dionysos and Ancient Polytheism* (Berlin and New York: De Gruyter, 2011), pp. 535–51.

The theme is taken further, and integrated into a broader context, in Seaford 1994b and Seaford 2012a. For the opposing view, that there is nothing Dionysiac about the content of tragedy, see Friedrich 1996, with my reply in the same volume (Seaford 1996b). A contrasting (or complementary?) account of the tragic representation of ruling families is by M. Griffith, 'Brilliant dynasts: power and politics in the *Oresteia*', *ClAnt* 14 (1995), 62–129.

A critique of various political interpretations of Attic tragedy (including mine) is by J. Griffin, 'The social function of Attic tragedy', *CQ* 48 (1998), 39–61 (see also my response, Seaford 2000d). Another critique of various political interpretations of tragedy (including mine) is by D. M. Carter, *The Politics of Greek Tragedy* (Exeter: Bristol Phoenix, 2007). See also the exchange between Rainer Friedrich and myself, on ritual and politics in tragedy, in *Arion* 7.3 (2000), 113–52; 8.2 (2000), 74–98; 9.1 (2001), 57–72; 9.3 (2002), 166–8.

A comprehensive account of intrafamilial violence in Attic tragedy is by E. Belfiore, *Murder Among Friends: Violation of Philia in Greek Tragedy* (Oxford: Oxford University Press, 2000). For the representation of Dionysos in drama see A. Bierl, 'Dionysos auf der Bühne: gattungsspezifische Aspekte des Theatergottes in Tragödie, Satyrspiel und Komödie', in R. Schlesier (ed.), *A Different God? Dionysos and Ancient Polytheism* (Berlin and New York: De Gruyter, 2011), pp. 315–41. Further recent work on Dionysos is listed in this volume in the postscript to Chapter 3.

For the extension of the theme to Vergil's *Aeneid* see E. Krummen, 'Dido als Mänade und tragische Heroine: Dionysische Thematik und Tragödientradition in Vergils Didoerzählung', *Poetica* 36.1/2 (2004), 25–69; V. Panoussi, *Greek Tragedy in Vergil's Aeneid: Ritual, Empire, and Intertext* (Cambridge: Cambridge University press, 2009), chapter 4.

CHAPTER 3

Dionysos, Money and Drama

The sixth-century Greek polis was almost certainly the first thoroughly monetised society in history. This radical transformation of social relations was accompanied by – and influenced – radical cultural transformation, notably the development of metaphysics and of sophisticated drama. This is the argument of my *Money and the Early Greek Mind* (Seaford: 2004c). Here I take the argument further by suggesting a new way of thinking about the Dionysiac that involves its relationship to monetisation. This does not, of course, include every aspect of the god. My main focus is on the Dionysiac thiasos and on the drama that developed out of its celebrations.

Money and the Dionysiac Thiasos

In the most powerful turning point in ancient drama, Dionysos in Euripides' *Bacchae* (811) asks Pentheus whether he would like to see the maenads sitting together in the mountains. Pentheus, suddenly abandoning his stubborn and aggressive resistance, replies 'Yes, very much so.' This is surprising enough. But he then adds, no less surprisingly, 'I would give an enormous weight of gold [to do so].' In my commentary on the play I called this offer odd, and failed to see its significance, referring only to contemporary evidence for the payment of fees for mystic initiation.

Why does this key moment focus on money? It cannot be explained as *merely* a way of expressing Pentheus' strong desire, like the modern 'I would give a lot of money to ...' (an expression relatively rare in ancient literature).[2]

The first step in an answer is to consider the reaction of the chorus in their next song. They ask 'What is the wise or the finer (κάλλιον) gift from the gods among mortals? Is it to hold the hand powerful over the head of your enemies? What is fine is dear always' (with 'always' emphasised by the word order). This means that power over enemies, being transient, is *not* what is wise and fine.[1] The chorus then utter a *makarismos* of the kind delivered in mystic initiation ('blessed is he who has escaped the storm …'), in which they compare the uncertainties of competition in *wealth and power* unfavourably with the blessedness (permanent happiness) of the here and now conferred by mystic initiation (902–11).

Whether we keep the comparative κάλλιον or read the superlative κάλλιστον, the sense of the chorus' question is 'what is best for humankind?' The same question is put by Midas to the old satyr Silenos (or simply to a 'satyr'), whom he has captured (Aristotle fr. 44 Rose). Silenos responds by calling Midas 'ephemeral', and reveals that for humankind the best thing is never to have been born, the second best to die as soon as possible. As a reward for releasing Silenos, Midas is offered by Dionysos (or by Silenos himself) the fulfilment of any wish,[2] which is in effect equivalent to the question 'what is best for humankind?' He chooses money – the power to transform all things by his touch into gold – and subsequently regrets the choice when his food becomes gold.

Midas' touch is the reaction of the Greek mythical imagination to the new (unknown in Homer) and astonishing power of precious metal as universal equivalent. A negative aspect of this power is that all things may be seen in terms of money: absorption in happiness in the abstract (money) may become incapacity for happiness in the concrete. But why is it the animalistic Silenos who is set against the man of money?

Silenos belongs outside and prior to the polis, to the world of nature, of use-value unmediated by money. And so he speaks to Midas 'about natural and ancient things'.[3] Plato (*Leg.* 7.815c) tells us that 'initiations performed by people imitating satyrs and silens' are 'not of the polis' (οὐ πολιτικόν).[3] The mystic initiate may acquire the pre-monetary identity and immortal happiness of the satyr or silen,[4] and the immortal Silenos disdains the mortality of even the wealthiest uninitiated. The question 'who is happiest?' might receive the answer 'the wealthiest' that Kroisos expects from Solon (Hdt. 1.30). But wealth, as Kroisos discovers, may be transient. Another answer is provided by the mystic *makarismos*: 'blessed (permanently happy) is he who …', as in the *Bacchae*. Midas is not only instructed by Silenos

[1] See Seaford 1996a: 218–19.

[2] Ov. *Met.* 11.100–4; Hygin. *Fab.* 191; Serv. *ad* Verg. *Aen.* 10.142; Max. Tyr. 11. Dionysos does not appear in the early versions of the story, but it was precisely the affinity of the satyrs with Dionysos that brought them so inseparably together.

[3] Serv. *ad* Verg. *Ecl.* 6.13, after Theopompus (*FGrH* 115 F75).

[4] See Seaford 1984b: 8–9.

but in one version actually initiated into the Dionysiac or Orphic mysteries, recognises Silenos as a fellow member of the thiasos, is saved from his own monetary power by Dionysos and thereafter dwells in the wild, worshipping Pan.[5] Similarly, the experiences of Pentheus in the *Bacchae* reflect those of the mystic initiand,[6] and he – like Midas facing Silenos – confronts in Dionysos a combination of humanity, animality and immortality. But Pentheus, who is unable to imagine that Teiresias' motive for embracing the new cult is other than monetary gain (257), remains the man of money even at the point of his apparent transformation, for he imagines in terms of money even the forbidden sight promised to him (812). This then is the point of his offer of gold.

Silenos' disdain for mortality has a special point in relation to Midas as the man of money. Money intervenes between humankind and nature, and this intervention has a temporal dimension. Money always embodies the deferral of the enjoyment of what it may subsequently purchase. As 'Money' says to Philip Larkin, 'I am all you never had of goods and sex / – you could get them still by writing a few cheques.' With money used as a store of wealth, deferral may even extend beyond the lifetime of its owner, especially as monetary value – in order to function – must be envisaged as permanent. The accumulation of money may therefore imply forgetfulness of mortality, in contrast to the eternity bestowed by the death-like ordeals of mystic initiation. Aristotle says that Silenos had in mind that existence after death is preferable to life. Nobody is more suitable to remind Midas of his [4] ephemerality than Silenos, who combines immortality with *immediacy* of enjoyment (and in some versions of the story he is drunk). Similarly, the chorus of the *Bacchae* praise the eternal happiness conferred by mystic initiation on the here and now.

In a fragment of Pindar (fr. 157), Silenos calls the famous pipe-player Olympos 'ephemeral' – as he did Midas – and adds 'you say foolish things to me in boasting of money (χρήματα)'. Similarly, in Aristophanes' *Clouds*, Sokrates addresses the money-seeking Strepsiades as 'ephemeral' and submits him to a kind of mystic initiation. In Plato's *Symposium*, part of the point of the comparison of Sokrates to a satyr or silen is that he despises wealth.[7]

[5] Ov. *Met.* 11.93–4, 134–47; Konon *FGrH* 26 F1; Clem. Al. *Protr.* 2.13.1; Justin 11.7.14; Luck 1969: 470–7. In one version Midas creates a spring of gold, which Dionysos transforms into water: Alexander Polyhistor *FGrH* 273 F76.

[6] See Seaford 1996a.

[7] 216d4–e4 (cf. 218e5–7). Usher 2002 compares the *Symposium* episode to a satyr play and to the Midas episode, but without considering the theme of money.

In the Pindar fragment, Silenos speaks probably as Olympos' teacher of the pipe (*aulos*), drawing a distinction between the use-value and the exchange-value of its music (though without, of course, using those terms). The *aulos* is in one version of the myth discovered but discarded by Athena, and then taken up by the satyr Marsyas, who teaches it to Olympos. This seems to have been the theme of a lost satyr play (*fr. trag. adesp.* 381). In satyric drama, the Dionysiac thiasos of Silenos and the satyrs is characteristically present at inventions, notably of the equipment of their revels: wine, the *tympanon* and the lyre, as well as the *aulos*. We can locate the thiasos not just between nature and culture but more specifically at the very point at which culture is extracted from nature – the sound of the lyre from the tortoise, wine from the grape and so on. Olympos, like the Dionysiac musician Arion who made money from music (Hdt. 1.24), is – in the human sphere – concerned with the exchange-value of Dionysiac music, whereas the immortal Silenos and satyrs, being present at its emergence from nature, are concerned only with its use-value. Silenos depicted on coinage, notably in Sicily, transcends the limitation inherent in money by suggesting the more immediate pleasure of the local wine.

Another very common theme of satyric drama is the captivity of the satyrs by a powerful or wealthy individual. This theme had the advantage of explaining the presence of the thiasos [5] in new contexts; but it did in fact pre-date the drama, for the capture of Silenos by Midas is shown in vase painting from the second quarter of the sixth century.[8] Its association in the Midas myth with money continues, in a different form, into satyric drama. In Euripides' *Cyclops*, for instance, the Homeric cannibal Polyphemos has become a sophisticated man of substance, equipped with slaves (the satyrs) and cattle in addition to his Homeric sheep. 'Wealth', he proclaims, 'is god for the wise; the rest is empty rhetoric' (316–17).

Earlier, Odysseus had arrived to find Silenos and the satyrs at Polyphemos' cave. He tells Silenos to 'sell' him food, and Silenos asks him how much gold he will 'give in return' (138). Odysseus replies that he has no gold but the 'drink of Dionysos'. Silenos, long without wine, tastes it and is so excited that, when Odysseus also offers currency (νόμισμα), he rejects it, maintaining instead that he would for a single cup of wine 'give in return' all the flocks of all the Kyklopes. Why does Odysseus first say he has no gold but then offer νόμισμα (160)? Because what he offers is fifth-century (and so *silver*) coinage? That would be a subtlety lost in the joke

[8] *LIMC* 8.850. See Roller 1984. Aristotle (fr. 44 Rose) says that the story has been popular for many years.

that Odysseus cunningly offers money only once it is unnecessary. Silenos is made to ask about gold so that he can then, once immersed in the immediate pleasure of wine and indifferent to all else, change his mind and say 'forget the gold coin' (161). Odysseus belongs to the fifth-century world of sale and coinage, whereas Silenos, who speaks of 'giving in return', seems to belong to the older world of gift exchange or barter. In fact, even barter is for Silenos too calculating, for after tasting the wine he loses all sense of *equal* exchange.

Euripides' *Cyclops* is the only satyr play to have survived complete. The fragments of satyric drama contain several suggestions of our contrast between the immediate pleasures of the Dionysiac thiasos and concern with money.

In Aeschylus' satyric *Theoroi*, the satyrs are said to waste their master's money (fr. 78a.35). In Sophocles' fragmentary *Ichneutai*, in which the satyrs are present at Hermes' invention of the lyre, the reward promised by Apollo to the satyrs for [6] finding his cattle consists of their freedom, and of gold. It is significant that the gold is welcomed by Silenos *not as money* but as a gold crown which he looks forward to *wearing*.[9] From another (probably satyric) play, we have the fragment 'for a hungry man barley-cake is more valuable than gold and ivory'.[10] In a fragment of Euripides' satyric *Eurystheus* (fr. 378), someone complains that a man with money has first place, and power over people better than himself: this suggests that the pre-monetary myth of the labours performed by Herakles in vassalage to Eurystheus has been transformed into a story of the power of money to command labour.

In Euripides' *Skiron*, the satyrs are the servants of the ogre Skiron. The longest fragment (fr. 675) is as follows: 'These you can take, if you give one young horse, those if you give a pair. These are going for four silver horses. They (the girls) like an Athenian if he brings a lot of virgins.' The horses and virgins are the images stamped on Korinthian (Pegasos) and Athenian (Athena) coins. There is mention in the fragmentary papyrus hypothesis of prostitutes.[11] And so the speaker (Silenos? a satyr?) of the fragment is probably the keeper of a brothel belonging to Skiron (robber turned businessman?), trying to sell the prostitutes' favours. It seems that there is

[9] Fr. 314.51 (cf. 162, 208). The incorruptibility of gold suits the eternity aspired to by Dionysiac mystery cult (e.g. the funerary gold leaves).

[10] Achaeus, *Kyknos*, *TrGF* I fr. 25.

[11] *P. Oxy.* 2455 fr. 6.86 (*TrGF* V.2, p. 660).

proposed, as in *Cyclops*, an exchange of money for something valued by the thiasos (in *Cyclops* wine, in *Skiron* sex). And in both cases a member of the thiasos affirms his belonging to the old world of (Dionysiac) use-value by distancing himself from the inherent uselessness of coinage, in *Cyclops* by rejecting it completely in comparison with wine, in Skiron by identifying the coins (as if unable to appreciate their merely monetary value) with the young horses or virgins stamped on them, both of which are appropriate in an erotic context.[12]

Given these various suggestions of our theme in the sparse remains of satyric drama, we may infer that the opposition [7] between the pre-monetary solidarity of the Dionysiac thiasos and the monetised world inhabited by the mortal individuals (especially the satyrs' captor) was a general theme of the genre. In both the extant dramas with a Dionysiac thiasos as chorus, *Cyclops* and *Bacchae*, the powerful individual is the failed captor of the thiasos and hostile to its celebrations, and yet eventually succumbs to it in a manner that reflects mystic initiation.[13] This too may have been a generic theme. In the *Bacchae* there is a striking contrast between, on the one hand, the solidarity of the thiasos, for whom the happiness conferred by mystic initiation involves 'merging the soul with the thiasos' (75 θιασεύεται ψυχάν), and, on the other, the stubborn isolation of Pentheus, impervious to both advice and manifestations of deity, and finally killed by his own mother. In *Cyclops*, Polyphemos praises wealth as allowing him self-sufficient isolation (316–46). Contemptuous of deity, he happily dines alone in his cave and then masturbates: isolation here reaches an extreme form.

It remains to mention one more similarity between Pentheus and the monstrous giant Polyphemos. Pentheus' father, Ekhion, one of the warriors that sprang from the dragon's teeth sown in the earth by Kadmos, is a shadowy figure who does not appear in the play. But he is mentioned by the chorus in their attribution of Pentheus' oppressiveness to his inhuman monstrosity: 'Ekhion the chthonic begot [Pentheus] a wild-faced monster (τέρας), not a mortal man, but like a slaughtering giant' (540–4) and 'an earth-born offspring' (996).

12 Desirable girls as young horses: Anacreon fr. 417; Alcman fr. 1.46–9; Thgn. 257–60; Eubulus fr. 82.2; Epicrates fr. 8.3–4. This is not of course to say that the practice of referring to coins by their images was *confined* to satyrs.

13 Note especially *Bacch.* 443–4; *Cyc.* 203–21; etc. See Seaford 1996a and 1984b: *ad locc.*

Tragic Isolation

According to Aristotle, tragedy developed 'from the satyr-play-like' (ἐκ σατυρικοῦ). Satyric drama and tragedy were creations of the polis, and performed in the city, but the initiations performed by satyrs and silens are, according to Plato (*Leg.* 7.815c), 'not of the polis' (οὐ πολιτικόν). In the predramatic myth, Midas captures Silenos under Mt [8] Bermion, in his gardens where wild roses grow (Hdt. 8.138). In satyric drama, the tension between the Dionysiac thiasos and the isolated individual is contained within the satyric milieu of rural remoteness. The traditional ogre in the wild, such as Skiron, becomes the isolated man of money. Polyphemos – free of respect for nature, contemptuous of deity and of reciprocity, self-sufficient (even sexually), worshipping only wealth (*Cyc.* 316–46) – is, despite his sophistication, isolated in his remote cave.

There is another factor that, in both *Cyclops* and *Bacchae*, contributes to the impervious isolation of the monstrous man of money. This is the mythical projection of the *isolation of the initiand*[14] in the preliminary stage of mystic ritual preceding the antithetical 'merging of the soul with the thiasos' (*Bacch.* 75) that the chorus mention as a blessing of initiation. Ritual isolation and monetary isolation converge.

But despite this similarity, tragedy, in contrast to the satyric, belongs entirely to the polis. The behaviour of Pentheus expresses not only the isolated resistance of the initiand and the isolated inhumanity of the monstrous ogre but also the impervious isolation of the political man of money, the tyrant. Both satyric drama and tragedy represent a synthesis of elements from ritual, performance traditions (notably choral lyric) and historical experience. But it was only in tragedy, the urban offspring of the 'satyr-play-like', that the mythical expression of the anxious resistance overcome in mystic ritual became (in a narrow sense) political. More precisely, it merged with a typical theme found in aetiological myths of polis cults, namely the initial unsuccessful resistance to the new cult.[15] An opposition within mystic ritual, between the recalcitrant isolation of the initiand and his eventual incorporation into the group, might come in tragedy to express a political opposition, between tyrant and people. Just as

[14] Seaford 1994b: 281–301; and note the mystic context of *Bacch.* 609. Initiation was, unlike many other rituals, a matter of individual choice (Hdt. 4.79.1, 8.65.4). We know of several mystic formulae uttered by, and others addressed to, the individual (notably inscribed on the gold leaves). At Eleusis the initiand was at one stage veiled, and there was a transition from the panic of a chaotic mass of individuals to communal joy (Plut. fr. 178; cf. Ar. *Ran.* 156–7).

[15] E.g. the cult of Dionysos in Attica: *Suda*, s.v. Melanaigis; Hygin. *Fab.* 225; Schol. Ar. *Ach.* 243.

the Athenian tyrant Peisistratos seems to have identified himself with the mythical Herakles,[16] so conversely the mythical individuals of tragedy tend to acquire the characteristics of historical tyrants.[9]

In contrast to older forms of socio-economic mediation (reciprocity, redistribution, even barter) money tends to isolate the individual.[17] Its general impersonal power to command the labour of others (together with its ease of total possessibility, of concealment, of storage, of self-reproduction and of transport) tends to reduce the importance of interrelations. This takes its extreme form – in the personal Greek imagination and quite possibly (up to a point) in their historical reality – in the figure of the tyrant represented in Herodotus, tragedy, Plato and various other texts. This figure is typically isolated from the gods by his perversion of the sacred, and from his own kin by violent conflict, even though he may practice endogamy. All this is for the sake of tyranny and individual possession of the money that obtains and sustains tyranny.[18] We refer to tragic 'heroes', but extant tragedy itself does not, nor does any ancient writer on tragedy. Tragedy rather uses the root *tyrann-*, even more frequently than *basil(eu)-*. We will confine ourselves here to three such 'tyrants': Pentheus, Oidipous and Kreon.

In the *Oedipus Tyrannus* of Sophocles, *tyrann-* appears fifteen times. Oidipous embodies, in the extreme form characteristic of myth, the historical ambivalence of the tyrant as both benefiting and harming the polis.[19] Like Pentheus, he suffers violent isolation from his closest kin as well as from deity. And like Pentheus, he imagines that any challenge to his outlook is motivated by money (124–5, 380–6, 388). For the chorus, the downfall of the tyrant results from hubris that is 'overfilled with many things in vain' and from unjust gain (κέρδος) associated with unholy things and touching the untouchable (873–91).

When Oidipous states (542) that it is with money and a host of friends that tyranny is obtained,[20] this seems odd, for he acquired his tyranny not in fact thus, but by solving the riddle of the Sphinx. Whereas mythical monsters are generally overcome by force, and with the help of deity, Oidipous solves the riddle merely by his own intelligence, without the

[16] Boardman 1972, 1975.
[17] E.g. Simmel 1978; Bloch 1989: 179; Parry and Bloch 1989: 4–6; Stirrat 1989: 100–1.
[18] See Seaford 2003d[5].
[19] E.g. Arist. *Pol.* 1313a34–1315b10; Thuc. 2.15.5, 6.54.5–6, but cf. 6.53.3; the conflicting traditions about Periander tyrant of Korinth.
[20] And having friends itself depends – as both comedy and tragedy observe – on having money: e.g. Ar. *Plut.* 834–8; Soph. fr. 88.1; Eur. *Phoen.* 402–5, *Supp.* 601–7.

help of deity.[21] In some versions he then kills her or she commits [*10*] suicide, but in tragedy his victory consists in solving the riddle, with emphasis on his intelligence.[22] The Sphinx, like Silenos, combines a wild location, humanity, animality, divinity and ancient wisdom transmitted through initiation.[23] In several vase paintings Oidipous confronts the Sphinx seated on a pedestal, but in one she is replaced by a seated satyr.[24]

However, in a reversal of the relationship between Silenos and Midas, the wisdom of the Sphinx is defeated by the intelligence of the isolated mortal. She, despite her ancient and divine origin (e.g. Hes. *Theog.* 326), ceases to exist, and he thereby obtains marriage, wealth and tyranny – but only at the cost of polluting the polis and eventually realising the catastrophe of his isolation. To this catastrophe the chorus respond 'alas generations of men, how I calculate you as equal to nothing', and deny the possibility of bestowing permanent happiness on any mortal by *makarismos*.[25] Oidipous should not have been born (according to the oracle given to Laios), and wishes that he had died as a baby (1354, 1391–2). The ancient wisdom of Silenos has in the end prevailed. It is in the appearance of omnipotent autonomy that the individual mortal is revealed – by his own autonomous intelligence – as in fact most wretched. It is *hybris* that begets the tyrant (873). Just as in Aristotle's account Silenos tells Midas that the most painless life requires ignorance, so Iokaste counsels ignorance (1068) and Kadmos reflects that by remaining permanently deluded the Theban maenads would be spared suffering (*Bacch.* 1259–62).

Whom does Oidipous represent? One answer has been that his autonomous, self-confident versatility represents the fifth-century Athenian.[26] These qualities depend in part, I suggest, on monetisation. The power conferred by money on the individual Athenian (as opposed to the moneyless Spartan) over a vast range of goods and services tends to reduce the need for interpersonal relationships such as reciprocity (even, it may seem, with deity) and kinship, and is limited only by the amount of money he possesses. The tragic tyrant takes this autonomy to its disastrous extreme.[*11*]

[21] *OT* 395–8 (seeming to reject 38). Cf. Eur. *Oedipus* frr. 548, 552. The importance of this is stressed by Goux 1993: 13–19.

[22] *OT* 37–8, 396–8, 509, [1525]; Eur. *Phoen.* 48–50, 1731, [1759].

[23] Initiation: Goux 1993: 40–59 (add that riddles are frequent in initiation). Wisdom: e.g. Eur. *Phoen.* 48; *RE* 3A.1725.

[24] *LIMC*, s.v. Eumas. In one version, occurring perhaps in Euripides, it is Dionysos who sends the Sphinx against Thebes: *RE* 3A.1707. Some coins of Chios have an ensemble of vine, amphora and Sphinx.

[25] 1186–96; cf. Oidipous' wedding *makarismos* at 420–3, 1281–4.

[26] Knox 1957: 67–77. Note especially also Thuc. 1.70.6, 2.41.1–2.

In as much as the tragic tyrant belongs – unlike the monster of satyric drama – to the polis, he must reproduce. He cannot be content, like Polyphemos, with the self-sufficiency of masturbation. To be sure, the monster Pentheus dies before reproducing. But his monstrosity is associated with the self-sufficiency of the household: his father, Ekhion, was born from dragon's teeth sown in the earth, an arrangement that introduced introverted autochthony into Kadmos' household. To have given Agaue to a husband from another household would have been to lose the tyranny. The preservation of wealth and power within the Greek household, ordinary or tyrannical, may require the introverted self-sufficiency of endogamy.[27] It is therefore appropriate that the only possible indications of Pentheus' sexuality are incestuous (957–8, 968–9). But the incestuous tyrant *par excellence* is Oidipous.

The tendency to self-sufficiency through familial introversion is no doubt very ancient, but with monetisation it acquires a new character. In the pre-monetary world of Homer, prestige objects and women belong to the inner chamber (θάλαμος) of the household, and yet are given to outsiders (the women as brides or slaves). With the advent of the regime of abstract (monetary) value, and of the regulation of the legitimate continuity of the household by the polis, this polarity between containment and circulation (of wealth and women) acquires new significance. The household is drawn into monetary circulation. It may continue to store valuable objects, but generally only as part of its overall wealth – including 'invisible wealth' (ἀφανὴς οὐσία) – imagined in terms of monetary value. The concealment of Homeric treasure within the inner chamber has been replaced by the greater degree of invisibility easily assumed by merely monetary value. The Homeric separation of goods into prestige and subsistence spheres is dissolved by monetary circulation, or rather replaced by a new separation – between abstract value and the circulation of concrete goods. But the association of wealth with women persists, in a new form. The [*12*] antithesis between, on the one hand, abstract value imagined as self-sufficient, permanent, controlling and, on the other, its actual dependence on the constant transformation and circulation of material goods is analogous to the antithesis between the perpetuated identity of the patrilineal citizen household and its dependence on the constant circulation of women, their transformation into wives as they pass from one household to another. Indeed, the household may aspire, or imagine

[27] For classical Athens see Seaford 1994b: 211 with bibliography; Cox 1998: 32–6, 210. In drama: Aesch. *Supp*. 338–9.

itself, to be self-sufficient both economically and in reproducing itself, even though in fact it participates in the circulation of both goods and women. Accordingly, there is fantasy about reproduction without women, for instance Hippolytos' preference for buying children from temples (Eur. *Hipp.* 618–24).

To enable the males to reproduce while supposedly preserving the self-sufficient identity of the household, there are two possible strategies. One is to imagine that the incoming brides contribute mere matter to, or are mere receptacles for, the offspring.[28] The other is endogamy (frequently practised in classical Athens) – producing offspring from women from within the household, which also retains the wealth which would otherwise be lost (as dowry).

As for self-sufficient reproduction of wealth, this may become, with the circulation of money, more difficult in reality. But the homogeneity and the isolating omnipotence of money may provide the desired illusion, by means of two strategies analogous to those just mentioned as used in sexual reproduction (there can be erotic desire for money).[29] One, analogous to the privileging of male over female, is to privilege monetary value over goods, so that purchased goods seem to embody monetary value belonging to the household. The other – analogous to endogamy – is to use the apparently self-increasing power of money. Whereas gift exchange, barter and purchase involve permanent relinquishment, money loaned at interest or commercially invested eventually produces more of *itself* for the originating household, as does endogamy.[30] Interest is called τόκος ('offspring'),[13] says Aristotle (*Pol.* 1258b), because offspring are similar to their parents, and τόκος is 'currency the child of currency' (νόμισμα ἐκ νομίσματος).

In this analogy between interest and offspring there are three inconcinnities. First, sexual τόκος is entirely natural reproduction, but Aristotle adds that interest (τόκος) is the most unnatural form of acquisition. Second, children generally derive from two different families, whereas the interest produced by money is completely homogeneous with itself. Third, whereas the bride is generally lost to her natal family, and her τόκος

[28] Philolaos DK 44 A 27; Aesch. *Eum.* 658–66, 735–6; Pl. *Ti.* 50c–d; Arist. *Ph.* 1.9.192a23; *Gen. an.* 738b. With Pl. *Leg.* 6.775d8, cf. Artem. 2.45; Martial 6.27.3; Aesch. *Supp.* 282–3; Macrob. *In Somn.* 1.6.63. Sexual reproduction is imagined as like stamping a coin: form, conferring abstract value, is male, material female.

[29] Eur. *Supp.* 178, 239; *Hec.* 775; *fr. trag. adesp.* 129.1–2.

[30] Interest first appears as a fact of life in Aristophanes, notably in the *Clouds*; cf. Pind. *Ol.* 10.7–9. It seems to have developed out of the practice (recommended by Hesiod) of reciprocating a gift with a better one: Millett 1991: 40–52, 99, 121.

belongs to her husband's family, money loaned or commercially invested returns to its owner together with its (homogeneous) τόκος.

It is when the girl is not lost to her natal family that her offspring is more than usually homogeneous with what produces it. Indeed, the form of reproduction closest to Aristotle's characterisation of interest – as 'currency from currency', and unnatural – is in fact incest. It is with horror that Oidipous calls himself 'ὁμογενής (of the same family, homogeneous) with those from whom I was born'.[31] In the case of the Theban royal family all three inconcinnities between monetary interest and human reproduction disappear. Money and females should circulate, and are transmitted together (the dowry), but the introverted household keeps, even conceals,[32] its money and its females for itself.[33] In a series of myths, many of them dramatised in tragedy, endogamy – of which the extreme form is incest – is associated with blindness and with the confinement of a female by her male blood-kin, whereas the opposite pole, consisting of exogamy and the liberation of girls from confinement, is associated with Dionysos.[34] Just as the mythical confinement of women in darkness or underground by their male kin expresses endogamy, so money may be hoarded by being made invisible, frequently underground.[35] These cautionary myths set the communality of Dionysos against the potentially anti-communal tendency to retain wealth and power within the household by means of endogamy.[*14*]

'The same great harbour sufficed son and father as θαλαμηπόλος' (*OT* 1207–10). θαλαμηπόλος is here translated 'bridegroom', but elsewhere means attendant of the θάλαμος, of the *storeroom*, in its only other fifth-century occurrence (Aesch. *Sept.* 359). In *OT* it evokes the dual meaning of θάλαμος as bridal chamber and storeroom of the household's wealth. Similarly, Antigone, confined by her male kin in her underground bridal

[31] Soph. *OT* 1361; cf. 1186–8, 1215; Seaford 1994b: 218–19. The importance of the analogy of biological with monetary reproduction in *OT* was recognised, from a different perspective, by Shell 1978: 95–6.

[32] E.g. Pind. *Isthm.* 1.67–8; *Nem.* 1.31–2.

[33] See Seaford 1990a. This combination is at the heart of Plautus' *Aulularia* (and presumably of its Greek model), especially the scene in which the young man's confession of making the girl pregnant is mistaken by her father as confessing to have stolen his pot of gold (731–57). The Lydian king Kandaules' concealment of his wife is completely reversed by his need for her to be admired naked (i.e. for enviability for himself), which results in him losing his wealth and power (Hdt. 1.8–12).

[34] See Seaford 1990a. Such mythical heroines are Danae, Alope, Antiope, Auge, Melanippe, Karya, Arsinoe, Hemithea, Amphissa, Philomela, Ino, Kleopatra, Elektra, Tyro.

[35] Apart from the numerous coin hoards found buried, see Ar. *Av.* 599–602 with Dunbar 1995: *ad loc.*; *Plut.* 237–8 (Wealth complains of being hidden in the ground); also e.g. Antiph. DK 87 B 4; Xen. *Vect.* 4.7; Dem. 27.53; Pl. *Leg.* 11.913a–b; Men. *Dys.* 812 ('invisible wealth' kept buried); Diod. Sic. 2.15.3; App. *B Civ.* 4.73 (Rhodes); Ael. *VH* 13.2.

θάλαμος (*Ant.* 804, 891), is compared to Danae confined by her male kin in her θάλαμος, in which 'she was treasurer of the gold-flowing seed of Zeus' (948–50). In Euripides' *Danae* (fr. 324), the pleasure in gold is said to be greater than that of parents and children in each other.

In *OT* 873–91 (paraphrased above), tyrannical gain (κέρδος) is associated with unholy things and touching the untouchable, which here cannot but suggest incest. And Antigone identifies her κέρδος (*Ant.* 462, 464) with the quasi-incestuous (73–6) loyalty to her own blood-kin that she explicitly prefers to marriage. Kreon professes devotion to the polis, but regards it as belonging to himself (736–8, 291–2). His obsession with the monetary motives of others (221–2, 289–301, 322, 1036–9, 1047, 1055, 1063) arises – even more clearly than Pentheus' and Oidipous' – from fear of the individual autonomy that money confers on them, a fear strengthened by projection onto them of his own typically tyrannical desire to concentrate money and power in himself alone,[36] which ends in extreme isolation – even from his closest kin. His money isolates him, like Midas, by making him find money everywhere.

Money is, for the tyrant, ambivalent. It is a crucial instrument in obtaining and maintaining autocracy. But it confers autonomy on others, and is in a sense egalitarian, for – as Aristotle notes – currency makes possible communality, and transactions involving currency imply equality between transactors (*qua* transactors).[37] Like Oidipous' denunciation of the unknown murderer whom he supposes to be motivated by money (*OT* 124–5, 216–75), the evil effects of [15] money that Kreon denounces – damage to cities, expulsion of men from their homes, teaching upright minds to do shameful things, making men know no limit to impiety (*Ant.* 295–301) – turn out to be suffered or perpetrated by himself. Teiresias, accused by Kreon of venality, retorts that it is characteristic of tyrants to love disgraceful gain (*Ant.* 1056), and Teiresias is always right (1092–4). The rigid isolation of Kreon, his single-minded illusion of self-sufficiency, is formed – politically and psychologically – in part by money, from whose circulation he nevertheless fiercely distances himself. In the end his only 'gain' (κέρδος) is to be led away in isolated lamentation.

Where, in all this, is the opposite pole to monetary individualism, the pre-monetary communality associated with Dionysos? In both *Antigone* and *OT*, he plays a symbolic role, in the imagination of the citizen chorus, just before the final disaster. In *Antigone*, after Kreon vainly orders Antigone

[36] Note especially 1062–3, and Seaford 1998c[4].
[37] Arist. *Eth. Nic.* 1133b15–18, 1132b34.

to be released from underground, Dionysos is invoked to come from outside to purify the city (1115–52). In *OT*, just before the revelation scene that causes Oidipous to blind himself, the chorus speculate that he may be the son of Dionysos who dwells on the mountaintops (1105–9). Both passages evoke – as an antithetical extreme to the tragic catastrophe – the communal rituals of the City Dionysia that commemorate the original arrival of Dionysos at Athens from outside (over the mountains from Thebes), and that together with satyric drama frame the performance of tragedy. Further, in *OT*, the idea of the god out there being Oidipous' father contrasts with the reality of Oidipous having been begotten at the centre, at the very place of his incestuous marriage. *Antigone*, too, is about incest, not only in that Oidipous' incestuous offspring (1–3) Antigone puts her quasi-incestuous attachment to her dead brother above marriage (73–6, 891–928), but also in the form of punishment: in contrast to the collective stoning originally announced as deterrent, Kreon decides that *he himself* (773–80) will confine his niece alive in the earth, in a bridal θάλαμος (804). The [16] invocation of Dionysos to come from outside to purify the polis, just after the order to liberate Antigone, must evoke his role as the enemy of endogamy and liberator of the female from confinement.

The historically unprecedented freedom conferred on the individual by money – freedom from kin, from reciprocity, even (it may seem) from deity – is taken by the mythical (still largely pre-monetary) imagination to its extreme in the figure of the tragic tyrant, whose *isolation* (from kin, even from deity) goes beyond anything found in Homer. Pentheus, Oidipous, Kreon: each one of them is a 'tyrant' who – like Greek tyrants in general – is violently alienated from his kin, has trampled on the sacred, has made deity hostile and seems obsessed with money. And they are all from the Theban family of tyrants whose reproductive introversion seems to express, in the pre-monetary logic of myth, the self-sufficient isolation that the new phenomenon of money allows to become an economic and political reality – in its most extreme form in the tyranny experienced by the Athenians (and many others) in the period leading up to the genesis of tragedy. The first Athenian coins may well have been minted under Peisistratos.

I have discussed only three tragedies.[38] And it is only sometimes that the fundamental importance of money is in tragedy made explicit, as for instance when Aigisthos announces that he will henceforth rule by means of the dead Agamemnon's money (Aesch. *Ag.* 1638–9), or when in

38 For further studies of money in tragedy see Seaford 1998c[4].

Sophocles' lost *Aleadai* someone says that it is money that creates – among other desirable things – friends, honours and tyranny (fr. 88). Tragedy depicts the pre-monetary, heroic world. But it does so, I suggest, in a manner influenced by the historical consequences of monetisation even when there is no mention of money. In a monetised society each possessor of money possesses a little autonomy, but it is only in tyranny that there survives anything resembling the heroic autonomy of the Homeric world, and tyrannical autonomy is based largely on money.[39]

POSTSCRIPT

The theme of this chapter is taken further and integrated into a broader context in Seaford 2006a and 2004c, especially 14§D. The influence of the myth of Midas and Silenos on Plato's *Symposium* is described by M. Usher, 'Satyr play in Plato's *Symposium*', *AJP* 123 (2002), 205–28. The traditional story patterns behind the myth are discussed by Davies 2004. The evocation of the myth in tragedy is the theme of Easterling 2013.

For Greek attitudes to money see D. Schaps, *The Invention of Coinage and the Monetization of Ancient Greece* (Ann Arbor, MI: University of Michigan Press, 2004); Malcolm Schofield, *Plato: Political Philosophy* (Oxford: Oxford University Press, 2006), index, s.v. money; S. von Reden, *Money in Classical Antiquity* (Cambridge: Cambridge University Press, 2010); T. van Berkel, 'Pricing the invaluable: Socrates and the value of friendship', in R. Rosen and I. Sluiter (eds.), *Valuing Others in Classical Antiquity* (Leiden: Brill, 2010), pp. 249–77.

There have been two substantial collections of papers on Dionysos: R. Schlesier (ed.), *A Different God? Dionysos and Ancient Polytheism* (Berlin and New York: de Gruyter, 2011), and A. Bernabé et al. (eds.), *Redefining Dionysos* (Berlin and Boston: de Gruyter, 2013). For the visual evidence see C. Isler-Kerenyi, *Dionysos in Archaic Greece* (Leiden: Brill, 2007) and *Dionysos in Classical Athens* (Leiden: Brill, 2014).

[39] My thanks go to Matthew Wright and Yana Zarifi for their comments on an earlier draft.

CHAPTER 4

Tragic Money

1. Introduction

Tragedy was a product of the classical polis, but took its themes (with very few exceptions) from an imagined earlier age, the heroic age that is also the subject of the Homeric poems. The result, it has been argued, is a creative tension, notably between the spirit of heroic autonomy and the rule of law characteristic of the polis.[1] The institutions of the polis make themselves felt, anachronistically, in the tragic representation of heroic myth.[2]

My aim here is to extend this argument by examining the influence of money, including coinage (an institution of the polis), on the tragic representation of heroic myth, and in particular through three case studies, one selected from each of the extant tragedians. My aim is to describe the part played by money in the texture of the plays, and to indicate the relation of this role to its cultural and historical background. I will be concerned only briefly with the definitional and theoretical problems of money and with the early history of the development of precious metal as money. Such topics will be treated at much greater length in the large-scale study of the cultural consequences of money on which I am currently engaged, and which will locate tragic money in its historical context.[3] For my present purpose it will be sufficient to use, as a historical foil to tragedy, Homeric epic. This is because, although both Homer and tragedy represent the heroic world, the creative phase of Homeric epic (roughly the eighth and early seventh centuries) occurred *before* – whereas tragedy came into being shortly *after* – the rapid development of coinage (the first ever

[1] E.g. Vernant & Vidal-Naquet 1988: 23–8.

[2] See e.g. Easterling 1985: 6–7, whose two paragraphs on coinage are the only treatment known to me of tragic money, apart from occasional remarks on money from a perspective very different from mine in von Reden 1995: 147–68.

[3] The cultural consequences of money in early Greece have received far less attention than those of literacy. Notable exceptions are Thomson 1961; Shell 1978; Kurke 1991.

widespread coinage) by the Greek city-states in the sixth century. The world represented by Homeric epic contains neither coinage nor even (except for a few indications) money,[4] nor is its representation of events influenced by money, whereas the world represented by tragedy does, anachronistically, contain (precious metal) money, occasionally explicitly in the form of coinage, and is, I will argue, in various non-obvious ways shaped by money. Like other institutions of the polis, coinage (and precious metal money generally) influences the tragic representation of heroic myth.

Money is, of course, a quite distinct category from wealth. If we say that the functions of money are to be a measure of value, a means of exchange, a means of payment and a store of value,[5] then in Homer there is nothing that is especially associated with, or regularly performs, any one of these functions, except that a measure of value is sometimes provided by cattle. And so there is in Homer nothing with a greater claim than cattle to be called money.[6] But even cattle do not perform any of the other functions of money, and even as a measure of value they *[120]* are used only occasionally and for a limited range of goods.[7] In the sixth and fifth centuries, on the other hand, we find precious metal performing all the functions of money. The *combination* of these functions in a single thing (gold or silver) produces a radical novelty. Furthermore, it seems that precious metal (whether gold, silver or even both simultaneously) became, at least in some of the city-states, generally acceptable as a means of payment and exchange. We may therefore call it a universal equivalent.

From the evidence for the development of a universal equivalent in this period I confine myself here to a small sample of texts. The function of money as a (universal) *means of exchange* is famously illustrated by Heraclitus:[8] 'All things are requital for fire and fire for all things, just as goods for gold and gold for goods.'[9] The supreme inherent value of gold, and its strange new power to (in a sense) embody all things, allows the poetic exaggeration by Pythermos, apparently a contemporary of Heraclitus, to

[4] See nn. 6, 76 and 78 below. The question of to what extent, if at all, there is money in Homer, and the crucial question (on which it depends) of how we define money (too broad a definition is useless), I will deal with in my larger study.

[5] For this analysis see e.g. Polanyi 1977: esp. 102–6. But on any reasonable definition of money, money barely exists in Homer.

[6] Despite the few indications of a special status for gold as representing wealth in general: e.g. *Od.* 3.301.

[7] The only cases involving trade are *Il.* 21.79 (sale of Lykaon); *Od.* 1.431 (purchase of Eurykleia). The others are *Il.* 2.449 (golden tassel on Athena's aigis), 6.236 (suits of armour exchanged), 23.702–5 and 885 (prizes); *Od.* 22.57 (compensation).

[8] DK 22 B 90.

[9] πυρὸς ἀνταμοιβὴ τὰ πάντα καὶ πῦρ ἁπάντων ὅκωσπερ χρυσοῦ χρήματα καὶ χρημάτων χρυσός.

the effect that 'the things other than gold were after all nothing'.[10] A universal means of exchange will also almost inevitably act as a *measure of value.*[11] A specified quantity of precious metal as a *means of payment* is frequent, for instance in Herodotus,[12] in early inscriptions,[13] or in the coins paid to Athenian officials and jurymen. The function of precious metal money as a *store of wealth*, and indeed the overall importance of money in the age of Sophocles and Euripides, emerges from the stress laid in various speeches, reported by Thucydides, on the importance of money in the Peloponnesian war.[14] Thucydides even makes Hermokrates the Syracusan refer to 'gold and silver, by which war *and the other things* thrive' (6.34.2 ... ὅθεν ὅ τε πόλεμος καὶ τἄλλα εὐπορεῖ). Perikles (2.13.3) is made to claim that the strength of the Athenians comes from the income of 600 talents from the allies, and to refer to 6,000 talents of coined silver on the Acropolis and much uncoined silver and gold of various kinds in the temples. Both uncoined gold and silver and the Athenian silver coinage could be used to defray the various expenses involved in warfare. Uncoined precious metal money existed before, and continued to exist alongside, the special form of precious metal money that is coinage. But coins, of which vast numbers have survived from the sixth century onwards, no doubt facilitated the combination of money functions, the increasing importance of money in the economy, and the sense of money as something separate from everything else.[15] In Aristophanes they are a regular feature of everyday life.[16] [*121*]

2. Does Money Have Limits?

Precious metal as a universal equivalent (money) has – despite its ease of storage, of concealment and of transport in high values, its homogeneity and its lack of use-value – the effortless power to acquire (or seemingly to be transformed into) things unlimited in kind and number. And so there seems to be no natural limit to the acquisition of it, whereas to the

[10] *PMG* 910. This fell on receptive ears, being referred to by Hipponax (or Ananius: Ananius fr. 2 West).
[11] As at e.g. Ar. *Pax* 1201.
[12] E.g. 2.180; 3.56, 58–9, 131; 5.51, 77; 6.79, 92.
[13] E.g. Jones 1993: nos. 46–9.
[14] Thuc. 1.80.3–4, 83, 121.3, 141–3; 2.13.2–3. Cf. e.g. [Xen.] *Ath. Pol.* 3.3; [Arist.] *Ath. Pol.* 27.3.
[15] A good recent overview of the problems of the early development of Greek coinage is by Howgego 1995: 1–7, 12–18.
[16] *Eq.* 797–800; *Vesp.* 787–93; *Nub.* 247–9; *Pax* 1201–2; *Av.* 301, 1105–8; *Ran.* 139–41, 718–33; *Eccl.* 601–2, 815–22.

acquisition of e.g. tripods there is a natural limit set by the use of tripods (to boil meat, as gifts, etc.) and by the problem of storing them.

'Of wealth', writes Solon, 'there is no limit that appears to men. For those of us who have the most wealth are eager to double it' (fr. 13.71–3). This sentiment probably precedes the introduction of coinage, but is certainly appropriate to a society in which precious metal money has become a focus of desire, and is quite unlike anything in Homer. The notion takes brilliant form in Aristophanes' *Wealth*: not only does Wealth have power over everybody and everything, it is also distinct in that of everything else (sex, bread, music, honour, courage, soup and so on) there is satiety (πλησμονή), whereas if somebody gets thirteen talents he desires the more strongly to get sixteen, and if he achieves this, then he wants forty and says that life is not worth living unless he gets them (189–97). To the apparently unlimited power and unlimited accumulation of money belongs a unique desire. Tragedy comments on this desire both in general[17] and in particular – notably in the figure of Polymnestor in Euripides' *Hecuba*, destroyed, like Polykrates of Samos,[18] by his passion for ever more gold.[19] The power of money to acquire all things, together with its ease of storage, of concealment and of deployment, concentrates the desire for each of those things on to itself, making itself seem more desirable than any particular thing that it can obtain. And indeed with the development of money the aim of commerce seems to be, in Greece as generally elsewhere, more and more the acquisition of money (rather than of the things that can be acquired by money).

This seemingly unlimited power of money, inspiring unlimited desire for its unlimited accumulation, extends itself outwards, and thereby threatens traditional non-monetary values. For instance, in choosing a spouse people prefer wealth to noble birth, complains Theognis (183–96). At the same time the seemingly universal power of money over all things (to acquire them, or to be transformed into them) is also the power to include them in a seemingly universal regime of comparative evaluation. Money requires and promotes the evaluation of every commodity against every other. This creates or encourages a mode of thinking inclined to comparative evaluation even of those things (if there are any such) which fall outside the power of money. In other words, the seeming universality of comparative monetary evaluation is unconsciously extended outwards into the

[17] E.g. Eur. *Supp.* 239: the useless wealthy are 'always passionate for more', πλειόνων τ' ἐρῶσ' ἀεί.

[18] Hdt. 3.123–5. See §3.

[19] 775 χρυσὸν ἠράσθη λαβεῖν, 1002–14, 1146–8, 1206–7.

universe of evaluation as a whole. And so the universalising dynamic at the heart of money, its need to extend its influence outwards, both sets up a contradiction between money/wealth and (say) noble birth – a contradiction of historical importance – and at the same time promotes a mode of thinking inclined to compare basic values (money/wealth, noble birth, health, virtue and so on) with each other. Money/wealth is not necessarily a term in the comparison.[20] But it frequently is, and in such cases we can say that money/wealth becomes a value, to be compared with other values, in a regime of comparative evaluation that it has itself (as a general measure of value) helped to establish. Health is best, says the drinking song, physical beauty second, honest wealth third and to be young among [122] friends fourth.[21] Such comparisons are missing from the moneyless world of Homer.[22]

At this point my use of the term 'money/wealth' requires clarification. When all or most goods can be obtained (and evaluated) by a single thing (i.e. money), wealth and money can be transformed into each other and so may tend to be denoted by the same term. For example χρήματα, defined by Aristotle as 'all things of which the value is measured by currency',[23] is variously translated 'things', 'wealth' and 'money'. It means, in the post-heroic age, both money and those things which money can measure and transform itself into, just as they can transform themselves into money. In this sense both the things and the money seem to belong to the same category (money/wealth). And so when tragedy compares (say) noble birth with χρήματα or πλοῦτος (wealth) or νόμισμα (currency) or ἄργυρος (silver, the material of Athenian coinage) or χρυσός (gold, the most valuable of commodities and associated with the wealth of the heroic age), these terms all refer to aspects or forms of the same thing, the money/wealth familiar to the Athenian audience. By the term 'money' I will henceforth mean this money/wealth, rather than the narrower category of currency or coinage.

[20] It is not in Sappho fr. 16; Xenophanes fr. 2 West = DK 21 B 2.

[21] *PMG* 890; also Archil. fr. 19 ('I don't care about the wealth of Gyges etc.', continued presumably by specifying what is more important than wealth); Thgn. 699–718; *PMG* 988; Eur. *Med.* 542–4, fr. 659.

[22] With the notable exception of the passage (discussed below in §3) of *Iliad* 9 in which Akhilleus compares numerous gifts with his life. We have, of course, to allow the possibility that the creator(s) of Homeric epic were not unfamiliar with money, but tended to exclude it from their heroic vision. Poetry that is not very much later than Homer, such as Sappho and Alcaeus, shows the influence of money (though not of coinage).

[23] *Eth. Nic.* 1119b26–7 χρήματα λέγομεν πάντα ὅσων ἀξία νομίσματι μετρεῖται.

The range of values or motivations to which tragedy explicitly or implicitly compares money is wide, especially in Euripides, and the comparison takes various forms.[24] It may be said that people honour money above freedom[25] or wisdom;[26] or that money is in fact more powerful than words[27] or family feeling;[28] or that it *should* be preferred to piety.[29] The advantage enjoyed by money may not be simply that it is more desirable, but rather that it is primary, in the sense that the other value may turn out to be one of the numerous things that are obtainable by money. For instance, noble birth (εὐγένεια) results from having wealth in the house over a long period.[30] Conversely, εὐγένεια is destroyed by poverty.[31] Everything is secondary to wealth, for, although some praise health, the poor man is always sick.[32] In a fragment (fr. 88) of Sophocles' *Aleadai*, money (τὰ χρήματα) is said to create friends, honours, tyranny, physical beauty, wise speech and pleasure even in disease.[33] Small wonder then that money is said to be the most honoured and powerful thing among men,[34] to be what they all toil for,[35] to *[123]* 'enslave'[36] and 'defeat'[37] them. 'Money' may even come to stand for something like 'an especially good or desirable thing', as in such expressions as 'it is money if one is pious to god', or '(I do not want money from you). It is money if you save my life, which is the dearest thing I have.'[38] In a fragment (fr. 324) of Euripides' *Danae* it is said that the pleasure given by gold is greater than that of parents and children in each other, and is like Aphrodite's look that inspires innumerable passions. Erotic passion for money reappears elsewhere,[39] notably in an anonymous fragment that is worth quoting in full:

[24] It should be noted that the frequency of money in the fragments is due to the interest in money of the writers who preserved them, especially the anthologer Stobaeus.
[25] Eur. fr. 142.
[26] Eur. fr. 327; cf. also *HF* 669–72.
[27] Eur. *Med.* 965.
[28] Eur. fr. 324.
[29] *Fr. trag. adesp.* 181.
[30] Eur. fr. 22; also fr. 95.
[31] Eur. *El.* 38; cf. on the other hand Eur. fr. 1066 (χρήματα depart but εὐγένεια remains).
[32] Soph. fr. 354.
[33] See nn. 87 and 105 below. See also Soph. *OT* 542 (tyranny caught by χρήματα, cf. Aesch. *Ag.* 1638–9); Eur. *Hec.* 818 (payment for rhetoric lessons, which bestow power); *El.* 428–9 (χρήματα permits hospitality (but cf. 394–5) and saves from disease).
[34] Eur. *Phoen.* 439–40; also *HF* 774–6, fr. 325; *fr. trag. adesp.* 294.
[35] Eur. fr. 580.
[36] Eur. *Hec.* 865, *Supp.* 875–6; cf. fr. 1092.
[37] Eur. fr. 341; cf. *Ion* 629.
[38] Eur. fr. 252, *Or.* 644–5; cf. also Aesch. *Cho.* 372; Eur. *Hec.* 1229, *Tro.* 432–3.
[39] Eur. *Supp.* 178, 239, *Hec.* 775. Conceivably the word may have lost erotic associations, however, in such passages.

> O gold, offspring of the earth, what passion (ἔρωτα) you kindle among humankind, mightiest of all, tyrant over all. For those at war you have greater power than Ares and enchant all things: for the trees and the mindless races of wild animals followed the Orphic songs, but you (are followed by) the whole earth and sea and all-inventive Ares.[40]

On the other hand, it is claimed that alongside money are needed virtue[41] and knowledge;[42] that money is powerless to prevent a military conflict,[43] or against death;[44] that it is not to be preferred to a trouble-free life,[45] a good wife,[46] a genuine friend,[47] the fatherland,[48] wisdom;[49] that (a person's) nature, not wealth, is what lasts;[50] that in choosing a spouse people prefer ἀξίωμα (rank, reputation) to money.[51] Sometimes the priority is expressed in terms of exchange: for genuine friendship one should give much money,[52] even an innumerable amount;[53] one would not exchange youth for any amount;[54] virtue (is the only thing that) cannot be acquired by money.[55] Such texts maintain that there is, after all, a limit to the power of money.

3. Aeschylus: *Agamemnon*

In a famous scene of Aeschylus' *Agamemnon*, Agamemnon is persuaded by Klytaimestra to walk to his house on a path of textiles. The economic aspect of this scene has been emphasised by John Jones: what Agamemnon is persuaded to do is to waste the wealth of the household. 'Clytemnestra's sentiment that the *oikos* is so rich that it need not bother with this kind of extravagance, while trivial-seeming to us, will have struck a fifth-century audience as [124] recklessly hubristic.'[56] In the same vein Simon Goldhill

40 *Fr. trag. adesp.* 129.
41 Eur. frr. 163, 542.
42 Eur. fr. 1066.
43 Aesch. *Supp.* 935.
44 Aesch. *Pers.* 842; Eur. *Alc.* 56–9.
45 Eur. *Ion* 629–31, *Med.* 598–9, *Phoen.* 552–4.
46 Eur. fr. 543.4–5 (the only thing preferable to wealth).
47 Eur. *Or.* 1155–6.
48 Eur. fr. 1046.
49 *Fr. trag. adesp.* 130.
50 Eur. *El.* 941.
51 Eur. fr. 405.
52 Eur. fr. 934.
53 Eur. *Or.* 1156–7.
54 Eur. *HF* 643–8.
55 Eur. fr. 527; cf. *El.* 253, 372.
56 Jones 1962: 82–93 (citation from 88).

writes that 'the wanton destruction of the household property' represented by trampling the textiles 'is in absolute opposition to the normal ethos of the household, which aims at continuity and stability of wealth and possessions'.[57] While in general agreement with this view, I want to take the argument further by focusing on the wealth as *money*.[58] What is shocking about the scene is not just the waste of wealth, but the seemingly infinite power of money (to acquire things from outside the household). Now, just as money can be transformed into a wide range of items, so the topic of money cannot (from one perspective) be separated from a host of others: wealth, exchange, production, signification and so on. But from another perspective money is quite distinct from all of these: not only is it conceptually distinct, but they may also all in fact exist without it. My focus is on the specific (and historically important) phenomenon of money. There has been, so far as I am aware, only one other discussion of this scene that picks out the monetary aspect.[59]

As Agamemnon walks into the house to his death, Klytaimestra justifies the dangerously extravagant use of the textiles as follows (958–65):

> ἔστιν θάλασσα – τίς δέ νιν κατασβέσει; –
> τρέφουσα πολλῆς πορφύρας ἰσάργυρον
> κηκῖδα παγκαίνιστον, εἱμάτων βαφάς.
> οἶκος δ' ὑπάρχει τῶνδε σὺν θεοῖς, ἄναξ,
> ἔχειν, πένεσθαι δ' οὐκ ἐπίσταται δόμος.

57 Goldhill 1986: 11.

58 The distinction between wealth and money is important. Although money is wealth, and wealth may take the form of money, with the result that the same word (e.g. χρήματα) may refer to both, nevertheless they are crucially distinct categories. Wealth and its dangers are themes of the *Agamemnon* (e.g. 773–81, 1575–6); but, apart from the lines discussed below (949, 959, 437), money occurs only in the allusion to (false) coinage at 780.

59 This is a passage in Sitta von Reden's discussion of the scene in terms of how 'commercial images convey meanings of social disruption in a complex sense' (von Reden 1995: 161–4). Because the passage is hard to summarise, I give it in full:

> it remains remarkable that the value of a symbol of power is described in monetary terms. The purple tapestry was certainly not bought with money. Given that the text has just raised the question how objects change their value in different contexts of exchange, the attribute ἀργυρώνητος seems to withdraw the tapestry from the sphere of sacred values circulating between men and gods and to transfer it instead into a human sphere of exchange. Moreover, if there is a metaphysical relationship between the colourful carpet and Clytemnestra's crafty web of words the redefinition of the carpet as a value in the monetary economy of humans carries over to Clytemnestra's speech.

I do not know why von Reden claims that 'the purple tapestry was certainly not bought with money' (her endnote does not help). Her general approach to the scene is influenced by Goldhill's reading of it in terms of the manipulation (and openness) of signification in Goldhill 1984: 66–79.

πολλῶν πατησμὸν δ' εἱμάτων ἂν ηὐξάμην,
δόμοισι προυνεχθέντος ἐν χρηστηρίοις
ψυχῆς κόμιστρα τῆσδε μηχανωμένῃ.

The sea exists – who will dry it up? – nourishing an ever-renewed gush, equal to silver [i.e. worth its weight in silver],[60] of much purple, the dyeings of garments. The household has a supply of these things, with the grace of the gods, for us to have, king. The house does not know how to be poor. Of many garments would I have vowed the trampling, had it been prescribed at the home of an oracle for me as I devised a means of recovering this man's life.

The textiles may be trampled because their purple dye comes in constant supply from the inexhaustible sea. But it does not flow directly into the house. ἰσάργυρος expresses the high value of the dye. Agamemnon has just remarked that the textiles are ἀργυρώνητος (949), [125] bought with silver, an epithet that would be inconceivable in the moneyless world of Homer. The inexhaustibility of the supply of dye is relevant only if there is an inexhaustible supply of money (silver) to pay for it, which by implication therefore there is. The emphasis on the (natural) inexhaustibility of the sea implies the inexhaustibility of the silver money (a human construction) used in equal quantities (ἰσάργυρον) to acquire the dye.[61] We noted earlier that money is both homogeneous and unlimited. In both these respects it is like the sea.

The power of money means that the textiles are infinitely replaceable. The textiles walked on by Agamemnon are in essence no different from the textiles that can so easily replace them. They are, in this respect, quite antithetical to the golden lamb which, in the previous generation of the house of Atreus, bestowed the royal power.[62] In Homer the Argive royal power is conveyed by a sceptre once held by Zeus and transmitted down the generations.[63] The functioning of such 'talismanic' objects requires them to be unique.[64] Despite the frequent references in the Agamemnon to the

[60] Commentators compare Theopompus, *FGrHist* 115 F117 ἰσοστάσιος γὰρ ἦν ἡ πορφύρα πρὸς ἄργυρον ἐξεταζομένη (at Kolophon), 'for the purple dye was being valued as equal in weight against silver' (i.e. as worth its weight in silver).

[61] It is interesting that the (potentially alarming and relatively novel) *manmade* inexhaustibility of money is envisaged in terms of the *natural* inexhaustibility of the sea – whether through reticence or anxiety or the need for a concrete analogue for a difficult abstraction. Cf. e.g. Soph. *Ant.* 1077 κατηργυρωμένος, meaning 'bribed with silver'.

[62] Eur. *El.* 699–746 with Cropp 1988: *ad loc.*; *IT* 196; *Or.* 812–13, 996–1000.

[63] *Il.* 2.101–8.

[64] The description is from L. Gernet's discussion of such objects in Greek myth (Gernet 1981: 73–111).

bitter struggle for the kingship in the earlier generation, neither the lamb nor the sceptre is mentioned.[65] How then does Aigisthos hope to exercise the power that he has, in conjunction with Klytaimestra, usurped? 'I will try to rule the citizens', he says, 'through this man's [i.e. Agamemnon's] money'.[66] And it is later in the trilogy repeatedly stressed that in enacting revenge Orestes is also reacquiring control of the χρήματα.[67] In Aeschylus the power of the royal household derives not from the talismanic object of myth, a divinely granted unique object in which alone is embodied the power to rule, but rather from its opposite: from the relatively novel power of money, with its homogeneous power to acquire and replace all objects.

In one version of the myth, then, the kingship depends on a unique talismanic object, whereas in the other it depends on the homogeneous, unlimited power of money. The polar opposition formed by these two kinds of value is implicit in various texts of the period, notably in Herodotus[68] and in tragedy:[69] I will concentrate here on one example from each – the Herodotean story of the tyrant Polykrates' seal-ring (3.40-3), and a passage from the tragedy *Rhesus* attributed (probably wrongly) to Euripides.

Amasis, alarmed by his friend Polykrates' success, advises him to avoid the jealousy of the gods in the following way: 'Think of whatever it is you value most – whatever you would most regret the loss of – and throw it right away.' The relinquishing of something valuable so as to [*126*] obtain safety is an ancient and widespread pattern of action.[70] Polykrates throws his seal-ring (σφραγίς) into the sea, whence however it returns to him (in the belly of a fish). Why is a seal-ring his most valuable possession? Because it is a source and symbol of sovereign power. Polykrates may, like many an autocrat, have used his seal-ring to implement his authority. However, his power was largely based on the control of precious metal money.

[65] *Ag.* 1095–7, 1193, 1217–22, 1242–3, 1583–1602.

[66] *Ag.* 1638–9 ἐκ τῶν δὲ τοῦδε χρημάτων ...

[67] *Cho.* 135, 250, 275, 301; *Eum.* 757–8.

[68] E.g. at 9.93–4, the story of Euenios, who after having failed in his duty to guard some sacred sheep thought to buy some more to replace them (ἀντικαταστήσειν ἄλλα πριάμενος). But he is found out and blinded. In return, the people are required by an oracle to make him whatever compensation he chooses for being blinded. He is asked, before he knows about the oracle, what compensation he would choose, and specifies certain pieces of property. But when the oracle is revealed to him, he is angry at the deception, even though the people buy the property from its owners and give it to him. His anger is presumably at having been tricked into confining his choice to something specific. Neither the specific sheep nor the specific property are replaceable by (the potentially unlimited power of) money.

[69] E.g. in Eur. *El.* (§5 below) or, in Sophocles' *Philoctetes*, the persistent contrast between the bow (talismanic object and gift) and the commercial ethos associated with the trickery of Odysseus (303, 578–9, 668–73, 978, etc.).

[70] Burkert 1996: 34–55.

Herodotus calls him 'very desirous of money' (3.123 καί κως ἱμείρετο γὰρ χρημάτων μεγάλως), and he is eventually (doomed by the return of his ring) lured to his death by the false promise of enough money in the form of gold to 'rule the whole of Greece'.[71]

The reign of Polykrates coincides with the early rapid development of coinage, and he certainly coined money.[72] And so, given the likely importance of royal seals in the development of coinage,[73] Polykrates' seal may also have been associated with his monetary power. But whereas the seal transmits power through its impression (with the recipient substance, say clay, being of no significance), the coin is powerful not only by virtue of the impression it has received but rather mainly by virtue of its substance, the value of which is guaranteed by the impression. And of course unmarked precious metal money has power by virtue of its substance alone. But if the widespread power of Polykrates is basically monetary, then the precautionary loss advised by Amasis cannot work: to throw away the object whose loss he most regrets is far less of a loss than it would be in a pre-monetary world. Rich textiles, notes Klytaimestra, can be replaced by means of money. What Polykrates chooses to throw away, his little seal-ring, might seem to be vital, as the source of his royal power and even of his control over coinage. But in fact his power depends not on his seal but on the inherent power of precious metal (coined or uncoined).

In order to abandon a small object irretrievably it makes sense to throw it into the sea. But what does it mean for it to come from the sea? Queen Klytaimestra's ability to replace the textiles from the 'inexhaustible' sea implies control not just over the wealth of the (unlimited, homogeneous) sea, but also – because the textiles are 'bought with silver' – over the unlimited homogeneity of money. So too in the popular tale of Polykrates, the sea, because it is the obvious concrete embodiment of unlimited homogeneity, may be a means of imagining the novel abstraction of money. To be sure, it is also relevant that Polykrates controls the sea literally, with his ships.[74] But his power is based to a large extent on money. What seems to bestow the power is not a unique seal-ring (as it might be for a ruler in the pre-monetary world), but the unlimited homogeneity of money, which, in stark contrast to the ruler's seal-ring, seems to be everywhere. And so in a world of money, in which everything seems infinitely replaceable, the

[71] Hdt. 3.122.4 εἵνεκέν τε χρημάτων ἄρξεις τῆς ἁπάσης Ἑλλάδος.
[72] Hdt. 3.56.2; Kraay 1976: 30, 36.
[73] Macdonald 1905: 44–52; Steiner 1994: 159–63.
[74] For the 'thalassocracy' of Polykrates see Hdt. 3.122.2; Thuc. 1.13.6, 3.104.2; also Hdt. 3.39, 44–5.

ruler cannot, despite (or rather because of) the unprecedented form of power given him by money, succeed in the ancient and vital precaution of sacrificing a single object of irreplaceable value. Even the homogeneous infinity of the sea, so far from being a means of losing the ruler's irreplaceable seal-ring, seems to confirm his power to replace by restoring it to him. Thucydides (1.13) associates the growing importance of money with the establishment of tyrannies in the cities and the development of sea power. Besides his unprecedented individual domination of the sea, Polykrates is one of the first autocrats in a world in which the increasing power of money is being marked by the rapid development of coinage. The return of the seal-ring from the sea may express the tension, in the popular imagination, between a [127] traditional instrument of autocracy (the seal-ring) and a relatively new one (money).[75]

As for the *Rhesus*, my interest is in a Homeric episode that has been reshaped, partly under the influence of money. In the *Iliad*, Hektor offers the horses and chariot of Akhilleus as a reward to elicit a volunteer for a dangerous exploit. The volunteer, Dolon, is described as 'a man of much gold and bronze' (10.315 πολύχρυσος πολύχαλκος). The only purpose of this description is to prefigure his later claim, when captured and asking to be ransomed, that 'there is inside (our house) bronze and gold and much-wrought iron' (378–9). In the tragic version the reward (or payment, μισθός) is mentioned only after Dolon has volunteered. Hektor suggests various possibilities, including gold, which Dolon rejects on the grounds that 'there is (gold) in (our) household; we do not lack livelihood' (170). The identity here assumed between gold and livelihood (βίος), an identification that barely occurs in Homer,[76] means that gold is envisaged as money. When Hektor a few lines later asks him which of the Greeks he would like to have so as to ransom, Dolon replies 'as I said before, there is gold in (our) house' (178). Dolon finally reveals that he wants the horses of Akhilleus, which Hektor grants him (even though they are not yet captured), not without expressing his own strong desire for them, immortal as they are, the gift of Poseidon to Peleus (184–8).[77] The Homeric version has been recast so as to elevate the horses of Akhilleus to the status

[75] As does, in a different way, the story of Gyges and his seal-ring: Seaford 1994b: 224–5.

[76] By far the closest is *Od.* 14.324–6 (= 19.293–5), in which it is said that the 'bronze and gold and much-worked iron' gathered by Odysseus as he travelled in search of gain 'would feed one man after another to the tenth generation'. See also *Od.* 3.301.

[77] As if to preclude the kind of dissent created between Ajax and Odysseus by the *arms* of Akhilleus, Dolon immediately consoles Hektor for the loss of the item of unique *quality* ('the finest (κάλλιστον) gift of the Trojans') by invoking *quantity*: Hektor should not be envious, for there are innumerable other things for him to enjoy (191–4).

of a uniquely desirable object, more desirable even – it is stressed – than money. And to that end the Homeric wealth of Dolon has become, in the tragic version, money. In the moneyless world of Homer there is no need to elevate a desirable object above the power of money.[78]

In the *Agamemnon*, we observed, money may replace luxury goods and convey political power. But that does not exhaust the functions attributed to it. Klytaimestra asks Agamemnon whether he would have vowed to the gods, in a moment of fear, to walk on the textiles, and Agamemnon agrees that he would have so vowed, had an expert prescribed the ritual (933–4). And as he walks into the house, 'destroying wealth and silver-bought weavings' (949), she declares, in the passage quoted above, that she would have vowed the trampling of many cloths to save Agamemnon's life, had it been prescribed by an oracle. Given that she has just alluded to the inexhaustible supply of dye for garments bought by the house's supply of money, it follows that the 'many garments' on which Agamemnon's life would depend would themselves depend on money.

Of course the expert prescriptions of ritual imagined by Klytaimestra are merely hypothetical, designed to show that walking on textiles cannot be unequivocally bad because it might in a certain circumstance be right – a way of pleasing the gods and saving Agamemnon's life. But would such prescriptions be given? In Euripides' *Alcestis* the figure of Death objects to the use of wealth to 'buy' long life (56–9). It is true that the destruction of valuable [*128*] things might, as we have seen, be considered conducive to safety. Indeed, on Agamemnon's entry into the house the chorus sing of their anxiety: an overloaded house is like a ship from which, to avoid disaster, wealth must be jettisoned into the sea, whereas[79] Zeus gives an abundant annual harvest to keep off hunger (1007–18). However, the wealth trampled by Agamemnon is no such sacrifice, for it is, as Klytaimestra boasts, inexhaustibly replaceable, and comes indeed from the sea (like the ominous return of Polykrates' ring), in sharp contrast to the seasonal crops

[78] This does not mean that gold is not used in payment in Homer. In fact, the least weak suggestions of money in the epics are some instances of gold by itself as substance (i.e. not in an artefact) given in payment (though it may be called a 'gift'): *Il.* 11.123–5, 18.507, 22.331–2; *Od.* 4.525–6, 11.327 (cf. 15.527), 14.448. But it is interesting that these transactions are either peripheral to the main narrative (e.g. in the decidedly non-heroic trial scene on the shield of Akhilleus) or negative in some way (e.g. Aigisthos' payment to his watchman) or (in most cases) both. Because gold-as-payment is in each case not the only unusual feature of the passage, no circularity is involved in suggesting that they are non-heroic intrusions from the incipient world of money.

[79] Denniston and Page 1957 on Aesch. *Ag.* 1015–17 write 'τοι [in 1015] is odd here, for this [i.e. the sentence about agriculture] is simply a further illustration of the same theme', failing to see the contrast, which makes τοι appropriate. Cf. e.g. Thgn. 197–202.

provided by Zeus to fulfil the basic need of hunger. Sea trade was in this period the main source of commercial wealth.

The ritual prescriptions hypothesised by Klytaimestra have in reality not been given. The effect of Agamemnon walking on the textiles is in reality the opposite of what is imagined in Klytaimestra's hypotheses. Trampling the infinitely replaceable 'silver-bought' textiles, which Klytaimestra had hypothesised as pleasing the gods and saving Agamemnon's life, in reality displeases the gods and so, we feel, seems to doom him. The dangerous power of money may produce quite opposite effects. Agamemnon regards himself as being treated as a god (921–5, 946) and is accordingly anxious (924). There is danger of resentment, φθόνος, from men (937–9) and from gods (947).

Of human φθόνος against him we have already heard – in the choral strophe (437–55) that describes the Greek deaths at Troy with the image of Ares as a 'gold-changer of bodies', who 'sends from Troy the fired heavy bitterly bewailed [gold] dust to their dear ones, filling the urns with easily placed (εὔθετος) ash in exchange for men'. Ares is envisaged as a trader who exchanges large things (goods/bodies) for small (gold dust/ash of cremated bodies – 'heavy' only in the grief it inspires).[80] A crucial advantage of precious metal as a medium of exchange, its ease of storage and of transport, is expressed in εὔθετος,[81] a word which also, it has been recognised, evokes the laying out of the body at a funeral.[82]

In the ninth book of the *Iliad* Agamemnon offers Akhilleus numerous valuable gifts as persuasion to return to the battle, but Akhilleus rejects them. All the wealth of Troy, and of Delphi too, says Akhilleus, is not equal in value (ἀντάξιος) to my ψυχή (soul or life). Cattle and sheep, he explains, can be plundered and tripods and horses can be obtained, whereas the ψυχή of a man cannot be plundered or captured to come back again once it were to exchange the barrier of his teeth (401–9). ἀμείβεσθαι elsewhere in the *Iliad* always refers to *exchange* (of armour). Uniquely in Homer, we have here an explicit comparative evaluation of basic categories

80 'Gold-changer' is χρυσαμοιβός, which occurs only here (and in Hsch.). Cf. ἀργυραμοιβός, a name given by Plato (*Plt.* 289e) to those free men who trade 'in the market-place or by travelling from city to city by sea or by land, exchanging currency (χρυσαμοιβός) for other things or currency for currency'. χρυσαμοιβός is more appropriate than ἀργυραμοιβός to the heroic age and to a god.

81 The mss. εὐθέτου ('of the ash') has been emended to εὐθέτους ('of the urns'), unnecessarily. And the corruption would be much more likely the other way (Denniston and Page 1957: *ad loc.*).

82 Phryn. *Praep. Soph.* 71.9 (von Borries) εὐθετεῖν νεκρόν· τὸ εὖ κοσμεῖν ἐν τάφοις νεκρόν; Dio. Cass. 40.49; *SEG* 1.449. Fraenkel's comment on *Ag.* 444 that this sense 'is irrelevant here, for the bodies have been cremated' misses the exquisitely bitter combination in a single word of opposites – impersonal commercial convenience and the ritualised love for a dead family member.

(wealth against life), perhaps as a heroic rejection of the incipient power of money.[83] Although life is too valuable to be exchanged for wealth, death is envisaged by Akhilleus as itself a kind of (irreversible) exchange of life, as it is sometimes in tragedy – for [*129*] example[84] in Euripides' *Suppliants* (775–7): 'this is the only expenditure (ἀνάλωμα) that you cannot obtain once it is spent – human life; whereas there are means of raising money'.[85] The image of the gold-changer in the *Agamemnon* combines these notions and takes them further. The death-as-exchange occurs, like the death-as-exchange mentioned by Akhilleus, in battle. And this is precisely the death (on behalf of the Atreidai at Troy) that is bitterly rejected by Akhilleus. Further, the idea of a trader (Ares) *presiding*[86] over warfare implies that the aim of the warfare is gain. In the anonymous tragic fragment quoted in §2 it is said that for those at war gold has more power than Ares, and that Ares follows the enchantment of gold. And so, given that in the *Iliad* Akhilleus complains that Agamemnon takes the most and best spoils of the war for himself (1.165–8, 9.330–3), it may even be that the Aeschylean image of dying as an exchange (of bodies for ash) implies the further notion that the exchange involves gain for the Atreidai, against whom the Greeks direct bitter φθόνος (450), angry talk and curses (456).

Because its power appears transcendent and unlimited, money seems able even *to exchange into their opposite* things (any commodity into money, large into small, life into death) as well as people, whether because they desire money (honest people into criminals at Soph. *Ant.* 298–9) or because they have it: a bad man into a good one (Thgn. 1117–18), a slave into an honoured man (Eur. fr. 142), a poor speaker into a clever one and an ugly person into a beautiful one (Soph. fr. 88), even, we saw in the *Agamemnon*, a man into something like a god.[87]

As well as this power of exchange into the opposite, money in the *Agamemnon* seems able to do opposite things: to save life and to destroy it, to please the gods and to offend them. The unlimited, out-of-sight power of the household's money, embodied in the invisible inexhaustibility of the sea and of the 'ever-renewed gush, equal to silver' of the dye produced in its depths, is ambivalent. On the one hand, in the hypotheses of Klytaimestra, it may please the gods and save Agamemnon's life. The trampling of the

[83] I will argue this in detail elsewhere [Seaford 2004d: 301–3].
[84] See also *Med.* 968, *Hipp.* 964–5; cf. Soph. *OT* 30.
[85] ... χρημάτων δ' εἰσὶν πόροι – a regular phrase for raising money: LSJ, s.v. πόρος ii.3.
[86] Because holding the balance (439), like Zeus at Hom. *Il.* 8.69, 16.658, 19.223–4, 22.209.
[87] Or, in the words of Soph. fr. 88.2–3, money can acquire 'the seat of highest tyranny that is nearest to the gods' (adopting Conington's θεοῖσιν for the nonsensical ἄκουσιν or τ' ἄγουσιν of the mss).

'many cloths', dyed with valuable but inexhaustible dye and bought with silver, is enclosed by the imagination of Klytaimestra within a ritual framework: anxiety is allayed by imagining the containment of material excess within ritual prescribed by experts. The hypothetical ritual is called by Agamemnon a τέλος. The basic sense of τέλος, which it certainly retains when applied to ritual, is that of *completion*. τέλος can also mean 'that which is paid for state purposes',[88] and τελεῖν can mean simply 'to pay'. As well as making rituals possible, money also *resembles* ritual in certain respects. The efficacy of both depends on collective trust in the efficacy of a detached paradigm that persists through everyday vicissitudes.[89] And rites of passage in particular may, like money, be agents of transformation into the opposite.

On the other hand, whereas the power of ritual may derive from its self-containment (as a paradigm of how things should be) and its function may be precisely to limit or to contain – for instance to mark the end of a period of hostility or of mourning, or indeed to mark a prudent limit to good fortune by an offering to deity – the power of money is (in the sense we have described) essentially unlimited. And this unlimited power, embodied in the trampled textiles, seems to doom Agamemnon. As he himself anxiously admits, they constitute an honour appropriate only for a god. He walks over them to his death. In this respect it is highly *[130]* significant that the textile in which Klytaimestra then traps Agamemnon so as to kill him is, it has been pointed out,[90] associated with the textiles that he trampled. They are both referred to by the same vocabulary.[91] And the murder-cloth on stage at the end of the *Choephori* was, if not the same prop, at least a strong visual reminder of the earlier sight of the trampled cloths, especially as it is said to have been *dyed* by Aigisthos' sword (the trampled textiles were πόρφυρος,[92] the colour of blood),[93] and stained by the κηκίς (gush) of blood, with its evocation of the κηκίς of dye referred to by Klytaimestra. It is as if the woven cloth which Klytaimestra imagined as saving Agamemnon's life has become what Orestes calls the 'father-killing woven cloth' (*Cho.* 1015 πατροκτόνον γ' ὕφασμα).

88 LSJ, s.v. τέλος v.
89 See e.g. Douglas 1966: 69: 'money is only an extreme and specialised type of ritual'.
90 E.g by Taplin 1978: 79–82.
91 εἷμα at *Ag.* 921, 960, 963, 1383; ποικιλ- at *Ag.* 923, 926, 936, *Cho.* 1013, *Eum.* 460.
92 *Ag.* 910, 957.
93 At Ach. Tat. 2.11.5–6 the dye πόρφυρος is mistaken for blood; Hom. *Il.* 17.361; Ap. Rhod. 4.668; Bion, *Epitaph.* 27; etc.

I have elsewhere argued in detail that various features of Klytaimestra's treatment of Agamemnon, including the cloth in which she traps him, form a coherent complex designed to evoke the death ritual given to a man by his wife.[94] Agamemnon is killed by the cloth in which normally a woman lovingly wraps her dead husband,[95] and which has normally been woven by the women of the household,[96] often presumably by his wife.[97] Death ritual encloses within a traditional, reassuring order[98] the brutality of death. In the *Agamemnon*, with death ritual as the expression of brutal violence, the enclosure is turned inside out. The temporal aspect of this reversal is the (anomalous) perpetuation of the ritual: Agamemnon, not yet laid to rest, continues (in the *Choephori*) to be lamented, and unsuccessfully appeased (by the libations of Klytaimestra).[99] The lamentation arouses the emotions needed for the matricide and so helps to perpetuate the reciprocal violence. The last lines of the *Choephori* ask despairingly: where will the might of destruction end?

Normally the grief inspired by death must not overturn the traditional limitations set by ritual and by legislation; such overturning may (in cases of murder) encourage uncontrolled vendetta, whereas it is vital for the polis that revenge too should be contained within traditional limitations.[100] In the *Oresteia* there is systematic subversion of such traditional limitations, and one agent of this subversion is the unlimited power of money. It is not just that the money of the household is what Aigisthos hopes to rule by, and what Orestes hopes to regain. Rather, the unlimited power of money is, we saw, embodied in the cloths trampled by Agamemnon, which are associated with the cloth that kills him. Further, of the cloth that kills him Klytaimestra says (*Ag.* 1382–3): [*131*]

[94] Seaford 1984c[II].

[95] See esp. Eur. *Tro.* 377–8 οὐ δάμαρτος ἐν χεροῖν πέπλοις συνεστάλησαν (and 390). On the link between φιλία and the handling (washing and dressing) of the corpse see esp. Soph. *Ant.* 897–902.

[96] Hom. *Il.* 22.510–11.

[97] In the *Odyssey* Penelope does so for the widower Laertes.

[98] Expressed e.g. in the word εὔθετος: see n. 82 above.

[99] It is also relevant to our theme to note that Klytaimestra's 'gifts' to her murdered husband are 'less than the offence. For someone to pour out everything in exchange for one blood [i.e. life] is labour in vain' (*Cho.* 519–21). Although both blood and offerings can be 'poured out', once again it is said that life is more valuable than all wealth. οὐκ ἔχοιμ' ἂν εἰκάσαι τάδε τὰ δῶρα· (a better reading than τόδε· ...) in the previous line has never been properly understood (e.g. Lloyd-Jones translates 'I do not know to what to liken these her gifts'). In fact it refers to the lack of equivalence between the offerings and what they are an attempt to compensate for. The phrase οὐκ ἔχω (προσ)εικάζειν occurs elsewhere in Aeschylus only at *Ag.* 163, where its meaning is interestingly similar (in the image of a balance).

[100] Seaford 1994b: 74–105.

> ἄπειρον ἀμφίβληστρον, ὥσπερ ἰχθύων,
> περιστιχίζω, πλοῦτον εἵματος κακόν.
>
> A covering without end, like [a net] for fish, I set around him, an evil wealth of cloth.

ἀμφίβληστρον is from the verb ἀμφιβάλλω, which is used for dressing the corpse, and so suggests a shroud. Why is it 'without end' (ἄπειρον)? Because, unlike garments worn by the living, the funerary garment was wrapped around the hands and feet of the corpse, and sometimes even the head. It encloses, like the net which is ἄπειρον in the sense that it has no πέρας, no end or limit past which the quarry can escape. And indeed in the hands of Klytaimestra it has in effect become such a net. All this has been argued in detail elsewhere.[101] The further point to make here is that from ἄπειρον also flows the description 'evil wealth of cloth'. The cloth comes from the household's unlimited 'silver-bought' supply, in sharp contrast to the ritualised specificity of the cloth normally woven within a man's household (presumably often by his wife) for his corpse. The unlimited money of the household that was earlier embodied in the cloths trampled by Agamemnon is now embodied in the cloth that kills him because it has no limit. In a manner characteristic of the astonishing imagination of Aeschylus, the abstraction of dangerously unlimited money is expressed in a concrete instrument of Agamemnon's death.

The unlimited money was in fact embodied in the cloth through its dye, the 'ever-renewed gush (κηκίς), equal to silver, of much purple, the dyeings of cloths'. Even in this particular the physical embodiment of the dangerous notion of unlimited wealth seems to turn against its owner, for the same word, κηκίς, is used of the gush of blood that (like the dye) stained the murder-cloth, displayed by Orestes as he stands in the toils of apparently ever-renewed vendetta at the end of the *Choephori* (1012). He has just decided, as he addresses the cloth, that it is not so much a shroud as a net (998–9), and indeed 'the kind of net possessed by a brigand, a cheater of travellers, leading a life that deprives people of money/silver' (1002–3 ἀργυροστερῆ βίον νομίζων). The detail here is puzzling. Perhaps we can make sense of it as flowing from the notion of the cloth as used to deprive the king of the unlimited money that it also embodies.

To conclude, the unlimited power of money, embodied in the cloth, is set by Klytaimestra within the limits of (hypothetical) ritual, but with the killing of Agamemnon subverts those limits and displays once again the

[101] Seaford 1984c[11].

power of money to exchange things into their opposite. This dialectic of money and death ritual I will now pursue in the *Antigone.*

4. Sophocles: *Antigone*

Kreon's first speech in Sophocles' *Antigone* announces the edict forbidding the burial of Polyneikes. It is followed by an interchange with the chorus that, despite its brevity, reveals much. Kreon asks them not to side with 'those who disobey these things' (219). And when they reply that nobody is foolish enough to have a passion for death, Kreon agrees that death is indeed the payment, but that gain (κέρδος) often ruins men through their hopes. There follows immediately the news that death ritual has been performed for Polyneikes, to which Kreon responds by being 'completely certain' (ἐξεπίσταμαι καλῶς) that his political opponents have bribed the guards to do it (289–94), adding a generalisation about the power of money, as follows (295–301): [132]

> οὐδὲν γὰρ ἀνθρώποισιν οἷον ἄργυρος
> κακὸν νομίσμ' ἔβλαστε· τοῦτο καὶ πόλεις
> πορθεῖ, τόδ' ἄνδρας ἐξανίστησιν δόμων,
> τόδ' ἐκδιδάσκει καὶ παραλλάσσει φρένας
> χρηστὰς πρὸς αἰσχρὰ πράγμαθ' ἵστασθαι βροτῶν·
> πανουργίας δ' ἔδειξεν ἀνθρώποις ἔχειν
> καὶ πάντος ἔργου δυσσέβειαν εἰδέναι.

> no currency ever grew up among human kind as evil as money: this lays waste even cities, this expels men from their homes, this thoroughly (ἐκ-) teaches and alters good minds of mortals to set themselves to disgraceful acts; it showed men how to practise villainies and to know every act of impiety.

In this striking statement of the unlimited impersonal power of money, which we have already mentioned (in §3) as an example of its power of transformation into the opposite, we should notice here three things. The first is that Kreon seems to mean not just money but specifically coinage. 'Silver' (rather than gold, as at 1039) was the material of contemporary Athenian (and most Greek) coinage. The word νόμισμα means something like 'custom', but could also mean coinage ('currency' has a similar range), and so could hardly fail to suggest coinage here. It is as if Sophocles has coinage in mind, but does not want to commit the anachronism of locating it in the heroic age. The second point of interest is the emphasis on the *psychology* of money: it is said to teach and alter minds, and enable us to 'know' impiety. Third, Kreon says that there is no act of impiety that money will not enable us to know (πάντος ἔργου). The power is unlimited even against the imperatives of religion. But how can performing death ritual be impiety? It is, rather, Kreon's denial of burial that would seem to most Athenians to be just such an act of extreme impiety.[102] It seems to be Kreon himself who is transforming things into their opposite, a transformation later expressed in the words of Antigone: 'I obtained impiety by being pious' (924 τὴν δυσσέβειαν εὐσεβοῦσ' ἐκτησάμην).

The episode ends with Kreon firm in his view that what he is contending with is the power of money (322, 326). He even accuses the guard of 'giving up his life/soul for money' (322 ἐπ' ἀργύρῳ γε τὴν ψυχὴν προδούς). Kreon is completely certain that the performance of the death ritual is to be attributed to the power of money, and so implicitly excludes the possibility that it has been performed for its inherent value – just as he excludes this inherent value also from his own decision to ban the death ritual, never even *weighing up* the importance of death ritual against the importance of not honouring traitors.

Kreon's attitude to money is explored further, much later in the play, in his intense confrontation with the seer Teiresias. Faced with Teiresias' exposure of the error of denying Polyneikes burial, Kreon replies that he has 'long been traded and made into cargo' (1036 ἐξημπόλημαι κἀκπεφόρτισμαι πάλαι) by the tribe of seers. The verbs used are striking, and they are precise. Kreon imagines himself as like a slave shipped off to be sold. Just as the cargo makes profit for the trader who controls it, so Kreon claims that he has in the past made profit (presumably unwittingly) for the corrupt seers by accepting their advice. This (mistaken) sense Kreon has of having been wholly in the power of money is a little later given an explicit psychological dimension, when Kreon says to Teiresias 'know that you will not purchase my mind' (1063 ὡς μὴ 'μπολήσων ἴσθι τὴν ἐμὴν φρένα). 'Purchase my mind' does not mean that Teiresias intends to bribe Kreon, rather that for Kreon to obey would be to sell his mind in the sense that it would be (indirectly and unwittingly) in the power of the money paid to Teiresias. The implication of 1036, that the power of money may be unseen by its victims, is in 1063 made a little more explicit in the notion of purchasing (and so controlling) the *mind*. *[133]* A similar phrase occurs elsewhere only in Sophocles' *Trachiniae*: Deianeira compares her reception of the youthful Iole into her house as 'like a sailor [receiving] a cargo, harmful merchandise of my mind' (537–8 φόρτον ὥστε ναυτίλος, λωβητὸν

[102] Cf e.g. Eur. *Supp*. 123, 520–63 (Theseus on the unburied dead at Thebes); Phylarchus, *FGrHist* 81 F45 *ap*. Ath. 12.521d.

ἐμπόλημα τῆς ἐμῆς φρένος). The rare word ἐμπόλημα refers to what is traded, or to the profit made by trade. Iole is to Deianeira as an ἐμπόλημα is to a sailor not only in that Deianeira has received her into her house/ship, but also in that the merchandise may harm (λωβητός) the sailor: the profitable merchandise on which the sailor is intent (paradoxically, for he does not want it for himself) may bring him to a watery grave.[103] Similarly the 'cargo' taken on by Deianeira may, though not for herself, destructively absorb her mind, an absorption expressed by the juxtaposition ἐμπόλημα τῆς ἐμῆς φρένος. As in the similar phrase in the *Antigone*, there is a sense of the power of monetary gain to absorb or invade the mind.

The context of Kreon's remarkable statement at 1063 deserves scrutiny. His continuing accusations of venality (1037, 1047, 1055) have been met with a *vos quoque* by Teiresias: to Kreon's view that all seers love money he responds (1056) that it is the characteristic of tyrants to love disgraceful gain (αἰσχροκέρδειαν). Teiresias is, as usual, correct. Wealth and tyranny are often mentioned together,[104] for instance of Kreon himself a little later (1168–9). Further, in Sophocles' *Oedipus Tyrannus* (541–2) it was pointed out, again to Kreon, that to obtain tyranny you need money (χρήματα),[105] and in fr. 88 it is said that with χρήματα people acquire tyranny.[106]

When a little later Kreon repeats yet again the charge of venality, 'Reveal, only speaking not for gain', Teiresias replies οὕτω ἤδη καὶ δοκῶ τὸ σὸν μέρος (1062). The meaning and interest of this line have never been realised. In order to bring out its subtle significance we will have to resort to detailed analysis and to what may seem rather ponderous paraphrase.

The line has been interpreted in two different ways, depending on whether δοκῶ is taken to mean 'I think' or 'I seem': first, as a grim understatement of Kreon's impending catastrophe, 'I think [to be about to speak] thus [i.e. with no gain] for you too already' or (amounting to the same meaning) 'I think your part [i.e. the outcome for you] too [to be] already thus [i.e. not gainful]', and second, as a question, 'Do I already seem in your view [to be speaking] thus [i.e. for gain]?' The most recent commentator (Brown), while admitting that neither interpretation is satisfactory, prefers (as does Jebb) the former. But the phrase τὸ σὸν μέρος can

[103] That is why, as we saw (§3) at Aesch. *Ag.* 1008–14, it may be advisable to jettison the cargo.

[104] E.g. Soph. *OT* 380, fr. 88; Eur. *Supp.* 450–1, *Ion* 625–30, *Or.* 1156, fr. 420. Note the τυραννικὴ οὐσία of Kimon ([Arist.] *Ath. Pol.* 27.3).

[105] See also Hdt. 1.61, 64; Pl. *Resp.* 1.338a–b, 8.567d, 8.568d. The sentiment in *OT* must have been strongly felt, for it applies in fact to the career neither of Oidipous nor of Kreon.

[106] Literally χρήματα 'finds' for people friends, honours and the seat of highest tyranny, nearest to the gods (see n. 87 above). The fr. was mentioned in §2.

mean neither 'for you' nor 'the outcome for you'. Nor on the other hand can it mean 'in your view'. It occurs twice elsewhere in Sophocles, in both cases in the same place in the line as here. Oidipous tells Kreon that his daughters are destitute πλὴν ὅσον τὸ σὸν μέρος, 'except in so far as your part', i.e. except for what you do for them (*OT* 1509). Secondly, Oidipous tells Polyneikes (*OC* 1366) that without his daughters he would not still exist, τὸ σὸν μέρος, i.e. 'as far as your part is concerned'. And the very similar adverbial τοὐμὸν μέρος occurs once in Sophocles, again in the same place in the line, when Hyllos tells his father Herakles that, in the preparation for his death, οὐ καμῇ τοὐμὸν μέρος, 'you will have no difficulty as far as my part is concerned'.[107] The phrase consistently means something like 'as far as your (or my) part is concerned'. The effect of your (or my) part is (or would be, [134] were there no other factors) what is described in the verb: Oidipous would not still exist; Herakles will have no difficulty.[108]

What is Kreon's part, such that (if the only factor) its result is that 'I seem (or think) to be speaking for gain'? It can hardly be other than his arrogant and suspicious behaviour, characteristic of the tyrant. Also characteristic of the tyrant, Teiresias has just pointed out, is love of gain (1056). And so Teiresias' words mean 'For [i.e. you say what you have said because] I too *seem* [as well as you, who however really are mercenary] [to speak] thus [for gain] already [even before having made the revelation], as far as your part in the situation is concerned [i.e. your tyrannical outlook].' That is to say, 'so far as your tyrannical outlook is concerned, yes, I must seem to you right from the start to be speaking for gain, because tyrants love gain'.[109] This interpretation gives point to every word in the line, as well as to Kreon's reply (discussed above) that Teiresias will not purchase his mind. This reply means, as argued above, 'my mind will not succumb to your attempt to control it by the power of money that motivates you'. But it can now be seen to be also appropriate specifically as a reply to (our interpretation of) the previous line: Kreon mentions his own mind to defend it against Teiresias' implication that it is under the power of money.

Teiresias' implication is crucial for the understanding of Kreon. From the beginning, the tyrant has seen in the resistance to him nothing other than the power of money, a power for which, he believes, people may give up even their lives (221–2, 322). His persistence in this vehement blindness

[107] Similarly Eur. *Heracl.* 678; [*Rhes.*] 405; Pl. *Cri.* 45d2, 50b2, 54c8, *Epist.* 7.328e1.

[108] In a more complex construction (with πλήν) the daughters of Oidipous would be destitute or not destitute.

[109] Even if δοκῶ means 'I think', this would give much the same meaning, with δοκῶ sarcastic.

is, Teiresias indicates, characteristically tyrannical. Tyrants are arrogant and suspicious, and see the world in terms of monetary gain. Kreon reacts to threat by angrily projecting the same narrowness of vision onto his opponents. He resembles, on this interpretation, the other Theban tragic tyrants Oidipous and Pentheus in that, like them, he spends the first part of the drama vehemently persecuting what he himself turns out to be. The narrowness of vision is in all three cases finally blown apart. Reporting the death of Haimon, the messenger reflects that household wealth and tyrannical *bella figura* (σχῆμα) are worthless ('I would not buy them for the shadow of smoke') without happiness (1168–71). In the end the only 'gain' (κέρδος) for Kreon is to be led away (1324–6). In fact, all the evil consequences of money noted by Kreon in the passage quoted above (295–301) may be said in the end to apply to himself: devastation of the polis (cf. 1015 νοσεῖ πόλις), the expulsion of men from their homes, good minds altered to perform disgraceful deeds, and extreme impiety. It is the money-obsessed tyrant who, as we saw Antigone implying in the matter of impiety and piety, has transformed things into their opposite.

This interpretation of what Teiresias says at 1062 is confirmed by his next words, the opening of his devastating final speech (1064–90). It will not be long, he says to Kreon, before

> you will have given in return (ἀντιδούς) a corpse from your own vital parts [i.e. Haimon], an exchange (ἀμοιβόν) for corpses, wherefore (ἀνθ' ὧν) you on the one hand have (ἔχεις μέν) [one] of those above, having thrust it below (τῶν ἄνω βαλὼν κάτω), having lodged a soul ignominiously in a tomb [Antigone], and you on the other hand have (ἔχεις δέ) [one] of those below,[110] a corpse dispossessed, without death ritual, impure [Polyneikes].

These lines are often rightly cited as expressing the dual perversion of ritual norms that is somehow at the heart of the *Antigone*. What has not attracted attention is the extent to which this involves *exchange*. The corpse of Haimon will be given *in exchange* for (it is thrice declared) the corpses *in the possession* of Kreon. Whether we translate ἀνθ' ὧν here 'because' (as most translators do) or 'wherefore' (its more frequent meaning), it must, as it does [135] elsewhere,[111] refer to exchange. Hence the emphasised (by

[110] The mss. θεῶν is suspect, and I have omitted it from my translation (this does not affect my argument).

[111] LSJ cite, under the meaning 'because' (A.i.3), this line of *Ant.* and Ar. *Plut.* 433–4, which however means 'you will pay the penalty *in return for* your attempt to banish me'. Under the meaning 'wherefore', LSJ cite [Aesch.] *PV* 31, Soph. *OT* 264, Thuc. 6.83.1, *Ev. Luc.* 12.3; and Jebb 1891 on 1068 cites Soph. *OC* 1295; but in all these cases too (except the much later *Ev. Luc.* 12.3) it is a matter of exchange.

position) and repeated ἔχεις. ἔχεις ... βαλὼν κάτω does not mean 'you have thrust the corpse below',[112] but rather 'you have (i.e. possess) the corpse, having thrust it below', just as the second (parallel) ἔχεις, which has no attendant participle, must refer to possession. In fact Kreon's perversion of death ritual is envisaged as a hideous exchange, in which because he controls and possesses the corpses (where they should not be) he has in return to pay with the corpse of his own son. This disastrous *possession* of the corpses whose death ritual he controls is of a piece with the tyrannical desire for gain to which Teiresias has directly (1056) and indirectly (1062) just referred. That is perhaps why Teiresias says that Kreon will have given only one (ἕνα) corpse in exchange for two.

The transaction is precisely antithetical to the one imagined earlier by Antigone (461–8), in which, balancing premature death against the evils of her life and the pain of not burying her own brother, she chooses premature death as representing a *gain* (κέρδος). Decisive is the (non-monetary) value of death ritual and of the good relations with her blood-kin in the next world[113] that her performance of their death ritual ensures (897–902).[114] By contrast, whatever Kreon gains by his perversion of death ritual he has to pay for with the bitter alienation and death of his blood-kin, 'a corpse from your own vital parts'. The girl innocent of money registers an overall gain, the money-obsessed tyrant an overall loss.[115]

The value to which Kreon professes allegiance is not of course monetary but the well-being of the polis. There is, nevertheless, a subterranean contradiction between this allegiance to the polis and his elaborate condemnation of silver as an evil 'currency' (νόμισμα). Coinage was a creation of the polis, and the word for it (νόμισμα) indicates the fact that coinage depended for its acceptability on the νόμοι, the conventions and laws, of

112 Thus Brown 1987, and similarly other translators. Translations of Greek tragedy regularly eliminate what seems awkward or unfamiliar, and thereby fail to reproduce precisely what is interesting.

113 Her location of value in Hades is sufficient to shed doubt on certain values in this world (521).

114 What may seem to some paradoxical – that this value produces an overall gain despite being non-monetary – is brought out by the word κέρδος.

115 Further, the replaceability of the spouse (or betrothed) – stressed by both Kreon (526) and Antigone (909) – is analogous to the replaceability of goods by means of money, whereas the *natural* tie of blood-kin may be, Antigone maintains (911–2), irreplaceable: see Murnaghan 1986: 199; Seaford 1994b: 216–18. Similarly Klytaimestra, who implies the unlimited power of money to replace goods (§3), has already replaced her spouse, while ironically praising his *uniqueness* (Aesch. *Ag.* 895–901 – in images associated with death ritual: Seaford 1984c[II]: 254), having just used (888) the same verb (κατασβέννυμι) of her tears for him having dried up as she later uses to express the *in*exhaustibility of the sea (as a metaphor, we have seen, for the unlimited power of money). I owe much in this note to Betty Belfiore.

the polis.[116] The very metaphor with which Kreon opens his elaborate profession of devotion to the polis assimilates the ruler[117] to a coin: you cannot know the soul, mentality and judgement of anybody, he says, until he is seen 'proved in rubbing against rule and laws' (177 ἀρχαῖς τε καὶ νόμοισιν ἐντριβής). ἐντριβής is a metaphor from rubbing precious metal against the touchstone. Its juxtaposition with νόμοισιν evokes the legislative concern of the polis to ensure by testing the *[136]* quality of its coins.[118] Now one aspect of the tyrants' use (noted above) of money to establish and maintain their power was their control of the novel power of coinage. To take an Athenian example,[119] Peisistratos not only used money to obtain (Hdt. 1.62.2) and confirm (Hdt. 1.64.1) his tyranny, but may well have presided over the introduction of coinage into Athens.[120] And there was a tradition that his son the tyrant Hippias, a contemporary of the older members of Sophocles' audience, manipulated the coinage.[121]

Kreon, then, expresses devotion to the polis, even though he also claims that the polis belongs to himself as ruler (738). He attributes desire for the uniquely harmful νόμισμα of silver to his enemies, even though members of the audience would be well aware that a tyrant relies on the νόμισμα of silver.[122] 'Do not', says Haimon to Kreon, 'keep only one disposition (ἦθος) within you, that what *you* say, and nothing else, is right' (705–6). We may perhaps regard the exclusive pursuit of a single value to be a habit of mind influenced by money, even though the single value pursued is not acknowledged to be money.[123] Indeed, how could it be? In a manoeuvre well known to modern psychology[124] and depicted (though not of course theorised) elsewhere in tragedy,[125] Kreon cannot allow himself

[116] See esp. Arist. *Pol.* 1257b, *Eth. Nic.* 1133a. Inscribed laws have survived enforcing the acceptability and use of local currency: the Attic inscription referred to below (n. 118); also *SIG*³ 218, 525.

[117] That the ruler is meant is clear from 177 ἀρχαῖς and 178.

[118] See e.g. the inscribed Attic law published by Stroud 1974: 157–8: *inter alia* the public tester is to neutralise silver coins which are bronze or lead underneath.

[119] From many other instances we may cite the tradition that Polykrates (cf. n. 72) manipulated the Samian coinage.

[120] Kraay 1976: 58–9.

[121] [Arist.] *Oec.* 1347a (fourth century).

[122] We may even be reminded of the tyrant described by Thrasymakhos in Plato's *Republic*, whose massive thefts and enslavement of the citizen body are sanctioned by the justice that he himself creates (justice being 'the interest of the stronger'): *Resp.* 1.338e, 1.344a–c.

[123] Nussbaum 1986: 58 writes 'By making all values commensurable in terms of a single coin – he is preoccupied with the image of coinage and profit in ethical matters – Creon achieves singleness, straightness, and an apparent stability.' This is perceptive, but money in the play does, I believe, far more than provide ethical imagery that is analogous to Kreon's habit of mind.

[124] See e.g. Rycroft 1968: 29–30, 125–6; Laplanche and Portalis 1988: 349–60.

[125] Notably in Pentheus in Eur. *Bacch.*, as shown by Parsons 1988, who also offers an excellent general defence of the application of psychoanalytic insights to tragedy.

to acknowledge the ambivalence within himself (as a tyrant) between devotion to the polis and self-seeking power; and so on the one hand he vehemently professes the former and on the other hand he subconsciously *denies* the latter within himself, vehemently *projecting* it onto others. There is a similar and related manoeuvre, shortly before his rejection of monetary control over his mind, in his angry remark to Teiresias: 'Make your profit, trade in electrum from Sardis and Indian gold. You will not cover that man with a tomb' (1037–9). Whereas earlier the corrupting element was, according to Kreon, the silver currency of the polis, now it is gold and electrum (a natural alloy of gold and silver) from distant parts. It is as if Kreon, now increasingly threatened, is so keen to keep money (which we know his position in the polis requires) separate from himself and his polis, that he projects money (together therefore with the allegiance of his enemies who seek it) onto foreign parts, well away from himself and his polis.

In *Agamemnon* the unlimited wealth of the tyrannical household, embodied in the murderous cloth, perverts death ritual into its opposite: the cloth with which a dead man is usually lovingly wrapped by his wife becomes an 'evil wealth of cloth' by which, precisely because it is 'unlimited', Agamemnon is trapped by his wife. The death ritual[126] of Antigone is, like that of Agamemnon, a means of killing her. And this, together with the opposite perversion [137] of keeping the dead Polyneikes unburied, is inflicted by the unlimited power of a tyrant for whom money is so important that his vision of its unlimited power seems to make him blind to the claims of death ritual, and whose consequent perversion of death ritual is expressed in terms of possession in return for which he must after all give up what is most dear to him. In both dramas the implicit contradiction between the unlimited impersonal power of money and the absolute personal claim for death ritual is expressed in catastrophic perversion of the ritual.

5. Euripides: *Electra*

The contradiction between on the one hand the impersonal, generalised value of money and on the other hand the individual significance of a kin-relationship (and of objects specific to it) will now be pursued in Euripides' *Electra*. The old man, who has arrived with meat and wine for Elektra's guests (as yet unrecognised as Orestes and Pylades), stares intently at Orestes. 'Why', asks Orestes, 'is he staring at me as if looking at a bright

[126] The procession to the 'tomb' clearly evokes a funeral procession (806–16, 891–4).

mark on silver? Is he matching me with someone/something?' (558–9 τί μ' ἐσέδορκεν ὥσπερ ἀργύρου σκοπῶν λαμπρὸν χαρακτῆρ'; ἢ προσεικάζει μέ τῳ;). As we saw also in the *Antigone*, it is as if the dramatist has coinage in mind, but does not want to commit the anachronism of naming it directly.

The old man is in fact 'matching' someone unknown to him (the stranger, who could be anyone) with a specific person whom he remembers (Orestes). Now 'matches' must also make sense in terms of the immediately preceding coinage metaphor, and so implies (whether or not προσεικάζειν was a technical term for it) the matching of the mark on this particular coin with the *type* of coin-mark that guarantees authenticity,[127] for that would be the point of intense staring at the mark on the coin, whether by ordinary people or by the testers called ἀργυροσκόποι[128] or ἀργυρογνώμονες.[129] But this implies a process antithetical to the matching of a stranger with Orestes. The stranger, who could be anybody, is identified as a unique individual, whereas to identify a coin as authentic by 'looking at the mark' means to identify the presence of the general type to be found also in any authentic coin. Perhaps then, we may be tempted to say, the point of the metaphor is confined entirely to the intentness with which the old man looks at Orestes.

But we cannot so restrict the metaphor, for in fact it extends throughout the process of recognition. A few lines earlier, on first seeing the strangers, the old man says (550–1) 'they are well-born (εὐγενεῖς) – but this is ἐν κιβδήλῳ: for many who are well-born are bad'. κίβδηλος means false or spurious, 'especially of coin' (LSJ). 'O Zeus,' says Euripides' Medea, 'why have you provided for humankind clear signs of what gold is κίβδηλος, but there is no natural mark (χαρακτῆρ ἐμπέφυκε) on the body of men by which to distinguish the bad' (*Med.* 516–19). This contrast is already in Theognis (119–24), with the difference that by the time of the tragedians it has been influenced by coinage.[130] Gold can be tested (e.g. by the touchstone), but in the late fifth century the most widespread means of guaranteeing the value of precious metal was the engraved or impressed mark (χαρακτῆρ – from χαράσσειν, 'to cut, engrave, inscribe') on silver coinage. Men, unlike gold, cannot be easily tested. And, unlike coins, they do not have a χαρακτῆρ on their bodies. Orestes however does indeed have such a

127 That is so whether the type is merely remembered or is to hand in a coin known to be genuine.
128 *IG* V.1390.47–8; Phryn. *Praep. Soph.* 30.10 (de Borries).
129 [Pl.] *Virt.* 378e.
130 Falsely stamped coin is a moral image already at Aesch. *Ag.* 780.

χαρακτῆρ. Elektra, still not yet persuaded by the old man that the stranger is Orestes, asks (572) 'what χαρακτῆρ can you see by which I will be persuaded?' The word χαρακτῆρ does not follow from what [138] precedes, but is rather chosen by Euripides to anticipate the old man's reply: a scar.

The novelty of coinage, from a semiotic perspective, is that the sign (the mark) authenticates its own material (the metal). In this respect coinage differs from such authenticating signs as, say, a token carried by someone to authenticate their identity, or even from a seal authenticating a document. Now the scar is a traditional token of identification, most famously in the Homeric homecoming of Odysseus.[131] But of all the traditional tokens of identification only the scar resembles the mark on coinage – as something inscribed or impressed, and so part of what it authenticates. The scar is, at least here at *El.* 572, a χαρακτῆρ.

Immediately before the recognition there is a long passage in which Elektra dismisses the tokens advanced by the old man as signs of Orestes: a lock of hair and a footprint found at Agamemnon's tomb, and a woven cloth. This has been much discussed, often with the justified assumption that the point cannot merely be criticism of the effectiveness of these tokens in Aeschylus' version. Although Elektra turns out to be wrong about hair, footprint and cloth, it is of course more sensible to be convinced by a scar. But why then were the tokens effective in Aeschylus, and why the emphatic difference in Euripides? The hair, footprint and cloth are invested with the personal identity of Orestes. The hair also embodies his relation with his father enacted in death ritual, and the cloth his relation with his sister. But the scar (unlike the other tokens, which are hard to match with certainty to what they authenticate) is like a coin-mark, part of what it authenticates. The convenience of self-authentication would have contributed to the rapid spread of coinage.

Elektra's dismissal of hair, footprints and cloth may have various functions, such as (it has been suggested) to express her nervous reluctance to accept such wonderful news. But we can also say that the old poetic notion of a thing so closely associated with an individual as to be an unmistakeable token may reflect a past world in which the impersonal power of money, and especially of coinage, has not yet largely replaced the power of objects that are envisaged as unique because invested with personal identity or 'talismanic' power. Examples of objects invested with personal identity would be the gift, or the shroud – or Akhilleus' shield, which is

[131] *Od.* 19.390–475; 21.217–23. Odysseus' scar was acquired in a hunt. So too was Orestes' but, as he was a small child, the hunt becomes a playful chase of a fawn inside the house (or courtyard).

to be found in the choral ode (432–86) preceding the recognition, with its 'signs in the circle' (ἐν κύκλῳ ... σήματα), antithetically to a coin-mark, terrifying in heroic battle.[132] Examples of objects invested with talismanic power would be a royal sceptre – or the golden lamb that bestowed sovereignty in Argos and is to be found in the choral ode (699–746) following the recognition.[133] In this way Elektra's dismissal of the tokens is of a piece with the monetary dimension of the recognition.

We are now in a position to re-describe the apparent ineptness of the phrase ἦ προσεικάζει με (559). The scar identifies Orestes as a unique individual, the long-lost brother. But the coin-metaphor, appropriate though it turns out to be to the identifying scar (χαρακτῆρ), implies the recognition not of a unique identity but of its opposite, of a type and of the quality guaranteed not (as in heroic myth) by a unique identity but rather by adherence to the type. Once again, somewhat as in the *Agamemnon* and *Antigone*, we find a combination of opposites, of the unique personal value of a family member with the general impersonal value of money. In the *Agamemnon* the opposites are combined in a cloth, in *Electra* in a scar.

The old man begins his revelation of Orestes' identity by telling Elektra to pray to get a dear treasure (λαβεῖν φίλον θησαυρόν). The dear treasure is of course Orestes. But θησαυρός, as well as sustaining the money metaphor, must remind us that, for Elektra, the regaining of *[139]* Orestes will mean the regaining of much else besides. In contrast to the Aeschylean and Sophoclean versions, the defining characteristic of Elektra in the first part of the play is the poverty about which she constantly complains. The situation of a princess married off to a penniless peasant provokes the kind of reflections that in §2 we described as encouraged by the apparently unlimited power of money. Elektra's poverty, she maintains, excludes participation in the ritual of the polis and the offering of hospitality.[134] Even noble birth (εὐγένεια) is, claims the peasant, destroyed (ἀπόλλυται) by poverty (37–8). Orestes too, it is emphasised, has nothing: 'everything depends on your own hand and chance, if you are to take your ancestral house and polis' (610–11). The poor, it is claimed, may be more virtuous, and even better hosts, than the rich.[135] But to obtain autocracy, in the post-heroic age and even according to views expressed in tragedy, you need money and

[132] On the resemblance of the shield-devices in Aesch. *Sept.* to coin-marks see Steiner 1994: 53–9.

[133] At Eur. *IT* 813–15 this golden lamb is actually depicted among the scenes woven on the cloth by which Orestes proves to his sister his identity.

[134] 184–92 (her tears are also a reason for not participating), 404–5.

[135] 253, 371–2, 394–5.

the following that comes with money.[136] Orestes, it is stressed (601–9), has no following because he has nothing. And so he must rely on the traditional individual heroism.

In this he is successful. Elektra accuses her mother of having 'bought' Aigisthos as husband (1090), and taunts the dead Aigisthos as follows: 'you prided yourself that you were someone, strong by means of money (τοῖσι χρήμασι σθένων). But money is only for short acquaintance. It is nature (φύσις) that is secure, not money' (939–41). The gold offered by Aigisthos as a reward for killing Orestes (33) proved ineffective. And the contrast between the poverty of the peasant's hovel and the luxurious wealth brought to it by Klytaimestra[137] forms a visually powerful context for the matricide. Money proves in the end to be less powerful and less basic than it seemed to be in the first half of the play.

The recognition of Orestes, with all its emotional power, is from its beginning tied to this competition of basic values, for, as we have seen, the old man, on first seeing the strangers, dissociates noble birth from virtue. He also implicitly compares noble birth without virtue to precious metal that is spurious (κίβδηλος). And so when, seven lines later, the recognition of Orestes is represented in terms of examining the mark on a coin, it must inevitably seem to be not just the recognition of identity but also of quality, of true value. What we have called a combination of opposites implied by this imagery – of the impersonal general value of money with the personal value of a unique individual – may also be seen as a symbolic resolution of contradiction. It may seem that Orestes cannot prevail, for he has nothing. Contrary to Elektra's heroic expectation (524–6), he has had to arrive secretly. As if in response to such realistic pessimism, the triumphal recognition of Orestes seems to be not only the traditional recognition of a person (a family member, a hero who will bring deliverance) but also of true value (money that is not κίβδηλος). In the person revealed seem to be combined all basic values that are elsewhere so problematically compared with each other: kinship, noble birth, heroic nature, the impersonal power of (genuine) money. It is as if the potential spuriousness (κίβδηλος) of money implies doubt about its power. And indeed the power of the tyrants' money proves to be a matter of mere temporary seeming, whereas true and lasting value resides in the nature (φύσις) of Orestes. Whatever we or the Dioskouroi (1244–6) may think of the eventual matricide, the transition,

[136] Soph. *OT* 541–2; cf. e.g. Eur. *Phoen.* 402–5, which makes it clear that, for keeping friends, money is more important than noble birth.

[137] Note esp. 994–5, 998–1001, 1006–7, 1107–8, 1139–40.

in the recognition scene, from appearance to reality is also a (temporary) symbolic mediation of the unresolvable conflict between basic values.[138]

POSTSCRIPT

Subsequent monographs on money are D. Schaps, *The Invention of Coinage and the Monetization of Ancient Greece* (Ann Arbor, MI: University of Michigan Press, 2004); S. von Reden, *Money in Classical Antiquity* (Cambridge: Cambridge University Press, 2010).

The relationship of money to the genesis, form and content of tragedy is explored in Seaford 2004c; see also Seaford 2000a.

Papers involving specific tragic passages are G. Bakewell '*Agamemnon* 437: *Chrysamoibos* Ares, Athens and empire', *JHS* 127 (2007), 123–32; H. Tell, 'Wisdom for sale? The Sophists and money', *CP* 104 (2009), 13–33 (27–31 are on the tragic Teresias); Y. Chang, 'On Sophocles' *Antigone* 1037–9: electrum, gold, and profits', *Concentric: Literary and Cultural Studies* 37. 1 (2011), 143–68; K. Ormand, 'Buying babies in Euripides' *Hippolytus*', *ICS* 40 (2015), 237–61.

For the idea that money influences dramatic form see Seaford 2017a (= Chapter 20 in this volume).

138 I am grateful to Betty Belfiore, Chris Gill and the anonymous *JHS* referees for their improvement of this paper.

CHAPTER 5

Tragic Tyranny

There has been some interest in comparing or combining the tyrant of Greek tragedy with the picture of the absolute autocrat to be found in historical and literary texts, notably the monarch described in Herodotus' famous Persian debate on forms of government and the tyrant described by Plato in the *Republic*. But there is much still to be said. This is partly because the division of intellectual labour has meant that the interpreters of tragedy have not been sufficiently historical, and the historians have not shown much understanding of tragedy. A recent book that can call itself *Die politische Kunst der griechischen Tragödie*, by Christian Meier, has nothing of interest to say about tyranny and contains not a single reference to tyranny outside the tragic texts. The still more recent collection of twenty-nine essays entitled *Tragedy and the Tragic*, including one by me, does not contain 'tyrant' or 'tyranny' in the index, though it does of course contain 'hero'.[1] One exception is George Thomson's (1932) pioneering work on the *Prometheus Bound*, and another is Bernard Knox (1957) on the *Oedipus Tyrannus*. But Knox's work seems to me to be misconceived, as I will go on to explain. The discussion that best transcends the division between history and literature is by Diego Lanza (1977), but even that fails to do justice to the theme.[2]

A small portion of the blame for this interpretative blind spot can be ascribed to Nietzsche, who in *The Birth of Tragedy* explicitly excluded the sociopolitical from tragedy, and another small portion to Aristotle, who in his *Poetics* implicitly excluded it.[3] This exclusion makes it easier for Aristotle to concentrate on the similarity between tragedy and Homer,

[1] Silk 1996.

[2] He does cover the greed and impiety of the tyrant but not the themes on which I focus: money, abuse of ritual and kin-killing, with concomitant isolation. See also e.g. Funke 1966; Cerri 1982: 137–55; Vernant 1982a: 19–38; Saïd 1985; and most recently Barceló 1993; Giorgini 1993; and the interesting remarks in McGlew 1993: 190–206.

[3] See Hall 1996.

in which he is at one with some ancient anecdote and much modern criticism.[4] But the Homeric monarch could hardly be more different from the tragic tyrant. Suffice it to say here that the tyrannical practices that I will show to be interconnected [96] and central to tragedy – killing family, abuse of ritual, power through money – are almost entirely absent from Homer.

Another way literary critics have of failing to understand the tragic tyrant is to imagine that he somehow embodies the community/polis and that his destruction or exile is somehow a disaster for the community/polis. This preconception I will illustrate in my discussion of *Antigone* and *Bacchae*.

For the Athenians the tyrant did not embody the polis. Tragedy reflects, among other things, the Athenian experience of, and continuing pre-occupation with, tyranny. Their attitude to it was generally hostile and at best ambivalent. Further, projected onto the extreme figure of the tragic tyrant may be anxiety at the general tendency towards the autonomisation, notably through money, of the individual. I must emphasis at the outset that my concern is largely with representations of tyranny in various texts rather than with what the tyrants actually did.

Three Tyrannical Characteristics

Among the typical characteristics of the tyrant are impiety, distrust of his close associates (*philoi*) and greed. I begin by defining each of these characteristics more narrowly, relating each of them directly to the obtaining and maintaining of tyrannical power. This point can be illustrated from the rise and fall of Polykrates, tyrant of Samos in the sixth century.

In an account preserved by Polyaenus, Polykrates seized power during a sacrifice for the whole people (πάνδημος) at the temple of Hera, which was preceded by an armed procession. He collected as many arms as the festival provided a pretext for and instructed his brothers Syloson and Pantagnostos to take part in the procession. After the procession, with the Samians about to sacrifice, most men laid aside their arms by the altars as they attended to libations and prayers. But those who formed a coherent group around Syloson and Pantagnostos retained their arms and killed everybody.[5] Herodotus (3.39) adds that Polykrates then divided up the polis with Syloson and Pantagnostos but subsequently exiled the former, killed the latter and controlled the whole island himself. He was eventually

[4] Seaford 1994b: 275.
[5] Polyaenus, *Strat.* 1.23.

lured to his death by the governor of Sardis, who, according to Herodotus, promised him 'enough money to get control of the whole of Greece'. Polykrates accepted, says Herodotus, because he used to desire money greatly.[6] His tyranny coincided in fact with the early and rapid development in the Aegean of an especially convenient form of money, coinage, and Polykrates himself certainly produced coins. One use of the [97] coins might have been to pay the numerous mercenary soldiers mentioned by Herodotus.[7]

The typical characteristics of the tyrant are generally represented, in Herodotus,[8] Plato and elsewhere, as if they were defects of character. But what we can see in the case of Polykrates is that his impiety, distrust of *philoi*, and greed all belong to the logic of obtaining and maintaining tyrannical power. We can define each of them more narrowly. His impiety is specifically the use (or rather abuse) of ritual to obtain power. His distrust of *philoi* takes the extreme form of exiling or killing family, his brothers, whose close relationship had qualified them to be trusty associates in the coup, with the result that they become associates in power and so obstacles to Polykrates' absolute power.[9] The claims of family, as of the sacred, are annulled by the individual desire for power that depends on violence – and on money, for his greed for precious metal money is not simply the vice of greed but, more specifically, the desire for the means of tyrannical power. All three of our tyrannical characteristics are not therefore just defects of character but instruments of power.

It is moreover important to see the interconnections between the distrust of *philoi* and the greed. Control over the relatively new phenomenon of money allows the tyrant to dispense with the ancient principles of solidarity through kinship and of reciprocity, for he is able to create his following by paying them. Of course, paying mercenaries involves reciprocity in the broad sense that the mercenaries fight in return for pay. But if we look at the means of creating a following in Homer, we do not find money, which (on any sensible definition of money) does not exist in Homer. We do not indeed find any single thing binding the Homeric

[6] 3.123.1 ἱμείρετο γὰρ χρημάτων μεγάλως. See also Diod. Sic. 10.16.4.

[7] 3.45.3 ἐπικουροί τε μισθωτοὶ καὶ τοξόται οἰκήιοι ἦσαν πλήθει πολλοί ('there were numerous paid auxiliaries and native archers'); also 3.54.2. Herodotus also recounts a 'silly story' (3.56.2) that Polykrates bought off an invading force of Spartans with gilded lead coins. Polykrates also attracted the doctor Demokedes by offering him a larger salary (two talents) than that offered by the Aeginetans (one talent) and the Athenians (100 minas) (Hdt. 3.131).

[8] On the complex representation of tyranny by Herodotus see Dewald 2003.

[9] Cf. esp. Eur. fr. 605; Arist. *Pol.* 1312b9–17.

leader to followers but a range of factors that include his accepted right to redistribute booty, his charisma, his martial prowess, his interpersonal relationships with his followers and his ability to lead, all of them creating a sense of gratitude or indebtedness among his followers.[10] What the mercenaries value, on the other hand, is the objective power of a single thing, money.

The presence and interconnection of our three specific tyrannical practices – abuse of the sacred, killing family and power through money – can be found in various historical and philosophical texts. Herodotus said that Periander the tyrant of Korinth killed his wife, Melissa, and suffered in consequence the hostility of his son, but also sent to his dead wife the clothes of all the women of Korinth by telling them to come to the temple of Hera. When [*98*] they came in their best clothes 'as if for a festival', he had them all stripped.[11] The festival is used to despoil the citizens. At Athens it was said that Kylon tried to become tyrant by seizing the Acropolis and robbing the temple of Athena (of its precious metal) during a festival of Zeus (schol. Ar. *Eq.* 445). And Peisistratos was said by Herodotus (1.60) to have re-obtained his tyranny through the trick of having himself led into the city by a woman dressed as Athena, an action designed to evoke a festival procession.[12] When Peisistratos subsequently has to leave Attica again, Herodotus stresses the importance of money to hire soldiers in both the final re-obtaining and the successful entrenchment of the tyranny.[13] The Hellenistic historian Baton of Sinope tells us that Pythagoras (the tyrant of Ephesos *c.*600) combined 'unlimited passion for money' with the practice of killing people in temples.[14] Various tyrants were said to have killed their opponents at sacrifices.[15] Kroisos, Kambyses and Kleisthenes, the sixth-century tyrant of Sikyon, were said to have killed their own brothers.[16] Many tyrants, it is claimed in Xenophon's *Hiero*, have killed, and been killed by, their own children and their own brothers, and many have been destroyed by their own wives and close companions.[17]

10 See most recently Donlan 1998.

11 Hdt. 3.50, 5.92η; Diog. Laert. 1.94. At Diog. Laert. 1.96 he plays the festival trick because he is short of gold.

12 Connor 1987: 42–6.

13 Hdt. 1.61.3, 64.1; [Arist.] *Ath. Pol.* 15.2.

14 *FGrH* 268 F3 ἔρως τε χρημάτων ἄμετρος.

15 Amphitres at Miletos (Nic. Dam. *FGrH* 90 F52); Kallippos at Syracuse (Plut. *Dion.* 56–7); Klearkhos at Byzantium (Diod. Sic. 14.12.3).

16 Hdt. 1.92.4, 3.30; Nic. Dam. *FGrH* 90 F61.

17 *Hier.* 3.8; similarly Isoc. 8.113. Thucydides (6.85.1) makes the Athenian Euphemos state that for a tyrant, as for an imperial city, self-interest is logical, and nothing is οἰκεῖον ('his own') unless trustworthy; that is, reliability not family association is the criterion for association.

In the description of the tyrant in Plato's *Republic* our three practices combine: the tyrant becomes like a wolf by virtue of tasting 'kindred blood' (8.565e7 φόνου συγγενοῦς) and eventually has to rely on the worst sort of people, people who 'will fly to him of their own accord in great numbers if he provide their pay' (8.567d). He supports them with sacred money (ἱερὰ χρήματα, i.e. temple treasures) and the property of his victims (8.568d) and then, when these run out, with the property of his begetter, the people, with the result that he becomes a kind of 'parricide' (8.569b). Plato also associates the tyrant with eating his children (*Resp*. 10.619c2).

In a famous fragment of Sophocles, money finds *philoi*, honours and 'the seat of highest tyranny, nearest to the gods',[18] and is 'strangely clever (δεινός) at getting to things not-to-be-trodden (ἄβατα) and things profane (βέβηλα)'.[19] What exactly is this power of money? The concrete polarity seems to imply the more abstract notion that money has the power to reach the sacred and the profane *indiscriminately*, to ignore or transgress the distinction between them.[20] We think of the tyrant using ritual and temple treasures to obtain and extend his secular power.

As for money obtaining the highest seat of tyranny nearest to the gods, the same triad – money, tyranny, deity – appeared in the very first reference to tyranny, by Archilochus (fr. 19), 'I do not care about Gyges with all his gold, nor did jealousy yet take me, nor do I envy the works of the gods, nor am I [*99*] in love with great tyranny.'[21] In Euripides tyranny is called 'equal to the gods' and 'the greatest of the gods'.[22] It is unsurprising that the tyrant Polykrates was warned (by Amasis) of the resentment of the gods.

Prometheus Bound and *Oresteia*

Just as the wealth and power of the tyrant may make him seem like a god, so the idea of deity may be shaped by the idea of the monetary power of tyranny. The most obvious case of god as tyrant is Zeus in the *Prometheus Bound*, who is not only repeatedly called *tyrannos* but also, it has been shown, embodies several of the typical characteristics of the tyrant: he is harsh, a law unto himself, suspicious of his friends, implacable and

[18] Soph. fr. 88; 'to the gods' translates Connington's (in my view, near certain) conjecture θεοῖσιν for the mss. ἄκουσιν (SM) or τ' ἄγουσιν (A); θακοῦσιν cj. Salmasius.

[19] βέβηλα is a generally accepted emendation of the mss. unmetrical τὰ βατά.

[20] Dem. 18.122 βοᾷς ῥητὰ καὶ ἄρρητ' ὀνομάζων.

[21] Fr. 19 οὔ μοι τὰ Γύγεω τοῦ πολυχρύσου μελει, | οὐδ' εἷλέ πώ με ζῆλος, οὐδ' ἀγαίομαι | θεῶν ἔργα, μεγάλης δ' οὐκ ἐρέω τυραννίδος· | ἀπόπροθεν γάρ ἐστιν ὀφθαλμῶν ἐμῶν.

[22] *Tro.* 1169; *Phoen*. 506; cf. fr. 250.

violent.[23] I want to take this point further by observing the manner in which Zeus comes to power. Prometheus, appropriately for the god of technological forethought, knew that the struggle between the Titans and Zeus would be decided not by force but by guile. Being unable to persuade the Titans of this, he allied himself instead with Zeus. 'By my advice', continues Prometheus

> the deep dark cavern of Tartaros covers Kronos together with his allies. And it is having had this benefit of me that the tyrant of the gods requited me with this foul punishment. For tyranny somehow has the disease of not trusting in its *philoi*.[24]

Prometheus and Zeus are united not only as allies but also by kinship.[25] We are reminded of Polykrates acquiring tyrannical power with the key assistance of his brothers, whom he then destroys. Zeus too can abandon the principle of reciprocity and dispense (once in power) with his closest allies. The report in Herodotus, cited by Dewald, of Polykrates robbing friends (so as to make them grateful when he returned what he seized) also expresses tyrannical trampling on the principle of reciprocity.[26]

This detail does not occur in the much earlier, pre-tyrannical version of the story to be found in Hesiod. Nor do two other details of the tragic version, each of which implies the abandonment of reciprocity by the tragic Zeus. One is his desire, after coming to power, simply to eliminate humankind. In Hesiod and in Homer, as in much of our evidence for Greek religion, the relations between mortals and immortals are imagined as shaped by reciprocity. A mortal may give sacrifice to deity and receive the goodwill of deity in return.[27] For Zeus in the tragic version to want to eliminate humankind is in effect to declare himself beyond the need for this reciprocal arrangement. Already in the sixth century Xenophanes had probably[28] maintained that the gods do not need anything, and the same view was certainly put in the fifth century by Antiphon and by Euripides' Herakles.[29] [*100*]

If deity does not need anything, it is beyond the reach of reciprocal relations with humans. It is made explicit by one Aristodemos, in

[23] Thomson 1932: 7–10; Saïd 1985.

[24] Aesch. *PV* 219–25; see also 305–6.

[25] Prometheus is the son of Earth (209–10); Zeus is her grandson; cf. 14, 289.

[26] Hdt. 3.39.4; cf. also 3.47.1, 3.48.2; Kurke 1999: 102–3.

[27] See most recently R. Parker 1998.

[28] The 'dubious authority' of the *Stromateis* in Eusebius to this effect (DK 21 A 32) is, Guthrie 1962: 373 argues, vindicated by Eur. *HF* 1341–6.

[29] Antiph. DK 87 B 10; Eur. *HF* 1345–6.

conversation with Sokrates, that the gods neither need sacrifice nor care for humankind.[30] Xenophanes lived during the high tide of tyranny, and I would suggest that his concept of deity is influenced by the experience of tyranny. The tyrant, in contrast to the Homeric leader, is to some extent freed from the principle of reciprocity by his control of money. The invisible but ubiquitous power of money was in the sixth century a strange and radical novelty, which is reflected, I suggest, in numerous aspects of sixth-century philosophy, including Xenophanes' strange and radically new notion of a single non-anthropomorphic deity staying in the same place while nevertheless agitating all things by the thought of his mind and (probably) needing nothing.

The third detail to imply the tragic Zeus' abandonment of reciprocity is as follows. In Hesiod Zeus defeats the Titans because he has the thunderbolt, given him by the Kyklopes in return for his freeing of them from captivity, and because he has physically powerful allies, the Hundred-handers, whom he obtained as allies by the service of freeing them (too) from captivity.[31] Zeus announces to the gods that whoever joins him in the fight against the Titans will keep or obtain honours and privileges.[32] In the tragic version, by contrast, the only ally of Zeus mentioned is Prometheus, who joins Zeus not in return for benefit but as representing the principle of guile that will prevail in the conflict. The Hesiodic Zeus is not without intelligence, but he defeats the Titans by what he has obtained through χάρις, reciprocity. The tragic Zeus on the other hand defeats them by guile; but the conflict itself is simply omitted from the narrative, and so we never learn how it was that the principle of guile prevailed. Of course, the king of the gods cannot be said to control the supply of money. Nevertheless, this fifth-century version, with its privileging of unidentified guile, reflects a world in which autocracy is no longer simply obtained, as it is in the world reflected by Hesiod, by doing favours to obtain allies in a conflict of mere physical force.

The only other extant plays attributed to Aeschylus in which the words *tyrannos* and *tyrannis* occur are *Agamemnon* and *Choephori*, notably of the regime established by Klytaimestra and Aigisthos. The chorus, as the murder of Agamemnon is being perpetrated, fear a tyranny (*tyrannis*) but are unable to prevent it.[33] The corpses of Aigisthos and Klytaimestra,

[30] Xen. *Mem.* 1.4.2, 10.
[31] *Theog.* 501–6, 624–63.
[32] 392–6; for the Hundred-handers see 735, 815–19.
[33] *Ag.* 1355, 1365, 1633.

slain by Orestes, are called a 'double tyranny', and Orestes is said to have 'liberated the whole polis of the Argives'.[34]

Aigisthos' and Klytaimestra's tyrannical coup involves in fact all three of [*101*] our tyrannical practices: killing family, power through money and the abuse (or perversion) of ritual. That family killing is involved is obvious: Klytaimestra kills her husband. As a result, the tyrannical couple does not seem to have any allies. They will, says the chorus, be hated by the people (1409–11, 1615–16); Klytaimestra will be 'away from the polis' (1410 ἀπόπολις). How then are they to maintain their tyranny? When, as the play ends, violent conflict with the chorus seems imminent, Aigisthos tells his squad of guardsmen to be ready, and the captain of the squad repeats the order.[35] The presence of these guardsmen, whether on stage or off, with a single crucial line spoken by the captain, is both highly dramatic and politically startling. Suddenly we are reminded that history, unlike myth, is decided by what Plato calls the worst kind of people, in the pay of ruthless autocrats. Aigisthos has said: 'I will try to rule the citizens by means of this man's money.'[36]

As for the abuse of ritual in the acquisition of tyranny, this is fairly obvious in Klytaimestra's invitation to Kassandra, just after the entry of Agamemnon into the house, to join the sacrifice that is just about to be performed there. Indeed, Klytaimestra subsequently uses sacrificial language to describe her murder of Agamemnon. But in fact she kills him in the bath, covering him with a cloth like a net. However, this too is abuse of ritual, of the ritual bathing and clothing of a dead man by his wife. Moreover, boasting of her deed, Klytaimestra says, 'An unlimited covering, like [a net] for fish, I set around him, an evil wealth of cloth' (1382–3). The cloth is unlimited (ἄπειρον) because, unlike the garments of the living, the shroud is wrapped around the hands and feet of the corpse and sometimes even the head and so can like a net trap the living Agamemnon. Now this cloth is also in various ways associated in the drama with the cloths on which Agamemnon hesitantly walked into the house,[37] cloths that were 'bought with silver' (949 ἀργυρωνήτους). They are, Klytaimestra attempts to reassure Agamemnon, replaceable, for the sea, from which the dye comes in an ever-renewed gush 'equal to silver', is, she says, inexhaustible, and the household does not know how to be poor. So, in the astonishing

[34] *Cho.* 973, 1046; cf. 824, 863–4.

[35] Unfortunately, most texts attribute line 1650 to the chorus, which is most unlikely.

[36] *Cho.* 1638–9 ἐκ τῶν δὲ τοῦδε χρημάτων πειράσομαι ἄρχειν πολιτῶν.

[37] See e.g. Taplin 1978: 79–82; Seaford 1998c[4]: 130.

imagination of Aeschylus, the cloth that Agamemnon walks on is a concrete embodiment of the unlimited money of the household, and so is the cloth that covers him in death, described as an 'unlimited covering ... an evil wealth of cloth'. And so all three of our tyrannical practices – abuse of ritual, killing family and power through unlimited money – combine in a single object displayed on stage, the murderous unlimited wealth of the shroud in which Agamemnon's corpse lies wrapped.[38] [*102*]

Democratic Ideology

'No mortal', says Euripides' Hekabe, 'is free. For he is the slave either of money or of chance; or the mass of people in the polis or the written laws prevent him from acting as he wants' (*Hec.* 864–7). In general the hero of myth (for instance, as represented by Homer) is constrained neither by money nor by democracy nor by written laws and so in these respects has an individual autonomy that is not found in the democratic polis. The major exception is tragedy, which represents the hero of myth in a world that is inevitably the world of the polis. How then can he continue in tragedy to have the autonomy that he has in myth? Only with being identified with the historical figure who both emerges from the polis and controls it, the tyrant. Tyranny, says Antigone, can say and do what it wants (she means unlike the Theban citizens, represented by the chorus).[39] In tragedy the word *tyrannos* (and its cognates) occurs more often than the Homeric word *basileus* (and its cognates), and this cannot be attributed merely to the greater metrical convenience of *tyrannos*. The autonomous hero of myth, when imagined in the polis, can retain his autonomy only by becoming a *tyrannos*. And so the tragic king embodies the Athenian experience of tyranny.[40]

That experience is ambivalent. On the one hand, the *tyrannos* is made possible by the polis. His kind of power is made possible by the advanced degree of political and economic organisation of the polis, which he himself may well advance still further.[41] Yet, certainly from the fifth-century

[38] For this argument in more detail see Seaford 1998c[4]: 123–31.

[39] Soph. *Ant.* 504–7.

[40] This experience may have been unusual: it is argued by V. Parker 1998, on the basis of Thucydides and Athenian drama, that the Athenians were unusual in making a sharp distinction between kingship and tyranny, as a result of remembering their tyranny as being distinct from their monarchy, which had melted away at an unusually early date.

[41] Thuc. 1.13, 6.54; Arist. *Pol.* 1314a29–1315b10. The ambivalence of tyranny is reflected in Aristotle's account of the two 'opposite' ways for a tyrant to stay in power (1313a34), one hostile to the community and the other beneficial to it.

Athenian perspective, his absolute personal power makes him antithetical to the polis. Indeed, the Athenians regarded their democratic polis as emerging out of the elimination of tyranny. It may well have been shortly after this elimination that tragic performances were organised at the City Dionysia, in honour of Dionysos Eleuthereus.[42]

This sense of ambivalence combines with this sense of transition from tyranny to create the tragic tyrant. The members of tyrannical families in tragedy frequently kill each other[43] and frequently abuse ritual. This also happens in the tyrannical families of historiography and philosophy. But there is a difference. Tragedy was a creation of the democratic polis and was performed along with elaborate polis rituals (in honour of Dionysos). The tragic tyrants are not permitted to abuse the rituals of the polis. Rather, their abuse of ritual tends to be expressed in their killing of family. The tyrannical horrors of family killing and abused ritual coalesce, as we have seen with the tragic killing of Agamemnon. Polis ritual in tragedy is typically instituted at *[103]* the end of the action, for instance the cult of the Furies in Athens at the end of the *Oresteia*. This gives as a typical pattern of tragedy family killing associated with the abuse of ritual, projected outside Athens (notably onto Thebes) and ending in the foundation of polis cult still celebrated by fifth-century citizens.[44] What I want to stress here is the historical genesis of the tragic tyrant, his derivation to some unknown extent from the actual experience of tyranny but more importantly from the reconfiguration of tyrannical practices by the democratic imagination. The result is that the isolation of the tyrant, even from his nearest and dearest, with the abuse of the rituals in which those family ties should be expressed, is taken to the extreme. Out of this situation emerges finally a polis cult in which the tragic victim, say Ajax or Herakles or Hippolytos, may seem to his devotees no less ambivalent than in the tragedy itself, inspiring the same mixture of awe, pity and relief that the time of the *tyrannoi* has been superseded.

Aetiological myth provides a basic pattern of perceiving the past. Once copulation occurred indiscriminately, and nobody knew who their father was, until marriage was instituted by Kekrops.[45] The original state of affairs is the opposite of civilised order. Once women voted, and outvoted the

[42] See Connor 1989: 7–32.
[43] Belfiore 2000.
[44] I have argued this at length in Seaford 1994b. For Thebes as representing the 'other' in Athenian tragedy see Zeitlin 1990.
[45] Schol. Ar. *Plut.* 773.

men on how Athens should be named (Athens not Poseidonia), and so Poseidon devastated the land and had to be mollified by the institution of patriliny and the removal of political rights from the women.[46] Here civilised order is preceded both by its reverse and by divinely caused havoc. In some aetiological myths the reversal and havoc may be the same: the daughters of Proiteus reject a deity and so are made to wander around the Peloponnese frenzied, imagining themselves to be cows, or diseased, before being released at a place where a cult is founded. In the *Bacchae* the royal rejection of Dionysos causes him to impose a multiple and chaotic reversal of the civilised order (women as men, humans as animals, and so on) which ends in the founding of his cult.

Tragedy was created, in my view, out of the ritual enactment of aetiological myth in Dionysiac cult, and a dominant pattern of tragic action derives from this genesis. I have even gone so far as to define tragedy as aetiological myth adapted to the needs of the polis – manifestly incomplete as is any definition of tragedy, but useful to correct an imbalance. In the *Oresteia*, for example, the divine embodiments of reciprocal violence, the Furies, threaten Athens with devastation before being persuaded by Athena to acquiesce in the civilised institutions of patriliny and the law court and to accept for themselves a polis cult. Clearly the Athenian audience was anxious about *[104]* the devastation that might be visited on its city by the ever-present threat of reciprocal violence, which is in the *Oresteia* projected back onto what might be called the aetiological past.

I suggest that tyranny too belongs to the aetiological past. Three factors cohere to put it there. One is that the Athenians believed that the present democratic order had indeed actually been created out of its tyrannical opposite. The second is the anxiety that the Athenians did feel about their democracy reverting to a tyranny.[47] It may even be that the far greater presence of *tyrannis* and the *tyrannos* in Sophocles and Euripides than in Aeschylus reflects an increase in anxiety in the last three decades of the century (e.g. Ar. *Vesp.* 488–92). Particularly interesting for my argument is that it was abuse of the sacred (mutilation of the Herms and profanation of the Eleusinian mysteries) that exacerbated in the Athenians anxiety about the possibility of tyranny.[48] The fact that the Eleusinian mysteries were an emotional polis ritual open to all may explain the democratic anxiety at

[46] Varro *ap.* August. *De civ. D.* 18.9.
[47] See Henderson 2003; Raaflaub 2003.
[48] Thuc. 6.28, 53, 60.

their hubristic (ἐφ' ὕβρει) performance in private houses.[49] Third, even if there had been no such anxiety, tyranny serves anyway to clarify and confirm the democratic order by signifying its opposite. This is particularly clear in the debate in Euripides' *Suppliants* between the good king Theseus and the arrogant Theban herald, with Theseus pointing out the various respects in which democracy is the best system and tyranny the worst.

Does the Tyrant Embody the Polis? *Antigone* and *Bacchae*

In my introduction I mentioned the scholarly preconception that the tragic tyrant somehow embodies the polis. Here, for example, are Oudemans and Lardinois on Thebes at the end of the *Antigone*: 'The city can only continue its existence by sacrificing those who are its most respected representatives, and there is no end to this persistent *self-sacrifice*'.[50] Charles Segal, defending his account of the *Bacchae* against my account, writes: 'It is ... true that the destruction of Thebes is reflected primarily in the ruin of the royal family.'[51] This is phrased as a concession to me, but still refers to the destruction of Thebes.[52] Dionysos has come to establish his cult in Thebes. If Thebes is destroyed, he will have no cult. I will now look at the *tyrannoi* of these plays, *Antigone* and the *Bacchae*.

Kreon in the *Antigone* embodies the historical ambivalence of the tyrant, as well as combining our three tyrannical practices. First, extreme isolation [*105*] from *philoi*. Early on, he expresses his disdain, commendable from a civic and even from a democratic perspective, for whoever puts his *philos* above his fatherland.[53] After all Polyneikes, to whom he denies burial, is his nephew. His principle is soon to be tested again. Faced with the infringement by his own niece Antigone, he says, 'But even if my sister's child, or nearer to me in blood than my entire Zeus Herkeios [i.e. my entire household], she and her sister will not escape the worst fate' (486–9). But, in the end, the principle is as a result of his actions realised in its extreme form, with the hostility and suicide of his closest *philoi*, his wife and son. The

[49] Note also that Thucydides' subsequent digression into the fall of the Athenian tyranny includes the abuse of a festival procession both by Hipparkhos to insult Harmodios and by Harmodios and Aristogeiton to avenge the insult by killing Hipparkhos.

[50] Oudemans and Lardinois 1987: 159, emphasis added.

[51] Segal 1997: 383. Cf. e.g. Friedrich 1996: 274: Dionysos in the *Bacchae* is 'destroyer of the polis'. But the only communities lastingly damaged in extant tragedy are barbarian (Aesch. *Pers.*; Eur. *Tro.*). When Phrynichus dramatised the sack of Miletos, the Athenians fined him.

[52] On this, see further Seaford (2000b).

[53] 182–3; cf. 187–90.

isolation of the tyrant from his *philoi* becomes catastrophic. What seemed at first to be civic principle turns into tyrannical vice.

Second, money. Early on, Kreon expresses the view, to which he constantly returns, that those who act against him have been bribed to do so, and he delivers a comprehensive attack on the evil effects of money. Here too the high-sounding principle becomes tyrannical vice. It was generally known that tyrants obtain and maintain their position at least partly through money. 'Oh wealth and tyranny ... how much are you envied', says Oidipous in the *Oedipus Tyrannus* (380–2), and he tells Kreon (541–2) that tyranny is obtained by a mass of people and by money (πλήθει χρήμασιν θ'). This must represent a general view because it is not in fact how Oidipous became a tyrant.[54] Oidipous also assumes that the power of money was behind the murder of the previous king (124–5). In the *Antigone* Kreon claims that the polis belongs to him (738). Teiresias, when accused by Kreon of venality, responds, 'No, it is tyrants who love disgraceful gain',[55] and Teiresias is never wrong.[56] When Kreon persists in the accusation, Teiresias says in effect, in a line (1062) that has never been properly understood, that he appears to Kreon to be intent on gain, because that is how Kreon himself is: that is, in effect, Kreon is projecting his own desire for gain onto him.[57] And then Teiresias says (1066–71), again in words that are generally mistranslated, that soon

> you will yourself have given from your own inward parts one corpse [his son Haimon] in exchange for corpses, and as a result of the exchange you have one of those above, having put below and lodged a living soul ignominiously in a tomb [Antigone], and you have up here one of those who belong to the gods below [Polyneikes].

This passage is often cited as embodying the dual abuse of death ritual that is somehow at the heart of the play. It does that, but it also presents this abuse as an *economic transaction* (ἔχεις ... βαλών does not mean, as it is usually translated, 'you have put' but rather 'you possess, having put', just as the second ἔχεις also means 'have' or 'possess'). Kreon will have given one (ἕνα), and gained *[106]* two. His tyrannical abuse of the death rituals of his own family is unmasked as being also a kind of hideous material gain: a

[54] Cf. e.g. Arist. *Pol.* 1311a9–11. The association of tyranny with wealth is very common and begins with the very earliest mentions of tyranny (Archil. fr. 19; Solon, fr. 33.5–6).

[55] 1056 αἰσχροκέρδειαν, the word used of Dareios' motive for violating a tomb at Hdt. 1.187; see further Kurke 1999: 84–6.

[56] Moreover, disgraceful gain is frequently attributed to tyrants: e.g. Eur. *Supp.* 450–1; Xen. *Symp.* 4.36, *Hier.* 7.12; Pl. *Grg.* 466b; Arist. *Pol.* 1311a4; Diod. Sic. 10.16.4.

[57] Rather as Oidipous in the *Oedipus Tyrannus* projects his own love of tyranny onto Kreon.

metaphor, but based on the reality of the devastating all-importance of money for tyranny. This description then, like that of the evil wealth of cloth in the *Oresteia*, combines our three (tyrannical) practices: killing family, abuse of (death) ritual and power as material gain.[58]

Towards the end of the *Bacchae* Kadmos gives a kind of funeral speech praising his grandson Pentheus. Here, if anywhere, it would be appropriate to praise the dead king for his championing of the polis. But Kadmos does not do so. Rather, he praises him for holding together the household (despite his conflict, in the drama, with all its living members over the new cult) and proceeding vigorously against the enemies of his grandfather in the city. 'To the polis', says Kadmos, 'you were a terror (τάρβος)' (1310). This τάρβος has been in evidence earlier, when the chorus says, 'I dread (ταρβῶ) to say free words to the tyrant. But nevertheless it will be said. Dionysos is second to none of the gods' (775–7). There is no indication anywhere of Pentheus representing the interests of the polis. He does rather illustrate the principle pronounced by the admirable Theseus in Euripides' *Suppliants*: 'There is nothing more hostile to a polis than a tyrant.'[59] It is true that Teiresias says to Pentheus, 'You rejoice when many stand at the gates, and the polis magnifies the name of Pentheus' (319–20). But his next words are '[Dionysos] too, I think, takes pleasure in being honoured', words that prefigure the polis festival of Dionysos founded at the end of the drama.

It is politically significant that Thebes does not seem to have room for both Dionysos and the tyrant. After the tyrant has been killed by his own mother in a kind of perverted sacrifice, Dionysos will replace him at the centre of the polis festival. At the Athenian City Dionysia, Dionysos was accompanied by a throng through the gates of the city, as he was also at another polis festival, the Anthesteria, on his way to the ancient house of the *basileus*. In a demonstration of his power to reverse the potential autonomy of the royal household, he copulated there with the wife of the *basileus*. At the City Dionysia the tragedies themselves were performed, and the tribute from the allies, which was so important to Athenian power, was displayed in the theatre.[60] It was the demise of the democratic polis that subsequently allowed powerful individuals to reverse the defeat of Pentheus, as it were, by identifying with the god in the festival: it is

[58] For this argument in more detail see Seaford 1998c[4].

[59] Eur. *Supp.* 429; see also *Phoen.* 560. For the tyrant serving his own interests as opposed to those of the polis see e.g. Arist. *Pol.* 1295a19–23.

[60] Parker 1996: 259.

because of his absolute power that, a century later, Demetrios Poliorketes is welcomed into Athens as Dionysos.[61] [*107*]

Might the Tyrant Symbolise the Polis? *Oedipus Tyrannus*

Negative characterisation of tyranny seems to have been a feature of Athenian tragedy throughout the period from which the plays are extant. To the plays I have already discussed, which cover a period of more than fifty years, we should add in particular Euripides' *Suppliants* (probably of the late 420s)[62] and his *Phoenician Women* (of 411, 410 or 409). This negative characterisation seems to express an anxiety about tyranny that, it has been claimed, was for at least some of this period not unjustified by the political situation. One response to this tragic preoccupation with tyranny might be, I suggest, to suppose that anxiety about a new kind of autonomy of the individual citizen, favoured by social developments that include the increasing monetisation of human relationships, is in tragedy projected onto its most extreme embodiment, the horribly isolated autonomy of the tyrant.[63]

Another response is what Bernard Knox argued for the *Oedipus Tyrannus*. When the play was written, tyranny as an institution was, claims Knox, a 'dead issue' (1957: 58). Moreover, Oidipous is not a typical tyrant: he does not banish or kill his co-regents, defy ancestral laws, outrage women, put men to death without trial, plunder his subjects, live in fear of his people or have an armed bodyguard; he is in direct touch with the Thebans, calls an assembly (*OT* 144), and so on (Knox 1957: 58–9). And yet the words *tyrannis* and *tyrannos* are especially common in this play. Knox's solution to this paradox of a democratically minded tyrant is that 'Oidipous' peculiar *tyrannis* is a reference to Athens itself', as the *polis tyrannos* known especially from Thucydides. Oidipous is like Athens: they both have wealth, skill, power given to them freely, vigour, faith in action, courage, speed of action and decision, intelligence, self-confidence, versatility, fear of conspiracy, and anger (64–77). Oidipous' hunt for the murderer of Laios 'is presented in terms of Attic private and public law' (78–98). His fall 'suggests … the fall of Athens itself' (99). The second *stasimon*, with its famous association of tyranny with the hubris that comes to grief, is, Knox

[61] Plut. *Demetr.* 12; Douris *FGrH* 76 F13; Parker 1996: 259. Mark Antony was also welcomed into Athens (and Ephesos) as Dionysos by the whole community.

[62] On tyranny in this drama see Raaflaub 2003.

[63] On the tragic tyrant as an extreme example of the individualising effect of money see Seaford 2004c: 292–317.

argues, a prediction that the tyrannical behaviour of Athens will lead inevitably to its downfall (99–106).

This case is worked out in great detail but is unconvincing. Of course tragedy is not incapable of an analogy between individual and city. Knox might have quoted Euripides' *Suppliants*, in which the people of Thebes, ruined by their own hubris, are explicitly compared in this respect to a man with newly acquired wealth (741–4). But this passage would not [*108*] have helped his case, for it confirms how easy it would have been for Sophocles to make explicit the analogy between *tyrannos* and tyrannical city. In the entire play, however, there is not the slightest suggestion of the idea of a tyrannical city.

Of course, the logic of tyranny may be the same whether the tyrant is an individual or polis. Both, for example, depend on money.[64] An example of a detail that I have not seen pointed out is as follows. You hold your empire like tyranny, says Kleon in the Mytilenean debate (Thuc. 3.37.2). Your subjects do not like it and plot against you, and you will not make them obey you by doing them a favour that will injure you. Your power over them depends on your strength, not on their goodwill. Compare the words of Kreon in Euripides' *Medea*, as he fatefully agrees to Medea's request to stay one more day in Korinth: 'My resolve is not at all tyrannical' (348). But elaborate political allegory is, in my view, quite alien to Greek tragedy. The notion of Athens as *polis tyrannos* in Thucydides is used either to denigrate Athenian foreign policy[65] or to persuade the Athenians or others to recognise the Athenian empire as a tyranny so that they may act realistically.[66] In either case, it has a quite specific political point, which would be out of place in Sophocles.

Less implausible is the weaker claim, also made by Knox, that the qualities of Oidipous make him similar to the typical Athenian citizen (as described by e.g. Thucydides). But this similarity, set in the anti-Athens of Thebes,[67] can hardly imply (ingenious) criticism of Athens. Rather, I have suggested, the tragic tyrant is indeed in a sense the autonomous citizen writ large. But he is also a tyrant, and Knox is in fact crucially wrong to suppose that at the time of its production tyranny was a 'dead issue'.[68]

64 See Kallet 2003.

65 1.122.3, 124.3.

66 2.63.2, 3.37.2, 6.85.1.

67 For this idea see Zeitlin 1990.

68 Knox relies on the odd argument that Aristophanic parody of accusations of tyrannical ambition shows that nobody took such accusations seriously. But cf. Henderson 2003; Raaflaub 2003.

Can we, from our perspective of aetiological myth and the typical characteristics of tyranny, make better sense of Oidipous as a democratically perceived tyrant?[69] The play ends with the implicit benefit for the polis (the cause of the plague is removed) but not with the founding of an institution or cult of the polis. That is left to the *Oedipus at Colonus*, in which the polis to be benefited by the cult of Oidipous will be Athens. Yet polis cult is also important for understanding the *Oedipus Tyrannus*. This is, first, because the influence of cult aetiology is, in my view, on tragedy in general, even on those tragedies in which no cult is founded. The second respect in which polis cult matters is as follows. I earlier noted, and so do other contributors to this volume [Morgan 2003],[70] the *ambivalence* of the tyrant: he is sometimes admired for his freedom or energetic beneficence to the polis and yet is almost universally detested; he is a creation of the polis and agent of its development and yet antithetical *[109]* to it. This ambivalence of the tyrant is embodied, to the extreme degree characteristic of myth, in the tragic Oidipous, who is saviour of the city, then would-be saviour but polluter (*Oedipus Tyrannus*), then saviour (*Oedipus at Colonus*). Here again, historical experience resembles, and so becomes shaped by, a mythico-ritual pattern: the ambivalence of the tyrant becomes assimilated to the extreme ambivalence of the *pharmakos*, the scapegoat, a slave or a king, whose expulsion or death brings salvation to the community. Indeed, it has been argued that the play contains allusions to the polis ritual of the expulsion of the *pharmakos*.[71] Similarly, the only point in the *Bacchae* at which the tyrant Pentheus is said to benefit the polis evokes the expulsion and killing of the *pharmakos*: it is when Dionysos says to him as he leaves the city for his death: 'Alone you κάμνεις on behalf of the polis, alone' (963), with κάμνεις meaning both 'toil' and 'suffer'.

Another factor supporting the notion of Oidipous as *tyrannos* is admitted by Knox himself: Oidipous is not (or rather does not seem to be) the hereditary successor to the throne of Thebes; he 'is an intruder, one whose warrant for power is individual achievement, not birth'.[72] To this we may briefly add our three interconnected tyrannical characteristics. First, we have already seen how Oidipous associates tyranny, and the obtaining of tyranny, with money. The disposal of the previous ruler was, however,

[69] A referee observed that my 'reading ... does not take into account the complexity of the play'. I readily admit that my brief discussion fails to perform this impossible task.

[70] See especially the contributions of Dewald, Raaflaub and Kallett in Morgan 2003.

[71] Vernant & Vidal-Naquet 1988: 131–3; Guépin 1968; on the ruler generally as *pharmakos* see Ogden 1997.

[72] Knox 1957: 54.

contrary to what Oidipous first assumes, not down to the power of money. It was rather another of our three characteristics: in his ascent to power, the tyrant kills family. At the end of the play Oidipous' tyrannical isolation from his closest *philoi*, even his daughters (1521–2), is total. It also, third, involves a ritual (marriage to the queen) that turns out to be the opposite of what it should be, an ἄγαμος γάμος ('non-marriage marriage'), with the wedding song a howl of pain, the wedding *makarismos* reversed, Oidipous' self-blinding at the bridal bed assimilated to the sexual act, and so on.[73] Incest, we may add, is another extreme version of an historical instrument of tyrannical power, namely endogamy.[74]

Finally, we must return to the second *stasimon*, with its famous association of tyranny with the hubris that is filled to excess with many things and falls to disaster. In arguing that this is about Athenian imperial policy, Knox focuses on the words,

> But if one goes on his way, contemptuous in action and speech, fearless of justice, not revering the seats[75] of the gods, may an evil destiny seize him, in return for his ill-fated proud luxury. If he will not gain profit justly and refrain from impious actions, or if he recklessly lays hold of the untouchable, [he will suffer divine punishment].[76]

'There is nothing in the play', writes Knox, 'which makes the remark about profit fit Oidipous.'[77] *[110]* The reference is in fact, he claims, to the tribute unjustly forced by Athens from its empire. From this tribute the Athenians had adorned the statue of Athena with gold, which Perikles said he was prepared to use for war purposes if necessary, thus (according to Knox) 'laying hold on the untouchable'.

Against this I insist on the typicality of the choral moralising. As we have seen, tyranny is generally associated with unjustly gained wealth, and Oidipous himself has at this point in the play already said how important money is in obtaining tyranny and has associated his own tyranny with wealth. Second, the combination of tyrannical excessive wealth with abuse of the sacred is elsewhere implicit not only in the passages we have discussed from *Agamemnon* and *Antigone* but also, for example, in the

[73] 420–3, 1275–85; Seaford 1987c[13]: 119–20.

[74] Gernet 1981; 289–302; cf. Hdt. 3.31; Pl. *Resp*. 9.571d1; Diog. Laert. 1.96; Vernant 1982a.

[75] Knox 1957: 103–4 translates ἕδη here as 'statues', in an implausible attempt to relate it to the impeachment of Pheidias for carving the portrait of Perikles on Athena's shield.

[76] 883–91: the words referring to the divine punishment are corrupt and are here merely paraphrased.

[77] Knox 1957: 104.

choral moralising of the *Agamemnon*[78] of 458, where it would be even more odd to regard it as a comment on the Athenian empire.

This does not mean, however, that the notion of Athens as a tyrannical polis is never relevant to the tragic *tyrannos*.[79] In Euripides' *Phoenician Women*, produced at a time when the *polis tyrannos* may have seemed to be suffering the consequences of its own hubris, Eteokles and Iokaste debate Eteokles' unwillingness to alternate sovereignty with his brother (499–567). I would do anything, says Eteokles, to have Tyranny, the greatest of the gods. It is cowardice to take less, and shameful to yield. I will not yield the tyranny, even at the cost of war. If one has to be unjust, the best thing is to be unjust for the sake of tyranny and pious in everything else. Iokaste replies that love of honour, *philotimia*, is the worst of gods, unjust and destructive. Equality, on the other hand, binds people to people and city-states to city-states, and lasts, whereas the less is always hostile to the more. Equality has created number, weights and the mutual yielding of day and night. Tyranny is an empty name. The wealth obtained by mortals really belongs to the gods, who take it back when they wish. The wealth you seek will be painful for Thebes.

This broad debate sees tyranny not just as rule by an individual but as a phenomenon to be located in the ethical and natural world. Euripides wrote it not long after the Melian debate (416), in which – in Thucydides' account (5.105) – the Athenians justify from a similarly broad perspective their domination of their empire as in accord with the divine and with the law of nature. Notice that equality, the implied opposite of tyranny, is said by Iokaste to bind city-states to each other and to be lasting. The implication therefore is that relations between city-states may be tyrannical and so unstable. Here at last we do have in tragedy the notion (albeit by implication) that a polis may behave tyrannically.[*iii*]

It is tempting to suppose that Euripides has been influenced in this by the tyrannical and currently unstable relation between Athens and the city-states of her empire. I am happy to yield to this temptation, provided that I am allowed to qualify it as follows. I have said that the Athenians' anxiety about the constant potential for tyranny within their own polis contributes to the projection of tyranny, in tragedy, onto the past and onto the elsewhere as a means of clarifying and confirming the current

[78] See esp. 367–84 (n.b. 371 ἀθίκτων, as *OT* 891), 773–82.

[79] As well as Eur. *Phoen.* one might mention *Hel.* 395 and *Or.* 1168, both associated by de Romilly 1969: 178 with Athens in relation to its empire.

democratic order. The time of the *Phoenician Women* (411–409) was certainly a time for such anxiety, perhaps also for anxiety at the consequences of Athenian tyranny over other city-states.

These anxieties may seem to us in a sense contradictory, for it was the democratic polis that had behaved tyrannically. Yet in the logic that projects tyranny onto the traditional Theban other, the two anxieties may cohere. Athens may project both the potential internal tyranny that it fears and the tyrannical foreign policy that it fears to give up, onto Thebes, where they cohere very nicely. In the *Phoenician Women*, as in the contemporary *Oedipus at Colonus* and the earlier *Suppliants*, it is the arrogance of internal Theban tyranny that produces conflict between city-states. It is contrary to the current spirit of the academy, and to the privilege we naturally accord to a certain kind of complexity, to suggest that Euripides does not here imply criticism of Athens. But it may indeed be that the novel, irresolvable and perhaps unbearable contradiction of a democratic *polis tyrannos* sought some symbolic resolution in a reassuringly traditional form of projection onto the chaotic past of a hostile city.[80]

POSTSCRIPT

I discuss the role of tyranny in the Athenian genesis of tragedy in Seaford 2012a: see the index s.v. 'tyranny'. For evidence of an early tradition of proclaiming awards to tyrant-slayers before the performances at the City Dionysia, see P. Wilson, 'Tragic honours and democracy: neglected evidence for the politics of the Athenian Dionysia', *CQ* 59 (2009), 8–29. For much more on the democratic hostility to tyranny, see D. A. Teegarden, *Death to Tyrants! Ancient Greek Democracy and the Struggle against Tyranny* (Princeton: Princeton University Press, 2014).

Further treatments of the dramatic representation of tyranny are B. Nikolsky, 'Slavery and freedom in Euripides' *Cyclops*', in R. Alston, E. Hall and L. Proffitt (eds.), *Reading Ancient Slavery* (London: Bristol Classical Press, 2011), pp. 121–32; D. DiLeo, 'Tragedy against tyranny', *Journal of Politics* 75.1 (2013), 254–65; D. K. Picariello and A. W. Saxonhouse, 'Aeschylus and the binding of the tyrant', *Polis* 32 (2015), 271–96.

Further work on tyranny includes S. Lewis, 'Καὶ σαφῶς τύραννος ἦν: Xenophon's account of Euphron of Sicyon', *JHS* 124 (2004), 65–74

80 My thanks go to the participants in the UCLA conference for lively discussion, and in particular to Greg Thalmann for his formal response.

(on the 'construction' of tyranny); G. Anderson, 'Before *turannoi* were tyrants: rethinking a chapter of early Greek history', *ClAnt* 24 (2005), 173–222; L. Mitchell, 'Tyrannical oligarchs at Athens', in S. Lewis (ed.), *Ancient Tyranny* (Edinburgh: Edinburgh University Press, 2006) 178–87; L. Mitchell, *The Heroic Rulers of Archaic and Classical Greece* (London: Bloomsbury Academic, 2013).

CHAPTER 6

Aeschylus and the Unity of Opposites

This is an essay in the interconnectedness of phenomena generally considered separately: verbal style, ritual, tragic action and cosmology. Their interconnectedness will emerge from the idea of the *unity of opposites* in each of them. I begin with the use of the stylistic figure I call antithetical *Satzparallelismus* in the ritual lament (§1) and in mystic ritual – in which it passes into expression (as oxymoron) of the unity of opposites, notably of life and death. Both these rituals, I have argued elsewhere, were factors in the genesis of Athenian tragedy,[1] and I argue here that their synthesised influence is felt both in tragic verbal style and in the form of tragic action (§2). The synthesis is deployed in Aeschylus' *Oresteia* to express, in lamentation, the cycle of revenge as a unity of opposites (§3). Various puzzling passages of the *Oresteia* can only be understood as expressing the need to differentiate the unity of opposites if escape from the cycle is to be achieved (§4). This escape comes, in the *Eumenides*, only after the emphatic differentiation of chthonic and Olympian deities, and the replacement of a Heraclitean model of the unity of opposites by a Pythagorean model of their reconciliation (§5).

1. Lamentation

I start with an example of the stylistic figure that I will call, after Norden, *Satzparallelismus*.[2] I define it, rather more narrowly than Norden, as the juxtaposition of sentences (which may be as short as a single word) that are distinct in *content* but resemble each other in *form*,[3] usually without

My thanks go to the anonymous referees for improvement of this article, as well as to my student Anthi Sambani for conversation on the topic.

[1] Seaford 1994b.

[2] Norden 1915: 15–29, 50–2, 813–24, 831–2; 1913: 254–63, 355–64.

[3] This formal resemblance later attracted the technical terms παρίσωσις (resemblance of length) and παρονομασία, παρομοίσωσις (assonance).

connecting words and at most with μέν ... δέ.[4] Its effect is a solemn staccato. The sentences generally describe (or prescribe) *actions*, and are often constituted by their content as an *antithetical pair*. The phenomenon is especially frequent in, although certainly not confined to,[5] two forms of ritual utterance – the lament[6] and formulae used in mystic ritual (§2); and it is in part through the influence of these rituals that this verbal form (and others closely related to it) occur [*142*] frequently in tragedy.[7]

I begin with instances of antithetical *Satzparallelismus* in the lament in Aeschylus.[8]

(1) Ξέρξης μὲν ἄγαγεν, ποποῖ
Ξέρξης δ' ἀπώλεσεν, τοτοῖ. (*Pers.* 550–1)

Xerxes led, alas.
Xerxes destroyed, alas.

(2)

– παιθεὶς ἔπαισας	– σὺ δ' ἔθανες κατακτανών
– δορὶ δ' ἔκανες	– δορὶ δ' ἔθανες
– μελεοπόνος	– μελεοπαθής
– πρόκεισαι	– κατέκτας
– ἴτω γόος	– ἴτω δάκρυα (*Sept.* 961–5)
– struck, you struck	– you died killing
– with a spear you killed	– with a spear you died
– having done wretchedly	– having suffered wretchedly
– you are laid out	– you killed
– let wailing flow	– let tears flow.

[4] And so excluded are expressions linked by ἄλλοτε ... ἄλλοτε or καὶ ... καί or οὔτε ... οὔτε *vel sim.*

[5] For instance it occurs (albeit only occasionally) in gnomic expressions (e.g. Thgn. 831; Diog. Laert. 1.98.1; Stob. 3.1.172.100). The presence of similar figures in the funerary encomium of Gorgias (DK 82 B 6) probably derives (given also the shared *topoi* of *enkomion* and lament) from the lament: Thomson 1953; Fehling 1969: 109 (poetry as the ultimate source of many of Gorgias' figures); see also their presence in Gorgias' *enkomion* of Helen (B 11), and antithetical *Satzparallelismus* in Agathon's *enkomion* of Eros at Pl. *Symp.* 197 and later in the Asiatic style of oratory.

[6] Alexiou 1974: 150–60; Thomson 1953: 82–3, including related genres such as Simonides' *enkomion* of the Spartan dead (*PMG* 531): ... εὐκλεὴς μὲν ἁ τύχα, καλὸς δ' ὁ πότμος, βωμὸς δ' ὁ τάφος, κτλ.

[7] Fehling in his study of the whole phenomenon of verbal repetition in early Greek literature pays special attention neither to the phenomenon I have defined nor to ritual nor to tragedy, but he does note that lyric and elegiac (except for the gnomic Theognis) have few *Wiederholungsfiguren* and that 'the tragic lyrics of Aeschylus differ considerably from other lyric, just as within ancient literature tragedy in general exhibits the most strikingly original developments in terms of *Wiederholungsfiguren*' (Fehling 1969: 101).

[8] Other instances in tragedy are Aesch. *Cho.* 436–7, 461; Soph. *El.* 193–4, 197, *Trach.* 950–1; Eur. *Supp.* 778, 833–4, *Hipp.* 836. Cf. Soph. *Aj.* 394–5; Eur. *Hel.* 198–9, *Phoen.* 1291–2.

In this lament for the dead brothers in Aeschylus' *Septem* each of the first four lines combines *Satzparallelismus* with antithesis between killing and being killed in return. In the first line the antithesis is contained within each of the symmetrical limbs.

Another example is from the great Aeschylean lament for Agamemnon:

(3) ὀτοτύζεται δ' ὁ θνῄσκων,
ἀναφαίνεται δ' ὁ βλάπτων. (*Cho.* 327–8)

There is bewailed the dead man,
There appears the avenger.

Here the antithesis expresses the movement within the lament from the passivity of being killed to the activity of revenge. Similarly (but in reverse order, for the revenge has been taken) Klytaimestra, as she stands over the corpse of Agamemnon, remembers the 'much-wept' Iphigeneia, and calls Agamemnon

(4) ἄξια[9] δράσας, ἄξια πάσχων (*Ag.* 1527)

having done what was deserved, suffering what is deserved.[10] *[143]*

A little later in the same passage, with the body of Agamemnon still on display, the chorus sing:

(5) ὄνειδος ἥκει τόδ' ἀντ' ὀνείδους,
δύσμαχα δ' ἐστι κρῖναι·
φέρει φέροντ', ἐκτίνει δ' ὁ καίνων·
μίμνει δὲ μίμνοντας ἐν θρόνῳ Διὸς
παθεῖν τὸν ἔρξαντα· θέσμιον γάρ. (*Ag.* 1560–4)

this insult has come in return for insult,
and they are hard to separate/judge;
he despoils the spoiler, and the killer pays;
it remains, while Zeus remains on the throne,
that the doer suffers: for so it is established.

9 Page retains τὴν πολυκλαύτην Ἰφιγένειαν ἀνάξια δράσας. And both he and Fraenkel object to the sense of Hermann's ἄξια δράσας governing Iphigeneia. But ἄξια δράσας removes the anomalous word division in the anapaestic dimeter (Ἰφιγένειαν is surely an intrusive gloss) and restores sarcastic sense. Klytaimestra's next utterance refers to Iphigeneia lovingly greeting her father in the next world, 1555–9: the chilling sarcasm is introduced by ἄξια δράσας, ἄχια πάσχων: 'he gave his daughter what she deserved – did he not? – and now accordingly he has what he deserves'. And cf. *Eum.* 868 (quoted in n. 94 below).

10 Though very close, this is not strictly an instance of antithetical *Satzparallelismus* as I have defined it, because it is not two sentences.

In the third line of this passage, as in the first line of (2), there is antithesis within each limb of the *Satzparallelismus*. In fact φέρει φέροντ' embodies even within itself something akin to antithetical *Satzparallelismus*: different inflections of the same word, referring to symmetrical but opposed deeds, are juxtaposed, giving the effect of antithetical *Satzparallelismus* collapsed into something akin to the oxymoron.[11]

What we see in these passages is that a stylistic figure, antithetical *Satzparallelismus*, expresses an antithetical movement at the heart of ritual, from the passivity of being killed to the activity of revenge. We are reminded that, among the Greeks and others, the lament is frequently a means of creating the emotions necessary for revenge.[12] Moreover, the two phases of this movement correspond to the action of the first two plays of the Oresteian trilogy. In the first play Agamemnon is killed; in the second his anger is enlisted, in the great lament, to support the act of revenge. The movement is also raised, in (5), to the level of an established universal principle guaranteed by Zeus. Antithetical *Satzparallelismus* may, as in Gorgias, become a mere rhetorical device, but in Aeschylus it expresses a fundamental reality.

2. Mystic Initiation

Although not confined to ritual, *Satzparallelismus* seems to have been especially common in various kinds of ritual utterance. A notable example, besides the lament, is mystic initiation.[13] Although not many of the formulae uttered in mystic initiations survive, a strikingly high proportion of them exhibit *Satzparallelismus*.[14]

From Eleusinian initiation we have:

(6) ἐκ τυμπάνου ἔφαγον, ἐκ κυμβάλου ἔπιον, ἐκερνοφόρησα, ὑπὸ τὸν παστὸν ὑπέδυν. (Clem. Al. *Protr.* 2.14)

From the tympanon I ate, from the cymbal I drank, I carried the *kernos*, under the bed-curtain I slipped.

[11] Rather different, though perhaps influencing Aeschylus, is Hom. *Il.* 18.309, the war god as killing the killer (κτανέοντα κατέκτα).

[12] Seaford 1994b: 74–105.

[13] For other kinds, see esp. the interrelated genres of funeral oration, *enkomion* and hymn: Thomson 1953: 77–83; Norden (n. 2 above).

[14] As do passages influenced by mystic initiation in both style and content, such as 1 Corinthians 13. The Eleusinian and Attis formulae are gathered and discussed by Thomson (1953).

(7) ὕε κύε (Procl. *In Ti.* 293c = 3.176.30D; Hippol. *Haer.* 5.7.34W)
Rain! Conceive! *[144]*

From the mysteries of Attis we have:

(8) ἐκ τυμπάνου βέβρωκα, ἐκ κυμβάλου πέπωκα, γέγονα μύστης Ἄττεως. (Firm. Mat. *Err. prof. rel.* 18.1Z)

From the tympanon I ate, from the cymbal I drank, I have become an initiate of Attis.

(9) ἔφυγον κακόν, εὗρον ἄμεινον. (Dem. 18.259)

I fled from the bad, I found the better.

And from the formulae of (Dionysiac) mystic initiation inscribed on the funerary gold leaves[15] we have:

(10) νῦν ἔθανες καὶ νῦν ἐγένου, ...
τα{ι}ῦρος εἰς γάλα ἔθορες·
αἶψα εἰς γ<ά>λα ἔθορες·
κριὸς εἰς γάλα ἔπεσ<ες>.

Now you died and now you came into being/were born, ...
a bull to the milk you rushed;
quickly to the milk you rushed;
a ram to the milk you fell.

(11) κύκλο<υ> δ' ἐξέπταν βαρυπενθέος ἀργαλέοιο·
ἱμερτο<ῦ> δ' ἐπέβαν στεφάνο<υ> ποσὶ καρπαλίμοισι.
δεσ{σ}ποίνας δ' ὑπὸ κόλπον ἔδυν χθονίας βασιλείας.

I flew out of the miserable circle of much grief.
I reached the lovely crown with swift feet.
I slipped under the lap of the royal mistress of the underworld.

All these formulae express the movement of the mystic initiand through initiation. All except perhaps (6) and (8) combine *Satzparallelismus* with *antithesis*, and in (9), (10) and (11) the antithesis expresses the passage

[15] GJ 26a.1–5 and 5.5–7.

through suffering or death to the eternal blessedness that we know from other texts to be the outcome of mystic initiation. Again, Pindar refers to the mystic transition with antithetical *Satzparallelismus*:

(12) ὄλβιος ὅστις ἰδὼν κεῖν᾽ εἶσ᾽ ὑπὸ χθόν᾽.
οἶδε μὲν βίου τελευτάν,
οἶδεν δὲ διόσδοτον ἀρχάν. (fr. 137)

Blessed is he who having seen those things will go beneath the earth.
He knows the ending of life,
He knows the god-given beginning.

One of the earliest pieces of evidence for Dionysiac mystic initiation is the report by Herodotus (4.79) that the Skythian king Skyles was initiated in the Greek colony of Olbia. From the same city have survived numerous polished bone plates, of which a group of three (first published in 1978), dated to the fifth century, are inscribed with the following words (GJ App. 1): [145]

(13)	βίος θάνατος βίος life death life	ἀλήθεια truth	Διό<νυσος> Dio[nysos]	Ὀρφικ[οί Orphic(s?)
(14)	εἰρήνη πόλεμος peace war	ἀλήθεια ψεῦδος truth falsehood	Διόν<υσος> Dion[ysos]	
(15)	Διό<νυσος> Dio[nysos]	ἀλήθεια truth	]α ψυχή (?) soul	

The 'truth' may be the truth revealed in Dionysiac or Orphic initiation. Does 'life death life' refer, like our other mystic formulae, to transition through death to eternal blessedness? Or does it, like the identity of opposites apparently being affirmed in (14), refer to the unity of life and death? There is a striking resemblance between these inscriptions and several fragments of Heraclitus, notably:

(16) ἀθάνατοι θνητοί, θνητοὶ ἀθάνατοι, ζῶντες τὸν ἐκείνων θάνατον, τὸν δὲ ἐκείνων βίον τεθνεῶτες. (DK 22 B 62)

immortals mortals, mortals immortals, living the death of those, and dying the life of those.

(17) ὁ θεὸς ἡμέρη εὐφρόνη, χειμὼν θέρος, πόλεμος εἰρήνη, κόρος λιμός … (B 67)[16]

God is day night, winter summer, war peace, satiety hunger …

This unity of opposites is explained as follows:

(18) οὐ ξυνιᾶσιν ὅκως διαφερόμενον ἑωυτῷ ὁμολογέει· παλίντροπος ἁρμονίη ὅκωσπερ τόξου καὶ λύρης. (B 51)

They do not understand how in being at variance it agrees with itself; backward-stretching *harmonia* as of bow and lyre.

The considerable influence of mystery cult on Heraclitus in various respects[17] makes it likely that here too the influence is from mystery cult rather than vice versa. Now for Heraclitus opposites are also subject to transformation into each other:

(19) τὰ ψυχρὰ θέρεται, θερμὸν ψύχεται, ὑγρὸν αὐαίνεται, καρφαλέον νοτίζεται. (B 126)

Cold things are warmed, warm is cooled, wet is dried, dry is made wet. [*146*]

The cycle of cosmological transformation involves the *soul*:[18]

(20) ψυχῇσιν θάνατος ὕδωρ γενέσθαι, ὕδατι δὲ θάνατος γῆν γενέσθαι· ἐκ γῆς δὲ ὕδωρ γίνεται, ἐξ ὕδατος δὲ ψυχή. (B 36)[19]

For souls it is death to become water, for water it is death to become earth: and from earth water comes into being, and from water soul.

[16] This may be a radical development of the use of antithetical *Satzparallelismus* to express the power of deity in transforming human fortunes into their opposite: Hes. *Op.* 1–10; cf. Pl. *Symp.* 197d; Hom. *Il.* 20.242–3; Nisbet and Hubbard 1970 on Hor. *Carm.* 1.34.12.

[17] The older arguments to this effect by Pfleiderer, Nestle, Macchioro, Cornford, Thomson and Guthrie were spectacularly confirmed by the discovery of the Olbian bone inscriptions and the Derveni papyrus: West 1983; Seaford 1986a[9]; Laks and Most 1997: 18–19, 133, 135. See now also Schefer 2000.

[18] For the importance of cosmology for the fate of the soul in mystic doctrine see Seaford 1986a[9]; Most 1997.

[19] Also B 77; Seaford 1986a[9]: 14–20.

This illuminates (13): βίος θάνατος βίος may refer both to the transition through death back to life and to the unity of life and death that is implied by this transition. The idea that death is also birth, expressed in the mystic formula (10), implies the unity of death and life expressed in (13) and (16). Reduced – as in (5) – to its bare minimum, antithetical *Satzparallelismus* becomes oxymoron. (Throughout this chapter I mean by oxymoron the juxtaposition, or near-juxtaposition, of two words antithetical in sense.[20]) And the oxymoron expresses the idea, associated with mystery cult, that we have an immortal soul contained or imprisoned in a mortal body, so that for our immortal soul life is a kind of death and death a return to immortal life. In mystic ritual this may involve the experience of a kind of death while still alive.[21]

This experience of death in mystic ritual is, along with numerous other features of mystic ritual, projected in the experiences of Pentheus in Euripides' *Bacchae*.[22] He experiences a kind of death while alive, first within the house[23] and then as wearing 'the adornment that he will take to Hades' (857). The costume referred to is also *female*. Indeed, it is striking that Pentheus seems to unite in himself, just before death, the basic oppositions of living and dead, adult and infant (968–9), male and female, human and animal (990, 1107–8). All these basic oppositions, each one crucial to identity, are likely – to judge from the surviving evidence – to have been united in the liminal phase of mystic initiation: the initiand becomes like a dead person, an infant,[24] of the opposite sex, a sacrificed animal.[25] The mystic unity of opposites contributes to the structure of tragic action.

In Aeschylus Agamemnon, just before his death, undergoes something similar: he is bathed and wrapped in a cloth by his wife as if already dead.[26] And he allows himself to be treated like a 'woman' (918), a 'barbarian '(919), a 'god' (925), and is 'sacrificed' as if an animal.[27] I do not claim that this is designed to reflect mystic initiation. It is, though, a characteristically tragic representation, which may owe something to the influence that – I have

[20] For a discussion of the oxymoron (more broadly defined) in early Greek literature see Fehling 1969: 286–92.

[21] Passage (10); Plut. fr. 178; Pl. *Phd.* 108a; [Pl.] *Ax.* 371d–e; Ar. *Ran.* 154–8, 313–459; *Nub.* 257; Seaford 1994b: 282.

[22] Seaford 1996a: 42.

[23] *Bacch.* 616–37; Seaford 1996a: 201.

[24] E.g. Fridh-Haneson 1987; Kingsley 1995: 267.

[25] Seaford 1996a: 43, 222.

[26] Seaford 1984c[II].

[27] *Ag.* 1118, 1278, 1433, 1504; Seaford 1994b: 369–70.

argued elsewhere[28] – mystery cult had on the genesis of tragedy. It is as alien as is mystery cult to the spirit of Homer.

More specifically, tragedy contains tragic oxymora uniting life and death,[29] for instance:

(21) (a) τὸν ζῶντα καίνειν τοὺς τεθνηκότας λέγω. (Aesch. *Cho.* 886)
I say that the dead are killing the living. [*147*]

(b) ζῶντα μ' ἔκτεινεν θανών. (Soph. *Trach.* 1163)[30]
Dead he killed me living.

(c) ἥδ' ἡμέρα φύσει σε καὶ διαφθερεῖ. (Soph. *OT* 438)
This day will give you birth and destroy you.

(d) μιᾷ σε τῇδ' ὁδῷ θανόντα τε | καὶ ζῶντα. (Soph. *El.* 1314–15)
You on this one journey dead and alive.

(e) ἔμψυχον ἡγοῦμαι νεκρόν. (Soph. *Ant.* 1167)
I consider [him] a living corpse.

Homer and Hesiod contain far fewer, and weaker,[31] oxymora than tragedy does.[32] It is no coincidence that the most striking oxymoron in all of Homer and Hesiod refers to Semele giving birth to Dionysos:

(22) ἀθάνατον θνητή. (Hes. *Theog.* 942)
a mortal to an immortal,

– a myth closely associated with death and rebirth in mystic initiation.[33]

Dionysos predicts that Pentheus will return from the mountainside 'carried … in the arms of your mother' (Eur. *Bacch.* 969). This suggests a baby carried by his mother, but actually Agaue will return carrying the severed head of her son. United here is the most intimate of all relationships

[28] Seaford 1994b.

[29] By far the closest expression in Homer is *Il.* 6.500 αἱ μὲν ἔτι ζωὸν γόον Ἕκτορα ᾧ ἐνὶ οἴκῳ, which, significantly, is from a passage that – it has been argued on various grounds – is a late passage of Athenian inspiration, with other affinities with tragedy: Bethe 1929: 318–20; Lorimer 1950: 442–7; Shipp 1972: 254–8; Sale 1987; Seaford 1994b: 330–8 (and cf. 166–72).

[30] 'Living' is there only for the sake of the oxymoron, just as at *Aj.* 1385, *Ant.* 871.

[31] Of the oxymoron I distinguish between two forms: a strong form, which expresses the identity of opposites, and a weak form, which merely draws attention to an opposition.

[32] I am aware of the following in Homer: *Il.* 1.299; 4.43 (sim. 7.197), 104; 6.484, 500; 9.378; 11.654 (sim. 13.775; *Od.* 20.135); 16.176; 21.483–4; 22.9; 23.116; *Od.* 1.242; 5.155; 8.329; 13.80 (?); 15.488–9; 17.466 (cf. 20.307; 4.346; 17.476); 18.73 (?), 404; 23.97. In Hesiod I am aware of *Theog.* 585, 609, 942; *Op.* 58, 179, 318.

[33] Seaford 1996a: 196–7.

(between mother and baby) with the most savagely hostile (the hunter with her victim's head). Similarly, the hostility between Orestes and his mother is expressed in his identification with the snake of her dream, which sucked at her breast:

(23) (a) ὥστ' ἐν γάλακτι θρόμβον αἵματος σπάσαι. (Aesch. *Cho*. 533)
so as to draw a clot of blood in the milk.

(b) θρόμβῳ τ' ἔμειξεν αἵματος φίλον γάλα. (Aesch. *Cho*. 546)
and mixed the dear milk with a clot of blood.

This may be described as an oxymoronic trimeter, i.e. a trimeter wholly devoted to expressing a unity of opposites. This is not uncommon in tragedy: other examples are (21a) and (21c).

The extreme isolation of the tragic individual (e.g. Pentheus, Agamemnon, Orestes), which may perhaps derive in part from the isolation of the initiand in mystic ritual,[34] is expressed in the *[148]* unity of the opposites φίλος and ἐχθρός, frequently embodied in oxymora such as the following:[35]

(24) (a) φίλου γὰρ ἐχθρά ... (Aesch. *Sept*. 695)
the hostile [curse of my] dear [father].

(b) ἀπέρωτος ἔρως. (Aesch. *Cho*. 600)
[sexual] love [that is] no love.

(c) μήτηρ ἀμήτωρ. (Soph. *El*. 1154)
mother [who is] no mother.

(d) φίλαι τε κοὐ φίλαι. (Eur. *El*. 1230)
dear and not dear.

(e) γάμον ἄγαμον. (Eur. *Hel*. 690)
marriage [that is] no marriage.

What I suggest is that the unity of opposites – of life and death, of φίλος and ἐχθρός – is manifest both in the verbal *style* of tragedy and in its representation of *action*. It is manifest also, we have seen, in mystic *ritual*, and in the *cosmology* of Heraclitus. It is also manifest in tragic cosmology. For instance the Sophoclean Ajax, just before dying, states that he has been

[34] Seaford 1994b: 281–327.
[35] Cf. also e.g. Soph. *OT* 416, 1214, 1256.

'feminised in speech', and then uses oxymora[36] to express the insight that in the cosmos the opposites alternate – summer and winter, night and day, and so on – and that accordingly he will act on the assumption that an ἐχθρός will become φίλος and vice versa. I have argued elsewhere that the passage also evokes mystery cult,[37] and so embodies the unity of opposites in all our four areas of *verbal style*, *ritual*, *action* and *cosmology*.[38]

3. Mystery Cult, Lamentation, Tragedy

I have argued elsewhere that important elements in the genesis of tragedy were mystery cult and hero cult. These two cultic forms were able to combine because of what they had in common, in particular lamentation (for Dionysos or the hero).[39] Lamentation, like mystery cult, unites death with life, both in the death-like state of the mourners[40] and in the life accorded to the mourned – as when Orestes says to his dead father (Aesch. *Cho.* 504) 'you are not dead even though you died' (οὐ τέθνηκας οὐδέ περ θανών). Here I expand the argument to include the style of ritual utterance: mystery cult and lamentation also had in common, as we have seen, antithetical *Satzparallelismus*.

The antithesis expressed in ritual *Satzparallelismus* may be sequential or simultaneous. In the mystic formulae it is in (6) and (8) sequential, although in these it is barely an antithesis. In *[149]* other mystic formulae – (7), (9), (10), (11), (12) – it is unclear whether it is sequential or simultaneous: for instance, the antithetical *Satzparallelismus* νῦν ἔθανες καὶ νῦν ἐγένου seems to refer to two distinct events of death and birth, and yet the repetition of νῦν implies that they are simultaneous – as in the lamenting *Satzparallelismus* at Aesch. *Cho.* 1014 νῦν αὐτὸν αἰνῶ, νῦν ἀποιμώζω παρών. This simultaneity of death and life is similarly implied in (13) βίος θάνατος βίος, which may also, however, as we have seen, imply *transition* from life through death to life.

Ambiguity between sequentiality and simultaneity in antithetical *Satzparallelismus* occurs also in our passages of Aeschylean lament. In (3) the emergence of ὁ βλάπτων (the dead Agamemnon) may follow or coincide with his being bewailed. In (2) the reciprocal death blows may have been simultaneous or (barely) sequential. (1) is sequential, but the

36 Soph. *Aj.* 647 φύει τ' ἄδηλα καὶ φανέντα κρύπτεται; 665 ἐχθρῶν ἄδωρα δῶρα; 676 λύει πέδησας.
37 E.g. the oxymoron at 692 … δυστυχῶ, σεσωμένον; see further Seaford 1994c[10].
38 For another example of the effect of mystic cosmology on tragic action see Seaford 1986a[9].
39 Seaford 1994b: 319, 322–7, 398; note esp. Hdt. 5.67.
40 Arist. fr. 101 Rose; Seaford 1994b: 86.

symmetricality of the *Satzparallelismus* implies that the expedition was doomed from the start. There is a similar effect in (4) and (5).

Let us look more closely at this effect in (5). Offence and counter-offence are sequential, but the antithetical *Satzparallelismus* – reduced to its most economical form (φέρει φέροντ', ἐκτίνει δ' ὁ καίνων ... παθεῖν τὸν ἔρξαντα) – expresses the symmetry and inevitability of the sequence, and thereby the unity of offence and counter-offence. Though opposites, they are 'hard (δύσμαχα) to separate' (κρῖναι) – i.e. hard to judge. And δύσμαχα may in this context imply that they are locked together like two fighters.[41] The result is, the chorus conclude, that the clan is stuck fast to destruction (1565–6). If each offence makes inevitable a counter-offence indistinguishable from itself, then there is no end to the chain of revenge. The indistinguishability of violent opposites makes resolution of conflict impossible. Seen as embodying the unity of opposites, the vendetta can have no end.

Antithetical *Satzparallelismus* may be reduced to the juxtaposition of two antithetical words, both in the lament (φέρει φέροντ') and in mystery cult: the oxymoronic βίος θάνατος βίος (13) and θνητοὶ ἀθάνατοι (16) express the unity of opposites implied by the mystic chant νῦν ἔθανες καὶ νῦν ἐγένου. And just as there is no end to the chain of offence and counter-offence, so too, in mystery cult, the passage of the soul seen as embodying the unity of opposites may seem endless, a 'miserable cycle' (11). Passage (16), taken together with other fragments of Heraclitus, implies a cycle of reincarnation:[42] the immortal soul enters a mortal body, leaves it at the death of that body, enters another body, and so on. But (11) indicates that in mystic ritual escape from the cycle is possible.[43]

What I am suggesting is that in the earliest extant tragedy the synthesis of mystery cult and lamentation involves the synthesis of their similar modes of verbal expression. The idea of the unity of opposites is in mystery cult expressed in antithetical *Satzparallelismus*, as it is also in Aeschylus, where it converges with the antithetical *Satzparallelismus* of the lamentation that drives on the reciprocal violence. And we shall suggest in §5 that the importance of escape from the cycle of reincarnation (in mystery cult) contributes to the Aeschylean representation of the importance of escape from the cycle of reciprocal violence.

[41] For μαχ- of athletic fighting, see LSJ, s.v. μάχομαι iii.

[42] Seaford 1986a[9].

[43] Seaford 1986a[9]; Zuntz 1971: 320–2; Aristoxenus *ap.* Diog. Laert. 8.14; *Orph. fr.* frr. 229 and 230K (= 348i–iii and 598B).

4. Differentiation of United Opposites in the *Oresteia*

In the lament from which (4) and (5) are taken it is said that lamentation by Klytaimestra for her husband would be ἄχαριν χάριν (*Ag.* 1545). Whereas φέρει φέροντ᾽ implies the unity of what are in fact *sequential* reciprocal acts, ἄχαριν χάριν is more completely oxymoronic, for it embodies an act of (positive) reciprocity (χάριν) that is *simultaneously* its own exact antithesis (ἄχαριν). Because Klytaimestra is a friend who is an enemy, her χάρις is ἄχαρις. *[150]*

The unity of opposites expressed by ἄχαριν χάριν is fundamental to the plot. In the next play Klytaimestra, 'intending χάριν ἀχάριτον' (*Cho.* 44), sends the chorus and Elektra to pour libations and pray at Agamemnon's tomb. The self-contradictory mission puts Elektra in a quandary: should her prayer accompanying the offerings be for positive reciprocity (89 παρὰ φίλης φίλῳ) or negative reciprocity (94–5 ἴσ᾽ ἀντιδοῦναι ... δόσιν γε τῶν κακῶν ἐπαξίαν)?

Persuaded to pray for the latter, i.e. revenge (144 τοὺς κτανόντας ἀντικατθανεῖν), she separates out, in cumbersome antithetical *Satzparallelismus*, the opposites unified in the χάρις ἀχάριτος, the prayer for blessings from the dead (for us) and the prayer for harm from the dead (for them):

(25) ταῦτ᾽ ἐν μέσῳ τίθημι τῆς καλῆς (Schütz: κακῆς M) ἀρᾶς,
κείνοις λέγουσα τήνδε τὴν κακὴν ἀράν. (*Cho.* 145–6)

These things I put in the middle of the good prayer,
speaking against them this evil prayer.

She then urges the chorus to sing a 'paian of the dead' (151 παιᾶνα τοῦ θανόντος) – an oxymoron in that the paian is often a song of triumph and certainly so in this context. Accordingly they sing a lament together with a celebration of the strength of the future avenger.[44] Once again, the sequence of violence and counter-violence that structures the trilogy is embodied in an oxymoron – here expressing a unity of opposites, paian and lament, in the same ritual song.[45] But the unity of opposites provides no release, no resolution. And so the wish is expressed for the differentiation

[44] At 154 κεδνῶν κακῶν expresses (however we read this problematic passage) the same unity of opposites.

[45] As also at Eur. *Tro.* 126.

of the opposites into a sequence: 'Instead of laments at the tomb may the paian …' (342–3).[46]

My hypothesis is that the need to differentiate united opposites is a dominant idea in the *Oresteia*.[47] Deriving from ritual, it is manifest in verbal style, in the shaping of events and intermediately in various statements, some of which have seemed cumbersome or puzzling, for example (25). What remains of this section explores this theme with further examples. It will illuminate not only passages whose meaning is disputed but also passages in which what is hard to see is Aeschylus' motive in writing them.

The omen of the eagles devouring the pregnant hare at Aulis, in the parodos of the *Agamemnon*, is described by Kalkhas as a unity of opposites: δέξια μὲν κατάμομφα δὲ … (145), 'favourable but inauspicious'. It is favourable because it means the sack of Troy, inauspicious because Artemis, resentful at the eagles

(26) αὐτότοκον πρὸ λόχου μογερὰν πτάκα θυομένοισι (*Ag.* 137)

sacrificing the poor trembling hare with offspring before birth,

will demand θυσίαν ἑτέραν, generally translated 'another sacrifice' but meaning in fact '*the* other sacrifice': and indeed the sacrifice of Iphigeneia both reciprocates the 'sacrifice' of the hare and is, as I have shown elsewhere, in various respects its polar opposite.[48] This being so, it is [*151*]
significant that, as Stanford notes,[49] every word of (26) could refer also to the sacrifice of Iphigeneia: 'sacrificing a trembling, cowering woman, his own child, on behalf of the army'. This description, by uniting the opposites, corresponds to Kalkhas' δέξια μὲν κατάμομφα δὲ. Faced with this symmetry of reciprocal opposite 'sacrifices', the latter to be reciprocated (151–5) by yet another 'sacrifice' (of Agamemnon, 1118, 1433, etc.), the chorus can conclude – in the hope to escape from the unity of opposites, to create positive sequentiality – only by repeating the starkly antithetical ritual *Satzparallelismus*

46 This occurs in reverse at Thuc. 7.75.7.

47 Compare the connection made by Girard 1977, in Sophocles and Euripides, between violence and the effacement of differences between the antagonists.

48 The 'meal of the eagles', their 'sacrifice' of the hare, is like a hunt ('hounds') by one species of another (extreme distance), whereas the 'no meal' sacrifice of Iphigeneia is not only same species but same family (extreme closeness) – with normal sacrifice (same household, different species) in between. See further Seaford 1989b¹: 90–1.

49 Stanford 1939: 143–4, whose translation I give.

(27) αἴλινον αἴλινον εἰπέ, τὸ δ' εὖ νικάτω (121, 138, 159)

sing the linos-cry (lament), but may the good prevail,

followed immediately by the famous hymn to Zeus, which begins thus:

(28) Ζεὺς ὅστις πότ' ἐστιν, εἰ τόδ' αὐ-
τῷ φίλον κεκλημένῳ,
τοῦτό νιν προσεννέπω·
οὐκ ἔχω προσεικάσαι
πάντ' ἐπισταθμώμενος
πλὴν Διός, εἰ τὸ μάταν ἀπὸ φροντίδος ἄχθος
χρὴ βαλεῖν ἐτητύμως. (160–6)

Zeus, whoever he is, if to be called by this name is pleasing to him, thus do I address him. I am unable to liken him to anything, putting everything on the scales,[50] except Zeus, if from my mind the vain burden must be cast genuinely.

The traditional doubt about the nature of deity is developed into a statement of his incomparability. Nothing may be likened to Zeus, except Zeus. From προσεικάσαι ('liken') we move rapidly to the similar notion of *equivalence*: nothing is like Zeus, and nothing (not even all things together) is equivalent to Zeus – in the way that equivalence is established by weighing on a balance.[51] Even were all things to be put on (ἐπι-) the scale, they would not be enough to remove the weight (ἄχθος) from the mind. Only Zeus can do that, as the god who, in Homer, inclines the fate-deciding scales.[52] Equilibrium in Aeschylus is not a dead metaphor,[53] but an image of the unity of opposites no less perfect than the bow and lyre used

[50] σταθμός may mean 'scales', and σταθμάω means 'measure' or 'weigh' (e.g. Ar. *Ran.* 797). ἐπισταθμάω occurs only here.

[51] The move is facilitated by (in a dynamic common in Aeschylus) the notion of equivalence being contained already in προσεικάσαι. It is not coincidental that in the third century εἰκάζειν is found meaning 'to estimate a *quantity*' (LSJ, s.v. iii). At Aesch. *Cho.* 518–19, θανόντι … δειλεία χάρις … οὐκ ἔχοιμ' ἂν εἰκάσαι τάδε | τὰ δῶρα· μείω δ' ἐστὶ τῆς ἁμαρτίας means not what it is usually taken to mean (e.g. 'I do not know to what to liken these her gifts', Lloyd-Jones) but 'I am not able to liken these gifts [as equivalent] to the offence against the dead man', which is then clarified in the words that follow.

[52] It is surprising that the commentators do not adduce Hom. *Il.* 8.69–72 and 22.209–13, where the fall of one side of the divine scales is caused by the (respective weights of the) two fates put on the scales by Zeus, and 19.223–4, where it is caused by Zeus himself (κλίνῃσι). Cf. Hom. *Il.* 16.658 Διὸς ἱρὰ τάλαντα; 14.99. At Aesch. *Pers.* 346 a god loads the scales (of battle) οὐκ ἰσορρόπῳ τύχῃ.

[53] Cf. e.g. *Ag.* 437–43.

as illustrations by Heraclitus in passage (18). The key to understanding the 'abrupt' (Page) transition to the hymn to Zeus is that only Zeus, who has established the principle of learning through suffering (177 πάθει μάθος), can resolve the dreadful unity of opposites implicit in the omen interpreted by Kalkhas.[54] The principle is restated at the end of the song: 'the skills of Kalkhas are not without fulfilment [152] (i.e. the cycle of violence will continue), but Justice for the sufferers inclines the scales to learning' (250–1 Δίκα δὲ τοῖς μὲν παθοῦσιν μαθεῖν ἐπιρρέπει).[55]

The sack of Troy, prefigured by the omen, is occurring as the dramatic action begins. Klytaimestra's lengthy description of this event derives entirely from her opening insistence on separating the two kinds of cry now heard in Troy:

(29) οἶμαι βοὴν ἄμεικτον ἐν πόλει πρέπειν·
ὄξος τ' ἄλειφα τ' ἐγχέας ταὐτῷ κύτει
διχοστατοῦντ' ἂν οὐ φίλως προσεννέποις·
καὶ τῶν ἁλόντων καὶ κρατησάντων δίχα
φθογγὰς ἀκούειν ἔστιν ... (*Ag.* 321–5)

I think an unmixed cry is clearly heard in the city:
vinegar and oil, having poured them into the same container,
you would call set apart in no friendly manner;
and the voices of the captured and conquerors
one may hear separately ...

She continues with a lengthy account of the sufferings of the Trojans, the release from suffering of the Greeks and the hope that the Greeks may not themselves come to grief (by offending the gods, or because of the sufferings of the dead), and concludes with the wish 'may the good prevail, to be seen not in equilibrium (διχορρόπως)'. Similarly, the herald arrived from Troy will optimistically say of the Trojan war 'the gain prevails, suffering does not outweigh (ἀντιρρέπει) it' (574).

Why does Klytaimestra insist on the cry (βοή) being 'unmixed', dwell on the simile of the liquids being unmixed (unlike the mixed milk and blood of passage 23b)[56] and emphasise the separate sufferings of the Greeks and

[54] Similarly at 182 the χάρις βίαιος of the gods (mss. βιαίως makes no sense) is an oxymoron that implies the unity of violent reciprocity with the positive reciprocity that, as a divine gift, emerges from it.

[55] Cf. Hom. *Il.* 14.99 αἰπὺς ὄλεθρος ἐπιρρέπῃ, and ῥέπειν at *Il.* 8.69–72 and 22.208–13; Ar. *Ran.* 1393.

[56] Cf. Eur. *Ion* 1016–17.

the Trojans? Because of the tragic focus on the unity of the opposites, of intensified utterance seeming to express both joy and grief, which gives rise to oxymora such as, for instance, our earlier 'paian of the dead', or Elektra's sobbing compared to laughter (*Cho.* 448), or the play on the ambiguity of βοή between joy and grief at Soph. *OT* 420,[57] or the wedding song that has to be re-learnt as a lament later in the *Agamemnon* (705–12) and which is said, in another evocation of the scales, to fall to (ἐπέρρεπε) the kinsmen of the *bridegroom* to sing.[58]

Like the chorus in (27), Klytaimestra's concluding wish 'that the good may prevail not in equilibrium' (349 μὴ διχορρόπως ἔχειν) uses the power of speech to resolve the 'equilibrium' of the unity of opposites. This suggests that, three lines earlier (346), the corrupt ἐγρήγορον qualifying the 'suffering of the killed' should be εὐήγορον, 'fair-spoken'.[59] Similarly, the herald insists that a 'fair-spoken' (εὔφημον, i.e. auspicious) day should not be polluted with the telling of bad news – he means the storm suffered by the Greek fleet on its return:

(30) εὔφημον ἦμαρ οὐ πρέπει κακαγγέλῳ
γλώσσῃ μιαίνειν· χωρὶς ἡ τιμὴ θεῶν. (636–7)

It is not seemly to pollute an auspicious day
with the voice of bad news. Separate is the honour [for the gods below]
from the [Olympian] gods. [153]

The allusive brevity of χωρὶς ἡ τιμὴ θεῶν implies the familiarity of the principle, unfamiliar to us, that gods above and gods below must be kept apart.

The herald continues by describing at length an example of what *would* be bad news, namely the sack of a city. In the case of such suffering, he adds, it is appropriate (πρέπει again) to utter παιᾶνα τόνδ' Ἐρινύων, 'this paian of the Erinyes' (645). This description is meant as hypothetical. But in fact a city (Troy) *has* been sacked, and so 'this paian of the Erinyes', referring to the hypothetical description, is a reality (hence the unusual role of the deictic τόνδε). We are reminded that a Greek paian means its opposite (lament) for the Trojans: whereas a paian, expressing triumph, belongs to

[57] Seaford 1987c[13]: 119. Cf. e.g. Soph. *Aj.* 976; Eur. *El.* 756, *HF* 751, 895.

[58] The point of the scales image may be that the anomalous absence of the bride's kin resolves the equilibrium inherent in the normal wedding (between sorrow and joy, bride's kin and bridegroom's kin) irreversibly into lamentation by bridegroom's kin: see further Seaford 1987c[13]: 123–7.

[59] Headlam's brilliant conjecture. Page ignores the decisive objections (Headlam, Fraenkel, Thomson) to ἐγρηγορός (Porson).

the gods above (notably Apollo), the Erinyes are of the world below, and agents of revenge.[60] This confirms, by the way, the interpretation I have given of (30) – following Thomson and Fraenkel – against Page's 'separate [i.e. from pollution] is the honour due to the gods'. The herald's attempt to keep the opposites separate is thwarted by his own choice of a detailed description of the sufferings of a sacked city as an example of what would be bad news. The oddity of this is the price paid for the manifestation of the power of the unity of opposites (of good news with bad, of victory with defeat, of the gods above with the gods below) over his intention to keep them separate. There is the same manifestation in his very next words, beginning the account of the storm that ravaged the Greek fleet:

(31) πῶς κεδνὰ τοῖς κακοῖσι συμμείξω, λέγων
χειμῶν' Ἀχαιοῖς οὐκ ἀμήνιτον θεῶν;
ξυνώμοσαν γάρ, ὄντες ἔχθιστοι τὸ πρίν,
πῦρ καὶ θάλασσα ... (648–51)

How shall I mix good with bad, telling
of a storm for the Akhaians that was not without the anger of the gods?
For fire and sea, being previously most hostile to each other, swore alliance ...

Despite the intentions of the herald, the opposites combine, even at the level of cosmology: sea combines with fire.

Agamemnon arrives. Rejecting Klytaimestra's invitation to walk on the textiles, he tells her not to spread cloths on his path, for it is gods who should be honoured thus, and for a mortal to walk on embroidered finery (923 ἐν ποικίλοις ... κάλλεσιν) is not without fear. He tells her to honour him as a man, not a god, and continues,

(32) χωρὶς ποδοψήστρων τε καὶ ποικίλων
κληδὼν ἀϋτεῖ. (926–7)
Separately proclaims the utterance[61] of 'footmats' and 'embroideries'.

Agamemnon is here emphasising the distinction he has just made: footmats (for men) are distinct from embroideries (for gods). However, Page

[60] Cf. *Ag.* 1075, 1078–9. For the juxtaposition of the paian with its chthonic opposite in tragedy, see Rutherford 1994–5.

[61] Or 'name', as at *Eum.* 418.

translates rather 'Fame shouts aloud, without footwipers and embroideries' (i.e. my fame speaks for itself), ignoring Fraenkel's decisive objections to this translation: in particular ποδόψηστρα are contemptible and so cannot be equivalent in this context to ποικίλα, which have just been said to be appropriate for a god not a man. Page objects that κληδών, ἀΰτεῖ and the strong coupling with τε καί are all inappropriate to the translation he rejects, failing to see that the strong coupling expresses a unity of opposites (between footmats for men and embroideries for gods, both mats) that the emphatically placed χωρίς and the strangely emphatic κληδὼν ἀΰτεῖ are needed to separate. Once again, an unexpected, seemingly cumbersome expression makes sense as emphatic differentiation of opposites. [154] τε … καί has a similar function earlier in the same scene:

(33) γνώσῃ δὲ χρόνῳ διαπευθόμενος
τόν τε δικαίως καὶ τὸν ἀκαίρως … (807–8)

You will know in time by investigating
the one who justly and the one who unseasonably …

– opposites which Agamemnon disastrously fails to separate, just as in the event he fails to separate ποδόψηστρα and ποικίλα, thereby also fatally uniting the opposites of man with god (922–3), male with female (918) and Greek with barbarian (919).

Just as Agamemnon is killed by a φίλος, Kassandra remembers how she was mocked (her prophecies disbelieved) by her own relatives:

(34) φίλων ὕπ' ἐχθρῶν οὐ διχορρόπως, μάτην. (1272)
by hostile friends not in equilibrium, in vain.

Page comments 'nothing whatever can be made of the words οὐ διχορρόπως μάτην'. Fraenkel takes them together as meaning 'not equivocally in vain', i.e. 'and their delusion clear beyond doubt', on the grounds that οὐ διχορρόπως goes harshly with ὕπ' ἐχθρῶν and 'does not add to the powerful phrase φίλων ὕπ' ἐχθρῶν anything essential'. But it does. Once again, what seems cumbersome and pointless acquires point as resolving the unity of opposites (expressed as equilibrium) – here of φίλος with ἐχθρός.[62] It is the hostility that prevailed.[63]

[62] Cf. Eur. *Phoen.* 1446 φίλος γὰρ ἐχθρὸς ἐγένετ', ἀλλ' ὅμως φίλος.

[63] μάτην then refers (if not corrupt) to the disastrous outcome of their mocking.

Like the bow and lyre of Heraclitus, scales in equilibrium embody the unity of opposites, but are also – unlike bow and lyre – an instrument of divine Justice. It is this that implies hope. Δίκα δὲ τοῖς μὲν παθοῦσιν μαθεῖν ἐπιρρέπει (*Ag.* 250–1; cf. *Cho.* 61): escape from the unity of opposites means Justice, or Zeus (passage 28), inclining the scales. The divine scales are fleetingly evoked, along with the idea of the gods as jurors voting 'not in equilibrium (οὐ διχορρόπως)' for the destruction of Troy (*Ag.* 815–16). In the trial of Orestes in the *Eumenides* the votes of the human jurors *are* equal – a potentially disastrous unity of opposites resolved by the casting vote of Athena.[64] Only one obstacle then remains to permanent escape from violence and suffering. The Erinyes, equally capable of causing devastation or blessings, remain angry. Athena addresses them thus:

(35) οὐκ ἂν δικαίως τῇδ' ἐπιρρέποις πόλει
μῆνιν τιν' ... (888–9)

> Not justly would you bring down (as in a balance) on this polis
> any anger ...

Here again ἐπιρρέπειν is not a dead metaphor: rather than meaning merely 'inflict', it expresses resolution of a unity of opposites, of a situation in the balance, of which the Erinyes may incline either side. [155]

5. Permanent Resolution

It was the unity of opposites – the indistinguishability of offence and counter-offence – that seemed to make resolution of the conflict impossible. Just as the killing of Agamemnon is assimilated – in (4) and (5) – to the killing of Iphigeneia, so the killing of Klytaimestra is assimilated to the killing of Agamemnon: offence and counter-offence form a unity of opposites. The assimilation is expressed in antithetical *Satzparallelismus*, for instance:

(36) (a) ἀντὶ μὲν ἐχθρᾶς γλώσσης ἐχθρὰ
γλῶσσα τελείσθω ...
ἀντὶ δὲ πληγῆς φονίας φονίαν
πληγὴν τινέτω. δράσαντι παθεῖν ... (*Cho.* 309–13)

[64] Seaford 1995.

In return for words of hate
let words of hate be paid …
In return for bloody blow
let bloody blow be paid. The doer must suffer …

(b) Ἄρης Ἄρει ξυμβαλεῖ, Δίκᾳ Δίκα. (*Cho.* 461)
Ares clashes with Ares, Justice with Justice.

This results in 'suffering that is hard to put a stop to' (470). Apollo tells Orestes to go after his father's murderers 'in the same way (τρόπον τὸν αὐτόν), meaning to kill them in return' (274). The display of a male and a female corpse will mirror the same display at the end of the *Agamemnon*,[65] and evokes the same ironical reference to their lying together in love (*Ag.* 1446, *Cho.* 906). And the identity of agency is expressed by the formal symmetry of stichomythia:[66]

(37) Klyt. ἡ Μοῖρα τούτων, ὦ τέκνον, παραιτία.
Or. καὶ τόνδε τοίνυν Μοῖρ' ἐπόρσυνεν μόρον. (*Cho.* 910–11)

Klyt. Fate is partly responsible, O child, for these things.
Or. And so it is Fate that brings this death too.

Similarly the same agents (the Erinyes) both impel Orestes to kill his mother and punish him for killing her:

(38) Klyt. ὅρα, φύλαξαι μητρὸς ἐγκότους κύνας.
Or. τὰς τοῦ πατρὸς δὲ πῶς φύγω παρεὶς τάδε; (924–5)

Klyt. Look, beware the angry hounds of your mother.
Or. How am I to escape those of my father if I fail to do this?

This threat of attack on Orestes by the Erinyes of his father had been proclaimed by Apollo (*Cho.* 283–4). To be sure, the Erinyes of the father may be thought to be in a sense distinct from those of the mother. But Orestes envisages his matricide as a third drink of unmixed blood for the Erinys (singular, *Cho.* 577–8): i.e. the same Erinys is actively involved in the whole chain of revenge.[67] [*156*]

[65] Taplin 1978: 125–6.
[66] Cf. the weighing of single tragic lines against each other at Ar. *Ran.* 1378–1413.
[67] See also *Ag.* 155, 1119, 1190, 1433, 1501, 1569, 1580; *Cho.* 402, 651.

Offence and counter-offence, dramatised in the first and second plays of the trilogy respectively, are assimilated to each other, and have failed to bring resolution (*Cho.* 1073–6). Accordingly, the third play brings resolution by distinguishing between them. The judicial decision is a 'separation' (διαιρεῖν: *Eum.* 472, 488, 630, 749), that must occur ἐτητύμως (488) – the adverb used of the definitive resolution in the hymn to Zeus (passage 28). Killing Agamemnon and killing Klytaimestra are 'not the same thing' (625).

A crucial precondition for this separation is that the superhuman involvement, which we have seen in the first two plays intensifying the unity of the opposed acts of violence, should be differentiated (as it is, vainly, in passage 30). Hence early in the *Eumenides* the repeated emphasis that the Erinyes, who in the *Choephori* were aligned with Apollo (283–4), are separate from – and detested by – the Olympian gods (69–73, 185–91, 197, 350–2, 365–6, 385–6). The physical presence of Apollo and the Erinyes underpins the differentiation of opposed principles that allows the judicial differentiation of the acts of violence. But differentiation is only the necessary first step. Permanent escape from the cycle of violence, like permanent escape from the cycle of life and death, requires reconciliation of the opposites in a new order.

How is this reconciliation to be achieved? First we should glance at Anaximander and Heraclitus, each of whom imagines a cosmology pervaded by opposites.[68] Anaximander imagines that the opposites 'give penalty and retribution to each other for their injustice according to the assessment of time', a process that also seems to be reabsorption and reuniting of the opposites into the 'unlimited' (ἄπειρον), from which they had been separated out.[69] For Heraclitus the tension between opposites, and the transformation of opposites into each other, is controlled by the *logos*. I argue elsewhere[70] that the cosmology constituted by the unity and interaction of opposites controlled by a third party – imagined in their different ways by Anaximander and Heraclitus – is in part a projection of *interpersonal* opposition that is controlled ultimately by the polis.

We have seen that central to the *Oresteia*, too, is the unity and interaction of opposites, which – though dominated by interpersonal oppositions – seems all-pervasive, even acquiring a cosmological dimension, and is

[68] Comparison of Aeschylus with the Presocratics has been surprisingly thin: most detailed is Rösler 1970.

[69] DK 12 B 1; Vlastos 1970: 77–80.

[70] Seaford 2004c.

eventually controlled, with the help of the gods, by the polis. And so the *Oresteia* dramatises the kind of social process that is, in Presocratic philosophy and even in the *Oresteia* itself, projected onto the cosmos. What distinguishes the civic optimism of the *Oresteia* is that the polis does not merely control an unending cycle of oppositions but permits an escape from the cycle into permanent well-being.[71]

We have noted the influence of mystery cult on Heraclitus, and in particular on his idea of the passage of the soul through the transformation of opposites into each other. Whether, like mystic doctrine, he also believed that the soul could escape from this cycle of cosmological transformation into permanent well-being is unknown (it is not indicated in the extant fragments). But the mystic doctrine is certainly analogous to the escape dramatised in the *Oresteia*, even if it did not influence it.

But perhaps it did influence it. The overall conception of events in the *Prometheia* (whether or not that trilogy was by Aeschylus) was influenced by the mystic idea of the passage of the soul through the cosmological cycle to eventual liberation.[72] Moreover, several passages of the *Oresteia* have been identified as evoking the mystic ritual at Eleusis.[73] To these I would add that the beacon in the darkness welcomed by the watchman as signifying 'release from sufferings' (*Ag.* 20–1) would have evoked the light in the darkness that signified salvation after sufferings in the Eleusinian ritual.[74] But firelight can be delusive (492) or even destructive (389). What the [157] watchman sees is generally translated 'light in the darkness' but actually means 'dark light' (21 ὀρφναίου πυρός).[75] It is only at the end of the trilogy that this unity of opposites is resolved by the direct association of the torchlight escorting the Erinyes with the permanence of their benevolence to Attica (*Eum.* 1029–31). The Eleusinian mysteries are a festival of the Athenian polis, and combine salvation for the individual initiand with the celebration of the gift of corn for all humankind. The liberation of Prometheus in the *Prometheia*, modelled on the mystic passage of the individual soul, brings permanent blessings for all humankind.[76] Similarly the liberation of Orestes brings to the Athenian polis blessings (the cult of

[71] This is not of course to say that punishment will become unnecessary: see e.g. passage (5) and *Eum.* 954–5.

[72] Seaford 1986a[9].

[73] Thomson 1966: index s.v. Eleusinian Mysteries; Seaford 1994b: 373–4.

[74] Seaford 1996a: 202; Thomson 1966 on *Ag.* 1.

[75] Cf. *Cho.* 319 σκότῳ φάος ἀντίμορον; Soph. *Aj.* 394 σκότος, ἐμὸν φάος; *OC* 1549 ὦ φῶς ἀφεγγές.

[76] Seaford 1986a[9].

the Erinyes, the law court, the alliance with Argos) whose *permanence* is repeatedly emphasised.[77]

This permanent resolution depends on reconciliation of the opposites that are early in the *Eumenides* so emphatically differentiated, the chthonian Erinyes and the Olympian gods. In the aetiological narrative of the Eleusinian mysteries, the *Homeric Hymn to Demeter*, Persephone is rescued from Hades by Zeus, but will have to spend a third of each year with Hades, an arrangement ratified by Zeus (445–8); and Demeter, though she fails to immortalise Demophoön, bestows on mortals happiness after death through initiation. Both outcomes incorporate the claims of death into the permanent victory over it. Death and life, the lower and the upper world, are reconciled so as to produce not a symmetrical unity of opposites but the predominance of the more desirable opposite. And this is also the incorporation of Persephone and Demeter into the male predominance of Hades and Zeus (414, 485). Similarly in the *Eumenides* the claims of the chthonian female Erinyes are incorporated into the permanent well-being of the male-dominated polis. But what form does this incorporation of the Erinyes take?

The chorus of the *Agamemnon*, in their anxiety as the king enters the house, sing:

(39) μάλα γάρ τοι τᾶς πολλᾶς
ὑγιείας ἀκόρεστον
τέρμα· νόσος γὰρ
γείτων ὁμότοιχος ἐρείδει. (1001–4)

Much health has an insatiable boundary. For disease, sharing a party wall, presses upon it.

The text is incurably corrupt,[78] but sense emerges. There are parallels, cited by the commentators, for the idea that it is damaging to pursue health too far. An excessive cargo – continue the chorus – causes the ship to founder on a reef; excessive wealth and famine are remediable, but (aptly for the context) blood once fatally shed cannot be restored. This introduces the idea that what produces unity of the opposites (by destroying the party wall between them) is excess.[79] Their differentiation is maintained by moderation. The desired state is situated between extremes. This applies to the

[77] *Eum.* 291, 484, 572, 670–2, 683, 708, 763, 853, 891, 965, 975, 977, 992, 1031.

[78] On metrical grounds. In particular, τᾶς πολλᾶς may be an intrusive gloss: West 1990: 207–9.

[79] An idea beautifully expressed in 1013 πημονᾶς γέμων ἄγαν, which should not be changed to πλησμονᾶς ...: Page's objection – 'what the ship is too full of ... is not "woe" but "wealth", "surfeit of goods"' – fails to recognise the unity of opposites.

basic goods of health and wealth as well as – we inevitably feel – to the impending act of revenge. Accordingly the same word ἀκόρεστος, 'insatiable', is used here of health, of the wealth that ends in disaster (1331), of the disaster that may spring from good fortune (756) and of the reciprocal violence (1117, 1484): things pass, through excess, into their opposite. The Erinyes will spell out the implication of this view: [*158*]

(40) μήτ᾽ ἄναρκτον βίον
μήτε δεσποτούμενον
αἰνέσῃς· παντὶ μέσῳ τὸ κράτος θεὸς
ὤπασεν, ἄλλ᾽ ἄλλᾳ δ᾽ ἐφορεύει. (*Eum.* 526–30)

approve neither an ungoverned life
nor a tyrannised one;
god gave power to every mean/middle,
though he oversees different things in different ways.

This principle has a psychological dimension: it is, continue the Erinyes, from 'health of minds that much-prayed-for well-being comes'. Their early enunciation of the principle (before the trial of Orestes) and its reiteration by Athena (696–7) prefigure the eventual reconciliation, in which they pray for the permanent exclusion of 'insatiable' (976 ἄπληστος) civil conflict, and praise the Athenians (1000) for having achieved σωφροσύνη (moderation, self-control).

The principle in passage (40) is *universal* ('*every* mean', with πάντι in emphatic position).[80] And so it is comparable to another strand of contemporary philosophy, namely Pythagoreanism. The earliest Pythagorean whose words survive is Philolaos (*c.*470–390). Among the very few authentic extant fragments we have:

(41) (a) Nature in the world order was fitted together [or 'harmonised', ἁρμόχθη] from unlimiteds and limiters (ἐξ ἀπείρων τε καὶ περαινόντων), both the whole world order and the things in it. (DK 44 B 1)

(b) ... since these beginnings (the unlimiteds and limiters) pre-existed and were neither alike each other nor even related, they could not have been ordered (κοσμηθῆναι) if ἁρμονία [fitting together, harmony] had not come upon them … (B 6)

[80] Even though the illustration they go on to give is, once again, of the excessively loaded ship foundering on the reef (of Justice).

This is followed immediately by a discussion of musical ἁρμονία.[81] In Plato's *Symposium* the Pythagoreanising doctor Eryximakhos speaks of concord brought to hostile opposites as a principle in both medicine and music.[82] Some Pythagoreans maintain, according to Aristotle (*Met.* 986a), that the fundamental constituents of the world are ten pairs of opposites (including good–bad). This idea seems to go back to the fifth century.[83] Other passages of Aristotle indicate that the first pair in the list – limit–unlimit – is (as it is for Philolaos) fundamental,[84] and that the list is (as suggested by the presence of the pair good–bad) *evaluative*: there is a 'column of the goods', and 'the bad belongs to the unlimited, the good to the limited'.[85]

We have then two models for the relation of opposites to each other. One is found in the Ionians Anaximander and Heraclitus. In this model the opposites may be thought to form a unity, in any of various ways: they constantly encroach on, or are transformed into, only each other; or they form a single continuum; or they depend on each other; or they are two aspects of the same entity or process. Neither opposite is superior to – or can ultimately prevail over – the *[159]* other. And so tension or strife persists. This is the model from which the *Oresteia* is constantly trying to escape.[86] The other model, associated with Pythagoreanism, is of opposites which retain their separate identities but combine to form an ordered whole. In this order one opposite may be superior to and dominate the other: for instance, Philolaos' idea of the fitting together of unlimiteds and limiters through *harmonia* is not an identity or mutual encroachment of limit and unlimited but a limitation of the unlimited;[87] and Plato in his

81 B 6A: for the authenticity and continuity of this fragment, see Huffman 1993: 147–60. Philolaos seems to have known of the harmonic mean, even if he did not call it 'harmonic': see DK 44 A 24 and Huffman 1993: 167–71.

82 186d–187a. This resembles the idea of health propounded by Pythagoras' fellow-Krotonian Alkmaion (DK 24 B 4), who was a contemporary of Aeschylus (see n. 83). With Eryximakhos' puzzlement over Heraclitus Plato satirises the confusion between Heraclitus and Pythagoreanism that persists even today (see n. 86 below). Heraclitean 'harmony', in contrast to Pythagorean, involves tension or strife between the opposites: Guthrie 1962: 435–7.

83 Aristotle says that he does not know whether it influenced Alkmaion of Kroton or vice versa. Alkmaion probably lived in the early to mid-fifth century: Guthrie 1962: 341–4, 357–9.

84 *Met.* 990a8; *Eth. Nic.* 1106b29; Guthrie 1962: 246.

85 *Eth. Nic.* 1096b15, 1106b29.

86 And so I regard the following incidental remarks in books on Aeschylus as profoundly misleading: at the end of the *Oresteia*, 'violence and counter-violence lead to harmony. There is a union of opposites. In this way a dialectical conception of the universe emerges ... which at the beginning of the fifth century comes into fruition ... in two quite different works of art, that of the dramatists and that of the philosopher Heraclitus' (Moreau 1985: 290). 'The basic ethical pattern or rhythm revealed by the action of the *Oresteia* is one of reciprocity and balance' (Gagarin 1976: 59).

87 Huffman 1993: 37–53. In the two extant fragments of Philolaos' cosmogony the first thing fitted together (ἁρμοσθέν), at the centre of the sphere, is called 'hearth' (DK 44 B 7), and the κόσμος

Pythagoreanising[88] ontology in the *Philebus* clearly believes that the limit should control the unlimited and 'put an end to the conflict of opposites', notably in health and music (25d–26b). This is the model in which the *Oresteia* finds a solution.[89]

The process envisaged in the first model – the alternating encroachment of opposites on, or their transformation into, only each other – is unlimited both in the sense that there is no limit to prevent the opposites successively annihilating each other and in the sense that the cycle has no end. But the second model implies – as does the Erinyes' notion of the mean (passage 40) – a limit preventing either opposite from prevailing – a limit like the party wall between health and disease. The unlimited with which the *Oresteia* is most concerned are those of reciprocal violence and the accumulation of wealth. They are related in that the reciprocal violence brought control of the wealth of the royal household.[90] Χαίρετ' ἐν αἰσιμίαισι πλούτου, uttered by the Erinyes (996), means in effect 'rejoice in the individual *limits* to wealth'.[91] But they stress the power of *every* mean, and Philolaos regards the fitting together of limiters and unlimiteds as *universal*.

Although there was an ancient tradition that Aeschylus was a Pythagorean (Cic. *Tusc.* 3.23), and attempts have been made to find evidence of this in his dramas, I do not assert the direct influence of Pythagoreanism on Aeschylus any more than I do the direct influence of Heraclitus. The point is that these ideas are not the recondite property of marginal researchers, but have – in varying forms – a widespread currency that derives at least in part from the similarity of social processes in the advanced city-states.[92] The (pre-Pythagorean) political origin of the importance of the mean is manifest in the poetry of Solon, who is – like Aeschylus – concerned with the cohesion of the polis, and sees that from the unlimited accumulation of wealth comes ruthlessly destructive civic conflict (frr. 13.71–6; 4.5–6), in which he mediates between rich and poor (frr. 5; 36.19–20; 37.9–10). He sees – again like Aeschylus – that what is required is moderation (fr. 4c.3 ἐν μετρίοισι τίθεσθε μέγαν νόον), and even universalises and projects onto the

comes to be from the centre outwards (B 17): i.e. fitting together produces a limited piece of the unlimited (fire): Huffman 1993: 42–3.

88 Huffman 1993: 106.

89 Aristotle records that, according to the Pythagoreans, supreme excellence and goodness are not present in the beginning, on the grounds that, although for plants and animals their beginnings are causes, excellence and perfection are in their outcome (*Met.* 1072b30). Cf. Guthrie 1962: 248–51.

90 *Ag.* 1574, 1638; *Cho.* 301.

91 Cf. αἴσιμος at Hom. *Od.* 21.294; 23.14.

92 Seaford 2004c.

cosmos the limits implicit in this attitude of moderation: 'It is very difficult to apprehend the mind's invisible measure (μέτρον) which alone holds the limits (πείρατα) of all things.'[93] And [*160*] just as Solon denies victory to both sides (fr. 5.6), so in Aeschylus the Erinyes are assured that they have not been defeated (*Eum.* 795): it is the city of Athens (901, 915, 1009) and the principle of permanent positive reciprocity[94] that has won the victory. Here again, we may add, there is escape from the unity of opposites, for the positive reciprocity is not also negative reciprocity and the victory is not also defeat, whereas in the *Choephori* Elektra's prayer (passage 25) combined positive and negative reciprocity (44 χάριν ἀχάριτον), and Orestes' 'victory' was simultaneously a defeat (1017, 1023).

In the Pythagorean table of ten oppositions preserved by Aristotle the good is associated with limit, male, still and light, the bad with unlimited, female, moving and darkness. The textile by means of which Klytaimestra kills her husband is called an 'unlimited ἀμφίβληστρον[95] ... a bad wealth of cloth' (*Ag.* 1382–3), and is associated with the textiles on which Agamemnon walks,[96] which were bought, Klytaimestra boasts, with the unlimited wealth of the house.[97] The unendingness of the murderous (*Cho.* 1015) textile is emphasised again by Apollo in the trial scene (*Eum.* 634–5 ἐν δ' ἀτέρμονι | κόπτει πεδήσασ' ἄνδρα δαιδάλῳ πέπλῳ). Klytaimestra's bathing and wrapping of her still-living husband is perverted death ritual,[98] and death ritual is a completion, a *limit*. Just as the Euripidean Elektra vainly calls the textile covering her murdered mother an 'end of the great sufferings of the house',[99] so the 'unlimited' textile with which Klytaimestra murdered her husband and covered his corpse evokes the unendingness of the sufferings

93 Fr. 16 γνωμοσύνης δ' ἀφανὲς χαλεπώτατόν ἐστι νοῆσαι | μέτρον, ὃ δὴ πάντων πείρατα μοῦνον ἔχει. Cf. fr. 13.52, the ἱμερτῆς σοφίης μέτρον of poetry. So too Philolaos seems to imply that in some way *knowing* involves limiting: DK 44 B 3 ἀρχὰν γὰρ οὐδὲ τὸ γνωσούμενον ἐσσεῖται πάντων ἀπείρων ἐόντων. This interpretation, with γνωσούμενον active in sense, is cogently argued by Huffman 1993: 118–20, who also compares Pl. *Theaet.* 161c–162d. Others have taken γνωσούμενον as passive (cf. the Aristotelian belief that an unlimited object is unknowable).

94 *Eum.* 974–5 νικᾷ δ' ἀγαθῶν ἔρις ἡμετέρα διὰ παντός. Note how *Eum.* 868, εὖ πάσχουσαν, echoes the antithetical *Satzparallelismus* of passage (4), ἄξια δράσας, ἄξια πάσχων. Cf. 984–6, 992 εὔφρονας εὔφρονες αἰεί, 999 φίλας φίλοι.

95 ἀμφίβληστρον is from the verb ἀμφιβάλλω, 'put around', which is used for dressing the corpse, and so suggests a shroud. It is 'unlimited' (ἄπειρον) because the funerary garment was wrapped around the hands and feet of the corpse, and sometimes even the head, and in the hands of Klytaimestra encloses, like a net, which is ἄπειρον in the sense that it has no limit past which the quarry can escape. But ἄπειρον is also associated with the 'bad wealth of cloth'.

96 Taplin 1978: 79–82; Seaford 1998c[4]: 130.

97 *Ag.* 949, 958–62; Seaford 1998c[4]: 124–31.

98 Seaford 1984c[11].

99 *El.* 1232; cf. *Ag.* 1107–9 ... τέλος.

of the house (as well as of its wealth). This unendingness is associated with the spirits of revenge, Klytaimestra's female champions the Erinyes, as is the covering textile (*Ag.* 1580 ἐν πέπλοις Ἐρινύων).

We have, then, an alignment of female with bad and with the unlimit that subverts the limit of ritual. This corresponds to the Pythagorean table of opposites. Given the opposition between on the one hand the Erinyes' permanent and universal mobility[100] and on the other the domestic fixity eventually achieved by Orestes (and indeed by the Erinyes), we may add the opposition still/moving. And we may also add the polarity light/darkness, given the association in the *Eumenides* of the Erinyes – and of the womb – with darkness,[101] together with the theme of light in the darkness described above.

Resolution of the conflict depends, we noted, on making a distinction between offence and counter-offence. This distinction is eventually found in the famous distinction between the male as parent of the child and the female as the mere environment for the seed to grow in. This argument, justifying Orestes in killing his mother to avenge his father, is put forward by Apollo with a reference to the motherless Athena (658–66), and then endorsed by Athena referring to her own motherlessness (735–8). Similarly, just as Philolaos envisages the creating of the world as a limiting of the unlimited, so – at the level of the microcosm – he envisages sperm as 'constructing' (κατασκευαστικόν) the animal that is constructed (τὸ κατασκευαζόμενον ζῷον), with the womb as the 'place' in which this occurs.[102] *[161]*

The casting vote in favour of this principle, and so for the acquittal of Orestes, is given by Athena, who thereby resolves the equilibrium of opposed votes. She is herself a unity of opposites, as a female who has no mother and, having just come from the battlefield (397–404, cf. 292–6), is probably dressed in armour (as she is in Homer and frequently in vase painting) – a female warrior. For her to announce that she favours the male in 'all things' (737) is female endorsement (and so more acceptable to the Erinyes) of a universal asymmetrical relationship between male and

100 Memorably described by Apollo at *Eum.* 76–7.

101 Womb: *Eum.* 665; Erinyes: *Cho.* 285–6, *Eum.* 72, 322, 370, 378–80, 396, 416, 844, 922.

102 DK 44 A 27; Huffman 1993: 298–9. Plato in his Pythagoreanising cosmogony divides the cosmos into three kinds of thing. There is what he likens to the mother: that which, itself formless, receives forms, which are imitations of what (permanently) exists. There is what he likens to the father: the source or model for what comes into being. And there is what comes into being: the offspring, which is in between father and mother (*Ti.* 50c–d).

female. The unity of opposites announced in the first oxymoron of the trilogy (*Ag.* 11 γυναικὸς ἀνδρόβουλον … κέαρ) is finally differentiated.

To conclude. Tragedy, performed at a festival of the polis, develops out of a synthesis of the rituals of mystic initiation and (lamentation in) hero cult. This synthesis, based in part on the antithetical *Satzparallelismus* common to both kinds of ritual, bequeaths to tragedy a focus on the unity of opposites – notably of life and death and of friend and enemy – manifest both in verbal expression and in the shape of action. Further, the synthesis is deployed, in the *Oresteia*, to express the *political* problem of the perpetuation of reciprocal violence. The identity of offence and counter-offence, expressed in antithetical *Satzparallelismus*, is an especially problematic instance of the unity of opposites, as it precludes the differentiation of opposites that would permit an end to the cycle of violence. The need to escape from this grievous cycle has a model in the need of the soul to escape, through mystic ritual, from the grievous cycle of reincarnation. The struggle to differentiate united opposites, which is a frequent theme of the *Agamemnon* and *Choephori*, succeeds in the *Eumenides* with the opening out to polis and cosmos: the gods of the upper and lower world are emphatically differentiated so as to enable the incorporation of the latter into a new order controlled by the former and of the female into a new order controlled by the male-dominated polis.[103]

The polis is constituted by the integration of potentially conflicting groups. The creation of the Athenian polis included – according to the version preserved in Plutarch's *Life of Solon* – both the control of reciprocal violence by the polis and the control of women (especially their funerary practice) by the men. Early Greek cosmologies, in imagining the universe in terms of society, imagined it as constituted by opposites whose interaction is controlled by an overall power – the 'assessment of time' (Anaximander), the *logos* (Heraclitus), *harmonia* (Philolaos). The *Oresteia* too projects onto the cosmos (as the Olympian and chthonian deities) a controlled interaction of opposites. At first it represents opposites – as do Anaximander and Heraclitus – as a unity, identical with or giving rise to each other; but finally it represents them – as does Pythagoreanism – as asymmetrically reconciled. But it differs from all three 'philosophical' cosmologists in its comprehensiveness: it represents the *relationship* between the social and the (anthropomorphic) cosmic order, as well as *transition* – under the influence of mystic and civic optimism – from the unity of the opposites to their differentiation and reconciliation in a permanent new order.

[103] Note esp. 973 ἀλλ' ἐκράτησε Ζεὺς ἀγοραῖος; 1045–6 Ζεὺς παντόπτας οὕτω Μοῖρά τε συγκατέβα.

Finally, my argument contributes incidentally to the debate between myself and Simon Goldhill on the question of whether we can say, as I have, that, despite the 'manifest complexity and ambiguity' of the *Oresteia*, in the end 'the questions are indeed answered and the conflicts resolved'.[104]

There is a sense in which, at the end of the *Oresteia*, anxiety remains. The well-being of Athens will continue to depend on the awe and fear (*Eum.* 517–25, 698–703) needed to ensure respect for the Areopagus and performance of cult for the Erinyes. In this sense we can indeed point to the failure of resolution. But for Goldhill, failure of resolution belongs to the text itself, in the form of persistent ambivalence. The crucial role of Athena as warrior female who chooses [*162*] the male is a paradox that contributes – as does the tied human vote that requires her intervention – to the failure of the civic discourse at the end of the *Eumenides* to 'repress a sense of its own insecurities'. In the ambivalent figure of Athena the tensions in the opposition between the sexes are 'displaced but not fully resolved'.[105]

To be sure, any spectator or reader of the drama may leave with a 'sense' that the tensions were 'not fully resolved'.[106] But it is in my view a mistake to see the ambivalences as (consciously or even unconsciously) devised to evoke this sense. The whole argument of this chapter suggests rather that the unity of opposites, both in the tied vote and in the gender of Athena, is a precondition for – and persuasive means of – reconciling the Erinyes to the transition to a final settlement in which the opposites are definitively differentiated and reconciled.

POSTSCRIPT

The relatively neglected subject of the relation between Aeschylus and the (Presocratic) philosophy of his time is taken further in Seaford 2010c, 2012a and 2013a, and in Seaford 2012a it is set in a broader context. For the economic basis of Presocratic philosophy and of tragedy see Seaford 2004c.

104 Seaford 1994b, 1995; Goldhill 2000.

105 Goldhill 1986: 31, 50–1.

106 For Goldhill (2000: 56) the choice of whether to read for closure or for ambiguity expresses a politicised position. I agree that the choice may well be (consciously or unconsciously) influenced by a basic orientation that is (in a broad sense) political. Goldhill allows that his political belief that 'commitment and openness are not necessarily mutually exclusive values' is reflected in his critical perspective on the *Oresteia*. I believe that our postmodern openness may in fact function (unconsciously) as a way of avoiding political commitment. And I allow that this belief of mine is not unconnected with my insistence on the political significance for Aeschylus of his construction of a transition from the unity of opposites (a strong form of ambiguity) to differentiation and clarity.

See also R. Rehm, *The Play of Space* (Princeton: Princeton University Press, 2003), Appendix ('Theories of space'); J. Allison, 'Cosmos and number in Aeschylus' *Septem*', *Hermes* 137 (2009), 129–47; and J. Allison, 'Antithesis and the one/many in Aeschylus' *Septem*', *Mnemosyne* 66 (2013), 566–92.

For the Presocratics and Sophocles see Vaios Liapis, *ΑΓΝΩΣΤΟΣ ΘΕΟΣ: ὅρια τῆς ἀνθρώπινης γνώσης στούς Προσωκρατικούς καὶ στὸν Οἰδίποδα Τύραννο* (Athens: Stigme, 2003).

A brief general survey is W. Allan, 'Tragedy and the early Greek philosophical tradition', in Justina Gregory (ed.), *A Companion to Greek Tragedy* (Malden, MA and Oxford: Blackwell, 2005), pp. 71–82.

PART II

Performance and the Mysteries

CHAPTER 7

The 'Hyporchema' of Pratinas

⟨ΧΟ⟩ τίς ὁ θόρυβος ὅδε; τί τάδε τὰ χορεύματα;
τίς ὕβρις ἔμολεν ἐπὶ Διονυσιάδα πο-
λυπάταγα θυμέλαν;
ἐμὸς ἐμὸς ὁ Βρόμιος,
ἐμὲ δεῖ κελαδεῖν, ἐμὲ δεῖ παταγεῖν
ἀν' ὄρεα σύμενον μετὰ Ναϊάδων
οἷά τε κύκνον ἄγοντα
ποικιλόπτερον μέλος.
τὰν ἀοιδὰν κατέστασε Πιε-
ρὶς βασίλειαν· ὁ δ' αὐλός
ὕστερον χορευέτω·
καὶ γάρ ἐσθ' ὑπηρέτας.
κώμῳ μόνον θυραμάχοις τε
πυγμαχίαισι νέων θέλοι παροίνων
ἔμμεναι στρατηλάτας.
παῖε τὸν φρυνεοῦ
ποικίλου πνοὰν ἔχοντα·
φλέγε τὸν ὀλεσισιαλοκάλαμον,
λαλοβαρύοπα <πα>ραμελορυθμοβάταν
†θυπα τρυπάνῳ δέμας πεπλασμένον
ἦν ἰδού· ἅδε σοι δεξιᾶς καὶ ποδὸς διαρριφά·
θριαμβοδιθύραμβε, κισσόχαιτ' ἄναξ,
ἄκου' ἄκουε τὰν ἐμὰν Δώριον χορείαν.

What uproar is this? What dances are these?
What outrageous behaviour has come to Dionysos'
tumultuous altar?
Bromius is mine, mine! It is I who must shout, I who must create
a clatter
as I rush over the mountains with Naiads,
like a swan producing its song of various plumes.
Pieris established song as queen; let the pipe
dance in second place, for it is a servant!
Let it aspire to be general only for

revelling and for the fist-fights of drunken
young men in front of doors.
Strike the one who has the breath of a spotted toad!
Set fire to the chatteringly-deep-voiced,
against-rhythm-and song-marching, spit-wasting-reed (pipe),
whose body is moulded by an augur!
Look at this! Here is a tossing of my right hand and my foot
for you!
Thriambos, *Dithyrambos*, ivy-crowned lord –
listen, listen to my Doric dance-song!
(trans. Olson 2011: 121–3, adapted)

This song is quoted by Athenaeus (14.617c–f). The text reproduced here is Snell's (*TrGF* 4 F 3, I 82 = *PMG* 708). I do not intend to provide a commentary on all the linguistic, textual and metrical difficulties. My concern is primarily with two problems: the identity of the object of Pratinas' hostility, and the kind of performance for which the song was written. This will require several digressions, one of which will lead to a new theory concerning dithyrambic language.

Pratinas is angry, as Athenaeus puts it, at the tendency of the new choruses (χοροί) to accompany the pipe-players (αὐληταί) rather than the other way around. Who are the [*82*] champions of this tendency? One suggestion has been Lasos of Hermione.[1] In chapter 29 of [Plut.] *De Musica* (1141c) we read:

> Lasos of Hermione, by altering the rhythms to the tempo of the dithyramb, and by taking the extensive range of the pipes (*auloi*) as his guide and thus using a greater number of scattered notes, transformed the music that had heretofore prevailed. (trans. Einarson and de Lacy 1967: 421)

Though far from winning universal acceptance,[2] this suggestion seems to me very likely to be correct.[3]

Lasos was born about 545 and lived in Athens under the patronage of Hipparkhos, who was murdered in 514. Pratinas competed in Athens in the seventieth Olympiad (500–497) and was probably dead by 467, when his

[1] E.g. Pickard-Cambridge 1962: 18–20.

[2] E.g. Lloyd-Jones 1966: 16.

[3] The source of the passage in Ps. Plutarch and in Athenaeus is probably Aristoxenus (Garrod 1920: 130). It is very likely that the Peripatetic school was well informed on the festival performances of the late sixth century. The *Didaskaliai*, in which Aristotle's research on the records of dramatic performances was preserved, may well have covered that period. We have also to reckon with the availability of such works as Hellanikos' *Karneonikai* (see *RE* VII.143) and Glaukos of Rhegion's 'On early poets and musicians'; see also Arist. *Poet.* 1449a28–31, 37–9; Kranz 1919. For our information on Pratinas *qua dramatist* a likely source is the Peripatetic Khamaileon's 'On satyrs'.

son Aristias produced one of his satyr plays. The high proportion among his plays of satyr plays, thirty-two out of fifty, suggests that he was active well before the rule of the tetralogy, which may have been instituted in 502/501[4] and certainly not much later.[5]

Athenaeus also describes the circumstances of Pratinas' anger: 'When the hired (μισθοφόρων) pipe-players and choral dancers dominated the dancing places.' The detail is not a simple deduction from the song itself, and so it has to be taken seriously. μισθοφόρων must mean *professionalism* rather than simply the payment of a fee, because the receipt of a fee by amateurs would have no effect on the relationship between elements of the performance. There is evidence for the existence of professional choral dancers in the fourth century in dramatic choruses.[6] If they did exist earlier[7] they would no doubt be dramatic rather than dithyrambic choral dancers, because the dithyrambic contest, unlike the dramatic, was tribal, and the dithyrambic leader of the chorus (χορηγός) had to select his chorus from among the members of his tribe.[8] It will be argued that Pratinas' song is from a satyr play. But of more interest for the moment is the observation on pipe-players (αὐληταί).

It seems that the state organisation of the City Dionysia was the work of Peisistratos, and that dramatic competitions were instituted about 534. 'Something like the state of affairs described by Athenaeus', writes Lloyd-Jones, 'may well have existed towards the end of the fifth century.'[9] We may add that it may well have existed towards the end of the *sixth* century, a generation after the state organisation of the City Dionysia, the very period of activity in Athens of both Pratinas and Lasos. But the appearance of a class of professional pipe-players in the dramatic and dithyrambic contests is not by itself sufficient, as Athenaeus appears to believe, to explain the phenomenon attacked by Pratinas.

At the dances in Phaiakia and on the shield of Akhilleus the singer is the *[83]* instrumentalist and also, at least in the former case, the poet.[10] The lyre-player (κιθαρῳδός) plays the lyre (κιθάρα) to his own songs. Alcman took some part in the choral dance.[11] Originally the dramatic poet acted

4 Pickard-Cambridge 1962: 66.
5 Pickard-Cambridge 1968: 79.
6 Pickard-Cambridge 1968: 90, 279–81.
7 χορευταί may be an inference from αὐληταί; cf. Garrod 1920: 131.
8 Antiph. 6.11; Pickard-Cambridge 1968: 76.
9 Lloyd-Jones 1966: 17.
10 Hom. *Od.* 8.256–64; *Il.* 18.569–71.
11 *PMG* 26.

in his own plays;[12] and Sophocles played the lyre in his *Thamyris* (*TrGF* IV Test. 28). But in fifth-century drama poet, singer and instrumentalist are in general distinct. However, even in these conditions the musical inspiration need be no other than the poet's own. When does it cease to be so? When the poet-composer becomes subject to the influence of a musical style alien to the tradition he has inherited. As a *channel* of such an influence we find in this case, as Athenaeus tells us, the professional pipe-player. Its *source* we may infer from our knowledge of the Lasian musical revolution: the dithyramb.

Of choral lyric in general the predominant instrument is the lyre, but of dithyramb and drama, as of Dionysiac religion in general, it is the pipe (αὐλός).[13] Because the singer cannot play the pipe, it is in this respect more naturally independent of song than is the lyre. But more importantly, the sound of the pipe, and in particular of the deep-toned *bombux*, is more suitable than the sound of the lyre to unrestrained music and dance, and indeed not just to accompany the dance but to excite it: 'I take up – I will not spurn – the pipe, oh tyrant of my mind.'[14] Aristotle would exclude from education the pipe as ὀργιαστικόν ('belonging to rites of a Dionysiac type'), along with the Phrygian mode:

> For both of these are ὀργιαστικά and excite the emotions. The poetry makes this clear: for of the instruments it is the pipe especially that accompanies Bacchic and all other such movement, and of the harmonies these things find their proper form in the Phrygian songs.

As an example he gives the dithyramb: 'such as the dithyramb, which is generally agreed to be Phrygian'.[15] Contrasted is the Dorian mode: 'In relation to the Dorian mode all agree that it is the most steady and has an especially manly character.' We may infer that the same contrast, albeit from a different perspective, is expressed by Pratinas' 'listen to my choral dance-song' (17), and that he is attacking the spread into drama, in the hands of professional pipe-players, of the dithyrambic style.

Pratinas was from Dorian Phleious, Lasos from Hermione, where the population was Dryopian, of pre-Dorian origin.[16] Lasos was credited in antiquity with the invention of the dithyramb, a misconception probably

[12] Pickard-Cambridge 1968: 93.

[13] See e.g. Roos 1951: 216–18.

[14] Soph. *Trach.* 216–7; cf. Aesch. fr. 57; Plut. *Quaest. conv.* 713a; Poll. *Onom.* 4.81; Lucr. 6.620.

[15] *Pol.* 1341a22–42b14.

[16] See e.g. Hdt. 8.43; the only festival known to us at Hermione was to Dionysos Melanaigis; it contained musical competitions (Paus. 2.35.1).

deriving from his part in introducing the dithyrambic contests into Athens under the tyrants.[17] There is no good reason to doubt the report in the *Suda* that he wrote the first treatise on music.[18] At Martianus Capella 9.936, of which the source is probably Varro, he is credited with the tripartite division of *mousikē* into the *hylikon*, the *apergastikon* and the *exangeltikon* (or *hermēneutikon*). Though the terms themselves are later than Lasos, it is argued by Privitera that the tripartite division itself does go back to Lasos, as the distinction, which reappears in Plato, between word, music and rhythm.[19] We need not follow Privitera so far as to suppose that Pratinas' song presupposes the tripartite theory. But if the Lasian musical innovations were accompanied and supported by the Lasian theory, that would give a special point to Pratinas' [81] insistence, in his attack on those innovations, on the right relationship between one element (ἀοιδά, 'song') and the other (αὐλός, 'pipe').

Before leaving the question of Pratinas' anger, we have to deal with a small point that might be employed against our argument. The only substantial extant fragment of Lasos (*PMG* fr. 702) refers to itself as in the Aeolian mode (ἁρμονία). But Pratinas too, despite calling this song Dorian, elsewhere declares his allegiance to the Aeolian mode (*PMG* fr. 712).[20] But even if we were to infer that Lasos and Pratinas composed only, or mainly, in the Aeolian mode, we certainly do not know enough about that mode to deny the possibility of a conflict within its parameters. The fact that Lasos calls it βαρύβρομος ('deep-thundering'), whereas Pratinas calls it the *middle* course, may not be, as Isobel Henderson suggests, simply a matter of relativity of pitch.[21] As Henderson herself concludes, 'we cannot understand such terms too exactly in a period of rapid development when the main styles were certainly losing any real association with the local schools and dialects from which they may originally have been named'.

We have tried to identify the object of Pratinas' wrath. Our second, closely related task is to determine the kind of performance for which the song was written. A once popular[22] but now relatively unfashionable,[23] candidate is satyric drama. In order to re-establish this view it will be necessary first of all to set down the positive arguments in favour of it.

[17] *Suda*, s.v. Lasos; *RE*, s.v. Lasos (col. 888); Pickard-Cambridge 1962: 13, 15; Privitera 1965: 86–8.

[18] Privitera 1965: 37–8.

[19] Privitera 1965: 39 ff.

[20] Similarly, his language is Doric, but with Aeolian elements (notably ἔμμεναι in v. 9).

[21] In Wellesz 1957: 382–3.

[22] E.g. Garrod 1920: 133–5; other refs. in Roos 1951: 232 n. 1.

[23] The fragment is printed by Page (*PMG* fr. 708), and studied in Oxford, as lyric poetry; see also Lloyd-Jones 1966: 16–18.

A. The external evidence. Thirty-two of Pratinas' fifty plays were satyric.[24] He was renowned in antiquity as a composer of satyr plays,[25] one of which survived to be produced by his son Aristias in 467.

B. The internal evidence. There can be little doubt that the singers are satyrs. This appears particularly in the intimate relationship they claim with Dionysos and in their desire to be singing and dancing with the Naiads on the mountains.[26] This was observed in 1912 by Becker,[27] who also remarked on certain verbal similarities with the satyric *Cyclops* of Euripides, notably the satyrs' description of Bromios as φιλοκισσοφόρος ('fond of wearing ivy').[28] We may add that the dance movement performed for Dionysos at v. 15 of Pratinas seemed to Roos[29] to be an apt description of the satyric *sikinnis* (a type of dance) as it is described in Athenaeus and Pollux and appears in fifth-century vase painting.[30] Second, it was suggested by Garrod[31] that in δέμας ('body', v. 14), an odd word to use of the pipe, there is an obscene secondary reference to erection.[32] This he regards as an indication of the satyric nature of the song. We may add that δέμας probably has the same obscene double entendre in the second line of the *Cyclops*,[33] and that it was a habit of satyrs to treat [85] drinking apparatus as sex object:[34] a being who calls his *phallos* a siphon (*Cyc.* 439) may well conceive of the pipe as a *phallos*.

We are now in a position to deal with the arguments advanced against the apparently inescapable conclusion that the song is from a satyr play.

1. Lammers makes four points of substance: (a) A song sung by satyrs is not necessarily from a satyr play. (b) Musical debate is well represented in choral lyric, but never found in tragedy or satyr play. (c) It seems that one chorus has performed in the new style, and is then driven out by another, which sings the extant song. 'Ist das ein Drama? Ist das eine dramatische

[24] *Suda*, s.v. Pratinas.

[25] Paus. 2.13.6; *Anth. Pal.* 7.707.

[26] Cf. Eur. *Cyc.* 1, 68, 74, 430.

[27] Becker 1912.

[28] *Cyc.* 620.

[29] Roos 1951: 178.

[30] Festa 1918.

[31] Garrod 1920: 135.

[32] Cf. Plat. Com. 189.10; Eustath. *in Il.* 1283.31–6; Hsch. s.v. δέμας (cf. Ar. *Vesp.* 1342; Ath. 14.621b5). For the corrupt θυπατρυπάνῳ Garrod proposed ῥυπαροτρυπάνως (cf. Hsch. s.v. παραπλασμός).

[33] On the roughly contemporary Pronomos vase (*ARV*^{2} p. 1336), Silenos and the chorus of satyrs have *phalloi*, of which only Silenos' is not erect.

[34] *Cyc.* 172 (reading κυνήσομαι), 439, 553–5; *ARV*^{2} 76 (Epictetus, in Tarquinia), 446 (Douris, in London).

Handlung?' (d) At [Plut.] *De Musica* 31 the name of Pratinas occurs in a list of non-dramatic lyric poets.[35]

To these points we may reply that (a) It is true that an early satyric song need not be dramatic, even if it refers to 'Dionysos' tumultuous altar';[36] but a satyric song by Pratinas almost certainly is (see A. above). (b) and (c) The musical debate, reference to the conditions of performance and absence of 'dramatische Handlung' are reminiscent of the parabasis of Old Comedy. These features of the parabasis are rightly regarded as primitive,[37] a relic of the transition from choral performance to drama. Why then should we be surprised to find them in the only substantial fragment of early (Phleiasian) satyric drama? In fact the similarity goes beyond content. It has been argued that the form of the first half of the parabasis – anapaests leading to an invocation – suggests, together with its name, that the Aristophanic 'parabasis' is derived from the original *entrance* of the chorus.[38] Pratinas' song also accompanies a choral entrance – that is generally agreed, and is apparent from the opening questions alone.[39] In its *form* also the satyric song resembles the parabasis: a partly (proceleusmatic) anapaestic passage is followed by an invocation of Dionysos. In its *action*, on the other hand, and in the accompanying words, it is reminiscent of the aggression of the *actual* entrance of the Aristophanean chorus.[40] Pratinas' song may be without complete dramatic illusion, but it is part of an agonic action, from which complete dramatic illusion may easily develop. If then the song stands at the transition from a satyric choral performance – σάτυροι ἔμμετρα λέγοντες[41] – to satyric drama, that may help to explain (d) the double tradition of Pratinas the dramatist and Pratinas the lyric poet.[42] From this apparent discrepancy Lloyd-Jones inferred a second Pratinas, a lyric poet of the late fifth century, to whom he appears to attribute all the fragments except fr. 4 (*PMG* fr. 711), largely on the basis of the marked interest they display in the history of poetry and music.[43]

35 Lammers 1931: 65 ff.

36 Cf. Pickard-Cambridge 1946: 9–10; Arnott 1962: 43–4.

37 E.g. Murray 1933: 12; further refs. in Sifakis 1971: 110 n. 3 (Sifakis' arguments on this point seem to me worthless).

38 Refs. in Sifakis 1971: 111 n. 21.

39 Cf. e.g. Polyphemos' opening questions at Eur. *Cyc.* 203.

40 With vv. 10, 12 cf. esp. Ar. *Ach.* 280–4, *Eq.* 247, *Av.* 365; Roos 1951: 231.

41 *Suda*, s.v. Arion.

42 At [Plut.] *De mus.* 31 (1142b) he is included, among other dramatists, in a list of 'fine composers of melodies for the lyre'. A further reason for this may be that it was inferred, rightly or wrongly, from the 'Hyporchema' that he was a champion of the lyre against the (dramatic) pipe.

43 Lloyd-Jones 1966: 18; as Lloyd-Jones observes, all our fragments of Pratinas owe their preservation to musical theory.

In advancing an alternative explanation of the double tradition [86] we do not mean to imply that Pratinas was uninterested in musical theory or that all his choral works were dramatic.

Pratinas' song stands at the transition from satyric choral performance to satyric drama. The point has been established partly by analogy with the predramatic content, form and action of the 'entrances' (parodos and parabasis) of Old Comedy. This suggests not that Old Comedy is derived from Phleiasian satyr play, but that they bear the marks of a similar origin in a certain kind of choral performance. The kind of choral performance in question has been inferred from the choruses of Old Comedy, independently of Pratinas, by Cornford.[44] Various considerations – the size of the chorus (twice that of tragedy), the persistence of their hostility from parodos to agon, the *antichoria* implied by the epirrhematic structure of the agon, the extant examples of antagonistic *antichoria* – lead him to conclude, with Zielinski, that 'there is thus a strong probability that in the earlier forms of comedy the *Agon* was a contest between the Leaders of two bands distinct and opposed in character, like the men and women in the *Lysistrata*'.[45] This conclusion is confirmed by an examination of the agonic form and the vestigial agonic content of the parabasis, from which the main conflict of the play, having been settled in the agon, has been eliminated. Analogous to this kind of choral conflict are the ritual *aischrologia*, choral contests in abuse sometimes combined with physical aggression, themselves derived from the combat of fertility ritual illustrated by Mannhardt and Frazer from various parts of the world.[46] 'Our hypothesis, then, is that the *Agon* and *Parabasis* have differentiated out of one original performance consisting of a ritual conflict between two parties, each with its champion.'[47] Presumably this undifferentiated choral agon consisted of two *choroi*, each combining the aggressive entrance of the parodos with the primitive features of the parabasis: self-presentation and self-praise,[48] invocation and invective, 'literary' polemics. These are the features found

44 Cornford 1968: 78–100.

45 Cornford 1968: 82; Zielinski 1885: 312. For further examples of antagonistic *antichoria* see Sifakis 1971: 118 n. 11.

46 Mannhardt 1905; Frazer 1907–13.

47 Cornford 1968: 98. Sifakis 1971: 108 regards the structure of the parabasis as deriving from the agon; why the influence, and what the parabasis was before it, he does not explain. Cornford's view would explain something that Sifakis cannot: Ar. *Ach.* 626, from the opening of the parabasis, is 'the only instance in which we find the chorus undressing without reason' (Sifakis 1971: 108). Elsewhere this undressing precedes agonic action by the chorus (e.g. Ar. *Lys.* 615, 662, 682). *Ach.* 626 is an example, in the oldest extant comedy, of the vestigial agonic contest of the parabasis.

48 Sifakis 1971: 42.

combined in Pratinas' song. We may therefore infer that one ancestor at least of Pratinas' song was the kind of ritual choral conflict investigated by Cornford. In the original ritual two *choroi* attack each other, physically sometimes as well as verbally, in a set and traditional ritual form. The poet inherits the agonic form of the *antichoria*, but may give it a new content, and the novelty may eventually effect such changes in the form as the growth in importance of the champion relative to the chorus itself. Between the *antichoria* of Cratinus' *Archilochoi* the contest of the agon is 'literary'. And so it is with Pratinas.

If the argument is accepted so far it will shed light on the immediate context of Pratinas' song. Various guesses have been made: that it follows on another kind of performance (Blass) – a tragedy (Ziegler); that it follows a performance by the chorus' own pipe-player (Dale); that the chorus attacks the leading performer (πρωταγωνιστής – Garrod); that it is 'simply a bit of harmless, burlesque banter among the participants in the performance' (Patzer); that another chorus has just performed (Pohlenz).[87] Clearly the last view must win our allegiance. One *antichorion*, representing one musical style, is attacked, physically perhaps (vv. 10, 12) as well as verbally, by another. The offending pipe-player may be the champion of the former *antichorion*, and doubly deserving of the hostility of the latter; or he may be the pipe-player of the performance as a whole, and so at the centre of the agon. Yet further into the realm of hypothesis it is inadvisable to proceed. We must rather pass to the second of the arguments advanced against the view that the song is from a satyr play.

2. A. M. Dale attacks 'those who insist that it must come from a satyr-play, though Athenaeus 14.617c is quite explicit that it was a Hyporcheme'.[49] However, on the very same page she observed that the word *hyporchema* has both a general and a technical sense, and that our ancient authorities are liable to pass from one to the other without warning, giving as an example Athenaeus himself (14.628–631). The attack on those who think the song is from a satyr play is effective only if we assume that Athenaeus, whose unpredictability in the matter she has just cited, is using the term in the technical and not in the general sense, an assumption which she makes no attempt to justify.

The criticism must be taken further. For Dale the general sense was nothing more than a song accompanied by a dance, applied in particular by Tzetzes' sources to certain dramatic odes, 'a necessary invention once

[49] Dale 1950: 19.

stasimon had come to be thought a motionless song'. To this she opposes the technical sense – 'a particular category of lyric performance' – of which, however, 'our ancient sources give contradictory accounts'. In one account the singers and dancers are separate performers; in another the dance of the *hyporchema* is 'an imitation of the things interpreted by the diction', and accompanies a singer-instrumentalist; and in another 'the genre of *hyporchemata*' is a paradigm of the unity of dancing and poetry.[50] Had Dale explained these contradictions rather than merely noting them, she would thereby have dissolved her distinction between the technical and the general sense of *hyporchema*. (a) The first account resembles the second only in so far as they are both songs to which others dance – the opposite of (b) Dale's general sense, in which 'the chorus dances while singing' (Ath. 14.631d). (c) In the third account, on the other hand, the interest is not in the conditions of performance but in the aesthetic unity of dance and song. What do these disparate accounts have in common?

The noun ὑπόρχημα first occurs in Plato (*Ion* 534c). It is never found in poetry; but in Aeschylus' *Choephori* (1024–5) we read πρὸς δὲ καρδίᾳ φόβος ᾄδειν ἕτοιμος, ἣ δ' ὑπορχεῖσθαι κρότῳ (ἠδ' ὑπορχεῖσθαι κότῳ mss.: corr. Abresch), 'Fear at the heart is ready to sing, and the heart to dance to the beat.' Here all three senses are combined: (a) the singer and dancer are separate; (b) the song is accompanied by dance; (c) the heart's dance is determined by the song of Fear. As the word itself suggests, *hyporchema* is not a genus[51] at all but an (ambiguous) description; and that is why the accounts of the 'genus' appear to be contradictory. This does not mean of course that the description could not come to be associated with a particular time and place, especially if, as appears from Athenaeus (14.628a) and Plutarch (*Mor.* 748a), the unity of dance and song to which it could refer was regarded as a lost ideal.[52] And in fact the *hyporchema* was associated with Thaletas and Xenodamos, the founders of the second organisation of music at Sparta, and with Pindar.[53]

So far then from assuming that Pratinas' song is a *hyporchema* in the technical sense, we must regard it as very likely that this 'technical sense' is a [88] creation of musical theory. It remains to explain why the satyrs' song is called by the name of *hyporchema* in Athenaeus. Which of its various meanings does the word have there? It may be based on some genuine

[50] Lucian, *Salt.* 16; Ath. 1.15d; Plut. *Quaest. conv.* 748a; etc.
[51] Koller 1954: 166–73.
[52] Koller 1954: 170–1.
[53] [Plut.] *De mus.* 9 (1134b); schol. Pind. *Pyth.* 2.127; Ath. 1.15d.

similarity with the lost 'Hyporchemata' of Thaletas and Xenodamos. More likely is that the identification as a *hyporchema* is based on nothing more than the song itself, either on the singers' description of their own dancing (vv. 15, 17)[54] or on their insistence, as they dance, on the primacy of their song against the pipe, an insistence which may have been thought to represent the 'hyporchematic' unity of song and dance. We owe the preservation of the song, after all, to an interest in *mousikē*, and that is why we read in Athenaeus 'in this *hyporchema*' and not 'from a satyric drama'.

3. According to Webster the song falls into the otherwise virtually unknown category of satyric dithyramb.[55] He adds that a dithyramb might well have been called a *hyporchema* in Alexandria. The positive arguments for regarding the song as dithyrambic consist first in the invocation θριαμβοδιθύραμβε (v. 16), and secondly in the style, which according to Webster is reminiscent of Aristophanic parody of the dithyramb. The first of these arguments is, taken by itself, of little significance: Dionysus may be called διθύραμβε outside the dithyramb.[56] The second is more serious, and will require a digression into the nature of dithyrambic language.

We can form some idea of the dithyramb after about 450 from the extant fragments,[57] from Aristophanic parody and from the occasional temporary observation. Of the language we are struck by three characteristics:[58] (a) the elaborately compound epithets;[59] (b) the frequency and aggregation of epithets;[60] (c) periphrasis, often of a riddling nature.[61] These three features occur also in Pratinas' song, and in particular in vv. 10–14, where they cohere: a string of various elaborately compound descriptions

[54] Cf. Cramer 1839: 20: ὑπόρχημα δ' ἂν εἴη μᾶλλον τῶν σατύρων, ἐκεῖνοι γὰρ ᾄδοντες ἅμα καὶ ὀρχοῦνται.

[55] In Pickard-Cambridge 1962: 20; see also Wilamowitz-Moellendorff 1913: 133.

[56] E.g. Eur. *Bacch.* 526.

[57] Of the fragments I treat as dithyrambic some are certainly so. From these and from ancient comments on the dithyramb we may form an idea of the dithyrambic style. The others are likely to be dithyrambic (as being dithyrambic in style, by a dithyrambic poet) or at least dithyrambic in style ([Plut.] *De mus.* 1132e reveals that Timotheus employed in his νόμοι the λέξις of dithyramb). I exclude Bacchylides (see below).

[58] We might be justified in adding a fourth: repetition (Pind. fr. 70b (lines 8, 10, 12, 15), fr. 75.16, fr. 85; *PMG* 760, 791 (lines 76, 129, 154–5, 158), 926e).

[59] Pind. frr. 70a, 70b (lines 1, 12, 13, 25, 26), 70c, 75 (lines 3, 5, 6, 6–7, 9, 14, 19), 82, 85; *PMG* 744, 745, 780, 791 (*passim*), 805, 806, 808, 810, 831, 832, 926a, 929d, 929f, 962, 963; Ar. *Nub.* 332–3, *Av.* 1385, 1389–90, 1394, *Pax* 831; Pl. *Crat.* 409c–d; Arist. *Poet.* 1459a8, *Rhet.* 1406b.

[60] Pind. frr. 70a, 70b, 75 (cf. Pickard-Cambridge 1962: 21), 76, 82; *PMG* 744, 745, 757, 760, 761, 778, 780, 791, 805, 806, 821, 831, 929f; Ar. *Nub.* 337, *Av.* 1379, 1385, 1389, 1394, *Pax* 298.

[61] *PMG* 744, 745, 760, 762, 780, 791 (lines 6, 12, 20, 25, 30–1, 62–3, 63, 64–5, 69, 76–7, 91, 93–4), 797, 798, 805c, 806, 808, 821, 827, 831, 832, 926c, 929f.

alludes to the *aulos*. The inference that the verses are dithyrambic in style is confirmed by the invocation θριαμβοδιθύραμβε two verses later. Returning to the dithyrambic fragments we discover this same coherence at *PMG* 744 (Ion of Chios):

ἄδαμον
παῖδα ταυρωπόν, νέον οὐ νέον,
ἥδιστον πρόπολον βαρυ-
γδούπων ἐρώτων,
οἶνον ἀερσίνοον
ἀνθρώπων πρύτανιν.[89]

Untamed bull-faced child, young but not young, most pleasant attendant of deep-thundering passion – wine, that bears men's minds aloft, their ruler.

Other dithyrambic descriptions of wine are similar in this respect: *PMG* 780 (Timotheos):

ἔγχευε δ' ἓν μὲν δέπας κίσσινον μελαίνας
σταγόνος ἀμβρότας ἀφρῷ βρυάζον,
εἴκοσιν δὲ μέτρ' ἐνέχευ', ἀνέμισγε
δ' αἷμα Βακχίου νεορρύτοισιν
δακρύοισι Νυμφᾶν.

Pour in one ivied cup teeming with the foam of the immortal dark drop, then pour in twenty measures, and mix up the blood of Bakchos with the newly wept tears of Nymphs.

PMG 831 (Philoxenos; see also 832) εὐρείτας οἶνος πάμφωνος ('the fair-flowing garrulous wine').

Similar also are the dithyrambic descriptions of musical instruments by Telestes:

PMG 805(c) – on pipe-playing:

ἃν συνεριθοτάταν Βρομίῳ παρέδωκε σεμνᾶς
δαίμονος ἀερόεν πνεῦμ' αἰολοπτέρυγον
σὺν ἀγλαᾶν ὠκύτατι χειρῶν.

which the breezy, quick-fluttering breath of the venerable goddess gave to Bromios to be his closest helper, together with the swiftness of her shining hands.

PMG 806.4:

πνεύματος εὔπτερον αὔραν ἀμφιπλέκων καλάμοις

interweaving a well-winged gust of breath with the reeds

PMG 808:

> ἄλλος δ' ἄλλαν κλαγγὰν ἱεὶς
> κερατόφωνον ἐρέθιζε μάγαδιν
> πενταρράβδῳ χορδᾶν ἀρθμῷ
> χέρα καμψιδίαυλον ἀναστρωφῶν τάχος.

> Each gave out a different strum and with a five-rodded joining of the strings aroused the horn-voiced harp, moving the hand up and down with the speed of a runner rounding the course.

Finally, in Antiphanes' parodic fragment (*PCG* fr. 55), in which each of our three features is well represented, one of the riddling periphrases refers to wine: Βρομιάδος δ' ἱδρῶτα πηγῆς (fr. 55.12 'sweat of Bromios' spring').

Most of these fragments owe their preservation in Athenaeus to their concern with wine and music. Nevertheless, it is clear from the remains of dithyrambic language as a whole that its characteristic features were associated in particular with the traditional agents of (Dionysiac) dithyrambic abandon: wine[62] and musical instruments, in particular the pipe. Of this phenomenon, Pratinas vv. 10–14 is the earliest and most striking example.[63]

In the fourth chapter of his *Poetics* Aristotle said both that tragedy developed 'from the leaders of the dithyramb' (ἀπὸ τῶν ἐξαρχόντων τὸν διθύραμβον), and that it developed from 'the satyr-play-like' (ἐκ σατυρικοῦ). The known Dionysiac origins of tragedy, together with the Dionysiac nature of dithyramb and satyr play, cohere with his view, even if they cannot be said to support it. If these three Dionysiac genera appear to be derived from the same kind of performance, is there anything in tragedy and satyr play to be compared with the Dionysiac language that we have discovered in the dithyramb?

There is only one surviving tragedy with a Dionysiac theme and a Dionysiac thiasos as its chorus: Euripides' *Bacchae*. We cannot say that vv. 89–135 of that play are a dithyramb. But they are certainly very like one. A mythical narrative is sung by the worshippers of Dionysos; the metre is unrestrained; ornamental epithets are frequent and often elaborately compound (100, 102, 108, 112, 117, 122, 123, 124); there is verbal repetition at 107 and 116; finally, there are the subjects of the narrative: 88–104 concerns Dionysos' double birth. In Plato's *Laws* (700b) we read καὶ ἄλλο,

[62] Cf. e.g. Archil. fr. 120; Epicharm. fr. 115.
[63] We note in passing that the hypothesis that line 10 refers to Phrynichus is unnecessary as well as improbable (Roos 1951: 210–14).

Διονύσου γένεσις, οἶμαι, διθύραμβος λεγόμενος ('and another type, the birth of Dionysos, I think, called the dithyramb'). According to Pickard-Cambridge, οἶμαι suggests that Plato is alluding playfully to the popular derivation of the word *dithyrambos* [90] from the double birth of Dionysos.[64] If so, the fantastic derivation could hardly have been popular unless the theme of the double birth was characteristic of the early dithyramb. The second narrative in these verses concerns the invention of the *tympanon* and its introduction into Dionysiac cult (120–34). But the *tympanon* is not mentioned directly; it is described in two periphrases: 'this hide-stretched circle' (124 βυρσότονον κύκλωμα τόδε) and 'a beat for the bacchants' cries of joy' (129 κτύπον εὐάσμασι βακχᾶν). The maenads have announced at the outset of their song 'I will always hymn Dionysos with songs that have been established' (71 τὰ νομισθέντα γὰρ αἰεὶ Διόνυσον ὑμνήσω). Taken together with the dithyrambic fragments, the evidence of this song suggests that periphrastic allusion to the properties of Dionysiac cult was a traditional feature of the dithyramb. The song suggests a further possibility, that a typical role for these properties was as *inventions*. Is this possibility strengthened by the dithyrambic fragments?

The pipe was invented by Athena, who discovered that it disfigured her face and threw it away, whereupon it was appropriated by the satyr Marsyas. The story was treated, probably in a dithyramb, by Melanippides (*PMG* 758);[65] of Telestes' verses on the same subject, which are preserved in Athenaeus as an answer to Melanippides, three fragments survive, one of which has already been quoted as describing pipe-playing in a typically dithyrambic periphrasis (*PMG* 805c). Telestes' periphrasis for the pipe (*PMG* 806, quoted above) occurs in a reference to the invention of the Lydian mode, and *PMG* 810 concerns the invention of the Phrygian mode. Verses 215–20 of Timotheus' *Persae* (*PMG* 791), which are dithyrambic in style,[66] are followed by references to the invention of the lyre (χέλυς) and to the kitharodic innovations of Terpander and of Timotheus himself. Finally, *PMG* 760 (Melanippides) concerns the invention of wine.

The *Bacchae* is the only extant tragedy on a Dionysiac theme. But before passing from tragedy to satyr play we have to mention a fragment (fr. 57) of Aeschylus' lost *Edonians*. The theme of the tragedy was the conflict between Dionysos and Lykourgos; and the fragment describes the Dionysiac thiasos:

64 Pickard-Cambridge 1962: 2.

65 At Xen. *Mem.* 1.4.3 Melanippides is presented as the dithyrambic poet *par excellence*.

66 On the dithyrambic λέξις of Timotheus' νόμοι see n. 57.

ὃ μὲν ἐν χερσὶν
βόμβυκας ἔχων, τόρνου κάματον,
δακτυλόδικτον πίμπλησι μέλος,
μανίας ἐπαγωγὸν ὁμοκλάν,
ὁ δὲ χαλκοδέτοις κοτύλαις ὀτοβεῖ ...

One holds in his hands the pipes, the labour of the drill, and fills out the finger-thrown song, the cry that brings on frenzy, while another crashes away with the bronze-bound cymbals.

The fragment is dithyrambic in mood (see n. 14) and in expression. And as in Pratinas, the periphrasis refers to the *making* of the instrument.

The chorus of satyric drama is always the thiasos of satyrs, the μαινόμενοι σάτυροι who in the parodos of the *Bacchae* are said to have introduced the drum (τύμπανον) into Dionysiac cult (just as it is the satyr Marsyas who received the pipe from Athena). Among the eight or nine certain cases of the theme of the invention in the remnants of satyric drama[67] we find the invention of wine, of the lyre and probably of the syrinx.[68] In Sophocles' *Ichneutai* the satyrs' inquiries about the source of the sound 'which no mortal has ever heard before' (144) are answered by Kyllene not, of course, with the name of the lyre, nor even with a direct description of it, but with a riddle: 'When the creature died it acquired a voice, but while it lived it had no speech' (300 θανὼν γὰρ ἔσχε φωνήν, ζῶν δ' ἄναυδος ἦν ὁ θήρ). The satyrs then approach the reality with a series of [91] conjectures. I have argued in a recent article that satyric drama, established as it was in the tetralogy to preserve the Dionysiac element disappearing from tragedy, is likely to have had some resemblance to the earlier, more Dionysiac tragedy, and that one point of resemblance is the *locus* represented by this passage of the *Ichneutai* – a *locus* derived ultimately from initiatory ritual, and found elsewhere in the exiguous remains of satyric drama and, in an attenuated form, in the stichomythia of tragedy.[69] I do not propose to repeat the argument here. The main point to be made is simply that the *locus* provides us with what we are looking for, a feature of the Dionysiac drama comparable with the feature we have already discovered in the Dionsyiac dithyramb: Dionysiac inventions are described in riddling terms. I will however add some minor points. First, the taste for etymology apparent in the

[67] Guggisberg 1947 72 ff.; Seaford 1976b. The multiplicity meets the demands of originality of plot.

[68] Soph. *Dionysiskos* (fr. 172): (wine) πόθεν ποτ' ἄλυπον ὧδ' εὗρον ἄνθος ἀνίας; Eur. *Cyc.* 37–40 probably refers to a previous satyr play (wine); Soph. *Ichn.* (lyre); Soph. *Inachos* (syrinx: see Carden 1974: 81).

[69] Seaford 1976b.

dithyrambic fragments, in one case of the word οἶνος ('wine'),[70] is clearly akin to the invention riddle; and it is actually found in one example of the satyric *locus* – the satyr's etymological reaction to the invisible syrinx in Sophocles' *Inachos*.[71] Second, Lasos was credited in antiquity with the invention not only of the dithyramb but also of *Lasismata*, sophisms akin to riddles.[72] Third, although the only completely extant satyr play, Euripides' *Cyclops*, has no place for the *invention* of wine, Euripides makes the land of the Kyklopes (unlike in Homer) entirely without wine. When this absence of wine is revealed to Odysseus, when he tells the satyrs that he has brought wine, when he offers the novelty of the wine to Polyphemos and when he instructs Polyphemos in the nature of the wine – on each of these occasions the wine is referred to not directly but in periphrasis.[73] Finally, we should mention the two extant fragments of Choerilus, probably the earliest Attic dramatic fragments, which are riddling: 'with his foot planted on [stones], the bones of the earth' (fr. 2 <λίθοισι> γῆς ὀστοῖσιν ἐγχριμφεὶς πόδα) and 'veins of the earth' (fr. 3 γῆς φλέβες). But we cannot confirm that they are of significance, even though they may refer to the creation of a spring by the dancing satyrs (cf. Aesch. *Amymone*; Gow 1965 on Theoc. *Id.* 7.8; Soph. *Ichneutai* 217–20). More interesting, paradoxically, is the riddling fragment of Thespis (fr. 4), which ends 'Look, I'm pouring you the [gleaming] flame of Bromios' (ἴδε σοὶ Βρομίου [αἴθοπα] φλεγμὸν λείβω), and which is undoubtedly a Hellenistic forgery. Forgeries may be significant if they are based on knowledge of what is being imitated; and forgeries of Thespis were ascribed by Aristoxenos (*ap.* Diog. Laert. 5.92) to Heraclides Ponticus, who wrote extensively on the history of literature. These lines of enquiry could be pursued further; but we must return to Pratinas.

The view that the language of Pratinas' song is dithyrambic conflicts with the assumption that the later dithyrambists invented *ex nihilo* the peculiarities of their language. The assumption is made, for example, by Pickard-Cambridge,[74] and it may be partly to blame for the lack of attention given to these peculiarities. The assumption seems to be supported by the relative rarity of these peculiarities in the 'dithyrambs' of Pindar and Bacchylides.

70 *PMG* 761; also Pind. frr. 85–85a; *PMG* 736, 759.

71 Fr. 269c.

72 Further, Lasos' asigmatic hymns are treated by Schultz as a form of riddle (*RE*, s.v. Rätsel, col. 113). The dithyramb itself is part of one version of the answer to a riddle at Ath. 10.456c (Schultz 1912: 113).

73 123–4, 141, 415, 519–29.

74 Pickard-Cambridge 1962: 49.

If it is to be retained, we will have to follow either Garrod, who dates the song to 'the very last years of Pratinas' life' (supposing that he lived into the period of the later dithyramb),[75] or Lloyd-Jones, whose arguments for the existence [92] of a lyric poet Pratinas towards the end of the fifth century we have already discussed. But there is in fact no good reason why we should retain the assumption, and several good reasons why it would be better to abandon it.

1. The innovations in the dithyramb effected by Melanippides and his followers are always described as musical by the ancient sources, not as linguistic.[76] We cannot, of course, deny that these musical innovations may have fostered a hypertrophy of pre-existing linguistic features.
2. There is no doubting the unrestrained nature of the early dithyramb. In attempting to reconcile the Phrygian mode and the music of the pipe with the comparatively quiet language of the dithyrambs of Pindar and Bacchylides, Pickard-Cambridge suggests that 'as the Bacchic rite to which it seems probable that the dithyramb at first belonged became part of the celebration of an orderly civic festival, the wildness of the music may have abated'.[77] The point of Pindar's distinction between his own and earlier (apparently Lasian) dithyramb is obscure (fr. 70b). But it seems to me very likely that, in respect of language at least, the deviants from the dithyrambic tradition were not the later dithyrambists but Pindar and Bacchylides. As the scholiast on Philostratus' *Life of Apollonius* (1.17) says of dithyrambic language, 'this is what dithyrambs are like, since they derive from Dionysiac initiation rituals (τελετῶν)'.
3. The fragments of Pindar's dithyrambs are in fact not without affinity with the language of the later dithyramb.[78] And the same is true of their metre.[79] Lost Pindaric dithyrambs may have been more consonant still with Horace's words on Pindar (*Carm.* 4.2.10–12):

[75] Garrod 1920: 132; we read at [Plut.] *De mus.* 30 (1141c–d) that until the time of Melanippides the pipe-players were paid by the poet and subordinate to the *didaskaloi*, 'since the poetry clearly played the leading role'. This looks like the object of Pratinas' hostility. Aristoxenus is probably the common source of the passages in Athenaeus and Ps. Plutarch. The point is important, but I have nothing to add to the convincing demonstration by Pickard-Cambridge 1962: 18–19 that 'until the time of Melanippides …' is an interpolation. With the deletion, Ps. Plutarch takes the change as part of the Lasian revolution. For the dates of Melanippides see Pickard-Cambridge 1962: 140.

[76] Pickard-Cambridge 1962: 40–3, 46, 51; Schönewolf 1938: 18–23.

[77] Pickard-Cambridge 1962: 32.

[78] See nn. 58–60 above.

[79] Pickard-Cambridge 1962: 22.

seu per audaces nova dithyrambos
verba devolvit numerisque fertur
lege solutis.

whether in his audacious dithyrambs he rolls down new words, or is carried away by rhythms freed from rules.

4. As an example of the schematisation inherent in the Alexandrian classification of lyric poetry, A. E. Harvey[80] cites the possibility that the 'dithyrambs' of Bacchylides were grouped together under the title *Dithyramboi* for no better reason than that they embody a continuous narrative.

Granted, then, that Pratinas' song is an example of the pre-Pindaric dithyrambic style, we are faced with three possibilities of interpretation. First, there is Webster's view, that it represents the otherwise virtually unknown satyric dithyramb. Second, it may be a case of dithyrambic influence on a satyric chorus or play. But what tells against both these possibilities is precisely the excessively dithyrambic character of vv. 10–14, which suggests caricature. Further, we have argued that it is the dithyrambic style of music that Pratinas is at pains to *attack*. These considerations lead naturally to the third hypothesis, which, though suggested over a century ago, has found *[93]* few adherents.[81] The abuse hurled at the dithyrambic instrument is *parody* of the dithyrambic style.[82]

Presumably there is also metrical parody. Although some similarity with Pratinas' metre is detectable in Pindaric and later dithyramb,[83] we must confess complete ignorance of the metre of Lasian dithyramb, except in so far as it was very likely unrestrained in character. Resolution on the scale of τίς ὁ θόρυβος κτλ. and φλέγε τὸν ὀλεσισιαλοκάλαμον κτλ. seems designedly ridiculous, concluding as it does with an attack on auletic polyphony: the pipe-player continues to play (v. 10) and the satyrs illustrate their insult by accommodating it to his trilling. Garrod points out that Marius Victorinus associates proceleusmatics with the entrance of the satyric chorus,[84] but fails to see that this is consistent with the view

80 Harvey 1955: 160.

81 Buchholtz 1871: 80. Roos 1951: 234–5 overstates the case, regarding the song as simultaneously a satirical picture of Pratinas' 'kitharodic' opponents and an attack on the Lasian dithyramb. There is no good reason to suppose that the satyrs are carrying lyres.

82 The imitations of the dithyramb at Ar. *Nub.* 333 and *Av.* 1388–90 are also explicit attacks on it.

83 Resolution (cf. esp. *PMG* 799; Marius Victorinus in Keil 1857: 99.1–2) and apparently random alteration of metrical units (cf. e.g. *PMG* 805a). I leave aside the difficult and for our purposes unrewarding question of strophic composition in dithyramb and satyric drama.

84 Garrod 1920: 134; Marius Victorinus in Keil 1857: 99.19–20.

that Pratinas is parodying precisely this (dithyrambic) tendency of satyric drama. The consequent run of short syllables is far longer than those found in the *Ichneutai* (see especially 176–8) and *Inachos* of Sophocles; it is in fact akin to those found in Old Comedy.[85]

We read in the *Suda* that Pratinas 'first wrote satyr plays' (πρῶτος ἔγραψε σατύρους). The notice is not above suspicion; it may derive from the fact that Pratinas was the first known writer of satyr plays, or one of the first to write words for the satyric performance.[86] From a survey of Attic vase paintings of the last quarter of the sixth century Buschor drew the conclusion that, although Pratinas may 'have been nourished by memories of the mimetic bustling of Peloponnesian satyric choruses', satyric drama grew up 'as an Attic plant in the Attic soil of these years'. The growth of the Attic satyr play coincided with the arrival of the Lasian dithyramb. Was the home-grown Dionysiac *genus* nourished by the imported? The inference seems very likely.[87]

We remember that Lasos effected a revolution in music by the introduction of dithyrambic rhythms and auletic polyphony. Luxuriant growth of this kind was uncongenial to the Phleiasian. His attack took the form of parody, but not mere parody of style. It is not hard to see how the periphrastic accounts of their own instruments might have a special place in the songs of the thiasos. So it is in the parodos of the *Bacchae*. Pratinas' parody goes to the very heart of the matter. He has inverted the *locus*. Indeed, the *locus* contains material for its own inversion. Just as in the *Ichneutai*, the entrance of Pratinas' satyrs is met by a novel sound – τίς ὁ θόρυβος ὅδε; (cf. *Ichn.* 142–4, 248–50), which [94] creates among them a violent reaction (παῖε … φλέγε – cf. *Ichn.* 131–3)[88] and is described in riddling terms. In Pratinas the satyrs' reaction is parodic and hostile. In the *Ichneutai* on the other hand, when Kyllene explains Hermes' use of the instrument (325–7 'a healer of pain and a consolation … the trilling of the lyre carries him away') the satyrs' attitude begins to change. Let us leave them with the last word (329–31):

85 Dale 1968: 54 ff.

86 Lloyd-Jones 1966: 15; Gilbert Murray in Harrison 1927: 344.

87 A similar conclusion was reached independently by George Thomson in respect of tragedy (Thomson 1946: 182–3); he explains the paradox that 'under the tyrants, Athens rapidly became a centre for the performance of dithyrambs, yet almost all the dithyrambic poets known to us are foreigners' by the hypothesis that the tyrants desired to make the dithyrambic tradition 'accessible to the Athenian dramatists, who were thus able to infuse it into their treatment of the tragic chorus'.

88 The τέρατα-εὑρήματα create vigorous reactions among the satyrs also in the following satyr plays: Aesch. *Prometheus Pyrkaieus*, *Theoroi*; Soph. *Inachos*; Eur.? (*P. Oxy.* 2455. fr.7 = *Sisyphus* satyricus, Test. iii *TrGF* V.2 p.657); see further Seaford 1976b.

ὀ<ρθο>ψάλακτός τις ὀμφὰ κατοιχνεῖ τόπου,
πρεπτὰ <δ’ αὖ> διὰ τόνου φάσματ’ ἔγ-
χωρ’ ἐπανθεμίζει.[89]

POSTSCRIPT

I integrate the Pratinas song into a broader context in Seaford 2012a: 106–21.

For a critique of my thesis on dithyrambic language see R. Hamilton, ‘The Pindaric dithyramb’, *HSCP* **93** (1990), 211–22 (and a brief response at Seaford 1994b: 268 n. 149); for important support for my thesis see Mendelsohn 1992; see also A. Ford, ‘The poetics of dithyramb’ in Kowalzig and Wilson 2013: 313–31. For more on the connection between the dithyramb and mystic initiation see S. Lavecchia, ‘Becoming like Dionysos: Dithyramb and Dionysiac initiation’, in Kowalzig and Wilson 2013: 59–75.

That the song comes from a satyr play ‘does now seem incontrovertible’ according to M. Griffith, ‘Satyr-play, dithyramb, and geopolitics’, in Kowalzig and Wilson 2013: 257–81 at 273. But the date remains controversial. For an early date see e.g. G. B. d’ Alessio, ‘Ἦν ἰδού: Ecce satyri (Pratina, *PMG* 728 = *TrGF* 4F3): alcune considerazioni sull’uso della deissi nei testi lirici e teatrali’, in F. Perusino and M. Colantonio (eds.), *Dalla lirica corale alla poesia dramatica* (Pisa: ETS, 2007), pp. 95–128; G. Hedreen, ‘Myths of ritual in Athenian vase paintings of Silens’, in E. Csapo and M. Miller (eds.), *The Origins of Theater in Ancient Greece and Beyond: From Ritual to Drama* (Cambridge: Cambridge University Press, 2007), pp. 150–93; A. d’ Angour, ‘Music and movement in the dithyramb’, in Kowalzig and Wilson 2013: 198–209. For a late date see e.g. B. Zimmermann, ‘Überlegungen zum sogenannten Pratinasfragment’, *MH* 43 (1986), 145–54; E. Csapo, ‘The politics of the new music’, in Murray and Wilson 2004: 207–48; J. C. Franklin, ‘Songbenders of circular choruses’, in Kowalzig and Wilson 2013: 213–36.

[89] I am grateful to R. Parker, T. Stinton and R. Stoneman for their comments on this paper.

CHAPTER 8

The Politics of the Mystic Chorus

The political significance of the ancient Greek χορός (a group that sings and dances) is based in part on its implicit claim to public space. My chapter centres on this general proposition, but has two specific focuses. One is on the special kind of solidarity in the chorus of mystery cult, and on the political significance of this solidarity. The other is on Athens of the classical period, about whose space and choruses we have especially good knowledge. But these focuses are not exclusive, for I also discuss (§6) a non-mystic choral performance in Sparta.

1. Capitalist Space

I start by sketching some features of space in advanced capitalist countries that contrast with the space of the classical polis, and that – however natural they may seem – we must think away if we are to understand the politics of the ancient Greek chorus. Most of our built environment consists of private space, and an aspect of this predominance of private space is the public invisibility of (real) political power. We also lack visible communal actions (as opposed to mere mass spectatorship), and of those that do occur almost none are transformative. Our public space is almost entirely given over to private purposes and commercial interests.[1]

By contrast, ancient Athenian private buildings were – at least in the classical period – relatively small,[2] and dwarfed by imposing communal buildings. [262] The Athenian assembly (in contrast to parliament) visibly embodied genuine political power. And, as an example of transformative communal action, spectacular processions not only displayed the purposive

[1] Indeed, our advanced process of capital accumulation includes an incessant tendency to encroach – if unresisted – on all available space (and time). The result is the pervasive fragmentation and incessant mutability that are at the heart of 'postmodern' experience.

[2] See e.g. M. H. Jameson (1993) in *OCD*[4], s.v. 'Houses (Greek)': 'The modesty of the Classical houses of all classes is striking'; Dem. 3.25–6, 23.207.

cohesion of the polis to itself and to others but were also imagined to maintain or transform the relationship between polis and deity.

Our power of abstraction has furnished us not only with maps but also with the idea of an abstract spatial framework in which all else is somehow contained, and which may even seem ontologically superior to any concrete marker of space. This superiority of abstraction may have particular applications. For instance, any concern I may have about the visible manifestations of the boundary between my land and my neighbour's is reduced by my knowledge that I possess a legal document containing a map. But in classical Athens there were few maps and no public register of land,[3] with the result that publicly visible markers (*horoi*, boundary stones) and publicly visible actions were all the more important. For instance, in a law preserved by Theophrastus we hear of the requirement that purchase be accompanied by a public sacrifice.[4]

2. Ancient Greek Processions

The public procession was transformative communal action (πομπή means 'escorting'). It often included the politically excluded: women, young people, metics (resident aliens) and perhaps sometimes even slaves.[5] Conversely, a procession expressing the solidarity of a *clan* might seem politically disintegrative: there were accordingly legal restrictions on funeral processions at Athens and elsewhere.[6]

The procession might express the communal occupation of space, whether urban space or – in the case of processions between urban and peripheral sanctuaries – the territory of the polis.[7] It might even, in the general absence of maps, serve to shape the conception of space outside the borders of the polis. A nice example is in Aeschylus' *Eumenides* (12–14): 'The path-making sons of Hephaistos escort him [Apollo, from Athens to Delphi] and greatly revere him, making the untamed land tame.' The scholia on this passage reveal that, when an Athenian *theoria* (sacred delegation) went to Delphi, it was preceded on the road by men carrying axes as intending to tame the land. A fourth-century *horos* in the Athenian *agora* [263] marked out 'the sacred road through which the *Pythaïs* [i.e. the

[3] Finley 1952: 13–15; Harrison 1968: 305–7.

[4] Fr. 97 (3) Wimmer; = fr. 21 Szegedy-Maszak 1981. For the role of ritual in early contract see Gernet 1981: 143–215.

[5] Kavoulaki 1999: 300; see also Graf 1996.

[6] Seaford 1994b: 74–86.

[7] Kavoulaki 1999: 297–9; de Polignac 1995: 24, 37, 40–3, 52–3.

delegation] journeys to Delphi'.[8] The Athenians' conception of the route is shaped by the procession.

Ancient processions bring offerings (sacrificial animals, a robe, etc.), and sometimes the deity himself, to a sanctuary. They are – unlike 'parades' – preliminaries.[9] They gather the community for focus on a temple, enhancing the power of such buildings to articulate public space. And they may be as pleasing to the deity as are the offerings and choral performances at its destination. For instance, according to Xenophon (*Eq. mag.* 3.2):

> I would think processions most pleasing to the gods and to the spectators if beginning from the Herms they move in a circle round all the shrines and images in the *agora* honouring the gods, and at the Dionysia the choruses give extra pleasure to the gods, especially the twelve gods [i.e. at their altar in the *agora*].

This reveals much. Processions have 'spectators', please the gods and may stop and give choral performances. These features reappear in other texts.[10] The procession may also sing as it proceeds.[11] Choral performance reinforces processional occupation of space. Herodotus reports that, when the Persians were ravaging an Attica empty of its inhabitants (in 480), there was seen 'a cloud of dust moving from Eleusis, as of about 30,000 men', and the 'mystic Iakchos [song]' was heard.[12] This was interpreted as a divine voice that would ensure victory for the Athenians. The purposive unison of the song of the vast[13] mystic procession that traversed the territory of the polis was of a kind to strengthen the will of the Athenians to survive, to reoccupy their land.

The procession of Eleusinian mystic initiates is represented in Aristophanes' *Frogs* as taking place in the underworld. They enter singing and dancing as they move in procession, and their repeated references to this combination[14] indicate that it occurred in the actual Eleusinian procession on the 'sacred road' between Athens and Eleusis.[15]

The procession escorted Iakchos, the Eleusinian Dionysos, and so the song sung in it is comparable to the dithyramb. For in its earliest detectable

[8] *Agora* 19 (1991) H 34; Parker 2005: 86.

[9] Kavoulaki 1999: 302.

[10] The Milesian Molpoi: *SIG*³ 57 = Sokolowski 1955: 50; Eleusis: *IG* II² 1078, Plut. *Alc.* 34.4; for 'spectators' see texts cited by Kavoulaki 1999: 294.

[11] On the various uses of the term *prosodion* ('processional song') see Rutherford 2003.

[12] 8.65.1; see also Aristid. *Or.* 22.6.

[13] Parker 2005: 348.

[14] *Ran.* 326, 335, 351–2, 372–5, 377–9, 396, 403, 440–1, 447–51.

[15] The building of bridges on this road is attested by inscriptions that express concern for the safety of the sacred objects: Parker 2005: 346–7.

phase the dithyramb was sung in the Dionysiac procession, which sometimes had the function of escorting Dionysos. At Athens the dithyrambic performance at [264] the destination of the procession grew in importance, and developed into tragedy at the Dionysiac festival, in which stationary dithyrambs were also performed.[16]

3. The Mystic Chorus

Robert Parker notes that 'hymning the god and dancing for the god are fundamental forms of Greek worship, and yet it is remarkably hard to find Athenian men engaging in them in their simple form in the classical period'. From the simple form he excludes the dramatic choruses as well as the (stationary) dithyrambs, and concludes that there was 'a transformation undergone [in Athens] by a traditional religious element, choral song, which lived on in Sparta in more or less its old form'.[17] I will return to this problem in §6 below.

Mystic ritual was secret, but the singing and dancing Iakchos procession of mystic initiates was in full public view, as was also presumably the dancing at Eleusis around the Kallikhoron well.[18] Mystery cult could include the movement of the initiates through the streets.[19] Similarly, the early dithyramb was sung in a public procession even though the earliest remains of the dithyramb are closely associated with the Dionysiac mysteries.[20] In Aristophanes' *Frogs* an aspect of the mystic experience, the exhilarated solidarity of the processional singing and dancing initiates, can be publicly displayed (§5 below) without revealing what was revealed only in the rite of passage. Much the same can probably be said of the early dithyramb. Besides public choruses associated with mystery cult, it seems that there were also choruses of which only the initiated had knowledge, and it is not always clear which type a chorus of initiates (what I will call the 'mystic chorus') belongs to. That the chorus might be a bridge between mystic secrecy and public display is suggested by the phrase 'to dance out the mysteries', frequent in much later texts.[21]

16 Seaford 1994b: 241–3, 267–8; D'Angour 1997.

17 Parker 2005: 181–2. He excludes the dithyrambs because they were performed for competition and 'not necessarily very religious in theme'.

18 Paus. 1.38.6.

19 Dem. 18.260 (Sabazios).

20 Seaford 1994b: 268; Lavecchia 2000: 11–12, 136; Kowalzig 2007a.

21 ἐξορχεῖσθαι τὰ μυστήρια: e.g. Lucian, *Salt.* 15; Alciphron 3.72; Ach. Tat. 4.8.3; *POxy.* 3.411.25.

The major public choruses at Athens, dithyrambic and tragic, developed out of the mystic chorus. What was it about the mystic chorus, whether Eleusinian [265] or Dionysiac, that gave it, paradoxically, such an important *public* role in Attica? An answer to this question will emerge in due course. But let us first note that mentions of the mystic chorus are plentiful, of various kinds and from different periods.[22] Categorical is the statement of Lucian that 'no ancient mystic initiation (τελετή) can be found that is without dance' (*Salt.* 15).

According to Plato in *Phaedrus*, we are sometimes reminded of a vision (of reality and beauty) that all human souls had in a previous existence. It is presented as a mystic vision ('the most blessed of mysteries') that we had while following gods, 'with a blessed χορός' (250b). Now χορός here is generally translated 'company' or 'band', but in fact means – as elsewhere – *chorus*.[23] The mystic chorus is impressive enough for Plato to associate it with our defining vision of reality and beauty. There is a hint – albeit no more than a hint – of this mystic vision as dependent on choral participation.

Moreover, the unison of the chorus was connected with a fundamental vision, six centuries later, by Plato's follower Plotinus – but merely as a metaphor for the vision of the individual soul. The χορός stays around its leader (*koruphaios*), sometimes turns away and loses sight of him, and when it turns back to him sings beautifully and is truly around him.

> So too we are always around him [i.e. the One], but not always turned to him. When we do look to him, then we have our goal and repose and do not mis-sing (ἀπᾴδειν) as we truly dance our god-inspired dance around him.[24]

Plato wrote of 'sharing in philosophical madness and *bakcheia*' (*Symp.* 218b3), where sharing in *bakcheia* is a metaphor referring to the ecstatic, music-driven movement of the group in Dionysiac (bacchic) cult. Here again, Plotinus takes a Platonic image and applies it to the inward vision of the individual: the ecstasy of the bacchic movement (ἀναβακχεύεσθε) is associated with the 'longing to be with yourselves, in gathering yourselves together apart from the body' (*Enn.* 1.6.5). In Plotinus, choral unison and Dionysiac movement unify – if only as metaphors – the individual, but in

[22] E.g. an inscription of 92 BCE provides evidence for choral dancing in the mysteries at Andania (Sokolowski 1969: no. 67.73, 98). See also e.g. Eur. *Bacch.* 21–2; Pl. *Leg.* 7.815c–d, *Euthyd.* 277d–e; Schol. Lycoph. *Alex.* 212; further passages in Burkert 1983b: 288 and Hardie 2004: 14–20.

[23] It can be used metaphorically, which is clearly not the case here. It never means just 'company' or 'band'.

[24] Plotinus, *Enn.* 6.9.8; cf. 3.6.2.

an earlier era they actually unified the mystic chorus (§5 below), and moreover this unity or unison could be a politically significant paradigm for the right relationship *between* individuals. [266]

4. Cosmos and Mystic Chorus

This defining mystic vision in Plato's *Phaedrus* is of what is above the sky.[25] Mystic ritual may provide for the initiates not only doctrine about the nature of the cosmos but also an experience of transcending cosmic divisions – for instance, of the sun shining in the underworld.[26] Experience of this kind, even a feeling of co-extensiveness with the cosmos, may be aroused in the chorus of initiates by their song and dance. It is this that may be hinted at by the souls in *Phaedrus* having their mystic supercelestial vision 'with a blessed chorus'.

Ancient Greek choruses are sometimes imagined as embodying heavenly bodies, in particular the stars. Such choruses are, in various texts and periods, especially – though not always (§6 below) – associated with mystery cult, not least in Attic tragedy. These texts have been assembled and discussed by Csapo.[27] My concern is with the relationship between this cosmic reach and the internal dynamic of the mystic chorus, as well as with the political significance of this relationship.

In a choral song of Sophocles' *Antigone* the Eleusinian (1120) Dionysos is called Iakchos (1152) and 'chorus-leader of the stars' (1147), on which the scholiast comments that 'it is according to a mystic *logos* that he is called chorus-leader of the stars'. In *Frogs* the chorus of initiates invoke Iakchos as brandishing torches, and then immediately call him 'light-bearing star of the nocturnal mystic ritual (τελετή)' (342). Torches in the darkness can easily be imagined as stars. A fragment of Aeschylus' *Bassarai* implies that the torches carried in Dionysiac cult could be imagined as lightning.[28]

Other instruments carried by the Dionysiac chorus of initiates could make a sound as of thunder. The dithyrambic fragment 70b of Pindar describes, as belonging to the Dionysiac mystic ritual (τελετά)[29] of the gods, the 'ῥόμβοι of drums' and a fire-breathing thunderbolt. Shortly afterwards

[25] *Phdr.* 247c2, 248b (quoted in §5).
[26] Seaford 2005b.
[27] Csapo 2008; see also Ferrari 2008.
[28] Fr. 23a τὸ τῆς ἀστραπῆς πευκᾶεν σέλας.
[29] τελετά here means mystic ritual, as the object of the chorus' 'knowing' (εἰδότες): cf. Eur. *Bacch.* 73–4 with Seaford 1996a: 157–8; Lavecchia 2000: 135–6, and 106 (on the assignment to this poem of fr. 346 with its mention of the Eleusinian mysteries).

the papyrus breaks off as it begins to narrate the birth of Dionysos. The ῥόμβος (*rhombos*) was an instrument, used in mystery cult, that made a roaring sound by being whirled, and ῥόμβοι is here generally translated 'whirlings'. The conflation of ῥόμβοι with drums implies a confusion of roaring sounds, easily imagined as thunderbolt or earthquake. A fragment (fr. 57) of Aeschylus describes, in the cult of Dionysos, 'the deep frightening sound of the drum, as of thunder beneath the earth'. The thunderbolt is brought down from heaven to earth, or even under the earth (like the roar of an earthquake), by the sound of *rhombos* and [267] drum in choral performance. The thunderbolt that was in mystic ritual[30] enacted here on earth was in all likelihood imagined as the thunderbolt that came down to earth at the birth of Dionysos. And the birth of Dionysos was strongly associated with the dithyramb.[31]

A similar experience of cosmic interconnection is indicated by the 'whirling circular aetherial shaking (*enosis*) of the *rhombos*', in a mystic context in Euripides' *Helen* (1362–3): *enosis* connotes earthquake,[32] and so to call it 'aetherial' implies a confusion of the roar of thunder with the subterranean roar of earthquake.[33] In the lost drama *Peirithous*, set in the underworld, the chorus – almost certainly of mystic initiates – refer to an aetherial *rhombos* around which dance night and the stars.[34] The most detailed reflection of the mystic re-enactment of the Dionysiac thunderbolt-with-earthquake is, we shall see (§7 below), in Euripides' *Bacchae*. Choral song and dance may create a sense of the earth moving. When the maenads dance and call on Dionysos 'in unison' (ἀθρόῳ στόματι), the 'whole mountain was joining in the bacchanal' (Eur. *Bacch.* 724–7). When the chorus of Sophocles' *Antigone* sing 'Let us go to all the temples of the gods with all-night choruses, and let Dionysos earth-shaker of Thebes lead us!' (152–4), it is the *dance* by which the earth is shaken. And we have seen that the mystic chorus may also, in imagining themselves as transcending cosmic boundaries, use their equipment – torches, *rhomboi*, drums – to make present phenomena that belong above or beneath the earth: stars, thunder, lightning and earthquake.

[30] Texts cited by Seaford 1996a: 195–7.

[31] Pl. *Leg.* 3.700b4–5; Eur. *Bacch.* 526–7; Seaford 1996a: 156.

[32] It means earthquake in the mystic passage of *Bacchae* (585), and in its only other fifth-century occurrence (Eur. *Tro.* 1326) is of the *earth*, as also in the common compound adjectives for Poseidon.

[33] Compare the earthquake and underground thunder in the mystic pattern in Aesch. *PV* (Seaford 1986a[9]), and in Soph. *OC* (Seaford 2012a: 335).

[34] Critias, *TrGF* I fr. 4, discussed by Csapo 2008: 273.

Why does a chorus imagine itself as having cosmic reach? The Andaman dance, as described by Radcliffe-Brown in 1922, has the following features:

1. It is an activity of the whole community: every able-bodied adult takes part.
2. The whole personality of each dancer is involved.
3. Each dancer is constrained by rhythm and custom to conform in his movements to the communal action.
4. This loss of self creates in the dance unusual energy and ecstatic harmony with the fellow-members of the community.[35] *[268]*

That synchronised movement increases rapport, liking and prosocial behaviour has been demonstrated by recent experimental psychology.[36] Rappaport, who cites Radcliffe-Brown, goes further in generalising about certain circumstances in which

> the boundary between individuals and their surroundings, especially others participating in ritual with them, may seem to dissolve. … such a sense of union is encouraged by the co-ordination of utterance and movement demanded of congregations in many rituals. To sing with others, to move as they move in the performance of a ritual, is not merely to symbolize union. It is *in and of itself* to reunite in the reproduction of a larger order. Unison does not merely symbolize that order but indicates it and its acceptance. The participants do not simply *communicate* to each other *about* that order but *commune* with each other *within* it. In sum, the state of *communitas* experienced in ritual is at once social and experiential. Indeed the distinction between the social and the experiential is surrendered, or even erased, in a general feeling of oneness with oneself, with the congregation, or with the cosmos.[37]

The dissolution of the boundaries around the self may create a sense of boundlessness, of the group extending into the cosmos. And the coordination may be enhanced by tempo:

> The tempos typical of such co-ordination, and perhaps requisite to it, are quicker than those characteristic of ordinary social interaction and the co-ordination itself is tighter. The rhythm of the drum may approximate to the rhythm of the heartbeats, and, as it synchronizes the movements of the dancers' limbs and unifies their voices into the unisons of chant or song, it may entrain their breaths and pulses, or at least be experienced as if it does.[38]

[35] Radcliffe-Brown 1922: 251–2.
[36] Miles et al. 2009; Wiltermuth and Heath 2009; Valdesolo and DeSteno 2011.
[37] Rappaport 1999: 220, emphasis in original.
[38] Rappaport 1999: 221.

Not only may such regular repetition occur within ritual, but the ritual itself may be repeated at precise intervals.

> That which is performed at rapid tempo and in tight coordination, and which through that tempo and coordination unites participants more tightly than they are under normal circumstances, is, *in being punctiliously repeated from one performance to the next, experienced as never-changing*.[39]

Moreover if, say, the dithyramb sung in the annual processional escort of Dionysos was experienced as never-changing, then the experience would have been amplified by the conviction that an ancient event is being re-enacted (the birth or original arrival of the god), and that it will continue to be re-enacted for ever. The solidarity of choral performance seems to extend indefinitely not only over space (as we have seen) but also over time.[*269*] This may have political significance: the spatial claim of the dithyrambic procession is – by means of myth – for all time.[40]

Myth may be re-enacted also by the secret mystic chorus. Plutarch's account of the initiands' wanderings in the dark (§5 below) may derive from the Eleusinian initiands' enactment of Demeter's search for Persephone.[41] But Eleusinian initiation is for the individual not regularly repeated; it occurs once in a lifetime. Its embodiment of permanence consists rather in pre-enactment of post-mortem participation in the eternal unison of the mystic chorus. The pre-enactment is of course temporary, but is united with post-mortem eternity by means of *memory*, which was of great importance for mystic initiates.[42]

5. The Solidarity of the Mystic Chorus

This group solidarity, expressed in the dissolution of the normal articulation of space (and of time), is a potential effect of choruses in general. There are three reasons why it may be found in the mystic chorus in particular. One reason is that mystic ritual, as a rehearsal of death and of post-mortem bliss, transcends cosmic divisions and aspires to eternity. Second, whereas on many occasions choral performance has a function external to itself (funeral, wedding, praise or escort of god or human victor, delighting audience and deity, etc.), the only function of the secret mystic chorus

39 Rappaport 1999: 221–2, emphasis in original.

40 For the 'timeless continuity' that mythical aetiology seems to establish see Kowalzig 2007b: 26–32; for time and performance see D'Alessio 2004: 292–4.

41 Seaford 2012a: 28 n. 27.

42 Especially on the gold leaves: GJ 1, 2, 8, 25; *Hymn. Orph.* 77.9–10 (Quandt).

is – we shall see – to enact (or pre-enact) its own blessed solidarity and eternal well-being: the sense of unlimited space and time, which in many contexts may be merely a by-product of intense unison, is in the mystic chorus closely associated with its function. Third, the ritual as a whole enacts the transition from individual suffering to choral happiness, and this surely intensified the solidarity of the chorus by a sense of contrast with its opposite.[43]

The contrast deserves our attention. Every Eleusinian initiand was required to sacrifice a pig 'on his own behalf'. Parker notes that this unusual individualism reflects the character of mystic initiation as preparation for [270] the individual experience of death.[44] But mystic ritual pre-enacts not only the isolation of death but also the subsequent blissful cohesion of the initiates in the underworld, which was accordingly imagined as containing choral dancing that is joined by the dead individual.[45] Mystic ritual dramatises individual isolation so as to transform it into its opposite – choral solidarity.

A famous fragment of Plutarch (fr. 178) compares the soul on the point of death to the transition in mystic ritual from ignorant fear in darkness to pure places and meadows in which there are a wonderful light, voices, choral dances (χορεῖαι), sacred sounds and holy visions: here the initiate 'is with (σύνεστιν) holy (ὁσίοις) and pure men'. Entry into this happy state is the consummation, τέλος, of a terrifying process of wearisome runnings around and movements through the darkness that are 'without τέλος' (ἀτέλεστοι) and 'viewed with suspicion': they seem endless, pointless and directionless. This preliminary stage dramatises the spatio-temporal boundlessness of the isolated individual: in the darkness he can discern neither spatial nor temporal end (τέλος) to his movements. Random movements in the darkness deprive the individual of all sense of social space: this is an apt expression of extreme isolation, for it is space on which social being primarily depends. Being ἀτέλεστοι, the movements also deprive the individual of social temporality. But eventually there is temporal completion (τέλος) that consists of entry into an eternal social space of purity and choral cohesion.[46]

[43] In one form of mystic initiation a group danced around a seated initiand or initiands (*thronosis*): Pl. *Euthyd.* 277d–e; Dio Chrys. 12.33; Lada-Richards 1999: 101.

[44] 'At collective rituals one animal or group of animals was commonly brought "on behalf of all"' (Parker 2005: 342).

[45] Plut. *Mor.* 1105b; epitaphs: Jaccottet 2003: nos. 112, 180, 29.

[46] In an epitaph from Philippi (third century CE?), Dionysiac initiates in the hereafter claim the dead man as *congrex*, to lead with torches the festal corteges: Jaccottet 2003: no. 29.19–21.

The other initiates whom the initiate joins are 'pure', and he has himself been purified by initiation. This mystic transition is alluded to by Plato in the *Republic* (8.560e) in his description of the degeneration of the democratic man:

> having emptied and purified of these things (virtues) the soul of the man who is ... being initiated with great initiation rituals, after this they bring in insolence and anarchy and profligacy and shamelessness, resplendent with a great chorus, crowned ...

Plato here describes degeneration, perversely, in terms of the positive psychic transition of mystic initiation that we have seen in Plutarch. The emptying or purification of the soul by individualising disorientation is followed by the impressive arrival of a chorus.[47] In Plato the chorus with its resplendent accompaniment is *brought in*. This corresponds (in Plutarch) to the wonderful light 'meeting' (ἀπαντᾶν) the initiand: the light is brought into the darkness (as in the orthodox Easter ceremony), and in the light there are *choreiai*. And, just as the initiates in Plutarch are pure, so in the Plato passage the initiate is purified. So too in Plato's *Phaedrus* choral initiates [271] are pure (250b–c). The homogeneous purity of the mystic chorus expresses its cohesion.

Any sense of purity and cohesion was surely enhanced by the contrast with the terrified isolation that preceded it. Mystic ritual rehearses the individual isolation of death so as to transform it into choral communality. Moreover in the Plutarch passage the initiate, even as he consorts with pure men, looks down on the 'uninitiated and unpurified mob of those here on earth, in much mud and mist driven together and trampling on each other'.[48]

Solidarity may be enhanced by exclusion.[49] But in this context the exclusion may seem paradoxical, for the Eleusinian mysteries, which Plutarch probably has in mind, were open to all.[50] The same contradiction, between universal access to mystic initiation and conflict between impure uninitiated individuals, reappears in a different form (adapted to his philosophical purpose) in Plato's *Phaedrus*: all human souls had pre-natal access to the mystic vision of reality (249e4–5), and indeed it is in the nature of immortal souls to fly upwards like winged chariots to the region where

[47] What follows, 'calling insolence good education, anarchy freedom, etc.', may be designed to evoke the mystic formulae expressing the unity of opposites: see Seaford 2003a[6]: 143–9.

[48] See also Plut. *De prof. virt.* 81d–e.

[49] Kowalzig 2007b: 169 suggests that mystic exclusivity could be a basis for creating civic identities.

[50] Provided that they knew Greek and were not polluted by murder.

the gods reside, and anyone who is willing and able follows their celestial movement, 'for resentment is excluded from the divine chorus' (247a7). However, some souls form a mass of chariots, 'trampling and jostling each other, each trying to get ahead of the other', and so depart 'uninitiated in the sight of reality' (248b4). As a result, not every soul can recollect its earlier (brief or partial) vision (250a). Here the cohesion and general accessibility of the mystic chorus are projected onto heaven, and it is only non-philosophical human weakness that prevents their universality.

The mystic solidarity that is enhanced by exclusion may have a political function, which is seen in fifth-century drama, most clearly in Aristophanes' *Frogs*. The initiated chorus of the dead in their underworld meadow are 'holy', ὅσιοι (327, 335), a model of joyful and egalitarian cohesion, with the unusual energy (345–9, 402–4) observed among the Andaman islanders by Radcliffe-Brown. We noted that the chorus might be a bridge between mystic secrecy and public display, and that the dithyramb, despite its association with mystic ritual, became a very public performance (giving rise to tragedy).[51] Similarly here the leader of the mystic chorus makes a public proclamation, excluding from the 'initiated choruses' (370) the impure and the uninitiated (354–7)[52] – as well as a wide range of *political* undesirables – for instance, 'anyone who does not dissolve hostile civil conflict (*stasis*) and is not at ease with citizens' (359).[272]

In Euripides' *Bacchae* Dionysos has come to initiate the whole polis (39, 208). The chorus state that mystic initiation means to 'join the soul to the thiasos' in the purifying dance. As for the maenads outside the city, even the mountain and its animals join in their dance (726–7), and they exhibit the cohesion of a flock of birds flying upwards (748). By contrast, the uninitiated *tyrannos* Pentheus displays a disastrously obstinate individualism. The members of the chorus are isolated from each other by the temporary loss of their god, and restored to joy by his epiphany (609), in a scene in which the impervious isolation of Pentheus is expressed in terms of the experience of the preliminary stage of initiation (the detailed similarity with Plutarch fr. 178 is astonishing). We will develop the political significance of this passage in §7 below.

In Sophocles' *Antigone* the Eleusinian Dionysos, mystic 'chorus-leader of the stars' (§4 above), is invoked to come to purify with dancing the polis

[51] Seaford 1994b: 241–3, 267–8.

[52] Hardie 2004: 20 notes the verbal parallels in Clement of Alexandria (*Strom.* 5.19.2), comparing the non-Christian to the uninitiated: he must 'stand outside the divine chorus'.

from a disease (1141) that has arisen from the mind (1015) of the isolated *tyrannos* Kreon.

In these three passages there is a contrast between the cohesion and purity of the mystic chorus and the individualism of one or more individuals outside the chorus. This contrast originates, I suggest, in the memorable and widely experienced transition, in mystic ritual, from competitive individual isolation to the cohesion and purity of the chorus. In our three passages, all from the dramatic performances of the democratic polis, the contrast has been adapted by the drama and has therein acquired a *political* significance (of various kinds). But how did this happen?

The chorus in general could be an image or agent of ordered political unity.[53] Especially significant in this respect was, I suggest, the mystic chorus. It is not just that – as we have seen – the mystic chorus both embodies and celebrates egalitarian unity imagined as all-pervasive (cosmic) and permanent. It is also that the Eleusinian cult involved mass participation, was a ritual of the polis[54] and, in the anecdote told by Herodotus (8.65), embodied victory for Athens over the invading Persians. The Athenians had a 'passionate sense … that their welfare was tied up with' the mysteries.[55]

Secret mystic ritual was sometimes celebrated in public festivals.[56] It was the *public* (processional) mystic chorus that in Herodotus' anecdote embodied victory. Whereas the only purpose of the *secret* mystic chorus is its own well-being, the *processional* form of the mystic chorus – whether Iakchos song or dithyramb – may acquire other functions, notably escorting the god (Iakchos, [273] Dionysos) or symbolically occupying territory. I suggest that the public form of the mystic chorus emerged – at least in part – from the tendency to extend the egalitarian solidarity of the mystic chorus to the whole community. This is manifest in the stationary dithyramb (§7 below), and even more so in drama. In *Frogs* the chorus of initiates embodies the unity of the polis. In *Bacchae* mystic initiation is secret, but the whole polis is to be initiated and Dionysos requires honour from all (35–40, 114, 208, 472–4). In *Antigone* it is 'the polis with all its people (πάνδημος)' that is to be purified by the mystic chorus-leader of the stars.

[53] E.g. Xen. *Oec.* 8.3; Polyb. 4.20–21; Paus. 5.16.5; *PMG* 713 (iii); Plut. *Lyc.* 4.1–2; Nagy 1990: 368; Wilson 2003; Kowalzig 2004.

[54] Sourvinou-Inwood 1997: 144–6.

[55] Parker 2005: 343, 348.

[56] For several Dionysiac instances see Seaford 2006a: 71–2.

In both *Bacchae* and *Antigone* the solidarity of the chorus contrasts with the impervious isolation of a *tyrannos* (Pentheus, Kreon) who at certain key moments of the drama is preoccupied with money. The significance of this will emerge in the next section.

6. Chorus and Powerful Individual

Kosmos can mean the political order as well as the cosmic order, and we have seen that the chorus can seem to embody both polis (social totality) and cosmos (physical totality). But the Olympian deities did not on the whole personify heavenly bodies, and the grounding of political practice in cosmic order was not a feature of Greek society to the extent that it was in, say, Egypt or Babylon.[57] In Greece the most striking conjunction of cosmos and polis was in the chorus.

An instance of this conjunction is provided by a song written in the seventh century for performance in Sparta, Alcman's *Partheneion*, as interpreted by Ferrari.[58] Although I am largely persuaded by it, this interpretation is far from generally accepted. I mention it here because it gives us a chorus that embodies both cosmos and (in a sense) polis and yet – in contrast to the solidarity of the mystic chorus – expresses rivalries. There is tension between two choruses, and between individual chorus members, expressed hyperbolically as combat: a rival chorus 'fights' with us, and Hagesikhora με τείρει (77), 'wears me down'.[59] Similar is the competition in beauty referred to by Euripides: 'May I take my place in the choruses … the ἁμίλλαι [conflicts, contests] in loveliness, with strife of delicately luxuriant hair.'[60] Hagesikhora ('Leader of the chorus') defeats me, effaces me, in the way that in other texts Artemis [274] outshines the nymphs, Aphrodite the Graces, Thetis her sisters and Helen her companions. 'Like the rising dawn … Helen shone among us', sing the dancing chorus at her wedding.[61] And Sappho writes of a girl who is now conspicuous among Lydian women as the moon surpasses all the stars.[62] These passages are adduced by Ferrari, who argues that the singing chorus are impersonating the Hyades, that the Pleiades are a rival chorus and that Hagesikhora is the

[57] The heavenly bodies influenced the timing of agricultural activity, of festivals, and of military activity. And cosmic order might be used to justify a political principle, e.g. at Soph. *Aj.* 668–75, Eur. *Phoen.* 541–7.

[58] Ferrari 2008: 17.

[59] τείρει is more often taken as erotic, but I follow Ferrari 2008: 80.

[60] *IT* 1143–8; Burnett 1985: 10, 160.

[61] Theoc. *Id.* 18.7–8, 26–8.

[62] Sappho fr. 96.6–9; cf. fr. 34.

moon.[63] Here co-extensiveness with the cosmos expresses not unison but rivalry.

In the *Partheneion* the *khorāgos* (chorus-leader) exercises authority within the chorus, and elsewhere Alcman applies the word to Agesidamos, 'leader of the people'.[64] The chorus may seem to embody the social totality, and accordingly the word *koruphaios* could refer both to chorus-leader and to political leader (e.g. Hdt. 3.82.3). In Sparta a central public space was called χορός.[65]

This brings us back to the 'transformation undergone [in Athens] by a traditional religious element, choral song, which lived on in Sparta in more or less its old form'.[66] We may add here that a factor in this transformation was the institution of the tragic and dithyrambic competitions at Athens at the City Dionysia[67] in the last decade of the sixth century, a time of democratic transformation.[68]

A crucial factor in this distinctively Athenian development was, I believe, the monetisation of festivals in the latter part of the sixth century, which resulted in choruses at the Dionysia being financed and controlled by powerful individuals. In democratic Athens the word *khorēgos*, 'chorus-leader', referred to a wealthy individual who did not belong to the chorus but provided the money to equip and train it.[69] The kind of tension exemplified by the *Partheneion* may have developed into tension between the dithyrambic chorus and the centralised monetary power of the tyranny. If so, then after the overthrow of the Athenian tyranny this tension was remembered in tragedy, as it emerged from dithyramb, and was assimilated to the ancient myth of the [275] rejection of Dionysiac cult by the king (as well as to the contrast between isolated initiand and initiated chorus).[70]

The tension between Dionysos and the *tyrannos* Pentheus in *Bacchae* includes the fact that they both want to be the focus of the pandemic festival. Pentheus rejoices 'when many stand at the gates, and the polis magnifies

63 Ferrari 2008: 83–105.

64 *PMG* 1.43–5; 10(b).11. For the connection between choral leadership and kingship in Sparta see Nagy 1990: 347–9.

65 Paus. 3.11.9. An account of the forging of 'religious space' by choral performance (on Delos) is by Kowalzig 2007b: 69–80.

66 Parker 2005: 181–2.

67 There is good reason to suppose that the choruses at the Thargelia were dithyrambs: Wilson 2000: 314 n. 22, 322 n. 115.

68 Perhaps these splendid new public choruses in a developing polis festival were thought to outshine the more private choruses that were an essential element of aristocratic education (Ar. *Ran.* 729).

69 'Athenian choral forms (dithyramb, tragedy, and comedy) strikingly plucked the *chorēgos* out of the chorus' (Kurke 2007: 100).

70 This paragraph states conclusions for which I have argued in detail in Seaford 2012a: 75–121.

the name of Pentheus. He too [Dionysos] … enjoys being honoured.'[71] In *Frogs*, and in the anecdote recorded by Herodotus, the mystic chorus seems to embody the whole polis, and in *Bacchae* the celebrations of the mystic chorus prefigure the initiation of the whole polis. The focus of the mystic chorus (on Iakchos or Dionysos) may become the focus of pandemic celebration. But Iakchos or Dionysos may be replaced there by the mortal potentate.

After Athens had lost its democratic autonomy, Demetrios Poliorketes was on one occasion welcomed as a god with processional choruses and with an *ithyphallos* (a hymn sung in festivals of Dionysos) that contained the verses

> Here the time has brought together Demeter and Demetrios.
> She comes to celebrate the solemn (σεμνά) mysteries of Kore,
> And he glad, as the god should be, and beautiful and smiling (γελῶν) is present.
> Something solemn (σεμνόν τι) he seems, his friends all in a circle and in the middle of them he himself.
> Similarly as if his friends are the stars, and he the sun.[72]

Demetrios has arrived at the time of Demeter's mysteries at Eleusis, in which Dionysos-Iakchos is celebrated in a choral procession. It has been argued that the ancient accounts of Demetrios have numerous details based on his assimilation to Dionysos.[73] Moreover, Plutarch tells us that the god whom Demetrios most emulated was Dionysos (*Demetr.* 2.3), that it was proposed that whenever he came to Athens he should be 'received with the ξενισμοί [welcoming entertainments] accorded to Demeter and Dionysos' (12.1), and that the Athenians renamed the Dionysia after him 'Demetria' (12.2). In the hymn, 'as *the* (τόν) god should be' (not '*a* god') probably refers to Dionysos,[74] who is elsewhere beautiful and γελῶν.[75] The repetition of σεμνός indicates, I suggest, that his identification with the sun is based on the identification of Dionysos with the sun in the mysteries. The Eleusinian Dionysos-Iakchos is in the fifth century 'light-bearing star of the nocturnal mystic ritual' and 'chorus-leader of the stars'. The Stoic Kleanthes, a contemporary of Demetrios and resident of [276] Athens, identified the sun with mystic torchlight[76] as well as with Apollo and with

[71] *Bacch.* 319–21; the *tyrannos* of Sophocles' *Antigone* thinks that he owns the polis (738).

[72] Demochares *FGrH* 75 F2, Douris *FGrH* 76 F13, both *ap.* Ath. 6.253b–f.

[73] Scott 1928: 226–39.

[74] Perhaps Demetrios was associated or identified with Dionysos in the lost beginning of the hymn.

[75] E.g. *Bacch.* 453, 439 (with Seaford 1996a: *ad loc.*). Similarly, Mark Antony was celebrated as Dionysos as he entered Ephesos and Athens: Plut. *Ant.* 24; Sen. *Suas.* 1.6.

[76] *SVF* 1.538.

Dionysos.[77] There are also later texts indicating the mystic identification of Dionysos with the sun.[78] The hymn states that of the gods only Demetrios can save them in the war: the Athenian polis is asserting its survival with a mystic chorus addressed not to Iakchos (as in Herodotus' anecdote) but to a more effective, human potentate.

In democratic Athens, on the other hand, the mystic chorus had been saved by their divine master from subjection to a human one. In Euripides' *Bacchae*, just as in his satyric *Cyclops* and indeed in many other satyr plays, it is in the anomalous absence of Dionysos from its dancing that the thiasos falls under the power of the man of money[79] – and is eventually liberated, just as in general the tragic chorus survives the downfall of powerful individuals.

The mystic chorus may embody the cosmos, but – in contrast to Alcman's *Partheneion* – is characterised by the cohesive anonymity of its members. Moreover, its allegiance is to deity rather than to any mortal: to Dionysos in *Bacchae* and (as 'chorus-leader of the stars') in *Antigone* (1147), to Iakchos in *Frogs*.[80] I suggest that the fifth-century tragic chorus – diverging from the aristocratic choruses of, for example, Sparta – retains the internal anonymity and egalitarian solidarity[81] of the mystic chorus from which it is in part ultimately derived.

7. The Politicisation of the Dithyramb

Why was such a large proportion[82] of the public *khoroi* in democratic Athens constituted by the dithyrambic and tragic *khoroi* at the polis festivals of Dionysos? Any answer cannot ignore the combination in the dithyramb of various features tending to promote a sense of community: its association with mystery cult (§3 above), its internal unity, its escorting into the city of a god who comes from outside[83] at a pandemic festival. In this combination of the mystic, the processional and the pandemic it resembled the Iakchos song. Pindar's dithyrambic fr. 70c contains what seems to have

77 *SVF* 1.540, 541, 546.

78 Seaford 2005b. Cf. the mystic saviour Dionysos as 'greatest light' at Eur. *Bacch.* 608.

79 Eur. *Bacch.* 547–59; *Cyc.* 73–81. For Pentheus and Polyphemos and other captors of the thiasos as men of money see Seaford 2003b[3].

80 Cf. also Eur. *Bacch.* 141.

81 Tension is, rather, with the *tyrannos*. The closest to internal tension is the spoken passage at Aesch. *Ag.* 1348–71, even though the variety of views does not in fact produce contradiction. Aesch. *Sept.* 1066–77 is a post-classical interpolation.

82 Parker 2005: 181–2.

83 Seaford 2012a: 44.

been a wish that [277] *stasis* (internal conflict) should be resolved, together with an invocation of Dionysos.[84]

The sense of community surely persisted even after the dithyramb became a stationary (rather than escorting) song as part of its development into tragedy. 'The characteristic circular dance of the dithyrambic chorus meant that it was endless and boundless – it had no head or leader.'[85] But it was tragedy that acquired, in connection with the developments described in §6 above, a new kind of political significance.

Another dithyrambic fragment of Pindar (fr. 70b) contains mention of the transition from processional to static dithyramb,[86] as well as mystic ritual in an (Olympian) μέγαρα (palace) with 'ῥόμβοι of drums' and a 'fire-breathing thunderbolt', and the birth of Dionysos (§4 above). The dithyrambs in *Bacchae* also embody the transition from processional to stationary dithyramb,[87] as well as – in the royal μέλαθρα (587–9) – mystic ritual containing a thunderbolt associated with the birth of Dionysos.[88] But they are also significantly different from the Pindaric dithyramb.

The entry-song of *Bacchae* exemplifies precisely the transition from processional to stationary dithyramb that was a crucial step in the development of tragedy. Dionysos tells his entering choral escort to go around the royal house and beat their drums, 'so that the polis of Kadmos sees' (61). Having called on anyone inside the μέλαθρα to come out, they pronounce the mystic *makarismos* and narrate the birth of Dionysos by the thunderbolt that killed his mother Semele. Whereas this is a *public* dithyramb, the second stasimon ('stationary song') has more affinity to the *secret* mystic chorus. First the chorus narrate, or rather dramatise, the birth of Dionysos, who is called 'Dithyrambos'. He was, they say, as a baby washed in the streams of Dirke.

> But you, O blessed Dirke, are thrusting me away when I have crown-wearing *thiasoi* in you [i.e. on your banks]. Why do you reject me? Why do you flee from me? In the future … Bromios will be of concern to you. (530–6)

Here the performance of the dithyrambic myth of birth embodies a claim to both time (past, present and future) and space. The dual claim is then implicitly repeated when, after their invocation of Dionysos to come from

[84] Wilson 2003 suggests that this 'represents a politicisation of the mystic, choral powers of Dionysos'.
[85] Kurke 2007: 100, based on Martin 2007.
[86] D'Angour 1997: 340–3.
[87] *Bacch.* 55–61; Seaford 1996a: 156.
[88] Seaford 1996a: 195–203.

afar, he appears along with earthquake and with the reactivation, at the tomb of Semele, of the flame that Zeus' thunderbolt once left when it killed Semele at Dionysos' birth (585–99, 6–9). The sounds as of thunder and earthquake were surely created here by drums, just as they were perhaps evoked earlier by the drumming 'around the royal house' in the first dithyramb.[89] [278]

Whereas in the Pindaric dithyramb it seems that the μέγαρα contain the mystic ritual as a context for the drumming enactment of the thunderbolt at the birth of Dionysos, in *Bacchae* this is directed *against* the μέλαθρα, which consequently collapses.[90] The cosmological power of the dithyramb, with drums making present the thunderbolt of Zeus, is – in the aetiological myth of resistance to the new cult – deployed on behalf of the polis against the resistant royal household. As the house collapses, Dionysos is greeted by the chorus as 'greatest light' and urges them to rise from the ground, where they have just fallen in terrified, individually isolated (μονάδα) desolation. The cosmological demolition of the royal house combines with the mystic transition from frightened isolation to (restored) choral solidarity. The cosmic reach that emerges from mystic choral solidarity acquires political power, by which mystery cult is established for the whole polis.[91]

8. Public and Private Space

This power of the dithyramb to extend cosmic-communal space into the household has to be seen in the context of our earlier account of the power of the performers of ritual – unknown in our society – to create and possess communal space. The extensive communal space of the polis contains places for numerous superhuman powers (deities, heroes). It was – in the imagination of the citizens – defined and maintained as public space not only by boundary stones but also by communal rituals associated with constructions such as sanctuaries, temples, altars and statues. Participation in ritual, and especially in choruses, creates – for both participants and onlookers – a memorable paradigm of the cohesive energy and consensual power needed to control and defend space. Εὐρύχορος, literally 'with broad choruses', is regularly translated 'with broad places'. The choral dance was

[89] βαρύβρομος ('heavy-roaring') of their drums (156) occurs also of thunder (Eur. *Phoen.* 182, cf. Eur. *Hipp.* 1201–2). And see §4 above.

[90] On the democratic polis physically demolishing the houses of its internal enemies see Connor 1985.

[91] Eur. *Bacch.* 39–40, 49; Seaford 1996a on 1329–30.

a vital instrument of military training,[92] and soldiers would march singing into battle.[93]

The space of the household too was a place of ritual and of gods. For instance, it is as protector of house and property that Zeus is called Ktesios. But his general presence in households qualifies the absolute possession of each household by its owner. In the polis all space is in a sense one space. 'Public ill goes into everybody's house, and the courtyard walls are no longer disposed to hold, but it leaps over the high wall, and finds him for sure, even if [279] he takes refuge in the inmost room.'[94] In Aeschylus' *Agamemnon* the whole household participates in sacrifice at the altar of Zeus Ktesios (1036–8), but at the end of the *Oresteia* it is Zeus Agoraios (of the *agora*) who 'obtained power' (*Eum.* 973). *Agora* could mean both assembly and a central public space. Zeus Agoraios had an altar not only in the *agora* (in Athens and elsewhere) but also on the Athenian Pnyx, where the Athenian assembly met.[95] In the same Oresteian movement from household to polis, the Erinyes in Argos are 'hard to send out' from the royal house (*Ag.* 1190), in Delphi beset Orestes inside the temple of Apollo, and in Athens obtain a place of public cult, without which no household will flourish (*Eum.* 895), and proceed to invoke in their choral song and dance blessings on the polis. Tragedy is frequently set at the point of confrontation between the private space of the household and the public space of choral dance. And it is above all the god of tragedy, Dionysos, who in both public ritual and myth irrupts into the private household.[96]

Finally, just as the inclusiveness of ritual solidarity may seem to extend itself outwards to include the cosmos, so conversely the exclusiveness of the ruling family is expressed by the inward movement of confinement in a small space. The endogamy that embodies this exclusiveness is often accompanied, especially in tragedy, by the spatial confinement of the isolated female by the male(s) of the household.[97] In *Antigone*, for instance, the spatial confinement of Antigone in her bridal tomb is associated with the reproductive introversion of the Theban royal family,[98] whereas – at the other extreme, just after it is decided to release Antigone – it is as

92 Pritchett 1974: 216–17; on the choral πυρρίχη, with some affinities to the dithyramb, see Ceccarelli 1998.
93 Rutherford 2001: 42–7.
94 Solon fr. 4.26–9.
95 He was also a patron of politicians: Sommerstein 1989: 269.
96 Seaford 2012a: 75–95.
97 Seaford 1990a.
98 Seaford 1990a.

chorus-leader of the stars that the mystic Dionysos is invoked by the chorus to come from afar to purify the polis with dancing.

To conclude, the singing and dancing group had in the classical polis an importance that is entirely unknown in mainstream monotheism. This importance was both religious and political, and was based on the implicit claim of the group to space (and time). In particular, the chorus of mystic initiates, in imagining themselves as coexistent with the cosmos as they prefigured their eternal solidarity, provided both for Platonic philosophy and (differently) for the polis a transcendent model of happy cohesion. It is as a result of this political significance that the mystic chorus developed at Athens into the public performance of dithyramb and tragedy, in both of which the chorus is marked by solidarity and anonymity. Rivalry and the naming of individuals, which in Alcman's *Partheneion* occur *within* the cosmic chorus, in tragedy serve to *contrast* the (autocratic) individuals with the chorus.

CHAPTER 9

Immortality, Salvation and the Elements

My theme is a certain pattern of mystic belief (and its synthesis with the Hesiodic tradition) as it appears variously in various texts, including the *Prometheia*, the funerary gold leaves, Empedocles and Heraclitus. Use will be made also of the recently published discoveries from Derveni and Olbia.

In the introduction to his recent commentary on the *Prometheus Bound* Mark Griffith makes two implicit, complementary assumptions about its relation to previous tradition. The first is that the play is a reworking of Hesiod. The second is that there is almost nothing that can be said to lie behind the 'bold process of selection, adaptation, and innovation' by which 'Hesiod's morality tale' is transformed into a 'drama of tragic tone and proportions' (1983: 5). The implicit picture is of the dramatist pondering the Hesiodic text in his attempt to imagine the bold changes and adaptations necessary to transform the story for the purposes of tragic production.

With the first of these assumptions, in which of course there may be some truth, I am not concerned here, except to say that there is no reason to suppose that the Hesiodic versions of the myth were more of a direct model for the *Prometheia* than some other early version or versions now lost. As for the second assumption, the only source (other than Hesiod) mentioned by Griffith in his introduction is Pindar, *Isthm.* 8.27–35, where Themis reveals the prophecy that Thetis will bear a son mightier than his father. Elsewhere, however, Griffith mentions dismissively fragment DK 31 B 115 of Empedocles:

> Attempts have also been made to link the period of Prometheus' punishment, quoted by a scholiast as being 30,000 years, to Empedocles' period of purification in *Katharmoi*. But this number possessed magical significance as far back as Hesiod *Op.* 252–5, and in *Prom.* the period is variously given as 10,000 years or a mere thirteen generations.[2] This avenue leads us no-where.[1]

[1] Griffith 1978: 116; Schol. *Prom.* 94; [Aesch.] *PV* 94, 774.

These objections carry little weight.[2] Furthermore, the parallel is not confined to the figure 30,000. What Empedocles says is that there is an ancient oracle of Necessity (Ἀνάγκη) to the effect that when a *daimon* sheds blood or breaches his oath he wanders for 30,000 years (or perhaps seasons, i.e. 10,000 years[3]) away from the blessed, being born in all manner of mortal shapes. He, Empedocles, is one such, 'an exile and a wanderer from the gods, because I put my trust in raving strife'. In other fragments he describes his experience either of the underworld or of this world imagined in terms of the underworld (B 118, 121)[4] and the final return of the *daimones* to a place of honour among the other immortals, where they feast, free from human miseries and weariness (B 147).

Despite obvious differences between Prometheus and the Empedoclean *daimon*, they are both immortals paying for an offence by many thousands of years of exclusion and suffering required by necessity (ἀνάγκη; cf. *PV* 105, 514–15, 1052), before final release and reinstatement. So much, together with some possibly Pythagorean elements in the *Prometheia*, has already been recognised.[5] It remains to develop the argument by focusing attention on three other non-Hesiodic features of the *Prometheia*: the association of Prometheus with the Titans in his parentage, punishment and release; the role of the cosmological elements; the crowning of Prometheus. But first, an [3] observation on methodology.

I will not, despite the linguistic evidence,[6] dispute Griffith's view that the *Prometheia* was not influenced by Empedocles. This 'avenue' will never lead us to certainty on that point. But taken together with various other avenues it converges on the following proposition: that the shape of the myth in the *Prometheia* has been created by a certain current of ideas which is manifest not at all in Hesiod's version, but in various other texts (among them Emped. B 115) which I intend to explore here. To react to similarities in ideas between two texts by assuming as the *primary* problem

2 30,000 in Hesiod does not refer to time; on *PV* 94 Griffith 1983 in his commentary remarks '"for ages", ten thousand used, as often, to denote untold numbers'; whereas the scholiast's 30,000 years (ascribed to the *Pyrphoros*, fr. 208a; 30,000 years also ascribed to Aeschylus in Hyginus *Poet. astr.* 2.15 = fr. 208a *app. crit.*) does seem more specific; and the inconsistency between *PV* 94 and 774 was clearly not felt.

3 O'Brien 1959: 85–6; cf. Zuntz 1971: 196–7. See also n. 23 below.

4 For the bibliography on this disputed question see Guthrie 1965: 254 n. 31. Guthrie himself opts for this world but adds 'that the description should recall the underworld is only natural, for true to the Orphic tradition Empedocles regards the life of the soul as belonging to a higher region, and banishment to earth as the equivalent of death'.

5 Thomson 1946: 319. Pythagoreanism: Thomson 1946: 326–7 and Thomson 1932 on *PV* 459–61, 551; cf. Griffith 1978: 110.

6 Traglia 1952: 41–60; cf. Griffith 1978: 111–13.

the (usually unanswerable) question 'Was X familiar with the work of Y?' is one symptom of the projection of modern conditions of literary production onto pre-Hellenistic antiquity. It is true that this question is often important. But, given the loss of the great majority of the texts of this period, as well as the vast scope for the oral dissemination of ideas, it is better to move on to safer and more interesting ground. Ancient poetical texts tend not so much to create ideas as to give them form. I will attempt to show that both Empedocles and the *Prometheia* draw on a certain sub-literary current of ideas: this is the basic explanation of the similarity between them, whether or not the dramatist and Empedocles knew each other's works. I should also make it clear at this point that I have nothing to contribute to the questions which have tended to monopolise scholarly attention: was the trilogy by Aeschylus? What was the order of plays? When and where was it written and performed? Nor does my argument depend on the answers to these questions.

1. The Association of Prometheus with the Titans in His Parentage, Punishment and Release

The Prometheia *and Hesiod*

In Hesiod Prometheus is the son of Klymene and the Titan Iapetos. In the *Prometheia*, however, he is himself a Titan, the son of Earth (also called Themis: 18, 209–10, 874, 1091). That his father is Ouranos is mentioned (in what survives of the trilogy) only indirectly: first, the Okeanids in their sympathy for Prometheus' suffering say that Zeus in his vengeance 'keeps the heavenly (οὐρανίαν) race subdued, and will not cease to' (*PV* 164–7; cf. 205); and there is a similar sense of [4] indignation also at 408–11, 'they lament the majestic and immemorial honour belonging to you and your brothers'. In both these passages the punishment of Prometheus by Zeus is closely associated with that of his fellow Titans,[7] and indeed Prometheus is in fact, like the Hesiodic Titans (but not the Hesiodic Prometheus!), hurled by Zeus' thunderbolt into Tartarus.[8]

[7] See also 425–30, 205. In what precedes his punishment, however, Prometheus is distinguished from his brothers; he is not called Titan (cf. Soph. *OC* 56; Eur. *Ion* 455, *Phoen.* 1122), perhaps to avoid an impression of brother betrayal.

[8] *PV* 1016–21, 1051–2, 1081–4 (cf. 154–5, 220, 1029); Hes. *Theog.* 687–712, 820 (victory depends on assistance from the hundred-handers: see West 1966 on 711–12); Hor. *Carm.* 2.13.37, 2.18.35, *Epod.* 17.67.

This association is apparent also in the other passage in which Ouranos' fatherhood of Prometheus is (indirectly) mentioned: fr. 193, in which Prometheus, still imprisoned but soon to be released, calls the already released Titans (in Cicero's translation) 'Race of Titans, my blood-relatives, offspring of Heaven' (Cic. *Tusc.* 2.10 *Titanum suboles socia nostri sanguinis, generata Caelo*). In the form of punishment the Hesiodic Prometheus has been partially assimilated to the Hesiodic Titans. The release from imprisonment of Prometheus and the other Titans is nowhere to be found in Hesiod,[9] true though it is that Herakles releases Prometheus from his torments by shooting the eagle at *Theog.* 523–31 (see West 1966: *ad loc.*). Some light will now be shed on these 'innovations'.

The Mysticism of Magna Graecia

On the three funerary gold leaves from the 'Timpone piccolo' at Thurii in southern Italy[10] the suppliant, who is almost certainly the dead person arrived in the underworld, makes the following claims (among others): that he is one of the race of the gods; that he was struck by thunder and lightning; that he has paid the penalty for unjust deeds; that he has flown off the circle of heavy grief and misery; and that he desires to be sent by Persephone to the 'seats of the pure'.[11] On three other similar and roughly contemporary leaves, from [5] Hipponion and Petelia in southern Italy and Pharsalos in Thessaly,[12] the dead man is urged to begin his supplication with the claim to be the child of Earth and starry Ouranos. And on the Petelia leaf he is told that he will 'rule among other heroes'.

It has been suggested that these claims are based on the Orphic myth of the origin of humankind in the sooty deposit of the smoke from the Titans, who were the children of Earth and Ouranos and who had been blasted by Zeus' thunderbolt for the crime of eating the infant Dionysos.[13] But nobody could claim to *be* a Titan, on the grounds that humankind was created from the soot from the smoke of their blasted bodies. Nor does the suppliant's claim to divinity have anything to do with Dionysos (as some have claimed): the view found in the neo-Platonist Olympiodorus

[9] On the spuriousness of Hes. *Op.* 173a–e (Kronos ruling in the isles of the blessed) see West 1978: *ad loc.*

[10] GJ 5–7. Probably fourth century: see Zuntz 1971: 293–4. The leaves will be cited according to GJ.

[11] Not every claim appears on every leaf, but the leaves are clearly based on the same overall conception.

[12] GJ 1, 2 and 25; the Cretan leaves GJ 10–14 and 16, and the Thessalian leaf GJ 29, also contain the phrase Γᾶς υἱός εἰμι καὶ Οὐρανοῦ ἀστερόεντος.

[13] E.g. Guthrie 1935: 174.

that we are part of Dionysos because the Titans have eaten of his flesh is almost certainly a later interpretation.[14] This does not mean, however, that the suppliant is not imagining himself as a Titan. Zuntz, for example, while granting that the Titans, 'rather than "the gods" in general, were "offspring of Heaven and Earth", in Hesiod as well as according to the Orphic Theogonies', nevertheless cannot allow the suppliant such a gross untruth: 'which is to say that, on this interpretation, the speaker actually was not killed by lightning – although he states that he was – and that he presents himself as a Titan; which he is not'.[15]

This objection carries no weight. The claim is not in fact to have been 'killed' but to have been subdued (ἐδάμασσε) by the thunderbolt. And more importantly, if the speaker does believe that he is a Titan he will also of course believe that he has suffered the thunderbolt of Zeus. Furthermore, the view favoured by Zuntz, that the reference is merely to an actual thunderbolt, seems most unlikely. It is possible, I suppose, that special ritual formulae and a common tumulus could be prepared for those struck by lightning. But where the reference to the thunderbolt is preceded immediately by a claim to be of the race of the gods and to have paid the penalty for unjust deeds,[16] and where there is also the claim, on leaves from elsewhere but almost certainly from the same matrix of belief, to be the child of Earth and Heaven, then very probably we are faced with a belief in [6] the dead man as a Titan.[17] The absence of the word Titan is of no consequence and might be compared with the failure to specify the nature of the 'unjust deeds'.[18]

These 'unjust deeds' were, I think, not, as is often supposed, the eating of Dionysos, but the ancient struggle against Zeus described in, for example, Hesiod's *Theogony*. That is to say, the infliction of the thunderbolt on an offending deity is the same event (excluding Prometheus) as is referred to at *PV* 164–5 δάμναται οὐρανίαν γένναν (cf. GJ 5.4 με μοῖρ' ἐδάμασε, 2.7

[14] See e.g. West 1983: 164–5.

[15] Zuntz 1971: 316, 365.

[16] GJ 6.4 and 7.4 (GJ 5 omits the unjust deeds).

[17] If a real thunderbolt was involved, then it may have been associated in some way with the defeat of the Titans. Burkert 1975: 94–5 follows Zuntz in imagining a real thunderbolt but also sees the punishment of the Titans for eating Dionysos: 'Humans, descended from the Titans, must await a similar punishment' (see below). Certainly it seems that individuals killed by lightning had a special status in Greek burial practice: see esp. Artem. 2.9: 'Nobody struck by lightning is without honour, inasmuch as he is honoured like a god'; Dodds 1960 on Eur. *Bacch.* 6–12; Bremmer 1983a: 106 n. 101.

[18] Similarly, West 1983: 23 n. 57 compares με μοῖρ' ἐδάμασσε in GJ 5–7 with Agamemnon playing down his misdemeanor at Hom. *Il.* 19.86–7. Cf. GJ 3.4 θεὸς ἐγένου ἐξ ἀνθρώπου.

αὐτὰρ ἐμοὶ γένος οὐράνιον): not incineration but consignment to Tartarus. What we have on the leaves is a mystic variation – involving the belief in the derivation of humankind from the Titans[19] – of a tradition found also in Hesiod. The suppliant claims the reinstatement due to a Titan, now that he has paid the penalty, apparently of confinement in Tartarus, to which he was consigned by the thunderbolt, and in the human body.[20]

The leaves do then have much in common with another mystic text in hexameters from Magna Graecia, the *Katharmoi* of Empedocles. In both cases concern with purity and ritual designed to ensure [7] post-mortem happiness[21] is based on the belief that human beings (or at least some of them) are deities who may escape from the underworld and cycle of reincarnation[22] into which they have fallen through their own violent misbehaviour. Empedocles seems to have been influenced by Hes. *Theog.* 793–806, where it is said that when discord arises among the gods any god who swears a false oath by the river Styx will suffer a coma for a year and then nine years of exile from the feasts of the gods.[23] This seems an insignificant episode, but it does contain the idea of the return of the deity from exile. The Hesiodic tradition found in the gold leaves, on the other hand, the defeat and imprisonment of the Titans, is very important in Hesiod for it results in the present order of the world ruled by Zeus; but the story in Hesiod, in contrast to the gold leaves, contains no hint of any release or return for the exiles: the Titans remain imprisoned in Tartarus to this day (*Theog.* 732). Mystic discontent with the suffering of humankind in the present order of the world adapts the tradition not only by imagining

[19] This is found as early as *Hymn. Hom. Ap.* 335–6 and as late as *Hymn. Orph.* 37.2, 4–6 (Quandt) – Titans as ἡμετέρων πρόγονοι πατέρων; see further Linforth 1941: 331–2. Dio Chrys. *Or.* 30.10 preserves the view that humans are punished by being born in the prison that is the world because of the ancient struggle against the gods of the Titans, from whose blood humankind derives, and that when we die we have been sufficiently punished and are released. On the Titans as themselves primordial (criminal) humans see Detienne 1979: 80–2.

[20] The details are of course obscure. κύκλος (see n. 22 below) may imply successive returns to the underworld after each life (cf. e.g. Pl. *Resp.* 10.614c). For the idea of the Titans imprisoned in men see below.

[21] See Seaford 1981a: 254; Parker 1983: 299–300.

[22] If the κύκλος βαρυπενθής ἀργαλέος of the leaves means the cycle of births (material in Zuntz 1971: 320–2; add ἀργαλέος also of the cycle of reincarnation at Emped. B 115.8); for Empedocles and reincarnation see e.g. Kirk et al. 1983: 314–17. The wealth of burials containing the gold leaves may suggest that here too, as in Empedocles, return to divine status is imagined as preceded immediately by high social status.

[23] The first year is described (799) as μέγας ἐνιαυτός, which although it refers here to a single year may have influenced later conceptions of thousands of years. Cf. *Orph. frag.* 295K = 345B, where 9,000 is a variant on nine years for the period of the god's punishment.

the suffering deities to be humankind but also by creating the prospect of release.

Pindar, who unlike Hesiod was certainly familiar with this current of ideas,[24] comforts the exiled Demophilos with the thought that 'immortal Zeus freed the Titans; after a while, when the wind has ceased, there is a changing of the sails' (*Pyth.* 4.291–3). The only other direct reference to a generalised release of the Titans is their appearance in the *Prometheus Unbound* to observe the sufferings of Prometheus (and in the parody by Cratinus, fr. 171). Elsewhere (fr. 133) Pindar says of 'those for whom Persephone will receive the penalty for an ancient grief' (οἷσι δὲ Φερσεφόνα ποινὰν παλαιοῦ πένθεος δέξεται) that 'in the ninth year she restores to the sun their souls, from which arise kings and men swift in strength and greatest in wisdom, who will be called by humankind for the rest of time pure heroes'. Plato, who quotes [8] this fragment, says that the truth expressed in it is maintained also by priests and priestesses (*Meno* 81a10–b1). The 'ancient grief' is usually taken to be the grief of Persephone at the eating of her child Dionysos by the Titans.[25] But there are difficulties in this interpretation and even greater difficulties in referring πένθος to the guilt of the Titans.[26] Turning to the Thurian gold leaves, we find that there too it is in Persephone's power to send the dead, if she accepts their penalty (ποινά GJ 7.4), to a place where they will be happy and pure.[27] The ποινά offered appears to be defeat by the thunderbolt and confinement in the 'grievous cycle of deep suffering' (κύκλος βαρυπενθῆς ἀργαλέος).[28] So too, I think, in Pindar the ποινὰ παλαιοῦ πένθεος offered to Persephone is a ποινά consisting in an ancient πένθος,[29] that is to say, the ancient defeat and confinement of the Titans. It appears, then, that the highest of humankind are imagined here as, like the occupants of the Thurian tumuli, eternally absolved Titans,[30] although the possibility cannot be excluded that

[24] E.g. West 1983: 110 n. 82.

[25] E.g. Rose 1947: 247–50; Burkert 1985: 298; Linforth 1941: 348–50.

[26] Linforth 1941: 346–50 (and Dionysos was after all quickly restored to life); on the other hand, see bibliography in Graf 1974: 74 n. 53.

[27] I.e. directly ἕδρας ἐς εὐαγέων, whereas Pindar is closer to Empedocles (B 146) and the Petelian leaf (GJ 2.11 καὶ τότ' ἔπειτ' ἄ[λλοισι μεθ'] ἡρώεσσιν ἀνάξει[ς]): she sends them, in their ninth year in Hades, to be great personages of the world, with a final destiny as ἥρωες ἁγνοί.

[28] See n. 22 above. This phrase appears only on GJ 5, mention of the ποινά only on GJ 6 and 7. Given the similarity of the three leaves, this may express a sense of equivalence between πένθος and ποινά.

[29] With ποινή compare e.g. [Aesch.] *PV* 268. The most serious objection to this view is that the genitive with ποινή elsewhere always refers to the crime. But an exception is unobjectionable: cf. e.g. Eur. *Hipp.* 764; [Aesch.] *PV* 900 (cf. Soph. *Aj.* 888); and the phrase θανάτου δίκην (compared by Long 1948).

[30] The apparent inconsistency with Pind. *Pyth.* 4.291 is of course of no consequence.

they are instead anonymous *daimones* such as we find in Empedocles both in the underworld and proceeding up the scale of life on their way back to bliss (B 115, 117, 118, 121, 146, 147).

The last passage to be mentioned, which is roughly contemporary with the gold leaves, is from Xenocrates, who appears to have held the view, or at least to have adduced it in explanation of Plato *Phaedo* [9] 62b, that the Titans are imprisoned in humankind,[31] as well as to have maintained that *daimones* are the disembodied souls of humans before birth and after death and that the class of *daimones* includes the Titans.[32] The *Phaedo* passage attributes to secret rites the doctrine that humans are in a kind of prison (ἐν ἀπορρήτοις λεγόμενος ... λόγος), and elsewhere Plato calls Orphic the view that the soul is imprisoned in the body.[33]

It would nevertheless be both questionable and irrelevant to my purpose to give to any of these texts the name 'Orphic', with its implications of that exclusivity which Zuntz misguidedly imposed on the gold leaves in the desire to exclude from them anything not Pythagorean.[34] My purpose is to trace the appearance in various texts of a mystic adaptation of Hesiodic tradition, in which humans (or some humans) are imagined as immortals (generally Titans) who in ancient times were punished for their violent misbehaviour by being cast down beneath the earth by Zeus' thunderbolt and who may nevertheless (perhaps after several reincarnations) be restored eventually, by supplication, purity or mystic ritual, to a happy state. This idea has influenced the form of punishment and eventual release of the suppliant[35] Titan of the *Prometheia*. The case for this proposition is a cumulative one, and we must proceed to the next stage.

2. The Cosmological Elements

The Prometheia

The first words of Prometheus are an appeal to the *aither* and the winds, to the rivers and the sea, to the earth, and to the sun (*PV* 88–92). And the play

[31] Fr. 20 Heinze (the reference to Dionysos is not necessarily Xenocrates': see West 1983: 21 n. 53). Diog. Laert. (4.11) places Xenocrates in Sicily with Plato. See also Plut. *Mor.* 996b–c; Linforth 1941: 338.

[32] Heinze 1892: 83, 94–6, 150–5. Titans confined in an unending cycle of misery seem implied by Pl. *Leg.* 3.701b–c (the syntax required by Linforth 1941: 341 is impossible; and with μὴ λεξαί ποτε κακῶν compare *Orph. fr.* 230K = 348B).

[33] *Crat.* 400c; cf. Arist. fr. 60 Rose.

[34] The Hipponion leaf (GJ 1) now rules out Zuntz's interpretation.

[35] Pherecydes *FGrH* 3 F17: (Herakles) οἰκτείρει ἱκετεύοντα.

ends in a confusion of the cosmological elements. (By 'cosmological elements' I mean the physical elements arranged each in its cosmological area.) Prometheus defiantly asks for fire (i.e. Zeus' thunderbolt) to be hurled against him, for the *aither* to be [10] roused by the thunderbolt and by the winds, for the wind to shake the earth from its foundations, for the sea to overwhelm the stars and for Zeus to throw him into Tartarus in the harsh whirlings of Ἀνάγκη ('Necessity'), 'for he will never do me to death' (1043–53). When the earth does indeed begin to shake, there is thunder, the fire of lightning, dust whirled by blasts, winds blowing against each other and the *aither* is confounded with the sea (1080–8); Prometheus appeals, in the very last words of the play, to his mother (Earth) and to *aither* who whirls round the light common to all (1091–2).[36] Each of these passages is about the four cosmological elements.[37] There is nothing comparable in the Hesiodic versions.

The Presocratics and Mystic Doctrine

1. Empedocles. The importance of the elements in the *PV* has not gone unnoticed. According to Herington, it is to be explained by Aeschylus' knowledge of the Presocratic doctrine of the four elements and in particular its Empedoclean form.[38] Emped. B 115 not only displays the similarities noted at the beginning of the previous section, it also contains the following lines (9–12) about the fallen *daimon*:

> For the force of the *aither* pursues him into the sea,
> while the sea spits him out onto the surface of the earth, and the earth casts him into the rays
> of the fiery sun, and the sun into the maelstroms of the *aither* –
> one receives him from another, and all abominate him.

'Aeschylus', according to Herington, 'was influenced by what he had learned from the thinkers of Western Greece, and added a new dimension. To the play of the Gods he fused a play of the Elements.'[39] This conclusion is unsatisfactory. To say simply that the dramatist has incorporated a philosophical theory into the myth is to leave the motive and effect of this

[36] *PV* 136–40, 1043–53 (cf. 994), 1080–93.
[37] Griffith 1978: 115 tentatively makes five elements by distinguishing *aither* from the wind. But cf. Rösler 1970: 46–9. The role of the elements in *PV* cannot, of course, be explained by Hom. *Il.* 3.276–80 and Solon fr. 13.17–24, as Griffith seems to imply. This is not to say that the former passage was not a factor in shaping *PV* 88–92.
[38] Herington 1963.
[39] Herington 1963: 195–6. Similarly Rösler 1970: 50–5.

incorporation entirely obscure. But in fact, as I have maintained in the previous section, it is not even [11] necessary to suppose that Aeschylus was familiar with the work of Empedocles. The *Prometheia* is the dramatisation of a myth already shaped by the same mystical current of ideas that we find in Empedocles and elsewhere.[40] Along with other 'innovations' in the myth, the role of the elements in the play has a mystical rather than a purely philosophical origin.

In a discussion devoted largely to post-classical evidence for the role of the four elements in the mysteries (e.g. Apul. *Met.* 11.23 *per omnia vectus elementa*, 'borne through all the elements') Samson Eitrem suggests that Empedocles' conception of the elements was influenced by mystic doctrine.[41] Although this is no more than a hypothesis, the case for it is stronger than Eitrem seems to have realised.

The fallen *daimon* (B 115) is required by the 'oracle of Necessity' (Ἀνάγκης χρῆμα) to be born in all manner of mortal beings for 30,000 years, exchanging one hard path of life for another; for (γάρ) he is pursued from the *aither* to the sea, from there to the earth, then to the rays of the sun and back to the maelstroms (δῖναι) of the *aither*.[42] This idea may be expressed by B 117, also from the *Katharmoi*, in which Empedocles claims to have been a boy (κοῦρος), a girl (κόρη), a bush, a bird and a fish. Whence did Empedocles derive it? Perhaps the closest parallel, despite some obvious discrepancies, is the view of metempsychosis ascribed by Herodotus (2.123) to the Egyptians. He records the view that the Egyptians were the first to say that the soul of man is immortal and that on the death of the body 'it enters ever again into a different creature. When it has passed through them all – land animals, sea animals and birds', it returns to a human body, the whole round taking 3,000 years. He adds that this idea is held by some Greeks, whom he says he does not want to name, as their own. This reticence may be to avoid disclosing ἀπόρρητα ('what must not be spoken');[43] and elsewhere (2.81) he associates Greek mysteries with the Egyptians. In fact the gold leaves, for example, do indeed betray Egyptian influence.[44] Or it may be, on the other hand, because the Egyptians do not seem to have had a doctrine of [12] metempsychosis, that at 2.123 Herodotus is projecting

40 As Pohlenz 1954: 31 points out, Prometheus must have been a Titan before 'Aeschylus'.

41 Eitrem 1926 and 1927 (see esp. 45–55). For further post-classical passages see Griffiths 1975 on Apul. *Met.* 11.23.

42 Cf. Prometheus looking forward to Ἀνάγκης στερραῖς δίναις (*PV* 1052).

43 Burkert 1972: 126 n. 38. Cf. Hdt. 2.47.2, 2.61.1, 2.170–1.

44 E.g. in the dead 'dry' suppliant's need for water; material in Zuntz 1971: 370–6.

Greek mystic belief onto foreigners.[45] Furthermore, we know from Plato that reincarnation was taught in Greek mysteries (*Leg.* 10.870d–e; cf. *Meno* 81a). Taken together, all this suggests that the idea of the immortal soul passing from one cosmological element to another has its origin not in philosophy but in mysteries; that is to say, that something like the experience of the initiand of Isis in Apuleius, *per omnia vectus elementa*, was taught or enacted in Greek mysteries, perhaps with an oriental origin,[46] in the classical period. We may add that even the gold leaves, if our earlier interpretation is correct, imply a passage of the immortal heavenly race (γένος οὐράνιον) from the sky, by the agency of fire, to beneath the earth and thence presumably to the ends of the earth. Partly because of the reticence of Herodotus and Plato, it is difficult to be more specific about the identity of the 'Greek mysteries' in question. Certainly the term 'mysteries' is not meant to imply a uniform phenomenon. But it does seem unlikely that the cluster of ideas with which we are concerned was confined to a single cult in a single place. Our knowledge of the mysteries in general reveals broad similarities even between mysteries belonging to different deities.

This hypothesis is supported by two other features, which may appear merely fantastical, of the passage of the fallen *daimon* in the fragments of Empedocles' *Katharmoi*. The first is the robing of the fallen *daimones* in an alien garment of flesh (B 126 σαρκῶν ἀλλογνῶτι περιστέλλουσα χιτῶνι), to which B 148 ἀμφιβρότην χθόνα may also refer. The assumption by the initiand of new clothing is a well-known feature of initiation; most of the evidence for it in the mysteries is late, but there is some from the fifth century.[47] In Empedocles the entry of the *daimon* into the alien mortal state is imagined in terms of the initiand's adoption of a strange and novel garment in the rite of passage.[48] *[13]*

2. Pherecydes. At this point I must make a brief digression into the fragments of Pherecydes of Syros (sixth century), in which we find another example of an event of physical creation being envisaged as the donning of a robe on a ritual occasion: *Chthoniē* ('Earth') puts on the robe, decorated

[45] As stated by Burkert 1972: 126.

[46] West 1971 argues for an oriental origin for certain beliefs about the elements (36–40, 94, 173–5, 223–4).

[47] Seaford 1981a: 259; for later evidence see e.g. West 1983: 27.

[48] Cf. the Orphic/Pythagorean notion of the body as the garment of the soul: Zuntz 1971: 405. Cf. also *Orph. fr.* 238K = 538 + 541B (a costume used in the rites of Dionysos and representing sun, stars and ocean): Eisler 1910: 106 and 1925: 283.

with the earth and its surroundings, given to her by her husband, Zas, on the third day of marriage (the day of the *anakalypteria*) and thereby becomes Earth.[49] Pherecydes was also said to have been the first to believe in the immortality of the soul and metempsychosis;[50] and according to Porphyry (*De antr. nymph.* 31 = DK 7 B 6) he spoke of 'caverns, ditches, caves, doors and gates', meaning in a riddling manner[51] the passage of souls to and from earthly existence. A clue to the origin of this concept is provided by a passage in the *Phaedo*, where Socrates infers from the rites and ceremonies practised here on earth (ἀπὸ τῶν ὁσίων τε καὶ νομίμων τῶν ἐνθάδε τεκμαιρόμενος λέγω) that the way to Hades has many forks and windings.[52] Socrates' idea of the passage of the soul to the next world derives from ritual; and so, I think, does Pherecydes'.[53] This is hardly surprising, as we know that the passage of the soul to the underworld was given expression in the mysteries,[54] an expression which may well have involved the caves, ditches and gates listed by Pherecydes.[55] This brings us to the second feature drawn *[14]* from the mysteries in the progress of Empedocles' fallen *daimon*: the robing in flesh seems to have taken place in a cave.[56]

3. **Heraclitus**. This is not the place to discuss the vexed question of whether the *Katharmoi* coheres with the rest of Empedocles' philosophy. There may be, as with Parmenides, a disjunction between his mystical vision and his cosmology.[57] With our next source, Heraclitus, on the other hand, the two appear to be integrated.

49 West 1971: 15–20.

50 References in West 1971: 25.

51 αἰνιττόμενος. 'Porphyry means that when Pherecydes speaks of souls going through gates, etc., we should attach a symbolic value to the physical structures' (West 1971: 25). See also n. 87 below.

52 Pl. *Phd.* 108a; Proclus (*In R.* 1.85.1–16 Kroll) derives this picture in the *Phaedo* ἀπὸ τῶν θυσίων καὶ τῶν πατρίων θεσμῶν ('i.e. Eleusiniorum' Kern, *Orph. fr.* 221).

53 For other examples of his imagery deriving from Greek ritual see West 1971: 68–75. The same may be true of his *cosmogonic* μυχοί.

54 See e.g. Burkert 1985: 437 on the Hipponian gold leaf; Festugière 1972: 60–1; Thomson 1966 on Aesch. *Cho.* 935–71.

55 Gates: cf. e.g. Plut. *De prof. virt.* 81e; Apul. *Met.* 11.23; ditches (βόθροι): cf. perhaps the βόθρος in the Anaktoron of the mysteries at Samothrace (Cole 1984: 27–8) or the mud of Plut. fr. 178, etc. (see Thomson 1966 on Aesch. *Cho.* 935–971). Caves: numerous examples (mostly Dionysiac) given by Boyancé 1960–1; Festugière 1972: 382 ff.; Burkert 1972: 151–2 (Pythagoras); at Eleusis Mylonas 1961: 99–100 associates a sixth-century cave shrine of Pluto with the mention of πύλαι Ἀίδαο at Eleusis in *Hymn. Orph.* 18.12 (Quandt); and cf. Dio Chrys. *Or.* 12.33 μυεῖσθαι παραδοὺς εἰς μυστικόν τινα μυχόν (Selden; μῦθον UBM; οἶκον P) (of Attic mysteries, probably the Eleusinian). Prometheus imprisoned in a cave: Arrian *Anab.* 5.3.2, *Ind.* 5.11.

56 B 120 ἠλύθομεν τόδ' ὑπ' ἄντρον ὑπόστεγον; Zuntz 1971: 254–5.

57 Parmenides and mysteries: e.g. Feyerabend 1984.

In the first quarter of the twentieth century it was argued, with considerable exaggeration, that the content of Heraclitus' philosophy was closely related to, and derived from, the Orphic mysteries.[58] A generation later it was demonstrated that the antithetical style of Heraclitus is hieratic, having its origins in the liturgical style that is found, for example, in the Eleusinian mysteries, and that his philosophy is presented in the manner of the Orphic *hieroi logoi* and the *legomena* of the Eleusinian mysteries.[59] These two lines of argument, one concerning content and the other form, were pursued independently of each other. Then in 1978 was published the well-known group of fifth-century inscriptions, on three small pieces of bone, from Olbia in south Russia (GJ App. 1).[60] Apart from a few squiggles, designs and individual letters, they contain the words ἀλήθεια, ψυχή, Διό(νυσος), Ὀρφικ[οί?], and three phrases: βίος θάνατος βίος ('life death life'), εἰρήνη πόλεμος ('peace war') and ἀλήθεια ψεῦδος ('truth lie'). The subject matter – truth (presumably revealed), the soul, life and death, Dionysos, Orphic(s?) – is what we would [15] expect of mystery cult,[61] while the antithetical phrases provide striking confirmation of the view that the style of Heraclitus originates in the mysteries. The alternative is to suppose that the mystics of Olbia were deeply influenced by the writings of Heraclitus. Such influence seems unlikely and, even were it so, would require an explanation – most obviously the mystic form and content of Heraclitus' *logos*. Even the revisers of Kirk and Raven's *The Presocratic Philosophers*, which is typical of modern treatments in excluding the mysteries from discussion of Heraclitus (except insofar as Heraclitus mentions them himself), have felt obliged by the Olbia discoveries to acknowledge in two footnotes the possibility of their influence on him.[62]

This does not mean, despite the appearance of Ὀρφικ(οί?) on the bone plate, that the arguments of Nestle and Macchioro must be resurrected. Their only contribution was to record the mystic provenance of Heraclitus' ideas of life and death. Macchioro developed the point in a false direction by attempting to explain a number of the fragments (notably DK B 52,

[58] Nestle 1905; Macchioro 1922. Cf. also e.g. Pfleiderer 1886. Most recently, Battegazzore 1979 has stressed the importance of the mysteries for understanding frr. B 1, 26 and 125.

[59] Cornford 1952: 113; Thomson 1953 and 1961: 273–5; Guthrie 1962: 425 n. 1. Cf. the autonomy which Heraclitus gives his discourse (*logos*): West 1971: 127.

[60] See e.g. West 1983: 17–19 and 1982: 19, where he suggests that the zigzag symbol may represent lightning.

[61] See e.g. West 1983: 18, who suggests that the numerous bone plates were membership tokens, expressing participation in common sacrifice. Cf. Hdt. 4.79.

[62] Kirk et al. 1983: 209 n. 1, 210 n. 1. There is still a tendency to assume implicitly that, except when they speak of deities, the Presocratics derive their doctrines largely from observing nature.

53 and 62) by reference to the myth of Zagreus. Much of the evidence he adduced is too late to be valuable, and the entire hypothesis is crudely formulated.[63] The case needs to be restated in a more acceptable form.

For Heraclitus the soul is composed, in part at least, of fire[64] and survives death.[65] Because (B 30) the world is an ever-living (ἀείζωον) fire, kindling in measures and going out in measures, the immortality of the soul would appear to be associated in some way with its fiery nature.[66] Heraclitus does speak of 'death' for souls (B 36 ψυχῇσιν θάνατος ὕδωρ γενέσθαι). But there is of course no contradiction here, as is sometimes supposed,[67] with the soul's immortality. 'Death' is not a ceasing-to-be but a transformation: compare B 30, [16] and Philo, *De aet. mundi* 21: '[Heraclitus] defines death not as total destruction, but as transformation into a different element'; and the cycle of transformations will bring the soul through its transformations into water, earth and water back to soul again (B 36).[68] Mortality is a transformation undergone by the immortal. Hence B 62 'immortals are mortal, mortals are immortal, living their death, dying their life', and B 88 'as the same thing there exists in us life and death, waking and sleeping, young and old. For these things change into those things, and those change back into these.' Somebody may be awake and conscious as a mortal but asleep and unconscious as an immortal, old as a mortal but young as an immortal – or vice versa.[69]

Some souls, apparently the predominantly fiery ones, appear to avoid even the 'death' of becoming water[70] and are perhaps united after 'death' with the aetherial fire. What distinguishes better portions after death (B 25; cf. B 136, 24) is not immortality – for that is in a sense common to all – but purity[71] and probably also continuity of consciousness. As one might expect from the association of soul and life with fire, diminution

[63] E.g. Macchioro 1922: 121: 'In reality the relation [between Heraclitus' philosophy and 'Orphism'] is one of identity, since Heraclitianism and Orphism are two different aspects of a single and unique impulse.'

[64] B 36 (cf. 31), 117, 118; Kirk et al. 1983: 203–4; Guthrie 1962: 466; cf. West 1971: 150.

[65] B 27, 98; cf. B 63.

[66] Guthrie 1962: 466; Kirk et al. 1983: 208.

[67] E.g. by Guthrie 1962: 476.

[68] Hence perhaps B 45 ψυχῆς πείρατα ἰὼν οὐκ ἂν ἐξεύροιο ... Cf *Orph. fr.* 226K = 437B ἔστιν ὕδωρ ψυχῇ θάνατος.

[69] See nn. 71 and 72 below; also Pind. fr. 131b3–4 εὕδει δὲ πρασσόντων μελέων, ἀτὰρ εὑδόντεσσιν ἐν πολλοῖς ὀνείροις | δείκνυσι τερπνῶν ἐφέρποισαν χαλεπῶν τε κρίσιν (i.e. his fate in the next world): see Thomson 1966: 82–3.

[70] B 25, 63, 136; Kirk et al. 1983: 207–8; Guthrie 1962: 481.

[71] Particularly if we can trust the versified B 136 ψυχαὶ ἀρηΐφατοι καθερώτεραι [sic] ἢ ἐνὶ νούσοις (cf. West 1971: 152 n. 2). See also the mystic idea of death as purification (material in Macchioro 1922: 113).

of the fiery element in the soul is caused by sleep or drunkenness,[72] both of which are states in which consciousness is diminished.[73] The 'dry' soul is not only best (ἀρίστη) but also wisest (σοφωτάτη) (B118). In B 63, … ἐπανίστασθαι καὶ φύλακας γίνεσθαι ἐγερτὶ ζώντων καὶ νεκρῶν ('they rise up and become wakeful guardians of the living and the dead'), a key word is ἐγερτί.[74] [17]

Recalling the mystic pattern of our earlier discussion, we find an analogy with the Heraclitean scheme in three points. First, a human being is a mortal who is also immortal (Titan, *daimon*, *theos*) and an immortal who is mortal, 'death' being a transformation undergone by the immortal. Furthermore, the phrase βίος θάνατος βίος ('life death life') on the Olbia bone plate constitutes a clear link[75] between the mysteries and Heraclitus in both style and substance, whether it signifies the progress of the immortal in us through 'death' (i.e. what we mortals call 'life') back to immortal life or (from our mortal perspective) the progress of the mortal through death to another life[76] or (predicatively) the identity of life and death (cf. B 62, quoted above).[77]

Second, there are better and worse fates after death. The better fate means escape from the cycle of becoming and is associated not only with purity[78] but also apparently with continuity of consciousness,[79] which may depend on abstention from a certain source of water. Similarly, in Plato's Myth of Er the souls must, as a prelude to reincarnation, drink of the waters of the rivers of Forgetfulness (ὁ Ἀμέλης ποταμός) on the plain of Lethe (Pl. *Resp.* 10.621a), and on the gold leaves from Petelia and Pharsalos the dead man is instructed to avoid a certain spring (presumably of Forgetfulness) and to drink instead 'from the lake of memory' (GJ 2.9 τῆς Μνημοσύνης ἀπὸ λίμνης; cf. 25.4) and then (GJ 2.11) 'you will rule among the other

72 B 26, 117; A 16 (Sext. Emp. *Adv. math.* 7.129); Kirk et al. 1983: 205–6.

73 See esp. B 117, the drunkard 'who does not see where he is going, since his soul is drenched' (οὐκ ἐπαΐων ὅκη βαίνει, ὑγρὴν τὴν ψυχὴν ἔχων); also B 1, 73.

74 It has also been suggested, and firmly denied, that Heraclitus may have believed that psychic survival as aetherial fire could be perpetual: Guthrie 1962: 481; West 1971: 188; cf. Kirk et al. 1983: 208.

75 Clearer than Sext. Emp. *Pyr.* 3.230, where the view attributed to Heraclitus, that when we live our souls are buried within us but when we die our souls revive and live, may be later interpretation influenced by mystic doctrine.

76 West 1982: 18–19.

77 West 1982: 18 notes the possibility that the first βίος was a later addition.

78 *Katharmoi* of Empedocles and DK 31 B 115.3 μιήνῃ; gold leaves: line 1 of GJ 5–7; etc.

79 Compare Empedocles, who says (DK 31 B 112.4) 'I go about as an immortal god, no longer mortal …' (ἐγὼ δ' ὑμῖν θεὸς ἄμβροτος, οὐκέτι θνητὸς πωλεῦμαι …) and remembers previous existences (B 117).

heroes' (ἔπειτ' ἄ[λλοισι μεθ'] ἡρώεσσιν ἀνάξει[ς), having escaped presumably from the cycle of reincarnation (cf. GJ 5.5).[80]

The third similarity with the Heraclitean schema is the importance, in our earlier hypothesis, of the cosmological elements in the cyclical passage of the soul. In Empedocles the fallen *daimon* is tossed around the four cosmological elements (B 115.10–13), whereas in Heraclitus the immortal (fire) in man is identified with one of the (three or four) elements, and its circular passage is one not *[18]* of rejection by the other elements but of transformation into them while simultaneously retaining in a sense its identity as fire.[81] Nevertheless, it seems that even in Heraclitus the soul is felt as subject to the elemental process and therefore as in a sense distinct from it. The immortal is elemental (fire) but also personal (fiery soul). B 66 πάντα γὰρ ... τὸ πῦρ ἐπελθὸν κρινεῖ καὶ καταλήψεται, if genuine, suggests fire as an agent of (punitive) transformation, especially perhaps for the watery soul; and together with B 64 'Thunderbolt (Κεραυνός) steers all things' may be compared with the thunderbolt as a punishment for the erring immortal in mystic doctrine. Clement reports that Heraclitus threatened mystics and others with what happens after death (τὰ μετὰ θάνατον) and prophesied fire for them.

Men (or some men) are identified by Heraclitus with the *daimones* of Hesiodic tradition: B 63 '... they rise up and become the wakeful guardians of the living and the dead' (ἔνθα δ' ἐόντι (ἐν θεοῦ δέοντι West) ἐπανίστασθαι καὶ φύλακας γίνεσθαι ἐγερτὶ ζώντων καὶ νεκρῶν) is generally agreed to be based on Hes. *Op.* 121–3 'but when he concealed this [golden] race beneath the earth, they are [now] *daimones*, guardians of mortal men' (αὐτὰρ ἐπεὶ δὴ τοῦτο γένος κατὰ γαῖαν κάλυψεν, τοὶ μὲν δαίμονές εἰσι ... φύλακες θνητῶν ἀνθρώπων). Here again, as with Empedocles and the gold leaves, we find a synthesis of a mystic pattern of belief with one of the few amenable passages of the Hesiodic tradition. For Heraclitus it seems that post-mortem existence (or persistence?) as a *daimon* requires a fiery (or daemonic?) soul in life, and this in turn depends on character and behaviour:[82] 'Character is *daimon* for man' (B 119 ἦθος ἀνθρώπῳ δαίμων).

We are faced, then, on the one hand with a linguistic style and mode of presentation derived apparently from mysteries and on the other hand with

[80] Cf. also the material in Rohde 1925: 543 and n. 151; Burkert 1985: 437.
[81] Kirk et al. 1983: 204; frr. B 36, 31, 30. Air is missing in B 36 and 31, though included in B 76: see Guthrie 1962: 453.
[82] Kirk et al. 1983: 207–8.

a content analogous to contemporary mystic doctrine. Taken together, all this suggests mysteries as an important source, though not necessarily of course the only one, of Heraclitus' philosophy.[83] As in the previous section, the point has been to identify a pattern of mystic belief rather than a particular sect. To complete the argument it remains to consider Heraclitus' declared attitude to the mysteries.[19]

'There awaits men when they die what they neither hope for nor expect' (B 27). Clement, in his *Protrepticus* (2.22.2, p. 16 Stählin), claims that Heraclitus directed this observation νυκτιπόλοις, [μάγοις,][84] βάκχοις, λήναις, μύσταις. Clement continues: 'he threatens these people with what happens after death, he prophesies fire for these people', and then, in words generally agreed to be Heraclitus' (B 14), 'the mystery rites practised among men are conducted in an unholy manner'. According to Kirk, Raven and Schofield, this 'implies that mysteries would not be utterly worthless if they were correctly celebrated'. Similarly Guthrie: 'Heraclitus was not hostile to initiations and Dionysiac *orgia* as such, but deplored the fact that they were carried out without any understanding of their true significance.'[85]

Further light on the matter comes from consideration of a traditional feature of mysteries: the deliberately confusing or riddling manner in which the secrets were revealed to the initiands.[86] That is why Heraclitus says that his *logos*, which he presents with riddling obscurity and as a mystic discourse, is incomprehensible to those who hear it for the first time.[87] From here it is a short step to the idea that mysteries might have a significance unrevealed even by the ritual revelations. This idea is in fact a philosophical commonplace. The mystery, because of its essential obscurity, can be interpreted as referring to something not revealed in the ceremonies. Furthermore, the uncertainty created in the mysteries seems at least sometimes to have surrounded revelations about the next world.[88] An example

[83] This means that Clem. Alex. *Strom.* 6.2.27.1 (p. 443 Stählin) 'I pass over in silence Heraclitus the Ephesian, who took most of his material from Orpheus' should not be simply dismissed (cf. Seaford 1981a: 260). See also the case made by West 1971: 11–13 that Heraclitus was only in a limited sense a philosopher.

[84] For deletion of μάγοις see Marcovich 1967: 466.

[85] Kirk et al. 1983: 209; Guthrie 1962: 476, based on B 14, 15, 68, 69.

[86] Seaford 1981a: 254–5; the confusion of the initiand was sometimes described as πτόησις (256 with n. 41; add Aristid. Quint. 3.25): this may underlie B 87 βλὰξ ἄνρθωπος ἐπὶ παντὶ λόγῳ ἐπτοῆσθαι φιλεῖ.

[87] B 1 ἀκούσαντες τὸ πρῶτον should be translated 'first', not (as it usually is) 'once'. Cf. *PDerveni* XX.2–3 = §66K οὐ γὰρ οἷόν τε ἀκοῦσαι ὁμοῦ καὶ μαθεῖν τὰ λεγόμενα (see below). See Thomson 1961: 273–5.

[88] Seaford 1981a: 254–5, 261–2 (where the omitted n. 84 should read 'F. Matz in *Ak. Wiss. Lit. Mainz* 1963, n. 5, 141 ff.; Nilsson 1957, 122 ff.'); cf. Pl. *Gorg.* 493a–b.

which bears on our argument is the remark of Plutarch that when the wise (οἱ σοφώτεροι) tell of the dismemberment and rebirth of Dionysos they are in fact telling riddles referring to his transformation into winds, water, earth, stars and the generation of plants and animals: this conception of the passion of Dionysos may well derive from its narration in the [20] mysteries.[89] Plato remarks that when the founders of the mysteries spoke about the next world they spoke in a riddling manner, their real meaning being that it is philosophers who are the initiated to be rewarded there (*Phd.* 69c). In a similar way Heraclitus seems to have believed that the mysteries as celebrated provide an inadequate conception of post-mortem experience. The truth about that experience is contained, of course, in his *logos*, which resembles a mystic doctrine in both form and content, differing from it in respects which we cannot recover (a greater degree of systematic abstraction? the denial of a permanent refuge from the cosmic process?[90]).

This discussion of Heraclitus has shown that, as with Empedocles, his doctrine of the elements and their relationship to the immortal soul appears to be influenced to some extent by mystic doctrine. It is, I would argue, to this mystic pattern of belief, rather than to Presocratic philosophy, that we must ascribe the role of the elements in the *Prometheia*. But before we return to the drama, the argument can be consolidated by pointing out that we are now in a position to understand more fully two texts of the fourth century, both found in graves.

4. The Derveni Papyrus. Here we must bear in mind the provisional nature of the available text.[90a] This 'commentary' on some Orphic verses combines a physical system of an Ionian type with a 'less rationalistic kind of concern with religious enlightenment', as remarked by West, who notes the oddity of the combination and explains it by the hypothesis that the writer was an (Orphic) initiate introducing his fellow initiates 'to a Diogenean cosmology in which he had been instructed elsewhere'.[91] But why should he want to do this? And why was the text placed on a funeral pyre, presumably to accompany the dead to the next world?

89 Seaford 1981a: 255. See also e.g. n. 50 above.

90 Note Clement's τούτοις μαντεύεται τὸ πῦρ. B 15 (Dionysos, unknown to his worshippers, is the same as Hades) may perhaps imply an absolute interpenetration of life and death which would preclude the mystic victory of the former over the latter. See in general Babut 1975.

90a See Postscript. References are to the *editio princeps* (Kouremenos et al. 2006), with paragraph numbers from Richard Janko's text in Kotwick 2017.

91 West 1983: 81, who discusses the text in detail.

In view of our argument so far, cosmology should not be regarded as an odd, alien kind of instruction for mystic initiates.[92] The Orphic [21] poem which the commentator expounds is said to be riddling (αἰνιγματώδης). For example, there are riddling references to cosmological elements: Zeus is interpreted as air (*PDerveni* XVII.3–6 = §53K); Moira as wind (τὸ πνεῦμα) (XVIII.2–3 = §57K); Demeter, Hera and Rhea as Earth (XXII.7–10 = §76K; cf. *PV* 209–10); Okeanos is said to be air, and air Zeus (XXIII.3 = §80K). We are reminded of the esoteric references attached to the names of the gods, not only in other Orphic texts but also in Heraclitus.[93] It is not only the mystic text which has for the Derveni commentator a hidden meaning. The Eumenides, to whom initiates sacrifice, are in fact souls (VI.8–10 = §18K). People are overcome by pleasure and remain ignorant of what is to come in the next world (V.6–10 = §15K). In a passage apparently from an unknown source quoted by the commentator with approval[94] it is said that people do not understand what is said in ritual when they first hear it (XX.2–3 = §66K οὐ γὰρ οἷόν τε ἀκοῦσαι ὁμοῦ καὶ μαθεῖν τὰ λεγόμενα; similarly Heracl. B 1; see also n. 86 above).

Along with this thematic similarity with Heraclitus there has also been observed a similarity of language. Our commentator even seems to know the works of Heraclitus, because at one point he appears to quote him (IV.5–10 = §12K).[95] At the same time and despite criticism of some aspects of cult, the text seems to be an initiate's exposition, of value to the dead, of an Orphic poem, and so is contained within the framework of mystic doctrine to an extent which our fragmentary evidence does not allow us to say of Heraclitus. Here then, as at Olbia, is another link between the mysteries and the style and content of the philosophy of Heraclitus. The problem of the precise relationship with Heraclitus is similar to the case of the Olbian plates. Some or all of the similarity may derive not from direct influence but from the shared tradition of mystic cosmology: truths about the cosmological elements and the next world are contained in mystic texts and mystic ritual, but in a riddling manner. Any direct influence is best attributed to the recognised mystic form and content of Heraclitus' *logos*,

[92] See also now Feyerabend 1984: 21–2, on Parmenides: 'das richtige Reden, die feste Begründung, ja die *philosophia* gehörten gerade dem bacchischen Kult des Dionysos. Seelenreinigungslehre …, Ontologie …, und Naturwissenschaft … standen eng zusammen.'

[93] B 15 (pun on Ἀΐδης?) 32 (pun on ζῆν?); cf. B 5 (praying to images indicates ignorance of deity). Cf. e.g. *Orph. frr.* 21a, 55, 56, 75, 237 (cf. Heracl. B 67), 297, 298K. West 1983: 79 compares the identification of gods with elements in Empedocles and others.

[94] Rusten 1985: 138–9. The paragraphos before line 11 precedes 'a feeble prose paraphrase of the last few lines'.

[95] Cf. Burkert 1983a.

transmitted perhaps by the followers of Heraclitus (Ἡρακλείτειοι). The Derveni text also called itself a *logos* (XXV.11 = §91K). [22]

5. Gold Leaf GJ 4 from Thurii. This text, which contained inside it leaf GJ 3, is puzzling by virtue of its thematic difference from its fellows.[96] It is also, unfortunately, so obscure that even where it can be read Zuntz can extract only two themes from it. Of these, one is the prayer to her mother uttered by Kore when abducted by Plouton; the other is the significant part (whatever it is) played in the text by fire, air and (probably) earth (but without any discernible mention of water). It might be added that it also seems possible to detect the ideas of the mixture of elements, of the activity of elements as deities and of conflict and perhaps also transformation between them.[97] Although little else can sensibly be said about the content of the text, it does present us with a clear case of a mystic text, one of a series of tomb texts whose conception of the next world derives in part at least from mystic ritual,[98] in which an eschatological myth associated especially with the mysteries is combined with a dominant concern about relations between three at least of the (divine) elements.

6. Euripides' *Bacchae*. A brief reference might be made, finally, to a third text of the classical period, the words of Teiresias to Pentheus in Euripides' *Bacchae* (274–85), in which Demeter and Dionysos are associated, in the benefits they have brought humankind, with the (Ionian) abstract opposition of the Dry and the Wet (τὸ ξηρόν and τὸ ὑγρόν). Much of what Pentheus is told elsewhere in the play is, as I have shown elsewhere, derived from the mysteries.[99] It may perhaps, in the light of our argument, be a mistake to regard what Teiresias says here as an exception, spoken from a perspective ('intellectual', or 'modernist' – Dodds 1960: 104) outside the mystic cult of Dionysos.[100]

This wide-ranging section now requires a conclusion. In Empedocles the immortal *daimones*, of which Empedocles himself is one, are punished by being tossed around the cosmological elements in a circle; [23] they also find themselves in the underworld and in a cave before their eventual

[96] Exposition in Zuntz 1971: 344–54.

[97] In line 5 αερι πυρ μεμ(ειγμενον)?, 1 Δημητρος ηττατι, 2 νικαι?, 4 παντα δαμαστα? ... βροντα δε παντ' ε(π' α)μοιβης?; 8 Δημητηρ πυρ Ζευ, etc. [Readings sometimes differ from GJ.]

[98] Seaford 1981a: 254.

[99] Seaford 1981a.

[100] Several points of similarity with mystic (notably 'Orphic') discourse (esp. at 275–9, 283, 284, 287, 289, 292) are noted by Gallistl 1979.

restoration from exile.[101] An important source for this pattern of events is mystic doctrine, perhaps as actually expounded in the celebration of the mysteries. This hypothesis coheres with the manner in which the cosmological elements appear, in various other texts, in a mystic form or context. The stages of the punishment are described by Empedocles in a manner influenced by a passage in Hesiod about exiled deity: Emped. B 115.12 ἄλλος δ' ἐξ ἄλλου δέχεται, στυγέουσι δὲ πάντες ('one after another receives him, and all abominate him') has been compared with Hes. *Theog.* 800 ἄλλος δ' ἐξ ἄλλου δέχεται χαλεπώτερος ἄθλος ('after the other another more difficult trial receives him'). In the *Prometheia* Prometheus is at first fettered to a lonely rock, where he makes his appeal to the cosmological elements. Second, and as a worse penalty (314, 1014–16), he is cast down into Tartarus by the thunderbolt of Zeus, to the accompaniment of a confusion of the cosmological elements, and the whirlings of Necessity, in defiance of which Prometheus proclaims his immortality: πάντως ἐμέ γ' οὐ θανατώσει (1043–53). Third, he emerges again to the light, is released and presumably is restored to Olympus. If the cosmological elements are borrowed from contemporary philosophy, it is a pointless and isolated borrowing. In fact the passage of the immortal through the hostile elements is part of a mystic pattern of ideas which emerged, in various forms, into Presocratic philosophy on the one hand and into the *Prometheia* on the other. The role of the elements must be added to those other features of the punishment and restoration of Prometheus which were described in the first section as originating in mystic doctrine.

3. The Crowning of Prometheus

The origin of the crown (στέφανος) is associated with Prometheus in a curious manner. Athenaeus (15.672f) reports that Prometheus accepted the crown from Zeus, after his release, as a voluntary, painless requital for having stolen fire. This suggests the idea of the crown as a kind of painless binding, an idea confirmed a little later (15.674d) when Athenaeus reports that Aeschylus in the *Prometheus Unbound* says that we wear crowns in honour of Prometheus 'in requital for his bond' (ἀντίποινα τοῦ ἐκείνου δεσμοῦ), and that in the *Sphinx* he describes the crown as [24] 'the best kind of bond on the basis of the story of Prometheus' (δεσμῶν ἄριστος

[101] The relation between elements, underworld and cave does not emerge from the fragmentary evidence.

ἐκ Προμηθέως λόγου).[102] At the end of the trilogy, then, as the aetiology of the crown, Prometheus wore it as a voluntary, painless alternative to his bond (δεσμός) – he moves from one kind of binding to another. But the conception of the crown as a (desirable) bond is a curious one and seems quite alien to most of the contexts in which it is worn (victory, symposia, etc.). Indeed, the Prometheus story is regarded in this respect as exceptional by Blech in his exhaustive study of the 'Kranz bei den Griechen'.[103]

There is, however, I think another example, missed by Blech, in the Thurii gold leaves: GJ 5.5–6 'I have flown off the circle of heavy grief and misery, and I have attained the desirable crown with swift feet' (κύκλου δ' ἐξέπταν βαρυπενθέος ἀργαλέοιο, | ἱμερτοῦ δ' ἐπέβαν στεφάνου ποσὶ καρπαλίμοισι). It seems that the στέφανος, worn by initiand and corpse, expresses here that release of the dead initiate which had been celebrated with these deliberately enigmatic formulae in his initiation into the mysteries. Whatever the primary reference of κύκλος (see n. 22 above), I detect a riddling contrast between two kinds of circle, the undesirable (βαρυπενθής etc.), imprisoning circle, and the desirable (ἱμερτός) circle of the crown. (That a crown might be imagined as a κύκλος is evident, if evidence be necessary, from Orph. *Arg.* 325 κύκλους ἐρόεντας ἐλαίης.[104]) The dead suppliant moves from one circle to another. The conception in the *Prometheia* is not identical, but it is sufficiently similar in its oddity – the resemblance of the στέφανος to that from which it celebrates release – to suggest a mystic provenance. This interpretation is supported by the fact that this aetiology of the στέφανος is associated[105] with an aetiology of finger rings: Prometheus wore a ring (of stone or iron and stone) as a mimetic memorial of his bondage. The point is that this too seems to have a mystic origin. The mystic initiates of Samothrace were given iron rings to wear, presumably to mark their transition.[106] Pausanias [25] relates that at Thebes Demeter entrusted the mysteries to one of the Kabeiroi called Prometheus (and his son Aitnaios),[107] and the Kabeiroi were also of course associated with the mysteries of Samothrace.

[102] Aesch. frr. 202 and 235; [Probus] *ad* Verg. *Ecl.* 6.42, etc. (see Brelich 1970; West 1979: 144; Blech 1982: 385).

[103] Blech 1982: 373. Hence perhaps the misunderstanding in the garbled version at Hyg. *Poet. astr.* 2.15 (Prometheus could hardly claim *impune peccasse*!).

[104] Also Hom. *Il.* 13.736; *Hymn. Hom. Ap.* 410; Pind. *Ol.* 8.32.

[105] Hygin. *Astr.* 2.15; [Probus] *ad* Verg. *Ecl.* 6.42; Serv. *ad* Verg. *Ecl.* 6.42; Plin. *HN* 37.2; Isid. *Etym.* 19.32.1; Etruscan mirror depicted in Roscher 1884–1937: s.v. 'Prometheus' 3094 (Gerhard Taf. 138). Cf. Catull. 64.295.

[106] Welcker 1824: 51–2; Hemberg 1950: 110 n. 2; Cole 1984: 30, 115.

[107] 9.25.6. For the association of Kabeiroi with Titans see *RE* 23.1 (s.v. 'Prometheus'), 692–3.

To conclude. The mysteries bring their initiands through death-like suffering into a state in which they may count on joyful immortality. Thus, discontent with the world, which produces both the idea of life as a punishment and the hope of release, asserts, when expressed in mystic doctrine, that a human being is an immortal, suffering punishment which will eventually come to an end. World order as presented in the Hesiodic tradition explains the sufferings of humankind but offers no hope for the future; it does, however, provide the material for its own subversion, for it is built on the apparently unending exile and imprisonment of offending immortals, notably the Titans and Prometheus, and also provides an example of the restoration of an offending *daimon* from exile. So in mystic doctrine we find the sufferings of mortality imagined as the punishment of these offending Titans or *daimones*, who will eventually, after a cycle of reincarnations, be released by death, of which the transition embodied in initiation is a rehearsal.

Prometheus is a special case.[108] He is associated with the sufferings of humankind even in Hesiod, where he is responsible for their plight but is also permanently imprisoned for ensuring their material advance; and his eventual release, in the *Prometheia*, was probably accompanied by further benefit for humankind (Justice?).[109] His story has been shaped by the same pattern of mystic hope that released the other immortal losers of the *Theogony*. Whereas the penalty imposed on them for their ancient crude dissension is ended with the transition from sufferings endured in human form, the penalty endured by Prometheus for ensuring material advance for humankind is ended with his release and the transition of humankind to civilisation.[110] In the mysteries the transition of the initiands to joy was sometimes associated *[26]* with the imparting of the gifts of civilisation to humankind: at Eleusis, for example, with the revelation of an ear of reaped corn.[111] The story in the *Prometheia* reproduces, indirectly, the same association: the transition undergone in the mysteries or taught in mystic doctrine has been consciously or unconsciously projected, through

[108] Though compare the Capitoline sarcophagus (Roscher 1884–1937: s.v. 'Prometheus' 3107), on which the release of Prometheus is envisaged as analogous to the death of humankind.

[109] See Griffith 1983: 303; Lloyd-Jones 1971: 99–103.

[110] This distinction is in one respect transcended by the idea, implicit in Oppian, *Hal.* 5.1–10, that the resourcefulness of humankind derives from his Titanic origin.

[111] Called by Hippolytus (*Haer.* 5.8.39–40) 'the great and most wondrous and most perfect mystery seen there by initiates' (τὸ μέγα καὶ θαυμαστὸν καὶ τελειότατον ἐποπτικὸν ἐκεῖ μυστήριον) and 'among the Athenians the great, perfect light from the unportrayable one' (παρὰ Ἀθηναίοις ὁ παρὰ τοῦ ἀχαρακτηρίστου φωστὴρ τέλειος μέγας). See further Seaford 1984b: 41–3. Hence perhaps the idea of Orpheus as εὑρὼν ἀνθρώποις γράμματα καὶ σοφίην (Alcidamas, *Odysseus* 24).

the figure of Prometheus, onto the transition embodied in the acquisition of civilisation.[112]

POSTSCRIPT

On cosmology as mystic initiation in the Derveni Papyrus see Obbink 1997. For allegory and salvational physics in the Derveni Papyrus see Most 1997 and Betegh 2004: chapter 9. For mystery cult and philosophy in southern Italy see Kingsley 1995. For mystery cult and Heraclitus see Schefer 2000. For cosmogony and mystery cult in Pindar see Hardie 2000. For mystery cult generally see Burkert 1987. On 'Orphism' see Edmonds 2013. There are now full editions of the gold leaves (GJ) and of the Derveni Papyrus (Kouremenos et al. 2006; still worth consulting for the *apparatus criticus* is R. Janko, 'The Derveni Papyrus: an interim text', *ZPE* 141 (2002), 1–62; see also Kotwick 2017.

112 I am grateful to Martin West and Albert Henrichs for their helpful criticisms of this article.

CHAPTER 10

Sophocles and the Mysteries

Greek tragedy has much in common with the ritual of the mysteries. In both, an enactment of a myth of suffering, accompanied sometimes by lamentation and containing a reversal,[1] creates great emotion among a group of onlookers,[2] who may be envisaged as in some sense purified.[3] That the mysteries were an important factor in the genesis of tragedy seems to me on various grounds very likely,[4] but is difficult to prove. Beyond doubt on the other hand is that tragedy alludes to the mysteries. The tragedians sometimes aim to evoke in their audience, many of whom were initiated, the powerful emotions associated with mystic initiation. In Aristophanes' *Frogs* Aeschylus' prayer, at the start of his contest with Euripides, is to 'Demeter the nourisher of my soul. Make me worthy of your mysteries' (886–7). A tradition that Aeschylus was prosecuted for revealing secrets of the Eleusinian mysteries is first mentioned by Aristotle.[5] And it has been shown by George Thomson that the *Oresteia* frequently employs the imagery of the Eleusinian mysteries.[6] As for Euripides, his *Bacchae* dramatises the aetiological myth of the foundation of the Dionysiac mysteries at Thebes, and its action prefigures the mystic ritual at several points.[7] The aim of this chapter is to extend the argument to Sophocles, in particular to his *Electra* and *Ajax*. [*276*]

[1] Suffering: Burkert 1987: 75. Lamentation in the mysteries: Seaford 1994b: 319 nn. 159–61, 323 nn. 177–82. Lamentation by the audience of tragedy: Pl. *Phlb.* 48a5–6, *Resp.* 10.605c–606c. For the enactment of death (or descent to Hades) and reversal in the mysteries see below. For further exploration of the analogy see now Schlesier 1995.

[2] For the mysteries as spectacle (θέα) see Pl. *Phdr.* 250b; *Symp.* 210e; etc.: Riedweg 1987: 2–4, 22–8, 37–42; Seaford 1994b: 270 n. 154.

[3] Mystic initiation as purification: Pl. *Phdr.* 244e, 250c, *Resp.* 2.364e, 8.560d–e, *Phd.* 69c; Plut. *Mor.* 1105b. Purification in the Eleusinian mysteries: Richardson 1974: 22, 211–13; Dionysiac: Eur. *Bacch.* 72–7. Tragedy causing purification: Arist. *Poet.* 1449b27–8.

[4] Seaford 1994b: chapters 7 and 8. For the history of this idea see Schlesier 1995.

[5] *Eth. Nic.* 1111a9; Athenaeus (1.21e) reports the tradition that the dignity of the Eleusinian mysteries officials' costumes was invented by Aeschylus.

[6] Thomson 1966 on *Ag.* 36–7, 336, 522, 1050–2, *Cho.* 583–5, 935–71, 963–4.

[7] Seaford 1981a, 1987a. Note also Zeitlin 1989.

In Sophocles' *Electra* Elektra laments over an urn containing what she thinks to be the remains of Orestes, and then, recognising him as in fact alive and in her presence, calls him 'Oh dearest light (ὦ φίλτατον φῶς)[8] ... dead by devices but now by devices saved (μηχαναῖσι μὲν θανόντα, νῦν δὲ μηχαναῖς σεσωμένον)', and breaks into song: 'Oh births, births of bodies [i.e. Orestes][9] dearest to me (ἰὼ γοναί, γοναὶ σωμάτων ἐμοὶ φιλτάτων)'. Somewhat later, on recognising the *paidagogos*, she calls him 'Oh dearest light (ὦ φίλτατον φῶς), Oh only saviour (σωτήρ) of the house of Agamemnon, how did you come? Are you he who saved him and me from many sufferings?' (1354–6).

The same complex of ideas is to be found in the mysteries. The appearance of (torch)light in darkness marked the transition of the initiands from ignorance and suffering.[10] There are fifth-century indications that Eleusinian torchlight was identified with a deity – whether Dionysos-Iakchos[11] or Ploutos,[12] who were in the Eleusinian context also by this time, it seems, identified with each other.[13] From much later writers we hear of the enactment, in the Eleusinian mysteries, of the abduction of Kore, with a night-long search for her concluded by thanksgiving and the tossing of torches.[14] We also hear of the dismemberment and rebirth of Dionysos enacted or celebrated in some way in the Dionysiac mysteries.[15]

In the fourth century CE Firmicus Maternus (*Err. prof. rel.* 22) describes a nocturnal ritual in which lamentation over an image is ended with the bringing in of light and the announcement to the initiands that the god has been saved and they will have salvation out of suffering (θαρρεῖτε μύσται τοῦ θεοῦ σεσωμένου | ἔσται γὰρ ὑμῖν ἐκ πόνων σωτηρία); but we do not know in which mysteries occurred this transition from lamentation to salvation marked by light in the darkness. At Eleusis the similar

8 Soph. *El.* 1224. This does not mean (or merely mean), as is generally supposed, 'dearest day': cf. her next two utterances, and the same words used of the *paidagogos* at 1354; Eur. *Bacch.* 608–9, *HF* 531; etc.

9 σωμάτων does not refer (as is sometimes supposed) to Agamemnon.

10 Plut. fr. 178, *Mor.* 81e; Dio Chrys. 12.33; Hippol. *Haer.* 5.8; Firm. Mat. *Err. prof. rel.* 22; Richardson 1974: 26. That this goes back to the classical period is clear from Pl. *Phdr.* 250b3–6, 250d1 (Riedweg 1987: 47–52); Aesch. *Cho.* 961 (Thomson 1966 on 935–71); Pind. *Ol.* 2.53–67.

11 Ar. *Ran.* 342–3; Soph. *Ant.* 1146–52 (note schol. *ad loc.* κατὰ γάρ τινα μυστικὸν λόγον, τῶν ἀστέρων ἐστὶ χοραγός); cf. Eur. *Ion* 1074–81, *Bacch.* 608.

12 At the outset of Pindar's famous account of life after death: *Ol.* 2.53–83.

13 Richardson 1974: 319–20.

14 References and discussion in Richardson 1974: 24–6 and Mylonas 1961: 261–72.

15 Late texts cited in Seaford 1994b: 283 n. 15; fifth-century indications are the Athenian 'Lenäenvasen' (Seaford 1994b: 264–5) and Hdt. 2.171.

transition[16] was associated, it seems from our meagre evidence, not so much with [277] *re*birth[17] as with *birth*, the birth of a child. The Gnostic quoted by Hippolytus says that during the night the hierophant announces, to the accompaniment of a great fire (ὑπὸ πολλῷ πυρί), the birth of a sacred child to the goddess (ἱερὸν ἔτεκε Πότνια κοῦρον). It has been pointed out that this ceremony is reflected in the words of a Euripidean chorus at the temple of Demeter and Kore at Eleusis: ἔτεκες καὶ σύ ποτ' ὦ Πότνια κοῦρον (Eur. *Supp.* 54). The child born to Demeter was identified in particular with Ploutos, who as we have seen was early identified with Dionysos and Iakchos. And Ploutos, Dionysos and Iakchos were each identified with a light (or star) in fifth-century poetry.[18] For our purposes it is of interest that Sophocles himself describes the Eleusinian mysteries in words which, once again including the title Πότνια, link torchlight and the role of Demeter and Kore as child-nurses with the benefit of the mysteries for mortals: ... λαμπάσιν ἀκταῖς οὗ Πότνιαι σεμνὰ τιθηνοῦνται τέλη θνατοῖσιν (*OC* 1049–51).

What Elektra says evokes the emotions experienced in the mysteries, for it alludes to a mystic complex of ideas: lamentation, fictive ('by devices') death and 'saving' from death, the birth of a child, identification of the saviour with light, release from suffering. The 'birth' of Orestes is prefigured in the lamentation: when holding the urn that she supposes to contain Orestes' remains Elektra laments him as if he were a child, her own child (1143–7), 'a small bulk in a small vessel' (1142).[19]

There is more. Elektra claims that she would never forget, even in suffering, the sight of Orestes when he appeared (1285–7), and that 'since I saw you, I will not cease weeping for joy. For how might I cease, who saw you both dead and alive on this one journey? You have done to me unfathomable things' (1312–5). In both passages it is the *sight* of Orestes that has brought permanent happiness, just as it is a *sight* that brings permanent happiness to mystic initiates: for example, Sophocles himself says of the Eleusinian mysteries (fr. 837) 'Thrice blessed (τρισόλβιοι) are those

[16] Although the words σῴζειν and σωτηρία are not found associated with the mysteries in the classical period, we do frequently find as a central element in our meagre early evidence the idea that mystic ritual (Eleusinian and Dionysiac) releases the initiands from sufferings that afflict the uninitiated, especially in the next world: Soph. fr. 837 (quoted below); *Hymn. Hom. Dem.* 480–2; Pl. *Resp.* 2.365a, *Phdr.* 250b–c; the Pelinna gold leaves GJ 26a–b (quoted below); the gold leaf GJ 5.5–6. See also n. 45 below.

[17] Despite Koerte 1915; cf. Burkert 1987: 100.

[18] See nn. 10–12 above.

[19] Eur. *Bacch.* 966–70 also plays on the mother holding her dead adult child as if a baby, again in the context of (potential) mystic (re)birth: Seaford 1981a: 267–8.

mortals who having seen these rites (ταῦτα δερχθέντες τέλη) go to Hades. For only these are able to live there. The others have all bad things.'[20] The rare word τρισόλβιος has been found on the two funerary gold leaves (GJ 26a–b) from Pelinna published in 1987, in the line *νῦν* ἔθανες καὶ *νῦν* ἐγένου, τρισόλβιε, ἄματι τῷδε, almost certainly a formula of mystic initiation. Orestes, 'by devices dead but now by devices [278] saved' (1228–9), 'on this one journey dead and alive' (1314–15), resembles not only the deity of mystery cult but also the Pelinna initiate, who 'now died and now came into being on this day'.[21]

The next line of the Pelinna texts is εἰπεῖν Φερσεφόνᾳ σ' ὅτι Βάκχιος αὐτὸς ἔλυσε. These are mysteries involving both Persephone (Kore) and Dionysos. Dionysos-Iakchos and Kore are also central figures, along with Demeter, of the Eleusinian mysteries.[22] The interpenetration of mystery cults, whether it produces a new ritual or merely imports a new deity, is favoured by their resemblance to each other in structure and function. And so sustained allusion to the mysteries may be, or may seem to be, to more than one cult. For example, Riedweg concludes his careful examination of Plato's *Phaedrus* as follows:

> The thematic layer of the mystery terminology is not a completely unified complex. Bacchic-Dionysiac elements (249c–d, 250a/252d–253c5) stand next to more extended descriptions of an Eleusinian imprint (250b–c/251a/254b). The common link is the idea of the ἐποπτεία (viewing), around which the mystery terminology of both imprints is organized.[23]

Again, the mysteries repeatedly evoked in the *Bacchae* are, naturally enough, the Dionysiac, and yet Pentheus' experiences in the stable exhibit numerous similarities, too numerous to be coincidental, with Plutarch's account of what is generally agreed to be Eleusinian initiation.[24] The mystic terminology in which Aeschylus presents the return of Orestes is Eleusinian (n. 6), and it seems that in this respect, as in so many others, Sophocles' play was influenced by Aeschylus'.[25] But in general the Dionysiac context of tragedy may have encouraged allusion to the Dionysiac mysteries. Another

[20] See also e.g. *Hymn. Hom. Dem.* 480–2. On the permanence of mystic εὐδαιμονία see e.g. Eur. *Bacch.* 897–911, with Seaford 1994b: 388–405.

[21] There would be this resemblance even with an original version with θεός (or μάκαρ) rather than the unmetrical τρισόλβιε: see Tsantsanoglou and Parássoglou 1987: 10–11.

[22] Graf 1974: 40–78.

[23] Riedweg 1987: 44–5.

[24] Seaford 1981a: 255–6.

[25] Apart from *OC* 1050–1 and fr. 837, both quoted above, and *Antigone* and *Ajax* (see below), Soph. also wrote a *Triptolemos*, which presumably concerned the Eleusinian mysteries.

possibility is that language may evoke mystery associations without being designed to evoke one cult in particular.

Ploutos is in Pindar 'conspicuous star, true light for a man'; Iakchos is in Aristophanes 'light-bearing star of the nocturnal initiation ritual (τελετή)', and in Sophocles 'chorus-leader of the fire-breathing stars' – 'according to a mystic λόγος' adds the scholiast.[26] So too Orestes predicts that from the pronouncement of his death he will see (δεδορκότα) – i.e. come alive[27] – and shine like a star over his enemies (65–6). This concludes his self-reassurance on the advisability of a [279] fictitious death (59 λόγῳ θανών),[28] which will be a detailed description of a chariot-race crash.

Why will the death of Orestes be told in such detail? And why does it occur in a chariot race? An answer, true as far as it goes, would be that Sophocles is elaborating the striking metaphor of the chariot-race crash applied by Aeschylus to Orestes as he first senses the onset of the Furies (*Cho.* 1021–4). But there is I think more to it than that. Elsewhere in Aeschylus' play Orestes' revenge is frequently described in terms of a contest,[29] sometimes in conjunction with mystic imagery. For example, Orestes concludes the planning of his revenge with the words τούτῳ δεῦρ' ἐποπτεῦσαι λέγω | ξιφηφόρους ἀγῶνας ὀρθώσαντί μοι (583–4). ἐποπτεύειν often refers to a stage (the *epopteia*, 'viewing') of the Eleusinian mysteries. That it has this association here is made very likely by the previous line, in which Orestes uses a phrase associated with mysteries to bind the chorus to silence.[30] The revenge is envisaged as both a mystery and a contest.[31] The ode that precedes the killings describes Orestes as a horse in a chariot race, needing control (794–9, cf. 939), and goes on to describe the desired outcome in terms of the mysteries: veiling, and then seeing a bright light (794–811).[32]

[26] See nn. 11–12 above.

[27] Cf. ταῦτα δερχθέντες τέλη in Soph. fr. 837 quoted above.

[28] To reassure himself he also says that he has frequently seen even wise men wrongly reported dead, who when they return home are honoured the more. Commentators compare Hdt. 4.95 (Salmoxis disappearing underground and mourned by the Thracians), but, as Kells 1973: 85 observes, this does not explain 'I have often seen'. And so there maybe a reference here to mystic initiation. Cf. Eur. *Hel.* 1050–6, where the puzzling 1056 may refer to the mystic sequence of lamentation (1054) followed by σωτηρία (1055).

[29] Aesch. *Cho.* 455, 584, 729, 794–9, 866–8, 939, with Thomson 1966: *ad locc.*

[30] 582 σιγᾶν θ' ὅπου δεῖ καὶ λέγειν τὰ καίρια. For detail see Thomson 1966: *ad loc.* Elektra is to look after things in the house (579–80) and the chorus are to remain outside (581–2; περὶ θύρας Plut. *De prof. virt.* 81d says of the initiands). That leaves Pylades (τούτῳ surely refers to him, cf. 900–2), who in contrast to the chorus enters the house for the revelation which is the next stage: hence δεῦρ' ἐποπτεῦσαι.

[31] ἐπόπτης could also mean a supervisor of athletic contests: Thomson 1966: *ad loc.* and on 728–9.

[32] If we read Headlam's ἀναδεῖν for ἀνιδεῖν in 808, this provides an element (the crown) common to contest and mysteries.

It seems unlikely that this association of mysteries with contest was the invention of Aeschylus. Mysteries and the contest are similar in structure: suffering (πόνοι) followed by *makarismos*[33] and crowning; athletic contests were embedded in ritual;[34] and epinician poetry often employs mystic terminology.[35] The agonic image 'attained to the lovely crown with swift feet', inscribed on a [280] Thurian 'gold leaf' of (probably) the fourth century, was probably a formula used in mystic ritual.[36]

Another text that combines mystic with agonic imagery is the passage of Plato's *Phaedrus* that contains the allegory of the soul as a charioteer with a pair of winged horses (246a–257d).[37] Of particular interest to us is 248a6–c2. Some souls, unable to reach the upper region,

> are carried around beneath, trampling (πατοῦσαι) and colliding with each other, with each trying to get ahead of the other. So there is a loud confusion (θόρυβος) and rivalry and utmost sweat (ἱδρὼς ἔσχατος) ...[38] And they all having much toil (πόνος) go away uninitiated (ἀτελεῖς) in the sight of reality ... The reason why there is much eagerness to see where the plain of truth is is that the fitting pasturage for the best part of the soul happens to be from the meadow (λειμών) there.

Several of the elements of this description reappear in Plutarch's accounts of the sufferings of the mystic initiands: in fr. 178 exhausting runnings around (περιδρομαὶ κοπώδεις), sweat (ἱδρώς), a crowd trampling on itself and driven together (πατούμενον ὑφ' ἑαυτοῦ καὶ συνελαυνόμενον), before being received by 'pure places and meadows' (λειμῶνες);[39] in *Mor.* 81e loud confusion (θόρυβος)[40] and mutual jostling (ὠθούμενοι). Although Plutarch may in such passages be influenced by earlier philosophical use of mystic imagery, there is no doubt that these passages are what they claim to be, namely accounts of the mysteries.[41] If what he describes goes back

[33] Note e.g. Orestes himself as athletic victor in Sophocles (693 ὠλβίζετο). For mystic *makarismos* see e.g. Soph. fr. 837 (quoted above): τρισόλβιοι ...

[34] E.g. Plutarch (*Thes.* 25.4) says that the Isthmian contests were originally held at night in the form of a τελετή (a word that in Plutarch generally refers to the mysteries) in honour of Melikertes. We also hear that this cult had ὄργια, a secret σεμνὸς λόγος (Philostr. *Imag.* 2.16) and ἀπόρρητα (Liban. *Or.* 2, p. 110 Först.).

[35] On this see most recently Garner 1992.

[36] GJ 5.6; in arguing against mystic content Zuntz 1971 was writing before the discovery of the Hipponion and Pelinna texts (GJ 1, 26a–b).

[37] Detail in Riedweg 1987.

[38] Cf. 247b5 πόνος τε καὶ ἀγὼν ἔσχατος.

[39] Note also the mystic initiates in the λειμών in Ar. *Ran.* (326, 344, 374), and in the gold leaves GJ 3.6 and 27.4.

[40] Note also *Mor.* 47a and 943c.

[41] Plutarch refers to his own initiation into the Dionysiac mysteries (*Mor.* 611d). On the detailed correspondence between fr. 178 and Eur. *Bacch.* 616–37 see n. 24 above.

to the fifth century, then the imagining of the sufferings of the initiands as the turmoil of a (chariot) race may not have been invented by Plato, but rather may have belonged to the traditional conception of mystic initiation as a contest. This conception, which we found applied to the struggle of Orestes by Aeschylus, would then be further alluded to in his metaphor of Orestes losing control of his horses at the point of winning the chariot race. The metaphor would then have the sinister connotation of a mystic transition in which the suffering of the initiand precludes rather than yields to the joyful transition.[42] If so, then Sophocles' detailed narrative of the same accident, resulting in the fictive death of Orestes, would have a similar connotation.

In the *Oresteia* Orestes' vengeance is one of a chain of transitions, each envisaged in mystic terms, which end not in the permanent happiness of mystic [281] initiation but in a new catastrophe. Only at the end of the trilogy will there be a permanent 'release from suffering'. Sophocles' *Electra*, on the other hand, is completed by the murders. The vengeance Orestes predicts with the image of himself as a star is successful. But this does not mean that the mystic imagery contributes to a representation of the murders as a triumphant act of justice leading to permanent well-being. There is an inevitable antithesis between mystic transition (to a place of peace and purity[43]) and the horror of matricide, and so it is hardly surprising that in both Aeschylus and Sophocles the mystic transition in terms of which Orestes' victory is imagined fails after all to bring happiness. Indeed the contrast, which we find elsewhere in tragedy (see below), between the permanence of mystic *eudaimonia* and the instability of vengeance makes their association seem especially perverse. The *permanence* of mystic *eudaimonia* is alluded to, we noted, in Elektra's claims that she will never forget the sight of Orestes and that she will never cease weeping for joy. But she adds, ominously perhaps, that 'you have done to me unfathomable things'. This excessive joy arises from a long-ingrained hatred (1311). She claims, in what seems to be a reversal of a mystic image, that her *suffering* is ἀνέφελον (lit. 'without clouds')[44] and cannot be forgotten (1246–50). And she says that the 'only release for my long suffering'

[42] As happens in e.g. the *Bacchae*: Seaford 1981a.

[43] See esp. Pl. *Phdr.* 250c4 ἐποπτεύοντες ἐν αὐγῇ καθαρᾷ; Ar. *Ran.* (initiands in Hades) esp. 155–7; Plut. fr. 178 τόποι καθαροὶ καὶ λειμῶνες. For mystic initiation as purification see n. 3 above.

[44] Correctly explained by the scholiast as 'manifest, uncovered' (φανερόν, ἀνακεκαλυμμένον). Failing to understand the ironic reversal, Kells 1973: 200 writes that 'it is not the habit of Greek imagery to represent *bad* things as bright', and gives ἀνέφελον the opposite of the meaning it always has elsewhere. At Eur. *Hipp.* 190–2 the afterlife promised by mystery cult (see Barrett 1964: *ad loc.*) is said to be hidden in clouds by darkness. Note also Aesch. *Cho.* 809–11 (with Thomson 1966: *ad loc.*).

(1489–90 κακῶν μόνον ... τῶν πάλαι λυτήριον) – a phrase suggestive of the mystic transition[45] – is the 'laying out' of Aigisthos 'for the buriers he deserves' (i.e. the birds and dogs): here the (mystic) 'release' becomes the explicit perversion of ritual – death ritual, in hideous revenge for the perversion of the death ritual of Agamemnon (278–85).

Whereas in Aeschylus there is a final, much postponed 'complete release from suffering',[46] in Sophocles' drama the hints of the mystic transition produce an implicit contrast between the mystic release from ignorant suffering and the horror of victory. Similarly, the arrival of Herakles as saviour from death in Euripides' *Heracles* is presented in mystic terminology that contrasts poignantly with what happens next: Herakles throws the head of his enemy to the dogs, and kills his own children in a frenzy that disrupts the purificatory sacrifice.[47] In Sophocles the contrast is to be found also in the *Antigone*: after the decision to release Antigone, [282] the chorus invoke Dionysos as the torch-bearing Iakchos of the Eleusinian mysteries,[48] although, in poignant contrast to Kore, Antigone will not in the end be released from her dark bridal chamber beneath the earth.[49] But the rest of this chapter will be devoted to the new light cast by the mysteries on the unsolved problem of the 'deception speech' in Sophocles' *Ajax*.[50]

After seeming to reject his wife's plea that he should stay alive, Ajax delivers the famous speech in which he says, among other things, that he 'was made female' (ἐθηλύνθην) by her (651), that he will go off to a meadow (655 λειμών) by the sea to purify himself, burying his sword 'where nobody will see', and that he 'will learn to revere (σέβειν) the Atreidai' (667). The chorus express their joy at his apparent decision to live. But Ajax will in fact reappear to curse the Atreidai and kill himself with the sword.

I agree with those scholars, notably Knox and Taplin, who believe that Ajax means throughout to kill himself, that the 'deception speech' hints at this (with the chorus perceiving only the surface meaning) and that the primary (or only) purpose of the speech is to express a new insight.[51] For

[45] For the mysteries as achieving release from suffering see n. 16 above, Pind. fr. 131a (the pious dead 'are all blessed through their share in the rites that deliver from suffering', ὄλβιοι δ' ἅπαντες αἴσᾳ λυσιπόνων τελετᾶν) and further passages quoted by Tsantsanoglou and Parássoglou 1987: 12.

[46] *Eum.* 83 ὥστ' ἐς τὸ πᾶν σε τῶνδ' ἀπαλλάξαι πόνων.

[47] Seaford 1994b: 368–82.

[48] Note 1120–1, 1146–7 (with schol., quoted at n. 11 above), 1151–2.

[49] For further detail (including the evocation of the Eleusinian ritual at 1204) see Seaford 1994b: 368–82.

[50] On the problem see most recently Stevens 1986; Crane 1990.

[51] Knox 1961; Taplin 1979.

Knox a rigidly immutable Ajax applies the insight to himself in a contemptuous and sarcastic spirit that serves to emphasise his magnificent isolation. To this Taplin makes some telling objections,[52] and maintains instead that Ajax adheres wholeheartedly to his insights, but is applying them to the time after his death, when so much will in fact be reversed from its present low ebb.[53] In this view there is undoubtedly some truth, but even Taplin fails to account fully for 'I was made female' and 'we will learn to revere the Atreidai', words extreme enough to seem to Knox sarcastic. And what exactly is the new insight? And why exactly should Ajax half-conceal it? A fuller understanding of the speech requires new considerations to be adduced.

The new considerations come from cult: from hero cult, to which I will return briefly, and from the mysteries. The practice of implying but also concealing (by riddling obscurity) a meaning beneath the surface occurred (or at least was imagined [283] to occur) in mystery cult.[54] This is a fact of great importance for understanding certain dramatic and philosophical texts, or quasi-philosophical texts such as the Derveni Papyrus commentary. The λόγος of Heraclitus, for example, is influenced by mystic discourse in its riddling style – but also in its content. For example the resemblance of the fifth-century Olbian bone inscriptions (containing the words Διό[νυσος] and Ὀρφικ[οί] and the phrases βίος θάνατος βίος, εἰρήνη πόλεμος and ἀλήθεια ψεῦδος) to Heraclitus in both style and content (cf. e.g. DK 22 B 62 ἀθάνατοι θνητοί, θνητοὶ ἀθάνατοι) is to be explained by the influence of mystic discourse, in this respect among many others,[55] on Heraclitus, rather than vice versa. Even if we were to suppose that the participants in the Olbian (Orphic–Dionysiac) cult had adopted the style and the philosophy of Heraclitus' λόγος, then this would require an explanation – most obviously the mystic provenance of the λόγος. The identity of life and death with each other seems in both mystic and Heraclitean thought to exemplify a general identity of opposites (described in the same antithetical style) and to result from the passage of the soul through the cosmological elements.[56] Ajax's insight is the mystic-Heraclitean one that

[52] There are none of the indications of tone found in sarcasm elsewhere in Sophocles. Why is the contempt unnoticed by the others? And 'the very poetry rebuffs the notion that Ajax's application of it to himself is sarcastic' (Taplin 1979: 124).

[53] His own honour, the prospects of his dependents, the friendship of Odysseus, etc.

[54] E.g. Seaford 1981a: 254–5. Cf. now the deliberate obscurity attributed to 'Orpheus' in *PDerveni*, esp. XIII.5–6 = §39K, XVII.13 = §56K [and VII.4–8 = §20K].

[55] Seaford 1986a[9].

[56] Seaford 1986a[9].

everything is eventually transformed into its opposite.[57] Further, its expression contains the following allusions (for those who understand[58]) to the mysteries.

The (mainly cosmological) transformations that Ajax lists in the beautiful lines 670–6 – winter into fertile summer, night into the light of flaming day, a storm at sea into calm, and sleep into waking – are all positive transformations; and at least two of them evoke the symbolism that we know was used to express the transition from anxiety to joy in the mysteries. One of these (674–5) is the transition from stormy sea to calm.[59] 'Blessed is he who has from the sea escaped the storm and found harbour', pronounces the mystic *makarismos* in the *Bacchae*.[60] A few lines later Ajax says τοῖς πολλοῖσι γὰρ βροτῶν ἄπιστος ἐσθ' ἑταιρείας λιμήν (682–3), 'for most men the harbour of friendship is false' (or '... there is a false harbour of friendship'). The emphatic position of 'for most men' implies that there is for a special few a *true* harbour (of mystic salvation). The other evocation of mystic [284] symbolism is night giving way to the light of day. As we have seen, the appearance of light in darkness in mystic ritual was a powerful symbol of the mystic transition. In his earlier despairing desire for death Ajax had identified the opposites of light and darkness (394–5 'Io! Darkness, my light, O gloom of the underworld, for me most bright!').

Of no less mystic significance is the transformation of Ajax himself into his opposite, a female. Anything can happen, he says, 'for I, who was before so terribly firm, like iron hardened in the dipping, was made female (ἐθηλύνθην) in my cutting edge (or mouth, στόμα) by this woman' (648–52). The change of identity required in the rite of passage is often expressed by an apparent change of gender (transvestism), which seems to have occurred in the Dionysiac mysteries of the classical age.[61]

Towards the end of the speech Ajax tells his wife to go in and pray for the completion, through to the end, of what his heart passionately desires (685–6 διὰ τέλους, γύναι, εὔχου τελεῖσθαι τοὐμὸν ὧν ἐρᾷ κέαρ). 'Through to the end/completion' (διὰ τέλους), in emphatic position, contrasts with that changeability of all things described at length in the preceding lines. In combination with τελεῖσθαι it alludes I think to the mysteries, which

57 Mystic doctrine (though not perhaps Heraclitus) may nevertheless allow a permanent refuge for the soul from the cycle of change: Seaford 1986a[9].

58 On the principle of μαθοῦσιν αὐδῶ: see n. 54 and Thomson 1966: on Aesch. *Ag.* 36–7.

59 Note also that the word for calming, κοιμίζειν, meaning 'put to sleep', not only introduces the following image of sleep yielding to waking but also prefigures Ajax's use of the very same word for his *death* at 832.

60 Eur. *Bacch.* 902–3; Seaford 1981a: 260; cf. Apul. *Met.* 11.15; Herm. Trismeg. 7.1; Vollgraf 1924: 178–85.

61 Seaford 1994b: 262–75 and 1981a: 258–9 on the transvestism of Pentheus.

as a ritual bringing completion were indeed sometimes called τέλος.[62] This is confirmed by the surprisingly strong word for desire, ἐρᾷ, which is then echoed by the chorus in their reaction to Ajax's speech: his last words, 'even if now unfortunate, I am saved (σεσωμένον)', with their allusion to the mystic transition, are immediately followed by the passionate desire of the chorus, ἔφριξ᾽ ἔρωτι ..., a combination of words that occurs elsewhere only in a fragment of Aeschylus (387), ἔφριξ᾽ ἔρωτι[63] τοῦδε μυστικοῦ τέλους, 'I shuddered with passionate desire for this mystic rite of completion (τέλος)'.[64]

φρίσσειν and its noun φρίκη occur frequently to describe the emotion of the initiand.[65] In this and all other contexts it means the shuddering of fear (sometimes akin to awe) or horror, never of joy. The other occurrences in Sophocles, for example, are as follows: of the reaction of the chorus to the screams of Klytaimestra (*El.* 1407), to the suffering of Herakles (*Trach.* 1044) and to the self-blinding of Oidipous (*OT* 1306), and of Kreon to the ominous words of Teiresias (*Ant.* 997). And so ἔφριξα at *Aj.* 693 does not mean what it is generally taken to mean, [285] namely a thrill of joy. Rather, ἔφριξ᾽ ἔρωτι suggests the contradictory emotions of mystic initiation (yet another example of the interpenetration of opposites). Plutarch says that those undergoing mystic initiation experience joy mixed with confusion and πτόησις, along with pleasant hope (*Mor.* 943c ... χαρᾶς οἷαν οἱ τελούμενοι μάλιστα θορύβῳ καὶ πτοήσει συγκεκραυμένην μετ᾽ ἐλπίδος ἡδείας ἔχουσιν). πτόησις, a state of anxious excitement, seems to have been, like φρίκη, characteristic of mystic initiands.[66] It is as part of a series of initiatory experiences that Pentheus in the *Bacchae* is described, as he arrives to attack the Dionysiac τελεταί, as ὡς ἐπτοήται (214).[67] And yet it seems to be part of his persistent πτόησις that he also, paradoxically, has a 'great ἔρως' (813) to see the τελεταί.[68] Maximus of Tyre (39.3), in mystic imagery influenced by the *Phaedrus*, writes of souls that are suffering and yet ἐρῶσαι τῆς τελετῆς. The contradictory emotions (including φρίκη)

[62] Examples in Richardson 1974: 314, and Seaford 1981a: 261 on τέλος at Eur. *Bacch.* 860 meaning mystic ritual (again ambiguously).

[63] ἔρωτι Brunk; ἔρως δὲ ms. This problem does not much affect my point.

[64] Their song also evokes (706–10) the mystic images of the removal of the cloud or darkness from the eyes (n. 43) and of calm after a storm for sailors (see n. 60). And so it resembles Soph. *Ant.* 1115–52 as a poignant choral evocation of mystic joy before the catastrophe. Much the same can be said of Aesch. *Cho.* 807–11 and 961–4: see Thomson 1966: *ad locc.*

[65] Pl. *Phdr.* 251a7; Plut. fr. 178, *Ages.* 24.7; Demetr. *Eloc.* 101; Aristid. *Or.* 22.2; Them. *Or.* 20.235a–b.

[66] Seaford 1981a: n. 42 (add Aristid. Quint. 3.25).

[67] Seaford 1987a.

[68] This is manifested in his desire to spend a lot of gold to see them (812). Cf. *PDerveni* xx.8–10 = §67K, in which those who pay money seem to be mystic initiands [cf. Seaford 2003b^3: 1–3].

of initiation are indicated also by the phrase used of Eleusis by Aristides (*Or.* 22.2): φρικωδέστατον καὶ φαιδρότατον.[69] And in Plato's *Phaedrus* (251a–252c) the newly initiated, 'on first seeing a godlike face ..., at first ἔφριξεν ... but then undergoes a change from this shuddering (ἐκ τῆς φρίκης μεταβολή) which becomes a mixture of pain and joy (ἀμφοτέρων μεμιγμένων), a longing which mortals call Ἔρως and the gods Πτέρως (the winged one)'.

The initiands suffer anxiety and confusion, but also (otherwise they would not be there) hope and passionate desire for something joyful. Accordingly, ἔρωτι at *Aj.* 693 means passionate desire. Just like ἔφριξα, it is generally taken to mean what it means nowhere else, namely 'joy'. But 'I shuddered with passionate desire' does not seem odd to those who recognise the evocation of the contradictory emotions of mystic initiation.

Given how little we know of the mysteries, it may be that there are further allusions lost on us, for example in the chorus' next words, περιχαρὴς δ' ἀνεπτάμην ('joyful I flew upwards'). In the *Phaedrus* the image of the winged soul flying upwards occurs along with mystic imagery (246a–7e), and in the passage just quoted the soul in its mixed emotions grows wings (251b–c).[70] It may be that this imagery of flying upwards represents, as we suggested earlier of his agonic imagery, Plato's development of ideas already associated with the mysteries; and the same is perhaps true even of his decision to describe ἔρως in mystic terms in *Phaedrus* and *Symposium*.[71]

Returning to Ajax's speech, we may say that the completion that his heart [286] 'passionately desires (ἐρᾷ)' is (unknown to the chorus) death, but that he desires it passionately because of his insight into mystic truth, a truth which may imply a hope concealed from the uninitiated. And so there are three layers of meaning, embodied for example in the bath with which he will purify himself (655 ἁγνίσας) – on the surface a mere purification, in fact in a sense a funeral bath,[72] but also, we may now add, suggestive of the purification that was a central idea (and practice) of the mysteries.[73]

As well as possible eschatological implications, Ajax's mystic insight into the interpenetration of opposites has ethical significance. From the mystic perspective of permanence implied by διὰ τέλους ... τελεῖσθαι he is able to

[69] Cf. Demetr. *Eloc.* 101, where φρίκη in the mysteries is associated with *darkness*.
[70] See also the gold leaf GJ 5.5 κυκλοῦ δ' ἐξέπταν κτλ. (n. 16 above), surely a mystic formula. [See Chapter 18 below.]
[71] Note esp. *Symp.* 209e5–210a1 ταῦτα μὲν οὖν τὰ ἐρωτικὰ ... κἂν σὺ μυηθείης.
[72] This is argued for by Knox 1961: 11.
[73] See n. 3 above. The Eleusinian initiands, like Ajax (654–5), purified themselves in the sea.

disengage from the changeability of reciprocal relations (679–83), whether of amity (φιλία) or hostility. The instability of *philia* is embodied in the gift of Hektor's sword (658–65). And he expresses the completeness of his disengagement from reciprocal hostility by claiming readiness to go to the extreme of 'revering' the Atreidai. This detachment is, he implies, moderation (677 σωφρονεῖν) that accords with the yielding of cosmic opposites to each other. So too Heraclitus regards his *logos* as a basis for the politically vital virtue of *sophrosyne*.[74]

The mystic allusions in the *Ajax* are undoubtedly there. It is much harder to explain *why* they are there, and their relation to the rest of the drama. I have attempted to do so in detail elsewhere,[75] and what remains of this chapter is a brief recapitulation of my argument.

The events of the *Ajax* were imagined to prefigure at various points the hero cult of Ajax, which was celebrated in particular in Attica. One such feature is Ajax's curse against the Atreidai just before his suicide: just as in Sophocles' *Oedipus at Colonus* and Euripides' *Heraclidae*, the future recipient of Attic cult dies angry against the forefathers of Athens' fifth-century enemies, and that anger would be remembered or even perhaps kept alive in the cult. But *within* the polis, hero cult is an agent of solidarity among citizens. And so it is appropriate that the future recipient of the civic cult should embody *sophrosyne* and respect for authority, as Ajax does in the 'deception speech'. His view that the changeability of amity and hostility should preclude absolute hostility is held also by Ajax's old enemy Odysseus as he persuades Agamemnon to allow a funeral for Ajax,[76] a funeral that prefigures the honours given to Ajax in civic cult. And so the ethical, political and cultic dimensions of the drama are closely interrelated. As often in tragedy, we find reflected the historical movement from one form of social relation [287] to another, from a network of reciprocal relations (characteristic of societies in which the state is weak or absent) to the organisation of citizens, in civic institutions and civic cult, around a centre or series of centres.

The importance of the chorus of 'Salaminians' in the drama may prefigure the special role played by the clan of 'Salaminians' in the Attic cult of Ajax.[77] In particular, after telling his wife, in words that allude to the mysteries, to pray for the fulfilment of his passionate desire, Ajax's next words

[74] See esp. DK 22 B 43, 101, 110, 112–14, 116–18. There may conceivably be a reflection of a mystic *sophrosyne* in Pl. *Phdr.* 250b2, 247d6, 254b7: cf. Riedweg 1987: 44, 61–2.

[75] Seaford 1994b: 123–39 and 388–405.

[76] Note esp. 1347, 1359, 1377.

[77] Seaford 1994b: 399 n. 129. For their role in the cult see Ferguson 1938.

are to the Salaminians: 'and you, comrades, perform with honour (τιμᾶτε) these same things for me as she does' (687–8), to which they respond with the mystic phrase ἔφριξ' ἔρωτι. This suggests the possibility that the hero cult prefigured by the drama contained a mystic element, and that this mystic element is prefigured in the 'deception speech'.

Given how little we know about the cult of Ajax, this can be no more than speculation. But there are two considerations in its favour. First, there are the connections and the structural similarity between hero cult and the mysteries. In both kinds of cult the human participants are associated, in a temporary death-like state (sometimes involving lamentation), with the death (or descent to the underworld) of the recipient of the cult, and this collective emotion might be of civic significance. Hero cult sometimes takes the form of mystery cult (or something very like it), heroes are sometimes honoured in mystery cult, and in myth heroes are initiated into the mysteries.[78] In Aeschylus' *Oedipus*, which seems to have ended with the foundation of the cult of Oidipous at Kolonos, Aeschylus was said to have revealed secrets of Demeter's mysteries; and so it has been suggested that fr. 387 (ἔφριξ' ἔρωτι τοῦδε μυστικοῦ τέλους) refers to Oidipous' initiation in Aeschylus' play. In Sophocles' version, the *Oedipus at Colonus*, Oidipous delivers a monologue similar to Ajax's 'deception speech', about the changeability of all things, especially human amity and hostility, with an implicit contrast to the permanent benefit to Athens of his own future cult (626), but says that he will not reveal the secrets (ἀκίνητ' ἔπη) of the cult.

The second consideration is as follows. If the deception speech was imagined as prefiguring mystery cult, then the *Ajax* resembles in this respect the *Bacchae*, in which the experiences of Pentheus were imagined as prefiguring the experiences of initiation into the τελεταί almost certainly founded by Dionysos in the lost part of the ending of the drama. In both cases the drama takes elements of the ritual to the extreme, as is characteristic of aetiological myth, so that for example both Ajax and Pentheus actually die, whereas death in mystic ritual is merely imagined. Further, both Ajax and Pentheus undergo sudden, strange transformations which produce an inconsistency of plot that is inexplicable without the mystic hypothesis. [288] The undoubtedly initiatory transformation of Pentheus has the following in common with Ajax's: (1) transition from excited aggression to meek subordination to the former enemy; (2) feminisation; (3) the acquisition of mystic insight (*Bacch.* 918–24); (4) the mystic image of the

[78] Brelich 1958: 118–24. See e.g. n. 34 above.

harbour (*Bacch.* 902–3); (5) an implicit contrast between the instability of human hostilities and the permanence of mystic happiness (*Bacch.* 897–911).[79] This contrast is important to the *Ajax*, and may prefigure the sociopolitical benefit of the cult. In the *Electra*, on the other hand, which (unlike *Ajax* and *Bacchae*) does not prefigure cult, the generally antithetical joys of vengeance and the mysteries are horrifically combined.[80]

POSTSCRIPT

The themes of this chapter are developed and integrated into a broader context in Seaford 1994b: chapter 10.

For mystic ritual in Ajax see E. Krummen, 'Ritual and Katastrophe: rituelle Handlung und Bildersprache bei Sophokles und Euripides', in F. Graf (ed.), *Ansichten Griechischer Rituale: Geburtstagssymposium für Walter Burkert* (Stuttgart and Leipzig: Teubner, 1998), pp. 296–325; J. Hesk, *Sophocles: Ajax* (London: Duckworth, 2003). For the 'deception speech' see A. Lardinois, 'The polysemy of gnomic expressions and Ajax' deception speech', in I. De Jong and A. Rijksbaron (eds.), *Sophocles and the Greek Language* (Leiden: Brill, 2006), pp. 213–23.

For hero cult in Ajax see V. Jay Ortiz, 'Athenian tragedy and hero-cult: a study of the Greek poetic and religious imagination', unpublished Ph.D. thesis, University of California (1993); A. Henrichs, 'The tomb of Aias and the prospect of hero cult in Sophokles', *ClAnt* 12 (1993), 165–80.

For mystic ritual in tragedy see I. Lada-Richards, 'Neoptolemos and the bow: ritual *thea* and theatrical vision in Sophocles' *Philoctetes*', *JHS* 117 (1997), 179–83; Hardie 2004; S. Tilg, 'Die Symbolik chthonischer Götter in Sophokles' Ödipus auf Kolonos', *Mnemosyne* 57 (2004), 407–20; V. Liapis, 'Zeus, Rhesus, and the mysteries', *CQ* 57 (2007), 381–411; Csapo 2008; M. Widzisz, 'The duration of darkness and the light of Eleusis in the prologue of *Agamemnon* and the third stasimon of *Choephoroi*', *GRBS* 50 (2010), 461–89; M. Widzisz, *Chronos on the Threshold: Time, Ritual, and Agency in the Oresteia* (Lanham, MD: Lexington Books, 2012). For mystic ritual in Aristophanes' *Frogs* see Lada-Richards 1999.

[79] The antithesis between reciprocal violence and mystic bliss is implicit in the (mystic ritual reflected in the) gold leaves: the initiand's claim to happiness in the next world is linked to the claim to have paid the penalty (being blasted by a thunderbolt) for unjust deeds (Zuntz 1971: 300–5). The most recent-known discovery, from Pherai, contains the words εἴσιθι ἱερὸν λειμῶνα· ἄποινος γὰρ ὁ μύστης (GJ 27.3–5).

[80] My thanks go to Judy Barringer for her comments on an earlier draft of this paper, and to the National Humanities Center in North Carolina, where this paper was written.

Subsequent overviews of mystery cult are M. Cosmopoulos (ed.), *Greek Mysteries* (London: Routledge, 2003); H. Bowden, *Mystery Cults in the Ancient World* (London: Thames and Hudson, 2010); J. Bremmer, *Initiation into the Mysteries of the Ancient World* (Berlin and New York: de Gruyter, 2014).

There are now substantial commentaries on *Electra* (2007) and *Ajax* (2011) by Patrick Finglass, both in the Cambridge Classical Texts and Commentaries Series.

PART III

Tragedy and Death Ritual

CHAPTER 11

The Last Bath of Agamemnon

Most of the work done on tracing persistent themes and images in the *Oresteia* has failed to take account of the associations of the theme or image for the original audience.[1] Some of these associations are with certain highly emotional rituals. In evoking the ritual the poet evokes also some at least of the emotion which generally accompanies its performance. I will take here as an example the association of the manner of Agamemnon's death, the fatal bath and the fatal robe, with the ritual of the funeral. This will I hope help to enrich our own emotional reaction to Aeschylus' presentation of this event, as well as to shed light on certain problematic passages.[2]

In Aeschylus Agamemnon is killed while being bathed by Klytaimestra. Fraenkel comments that 'the whole conception of Agamemnon's murder in the *Oresteia* rests on premises that are characteristically "Homeric". In the world of Epic, though not in Athens, women in high society do occasionally themselves attend a man in his bath.'[3] But in Homer Agamemnon was killed 'at a feast, as an ox is killed at the manger' (δειπνίσσας ὥς τίς τε κατέκτανε βοῦν ἐπὶ φάτνῃ), and his companions were killed like swine at a festive meal.[4] And this suggests that in the lost *Nostoi* the killing of Agamemnon was described in terms of a sacrifice of an animal. This version would have been highly appropriate to tragedy, in which killing is generally presented as sacrifice;[5] indeed, even the killing of Agamemnon in the bath in Aeschylus is described as a sacrifice (1118, 1433, 1504).

[1] E.g. Gantz 1977 virtually ignores the mysteries (cf. Thomson 1966: on *Ag.* 1 (cf. 20–1), 522, *Cho.* 935–71). Other typical treatments are e.g. Peradotto 1964; Lebeck 1971; Macleod 1975; Taplin 1977: 314–15.

[2] I would like to thank David and Su Braund, Margaret Alexiou, Peter Levi, Ewen Bowie, Pat Easterling and Oliver Taplin for their comments on this paper.

[3] Fraenkel 1950 on *Ag.* 1382; that this is an anachronism in Aesch. is confirmed by Ginouvès 1962: 162 n. 4.

[4] *Od.* 11.411–15 (and 4.535); also Soph. *El.* 203; Sen. *Ag.* 875–86; Paus. 2.16.6; Philostr. *Imag.* 2.10; Juv. 8.217.

[5] Burkert 1966: 116.

Furthermore, δειπνίσσας in Homer may be a trace of the version preserved in Hyginus[6] and Servius,[7] in which Agamemnon is killed while a participant in the sacrifice of animals. We might expect a sacrifice and consequent banquet to mark Agamemnon's return. Indeed, Klytaimestra in Aeschylus, on entering the palace to kill Agamemnon, says that she has to go in because there are sheep standing at the altar waiting to be sacrificed (1056–7; cf. 1310). This is the sacrifice to which she invites Kassandra, 'since Zeus, without anger, has made you share in the lustral waters (χερνίβων) of our house, standing near the altar of Zeus Ktesios among the many slaves' (1036–8), where the irony, missed by the commentators, is that the sacrificial victim too was sprinkled with the lustral waters (χέρνιβες):[8] the killing of Kassandra, as of Agamemnon, is presented as a sacrifice.[9] *[248]* Our expectation then must be that Kassandra and Agamemnon are to be sacrificed while participating in the sacrifice, as perhaps in the epic version. In the same way in Euripides Aigisthos is sacrificed while sacrificing and so is Klytaimestra.[10]

Why then did Aeschylus abandon the version, traditional and highly apt for tragedy, of the killing (expressed perhaps as sacrifice) of Agamemnon at the banquet (perhaps while himself sacrificing)? The slightly greater degree of vulnerability, and perhaps of dishonour, attaching to a victim in the bath seems sufficient to explain neither the switch to this unusual and remarkable location nor the manner in which Aeschylus, whether or not he invented the version,[11] returns insistently throughout the trilogy to its details.[12] The bath, and the cloak thrown over the victim, acquire a notoriety which may make us take them for granted, but should in fact suggest a significance additional to convenience for the murderers

[6] 117: Hyginus was familiar with material from lost epic (Rose 1963: ix).

[7] Serv. *ad* Verg. *Aen.* 11.267, where Ag. is killed *prima inter limina*: perhaps in Virgil's source he was sacrificing there (cf. Pl. *Resp.* 1.328c); and it may be relevant that there is evidence that in sixth- and fifth-century Attica at least the body was laid out in the porch (cf. Dem. 43.62; Phot. *Bibl.* s.v. πρόθεσις; schol. Ar. *Lys.* 611; cf. Suet. *Aug.* 100?; Boardman 1955: 55–8), as sometimes also, especially after a violent death, in modern Greece (Politis 1931: 328).

[8] Cf. e.g. Eur. *IA* 675, 1513–8, *IT* 705. Lucas 1969 sees the same allusion in ἐπισπένδειν νεκρῷ (Agamemnon's) at *Ag.* 1395.

[9] *Ag.* 1118, 1297–8, 1433, 1504.

[10] Eur. *El.* 839–41 (e.g. with τοῦ δὲ νεύοντος κάτω cf. e.g. Burkert 1966: 107), 1141, 1143–4, 1221–32. The context of killing in tragic versions of this story tends to be grimly apt: e.g. Aesch. *Cho.* 904 (cf. 571–6); Soph. *El.* 1401, 1495–6.

[11] More likely he did not, for the fatal bath is a theme of myth (Pelias, Minos and the daughters of Kokalos). Or was the 'bath' originally a coffin (Murray 1934: 210; cf. Deuteronomy 3.11), or a σφαγεῖον (Duke 1954: 327)? The origin of the theme is a separate question from Aeschylus' use of it, despite *Cho.* 999.

[12] *Ag.* 1109, 1115, 1126–9, 1382, 1492, 1540, 1580, 1611; *Cho.* 491–3, 981–4, 1011–13, 1071; *Eum.* 460–1, 633–5.

and dishonour for the victim. Is there anything apt about this manner of Agamemnon's death?

In Homer the bathing, anointing and dressing of living men by women is described in a manner almost identical to the bathing, anointing and dressing by the women of the dead Hektor.[13] The Attic male of the fifth century, on the other hand, was not apparently bathed by women during his life; but his corpse was washed and dressed by his female relatives.[14] Hence the ease with which Euripides envisages the bath that Klytaimestra gives the living Agamemnon as the washing of his corpse, λουτρὰ πανύστατα.[15] As elsewhere,[16] Euripides makes explicit what is powerfully implicit in Aeschylus. Consider the foreboding riddles (αἰνίγματα: *Ag.* 1112) uttered by Kassandra (1107–11):[17]

> ἰὼ τάλαινα, τόδε γὰρ τελεῖς;
> τὸν ὁμοδέμνιον πόσιν
> λουτροῖσι φαιδρύνασα, πῶς φράσω τέλος;
> τάχος γὰρ τόδ᾽ ἔσται· προτείνει δὲ χεὶρ ἐκ
> χερὸς ὀρέγματα.
>
> Oh, wretched woman – will you *do* this? Having washed in the bath the husband who shares your bed – how am I to tell the end? For it will come too soon: hand after hand reaches and stretches out.

προτείνει ... ὀρέγματα has been taken to refer to the repeated blows of the murder. Certainly, one is reminded of the repeated self-inflicted blows of the mourning women at *Cho.* 426 (ἐπασσυτεροτριβῆ τὰ χερὸς ὀρέγματα). But the murder-blow (τύπτει) is first sensed by Kassandra at 1128. προτείνει ... ὀρέγματα, however sinister, must refer to the bath. Kassandra is horrified at the details of an apparently commonplace and innocent event, the bath, because she envisages it, however obscurely, as the washing of Agamemnon's corpse. The handling of the body (χεὶρ ἐκ χερὸς) expresses the [*249*] intimacy between husband and wife (τὸν ὁμοδέμνιον ... φαιδρύνασα). But it is the handling of the body (αὐτόχειρ, ἐν φίλαισι χερσίν) that is stressed by Antigone and by Elektra[18] in the washing of

[13] *Il.* 24.587–8; *Od.* 3.464–5, 4.49–50, 10.364–5, etc. For the washing and dressing of the dead Sarpedon and of the dead Patroklos see *Il.* 16.669, 18.350.

[14] Soph. *Ant.* 901, *El.* 1139, *OC* 1602–3; Eur. *Phoen.* 1319, 1667, *Tro.* 1151–2; Pl. *Phd.* 115a6–9; see also n. 21 below. For the persistence of this practice into present-day Greece see e.g. du Boulay 1982: 224.

[15] *El.* 157, *Or.* 367; cf. e.g. *Hec.* 611.

[16] See e.g Thomson 1966 on Aesch. *Cho.* 794–9; or with *Ag.* 1441–2 (see n. 34 below) cf. Eur. *Tro.* 445, 313, 357–8.

[17] The question mark after τελεῖς may be unnecessary. ὀρέγματα Hermann for mss. ὀρεγμένα.

[18] Soph. *Ant.* 900, *El.* 1138 – both expressions in emphatic position; cf. e.g. Eur. *Med.* 1034, *Supp.* 175, *Hec.* 50; Soph. *Aj.* 1410.

the beloved corpse. Indeed, it is precisely because she has performed with her own hands (αὐτόχειρ) the funeral washing and dressing, and poured libations at their tombs, that Antigone expects to come as φίλη to her father, mother and brother.[19] Aristotle recommended that tragic sufferings (πάθη) should be among one's own (ἐν φιλίαις), such as when one member of a family kills another (*Poet.* 1453b19). It is a refinement of this principle that such an intimate and important expression of *philia* as the washing of the corpse should here in the *Agamemnon* become a means of expressing absolute hostility.

The bathed corpse in funeral ritual was adorned with its κόσμος: a crown (or headband) and a long garment.[20] Sometimes the washing and dressing was performed before death. Sokrates bathed before drinking the hemlock 'to save the women the trouble'. Alkestis washed and dressed herself just before dying. And Oidipous, before his final disappearance, was washed and dressed by his daughters.[21] The washing and dressing of Agamemnon is different in two respects. First, the death it precedes involves bloodshed. Consider the words of the chorus:

> 1455: ... Ἑλένα,
> 1459: νῦν [δὲ] τελέαν πολύμναστον ἐπηνθίσω
> [δι'] αἷμ' ἄνιπτον ...
>
> now thou hast crowned thyself with the last and perfect garland unforgettable, blood not to be washed away.

This is the text and translation for which Fraenkel argues in his commentary, taking the blood to be Agamemnon's. My only disagreement is with the (traditional) translation 'not to be washed away'. In fact ἄνιπτον means 'unwashed'. The chorus have before their eyes the body of Agamemnon in its funeral robe (1492). The unwashed blood on the robe (cf. *Cho.* 1012–13) is an anomaly, expressing the anomalous relationship between husband and wife: normally blood would be washed away in the funeral bath. And so the chorus are shocked into seeing the red blood as the flowers (1459 ἐπηνθίσω) of the consummating (τελέαν) funeral crown (στέφανος), imagined also as a triumphal crown for Helen. If the association of blood with the crown was a *topos* of the lament for a violent death,[22] and so an

[19] *Ant.* 898–902; cf. also 73, 99, 524, and n. 35 below. Hence φίλαι τε κοὐ φίλαι at Eur. *El.* 1230–1, and even φίλως (deeply ironical) at Aesch. *Ag.* 1581 (cf. 1491–2). Also cf. ἀγαπᾶν, ἀγαπάζειν of washing and dressing the dead (Eur. *Supp.* 764, *Hel.* 937, *Phoen.* 1327 with schol.).

[20] Previously unworn? See esp. Hom. *Od.* 2.97–100; Eur. *Alc.* 160–1; Alexiou 1974: 27, 39.

[21] Pl. *Phd.* 115a6–9; Eur. *Alc.* 159–61; Soph. *OC* 1602–3; cf. also Eur. *HF* 332–4, 526, 549, 702, *Hec.* 432. Soph. *Aj.* 654 εἶμι πρός τε λουτρά may well be ambiguous (cf. *Ant.* 1199–1202).

[22] See n. 32 below; cf. Bion 1.35, 41, 66, 75; also Eur. *Cyc.* 517–8, *Tro.* 564–5, *Hec.* 126–7.

idea already familiar to the audience, this would explain the briefness with which Aeschylus can allude to it here. Specific to this situation, though, is that the crown of blood is presumably the only one that Agamemnon will receive. Not washed away, it is permanent and unforgettable.

Second, Agamemnon is of course unaware of his impending death. His bath, and the cloak thrown over him after it, not only precede his death; they help to bring it about. Similarly in the *Bacchae*, Pentheus is unaware that the maenadic adornment (κόσμος) put *[250]* on him (προσάψων) by Dionysos is his funerary dress:[23] κόσμον ὅνπερ εἰς Ἅιδου λαβὼν ἄπεισι (*Bacch.* 857–8). Much of the dramatic power of the subsequent 'robing scene' would have derived, for the original audience, from the funerary aspect of Pentheus' 'disguise'.[24] A similar horror attaches to the change of clothes in Seneca's version of the murder of Agamemnon, which may derive from Ion of Chios:[25] Kassandra envisages Klytaimestra telling Agamemnon to take off his oriental costume and (882–3) 'to put on instead the clothing woven by the hand of a faithful wife – I shudder and tremble in my soul ...'. And then 'the death-bearing garment of a faithless wife, once put on, consigns the fettered man to slaughter' (887–8).

Dionysos puts on Pentheus the 'adornment with which he will go to Hades' (κόσμον ὅνπερ εἰς Ἅιδου λαβὼν ἄπεισι). And the lethal crown sent by Medea to Jason's bride is called 'the adornment of Hades' (Eur. *Med.* 980–1 τὸν Ἅιδα κόσμον): that is to say, just as the unmarried were buried in wedding κόσμος,[26] so here the bridal crown is envisaged as a funerary one. In Euripides Herakles arrives to find his family dressed in their funerary attire, and says 'will you not cast off these wreaths of Hades around your hair?' (*HF* 562 οὐ ῥίψεθ' Ἅιδου τάσδε περιβολὰς κόμης ...;). In all cases of Ἅιδου describing a noun, the noun refers either to a feature of Hades (e.g. δόμος) or to something already associated with Hades (e.g. funerary κόσμος, song). And so an expression such as Ἅιδου μητέρα ('mother of Hades', transmitted at *Ag.* 1235) is corrupt.[27] Consider, on the

[23] Seaford 1981a: 260–1.

[24] Seaford 1981a: 258–61; Maenads in the underworld: e.g. *Arch. Anz.* 1950, 170–1; *CIL* III.686; headband of the dead (cf. *Bacch.* 833): Kurtz and Boardman 1971: 364.

[25] Tarrant 1976: 11.

[26] Alexiou 1974: 5, 27, 39, 120.

[27] Despite the defences by Fraenkel 1950 and Denniston and Page 1957. See Thomson 1966: *ad loc.*, who suggests μαῖαν (the largest of the crustaceans, which preyed on its own kind, and might be glossed μητέρα). There is much to be said also for μαινάδ' (Weil): cf. Eur. *Hec.* 1077; Aesch. *Cho.* 698 βακχείας κακῆς (surely *about* Klyt.). Maenads occur in Hades (n. 24 above), are known as θυιάδες (e.g. Aesch. *Sept.* 498: cf. θυίουσαν here) and might tear apart their own kin. For vase paintings of a Dionysiac Klytaimestra see Kossatz-Deissmann 1978: 91, 99.

other hand, the second stage of Kassandra's vision of Agamemnon's bath (*Ag.* 1114–15): 'What is this that appears? Surely it is some kind of net of Hades?' (τί τόδε φαίνεται; ἦ δίκτυόν τί γ' Ἅιδου;). Here the phrase δίκτυον Ἅιδου is above suspicion, partly because of course a net may be lethal, but also because this particular net is in fact the robe thrown over Agamemnon after his bath. Made vulnerable by his funeral bath, Agamemnon is then trapped by his funeral robe. His dead body will later in the play be seen wrapped in it (1492, 1580), with the bath now acting as a bier.[28] Here, though, the body is still alive, and so the κόσμος Ἅιδου is a δίκτυον Ἅιδου.[29]

'What is this that appears?' The object is seen only dimly by Kassandra, and she senses its nature as 'a net of Hades'. Her next phrase (1116), ἀλλ' ἄρκυς ἡ ξύνευνος, ἡ ξυναιτία φόνου, apparently identifies net and wife. But because the net is also the robe, this has puzzled the commentators,[30] some of whom have been driven to giving ξύνευνος a reference it has nowhere else, namely to a robe (e.g. 'vestis dormitoria' Schutz). Of course Kassandra is using riddling language (1112 αἰνίγματα) to express what is obscure even to her. It is obscure, but it is becoming clearer. ἀλλά (1116) introduces a clearer perception of the net. 'ἡ ξύνευνος is the net'. What does this mean? The association of net with εὐνή ('bed') might suggest that it is a robe, and indeed a robe for the dead man [251] on his bed,[31] here with the unusual role of trapping as well as covering him (ξυναιτία φόνου). This suspicion is confirmed at 1126–7. But ἡ ξύνευνος must also suggest the wife in her role as bedfellow. This ambiguity suggests a close association between bedfellow and bed-robe. To what purpose? In order to evoke and exploit an ambiguity inherent in this very association. A wife sleeps on a bed (εὐνή) with her living husband under a robe, and when he dies she puts a robe over his body on a bed (εὐνή). Bed and robe play a central role in the intimate relationship between husband and wife, not only in life but also in death. Their role in life is evoked here by the word ξύνευνος: the robe is put over her living husband by his bedfellow. But in fact its role is funerary, to trap as well as to cover her still-living husband: ἄρκυς ἡ ξύνευνος, ἡ ξυναιτία φόνου.

[28] δροίτη (1540) can mean both: cf. *Cho.* 999, *Eum.* 633; Parth. fr. 49 (Lightfoot); etc.

[29] Similarly Night, from her stock of embroidered robes (κόσμοι), threw a net over Troy (*Ag.* 355–8).

[30] E.g. Fraenkel 1950: III.504 with n. 3 considers 'referring ξύνευνος to the use of the garment later for covering Agamemnon's dead body' as a possible 'solution of the puzzle', but rejects this as too far in the future. But the robe is the funerary one (and so ξύνευνος).

[31] εὐνή (or δροίτη etc.: n. 28 above) as 'bier': e.g. Eur. *Supp.* 766; *Il.* 18.352–3; n. 40 below. Agamemnon also has a εὐνή below: Aesch. *Cho.* 318; Soph. *El.* 436. The body in its robe might be covered by another robe (ἐπίβλημα), but this distinction plays no part here.

It seems likely that here, as elsewhere in Aeschylus,[32] the brief and elliptical wording was easier for the audience than it is for us, because it evoked a commonplace: the association of death with marriage, of the tomb with the bridal chamber, of the grave or bier with the marriage bed.[33] This association thrives on the practice of not using a special terminology (e.g. our 'shroud' or 'bier') to set apart the equipment of the funeral. The dead Adonis, for example, is to be placed in his bed-robes on Aphrodite's bed (Bion 1.70–3). And εὐνή can mean 'bier' (e.g. Eur. *Supp.* 766) or marriage bed (see especially Soph. *Ant.* 1224). Later in the play it seems that Klytaimestra evokes this commonplace, bitterly, when she refers to the dead Kassandra, who is probably lying alongside the dead Agamemnon, as κοινόλεκτρος τοῦδε … πιστὴ ξύνευνος ('she who shares a bed with this man … his faithful bedfellow').[34] Here at 1116 death and marriage are associated not, as is generally the context of the commonplace, because of death before marriage, but because the man is killed by his wife. A wife shares a man's εὐνή. She also dresses his beloved corpse, an act no less intimate than its washing. The Greeks killed at Troy had to forgo this: 'They were not wrapped with robes in the hands of their wives' (οὐ δάμαρτος ἐν χεροῖν | πέπλοις συνεστάλησαν).[35]

The third stage of Kassandra's vision (1125–8) has also puzzled the commentators:

> ἆ ἆ, ἰδοὺ ἰδού. ἄπεχε τῆς βοὸς
> τὸν ταῦρον. ἐν πέπλοισιν
> μελαγκέρῳ λαβοῦσα μηχανήματι
> τύπτει …

> Ah, look, look! Keep the bull away from the cow! Taking him in robes, the [a, her] black-horned one's trap, she smites …

The previous hint that the net is a robe[36] is here confirmed. μελαγχέρῳ is a variant in the M scholia, FG and (before correction) M having

[32] See above, and n. 22; Thomson 1966: on *Cho.* 935–71.

[33] See e.g. Soph. *Ant.* 891, 1224–5, 1236–41 (cf. Aesch. *Ag.* 1440–2, *Cho.* 976!); *Anth. Pal.* 7.507 (attributed to Simonides); Bion 1.70–3; etc. (see Alexiou and Dronke 1971: 825–41); for the present day see Danforth 1982: 74–91. For similar *syntax* cf. e.g. *Ach. Tat.* 1.13 τάφος μέν σοι τέκνον ὁ θάλαμος (marriage chamber).

[34] *Ag.* 1441–2; cf. *Cho.* 976; Eur. *Tro.* 445; Soph. *Ant.* 1240–1. And of course the bath was common to wedding and funeral.

[35] Eur. *Tro.* 377–8 (cf. 390); cf. Eur. *El.* 1230–1 and n. 19 above; for the comforting prospect of this kind of attention see Eur. *Hec.* 430 ζῇ καὶ θανούσης ὄμμα συγκλῄσει τὸ σόν.

[36] The robe is called πέπλος (here, *Eum.* 635) and φᾶρος (*Cho.* 1011–13, *Eum.* 634). πέπλος in Aeschylus and Sophocles (and also perhaps in Homer) refers only to barbarian, female, ceremonial or solemn robes; in Euripides it is the regular word for the attire of the dead, besides being used for ordinary male and female dress. φᾶρος is a broad cloak worn by the living and the dead.

the accusative. T. C. W. Stinton has made a detailed case for reading μελαγχέρῳ (genitive), referring to 'Klytaimestra's [252] cow-guise', with an (obscure) secondary reference to Death: 'taking him in robes, the [a, her] black-horned one's trap, she smites …'.[37] If this is right, it coheres with our interpretation of the passage as a whole: μελαγχέρῳ μηχανήματι would restate the idea implicit in 1115 δίκτυον Ἅιδου (the κόσμος Ἅιδου in an active role), and develop the idea of the actual participation of Death,[38] to whom Klytaimestra is assimilated via τῆς βοός and μελαγχέρῳ (cf. e.g. 1500). Kassandra's vision passes from the bath to the net (robe), and then to the person wielding the robe.

After the murder the robe is called by Klytaimestra a 'limitless covering … an evil wealth of blood' (1382–3 ἄπειρον ἀμφίβληστρον … πλοῦτον αἵματος κακόν). The latter phrase is of course one of several indications of the wealth of the household (e.g. 949). But this does not mean that it is not designed to associate the rich robe, as a funeral garment, with Pluto (Πλούτων): cf. e.g. Soph. *OT* 30 'Hades is rich (πλουτίζεται) in groans and laments'. The choice of ἀμφίβληστρον (from all the words meaning 'net') seems designed to suggest ἀμφιβάλλειν, the verb used in Homer for dressing the guest after his bath (as Fraenkel points out), but also for dressing the corpse.[39] The sense of encompassment in ἀμφίβληστρον is strengthened by ἄπειρον: an effective net has for the victim no boundary (πέρας) by which to make his escape.[40] Normally the dress of Greek males, in the fifth century at least, did not reach the feet. That is why the (funerary) maenadic robes of Pentheus are specified as 'reaching the feet' (Eur. *Bacch.* 833 ποδήρεις; cf. 936–8). And as for the dead Patroklos (*Il.* 18.352–3), 'having placed him on the bier they cover him from the head to the feet (ἐς πόδας ἐκ κεφαλῆς) in fine linen, with a white robe wrapped over it'. Representations survive of the robe or robes wrapped around the

37 Stinton 1975. Burkert 1966: 120 refers to the bronze-age Vaphio cup, and to the possibility of Agamemnon's death being connected with a ritual βουφονία.

38 Cf. Eur. *Alc.* 74–6, *Med.* 1110–11; Phrynich. fr. 3; Aesch. fr. 255; Soph. *Aj.* 854, *Phil.* 797; Aesop, *Fab.* 90H; Kaibel, *Epigr. Gr.* 89.3–4; *SEG* 1.454.2; etc. Cf. Hom. *Il.* 16.853, *Od.* 11.134–6.

39 E.g. *Od.* 3.467; *Il.* 24.588. In Aesch. ἀμφιβάλλειν occurs elsewhere only of ζύγον (*Pers.* 50, 72) and in fr. 153 λεπτὸς δὲ σινδὼν ἀμφιβαλλέσθω χροΐ – probably of the dead Patroklos (cf. Soph. fr. 210.67 σινδών of shroud). Cf. Eur. *El.* 1231–2 φάρεα τάδ' ἀμφιβάλλομεν on the dead Klytaimestra; Kaibel, *Epigr. Gr.* 89.4 Ἅιδης οἱ σκοτίας ἀμφέβαλε πτέρυγας; *fr. trag. adesp.* 127 (Hades) ὁ δ' ἀμφιβάλλει ταχύπους κέλευθον ἕρπων σκοτίαν.

40 Cf. [Aesch.] *PV* 1078 εἰς ἀπέραντον δίκτυον ἄτης; Ibycus, fr. 287.3–4 ἐς ἄπειρα δίκτυα; and of the same robe: Aesch. fr. 375 ἀμήχανον τέχνημα καὶ δυσέκδυτον, *Eum.* 634 ἀτέρμονι; Eur. *Or.* 25 ἀπείρῳ περιβαλοῦσ' ὑφάσματι. For the later tradition of a χίτων ἀτράχηλος see Fraenkel 1950 on Aesch. *Ag.* 1382; also Beazley, *ARV*[2] 1652 (Vermeule 1966).

hands and feet of the corpse, and sometimes even covering the head.[41] Like the net, the funeral robe encloses. A fragment of Sophocles' *Polyxena* (fr. 526), 'a tunic without limit, a garment of woes ... you' (χίτων σ' ἄπειρος, ἐνδυτήριον κακῶν), almost certainly a prophecy of Agamemnon's death, seems to allude to funerary dress, because ἐνδυτήριος implies solemnity.[42] The σε ('you') was probably governed by e.g. ἀμμένει ('awaits'): compare Polymestor's prophecy of Agamemnon's death (Eur. *Hec.* 1281), φόνια λουτρά σ' ἀμμένει ('a bloody bath awaits you'), in which ἀμμένει makes surface sense only by suggesting the funeral bath for the bloody corpse of the warrior; what it really means Agamemnon will of course discover too late.

The horror of the murderous funeral dress persists throughout the trilogy. Wrapped around the dead Agamemnon it is a 'spider's web' (ἀράχνης ὕφασμα) and 'woven robe of the Erinyes' (ὑφαντοὶ πέπλοι Ἐρινύων).[43] In the *Choephori*, when Elektra attempts to arouse her father by [253] reminding him that he was killed 'shamefully, in coverings devised for the purpose' (494 αἰσχρῶς τε βουλευτοῖσιν ἐν καλύμμασιν), the point of the emphatically placed βουλευτοῖσιν is the hideous irony that the funeral καλύμματα[44] helped to *effect* the death. When the robe is displayed together with the bodies of Klytaimestra and Aigisthos, Orestes wonders whether he should call it a net or shroud: 'a snare for a wild beast, or the foot-wrapping covering of a corpse's bier' (ἄγρευμα θηρός, ἢ νεκροῦ ποδένδυτον | δροίτης κατασκήνωμα).[45] In ποδένδυτον are combined two characteristics of the attire of the dead: solemnity[46] and the enclosure of the feet. The latter influences Orestes' decision to call the robe a net after all, for he continues 'You would call it a net and a snare and foot-entangling robe' (δίκτυον μὲν οὖν | ἄρκυν τ' ἂν εἴποις καὶ ποδιστῆρας πέπλους). The *hapax legomenon* ποδιστῆρας[47] picks up ποδένδυτον: the robe was

[41] E.g. the clay model of an *ekphora*: Kurtz and Boardman 1971: plate 16, also plate 37; *ABV*² 346, 7–8; Vermeule 1979: 14, fig. 8a; cf. Sokolowski 1969: no. 97; κρύπτειν in Eur. *Heracl.* 561, *Tro.* 627, *Hipp.* 1458; Eur. *Hec.* 432; Soph. *El.* 1468–9.

[42] Cf. Pearson 1917: *ad loc.*; Easterling 1982 on Soph. *Trach.* 674 τὸν ἐνδυτῆρα πέπλον. The robe in which the corpse was wrapped might be called an ἔνδυμα (Prott and Ziehen 1906: no. 93a.3).

[43] *Ag.* 1492, 1580 (παγαῖς Nauck); cf. e.g. Penelope weaving the shroud for her father-in-law, and Sen. *Ag.* 882–3 (quoted above).

[44] καλύμματα of funerary coverings: Soph. *El.* 1468.

[45] *Cho.* 998–9. δροίτη can mean bath or bier (see n. 28 above). And cf. *Ag.* 1540, *Eum.* 633–5 ... δροίτῃ περῶντι λουτρὰ κἀπὶ τέρματι | φᾶρος παρεσκήνωσεν, ἐν δ' ἀτέρμονι | κόπτει πεδήσασ' ἄνδρα δαιδάλῳ πέπλῳ.

[46] See n. 42 above.

[47] It may be intended to suggest ποδοστράβη, a kind of hunting net: Thomson 1966: *ad loc.* cites Xen. *Cyn.* 11.11. And cf. Eur. *Bacch.* 833.

not just wrapped around Agamemnon's feet (ποδένδυτον) but because he was alive it actively entangled them (ποδιστῆρας), and that is why it is to be called a net.

Over the corpse of Agamemnon the chorus had asked who will bury him, who will lament him and who will deliver the praise at the tomb (ἐπιτύμβιος αἶνος) with tears and with sincerity. Klytaimestra replied that she will bury him, without lamentation.[48] In the *Choephori* the great ἐπιτύμβιος θρῆνος (334–5), with its anger at the griefless, dishonourable funeral of Agamemnon (429–50), cannot repair the absence of Orestes from the placing in state (*prothesis*) and carrying out (*ekphora*) of the body itself (8–9):[49] 'I mourned your death, father, but I was not there, nor did I stretch out my hand at the carrying out of your corpse' (οὐ γὰρ παρὼν ᾤμωξα σόν, πάτερ, μόρον, | οὐδ' ἐξέτεινα χεῖρ' ἐπ' ἐκφορᾷ νεκροῦ). It is only at the end of the play, with his attention on the funeral robe, that Orestes declares (1014) 'Now I am here and praise him, now I am here and mourn for him' (νῦν αὐτὸν αἰνῶ, νῦν ἀποιμώζω παρών). The repeated emphatic νῦν means 'now at last',[50] αἰνῶ refers to the funeral praise (αἶνος)[51] and ἀποιμώζειν elsewhere in Aeschylus means lamentation over the body itself[52] – as παρών here and at v. 8 suggests. But whereas the lament of Andromakhe, for example, takes the form of a direct address to the dead Hektor,[53] Orestes here cannot address the man himself. Instead, he addresses the shroud (net): 'and addressing this father-slaying textile, I grieve' (1115 πατροκτόνον θ' ὕφασμα προσφωνῶν[54] τόδε ἀλγῶ). But the grief (ἄλγος) must be for more than his father: 'I grieve for what has been done and what has been suffered and for the entire family' (1016 ἀλγῶ μὲν ἔργα καὶ πάθος γένος τε πᾶν); and any attempt to praise or lament is cut short by the onset of the Erinyes.

At this point another victim of her own funerary ritual deserves mention: Sophocles' Antigone. The cave in which she is to be imprisoned

[48] *Ag.* 1547–50 (the textual problem does not concern us here).

[49] For the distinction between lamentation over the body and at the tomb see Alexiou 1974: 5–8.

[50] See Thomson 1966 on *Ag.* 1475 and *Cho.* 1014.

[51] Praise over the body: Hom. *Il.* 24.749, 767; Soph. *Aj.* 923–4; Bion 1.71; Alexiou 1974: 34, 40, 122, 175, 182.

[52] *Ag.* 329, fr. 138. Although lamentation tended to be female, it did not exclude male close kin: Alexiou 1974: 6.

[53] Hom. *Il.* 24.725, cf. 748, 762; 23.19; Eur. *Tro.* 1167; Alexiou 1974: 106, 109–10, 140, 174–6, 182–4, etc.

[54] Cf. also 997 τί νιν προσείπω, of the robe; such hesitancy expressed in the form of a question is characteristic of the lament: cf. e.g. *Ag.* 1489–91, and numerous examples in Alexiou 1974: 161–5; Thomson 1953: 81–2. See also the inversion of this device at Eur. *El.* 907–8, where it is used by Elektra to express her *hatred* over the corpse of Aigisthos.

is called her tomb,[55] and her movement towards it is imagined as a funeral procession.[56] Uniquely, she takes part [254] in this movement while still alive.[57] She will go to Hades αὐτόνομος ζῶσα μόνη δὴ θνατῶν (821–2 'alone among mortals of my own accord and whilst alive'). Agamemnon too was a victim of part of his funerary ritual, and he was buried without the normal lamentation and praise. But Antigone also suffers the *awareness* of being buried without lamentation (ἄκλαυτος) and without family (876 ἄφιλος; cf. 881–2); and the chorus point out to her the absence of praise.[58] She is lamented only by herself. Some critics have been puzzled that she should lament so bitterly, given her earlier defiance of death. Antigone, it is felt, should be made of sterner stuff. Most recently, Winnington-Ingram has suggested that the change in Antigone is brought about by her discovery of how she is to die: 'the thought of being buried alive has always had a peculiar horror for the human mind'.[59] This misses the point. She laments because it is her funeral.[60]

What then of the lamentation and praise due to Agamemnon? Orestes was not present to utter them over his father's body. And Klytaimestra, who wrapped the body in its robe, uttered no praise or lament over it. But as Agamemnon entered the house to his death, she compared his presence there with the living root of a tree shading the house.[61] The use of a striking image as praise at the moment of arrival is appropriate,[62] but must of course have seemed to the audience deeply ironical. Comparison of the beloved dead to a tree is a commonplace of the Greek lament from Homer to the present day.[63] And the idea of the lost one as a *shading* tree is found in an early version of the lament of the virgin as well as in the modern lament.[64] Furthermore, the notion of uprooting occurs as early as Homer as an image of death, and in the lament of the chorus of Sophocles'

[55] Soph. *Ant.* 849, 888, 891, 920.

[56] 807 νεάταν ὁδόν, 892, 920; cf. Soph. *Trach.* 874–5 τὴν πανυστάτην ὁδῶν ἁπασῶν; *Anth. Pal.* 7.203; etc.

[57] Stressed at 811, 821, 851, 888, 920. Both Kassandra (*Ag.* 1322–3) and Klytaimestra (*Cho.* 926) θρηνοῦσι for themselves (in a sense).

[58] 817, reading οὔκουν (not οὐκοῦν), Knox's case for which (1964: 176–7) is supported by the point being made here – that had Antigone died in any normal way she would have had a funeral ἔπαινος.

[59] Winnington-Ingram 1980: 139.

[60] Cf. e.g. Eur. *Bacch.* 1302–22, Kadmos' praise of Pentheus, where, as at Eur. *El.* 907–8, the commentators fail to mention the convention of praise over the dead body (see also n. 50 above).

[61] *Ag.* 966–7. Thomson 1966 puts these lines after 971.

[62] See e.g. Cairns 1972: 22, 25–7.

[63] *Il.* 18.55–7; Alexiou 1974: 198–201. This does not mean of course that it cannot be employed on the living (e.g. *Od.* 6.162–3).

[64] Alexiou 1974: 198, 204.

Electra for the royal house.[65] Despite the general thematic continuity of the ritual lament demonstrated in detail by Alexiou, we cannot infer that the specific comparison of the beloved to a shade-giving tree now uprooted by death was a theme of the ancient lament.

It is nevertheless striking that in fact most of the images applied 'with a griefless mind' (895 ἀπενθήτῳ φρενί) by Klytaimestra to Agamemnon at the climax of her welcoming speech are found also in the modern lament.[66] It seems not unlikely that Klytaimestra's emotional praise of Agamemnon would have been associated by the audience not only with his arrival but with his death, not only with the *encomium* but with the lament. In fact the formal and thematic similarities between the *encomium* and the lament[67] are exploited by the dramatist, just as he exploits the similarities between bathing and dressing a man for a feast on the one hand and for his tomb on the other. Klytaimestra employs the funeral praise (αἶνος), as well as the funeral bath and the funeral robes, on her living husband.

POSTSCRIPT

There is further discussion of death ritual in Aeschylus, in a broader context, in Seaford 2012a. See also K. J. Hame, 'All in the family: funeral rites and the health of the *oikos* in Aischylos' *Oresteia*', *AJP* 125 (2004), 513–38, and 'Female control of funeral rites in Greek tragedy: Klytaimestra, Medea, and Antigone', *CP* 103 (2008), 1–15; L. McNeil, 'Bridal cloths, cover-ups, and *kharis*: the "carpet scene" in Aeschylus' *Agamemnon*', *G&R* 52 (2005), 1–17.

More generally see H. P. Foley, *Female Acts in Greek Tragedy* (Princeton: Princeton University Press, 2001); L. Swift, *The Hidden Chorus: Echoes of Genre in Tragic Lyric* (Oxford: Oxford University Press, 2010), chapter 7.

For other murders in the bath see J. N. Bremmer. 'Agamemnon's death in the bath: some parallels', *Mnemosyne* 39 (1986), 418.

For the perversion of ritual in tragedy see A. Henrichs, '"Let the good prevail": perversions of the ritual process in Greek tragedy', in

65 *Il.* 14.414–5; Soph. *El.* 764–5; cf. a third-century CE consolatory inscription from Amorgos (*BCH* for 1891: 586–9); all from Alexiou 1974: 198–201.

66 See esp. Alexiou 1974: 91–4, 123, 153, 188, 203. For the lament for the man still alive see Hom. *Il.* 6.500, 18.51, 24.328.

67 Thomson 1953 and 1961: 133–4; cf. e.g. the chorus' greeting at *Ag.* 785–7 with their lament at 1489–91.

D. Yatromanolakis and P. Roilos (eds.), *Greek Ritual Poetics* (Washington, DC: Center for Hellenic Studies, 2004), pp. 189–98.

For death ritual see Garland 1985.

For Homer see J. Grethlein, 'The poetics of the bath in the *Iliad*', *HSCP* 103 (2007), 25–49.

CHAPTER 12

The Destruction of Limits in Sophocles' Electra

Greek tragedy is full of rituals perverted by intrafamilial conflict. To mention some examples from the house of Atreus: the funeral bath and the funeral covering, normally administered to a man's corpse by his wife as an expression of *philia*, have in Aeschylus' *Oresteia* become instruments in the killing of Agamemnon;[1] the pouring of libations at the tomb, normally a θελκτήριον ('appeasement') for the dead, becomes in the *Choephori* an occasion for his arousal;[2] Euripides has Klytaimestra 'sacrificed' while performing the sacrifice for her (fictitious) newly born grandchild.[3] On the important question of why it is that tragedians pervert ritual I hope to shed some light in future publications. The purpose of this chapter is to examine the radical form taken by the perversion of mourning in Sophocles' *Electra*.

In the first decade of the twentieth century the comparative anthropologists Hertz and van Gennep discovered as a widespread feature of the period of mourning its character as participation in the transitional state of the recently dead, to be ended by the incorporation of the dead person into his or her proper destination and the reincorporation of the mourners into the flow of everyday social life. The mourning relatives in a sense share the condition of the dead. They are separated from the rest of the community and may not eat, dress, etc. like other members of the community, a condition from which they are liberated by the eventual incorporation of the dead into the world of the dead.[4] This analysis has been exemplified in, for example, a recent study of the ideas and practice of modern rural death rituals in Greece: the seclusion of the mourners is a 'reflection of the isolation of the corpse lying buried in the ground', and their conversation with the dead

[1] Seaford 1984c[II].

[2] E.g. Eur. *IT* 166; Aesch. *Cho.* 42–5; cf. 87–105, 123, 456, etc. For funerary ritual stirring up feelings of revenge against outsiders see Alexiou 1974: 21–2.

[3] Eur. *El.* 1125, 1133, 1141–4.

[4] Hertz 1960; van Gennep 1960: 146–65; a recent assessment is Huntingdon and Metcalf 1979.

> draws to a close with the rite of exhumation, when the deceased is fully incorporated into the world of the dead. Over the course of the liminal period following death, the religious perspective within which the conversation between the living and dead is sustained is gradually replaced by a common sense perspective in which the finality of death is accepted.[5]

As for ancient Greece, continuity with modern mortuary ritual and lamentation is manifest in numerous details.[6] To take some examples relevant to our argument: the direct address to the dead was an element in the ancient Greek lament no less than it is in the modern;[7] Aristotle refers to the 'homoeopathy' of the mourners with the [316] dead;[8] ancient mourners, like the mourning women of rural Greece today, wore distinctive dark clothing and did not participate in communal religious life;[9] we also hear, as might be expected, of rituals marking the end of the period of mourning.[10] That ancient mortuary rituals 'fit neatly enough into van Gennep's scheme' has been noted recently by Robert Parker.[11] And so in the words addressed to Sophocles' Elektra (*El.* 1085–6), 'you have chosen a lifetime (αἰών) shared [with your dead father] and full of weeping',[12] there is nothing anomalous about sharing with the dead. What is anomalous is the αἰών:[13] Elektra is determined never to cease from mourning (104, 211, etc.).

5 Danforth 1982: esp. 54–6, 60–1, 140–1. For the concept of 'liminality' see e.g. Turner 1967: 93–111; Danforth 1982: 35–7.

6 See esp. Politis 1931: 323–6, and Alexiou 1974, whose treatment demonstrates *continuity* rather than mere similarity, both in the basic pattern of the ritual and in numerous (though not all) details, and illuminates the tenacity of the tradition in ritual and lament even in periods of historical and religious change.

7 Alexiou 1974: 8, 31, 46, 59, 109–10.

8 Fr. 101 Rose, *ap.* Ath. 15.675a; see further Parker 1983: 64. Soph. *El.* 847 τὸν ἐν πένθει (of the dead) assimilates their state to the mourners.

9 Danforth 1982: 54; Parker 1983: 37; Alexiou 1974: 8; etc.

10 Harp. and *Suda*, s.v. τριακάς; Poll. *Onom.* 1.66; Plut. *Lyc.* 27, *Mor.* 297a; cf. Lys. 1.14.

11 Parker 1983: 60; he quotes Hom. *Il.* 23.49–53, but it should also be remembered that the period of mourning/exclusion from shrines or festivals (Parker 1983: 37, 65 n. 110) does not necessarily end with the funeral.

12 σὺ πάγκλαυτον αἰῶνα κοινὸν εἵλου. Many have suspected κοινόν. But (1) consider what precedes. The song moves from the theme of (birds') care for parents (or 'family solidarity', Kells) to the dead Agamemnon (whether or not we read πατρὸς in 1075) and the lamenting Elektra as εὔπατρις (1081, with a secondary reference to her loyalty to her father). All this facilitates the sense 'in common with your dead father' in 1085. (2) κοινός is frequent of suffering (e.g. *Aj.* 267), of sharing in death (e.g. *Aj.* 577) and of kinship (e.g. *OC* 533–5). But much more significant is that in Sophocles the senses may be combined to express the shared death of kin (*Ant.* 57, 146, 546; cf. 1, 202), even by Elektra herself fifty lines later (1135 τύμβου πατρῴου κοινὸν εἰληχὼς μέρος). (3) The idea of association with the dead father is what we might expect (n. 8 above), and indeed has already been expressed recently by Elektra (986 συμπόνει πατρί).

13 αἰών means her whole span of life: cf. e.g. Soph. *Trach.* 2; also Aesch. *Cho.* 442 (see below n. 18).

In terms of the scheme discovered by Hertz and van Gennep, one aspect of this anomaly is the absence of a group into which to be reintegrated: Elektra cannot feel at one with the killers of her father. Another aspect is the failure of Agamemnon to be properly incorporated into the world of the dead. Such incorporation depended traditionally on the performance of funerary ritual.[14] Whether or not it was possible to appease successfully a murdered husband,[15] in none of the three tragic versions is even the normal funerary ritual properly performed,[16] and in Aeschylus and Sophocles Klytaimestra is prompted by a dream to appease her victim with libations which are claimed by her enemies to be ineffective.[17] In Aeschylus the ritual was carried out, but without lamentation, praise and honour; Elektra was not allowed to take part; Agamemnon's body was subjected to mutilation (μασχαλισμός);[18] and Orestes and Elektra eventually address their dead father, whose anger has outlived his cremation.[19] In Sophocles the situation is even worse (*El.* 445–6): Klytaimestra subjected the corpse to μασχαλισμός and wiped the bloodstains on his head to serve as a bath (ἐπὶ λουτροῖσιν);[20] and the only *[317]* other rites we hear of are choral dances (χοροί) and monthly sacrifices to the saviour deities on the day of Agamemnon's death (278–81).[21] It is therefore quite understandable that the Sophoclean Elektra justifies her excessive lamentation by the sight of her father's woes (πήματα) constantly 'increasing instead of diminishing' (258–60 θάλλοντα μᾶλλον ἢ καταφθίνοντα), and that Agamemnon 'comes to the light' (419) to appear to Klytaimestra in a dream, rather as in rural Greece today dreams are considered to be a channel through which the dead may make demands of the living – but only, on the whole, in the limited transitional period following death.[22]

14 Hom. *Od.* 11.72–3; *Il.* 23.71; etc.

15 μασχαλισμός (see n. 18 below) was an attempt to control the ghost. On the victim's anger see now Parker 1983: 104–43.

16 See Eur. *El.* 289, 323–31; for Aeschylus and Sophocles see below.

17 Aesch. *Cho.* 519; Soph. *El.* 442–3.

18 See n. 15 above; *Ag.* 1553–4, *Cho.* 429–39 (of which the continuation, ἔπρασσε δ' ἅπερ νιν ὧδε θάπτει, | μόρον κτίσαι μωμένα | ἄφερτον αἰῶνι σῷ, seems to imply that the dishonour done to Agamemnon was intended to produce a lifetime (αἰών, see n. 13 above) of lamentation for his surviving children); 444–50.

19 *Cho.* 315–23, 324–7, 332–9, etc.

20 I.e. to cleanse herself, with the implication also that this was the only funeral bath Agamemnon got. For the possibility of the water in which the mourners washed being offered to the dead see Parker 1983: 36 n. 15.

21 It is true that Agamemnon has a tomb, which implies that he was buried. But cf. Eur. *El.* 289 (burial denied) with e.g. 323 (his tomb). The story needs a tomb. The question does not arise of whether Elektra was prevented from performing the rites (cf. Aesch. *Cho.* 444–50).

22 Danforth 1982: 135. Cf. Akhilleus and Patroklos.

Elektra says that when she sees the monthly choral dances and sacrifices instituted by Klytaimestra, 'All by myself I lament, I pine and I groan over the wretched feast named after my father' (283–5). Rites were performed, in the classical period, on the thirtieth day after death.[23] And there is lexicographical evidence for a meal shared by the relatives in honour of the dead person 'on the thirtieth day'.[24] If the Attic thirtieth-day rite did include such a meal, then the consumption which presumably accompanied Klytaimestra's monthly choral dances and animal sacrifices is a specific perversion of this ritual meal; and this (rather than, as is supposed by the latest commentator, the meal at which Agamemnon was killed[25]) is the meal which Elektra means by 'the wretched meal named after my father': the usurpers even named their celebratory feasts after Agamemnon, like a hero cult.[26] Perhaps they also envisaged them as a celebration of the fatal meal. When Elektra sees all this she weeps all alone.

There is reason to believe that in classical Athens the thirtieth-day rite concluded the period of mourning, or at least was a significant stage in the separation of the mourners from the dead.[27] If so, then another dimension of the perversion of Klytaimestra's celebration consists in its monthly repetition. So far from contributing to the restoration of normality, it renews every month the insult to Agamemnon, and thereby contributes to the dual impossibility of incorporating Elektra back into the world of the living on the one hand and her angry, suffering father into the world of the dead on the other. She must respond to the perverted and protracted rites of her mother with anomalously protracted lamentation of her own: δείν' ἐν δεινοῖς ἠναγκάσθην (221).

Klytaimestra responds, in her turn, by using a traditional consolation (cf. 153–4) – 'you are not the only one to suffer bereavement' – as a reproach, and adds the malicious hope that 'the gods below' may never release Elektra from her lamentations. As we have seen, Elektra shares her life (αἰών) with her dead father. There are even plans to put her, if she does not cease lamenting, in a place where she will not see the sun, 'living in an enclosed room, outside this land (379–82 ζῶσα … ἐν κατηρεφεῖ |

[23] *IG* XII 5.593 = *SIG*³ 1218 = Sokolowski 1969: no. 97; cf. Harp. and *Suda* s.v. τριακάς; Poll. *Onom.* 1.66.

[24] Phot. *Bibl.* s.v. καθέδρα; Bekker 1814: 268.19–23; Rohde 1925: 195 n. 86.

[25] Kells 1973: *ad loc.*; cf. Soph. *El.* 203–4; *Od.* 4.531–5; Eust. *Od.* p. 1507 says that Soph. meant by Ἀγαμέμνονος δαίς a (yearly) celebration.

[26] There were e.g. monthly sacrifices to Herakles in fifth-century Attica: Polemon *ap.* Ath. 6.234e; cult of Agamemnon: Roscher 1884–1937: 1.96. For (later) monthly celebrations or sacrifices see Diog. Laert. 10.18; Gow 1965 on Theoc. *Id.* 17.127; Wissowa 1902.

[27] Lys. 1.14 ἔδοξε … τὸ πρόσωπον ἐψιμυθιῶσθαι, τοῦ ἀδελφοῦ τεθνεῶτος οὔπω τριάκονθ' ἡμέρας.

στέγῃ, χθονὸς τῆσδ' ἐκτὸς)[28]. This [318] will suit her position between the living and the dead. In the same way Antigone, as a result of what is regarded as undue attachment to the dead, is put alive into an enclosed tomb (κατηρεφὴς τύμβος),[29] where, says Kreon, she can pray to Hades, 'the only god she worships' (777).

Already Elektra is suffering deprivation (187–92): 'I waste away without children, I have no loving husband to watch over me; instead, like some worthless outsider I tend the rooms of my father, in these squalid clothes, and stand around an empty table.' Are these sufferings self-imposed, or are they inflicted on her directly by her enemies? This ambiguity seems to me unresolvable, but significant. On the one hand they are appropriate to the condition of the mourner,[30] and may seem therefore to be self-imposed. Why then does Elektra seem to imply here that the sufferings are inflicted on her by her enemies? In the same spirit perhaps as Euripides' Elektra adopts humble tasks entirely voluntarily in order to display to the gods the hubris of Aigisthos (Eur. *El.* 58). On the other hand, the imprisonment with which Elektra is threatened has provided a clear example of a punishment which is imposed by her enemies but also appropriate to the condition of the mourner. Indeed the welcome she extends to this prospect of a living death, and even her bitter desire to be far removed from her sister (391), are based on the realities of mourning: participation in the state of the dead and seclusion from the non-mourners. And although it may appear paradoxical to punish Elektra's excessive mourning by inflicting on her sufferings which are a more extreme manifestation of the same condition, we find the same paradox in a third-century law from Gambreion, which imposes certain restrictions on funerals, requires the women to 'take part in the processions written in the law' after the official period of mourning is over, and at the same time imposes on the women a ten-year exclusion from sacrifice and from the Thesmophoria as a penalty for ignoring the restrictions.[31] That is to say, the penalty for excessive mourning is a further long period of the kind of exclusion that is appropriate to the condition of mourning.

[28] Kaibel reads ἐν κατηρεφεῖ χθονὸς στέγῃ τῆσδ' ἐκτὸς, i.e., ἐκτὸς τῆσδε (στέγης), 'not in the palace but underground'. [I now prefer to read ἐντὸς.]

[29] Soph. *Ant.* 885–6; cf. 888 εἴτ' ἐν τοιαύτῃ ζῶσα τυμβεύειν στέγῃ, 774–80, etc. Houses sealed off when death imminent? (Parker 1983: 35 n. 10, citing Men. *Asp.* 466–7).

[30] Obviously a wedding could not be held in mourning; less obvious is the idea that contact with death might endanger the female reproductive processes: Parker 1983: 53; some evidence for fasting: Parker 1983: 36 n. 16, and Hom. *Il.* 24.612–13; torn clothes: e.g. Sokolowski 1955: no. 16.

[31] Sokolowski 1955: no. 16; Alexiou 1974: 17.

It may indeed be supposed that Elektra's enemies fear the threat that might be posed by her offspring (as Elektra at least claims, at 964–6), as in Euripides' version. But it is anyway unthinkable that Elektra should want to be married while absorbed in mourning. Husbandless, she lives like an outsider in the rooms (θάλαμοι) of her father (190). Now the word *thalamos*, which refers here to an inner room of the palace, refers in three of its four other occurrences in Sophocles either to a bridal chamber or to a tomb.[32] And however incompatible these two places may seem, the traditional association of the death of an unmarried girl with her wedding[33] allows Sophocles to exploit in *Antigone* the ambiguity of *thalamos*: the tomb in which Antigone is to be put alive, and where she dies in a kind of wedding ritual with Haimon (1240–1 νυμφικὰ τελή), is compared to the 'tomb-like chamber' (τυμβήρης θάλαμος) in which Danae was united with Zeus (947); and in the hymn to Eros Antigone is said to be on her way to 'the chamber that receives all' (804 τὸν παγκοίταν θάλαμον; *[319]* cf. 813–16).[34] In the *Electra* passage too, it seems to me, the word is chosen for its association with both the tomb and the bridal chamber. The primary reference of θαλάμους πατρός is of course the palace, but it cannot avoid connoting in this context the abode of the dead,[35] with the result that Elektra seems to belong both to the world of the dead and (but as an outsider) to the world of the living. This is the paradox of mourning, sharpened here by the isolation of the mourner.

This isolation is expressed by a further layer of ambiguity. Any *thalamos* of death occupied by an unmarried girl would readily be imagined also as bridal, as for example in *Antigone*. This connotation is particularly likely here, where Elektra is complaining that she has no husband. Normally it is at her wedding that a girl feels isolated from her father's home, an isolation associated apparently with death,[36] as the necessary prelude to incorporation into the *bridal thalamos*. The bride undergoes a temporary, solitary liminality, between the two households.[37] Elektra, however, suffers a comparable isolation in mourning. The unusually solitary liminality of Elektra's mourning has in this passage been assimilated, albeit faintly, to

[32] *Ant.* 804, 947 (see below), *Trach.* 913, *OT* 195. On the chthonic and bridal associations of θάλαμος generally see Vernant 1983: 149.

[33] And of the wedding with death: see e.g. Alexiou and Dronke 1971.

[34] Cf. also e.g. Eur. *Supp.* 1021–2 χρῶτα χρωτὶ πέλας θεμένα Φερσεφονείας ἥξω θαλάμους; Simon. 81 Page (*Epig. Gr.*) οὐκ ἐπιδὼν νύμφεια λέχη κατέβην τὸν ἄφυκτον Γόργιππος ξανθῆς Φερσεφόνης θάλαμον; Vernant 1983: 149.

[35] Cf. e.g. n. 34, and Aesch. *Cho.* 315–18, where Orestes speaks of the εὐναί of his dead father.

[36] See Jenkins 1983: 142; Alexiou 1974: 58, 120–2; etc.

[37] Seaford 1986b.

the solitary liminality of the bride. But for Elektra it is permanent. She lives in the *thalamoi* of the palace. But she does not belong there. She should have made the transition to the *thalamoi* of her husband. But because she belongs to the dead, to the *thalamoi* of her dead father, she cannot make this transition. There is something similar in Euripides' version, where she is a married *parthenos* ('maiden'): being in mourning, she rejects participation in the celebrations of the *parthenoi* (167–83), but she also says of herself 'with no share in the festive rites and deprived of the choral dances, I shun the company of women, being a maiden' (310–11 ἀνέορτος ἱερῶν καὶ χορῶν τητωμένη | ἀναίνομαι γυναῖκας οὖσα παρθένος),[38] and so is in a sense permanently in the transitional position ascribed by John Chrysostom to the bride: 'the bride is in between these two groups [i.e. the chorus of women and the choruses of maidens], neither unmarried nor a wife, for from there she comes out ...' (*PG* 62.386).

To return to the main line of argument: it appears that the deprivations characteristic of mourning are inflicted on Elektra, in an intensified form, by her enemies. Or so at least she seems to suggest for some of them. Ritual liminality appears as what might be called social liminality. And it might be added here that this liminality or exclusion is provided with a visual dimension by the conditions of performance: Elektra spends *[320]* almost the entire play outside the door of the palace, and on the news of the death of Orestes she resolves to wither away 'without dear ones' (ἄφιλος) and 'by this door' (τῇδε πρὸς πύλῃ) (818–19). Now according to the analysis proposed by van Gennep and Hertz, death rites, by maintaining temporarily the reality of the dead person, articulate an ordered integration of the dead into the next world and of the mourners back into society. 'In the final analysis', writes Hertz at the end of his study, 'death as a social

[38] γυναῖκας in 311 is Triclinius' correction of γυμνὰς (though he left the δὲ). Kovacs 1985 reads ἀναίνομαι γὰρ γυμνὰς οὖσα παρθένους (he also deletes 308, and reads Scaliger's Κάστορ(ε) ὃ in 312, for which see Kovacs 1985: 308 n. 9). But (1) He dismisses Zuntz's view that Triclinius derived the correction from another MS, but without mentioning one of the two pillars of Zuntz's argument (see Zuntz 1965: 107, on *El.* 168). (2) More importantly, Elektra cannot mean by γυμνὰς 'without festal attire'. The examples Kovacs gives of γυμνός meaning 'something less than total nakedness' all refer to the absence of an (outer) garment – a very different matter from poor *quality* of clothing. (The modern 'I've nothing to wear' is irrelevant.) And of course Elektra has just stated that she weaves her own πέπλοι (307). The corruption may have entered from 309. (3) It is not true that 'lack of clothing was precisely the reason she gave the Chorus in 175–9 for declining their invitation' to the festival. The reason she gave there was lamentation, to which she added (184–9) the complaint that her clothes were unsuitable for the daughter of Agamemnon. And so the chorus' offer of fine clothes (190–3) is of course not taken up. (4) It is not true that Elektra's other complaints at 307–10 'describe real and not imaginary or self-inflicted injuries'. With 309 cf. 55–9. (5) Kovacs' objections to the sense of 311 underestimate the isolation inherent in Elektra's position.

phenomenon consists in a dual and painful process of mental disintegration and synthesis. It is only when this process is completed that society, its peace recovered, can triumph over death.'[39] What happens in Sophocles' *Electra* is the reversal of this function of death rites. Deprivation, separation and association with the dead, which are normally preliminary responses to the disruption caused by death, and so agents of an articulated restoration of social cohesion, have in this case become instruments in the struggle, agents of disruption within the family. In the same way Elektra, for her part, gives as one reason among others for her continued lamentation (355–6): 'I cause them grief (λυπῶ δὲ τούτους), and in doing so attach honour to my dead father, if there is any gratitude down there.' It is an instrument in the apparently endless conflict with her mother and stepfather, a response, certainly, to the disruption caused by death, but also an agent of disruption in the family. It is true that she attributes to her lamentation the orthodox purpose of honouring the dead; but in this case the honour derives from the grief (λύπη) caused to other members of the family. So far from being a response by the kinship group to the disruption caused by death, a response which though relatively unrestrained is nevertheless contained within an articulated framework of separation and reintegration, the ritual of mourning has been perverted by both sides into a weapon in a conflict within the kinship group, a conflict which is uncontained by any temporal, moral or ritual limit, and which is intensified by the perversion of the natural relationship between mother and daughter. The blood which Elektra drinks from the soul of her mother is 'unmixed' (786). So far from containing disorder, the ritual is employed in its service.

In its provision of an articulated framework for a grief which has no natural limits, ritual may be supported by exhortation[40] or legislation. For example, Lykourgos was said to have prescribed for the Spartans a period of mourning (χρόνος πένθους) of only eleven days: on the twelfth day they had to sacrifice to Demeter and 'let their grief go' (λύειν τὸ πάθος).[41] (As is so often the case in tragedy, Sophocles' *Electra* represents the prevalence, in exotic circumstances, of a tendency which in life had to be kept under control.[42]) Inherent in death ritual are socially constructed limits on the potentially unlimited, natural expression of grief. The conflict in the house

[39] Hertz 1960: 86; Danforth 1982: *passim*.
[40] E.g. Hom. *Il.* 24.549; Soph. *El.* 154, 289; Cic. *Tusc.* 3.79.
[41] Plut. *Lyc.* 27.2; see also Alexiou 1974: 16–17.
[42] Cf. the *pleasure* of lamenting: Eur. *Tro.* 608–9, *El.* 125–6; [Aesch.] *PV* 637–9; Alexiou 1974: 230 n. 69.

of Atreus, on the other hand, is without measure or limit. To the chorus, who urge restraint, Elektra replies (236–7): 'And what natural measure is there of wickedness? Tell me, how can it be good to be unconcerned for the dead?' (καὶ τί μέτρον κακότατος ἔφυ; φέρε, | πῶς ἐπὶ τοῖς φθιμένοις ἀμελεῖν καλόν;). κακότας here refers to the wickedness of the usurpers, perhaps also to the resulting suffering of Elektra. The point of ἔφυ is that there is no *natural* limit in it. The absolute, unrestrained κακότας of her enemies must produce in Elektra misery which is absolute and unrestrained and lamentation without end. Where socially constructed ritual norms are swept away, or perverted into the service of a natural, unrestrained conflict, there are no limits. Elektra is drawn into the paradoxical state of absolute liminality.

The eventual victory over Klytaimestra and Aigisthos constitutes a further stage [321] in the reciprocal perversion of death ritual. Klytaimestra is struck down at the very moment when 'she is arranging the urn for burial, while those two stand over her nearby' (1400–1 ἐς τάφον | λέβητα κοσμεῖ, τὼ δ' ἐφέστατον πέλας). κοσμεῖν is often used of the ordered beauty of death ritual, as just recently by Elektra of the rites that she could not perform for Orestes (1139; cf. e.g. Soph. *Ant.* 396, 901). In τὼ δ' ἐφέστατον πέλας there is a sinister ambiguity: on the one hand it signifies attendance at the solemn deposition of the urn,[43] on the other hand the imminent attack.[44] As in the *Oresteia* (see n. 1 above), death ritual has become an instrument of murder. A few lines later Aigisthos arrives and sees the covered body which he thinks is Orestes'. The concealment of the head would arouse no suspicion, as this was not unknown in the funeral.[45] Aigisthos declares his desire to lament his kin (1469), a declaration which has the same effect as the earlier κοσμεῖ (1401) about Klytaimestra: after the reciprocal perversion of death ritual, here at last appears the (false) prospect of the restoration of ritual order. The critics react either by suspecting hypocritical piety (e.g. Jebb) or by supposing that Sophocles has decided to give the villains decent emotions after all (e.g. Kells). Both these reactions are wrong because they both miss the point, which is that the suggestion of ritual order is introduced only so that it may once again be horribly subverted. A further stage is reached in the reciprocally perverted use of death ritual in absolute conflict.

[43] Cf. e.g. Eur. *Andr.* 1102 ἐσχάραις τ' ἐφέσταμεν (at Delphi), *Supp.* 1009–10 τὴν ἧς ἐφέστηκας πέλας πυράν (of an anomalous situation, but perhaps employing a familiar phrase).

[44] Cf. e.g. Hdt. 3.78.4–5; Thuc. 8.69.4.

[45] Seaford 1984c[II]:252 n. 41. For lamentation though it seems always to have been uncovered, cf. 1468 χαλᾶτε πᾶν κάλυμμα ..., ὅπως κτλ. Notice the bitter ambiguity of προσηγορεῖν φίλως (1471): see also Seaford 1984c[II]: 249 n. 19.

It is true that this further stage does at least put an end to the anomalous lamentation of Elektra. Her 'unresolvable (ἄλυτα) woes' (230) was too pessimistic, and after the victory she finds the 'only deliverance (λυτήριον) from these longstanding woes' (1489–90). But just as, earlier in the play, she denied that the offerings sent to the tomb could constitute 'deliverance for the murder' (λυτήρια τοῦ φόνου) for the anxious Klytaimestra (447; cf. 635), so here the 'only λυτήριον' of her own sufferings involves (unlike e.g. the Spartan λύειν τὸ πάθος) neither ritual nor reintegration. Quite the reverse. It consists rather in giving the corpse of Aigisthos 'the kind of burial he deserves' (1488), that is to the birds or dogs.[46] The victory has only confirmed the mutual destruction of limits normally imposed on emotional behaviour by ritual.

Indeed, despite the deliverance (λυτήριον) devised at 1488–9, and despite her joy, Elektra says (1246–55) of her (inherently unlimited) suffering (οἷον ἔφυ κακόν; cf. 236) that it is never resolvable (οὔποτε καταλύσιμον), that it will never forget (οὐδέ ποτε λησόμενον); that it would be appropriate to speak of it constantly and without end (ὁ πᾶς ἐμοὶ ὁ πᾶς ... παρὼν ... χρόνος). The prospect of unending weeping, this time for joy – οὔ ποτ' ἐκλήξω χαρᾶς | δακρυρροοῦσα (1312–13)[47] – is the reverse image of her earlier 'I will not cease from laments' (103–4 οὐ μὲν δὴ λήξω θρήνων); again, it confirms the destruction of the limits inherent in the cyclical ritual process of mourning followed by the reintegration of the mourners back into society. And as for the anomaly of her apparently permanent, miserable virginity (187, see above), this too is reaffirmed by the appearance, after her recognition of Orestes, of its reverse image: it moves on to a triumphant offensive (1239–42): 'By Artemis, the ever untamed, I shall not deign to tremble before the excessive burden of women ever present within the house (περισσὸν ἄχθος ἔνδον γυναικῶν ὂν αἰεί).' Elektra was once 'excessive among those in the house' (155 τῶν ἔνδον περισσά); [322] but now it is the women whom she envisages as a permanent 'excessive burden in the house' (περισσὸν ἄχθος ἔνδον), in contrast to herself, for she associates herself by her oath with the fearless, homicidal,[48] extra-mural, permanent (ἀεί) virginity of Artemis.[49]

[46] Cf. e.g. Hom. *Od.* 3.259; Aesch. *Sept.* 1020–1; Eur. *El.* 895–6.

[47] χαρᾷ (Schaefer) is generally printed: but the mss. χαρᾶς appropriately (cf. 1311) emphasises her feeling of joy, reassures Orestes (cf. 1309–10) that weeping will require no pretence and intensifies the irony that Klytaimestra will misinterpret her tears.

[48] Cf. e.g. Hom. *Il.* 21.483–4 σὲ λέοντα γυναιξὶ | Ζεὺς θῆκεν, καὶ ἔδωκε κατακτάμεν ἥν κ' ἐθέλῃσθα.

[49] Cf. the Danaids rejecting marriage: ... ἀδμῆτος [i.e. Artemis] ἀδμήτᾳ ῥύσιος γενέσθω (Aesch. *Supp.* 149–50). For the deity expressing state of swearer see e.g. Ziebarth 1892: 13. It is almost as if the γοναὶ σωμάτων ἐμοὶ φιλτάτων (1233) sublimate Elektra's need for children; cf. also Plut. *Quaest. Rom.* 265a; Hsch. s.v. δευτερόποτμος.

Corresponding to the reintegration of the mourners back into society is, as we have seen, the integration of the dead into the world of the dead. How does Agamemnon fare? In Aeschylus' *Choephori* Orestes complains in the prologue, on his arrival in Argos, that he was not present (παρών) to perform the rites over the body (8–9); and after his victory over the usurpers he says 'Now I am here and praise him, now I am here and mourn for him' (1014). But there is of course even now no body;[50] and so he continues, 'addressing this father-killing robe I grieve', addressing not the body but the cloak in which it was wrapped. But this cloak, as Orestes has himself said in a style characteristic of the funeral eulogy (αἶνος),[51] should be called a net rather than a funerary cloak; and his attempt to praise and lament his father descends immediately into madness. This failure to perform the ritual, and thereby perhaps to establish his succession,[52] is of course the work of the Erinyes. But it seems also to proceed from the original perversion of Agamemnon's funerary ritual arising from the conflict within the family and embodied in the funerary cloak which has functioned as a net.[53]

In Sophocles' version, on the other hand, there is no such attempt after the victory to perform the rites. Quite the reverse. After proclaiming her intention never to cease crying for joy, Elektra goes on to say that 'if our father were to come here alive I would not consider it a prodigy, but would believe what I saw' (1316–17). So far from passing, after his prolonged sufferings, into the world of the dead, Agamemnon might even, so Elektra says, now reappear, as Orestes has seemed to do (1314–15), in the world of the living. This is of course an ἀδύνατον ('impossibility'), expressing her amazement. However, the content of the ἀδύνατον is not chosen arbitrarily. Rather, it must be seen in the light of her anomalous lamentation, which, apart from inflicting pain directly on the usurpers (see above), also had the role of sustaining the reality of the dead Agamemnon. This is a more defensive role than the lament has in Aeschylus, where the assistance of the dead Agamemnon, whose independent reality is not at stake, is invoked for the coup. The Sophoclean Elektra on the other hand implies that if she does not lament, 'the dead man will lie there as earth and nothing more, poor wretch' (245–6 ὁ μὲν θανὼν γᾶ τε καὶ οὐδὲν ὢν |

[50] Praise (αἶνος) and lamentation (ἀποιμώζειν) normally require a body: Seaford 1984c[ii]: 253 nn. 51 and 52.

[51] Seaford 1984c[ii]: 253 n. 54.

[52] Cf. e.g. Isaeus 2.36–7, 4.19, 4.26, 8.21–7, 9.4–5.

[53] See also the point made in n. 18 above.

κείσεται τάλας). This does not mean merely that the dead man will be *treated as if* he were nothing: there is also the implication that without her lamentation he will actually *be* no more than earth.[54] It is on these lines that we can resolve the contradiction between her reference to the sufferings of Agamemnon and her conception of her own desired death (by entering the house of Orestes, i.e. the urn in which she supposes his ashes to be) as 'she who is nothing into that which is nothing' (1166 τὴν μηδὲν ἐς τὸ μηδέν), to which she adds that the dead suffer no distress. Whereas Agamemnon had been lamented by her, she is now left with nobody in the world (1150–2), and so when she is united in death with Orestes they will have nobody in the world above to lament them. [323]

In rural Greece today a woman in the early period of mourning can 'inhabit the socially constructed reality that existed prior to the death of the relevant significant other. She can continue to interact with the deceased; she can carry on a reality-sustaining conversation with him through the performance of death rituals in his memory'.[55] Elektra seems to move between (subjectively) sustaining the reality of the dead man on the one hand and reacting to his (objective) sufferings on the other. And the specific capacity of the lament to sustain the reality of the dead person is no longer the necessary first stage (reaction to the shock caused by death) in an articulated process leading to the acceptance of death and the restoration of normality; it takes rather the form of a defensive move in a bitter struggle. Here again, then, the role of ritual is perverted. And after the recognition of Orestes, it is almost as if the abnormally antagonistic subjective element has moved, now that victory is in sight, on to a triumphant offensive, as if Elektra, who is sometimes thought to be losing her mind in this scene, is ready to believe in the actual return of Agamemnon from the dead. Here too, then, the destruction in conflict of the limits inherent in ritual is confirmed in the eventual reversal of circumstances.

In conclusion, these considerations seem to me central rather than peripheral to the understanding of the play. They also shed some light on the controversial problem of how Sophocles evaluates the revenge. Furthermore, this kind of analysis produces fruit elsewhere in tragedy. For example, the horror surrounding the destruction of the limits of (wedding) ritual is central to Sophocles' *Trachiniae*.[56] Limited progress can be made

[54] See also 356, 833–6. Dead person as earth: Peek 1955: no. 1702.2; Hom. *Il.* 7.99, 24.54; Eur. fr. 757.7, *Supp.* 531–6.

[55] Danforth 1982: 140.

[56] Seaford 1986b.

towards understanding the emotional effect of tragedy on the original audience. Literary criticism, if it ignores contemporary ritual, cannot make even this limited progress.[57]

POSTSCRIPT

For Sophocles' *Electra* see R. Kitzinger, 'Why mourning becomes Elektra', *ClAnt* 10 (1991), 298–327; H. Foley, *Female Acts in Greek Tragedy* (Princeton: Princeton University Press, 2001), chapter 3.2; G. Wheeler, 'Gender and transgression in Sophocles' *Electra*', *CQ* 53 (2003), 377–88; M. Wright, 'The joy of Sophocles' *Electra*', *G&R* 52 (2005), 172–94; E. Karakantza, 'Throwing out the *menos* with the bath water: the Sophoclean text vs Peter Stein's *Electra*', in A. Bakogianni (ed.), *Dialogues with the Past. Classical Reception: Theory & Practice*, *BICS* Supplement 126 (2013), 61–78; L. Swift, *The Hidden Chorus: Echoes of Genre in Tragic Lyric* (Oxford: Oxford University Press, 2011), chapter 7. There is now a substantial commentary on the play by P. Finglass, *Sophocles: Electra* (Cambridge: Cambridge University Press, 2007).

For the female lament in Greek tragedy see A. Suter, 'Lament in Euripides' *Trojan Women*', *Mnemosyne* 56 (2003), 1–28; C. Dué, *The Captive Woman's Lament in Greek Tragedy* (Austin: University of Texas Press, 2006). For the Greek female lament, both ancient and modern, see G. Holst-Warhaft, *Dangerous Voices: Women's Laments and Greek Literature* (London and New York: Routledge, 1992). A cross-cultural collection on the lament is A. Suter (ed.), *Lament: Studies in the Ancient Mediterranean and Beyond* (Oxford: Oxford University Press, 2008). For a theoretical perspective on tragic lamentation see B. Honig, *Antigone Interrupted* (Cambridge: Cambridge University Press, 2013).

[57] I would like to thank Robert Parker for his helpful criticisms without incriminating him in my argument.

PART IV

Tragedy and Marriage

CHAPTER 13

The Tragic Wedding

1. Introductory

Wedding ritual in tragedy tends to be subverted. In explaining and arguing for this generalisation I hope also to shed new light on some of the passages deployed.

My starting point is the actual wedding ceremony. How did the Athenians of the classical period imagine that it was celebrated? Our evidence derives largely from contemporary drama and vase painting. The picture presented by this evidence coheres very well in certain respects with that derived from other periods and places: Sappho, Catullus' imitation of the Greek, the lexicographers and so on. For example, one important element that is found in the Attic and the non-Attic evidence alike is the ambiguity, for the bride, of the transition. The abrupt passage to her new life contains both negative and positive elements. On the one hand it is like the yoking of an animal or the plucking of a flower.[1] It means isolation, separation from her friends and parents.[2] It is an occasion of resentment and anxiety,[3] comparable to death.[4] And on the other hand she is also subjected in the ceremony to praise and *makarismos* ('blessing').[5] The

[1] See nn. 58, 62, 63, 64 below.

[2] Sappho fr. 104(a); Soph. *Trach.* 527–30, 583; Theoc. *Id.* 18.38–9; Poll. *Onom.* 3.42; Catull. 62.21–2, 32; Dracontius, *Rom.* 6.92–5; Claud. *Epithal. in Pall.* 125; cf. e.g. Politis 1931: 281; Campbell 1964: 121; Sourvinou-Inwood 1987: 140.

[3] Sappho fr. 114; Poll. *Onom.* 3.42; Theoc. *Id.* 8.91; Schol. Theoc. *Id.* 18.34; Plut. *Lyc.* 15, *Mor.* 289a. For fifth-century Attic vase painting see Jenkins 1983; Sourvinou-Inwood 1987: 139–41. See also n. 2 above, and Claud. *Fesc. Hon. Aug.* 4.3–4, *Cons. Stil.* 2.357–8; Auson. *Cent. Nupt.* 91–3; [Varro], *Sent.* 11 Riese.

[4] See nn. 82–92 below; also Jenkins 1983; Williams 1984: 279 (on *ARV*^{2} 89.13); Antiph. DK 87 B 49 (cf. Thomson 1949: 338).

[5] Praise: Sappho frr. 108, 113; Ar. *Pax* 1330; Theoc. *Id.* 18.20–38; Himer. *Or.* 1(9).19–20; Men. Rhet. 403.26–404.14 Spengel; [Dion. Hal.] *Rhet.* 265, 270 Radermacher; Catull. 61.16–25 etc.; Politis 1931: 278–89. *makarismos*: Hes. fr. 211.7; Sappho fr. 112; Eur. *Alc.* 918–19, *Tro.* 311–12, *Hel.* 375–6, 640, 1434–5, *IA* 1076–9, 1404–5, *Phaeth.* 240; Ar. *Pax* 1333, *Av.* 1722–5, 1759; Theoc. *Id.* 18.16, 52; Hom. *Od.* 4.208; Pind. *Pyth.* 3.88–9; Antoniad. Cret. 66 (Politis 1931: 284 n. 3).

relationship between the negative and the positive tendency of the ritual is a delicate one: the negative tendency must not be denied, but it must of course eventually be overcome. For example, the negative image of nature destroyed may be met by the positive image of its taming and cultivation.[6] The 'death' of the girl (or her abandonment of virginity) may be expressed by the sacrifice of a substituted animal.[7] The wedding expresses not only the victory of a positive over a negative tendency, but also in a sense the victory of culture over nature.[8] The wild animal is tamed; sexual union is legitimised; the field is ploughed.[9] And because the wedding constitutes one of the two or three most fundamental transitions in the life of an individual, particularly perhaps for a woman,[10] the failure to complete the transition is profoundly anomic. This failure, which may occur in various ways, is constantly explored by tragedy.

The most obvious form of this failure is of course death before marriage. Such a death is constantly imagined, particularly in epitaphs, as a kind of marriage, notably (for the girl) with Hades.[11] That is to say, a transition effected by nature (death) is enclosed by the imagination within a similar transition effected by culture (marriage). It is important to observe that this [*107*] enclosure is facilitated by the presence in the wedding of elements associated with death, to some extent perhaps actual lamentation, but more importantly 'equivocal' elements common to the two rites of passage:[12] in both wedding and funeral the girl is washed, anointed and given special robes (πέπλοι) and a special crown (στέφανος) in order to be conveyed on an irreversible, torchlit journey (on a cart)[13] accompanied

[6] Notably at Catull. 62.39–56 (a poem largely Greek in inspiration); see also n. 9 below.

[7] At the *proteleia*: Burkert 1983b: 62–3; cf. Eur. *IA* 433 with 718–19.

[8] See esp. Redfield 1982: 192–4 (add e.g. [Dion. Hal.] *Rhet.* 262: 'They left a bestial and wandering life, and through marriage attained a tame and ordered life').

[9] See e.g. Magnien 1936: 129–31, 133–4; Vernant 1982b: 138–9, 150; Detienne 1977: 116–17; Redfield 1982; the formula γνησίων παίδων ἐπ' ἀρότῳ, 'for the ploughing of legitimate children' (Men. *Sam.* 727, *Dys.* 842; etc.); Ael. *NA* 12.24; n. 58 below.

[10] Cf. Hipponax fr. 68: 'Two days are pleasantest for a woman: when someone marries her, and when he carries out her corpse.'

[11] E.g. Peek 1955: nos. 658, 1162, 1238, 1551, 1553, 1989; cf. e.g. Soph. *Ant.* 810–16; Eur. *IA* 461; Ael. fr. 50 Hercher. For a striking modern example see the Greek newspaper *TA NEA* for 16 March 1987.

[12] On wedding lamentation etc. see §4 below and n. 4 above; on equivocal elements (and wedding laments) in Greece today see Alexiou 1974: 120–2. Note that such ambiguity within the wedding does *not* for the audience underlie the lament of Capulet (*Romeo and Juliet* IV.v.84–90): 'All things that we ordained festival / Turn from their office to black funeral: / Our instruments to melancholy bells, / Our wedding cheer to a sad burial feast; / Our solemn hymns to sullen dirges change, / Our bridal flowers serve for a buried corpse' (quoted by Alexiou and Dronke 1971: 831).

[13] In fact the corpse might be carried either on foot or on a cart (see e.g. *ABV* 346.7 and 8 = Vermeule 1979: 20, figs. 15 and 16). Equally unsurprisingly, the bridal pair sometimes went on foot (see e.g. Poll. *Onom.* 2.195).

by song, and to be abandoned by her kin to an unknown dwelling, an alien bed and the physical control (χεὶρ ἐπὶ καρπῷ, 'hand on wrist') of an unknown male.[14] The unmarried girl is buried in her wedding attire;[15] she is imagined as a bride taken off by Hades;[16] and so on.[17] The wedding attire is of course not a mere symbol. It would have been worn in the actual marriage that she has been denied: 'For the clothes in which I was going to dress as a bride, with these I have gone to Hades.'[18] The actual wedding may have been imminent.[19] Indeed, this interpenetration of the two basically similar transitions is sometimes intensified to the point at which the girl (or sometimes the man) dies after preparations for the wedding have begun or even during the ritual itself.[20] The surprising frequency (or at least the survival) of such cases is perhaps attributable to a tendency of the imagination to intensify the interpenetration.[21] In these cases it is as if one of the negative elements in the wedding ceremony (marriage as death) has triumphed over the positive, as if the pattern of the wedding ceremony has been disrupted so as to turn into its opposite.

Tragedy is intensely interested in this kind of disruption. I will begin by noting three examples of the death of an unmarried girl which is clearly associated with her imminent wedding (Antigone, Iphigeneia, Glauke). Second, as the centrepiece of the argument, I will discuss at length the case of the Danaids, in which the prevailing negative element is not the death of the bride but her hostility to the groom. Third, in Section 3, I will discuss examples of the death of a married woman imagined as the re-enactment of her marriage (Deianeira, Iokaste, Euadne, Medea). Finally, in Section 4, I examine cases of extramarital sexual union imagined as marriage: i.e. a merely natural union is shaped by the imagination into a transition effected by culture[22] (Paris and Helen, Agamemnon and Kassandra, Herakles and

[14] Description of the funeral: Vermeule 1979: 11–21; Kurtz and Boardman 1971: chapter 7; Garland 1985: chapter 3; of the wedding: Erdmann 1934: chapter 5; Daremberg and Saglio 1877–1919: s.v. 'Matrimonium'. On χεὶρ ἐπὶ καρπῷ see Jenkins 1983.

[15] E.g. Peek 1955: nos. 683, 1238; Alexiou 1974: 230 n. 63; cf. Eur. *Tro.* 1218–20.

[16] E.g. Peek 1955: nos. 658, 1238, 1553; Jenkins 1983.

[17] E.g. *Anth. Pal.* 7.185 (torches), 487 (bed), 489 (θάλαμος); Peek 1955: nos. 1450 (house), 1823 (torchlit journey); cf. e.g. Soph. *Ant.* 806–16 (journey, bed).

[18] Peek 1955: no. 683.7–8.

[19] E.g. *Anth. Pal.* 7.291, 568; Peek 1955: nos. 988, 1976, 1989; *Ach. Tat.* 1.13.

[20] *Anth. Pal.* 7.182, 183, 188, 568, 610 (obviously imaginary), 711, 712; Peek 1955: nos. 228, 1238, 1522, 1801, 1825, 1910, 1989.19, 2038; cf. *Anth. Pal.* 878; Ap. Rhod. 3.656–61; Hor. *Carm.* 4.2.21; Heliod. *Aeth.* 2.29.

[21] E.g. Peek 1955: no. 1238 is an epigram which illustrates how easily the idea of death just before the wedding might arise from the practice of burying the unmarried girl in bridal attire.

[22] I.e. the same shaping as operates on the natural event of death (see above).

Iole, Neoptolemos and Andromakhe). Reference will also be made to various other couples on the way. In all these categories the negative tendency of the ritual prevails.

2. The Girl About to Be Married

§1. The death of **Antigone** is presented by Sophocles in a manner suggestive of a wedding, in part with Hades or Akheron, in part with her betrothed Haimon. The place of her imprisonment *[108]* is both a tomb and a bridal chamber (816, 891; cf. 804, 886, 947). Hades 'who puts all to bed' (ὁ παγκοίτας) is taking Antigone off alive (810–11). Less obviously, it should be noted that the hymn to Eros that introduced Antigone's burial lament is appropriate to a hymenaial context. In particular, its theme is the power of sex in nature and in the cosmos, which was a *topos* of the later wedding ceremony at least (see n. 117 below), constituting praise of the mighty power that has brought the couple together. But here, inasmuch as Haimon and Antigone are brought together in death (described in terms of sexual and marital union: see §6), the *topos* is in part reversed. Failure to realise this point has produced among critics puzzlement about the introduction of the theme and misunderstanding of its significance.[23] As so often, deviation from what we expect arises from the presence of a *topos*. Another example of this phenomenon is in fact provided by the 'marriage' in the tomb of Antigone and Haimon, which produces certain inconsistencies of plot.[24]

§2. **Iphigeneia**. We know several cases of girls before marriage traditionally lamenting for – or offering sacrifice, their hair or libations to – a mythical young person who had died a virgin.[25] Surely this mythical death is at least partly an expression of the death associated with the marital separation from maidenhood. The mythical figure embodies, albeit indirectly, the loss experienced by the bride, and provides an object for her emotions. It appears therefore that the subversion of the marital transition is a feature of myth. It is not invented by tragedy, though tragedy exploits it and probably extends its scope.

[23] E.g. von Fritz 1934; Winnington-Ingram 1980: 92–8 (similar to the failure to see that Antigone laments because it is her funeral: Seaford 1984c[II]: 254).

[24] Notably in the behaviour of Haimon: the inconsistencies are described by Tycho von Wilamowitz-Moellendorff 1917: 21–3 ('it is clear that for the poet there is no doubt from the beginning that Haimon will commit suicide in Antigone's tomb. He is as little concerned as the audience is with how and for what purpose Haimon could have entered it, and and does not think to give any particular justification for his entrance'); and cf. 36 with 773–80.

[25] E.g. Hdt. 4.34; Paus. 1.43.4; Plut. *Arist.* 20; Paus. 2.32.1–4 (and Eur. *Hipp.* 1425–7).

This is particularly clear in the case of Iphigeneia, who combines these two forms of substitute death (of a mythical maiden, of a sacrificial animal). In one version she is actually sacrificed to Artemis; in another she is replaced by an animal (a hind, or a bear). The substitution of (or perhaps the metamorphosis into) a bear is reported by Phanodemos of Athens,[26] and is clearly related to the importance of Iphigeneia and Artemis at Brauron, where young girls ritually imitated bears (ἀρκτεύειν). In the scholium on Ar. *Lys.* 645 we read that Iphigeneia was to be sacrificed at Brauron but was replaced by a bear, and that as a result 'they celebrate a secret rite for her' (μυστήριον ἄγουσιν αὐτῇ).[27] 'To serve as a bear' (ἀρκτεύειν) was regarded as a preparation for marriage.[28] And so the death (or escape from death) of Iphigeneia seems to have been, at least in part, an expression of the association of death with the loss of girlhood in marriage. Wilamowitz regarded the luring of Iphigeneia to Aulis by the prospect of marriage as inessential to the story ('nur eine Zuthat zu der eigentlichen Geschichte') and guessed that it was an innovation by the poet of the *Cypria*.[29] The question of who made the 'innovation' is unanswerable. But what we can say is that the 'innovation' was unlikely to have been absolute: like most unnecessary innovations, it was probably a development of an existing theme, namely that of Iphigeneia as bride. It is of interest here that in one version she was actually married to Akhilleus and had a son by him.[30]

In Euripides' *Iphigeneia in Aulis* the marriage to Akhilleus for which she is summoned by her father is of course only a device to encompass her sacrifice. But the persistent presentation of this sacrifice in terms of marriage is due only in small part to the needs of the deception. The normal role of the *proteleia*, the sacrifice preliminary to marriage, appears to have been to give to the deity the life of an animal as a substitute for the life of the bride (n. 7 above). The rumour in the *[109]* Greek camp is that 'they are offering the girl as a preliminary sacrifice to Artemis' (433 Ἀρτέμιδι προτελίζουσι τὴν νεάνιδα). And Agamemnon pretends that the impending sacrifice to Artemis is the 'premarital sacrifice for his child' (718 προτέλεια … παιδὸς). The irony of the bride transformed from participant in the sacrifice to victim is sustained at 675, 'for you will be standing near the χέρνιβες [lustral water]', which could apply equally to bride and to victim,[31] and at 1475–9

[26] *FGrH* 325 F14(a) and (b) (fourth century BCE).
[27] Cf. e.g. Eur. *IT* 1450–61 and in general Brelich 1969: 241–78.
[28] Krateros *FGrH* 342 F9; Schol. Ar. *Lys.* 645; Burkert 1985: 263.
[29] Wilamowitz-Moellendorff 1883: 250.
[30] Nicander *ap.* Ant. Lib. *Met.* 27 (cf. Eur. *IA* 1355–6, 940); Lycoph. *Alex.* 183, 324; Duris *FGrH* 76 F88.
[31] Cf. 1479, 1518, *IT* 58 etc., and a similar ambiguity at Aesch. *Ag.* 1036–8 (cf. §10). Cf. also Eur. *IA* 1080–8.

'Lead me away... come, give me wreaths to put on – here is my hair to wreath – and streams of χέρνιβες' (both bride and victim are adorned and led in procession).[32] She will be sacrificed as an 'undefiled heifer' raised not by cowherds but 'with your mother, ... decked out as a bride for marriage with a descendant of Inakhos' (1080–9): here the irony deploys a traditional comparison of the bride to a young animal leaving her mother.[33] As in Aeschylus (see §9a), the death of Iphigeneia in her *proteleia* is not imagined but real. The negative element prevails.

Second, the arrival and final departure of Iphigeneia are presented in a manner evocative of the wedding. The elements of a normal wedding particularly relevant here are the *makarismos* ('blessing') of the nuptial pair (n. 5 above) and their arrival at the house of the groom in a cart accompanied by the mother of the bride and other women.[34] The moment of this arrival was a poignant stage, often depicted in Attic vase painting,[35] in the transition of the bride to her new life, for it was here presumably that she was abandoned by her kin.

Klytaimestra arrives as 'leader of the bride' (610) with Iphigeneia and her 'bridal gifts' (611) in front of the halls (685) of Agamemnon, in a cart or chariot (610, 616), to the accompaniment of a choral *makarismos* (590–7). Much concern is shown for the descent of Iphigeneia from the chariot (614–16).[36] In the subsequent dialogue Agamemnon speaks of a 'voyage' (πλοῦς)[37] which Iphigeneia is to undertake 'alone, separated from your father and mother' (669), and which she takes to mean that she is to live in another household. He then bids her farewell, 'go within the hall, ... kissing me and giving me your right hand, since you are going to dwell apart from your father for a long time' (678–80), and disguises his grief as that felt by a father at the marriage of his daughter (688–90).

The next episode, in which Klytaimestra meets with Akhilleus and discovers the truth from the old man, is followed by a choral song celebrating the marriage of Peleus and Thetis. The aptness of this theme is

[32] For other parallels between marriage and sacrifice see Vernant 1982b: chapter 7; Foley 1982 (on the *IA*; a longer version in Foley 1985: chapter 2).

[33] Seaford 1986b: 50–4; Sappho fr. 104(a); Soph. *Trach.* 527–30.

[34] Eur. *IA* 732; schol. Eur. *Tro.* 315; Ov. *Her.* 8.96; Nonnus, *Dion.* 46.304; and the vase paintings referred to in n. 115. I find that the evocation of the wedding by the chariot is suggested also by Foley 1985: 70–1.

[35] Daremberg and Saglio 1877–1919: s.v. 'Matrimonium' 1652–3.

[36] There may well be much (early) interpolation or rewriting in this scene (Page 1934: 160–9); but even (early) interpolated lines are not necessarily thereby excluded from our argument, which is not concerned with the personality of Euripides.

[37] See also §9a below.

obvious. The offspring of the marriage was Akhilleus; and it forms a contrast with the present 'marriage' (note especially the reference to the *makarismos* at 1076–80: 'Blessed did the gods make the wedding then ... and your head too the Argives will wreath'). But it should also be noted that the practice of referring to a paradigmatic mythical or divine marriage seems to have been a practice of the contemporary wedding ceremony.[38]

The arrival of the Greeks to take Iphigeneia to her death produces the prospect of a scene familiar from certain descriptions of the wedding, the bride torn from the embrace of her mother (1367, 1460).[39] Finally, the very last words of Iphigeneia evoke the predicament of the bride (1505–9): 'torch-bearing day (λαμπαδοῦχος ἁμέρα) and light of Zeus, another life (αἰῶνα), another fate (μοῖραν) will I live in. Farewell dear light! (φάος)' The faint suggestion in λαμπαδοῦχος of the wedding torches *[110]* of which Iphigeneia has been deprived[40] is strengthened by the subsequent suggestion of a change of dwelling place.[41]

§3. **Glauke** in Euripides' *Medea*. The dress and crown sent by Medea to the princess Glauke are a wedding gift, contributing to the traditional *eudaimonia* ('blessedness') of the bride (952–8). They are donned by the bride, who then admires herself in the mirror.[42] But they turn out to be 'an adornment of Hades' (908 Ἅιδα κόσμος), i.e. funerary dress.[43] The unmarried girl was buried in her wedding dress and crown.

In the wedding of Glauke the association of the wedding adornment (κόσμος) with death has become a reality. And the same is true of the journey: in 985 'she shall wear her bridal gown (νυμφοκομήσει) among the dead' and in 1234–5 (significant even if interpolated) 'she shall go to

[38] Ar. *Av.* 1731–44; Sapph. fr. 44 (if hymenaial), cf. fr. 218; Men. Rhet. 400.7–402.20 (includes Peleus and Thetis) etc.; [Dion. Hal.] *Rhet.* 262; Claud. *Epithal. Hon. Aug.*, *praef.* and Sid. Apoll. *Carm.* 14.26–30 (Peleus and Thetis); cf. Catull. 64. Note also the popularity of the wedding of Peleus and Thetis in vase painting, e.g. on a nuptial *lebes* (*ARV*² 585.33).

[39] Catull. 62.21–2 (surely based on a Greek model); cf. Sappho fr. 104; Soph. *Trach.* 527–31; Eur. *Hec.* 90–1, 207–9, 418, 611–12; Plut. *Lyc.* 15; Politis 1931: 281. Cf. Eur. *IA* 1087.

[40] The absence or the extinguishing of the wedding torch was a *topos* of the death-instead-of-marriage theme (see above; e.g. *Anth. Pal.* 7.185; Bion 1.87; Daremberg and Saglio 1877–1919: s.v. 'Hymenaios'), and may be associated, as it seems to be here, with the darkness of Hades (e.g. Peek 1955: no. 804). On the association of φῶς, and especially torchlight, with σωτηρία, see Fraenkel 1950 on Aesch. *Ag.* 522; Thomson 1966 on *Ag.* 522, 935–71.

[41] Meaning lifetime, αἰών might easily refer to the (new) lifetime that begins at marriage: Eur. *Or.* 603, *Med.* 243, *Supp.* 1005 (see §7d below), *Alc.* 475. For μοῖρα and marriage see Ar. *Av.* 1734; Poll. *Onom.* 3.38. And cf. Antiph. DK 87 B 49.3 (p. 357.15) καινοῦ δαίμονος ἄρχει, καινοῦ πότμου.

[42] A scene depicted in Attic vase paintings (e.g. *ARV*² 1476.3).

[43] Cf. e.g. Eur. *HF* 562, *Bacch.* 857. See also the attention paid to Pentheus' dress (*Med.* 1161–2 with *Bacch.* 928–34, 1165–6 with 937–8). I suggest that Pentheus too is looking at a mirror (1987b).

the house of Hades due to her marriage with Jason' – the destination of the bride's journey is the house not of her husband but of Hades.[44] The association with death, one of the negative tendencies which in a normal wedding would be overcome in the rituals of transition and incorporation, has in the tragedy emerged as a triumphant reality.

§4. The **Danaids**. Aeschylus' *Suppliants* presents two central, closely related and unresolved problems. First, is the aversion of the Danaids to marriage in general or to marriage with their cousins in particular? Numerous passages may be deployed to support each alternative.[45] Second, on what is the aversion based? On the one hand, for Thomson, the conflict is between the rule of exogamy and the principle embodied in the Attic law of the heiress, by which heiresses without brothers could be claimed in marriage by their kin, so as to keep the estate within the family.[46] At the other extreme, Garvie maintains that 'we must look for the Danaids' motivation purely in their own character, and not in any simple obedience to a supposed moral or social principle'.[47] Most recently, Friis Johansen and Whittle (henceforth FJW), while accepting the importance of the Attic law for evaluating the action of the Aigyptiads, insist that the Danaids do not in fact invoke the principle of exogamy or denounce the principle of endogamy.[48] And so what motivates them? Here, FJW, while stressing the importance of the violence of the Aigyptiads, nevertheless implicitly admit puzzlement.[49]

It seems to me that progress on this front can be made only by the adoption of a new perspective. The attitude of the Danaids resembles in several respects the attitude associated with the Greek bride or her female companions, but taken to an exotic extreme. We are of course hampered in this comparison by the scarcity of direct evidence for the attitude and experience associated with the bride in fifth-century Attica. However, the coherence in various respects of the evidence for wedding ritual from

[44] See also nn. 11–17 above.
[45] Garvie 1969: 221; Friis Johansen and Whittle 1980: 1.30–4.
[46] Thomson 1946: 279–95.
[47] Garvie 1969: 221.
[48] Friis Johansen and Whittle 1980 (henceforth FJW): 1.34–7.
[49] 'The reader may, at his or her own risk, take the themes of general aversion to marriage, *hybris* in the Aigyptiads and legally prescribed endogamy as suggesting various motives for the Danaids' flight from their cousins, but the function of these themes in *Supp.* (and perhaps in the trilogy as a whole) is only that of placing the action in a complex and shifting perspective' (FJW: 1.37).

different times and places[50] is such that the cautious use of evidence from one area to complement evidence from another is not necessarily illegitimate.

The Danaids, lamenting and fearful of isolation from their kin, claim to have a 'heart' which [III] is 'without experience of tears'.[51] In a passage of Sophocles' *Trachiniae* heavily influenced by the wedding song[52] Deianeira expresses to the leader of the chorus of girls the hope that they will not suffer what marriage has brought her, 'but at present you are without experience', and proceeds to illustrate the point by comparing the unmarried girl to a protected or untroubled young animal or blooming plant. This image seems to have been a *topos* of the wedding song. For example, Sappho fr. 104(a), whatever precisely the original text, probably compares or contrasts the separation of the bride from her mother with the life of pastoral animals. Later in the *Trachiniae* Deianeira as a bride is compared to a 'lonely heifer' suddenly separated from her mother.[53] In the *Suppliants* the Danaids call themselves 'a heifer (δάμαλιν) pursued by wolves on sheer ridges' (351–2), and associate themselves with the sufferings of their ancestor, the heifer Io (41), whom they twice call 'mother'.[54] To the pastoral scene of her sufferings they regard themselves as having returned.[55] Mention should perhaps also be made in this context of the image of the hawk preying on the nightingale (62) or dove (223–6; cf. [Aesch.] *PV* 857). It is true that this image does not appear in the meagre remains of the ancient wedding song; but it may be significant, in view of the demonstrable continuity of similar images in the wedding as well as of details of the ritual itself,[56] that the image of the bird of prey catching a weaker bird (e.g. the partridge) is a feature of the Greek wedding song in the mediaeval and modern period.[57]

The grazing animal may have to face not only isolation and beasts of prey but also subjection by humans. The verb ζεύγνυμι ('yoke'), in active

[50] See §1 above; also the general treatments of the ceremony mentioned in n. 14.

[51] *Supp.* 69–76; see also e.g. 748–9.

[52] *Trach.* 141–9; Seaford 1986b.

[53] 529–30; see also Lycoph. *Alex.* 102; Eur. *IA* 1083–8, *Hel.* 1476–8, *Hec.* 205–10 (cf. 90–1, 416–18, 526, 612); Pind. *Isthm.* 8.48.

[54] 141, 539; cf. 51, 275. This appeal (1) expresses the Danaids' claim on the Argives; (2) may express, according to the psychoanalytic analysis of Caldwell 1974: 45–70, their desire for a 'fantasised mother'; (3) is highly apt for their quasi-hymenaial position, particularly given the hymenaial *topos* of the heifer parted from her mother. See also [Aesch.] *PV* 665–82.

[55] 40–56, 538–40, 1063–6. Cf. *PV* 665–82, where Io is forced out (ὠθεῖν) of the parental home to become a heifer on the margins of the land. Murray 1958 ignores the ritual dimension.

[56] Seaford 1986b: esp. nn. 10, 14, 20, 24; Koukoules 1951: 88–92, 101–19, 148–85; Politis 1931: 281.

[57] Politis 1931: 283; Danforth 1982: 114; Zakhos 1966: 66, 132; cf. Alcman fr. 82.

or middle form, is regularly used in tragedy to express what a man does to a woman in marrying her.[58] Zeus in giving Thetis as wife to Peleus 'subdued her to her husband' (*Il.* 18.432 ἀνδρὶ δάμασσεν). 'Thus', runs a bucolic simile, 'would a tamed bride (νύμφα δμαθεῖσ') grieve' (Theoc. *Id.* 8.91). The Danaids compare themselves to a δάμαλις ('heifer', see above), a word cognate with δαμάζω ('subdue', 'tame') and applied to an animal (generally female) not yet tamed or subdued. At 144–53 they invoke Artemis to help ἄδμητος ἀδμήτᾳ ('she untamed for me untamed'),[59] and express the desire, as the offspring of Io, 'to escape the beds of men, unmarried, untamed (ἀδάματον)'. They do not want to be the 'servants' (δμῶϊς[60]) of the sons of Aigyptos (335); and the threat of seizure makes them shout 'I am being subdued!' (905 δάμναμαι). The image of the murderous Danaids as 'lionesses who have chanced upon calves' (Hor. *Carm.* 3.11.41) expresses not only savagery but also the reversal of the hymenaial image of the heifer subdued.

When Deianeira praises the life of the unmarried girl, she alludes to the hymenaial imagery not only of the untroubled animal but also of the protected, flowering plant.[61] We find plant images used on the one hand to praise bride or groom,[62] and on the other hand, like the animal imagery, to express the negative aspect of the loss of girlhood: in Sappho a hyacinth trodden [*112*] down by herdsmen, and an apple threatened by the apple-pickers; in the *Trachiniae* a plant growing up 'in its own place' (χώροισιν αὑτοῦ), protected from the weather; in Catullus a flower plucked from a sheltered garden.[63] We should compare those epitaphs such as the one from Leontopolis (first century CE)[64] in which the girl, buried in her wedding attire, was about to leave her father's house to be wed when 'like a rose in a garden flourishing from the dew's moisture, Hades has suddenly come and snatched me away'.

[58] Eur. *Bacch.* 468, *Phoen.* 337, 1366, *IA* 698, *Tro.* 676, *Alc.* 994; cf. Soph. *Trach.* 536; Eur. *El.* 99, *Hipp.* 549, *Supp.* 822; and esp. Soph. fr. 583. Cf. Xen. *Oec.* 7.18–19; Ap. Rhod. 4.96; *Suda* and Hsch. s.v. ζυγόν; [Dion. Hal.] *Epid.* 262; etc. (Magnien 1936: 130–1).

[59] Cf. Timarete before her wedding dedicating her childish things to Artemis Limnatis, κόρᾳ κόρα, ὡς ἐπιεικές (*Anth. Pal.* 6.280); Seaford 1985[12]: 321–2 on Soph. *El.* 1238–9. The Danaids' devotion to Artemis (see e.g. 1031) is of course not an explanation of their hostility to marriage (as believed by some) but a consequence of it.

[60] A word associated with δάμναμαι (see FJW: *ad loc.*).

[61] See Easterling 1982: *ad loc.*; Seaford 1986b.

[62] E.g. Sappho fr. 115, and 117[A] (L-P Addenda); Theoc. *Id.* 18.30; Seaford 1986b: 52 n. 10; add Eur. *Hipp.* 630, *Med.* 231 (cf. 242); Greg. Naz. *PG* 37.1493.186 νυμφίον ὑμνείοντες ἐοικότα ἔρνει καλῷ; Galavotti 1935: 234.29–30 and 235.64.

[63] Sappho frr. 105a, b; cf. Himer. *Or.* 9 (Colonna); Soph. *Trach.* 144–7; Catull. 62.39–47; cf. e.g. Politis 1931: 281.

[64] Peek 1955: no. 1238; cf. e.g. nos. 1162.8, 1801; Alexiou 1974: 195.

It is in the light of this tradition that we should understand the word ὠμόδροπος ('plucked unripe') at Aesch. *Sept.* 333 (see §12 below), as well as three passages from the *Suppliants*. Danaos, concerned with the possibility of male admiration in Argos, says of his daughters 'the tender bloom is not at all easy to guard: man and beast destroy it' (998–9). And when the Danaids sing about the possibility of war, 'let the flower of youth remain unplucked, let mortal-destroying Ares, Aphrodite's bedfellow, not shear away its bloom' (663–6),[65] the reference to Aphrodite implies the familiar idea that what warfare is for the young man marriage is for the girl,[66] and therefore the hope in this case that the plucking of the bloom of youth can be avoided for both sexes.

About their prospective Egyptian bridegrooms, on the other hand, the Danaids sing 'Let [Zeus] look upon human violence, with which the stem thrives (νεάζει[67]) and flourishes by means of marriage with us' (104–6). Normally the bridegroom is praised by a comparison with a plant (see n. 62 above). But here the comparison has been reversed to express female disapproval. I suspect that this kind of reversal derives from the amoebean form exemplified by Catullus 62, in which the male chorus respond to the girls' complaints (cruel Hesperus, the bride as a plucked flower) by praising Hesperus and comparing the bride to a vine needing the support of an elm. I will return to this point below.

Many of the passages discussed, in the *Suppliants* and elsewhere, seem to impute brutality to the male. There are in fact scattered pieces of evidence for the expression of fear in the ceremony by the bride (see n. 3 above). Certain features of the fifth-century Attic wedding ceremony (lifting the bride, χεὶρ ἐπὶ καρπῷ) have been interpreted as a rite of abduction.[68] And in certain vase paintings (notably an Attic skyphos of *c.*430) the abduction of an obviously reluctant Persephone by Hades in his chariot resembles the wedding scenes in so many respects that it has been suggested[69] that her reluctance reflects a real-life marriage ritual, in which the bride may be imagined as a departing soul. If so, this is further confirmation that the wedding was associated with death, and further light on the ease with

[65] Cf. Pind. *Pyth.* 9.37 ἐκ λεχέων κεῖραι μελιαδέα ποίαν, 109–11 χρυσοστεφάνου δέ οἱ Ἥβας καρπὸν ἀνθήσαντ' ἀποδρέψαι ἔθελον (Carson 1982).

[66] Vernant 1982b: 23.

[67] Cf. τὸ γὰρ νεάζον ... at Soph. *Trach.* 144–50 (and n. 33 above).

[68] Jenkins 1983 and Sourvinou-Inwood 1987. It is interesting that at Iambl. *VP* 18.84 certain rituals to which the bride is subjected are explained by her position as *suppliant*.

[69] Jenkins 1983: 142.

which the death of the unmarried girl is imagined as seizure by Hades as husband (see above).

The Danaids face abduction by the black[70] Aigyptiads. They also describe themselves as lamenting, firstly in fear of being without φίλοι (family and friends) in Argos (69–76), and then again, following their description of the Aigyptiads as 'a stem flourishing by means of marriage with us, their minds deaf to persuasion, with a frenzied purpose and inescapable goad' (κέντρον ἄφυκτον) (105–10), they continue[71] 'such wretched sufferings I shriek ... while still living I honour myself with lamentations' (112–16): that is to say, their lamentation for themselves as if already dead[72] seems to emerge from consideration of the sexual aggressiveness of the Aigyptiads. κέντρον ('goad') is an image of sexual desire, ambiguous here[73] inasmuch as [113] ἔχων can mean both 'feeling' and 'wielding'. ἄφυκτον ('inescapable') with its connotation of death[74] provides a bridge between the demands of male sexuality (more specifically the phallic κέντρον ἄφυκτον) and lamentation.[75] In addition, the association of death (particularly of a virgin) with marriage sometimes extends to an assimilation of the destruction of the body to the first physical contact of the married pair.[76] Accordingly, the Danaids' threat of suicide is presented as a preference not only for one husband (Hades) rather than another, but also for one kind of physical contact rather than another. For that seems to be the point of the corrupt lines 788–92 θέλοιμι δ' ἂν †μορσίμου | βρόχου τυχεῖν† ἐν σαργάναις, | πρὶν ἄνδρ' ἀπευκτὸν τῷδε χριμφθῆναι χροΐ | πρόπαρ θανούσας [δ'] Ἀίδας ἀνάσσοι ('I wish I could †obtain a deadly noose† among my woven clothes, before a loathed man draws near to my skin – before that may Hades lord it over me in death').[77] The basic meaning of σαργάνη seems to be 'plaited work' (FJW). And so its point here may be to assimilate the

[70] The emphasis (719, 745) on their blackness, as they approach intent on abduction, may connote death. If it is thought that this can be no more than realistic detail, cf. the black Egyptian Zeus-Hades gaining access to Io in Soph. *Inachos* (Seaford 1980). And other references in *Supp.* to black skin (of the Danaids) certainly connote death (154; Seaford 1980: 24; cf. also 785, 790–1, 778).

[71] I omit the very corrupt line 111.

[72] Cf. Soph. *Ant.* 806–16; Seaford 1984c[II]: 254.

[73] As noted by FJW, who also suggest an allusion to Io.

[74] Cf. e.g. Simon. *PMG* 520.4; Soph. *Ant.* 361–2; Peek 1955: nos. 1039.7, 1593.1.

[75] Cf. Simon. (*FGE* 406–7) οὐκ ἐπιδὼν νύμφεια λέχη κατέβην τὸν ἄφυκτον | Γόργιππος ξανθῆς Φερσεφόνης θάλαμον. And Soph. *Ant.* 788, 799 mentions the inescapability of Eros in a context which combines the themes of marriage and death (cf. e.g. 804 τὸν παγκοίταν ... θάλαμον). See also Eur. *Med.* 531, 634–5 (the ἄφυκτος arrows of love); also perhaps Aesch. *Supp.* 784.

[76] Cf. Eur. *Supp.* 1019–30, *Heracl.* 913–16, *Cyc.* 514–15; Pind. fr. 128c.7; Soph. *Trach.* 662 (cf. 833, 857–8, etc.); Eur. *Hec.* 367–8. See also below on Soph. *OT*, *Trach.* and *Ant.*, and Aesch. *Ag.* (§6).

[77] The text as printed by FJW. With ἀνάσσοι they compare 906 ἄνακτας meaning husbands. Cf. also 804–5 (with κοίτα cf. e.g. Soph. *Ant.* 804, *OC* 1706; Aesch. *Ag.* 1494).

noose to something woven or plaited[78] which would touch, surround or clasp the head or body of the bride (the crown? the girdle?). If this seems far-fetched, three considerations should be noted. First, σαργάναις is, as FJW argue, unlikely to be corrupt.[79] Second, in a story told by Plutarch (*Mor.* 253d) a virgin undoes her girdle (ζώνη) and uses it to hang herself in order to avoid rape. This form of death is interpreted by Helen King as an inversion of marriage: the undoing of the girdle is associated with marriage, but hanging, unlike marriage, produces no bloodshed.[80] Third, there is a similar perversity in the stress laid on the fineness of the woven cloth in which Antigone is found hanged (Soph. *Ant.* 1222 βρόχῳ μιτώδει σινδόνος καθημμένην), clasped by Haimon. Indeed, the presentation of the death of Antigone as a wedding, both in her passage to the tomb/bridal chamber (891 τύμβος ... νυμφεῖον) and in the messenger's narrative, is so pervasive that I believe that the attire in which she goes there, and with which she hangs herself, is bridal. Then as now in Greece, the unmarried might go to their tombs dressed for the wedding.[81]

The association between marriage for a girl and death, based as it is largely on a manifold resemblance (details of the ceremonies, abduction by a male, fear of the unknown, etc.), facilitates the association here of the sexual aggression of the suitors with self-lamentation and death. If the ancient Greek wedding also sometimes included elements of lamentation, this would be one of a large number of points of continuity with the modern Greek wedding.[82] An (apparently Hellenistic) epitaph[83] speaks of a girl who neither came to the bridal chamber nor heard the wedding song. Catullus in his free translation of Callimachus speaks of the 'feigned tears' of brides, 'which they pour out abundantly at the threshold of the bridal chamber'.[84] Proclus says that the wedding song was sung 'from a sense of loss of, and in search of, Hymenaios ... whom they say disappeared after marriage'.[85] Hymenaios is often depicted in art with a sad expression.[86] And

[78] Cf. πλεκταῖς at Soph. *OT* 1264 and μιτώδει at *Ant.* 1222 (see below).
[79] In fact the only plausible replacement I can think of is the slight change ζαργάναις (occurs elsewhere only in schol. Opp. *Hal.* 1.100 meaning ταινία), which would in fact suit my argument somewhat better. θανεῖν for τυχεῖν in 789 would remove all the problems noted by FJW, but the corruption would be hard to account for.
[80] King 1983: 118–21; Loraux 1985: 34–5, 41–5, 105 n. 15.
[81] Peek 1955: no. 1238.3; Eur. *Tro.* 1218–20.
[82] See e.g. Politis 1931: 278–9; Danforth 1982: 74–9; Alexiou 1974: 120–2.
[83] Peek 1955: no. 947.4: from the second or first century BCE, provenance unstated.
[84] Catull. 66.16–7; cf. also 61.81 *flet quod ire necesse est*; etc. (nn. 2 and 3 above).
[85] Procl. *Chrest. ap.* Phot. *Bibl.* 239 (321.1.19–22 Bekker); cf. also Tzetz. *Chil.* 13.606 (the wedding song sung by ἐξαπευχόμενοι ἀφάνισιν παστάδος; cf. 600).
[86] Daremberg and Saglio 1877–1919: s.v. 'Hymenaios' 335.

he has a habit of turning wedding celebrations into funeral lamentations.[87] Pindar groups together three kinds of song for the untimely deaths of, respectively, Linos, Hymenaios, 'whom the last of hymns [i.e. lamentation] snatched away at night as his skin was first touched in marriage' (ἐν γάμοις χροϊζόμενον), and [114] Ialemos.[88] It has been argued that this means that Pindar regarded these three kinds of song as various forms of the dirge (θρῆνος).[89] In a comparable focusing of the negative emotions of the wedding onto a mythical figure, the girls of Troizen cut their hair before their weddings (in mourning) and shed tears for Hippolytos.[90] The Danaids return to the association of the proposed marriage with death in the song that concludes the play: 'not by compulsion may the τέλος [consummation] of Aphrodite come. May this prize be a Stygian one' (μηδ' ὑπ' ἀνάγκας τέλος ἔλθοι Κυθερείας. Στύγιον πέλοι τόδ' ἆθλον).[91] Marriage and death are both consummations (τέλη).[92] The Danaids desire the τέλος of this marriage (if inevitable) to be the τέλος of death.

This final song, it is generally agreed, is divided between two parties. FJW have recently produced a very powerful case for assigning the other part to a chorus consisting not, as often believed, of the Danaids' maids, but of the Argive bodyguards. I would like to add the suggestion that the song is influenced by, and would evoke in the minds of the audience, the wedding song. The only surviving wedding song that consists of a dialogue between a male and a female chorus is the very Greek Catullus 62. But there are suggestions of the practice in the fragments of Sappho.[93] And in one of the two surviving fragments of the Danaid trilogy itself there is mention of young men and young women singing the song sung on the morning after the wedding night (see below).

In Catullus 62 the young men take up and reverse the themes of the girls' complaints (cruel Hesperus, the bride as a plucked flower), and thereby attempt to persuade them and the bride of the desirability of marriage (Hesperus is praised, the girl is like a vine needing support). Persuasion

[87] Alexiou and Dronke 1971: 830–7; see also n. 20 above.

[88] Fr. 128c.7–8 (the text is uncertain); with χροϊζόμενον cf. n. 76 above.

[89] Cannatà Fera 1980; cf. Alexiou 1974: 57–8.

[90] Eur. *Hipp.* 1425–9; Pausan. 2.32.1; 'The tears which they weep for him flow at the same time for that part of their own selves which, with that gesture and on that day, has gone forever' (Fauth 1959: 392–3); cf. Wilamowitz-Moellendorff 1891: 27; Séchan 1911: 115–20. On the hair see Fauth 1959: 389–93.

[91] 1031–3; for the text and interpretation see FJW: *ad loc.* I discuss this song in more detail in Seaford 1984–5.

[92] This point is made explicit by Artem. 2.49; see also Fischer 1965: 52, 56–7.

[93] Frr. 27.10, 30.6–7, 43.8–9; Burnett 1983: 218; see also Sen. *Med.* 108; Himer. *Or.* 9.21; Procl. *Chrest. ap.* Phot. *Bibl.* 239 (321.1.17–19 Bekker). There are choirs of youths and maidens in the wedding procession in [Hes.] *Sc.* 276–84.

(Peitho) was according to Plutarch one of the deities needed by people about to marry (οἱ γαμοῦντες), the others being Zeus Teleios, Hera Teleia, Aphrodite and Artemis.[94]

Turning to the final song of the *Suppliants* we find that Zeus, Hera, Aphrodite, Artemis and Peitho are in fact all mentioned within lines 1030–41, along with Pothos ('Longing') and Harmonia. The Danaids have praised the fertility of Argos and then appealed to Artemis and rejected the consummation (τέλος) of Aphrodite (1023–33). The young men's response begins 'This kind-hearted swarm, not unmindful of Kypris' (1034 Κύπριδος δ' οὐκ ἀμελὴς ἑσμὸς ὅδ' εὔφρων).[95] ἑσμὸς ὅδ' ('this swarm') is always taken to refer to the young men. But the possibility should be considered of at least a secondary reference to the Danaids. At 223 the Danaids are called ἑσμὸς ὡς πελειάδων ('a swarm as of doves'). The young men may be almost playfully picking up the Danaids' praise of fertility (see esp. 1028 πολύτεκνοι, 'having many children') as an indication of their interest in Aphrodite despite their explicit rejection at 1031–3. This interpretation coheres well with the association by Aphrodite herself of the fertility of nature with marriage later in the trilogy (probably indeed in the act of persuading the Danaids of the desirability of a marriage: see below). And with the almost playful spirit compare Catullus 62.37, where the young men say of the girls' complaints 'What then if they carp at the one they silently want?'

The Argive soldiers then go on to praise Aphrodite and associate her with the other deities of marriage (see above). They also respond to the Danaids' association of the τέλος of marriage with death by observing, in the corresponding place in the verse,[96] that the τελευτά[97] ('end') of [*115*] marriage has happened to many women in the past. The Danaids respond by invoking Zeus on their own side (1052–3) and rejecting persuasion (1055 'you would charm the uncharmable'; cf. 1040 'Persuasion the charmer'). Still, the girls do then admit that the mind of Zeus, which for the young men is associated with marriage, is obscure (1057–8), and the manner of their second appeal to Zeus to avert the marriage 'implicitly admits the existence of acceptable forms of marriage (γάμος)'.[98]

[94] *Mor.* 264b; cf. also Diod. Sic. 5.73.2; schol. Ar. *Thesm.* 973. Peitho and marriage: refs. in Buxton 1982: 35 (add Pind. *Pyth.* 9.39; Himer. *Or.* 9.19); Sourvinou-Inwood 1987: 145–6.

[95] θεσμὸς mss.; for the case for ἑσμὸς see FJW. See also n. 106 below.

[96] 1050–1; and note 1033 πέλοι = 1051 πέλει.

[97] On the ambiguity of τελευτά see nn. 161, 197 below.

[98] FJW on 1062–7. I adopt their distribution of the lines in this passage, which is in essentials certainly correct.

As in Catullus 62, the male chorus picks up and reverses what has been said by the female. But whereas in Catullus, as in a normal marriage, the male persuasion is imagined to be successful, in Aeschylus it is at best partially so, as we see more clearly of course in the sequel. The only Danaid to spare her husband is Hypermestra, who then, according to Pausanias (2.21.1), dedicated a temple of Artemis Peitho in Argos. The *Suppliants* ends on a note of anxiety[99] comparable to the ending of *Agamemnon* or *Choephori*, except that here the anxiety is enriched by the subtle evocation of a familiar process which would normally, outside the theatre, end with the acquiescence and incorporation of the bride.

To the other two plays of the trilogy there are only two fragments which can be confidently assigned. One of them (fr. 43) is transmitted as follows:

κἄπειτα δ᾽ εἰσὶ λαμπρὸν ἡλίου φάος
ἕως ἐγείρω πρευμενεῖς τοὺς νυμφίους
νόμοισι θέντων σὺν κόροις τε καὶ κόραις.

Although the theme seems reasonably clear, the *hymenaios diegertikos* sung the morning after the wedding night, the fragment appears badly corrupt. The replacement of εἰσὶ with εὖτε and of ἐγείρω with ἐγείρῃ (Wilamowitz) is an improvement; but the latter part of the fragment has remained obscure. We should read πρευμενεῖς τοῖς νυμφίοις νόμους[100] μεθέντων, and translate 'and then when dawn arouses the radiant light of the sun, let them sing with the youths and girls songs to propitiate the bridegrooms'. Compare e.g. Aesch. *Pers.* 609 πατρὶ (i.e. the dead Dareios) πρευμενεῖς χοάς, *Cho.* 823–4 νόμον μεθήσομεν. When the young men (κόροι) and young women (κόραι)[101] come to sing the *diegertikos*, the bridegrooms will be dead, murdered by the brides, rather as in Euripides the girls come to sing a wedding song for the dead Phaithon which, because he has in fact just been killed, is soon followed by a lament.[102] What is envisaged (by Danaos?) in this fragment is that the brides are to sing a song to propitiate[103]

[99] A comparable point is made about the metre of the exodus by Rash 1981: 194, 199: 'the [thematic] clash is summarised a final time in metrical form … The decisive "victory" of the Danaids' attitude is reflected … by the appearance of the lekythion which represents suicide, death, and murder to come'.

[100] One ms. (B) has νόμοις (rather than νόμοισι).

[101] Interpretation of the fragment has been hindered in part by the mistaken view, derived from the scholiast on Pindar (*Pyth.* 3.27) who quotes the passage, and Hsch. II.526 Schmidt, that σὺν κόροις τε καὶ κόραις was a stereotyped wish for children of the marriage. Cf. Lambin 1986, which appeared too late for consideration here.

[102] Eur. *Phaeth.* 227–44, 270–83; cf. *IT* 365–8, *Tro.* 351–2; Soph. fr. 725; Alexiou and Dronke 1971: 833, 835.

[103] Propitiation was a function even of the normal lament: Alexiou 1974: 55, 182.

the husbands they have murdered. Whether this is imagined as being sung alongside or instead of the *diegertikos*, the result is a fine example of an idea to which tragedy constantly returns: the often horrific contrast between songs opposed in mood.[104]

We do not know, of course, how the trilogy ended. One suggestion is that the confirmation of the institution of marriage was accompanied, perhaps as a means of reconciling women to marriage, by the foundation of a festival conducted by married women in the interests of fertility, the Thesmophoria. It has been pointed out that according to Herodotus the ritual (τελετή) called Thesmophoria by the Greeks was brought from Egypt by the Danaids, and that the Danaids [*116*] are independently associated with the watering of the Argolid.[105] One further connection remains to be suggested. On the one hand the Thesmophoria is a festival in which, as in Aphrodite's speech in the Danaid trilogy (see below), agricultural fertility is associated with the fertility of women.[106] But on the other hand the festival is characterised by an 'emphatic anti-sexual ethos' (abstinence, violence against male intruders),[107] which can be seen as the negative side of its function as a fertility rite,[108] and which may perhaps have been associated with the ethos and behaviour of the Danaids, particularly if they were eventually reconciled to marriage by Aphrodite's linking of marriage with the agricultural fertility produced by the union of heaven and earth (see below).

This is of course speculative. But if there is any truth in it, it would exemplify a phenomenon found elsewhere in tragedy: the pitiable events of the play provide the original reason (αἴτιον) for the negative tendency of a ritual. The most obvious example is from the *Hippolytus*: girls before their marriage will henceforth lament for Hippolytos (see above). Less obvious is the *Bacchae*: the sufferings of Pentheus represent in an extreme form the sufferings of the initiand into the Dionysiac mysteries, which are founded at the end of the play.[109] As for Aeschylus, the only genuine extant ending

[104] E.g. Aesch. *Ag.* 707–11, *Cho.* 342–3, *Sept.* 868–70, 915–21, *Pers.* 605; Soph. *Phil.* 212–19, fr. 861; Eur. *Alc.* 760 (δισσὰ δ' ἦν μέλη κλύειν), 922, *Supp.* 975–6, *Hec.* 685–7, *HF* 751–2, *IT* 184–5, 221–8, 365–8, *Tro.* 121, 148–52, 336 (cf. 351–2); fr. 122; *fr. trag. adesp.* 663.16–18; cf. e.g. Ov. *Her.* 12.139–40; *Anth. Pal.* 7.711. The contrast is particularly effective if the songs also have elements in common.

[105] Hdt. 2.171.2–3; Hes. fr. 128. Robertson 1924: 51–3; Thomson 1946: 279–95. The Thesmophoria was apparently first suggested in 1838 by A. Tittler (Garvie 1969: 227).

[106] See e.g. Nilsson 1967: 465. It is interesting in this connection to consider the mss. reading θεσμός at Aesch. *Supp.* 1034.

[107] Parker 1983: 81; Burkert 1985: 244; Detienne 1977: 78–81.

[108] 'The ritual focuses attention on the idea of productive sexual union by a paradoxical temporary insistence on its opposite' (Parker 1983: 83).

[109] Seaford 1981a; cf. also Eur. *Med.* 1382 with Brelich 1969; and *IT* 1454, 1459 with Brelich 1969: 242–6.

of a trilogy, in the *Eumenides*, is in this respect barely comparable: the cult of the Eumenides is founded in Athens. But it does provide a parallel to reconciliation of the defeated party by πειθώ ('persuasion') and to the resolution of conflict in the foundation of a cult associated with the fertility of the land. On the other hand, a major objection to this view is that no evidence survives for a substantial connection between the Thesmophoria and marriage.[110] I would like therefore to make another suggestion.

Hyginus (273) mentions games at Argos founded by Danaos 'with song at the marriage of his daughters, whence the word *hymenaeus*'.[111] Much in Hyginus derives from tragedy.[112] If the trilogy concluded with the institution of the wedding song, perhaps in the context of a remarriage of the Danaids, this would be a good example of the kind of tragic αἴτιον just described. In the trilogy pitiable events and female reluctance and lamentation are expressed in songs which *resemble* formal wedding songs. The antithetical character of these songs, which arises naturally out of the story, may, in the context of the successful hymenaial transition at the end of the trilogy and the foundation of the formal wedding song, have been adduced to explain the antithetical character of the formal wedding song.

The case for supposing that the remarriage (with Greeks this time) was represented, or at least prepared for, at the end of the trilogy is much stronger than is realised by those who support it.[113] This is because a remarriage provides such an excellent context for the only other fragment that certainly belongs to the trilogy (fr. 44), in which Aphrodite describes the action of desire (ἔρως) in uniting heaven and earth and thereby producing the fertility that benefits mankind. She concludes '[the earth] … is brought to fulfilment by the marriage with rain: I am in part the cause' (ἐκ νοτίζοντος γάμου | τέλειός ἐστί. | τῶν δ' ἐγὼ παραίτιος – the textual problem does not affect my point). This time, as opposed to the ending of the first play of the trilogy, the persuasion, uttered by the goddess herself, is successful. The presence of *[117]* Aphrodite even at the ordinary weddings of mortals is imagined by, among many others, Sappho, and in the *topoi*

[110] Although cf. Robertson 1924: 53, who cites Callim. *Hymn* 6.19; Verg. *Aen.* 4.58; Calvus *ap.* Serv. *ad* Verg. *Aen.* 4.58; Plut. *Mor.* 138b. Cf. Hom. *Od.* 23.296. And the participants in the Thesmophoria are (mainly or) entirely married women: Parker 1983: 83; Detienne 1977: 76–82; Burkert 1985: 242.

[111] *filiarum nuptiis cantu, unde hymenaeus dictus.* Cf. Pind. *Pyth.* 9, where the Danaids' (second) husbands are chosen by an athletic contest (also in Pausan. 3.12.2; Apollod. *Bibl.* 2.1.5). The disappearance of Hymenaios on his wedding night is associated with Argos at Tzetz. *Chil.* 13.599; schol. *Il.* 18.493; etc. (Roscher 1884–1937: 1.2801).

[112] E.g. for a detail of Aeschylus' *Lycurgus* trilogy preserved only in Hyginus see Sutton 1975b: 356–60.

[113] Listed by Garvie 1969: 226.

prescribed by Menander Rhetor;[114] her characteristic role is to persuade the bride or to bring her to the groom.[115] We sometimes find Aphrodite depicted with the bride in classical Attic vase painting.[116] And the role of sexual union in the cosmos and in nature, for example in the union of heaven and earth, was a *topos* at least of the later wedding ceremony.[117]

We may now return to the problem of the motivation of the Danaids, which can be seen in a new light. Given that their attitude and actions exemplify that apparently fascinating disruptive victory of the negative over the positive tendency in marital ritual that is a general feature of tragedy, the theme of endogamy is particularly well chosen as an agent of the disruption. It is not that a man claiming a bride under the law of the heiress might do so with a special degree of selfish and dominating urgency, conceivable though this is. More important is the motivation made explicit in 335–9:

Χο.	ὡς μὴ γένωμαι δμωῒς Αἰγύπτου γένει.
Βα.	πότερα κατ' ἔχθραν, ἢ τὸ μὴ θέμις λέγεις;
Χο.	τίς δ' ἂν φίλους ὠνοῖτο τοὺς κεκτημένους;
Βα.	σθένος μὲν οὕτως μεῖζον αὔξεται βροτοῖς.
Χο.	καὶ δυστυχούντων γ' εὐμαρὴς ἀπαλλαγή.

Chorus:	So that I might not be enslaved to the clan of Aigyptos.
King:	Do you say this because of hatred, or because of unlawfulness?
Chorus:	Who would buy their kin as masters?
King:	In this way there is a great increase in strength for men.
Chorus:	And an easy separation, if things go wrong.

At 337 the mss. have ὠνοιτο, and editors are divided between ὤνοιτο and ὠνοῖτο. FJW print φιλοῦσ' ὤνοιτο, with a lacuna of two lines after 337 to account for οὕτως in 338. But with this one might expect the singular τὸν κεκτημένον. And φίλους ὠνοῖτο makes good sense without the need for a lacuna: 'who would buy (cf. Eur. *Med.* 232–4) φίλοι as masters?', implying

[114] Sappho fr. 194; Men. Rhet. 412.12 εἰκὸς παρεῖναι ..., 407.7 (cf. 404.19–25, 406.19–24; Dracontius 6; etc. (Reitzenstein 1900: 97–9).

[115] E.g. Men. Rhet. 407.7; Claud. *Epithal. Hon. Aug.* 251–85; Stat. *Silv.* 1.2 etc. (Reitzenstein 1900: 97–9); cf. Eur. *Hipp.* 553 (at the 'wedding' of Herakles and Iole) Ἀλκμήνας τόκῳ Κύπρις ἐξέδωκεν. *ARV*^{2} 1317.1 and 1317.3 both probably depict a bride with Aphrodite and Peitho (cf. also e.g. 1325.27, 1328.99). Cf. Eur. *Hel.* 1120–1 (quoted at n. 191 below).

[116] E.g. *ARV*^{2} 1126.6, 1133.196.

[117] Men. Rhet. 401, 408.13–19; [Dion. Hal.] *Rhet.* 262; Himer. *Or.* 9.8 etc. (Reitzenstein 1900: 97–9). If it dates back to the fifth century, then Aphrodite's speech might even have been presented as an *aition* for it. Cf. §1 (*Antigone*); Procl. *In Ti.* 293c (III.176.26–8 Diehl) ὃ δὴ (Heaven–Earth union the first γάμος, etc.) καὶ οἱ θεσμοὶ τῶν Ἀθηναίων εἰδότες προσέταττον οὐρανῷ καὶ γῇ προτελεῖν τοὺς γάμους.

(in response to 336) paradoxical hostility (ἔχθρα) against φίλοι, 'kin', who would normally also be 'dear'.[118] Now whatever the truth of this much disputed problem, it is undisputed that 338 is an argument in favour of the marriage. But if so, then the Danaids' reply (339) must express agreement with and development of Pelasgos' observation;[119] and so it cannot refer, as Garvie would have it, simply to the ease with which Pelasgos can abandon the Danaids.[120] The 'release' (ἀπαλλαγή) must rather be a feature of the marriage, clearly divorce?[121] The objection that 'divorce would be the very thing that the Danaids would presumably want'[122] has no weight, for it is perfectly consistent for a woman to point to the ease with which she may be abandoned (and thereby perhaps isolated and disgraced) as one of a number of objections to entering in a marriage, particularly if [*118*] it is a specific response to the specific point made by Pelasgos. Another objection, that the Danaids' murder of their husbands is even more disreputable than divorce,[123] is equally irrelevant, as it ignores the Danaids' various possible motives for the murder, e.g. resistance to defloration, revenge, certain and immediate freedom from the Aigyptiads. If 338 refers to the accumulation of property within the household by kinship marriage,[124] then it coheres very well with our reading not only of 337 but also of 339. For a girl who marries one of her father's kinsmen will of course encounter loyalty between them and her husband. She will be without separate kinsmen of her own to support her in a conflict.[125] Hence perhaps the particular

[118] Perhaps *also* therefore τὸ μὴ θέμις: see in detail Thomson 1971 and 1946: 302–6, 450. There is no substance in the objection of FJW that 'φίλους can hardly mean "relation", as the idea of intermarriage is not alluded to until 387ff.' (it is mentioned there by *Pelasgos*!). They also object to ὠνοῖτο by comparing 202; but the Danaids need not have been penniless in Egypt. ὄνομαι does not seem to occur elsewhere in Attic (though cf. ὀνοταζόμεναι at Aesch. *Supp.* 10).

[119] Denniston 1954: 157–8; καί … γε is found in the play also at 296, 313, 468.

[120] Garvie 1969: 220; similarly FJW: *ad loc.*, who find an implausible link with 338 in the idea of male domination, which both gives the husband power and allows Pelasgos to abandon the Danaids easily! FJW also object that δυστυχούντων should refer to their *present* misfortune, and that it is hard to see 'what sort of misfortune they can envisage as inducing their cousins to dissolve the union'. But the point is that the Danaids seem to envisage their present misfortune, isolation and hostility as continuing into the marriage.

[121] So Tucker, Headlam, Thomson etc. Cf. Page 1938 on Eur. *Med.* 236–7; Stevens 1971 on Eur. *Andr.* 592.

[122] Garvie 1969: 220; similarly FJW: *ad loc.*; this pseudo-problem prompts Mackinnon 1978: 78 to take the line as an indignant question implying that divorce is *not* easy.

[123] Mackinnon 1978: 77.

[124] Thomson 1971: 29 compares Pind. *Isthm.* 3.2. and Eur. *El.* 427.

[125] Thomson 1971: 29 cites Plut. *Quaest. Rom.* 289e (the Romans, unlike the Greeks, prohibit such marriages) '… or because, seeing that women need many supporters due to their vulnerability, they did not want them to live in marriage with relatives, in order that if their husbands did them wrong their relatives would come to their aid'. And see also the protection offered by the Attic *state* (together with ὁ βουλόμενος): n. 129 below.

aptness of the plural φίλους … κεκτημένους. Furthermore, a dowry normally protected a woman from easy divorce, because it had in Attic law to be returned, in the event of a divorce, to her former *kyrios* (male legal guardian).[126] However, 'the *epikleros* ['heiress'] had no such leverage; she could not take her fortune and return to her former *kyrios*, for it was to him that she was married'.[127] She was therefore in an exposed position.

> The *epikleros* was in a sense an heiress, in that the estate always passed to the *oikos* of which she was a member; but the property was her husband's, and the only check upon her husband's ability to spend it was the danger of a lawsuit when her children came of age and took it over.[128]

Vulnerable in these and various other ways, the *epikleros* was in fact put under the protection of the *archon*.[129] But of course this civilised protection by the Attic state was not imagined as available to the Danaids. Indeed, the Danaids, not unlike Orestes in the *Oresteia*, represent the kind of problematic case which required, historically, the intervention of the state in an area originally regulated by the kin.

What this problematic case means for the Danaids is an enhanced degree of the isolation and subjugation associated even with the unproblematic marriage. The normal bride in moving from one household to another is resentful, but she nevertheless preserves with the family she has left links which will re-emerge to support her in the event of divorce or conflict with her husband or his family.[130] But the *epikleros* cannot look to any such support (and her *mother's* kinsmen do not of course even belong to her former *oikos*[131]). To put it another way, the *epikleros* does in a sense fail, in her marriage, to make the marital transition to another family; she remains in her own family,[132] but in a role even more isolated and subordinate (337 κεκτημένους) than that of the normal bride in her new family.

[126] See e.g. Schaps 1979: 76. Add Isae. 3.28, the one who gave her in marriage would have wanted a receipt for the dowry 'so that the husband might not easily be able to divorce his wife whenever he wanted'.

[127] Schaps 1979: 26.

[128] Schaps 1979: 57; cf. 27–8.

[129] Schaps 1979: 38; he notes that the *archon* had power over all possible abuses to which *epikleroi* were subject. See also [Arist.] *Ath. Pol.* 56.6; *Suda* and Harp. s.v. κακώσεως; Harrison 1971: 43. It was made easy for ὁ βουλόμενος to bring an εἰσαγγελία κακώσεως against the husband of an *epikleros*.

[130] Cf. the loyalties of the wife reverting to her old household in myth (Althaia, Psykhe, Eriphyle).

[131] It is interesting in this connection that no mention is made in the play of the Danaids' mother(s), although they do claim kinship with the Argives through their ancestress Io, whom they call 'mother' (15–18, 51, 141, 533, 539). They also appeal more than once to their immortal ancestor (on the maternal side) Zeus, who is however associated with marriage: note their quandary at 1057–8 (cf. 40–175, 1035, 1052–3, 1062–7).

[132] On this point see esp. Vernant 1983: 143–6.

This does not mean that the play is about the problems of the *epikleros*. There is, for example, no mention (except perhaps at 979) of an inheritance to be transmitted by the Danaids. The vulnerable isolation of women married to their agnatic cousins is alluded to only at 335–9. This anomaly does however play a subtle role in the victory of the negative tendency in the marriage ritual. In the other examples discussed in this chapter, the victory is effected by a factor external to the marriage itself (another woman, Kreon's edict, etc.). In the *Suppliants* on the other hand, as in the normal wedding, the negative tendency derives entirely from the bridal *[119]* perception of the groom and of the transition.[133] But how then in the *Suppliants* can the negative tendency credibly prevail? Largely because the Danaids and their cousins are exotic semi-barbarians in a mythical era. By itself, however, this exotic factor is no more than a simple reversal in fantasy of Greek norms,[134] whereas the endogamous isolation of the woman, with which it is combined, is both familiar to the Greeks and ideally suited to heighten the fears and reluctance of the bride.

3. The Death of the Wife

§5. **Deianeira.** The anxiety of the bride at isolation and loss of the bloom of youth (nn. 1–3 above) is expressed also in Sophocles' *Trachiniae* (141–9). Deianeira's negative emotions at her marriage persist into her married life,[135] first because of her husband's absence on his labours, but then through her own fatal mistake, with the result that finally she complains that she is alone (ἐρήμη), makes up the marriage bed, gets into it, addresses bed and bridal chamber, undoes her dress and plunges a sword into herself.[136] The word ἐρήμη has earlier been used to describe the position of Deianeira as a bride, isolated from her kin but not yet incorporated into her new

[133] In this respect the remark of FJW: 1.40 that the play is the earliest-known text in European civilisation to have dealt with the problem of arranged marriage is misleading to the extent that it ranges the Danaids alongside the bride forced to marry someone she does not love, usually to the exclusion of the man she does love. Such a bride has feelings *opposite* to what we imagine to be the normal bridal ones of joy, love for her groom, affection for her parents, whereas the feelings of the Danaids are an *intensification* of normal bridal ones (attachment to the father, resentment, fear of isolation and of male domination, etc.). Hence, incidentally, the problem of Danaos, who though sympathetic to his daughters neither asserts his paternal rights nor even expresses great hostility to the marriage (see FJW: 1.35–6, who offer a different solution): he is in these respects just like the father of a normal bride. Cf. Sourvinou-Inwood 1987:143–4.

[134] Cf. e.g. the Amazons. Even the Lemnian women require an external stimulus (as of course does Lysistrata).

[135] Esp. ὄκνος, uncertainty: 7, 181; cf. 37.

[136] 904–31; Seaford 1986b.

home.[137] As I have argued in detail elsewhere,[138] Deianeira never achieves the *eudaimonia* of incorporation. The negative tendency in the rite of passage has emerged as a reality, the actual isolated death of Deianeira.

§6. *Eudaimonia* is also denied, of course, to **Oidipous** and **Iokaste**. There is a sense in which their marriage only appeared to be properly completed. Teiresias predicts to Oidipous (Soph. *OT* 420–3):

> βοῆς δὲ τῆς σῆς ποῖος οὐκ ἔσται λιμήν,
> ποῖος Κιθαιρὼν οὐχὶ σύμφωνος τάχα,
> ὅταν καταίσθῃ τὸν ὑμέναιον ὃν δόμοις
> ἄνορμον εἰσέπλευσας εὐπλοίας τυχών;

> What kind of harbour will not receive your cry, what part of Kithairon will not soon resound with it, when you perceive the harbourless wedding into which you sailed in this house, after fair sailing?

The word here for wedding (ὑμέναιον) can also mean wedding song. Dawe prints a lacuna after 422. This is unnecessary. The ellipse would be acceptable given the familiarity of the processional wedding song and perhaps also of nautical imagery surrounding the wedding procession.[139] Familiar too is the idea that the joyful wedding song will be replaced by the cry of suffering, βοή, a word which can also refer to songs of joy (Eur. *El.* 879; Pind. *Nem.* 3.67; Ar. *Ran.* 212). Even the expression 'what part of Kithairon will not soon resound with your cry?' may have its equivalent in what is sung or said at the wedding.[140] And when the truth is revealed, Iokaste, intent on suicide, 'rushed straight towards the bridal bed' (1242–3) and 'bewailed the bed, where in her wretchedness …' (1249). Oidipous, finding her hanged, 'roars out terribly, wretched, and loosens the noose. And when the poor woman is lying on the ground' (1265–7) he puts out his eyes with her brooches, giving as he does so his reasons. The narrative continues (1275–84):

> τοιαῦτ᾽ ἐφυμνῶν πολλάκις τε κοὐχ ἅπαξ
> ἤρασσ᾽ ἐπαίρων βλέφαρα· φοίνιαι δ᾽ ὁμοῦ *[120]*
> γλῆναι γένει᾽ ἔτεγγον, οὐδ᾽ ἀνίεσαν
> φόνου μυδώσας σταγόνας, ἀλλ᾽ ὁμοῦ μέλας
> ὄμβρος χαλαζῆς αἵματός σφ᾽ ἐτέγγετο.

[137] 530; cf. Soph. *Ant.* 887; Eur. *Andr.* 854–5, *Tro.* 563–5, *IA* 1314; John Chrys. *PG* 62.386 *ad fin.*
[138] Seaford 1986b; cf. §11 below.
[139] See §9a. The rare word εὐπλοία ('fair sailing') occurs also at Aesch. *Supp.* 1045, again in the context of a disastrous marriage.
[140] [Dion. Hal.] *Rhet.* 271; Men. Rhet. 399.29, 404.17; Catull. 64.35–42; [Hes.] *Sc.* 284–5; Xen. *Hell.* 4.1.9; Diod. Sic. 13.84.1–3 (Tim. *FGrH* 566 F26); Sappho fr. 44.13–14.

> τάδ᾽ ἐκ δυοῖν ἔρρωγεν, οὐ μονούμενα,[140a]
> ἀλλ᾽ ἀνδρὶ καὶ γυναικὶ συμμιγῆ κακά.
> ὁ πρὶν παλαιὸς δ᾽ ὄλβος ἦν πάροιθε μὲν
> ὄλβος δικαίως· νῦν δὲ τῇδε θἠμέρᾳ
> στεναγμός, ἄτη, κτλ.

> Chanting such things, not once but many times did he raise his hand and strike his eyes. The bloody eyeballs together drenched his cheeks, nor did they send forth oozing drops of gore, but all at once a dark shower of blood, like hail, soaked him. These things broke out from two, not from one alone, but evils commingled for man and woman. Their former prosperity of bygone days was justly prosperity, but now, on this day, there is lamentation, there is ruin …

ἐφυμνῶν (1275) imparts a suggestion of ritual song, thereby reminding us of Teiresias' prophecy at 420.[141] And there runs through the narrative the suggestion of sexual union, of a re-enactment of the ἄγαμος γάμος (1214 'non-marriage marriage'): in the νυμφικὰ λέχη (1242–3 'bridal bed'), in χαλᾷ (1266 'loosens'),[142] in ἔκειτο (1267 'he lay down'), in πολλάκις τε κοὐχ ἅπαξ ἤρασσε (1275–6) and in particular in 1278–81: a shower of blood comes (no longer in separate drops but) all at once; the metaphorical ἔρρωγεν ('broke out') then proceeds naturally from the reality, as it too can refer to an outburst of liquid (a cloudburst, tears).[143] Given the association between rain and semen,[144] together with the description of what has burst forth as ἀνδρὶ καὶ γυναικὶ συμμιγῆ κακὰ, the suggestion of sexual union seems to me inevitable, particularly as συμμείγνυμι is a standard word for it. It is a pity that in his recent commentary Dawe not only fails to rectify the Victorian Jebb's omission of this point, but even removes one element in it by replacing the transmitted ἐκ δυοῖν ('from two') by Pearson's εἰς δυοῖν … κάρα ('onto the head of two').[145] Finally, the prosperity (ὄλβος) brought to Oidipous by his marriage, and which has now changed into its

[140a] [mss. †μόνου κακά. Cf. n. 145 below.]

[141] βρυχηθείς (1265) on the other hand denotes an unrestrained noise associated with animals, and is used of Deianeira when she feels again the negative emotion of her wedding (Soph. *Trach.* 904; cf. 1071–2; Seaford 1986b: 58).

[142] Cf. e.g. Hom. *Od.* 11.245; Eur. *Tro.* 501, 665; Plut. *Lyc.* 14; and esp. Soph. *Trach.* 924. At Plut. *Mor.* 253d a virgin undoes her girdle (ζώνη) and uses it as a noose for herself: this is interpreted by Helen King as an inversion of marriage and death (see §4 and n. 80).

[143] Plut. *Fab.* 12; Ar. *Nub.* 378; Philostr. *Imag.* 2.27; cf. West 1981: 68 on καταρρήγνυμι; Soph. *Trach.* 851, 919.

[144] Fertilising rain in e.g. Aesch. fr. 44 (see above); δρόσος ('dew') can mean drizzle as well as semen (Dover 1968 on Ar. *Nub.* 977; Callim. fr. 260.19Pf.); the same association between rain, blood and semen occurs at Aesch. *Ag.* 1388–92.

[145] Dawe 1982. Better at the end of the verse would be μονούμενα (Bruhn, Wilamowitz), μόνου κάτα (Otto); μόνας κάτα (Bruhn; cf. Thuc. 1.32.5, 37.4; Pl. *Leg.* 9.873d6). [In his revised edition Dawe 2006 prints ἐκ δυοῖν and μονούμενα.]

opposite (1282–4), may in this context suggest the doomed *makarismos* of the wedding ceremony (see also §7 and §12).[146]

Two further points can be made in support of this conclusion. First, it has been reached quite independently of Freud's view of the self-blinding of Oidipous as a symbolic self-castration in which the eyes represent the genitals.[147] I am not concerned with the truth or falsity of this view.[148] More to my point is the evidence adduced in its support by Devereux for the Greek association of eye and penis.[149]

Second, we have already noted in various passages of tragedy that unity of opposites which associates the destruction of the body with the first physical union of the married couple (§4 and n. 76 above). Particularly relevant here is the death of Haimon over the body of the hanged Antigone (Soph. *Ant.* 1237–41):[150]

> ... παρθένῳ προσπτύσσεται·
> καὶ φυσιῶν ὀξεῖαν ἐκβάλλει ῥοὴν
> λευκῇ παρειᾷ φοινίου σταλάγματος.
> κεῖται δὲ νεκρὸς περὶ νεκρῷ, τὰ νυμφικὰ
> τέλη λαχὼν δείλαιος εἰν Ἅιδου δόμοις.[151] *[121]*

> ... he clings to the maiden. And, panting, he shoots forth a swift flow of bloody drops upon her white cheek. Corpse lies around corpse, the wretched man having obtained his nuptial rites in the house of Hades.

The same *topos* is found also at Aesch. *Ag.* 1389–92:

> κἀκφυσιῶν ὀξεῖαν αἵματος σφαγὴν[152]
> βάλλει μ' ἐρεμνῇ ψακάδι φοινίας δρόσου,
> χαίρουσαν οὐδὲν ἧσσον ἢ διοσδότῳ
> γάνει σπορητὸς κάλυκος ἐν λοχεύμασιν.

> Panting out a sudden spurt of blood from his slaughter he hits me with a dark drizzle of bloody dew, and I delight in this no less than the sown crop delights in the gleam of Zeus-given rain when the husk is giving birth.

[146] Also 1195; and e.g. Eur. *Andr.* 1218 'It was in vain that the gods blessed you at your wedding' (μάτην δέ σ' ἐν γάμοισιν ὤλβισαν θεοί); Seaford 1986b: 55; cf. n. 5 above.

[147] Freud 1935: 398.

[148] Though see the striking evidence adduced in its support by Devereux 1973: 36–9. See also Buxton 1980: 25.

[149] Devereux 1973: 42 and 1976: 33–6; notably representations of *phalloi* with eyes, and cf. [Aesch.] *PV* 654.

[150] Cf. also *Trach.* 917–18, 924, 931, etc. (Seaford 1986b: 57–8).

[151] Cf. also 1205 νυμφεῖον, 1207 παστάδα, etc., and §1 above.

[152] σφαγὴν has been widely suspected. Fraenkel's ῥαγὴν is in fact supported by the erotic undertone, which he ignores (see above on *OT* 1279 ἔρρωγεν; West 1981: 68). ὀξεῖαν, whose basic meaning is 'sharp', then has a special point, because a ῥαγή may be γλυκύπικρος (of semen) or painful (of blood). Cf. the similar common use of πικρός (esp. Seaford 1984b on *Cyc.* 589).

The similarity of wording with the death of Haimon is clear enough. And as in the blinding of Oidipous, the comparison involves three terms: the blood is explicitly compared with rain, implicitly with semen.[153] The association of (διόσδοτος) rain with semen is implicit in the idea of the sexual union of Heaven and Earth, as in Aphrodite's speech from the Danaid trilogy (fr. 44; see above): 'And the rain from her bedfellow sky falls and wets the earth, and she gives birth.' And this idea seems to have been a commonplace of the wedding ceremony, at least in antiquity.[154]

§7. **Euadne** in Euripides' *Suppliants*, dressed as a bride, sings a song which explicitly recalls her marriage and is itself suggestive of the wedding song, and envisages her proposed suicide on the pyre of her husband Kapaneus as an erotic union. So much is clear enough, and well described by Collard.[155] But certain further details in which the scene evokes the wedding remain to be exposed.

(a) As Euadne first appears the chorus refer to the tomb of Kapaneus: 'Now I look upon these lairs (θαλάμας) and the sacred tomb of Kapaneus' (980–1). Nowhere else, so far as I know, does θαλάμη have any connection with death. Perhaps then it has here displaced θαλάμους,[156] which is elsewhere exploited for its ambiguity between tomb (or underworld) and marriage chamber.[157]

(b) Collard seems to me almost certainly right to suggest that the corrupt lines 992–3 λαμπάδ' ἵν' ὠκυθόαι νύμφαι ἱππεύουσι δι' ὀρφναίας ('where the swift brides ride the torch through the darkness') are a reminiscence of the torchlit wedding procession (of Euadne and Kapaneus). If so, then the point of ὠκυθόαι,[158] which refers to the (presumably joyful) urgency of the procession,[159] is an implicit association with the speed with which Euadne has now left her home

[153] The erotic undertone of this passage of *Ag.* has always seemed to me clear, ignored though it is by the commentators. I now find it argued in detail by Moles 1979: 179–89, who points to the sexual occurrences of δρόσος and βάλλω etc., but ignores the same *topos* in Soph. *Ant.* and *OT*, as does O'Daly 1985: 8, who is also I think mistaken in regarding λοχεύμασιν (1393) as ruling out erotic associations.

[154] See n. 117 above.

[155] Collard 1975: II.358; *Supp.* 990–1030, 1063–71. See also n. 76 above.

[156] For the reverse displacement see Eur. *Bacch.* 95, 561.

[157] Soph. *Ant.* 947, 804 (cf. *Trach.* 913, *El.* 190; Seaford 1985[12]: 318); cf. Eur. *Supp.* 1022. Even if we keep θαλάμας, there would surely be a play on θάλαμος (cf. Collard 1975: *ad loc.*).

[158] Collard 1975: *ad loc.* notes that this word is transmitted paroxytone, incorrectly if the adj. is nom. plur., but perhaps a sign that the dat. sing. was at one time understood.

[159] Cf. Sappho fr. 44. 11, 23(?); this does not mean that it was joyful for the *bride*! Eur. *Hel.* 724 τροχάζων describes running quickly beside the bridal chariot.

(1000 δρομάς, 1039 πηδήσασα). There is a comparable irony in Iole as a 'swift bride' (θοὰ νύμφα) at Soph. *Trach.* 857 (see §11). And it is interesting that, although she lives of course in her husband's house (1097–8), she in fact leaves, as in her wedding, the house of her father (1038–42, 1049). Similarly, the torches which contributed so much to the splendour of a wedding are associated with the fire in which she and her husband are now to be consumed.[160]

(c) The word τελευτά ('completion'), with which Euadne describes her approaching death, is commonly used of the wedding. Compare the same ambiguity at Aesch. *Ag.* 745 γάμου πικρὰς τελευτάς, 'a bitter completion of the wedding' (see below §9c).[161]

(d) After remembering her wedding *makarismos* (996–8 'the city of Argos raised [122] their happiness to the sky with songs'), Euadne expresses the desire to end her 'life of toil' and 'the troubles of her life' (1003–5). Collard rightly calls this latter phrase an exaggeration ('Ev.'s whole life has not been full of πόνοι, but only since the recent death of Cap.'). His explanation is that it is 'to suit the *sententia* 1006–8'. But in fact we should see it in the context of the failed wedding *makarismos*. The *makarismos*, employing the words μάκαρ, ὄλβιος or εὐδαίμων, bestows *permanent* felicity.[162] But of course permanent happiness in life can never be safely predicted. There can be no foolproof *makarismos*.[163] As Solon said to Kroisos (Hdt. 1.32.7), you can call someone fortunate (εὐτυχής) before he dies but not blessed (ὄλβιος); the latter depends on a successfully completed life, αἰών (1.32.5). Despite earlier appearances, the life of Euadne has turned out to be one of suffering. In the opening lines of Sophocles' *Trachiniae* Deianeira refers to the saying that you cannot evaluate somebody's life (αἰών) until they are dead; she on the other hand knows already that hers is bad, and goes on to explain how her married life has been one of constant suffering.[164] Despite the sometimes apparently joyful tone of Euadne's song, she too, no less than Iokaste and Deianeira, has failed to complete the hymenaial transition to happiness (*eudaimonia*), with the

[160] 1002 πυρὸς (πυρᾶς Bothe) φῶς τάφον τε ~ 1025 ἴτω φῶς γάμοι τε, 1019, 1029, 1071, also 1010–11. Perhaps this association of celebratory and destructive fire gives point to her opening question (990) τί φέγγος, τίν'αἴγλαν ...; (cf. *Tro.* 319–21 ἐγὼ δ' ἐπὶ γάμοις ἐμοῖς ἀναφλέγω πυρὸς φῶς ἐς αὐγάν, ἐς αἴγλαν).

[161] Also n. 197 and §8 below. τελευτά of the wedding also at Aesch. *Supp.* 1050; Pind. *Pyth.* 9.66; Hom. *Od.* 1.249–50 = 16.126–7, 24.126.

[162] See e.g. Ar. *Ran.* 1182–6, and in general de Heer 1969. See also n. 5 above.

[163] ὀλβίσαι δὲ χρὴ βίον τελευτήσαντ' ἐν εὐεστοῖ φίλῃ (Aesch. *Ag.* 928–9). See also §6 and §12.

[164] See Seaford 1986b.

result that her actual death is now imagined as a re-enactment of the wedding,[165] albeit in her case all that comes between husband and wife is the death of the husband.

§8. In despair at Jason's intention to marry Glauke, Euripides' **Medea** expresses a desire for death. The chorus reply as follows (148-53):

ἄϊες, ὦ Ζεῦ καὶ Γᾶ καὶ φῶς,
ἀχὰν οἵαν δύστανος
μέλπει νύμφα;
τίς σοί ποτε τᾶς ἀπλάτου
κοίτας ἔρος, ὦ ματαία;
σπεύσεις θανάτου τελευτάν;

'Do you hear, O Zeus and Earth and light, what sort of cry the wretched bride sings out? What desire for the terrible bed has come upon you, poor woman? Are you rushing towards the completion of death?

Four factors combine here to suggest the death-wish of a bride.

(a) As we have seen in Euripides' *Suppliants* and will see in Aeschylus' *Agamemnon*, the word τελευτά, like τέλος, is associated with the completion inherent in marriage as well as the completion inherent in death.[166] We find the same ambiguity indeed later in the *Medea* (1388 'beholding the painful completion (πικρὰς τελευτὰς) of your marriage with me').

(b) τᾶς ἀπλάτου κοίτας ἔρος ('desire for the terrible bed') expresses the familiar association of marriage bed and deathbed.[167]

Consider in this context the words of the nurse in the prologue (39–41), 'I fear that she might thrust a sword through her liver, silently entering the house to where the bed is made', in a passage which is generally condemned. For example Dindorf, followed by Page and by Diggle, brackets 38–43. The main reason[168] for doing so is the repetition (with ἢ for μὴ and ὤσω for ὤσῃ) of 40–1 at 379–80, in the deliberations of Medea on revenge. But the interpolation seems to me much more likely at 379–80. If so, the original text there ran:

165 That is why at 995 Collard is wrong to reject Haupt's αἰνογάμων on the grounds that 'discrepat cum gaudio Evadnae'.
166 Eur. *Supp.* 1012; Aesch. *Ag.* 745; and see n. 161 above.
167 Seaford 1984c[n]: 251; cf. Eur. *Med.* 141 ἡ δ' ἐν θαλάμοις τήκει βιοτὴν.
168 Page also objects to (a) ἢ καὶ τύραννον (42), and (b) the proximity of 'δέδοικα δ' αὐτὴν and δειμαίνω τέ νιν, *as well as* βαρεῖα γὰρ φρὴν and δεινὴ γάρ'. But for (a) replace καὶ with τὴν, and (b) expresses the nurse's anxiety. There may conceivably be radical corruption here, but there are no good reasons for wholesale deletion.

376 πολλὰς δ᾽ ἔχουσα θανασίμους αὐτοῖς ὁδούς,
οὐκ οἶδ᾽ ὁποίᾳ πρῶτον ἐγχειρῶ, φίλαι·
378 πότερον ὑφάψω δῶμα νυμφικὸν πυρί;
381 ἀλλ᾽ ἕν τί μοι πρόσαντες· εἰ ληφθήσομαι
δόμους ὑπερβαίνουσα καὶ τεχνωμένη,
θανοῦσα θήσω τοῖς ἐμοῖς ἐχθροῖς γέλων. [123]
κράτιστα τὴν εὐθεῖαν, ᾗ πεφύκαμεν
σοφοὶ μάλιστα, φαρμάκοις αὐτοὺς ἑλεῖν.

Though I've many paths I might take to kill them, friends, I do not know by which one I am to make the first attempt. Should I set the bride's house on fire? But one thing holds me back: if I'm caught entering the house and devising the crime, I'll be put to death and make myself an object of ridicule to my enemies. Best to choose the straight path, the one in which I'm most skilled by nature: to kill them with poison.

For the structure (πότερον ...;, then an objection, then an alternative) compare the words of the no less disturbed Iphigeneia (Eur. *IT* 884–91):

πότερον κατὰ χέρσον, οὐχὶ ναΐ
ἀλλὰ ποδῶν ῥιπᾷ;
θανάτῳ πελάσεις ἄρα βάρβαρα φῦλα
καὶ δι᾽ ὁδοὺς ἀνόδους στείχων· διὰ κυανέας μὰν
στενοπόρου πέτρας μακρὰ κέλευθα να-
ΐοισιν δρασμοῖς.

Are you to go by land – not by ship but by a rapid journey on foot? Then you will risk death by passing through barbarian tribes and going by roads that do not warrant the name. Yet the path through the dark rocks of the strait is a long way for escape by ship.

But the interpolator of *Medea* 379–80 wanted to supply another alternative, immediately, with the usual ἤ after πότερον. He was influenced perhaps also by πολλάς (376) and, in his choice of lines to interpolate, by δῶμα νυμφικόν (378). His interference is understandable, but it dilutes the point: Medea rules out the personal presence required by arson so as to choose the alternative of working from a distance with poison.

Page (1938: 68) writes 'at 41 the phrase [sc. ἵν᾽ ἔστρωται λέχος] comes suddenly and obscurely'. But not for those familiar with the *topos* of the wife's suicide with a sword on the marital bed.[169] Here

[169] Soph. *Trach.* 915–31 (esp. 918, 920, 924, 930–1); Verg. *Aen.* 4.648–65; cf. Eur. *Alc.* 175–84; Winnington-Ingram 1980: 81 n. 28. For (apparently) abrupt statements of (other) *topoi* see Seaford 1984c[II]: 249, 251; see also n. 195 below.

the *topos* contains the extra pathos that the bed has been prepared to receive a new bride (Greek marriage is patrilocal). Page continues 'In 379 it is clear to whose heart δι' ἥπατος refers: in 40 it is not so clear.' This is the reverse of the truth. It is clear enough in 40 from the *topos*, and anyway Jason and Glauke are mentioned as an alternative in 42, whereas the omission at 379 is odd. Lines 40–1 make much better sense here than at 379–80. And Medea's very first words are indeed a wish to die (96–7; also 144–7, etc.).

(c) νύμφη is used primarily of a young woman envisaged in relation to marriage, normally therefore of a bride, and, although the designation may continue into the marriage (e.g. Eur. *Or.* 1136 'she bereaved the wives (νύμφας) of their husbands'), in this context it cannot fail to have a bridal overtone.[170]

(d) μέλπει suggests a ritual context,[171] and is particularly apt if we suppose that bridal lamentation did occur in the wedding (see §4 above).

Further examples might be described of the death of a wife imagined in terms of her wedding, notably Phaidra[172] and Alkestis.[173] But instead we will proceed to the next category, in which an extramarital or merely natural union is imagined as a marriage in which the negative element prevails.

4. The Extramarital Union

§9. At Aesch. *Ag.* 686–771 the union of **Paris** and **Helen** is imagined by the chorus as a marriage which brings disaster.[174] From the numerous elements of this picture I select six.[175] *[124]*

[170] As also at Eur. *Andr.* 136–41 'Know that you, a slave from another city, are on alien soil, where you see none of your friends, most unfortunate, most wretched νύμφα – for your coming to this house is so extremely pitiable.'

[171] Page 1938 on *Med.* 150 calls this a metaphorical use of μέλπειν very rare in tragedy, and compares Aesch. *Ag.* 1445 and Eur. *Andr.* 1037–8 (both in fact of the lament).

[172] Eur. *Hipp.* 755–6 ἐπόρευσας ἐμὰν ἄνασσαν ὀλβίων ἀπ' οἴκων κακονυμφοτάταν ὄνασιν (i.e. instead of εὐδαιμονία), 768–72 τεράμνων ἀπὸ νυμφιδίων κρεμαστὸν ἅψεται ἀμφὶ βρόχον λευκᾷ καθαρμόζουσα δειρᾷ (cf. Soph. *Ant.* 1239 λευκῇ παρειᾷ – see above; Eur. *Med.* 1189, *IA* 875). For hanging as suicide cf. Antigone, Iokaste, Erigone (imitated by Athenian virgins).

[173] Eur. *Alc.* 866–7, 880–1, 898–9, 915–25.

[174] Given the tendency to describe adulterous union in terms of marriage ritual (cf. e.g. §11 (Iole), or the paradoxical phrase ἰδίοισιν ὑμεναίοισι of Aigisthos and Klytaimestra at Eur. *Or.* 558), it makes sense to ask whether Paris and Helen were *actually* married or not (cf. Hom. *Il.* 24.763, 3.140). Like the other cases in this category their union is extramarital in the sense that it violates the marriage of one of the partners, and 'natural' in the sense that it is effected by lust or violence or both.

[175] Cf. also 686 δορίγαμβρον, 720 προτελείοις, also (earlier) ἄγουσά τ' ἀντίφερνον Ἰλίῳ φθορὰν (406). Lebeck 1971: 48–9, 69–70, collects some of the obvious references to marriage in the trilogy.

(a) 690–2: Helen 'sailed forth from the finely woven *prokalummata* on the breeze of giant Zephyos [i.e. the west wind]' (ἐκ τῶν ἁβροπήνων προκαλυμμάτων ἔπλευσε Ζεφύρου γίγαντος αὔρᾳ). The *prokalummata* here are generally assumed to be 'curtains' (of bed, chamber or palace). But the reference is I think rather to the ritual unveiling of the bride. Nowhere else does *prokalumma* mean 'curtain'. True, it is a rare word. However, the verb *prokaluptein* does occur three times in tragedy: of the bride Glauke covering her eyes (Eur. *Med.* 1147), of Pylades covering Orestes with robes (Eur. *IT* 312) and of Antigone casting off her veil in a passage containing hymenaial associations (Eur. *Pho.* 1485–92; see n. 185 below).

Furthermore, *kalumma* regularly refers to what covers the *head*,[176] generally in the plural *kalummata*. Eur. *IT* 372 λεπτῶν ὄμμα διὰ καλυμμάτων ἔχουσα ('looking through the fine *kalummata*') refers to the bridal veil. The phrase ἐκ καλυμμάτων occurs later in the *Agamemnon* to refer to the bridal veil (1178); its only other occurrence is at Soph. *Trach.* 1078, where I have argued (elsewhere) that there is a secondary allusion to the bridal veil.[177] Mention should also be made of Aesch. *Cho.* 811 ἐκ δνοφερᾶς καλύπτρας ('from a veil of darkness'), which alludes to the ritual unveiling not of the bride but of the mystic initiand.[178]

It may be objected that 'she sailed from out of the veil' is an odd sense. But it is no more odd than 'she sailed from out of the curtains'. The abruptness may perhaps be explained in part by the existing association of the phrase *ek* (*pro*)*kalummatōn* with the bridal veil.[179] The ritual of the *anakalypteria*, the unveiling of the bride, seems to have occurred at the end of the wedding banquet, just before her departure on a chariot to her new home.[180]

I suspect that this departure may have been associated with a nautical image. If so, the association would underlie various passages of tragedy, for example[181] (1) Eur. *IT* 370–1 'You ferried me in a

[176] See LSJ. In both the apparent exceptions (Aesch. *Cho.* 494; Soph. *Trach.* 1078) it may have the same sense (cf. Seaford 1984c[II]: 252–3, and 1986b: 56–7).

[177] Seaford 1986b: 56–7.

[178] See Thomson 1966: *ad loc.*; add Parmen. DK 28 B 1.10 (Thomson 1961: 289–90).

[179] For this kind of abruptness see n. 169 above.

[180] Oakley 1982: 113–14; Toutain 1940. This fact underlies also *Ag.* 1178–81 (see below) and Eur. *Phoen.* 1485–92 (see n. 185 below).

[181] See the passages quoted in n. 183 below, also Aesch. fr. 154a.3 ἀλίμενον γάμον; *Ag.* 227 προτέλεια ναῶν. Dionysos apparently travelled to his wedding at the Anthesteria in a ship cart: Seaford 1984b: 8 with n. 23.

chariot to a bloody wedding' (ἐν ἁρμάτων ὄχοις ἐς αἱματηρὸν γάμον ἐπόρθμευσας); (2) Eur. *Tro.* 569–70 (see §12); (3) Soph. *OT* 420–3 (§6); (4) later in the *Agamemnon* itself Kassandra says (1178–81) 'No longer will the oracle peer from behind a veil like a newly wedded bride, but seems bright as it rushes on, blowing towards the risings of the sun, so that like a wave ...' (καὶ μὴν ὁ χρησμὸς οὐκέτ' ἐκ καλυμμάτων ἔσται δεδορκὼς νεογάμου νύμφης δίκην, λαμπρὸς δ' ἔοικεν ἡλίου πρὸς ἀντολὰς πνέων ἐφήξειν, ὥστε κύματος δίκην ...). This curious conjunction of images (unveiling, wind and wave) cannot be explained merely by the multivalency of the word λαμπρός.[182]

At 690–2, as at 1178–81, we pass from unveiling to wind. Both passages are set in the context of the abduction of a woman (Helen, Kassandra – see §10 below), and at 691 ἔπλευσεν κτλ. is clearly more than a mere image.[183] In both cases that which corresponds to the *anakalypteria*, the sudden dissolution of contrived obscurity, is its opposite in mood: the discovery of the secret departure of Helen with Paris, the revelation (1183 οὐκέτ' ἐξ αἰνιγμάτων) of death in the palace. This irony occurs, I believe, in other plays: in the uncovering of the wounded Herakles towards the end of Sophocles *Trachiniae*,[184] and in the unveiling, induced by grief, of Euripides' Antigone.[185] But it occurs also elsewhere in the *Agamemnon* itself. It has been argued recently by M. L. Cunningham that 239 κρόκου βαφὰς δ' ἐς πέδον χέουσα ('pouring down dippings of saffron to the ground', of Iphigeneia being sacrificed) refers to the bridal veil. She points in particular to the likelihood that the Greek bridal veil was saffron in colour, to the force which this interpretation gives to the following words 'she struck each of her sacrificers [125] with a piteous missile from her eyes', and to a fifth-century vase showing Iphigeneia being led to the sacrifice holding up what seems to be a bridal veil.[186] Four further

[182] 'Clear' of oracles, 'bright' of the bride's complexion, 'keen' of the wind and 'bright' of the sunlight: Silk 1974: 197; Goldhill 1984: 85.

[183] Cf. the attention focused on a sea voyage in a hymenaial context at Eur. *IA* 667–70, *Hipp.* 752–63 (esp. 755–6, see n. 172 above), *Tro.* 455–6.

[184] Seaford 1986b: 56–7.

[185] Eur. *Phoen.* 1485–92. She overcomes her maidenly shame (1487–8), emerges from the women's rooms, παρθενῶνες (cf. 1275), sheds her veil, but is led not in a bridal procession but by the dead (1492 ἁγεμόνευμα νεκροῖσι – constantly mistranslated as active). See also n. 180 above. Her solitary, lamenting procession is similarly ambiguous (cf. §1 above) in Sophocles' version (§2). This is not to ignore the influence of Hom. *Il.* 22.468–72 (also a wedding veil!).

[186] Cunningham 1984; *ARV*^{2} 466 n. 266. So too Armstrong and Ratchford 1985, which appeared too late for consideration here.

points need to be made. First, the hymenaial association is in fact first introduced a little earlier, in the description of the sacrifice as 'the preliminary rites (*proteleia*) for the ships' (227). The *proteleia* were associated in particular with the wedding.[187] And as we find elsewhere (see n. 198), the Aeschylean irony is made more explicit by Euripides (see §2). Second, the line immediately preceding 239, 'by force and the muting strength of bridles' (238), contains a hymenaial image, the control over the bride as over an animal,[188] which is picked up again at 245 with the description of Iphigeneia the virgin in her father's house as 'unbulled' (ἀταύρωτος). Third, ἔβαλλε κτλ. is of a very subtle pathos: the reversal of the mood of the wedding is perhaps not absolute, for at the *anakalypteria* the newly revealed face at the centre of attention may have been to some extent fearful or even φίλοικτος; at the same time ἔβαλλε ... ἀπ' ὄμματος βέλει cannot fail in a hymenaial context to retain an erotic association, as does the phrase μαλθακὸν ὀμμάτων βέλος used later in the play, in the song under discussion, of Helen coming to Troy as a bride (742).[189] Fourth, this interpretation avoids the serious difficulties in interpreting κρόκου βάφαι as blood or as the robe.[190]

As the song proceeds, other features of the marriage of Paris and Helen also turn into their opposite.

(b) The deity bringing the marriage to completion is not, as normally, Zeus Teleios, Hera Teleia or Aphrodite,[191] but *telessiphron Mēnis*

[187] Defined by Hesychius as of Helen 'the sacrifice and celebration before the wedding'. Cf. 720 ἐν βιότου προτελείοις of Helen. In *Ag.* 65 and 227 Fraenkel 1950: II.41 sees an inversion of its cheerful wedding associations. Similarly Zeitlin 1965: 465–6 ('unpropitious use'). Lebeck 1971: 186 notes that 'it is precisely because she is sacrificed to Artemis that Iphigenia can be called προτέλεια ναῶν with a play on προτέλεια γάμων'. It should be added that the story of this sacrifice had long been associated with marriage (see §2 above). Further dimensions of (ironic) aptness are that the sacrifice of Iphigeneia is, like the marriage *proteleia*, a necessary prelude (cf. also *Ag.* 65) to a man (Menelaos) taking off his wife (cf. the previous line, γυναικοποίνων πολέμων ἀρωγάν), and that ναῶν perhaps owes something to the nautical image discussed above (cf. Eur. *IA* 667–70).

[188] See nn. 53 and 58; Sourvinou-Inwood 1987: 137–9, 145.

[189] Cf. also e.g. Aesch. fr. 242, *Supp.* 1004–5 etc.; Thomson 1932 on [Aesch.] *PV* 590–1 (his 614–15), Barrett 1964 on Eur. *Hipp.* 525–6 and 530–4.

[190] The slaughtering must come later; *why* nakedness?; etc. (see Lloyd-Jones 1952: he suggests the robe hanging down to the ground). The objection to the robe might be avoided also by the view of Sourvinou-Inwood 1971 that there is a reference to a (hypothetical) ritual derobing at the *arkteia*. But the *anakalypteria* (enforced perhaps by the gagging) makes more sense in the context, and unlike derobing would be consistent with Maas' view of πέπλοισι περιπετῆ and προνωπῆ (233–4; Maas 1951).

[191] Aesch. *Eum.* 214 (cf. *Ag.* 973; Salviat 1964); Plut. *Quaest. Rom.* 264b; Diod. Sic. 5.73.2; Men. Rhet. 407.7; [Dion. Hal.] *Rhet.* 262; cf. also nn. 94 and 192. Cf. Eur. *Hel.* 1120–1 Πάρις αἰνόγαμος πομπαῖσιν Ἀφροδίτας.

('Wrath who brings her purpose to completion' – marriage is of course a *telos*, 'completion') and an Erinys (700, 744–9). Indeed the common idea that deity is actually present at the wedding[192] gives a special point to the presence of Wrath and the Erinys here.

(c) The completion brought about by the Erinys is a bitter one (744–5 'swerving aside she brought to completion a bitter end of the wedding').[193] She seems on the one hand, in the context, to be identified with Helen; but on the other hand, as νυμφόκλαυτος (749), which may mean 'bringing tears for the bride' or 'bewept by the bride' but hardly 'a weeping bride',[194] she seems to be distinct from Helen. It seems best to allow Aeschylus the sinister ambiguity. But whatever the truth of that, νυμφόκλαυτος would seem less awkward and obscure to the original audience than it does to us, because for them it would evoke something familiar to the audience:[195] the element of lamentation by or on behalf of the bride.[196] Normally of course this negative [126] tendency would be overcome in the rite of passage. But here the deity who brings the marriage to completion (ἐπέκρανεν) is an Erinys, so that anomalously it *ends*, in the long term, in tears (γάμου πικρὰς τελευτάς),[197] the tears not necessarily of Helen but of the Trojan wives in general. In Euripides (*Hec.* 946–9; cf. 483) the Trojan women sing 'since there took me ruinously from my ancestral land and uprooted me from my home a marriage – not a marriage but some kind of torment from a vengeful spirit' (ἀλάστορος). Like brides they have been removed by marriage from their homes, but the marriage is not their own but Helen's and so not a marriage at all but suffering inflicted by a vengeful spirit (ἀλάστωρ). As at *Ag.* 744–9, it seems that a demon employs the marriage of Helen to inflict the subversion of marriage on the Trojan women. As elsewhere,[198] Euripides makes more explicit the irony of Aeschylus.

192 See nn. 114–16.

193 Cf. Pind. *Pyth.* 9.66 τερπνὰν γάμου κραίνειν τελευτάν; Aesch. *Supp.* 138–40 (The Danaids:) τελευτὰς δ' ἐν χρόνῳ πατὴρ ὁ παντόπτας πρευμενεῖς κτίσειεν (cf. 1050–3); Eur. *Phaeth.* 99–100 (hymenaial) θεὸς ἔδωκε, χρόνος ἔκρανε λέχος; *Supp.* 1008 εἰ δαίμων τάδε κραίνοι (see §7). At Aesch. *Ag.* 701 we should read Headlam's ἤνυσεν (see Thomson 1966: *ad loc.*).

194 See Fraenkel 1950: *ad loc.*, with Denniston and Page 1957; also Eur. *Hec.* 948–9 (see §12 below).

195 For the critical principle involved see n. 169. Note also Fraenkel's remark 1950: III.594: 'Everything is compressed, hinting … rather than describing fully. Time and again in Aeschylus, above all in the *Oresteia*, do we encounter this "parodying" of sacred rites.'

196 See nn. 82–90.

197 Cf. Eur. *Med.* 1388 πικρὰς τελευτὰς τῶν ἐμῶν γάμων ἰδών. The point is that τελευτά, like τέλος, can refer both to marriage and death: n. 166; Eur. *Med.* 153; cf. e.g. Artem. 2.49.

198 Seaford 1984c[II]: 248.

(d) It has in fact been directly stated by the chorus that the Trojans, who earlier sang the wedding song, have now had to learn instead the song of lamentation (705–16). At the wedding it is normal to compliment bride and bridegroom.[199] Sophocles applies the word εὔλεκτρος ('good for the marriage bed') to the bride (*Ant.* 796), and to Aphrodite at the contest for the bride Deianeira (*Trach.* 515). But Troy, in having to learn the lament instead of the wedding song, 'groans, calling upon Paris, disastrous for the marriage bed' (711–13 στένει κικλήσκουσα Πάριν τὸν αἰνόλεκτρον). κικλήσκουσα ('calling upon') here suggests the direct address that occurs in both the lament and the wedding song.[200] There may also perhaps be a faint suggestion of the funerary bier (λέκτρον).[201]

(e) What comes to Troy is described as 'a gentle missile from the eyes, a flower of desire that bites the heart' (742–3 μαλθακὸν ὀμμάτων βέλος, δηξίθυμον ἔρωτος ἄνθος). The image of the flower is traditionally applied to the bride in the wedding.[202] In Aeschylus' *Suppliants* it is associated simultaneously with the unwilling brides and the young men threatened by war (663–6, §4 above). Here the words βέλος and δηξίθυμον are appropriate to the praise of the beauty of Helen (see Fraenkel 1950: *ad loc.*), but acquire in the context a sinister double meaning.

Comparable is the ambiguity of κῆδος (699), recognised by the commentators, between connection by marriage and grief. It is of interest to compare also Eur. *Phoen.* 340–3, where the marriage of the Theban Polyneikes to an Argive is called ξένον κῆδος and γάμων ἐπακτὸν ἄταν. There is ambiguity not only in κῆδος but in ἐπακτὸν, a word applied to the wealth brought by a wife to the home of her husband (Eur. fr. 502.5), but which has two extra senses here: first, the bride comes not just from another household but from another city; and second, ἐπακτός in Aeschylus refers to the foreign army brought by Polyneikes,[203] and so cannot fail to suggest here the connection between the marriage of Polyneikes to an Argive and the

199 E.g. Sappho frr. 108, 110, 111, 112, 115, 116; Ar. *Pax* 1351–2; Eur. *Alc.* 920–1; Theoc. *Id.* 18.19–38, 49; Men. Rhet. 402.22–404.14; Greg. Naz. *PG* 37.1493–5.

200 *Il.* 24.725, 748, 762; Aesch. *Cho.* 315; Eur. *Tro.* 1167–72; Sappho frr. 108, 112, 113, 115, 116, 117; Ar. *Pax* 1346–8; Catull. 62.59, etc.

201 Cf. the same story at Aesch. *Ag.* 1440–1 (quoted in §10 below) and Bion 1.70; cf. Aesch. *Cho.* 318; Eur. *Hel.* 1261; and in general Seaford 1984c[II]: 251 (on *Ag.* 1116); also perhaps the sepulchral *Anth. Pal.* 7.649 ἀντί τοι εὐλεχέος θαλάμου ...

202 See §4 above and nn. 61–4.

203 *Sept.* 583; cf. e.g. Soph. *Trach.* 259, *OC* 1525; cf. Eur. *Phoen.* 580–2.

Argive invasion of Thebes. And when Iokaste goes on to complain that the marriage was not celebrated in Thebes, and in particular that 'throughout the city of Thebes the entry (ἔσοδοι) of your wife was conducted in silence' (348–9), this serves to reinforce the association of the intended military entry into Thebes with a bridal procession.

(f) The dire consequences of the impious union between Helen and Paris are described as offspring (750–72). Here too we find, it seems, the perversion of a wedding *topos*, the desire for children resembling their parents.[204] This gives a special point to 758–60 'for the impious deed afterwards gives birth to more, and they resemble their own kind', and to 770–1 'Ruin, resembling her parents'.

To conclude, *Ag.* 686–771 exhibit a multiple perversion of wedding ritual, in which the [127] positive elements are perverted into negative elements and the negative elements prevail. Comparable, in microcosm, is Sophocles' *Electra* 193–9:

> οἰκτρὰ μὲν νόστοις αὐδά,
> οἰκτρὰ δ᾽ ἐν κοίταις πατρῴαις,
> ὅτε οἱ παγχάλκων ἀνταία
> γενύων ὡρμάθη πλαγά.
> δόλος ἦν ὁ φράσας, ἔρος ὁ κτείνας,
> δεινὰν δεινῶς προφυτεύσαντες
> μορφάν.

> Pitiable was his cry upon his return, pitiable, on his ancestral couch, when the blow of the bronze-jawed axe rushed straight for him. Treachery was the one that planned it, lust the one that killed, the two of them generating terribly a terrible form.

Here the homecoming of Agamemnon and his death at the hands of Klytaimestra and Aigisthos is described in terms suggestive of a wedding. δόλος ἦν ὁ φράσας, ἔρος ὁ κτείνας seems to echo the kind of expression found in the wedding song at Eur. *Phaeth.* 99–100 θεὸς ἔδωκε, χρόνος ἔκρανε λέχος ('God bestowed, time fulfilled, the marriage').[205] The deities presiding over the marriage or bringing it to completion have become sinister ones, treachery and lust, who seem half-identified with the human

[204] Emphasised by Men. Rhet. 404.27, 407.9, 23; Catull. 61.214–18; cf. Theoc. *Id.* 18.21, 50–53; Sid. Apoll. *Carm.* 15.191; [Dion. Hal.] *Rhet.* 266. Cf. also Hes. *Op.* 235 and West 1978: *ad loc.* (add. Pl. *Crit.* 112c and Plut. *Mor.* 824c).

[205] Cf. also Men. Rhet. 400.18–20, 406.22–4; on the origin of this style in ritual formulae see Thomson 1953: 82–3; cf. esp. Zen. *Prov.* 3.98.

agents (Aigisthos and Klytaimestra),[206] and give birth through a terrible breeding to terrible offspring (the murder). Lust (ἔρος) is of course not inappropriate to a normal marriage,[207] but here assumes a sinister function. The reunion of husband and wife[208] becomes the occasion for murder by the united wife and lover. Two further elements complete the picture. By an irony that should by now be familiar, the cry (αὐδά) at Agamemnon's return is pitiable rather than joyful (cf. the joyful cry in the wedding procession at [Hes.] *Sc.* 278); and he is killed ἐν κοίταις πατρῴαις ('on his ancestral couch'), an expression which, though consistent with the tradition that Agamemnon was killed at a banquet (cf. 203–4), cannot fail to suggest here a marriage bed.[209] Every one of these ironies has its counterpart in Aesch. *Ag.* 690–771.

§10. **Kassandra**. In Aeschylus as Agamemnon enters the palace, his wife prays to Zeus Teleios (973), the 'accomplisher'. She wishes Zeus to bring her prayers to completion (τὰς ἐμὰς εὐχὰς τέλει). Now Zeus Teleios is also associated with the *telos* ('completion') of marriage,[210] to which there is a secondary reference here. The death of Agamemnon is envisaged as a kind of marriage, which Zeus Teleios is being asked to bring to fulfilment. It is described by Kassandra as a *telos* (1107 τόδε γὰρ τελεῖς; 1109 πῶς φράσω τέλος) in a passage which alludes to the common association between death and marriage,[211] and by Klytaimestra herself in terms which allude to sexual union (see §6 above). τέλει ('fulfils') in 973 picks up the same word in the previous line, ἀνδρὸς τελείου δῶμ' ἐπιστρωφωμένου ('the *teleios* man moving about his house'), where the primary sense of *teleios*, 'with authority', conceals a secondary reference, as in 973, to marriage: *teleios* with a passive sense, 'brought to completion', is applied to those who have entered into marriage.[212]

[206] Jebb 1894 on Soph. *El.* 198f. compares Klytaimestra as ἀλάστωρ at Aesch. *Ag.* 1501. We of course think of Helen as Erinys at 737–49.

[207] E.g. Men. Rhet. 404.18–20, 407.19, 411.13.

[208] This bloody reunion is envisaged as a grotesque marriage by Aeschylus (see §10).

[209] Cf. esp. seventy-eight lines later (272–3) τὸν αὐτοφόντην ἡμὶν ἐν κοίτῃ πατρός ξὺν τῇ ταλαίνῃ μητρί; also Soph. *Trach.* 922; etc. (LSJ s.v. κοίτη).

[210] Schol. Ar. *Thesm.* 973; Diod. Sic. 5.73.2; Plut. *Quaest. Rom.* 264b; cf. esp. Aesch. *Eum.* 214; in general see Salviat 1964, who sees a reference to marriage in *Ag.* 973, but regards the point as being that Zeus in his association with marriage is the right deity to pursue a wicked father or husband. See also Lebeck 1971: 68–73.

[211] Cf. Seaford 1984c[II]: 251.

[212] See LSJ s.v. τέλειος 2b, and esp. Paus. Gr. fr. 306 τέλειοι οἱ γεγαμηκότες; add Aesch. *Supp.* 80, and cf. fr. 44.6–7.

Interpenetrating this grotesque union of Agamemnon with Klytaimestra is the no less grotesque union in death of Agamemnon and Kassandra. As in the *Trachiniae* (§5 and §11) and the *Medea* (§3 and §8) the husband's new attachment creates a situation in which the mutual subversion of the two incompatible unions issues in the death of one or more of the three parties. Klytaimestra describes the dead Kassandra, displayed alongside the corpse of Agamemnon,[213] as 'sharing a bed with this man, speaking oracles, his faithful bedmate, and a mast-rubber of the ships' benches' (1441–3 ἡ κοινόλεκτρος τοῦδε θεσφατηλόγος πιστὴ ξύνευνος, ναυτίλων δὲ σελμάτων ἰστοτρίβης),[214] *[128]* and adds 'she lies dead, the lover of this man' (1446). Furthermore, one of the threads of the famous 'Kassandra scene' is a sustained evocation of the negative elements in the situation of a bride: (a) like the bride, Kassandra has been taken from her father's home[215] and has arrived in a chariot with her man at his home;[216] (b) like the bride (apparently), she laments (1322);[217] (c) whereas for the bride capture and death are at most fictions,[218] for Kassandra they are a reality; (d) the bride was apparently welcomed on arrival outside her new home;[219] in attempting to make Kassandra leave her seat in the chariot (1054 ἁμαξήρη θρόνον)[220] Klytaimestra and the chorus use persuasion;[221] (e) they also compare her to an animal newly caught or unwilling to bear the bridle or the yoke;[222] the image Kassandra employs to express the emergence of her speech out of deliberate obscurity, the image of the unveiling of the bride (1178–83, see §9 above), is therefore not chosen arbitrarily.

[213] I suspect that she appeared with Agamemnon in the fatal cloth (1492, 1580), and therefore huddled in the bath (1540), which is described as a bed on the ground (χάμευνα).

[214] To the defence of ἰστοτρίβης (with an erotic sense) by Young 1964: 15 [and Sommerstein 2002: 155–6] add Aesch. *Supp.* 1042 τρίβοι τ' ἐρώντων (τρίβοι in an erotic sense, I believe, and a hymenaial context: see §4).

[215] Note the stress on the paternal home left behind at 1277 βωμοῦ πατρῴου δ' ἀντ' ἐπίξηνον μένει (and cf. ἀμμένει referring to hymenaial consummation at Soph. *Trach.* 528; Eur. *Cyc.* 514 with Seaford 1984b: *ad loc.*).

[216] I find the suggestion that 'the arrival of Agamemnon and Cassandra like a bride and groom at the door when Clytemnestra stands waiting to welcome her husband home has a blatant irony' made independently by Jenkins 1983: 138 on the basis of the fact that 'Agamemnon's arrival at the palace on a chariot with Cassandra by his side, and Clytemnestra waiting to greet them, corresponds pictorially with the vase painter's formula for the arrival of bride and groom'. He refers to Taplin 1977: 302–6, who successfully argues that Agamemnon and Kassandra were in the chariot.

[217] See above nn. 3, 82–92.

[218] See above nn. 4, 68–9.

[219] Schol. Eur. *Phoen.* 344; Jenkins 1983: 138 continues: 'The position of Clytemnestra at the doorway of the house is occupied by the groom's mother in the vase scenes of bride-fetching.'

[220] The bride had a special seat in the chariot: Hsch. s.v. κλινίς; Poll. *Onom.* 10.33, 52.22.

[221] 1052 ἔσω φρενῶν λέγουσα πείθω νιν λόγῳ, 1049, 1054. Cf. persuasion in the wedding: see §4 and n. 94.

[222] 1048, 1063, 1066, 1071; cf. §4 and n. 58.

This implicit allusion by Aeschylus to ritual is, as elsewhere,[223] made explicit by Euripides. Kassandra in the *Trojan Women* enters with a wedding torch (or two) and sings a wedding song (308–41). She is herself of course aware that the destination of the transition is Hades,[224] and that her body will be thrown out 'near my husband's tomb'.[225] This does not mean that the (traditional) *makarismos* of the bride[226] is entirely false, for there is a genuine albeit horrific joy at the prospect of the death of her husband that will accompany her own.[227] It is perhaps an exact reversal of normal practice first that the (inspired) bride takes the initiative (308, 325, 332–41), lighting her own torch[228] and uttering her own *makarismos*, and second that her joyful singing contrasts with the lamentation of everybody else (315–19, 332, 351–2). Certainly her mother envisages the torch as funereal,[229] an ambiguity well known from the Anthology.[230]

§11. **Iole.** On discovering that Herakles is about to return home, the women of Trakhis sing (Soph. *Trach.* 205–7) 'Let the house, about to celebrate a wedding, raise the cry with cries at the hearth' (ἀνολολύξατω[231] δόμος | ἐφεστίοισιν ἀλαλαῖς | ὁ μελλόνυμφος). The idea that the house is about to celebrate a wedding has of course offended some textual critics. But it is in fact, as I have argued in detail elsewhere,[232] one of a coherent series of allusions to wedding ritual throughout the play, some of which I have mentioned in §5 above. The return of Herakles is envisaged here as the re-enactment or final completion of the marital transition of Deianeira. But at the end of the song there arrives at the house a group of female captives, one of whom is noticed from among the others[233] by Deianeira, who remarks on her apparent virginity [129] (ἄπειρος) and nobility (307–13). This is Iole, the bride[234] of Herakles. Deianeira is, without yet realising it,

[223] See §9a, §9c and n. 198.
[224] 445 ἐς Ἅιδου νυμφίῳ γημώμεθα; cf. Aesch. *Ag.* 1291 Ἅιδου πύλας δὲ τάσδ' ἐγὼ προσεννέπω.
[225] 449; cf. the possibly ambiguous τὸν πεπρωμένον εὐνᾷ πόσιν ἐμέθεν (340–1): see Seaford 1984c[II]: 250–1.
[226] 312–13; cf. 311, 327, 336, 365; cf. n. 5.
[227] 311, 356–60, etc.; also at the other Argive and Greek sufferings: 365–9.
[228] 308, 320; cf. e.g. Eur. *Phoen.* 344–6, *IA* 732. So far as I know the bride never carries a torch in vase painting.
[229] 343 λυγρὰν ... φλόγα; with λυγρὰν cf. e.g. *Med.* 399 λυγροὺς θήσω γάμους; *HF* 1376–7 λυγραὶ φιλημάτων τέρψεις; *Supp.* 70 λυγρὰ μέλη.
[230] E.g. *Anth. Pal.* 7.185 (sepulchral): πῦρ ἕτερον σπεύδουσα.
[231] ἀνολολυξάτω Burges; -ξετε LRAUY: -ξατε KZg.
[232] Seaford 1986b.
[233] Cf. Theoc. *Id.* 18.25–8; Sappho fr. 34.
[234] 546, 843, 857, 894; with 536 ἐζευγμένην cf. Eur. *Hipp.* 544–5 (Iole as a filly yoked by Herakles in marriage).

in the position of Klytaimestra, standing in front of the house to which the new bride has been forcibly brought. μελλόνυμφος ('about to celebrate a wedding') begins to take on a fatal ambiguity. When Deianeira's suspicions are subsequently aroused, she praises her again, this time for her beauty (379).[235]

Later in the play the chorus, reflecting on the origin of Herakles' sufferings, mention his spear 'which back then brought this swift bride (θοὰν νύμφαν) away from lofty Oikhalia with martial valour. But the attendant Kypris was revealed as the silent but manifest agent of these events' (857–61). Two points need to be made here. First, θοὰν is emended away by some, and defended by others as meaning 'swiftly'. Both alternatives miss the point. The 'swift bride' reappears at Eur. *Supp.* 993 ὠκυθόαι νύμφαι. In both cases there is a poignant association between the urgency of the wedding procession which ends happily and the present arrival of the bride (§7). Euadne comes quickly to her husband's pyre. Iole is seized with ruthless urgency from her father's home; and the speed of her arrival is inflicted also on Deianeira: 'Without fear of these things this wretched woman, beholding great harm to the house, with a new marriage rushing in upon it …' (841–3 ὧν ἅδ' ἁ τλάμων ἄοκνος, | μεγάλαν προσορῶσα δόμοισι βλάβαν | νέων ἀϊσσόντων γάμων). I have reproduced ἄοκνος (Musgrave), which is generally accepted. But the mss. ἄοκνον may be right. Iole will not be allowed to delay her arrival with bridal ὄκνος ('fearful hesitation').[236] And ἀϊσσόντων should probably not be changed to ἀΐσσουσαν (Nauck). προσορῶσα ('beholding') suggests actual visual perception,[237] and evokes therefore the position of those waiting at the house of the groom for the bridal procession.

Second, the sinister epiphanic role of Aphrodite (860–1), expressing the destructive carnality of this union, is given special point by her (silent) presence even at a normal wedding.[238] She plays a similar role in Euripides' description in the *Hippolytus*[239] of the brutal 'wedding' of Herakles and

[235] For the praise of the bride (usually for beauty) see §4 and nn. 61–4 above.

[236] See in detail Seaford 1986b.

[237] προσορᾶν generally refers to actual seeing; the only possible exception in Soph. is at *OC* 142. Cf. *Trach.* 1139 ὡς προσεῖδε τοὺς ἔνδον γάμους.

[238] See nn. 114–16.

[239] 545–54 'The filly from Oikhalia, unyoked to the marriage bed, until then without husband and unwed, Kypris yoked from the house of Eurytos, like a running naiad and a bacchant, and gave her to the son of Alkmene, along with blood, smoke, and nuptials of slaughter. Alas for the wedding songs!' Cf. n. 58 (yoking) and, on the bride as maenad, Eur. *Supp.* 1000–1 (§7) and *Tro.* 307, 342, etc. (§10).

Iole. In the *Agamemnon* the deities bringing the union of Helen and Paris to completion are Wrath (Μῆνις) and an Erinys (§9b). An Erinys is present at the union of Herakles and Iole too, but as offspring: 'This bride (sc. Iole) has given birth, without ritual celebration (ἀνέορτος[240]) she has given birth to a great Erinys for this house' (893–5). This is comparable to the perversion we found in the *Agamemnon* of the desire expressed at the wedding for children resembling their parents (§9f).

§12. **Andromakhe** opens the play of Euripides that bears her name by calling on the city of her birth, Thebe, from which she came to Troy to be the enviable (ζηλωτός) wife of Hektor. Somewhat later, lamenting the loss of her city and her husband, and her consequent yoking (συνέζυγην) to a harsh fate (96–9 στερρὸς δαίμων), she adds that no mortal should be called prosperous (ὄλβιος) while still alive (100–2), a proverb which in this context must suggest the failed *makarismos* of the wedding ceremony (cf. §6 and §7). We are reminded of the *Iliad*, when the news of Hektor's death makes her shed her wedding veil, the veil she wore 'on that day when Hektor of the shining helmet led her from her home' (*Il.* 22.471–2). This bridal journey of Andromakhe was described in rich detail by Sappho, and may even have been paradigmatic.[241]

Andromakhe continues, 'Paris brought Helen into the bridal chamber not for a wedding but as a bed of destruction for lofty Ilion' (*Andr.* 103–4), and then, after mentioning the destruction of Troy and of Hektor, 'I myself was led from my bridal chamber to the shore of the sea' (109). Here again, as in the *Agamemnon* and the *Hecuba* (§9c), the 'marriage' of Helen and Paris is associated both with a destructive deity and with a Trojan marriage that it has destroyed. Whereas at *Hec.* 946–9 the Trojan brides are taken by marriage from their homes, but the marriage is Helen's, here in the *Andromache* it is as if one bridal journey to Troy (Helen's) has put another (Andromakhe's) into [130] reverse (ἀγάγετ' ... ἐς θαλάμους ... ἐκ θαλάμων ἀγόμαν). Appropriately to this reversal, Andromakhe as she was led out 'put around her head' slavery (110 ἀμφιβαλοῦσα κάρᾳ), like the veil normally shed by the departing bride. A little later the chorus sing of Andromakhe's servitude and isolation from her φίλοι in the house of Neoptolemos, concluding '... most wretched bride. For your arrival at the house of my master, Trojan lady, is most pitiable' (136–42). The idea

240 This is the mss. reading (cf. ἀδᾳδούχητος of clandestine marriage). ἁ νέορτος is generally printed [OCT now has ἀνέορτος].
241 Sappho fr. 44 (composed perhaps to celebrate a real wedding).

of the departure of the bride as physical abduction (§4 and n. 3; note especially Catull. 62.24 'What crueller thing do enemies do after the capture of a city?') facilitates the implicit association here of the abduction of Andromakhe with a wedding. So it is also with Kassandra and Iole (see above), and with the fearful women of Thebes (Aesch. *Sept.* 333–5): 'It is lamentable for young women, before the marriage rites in which they are plucked while young, to travel the hateful road from their homes' (κλαυτὸν δ' ἀρτιτρόποις ὠμοδρόπων νομίμων προπάροιθεν διαμεῖψαι δωμάτων στυγερὰν ὁδόν).[242]

The idea of Andromakhe's departure from Troy as a perverted bridal journey reappears in the *Trojan Women*. Forced to go as wife (660 δάμαρ) with Neoptolemos, she appears 'travelling in an alien cart. And at the rowing of her breasts (παρὰ δ' εἰρεσίᾳ μαστῶν) there follows her dear Astyanax' (569–71). The expression εἰρεσίᾳ μαστῶν[243] appears strange to modern commentators, possibly because it is an ironic development of the idea, familiar perhaps to the original audience, of the bridal cart as a boat (§9a).[244] Andromache is πάρεδρος ('one who sits beside') not, as in a bridal journey, to her husband, but to her dead husband's weapons (573). She calls on him to come, but is told that he is in Hades (587–8); and so she asks to be taken to Hades herself (594).[245] Finally, she reflects on the prospect of union with Neoptolemos: 'And yet they say how one night undoes a woman's hatred towards her husband's bed' (665–6). This is a sentiment associated with marriage in general: compare Soph. fr. 583, of the sufferings of marriage for the woman, 'and, once one night has yoked us, we must consent to this situation and think that it is well'. Interestingly, Andromakhe then rejects this piece of wisdom with an image usually used to legitimate the subordination of the bride, the image of the yoked animal: 'Not even a filly, parted from her stablemate, bears the yoke with ease' (669–70).[246] We noticed in Aeschylus' *Suppliants* a similar reversal of hymenaial imagery by women resisting marriage (§4).

POSTSCRIPT

The most comprehensive development of the theme of the interpenetration of wedding and funeral in tragedy is by R. Rehm, *Marriage to*

[242] The text is here disputed (I give the main mss. tradition), with suggestions including ἀρτιτρόφοις, ἀρτιτρόπων and ὠμοδρόποις. But this does not affect my point.
[243] The sense of εἰρεσίᾳ μαστῶν is disputed (see Lee 1973: *ad loc.*); but this does not affect my point.
[244] In particular cf. ὄχοις … πορθμευομένην with ὄχοις … ἐπόρθμευσας at Eur. *IT* 370–1.
[245] On the bridal journey imagined as to Hades see Jenkins 1983.
[246] Cf. Eur. *Andr.* 98 (quoted above) and 178; also n. 58 above.

Death: the Conflation of Wedding and Funeral Rituals in Greek Tragedy (Princeton: Princeton University Press, 1994). For a further specific example (involving vase painting) see Seaford 2005a. For a broad context (outside Athens) see J. Redfield, *The Locrian Maidens: Love and Death in Greek Italy* (Princeton: Princeton University Press, 2003). For painting see J. Barringer, 'Europa and the Nereids: wedding or funeral?', *AJA* 95 (1991), 657–67.

Further work on the representation or evocation of wedding ritual in tragedy includes D. Armstrong and A. Hanson, 'Two notes on Greek tragedy', *BICS* 33 (1986) 97–102; M. Halleran, '*Gamos* and destruction in Euripides' *Hippolytus*', *TAPA* 121 (1991), 109–21; K. Ormand, 'More wedding imagery: *Trachiniae* 1053ff.', *Mnemosyne* 46 (1993), 224–7; E. Contiades-Tsitsoni, 'Euripides *Pha.* 227–244, *Tro.* 308–341, *Iph. Aul.* 1036–1079', *ZPE* 102 (1994), 52–60; A. Kavoulaki, 'Staging the wedding: the nuptial *pompe* in Greek tragedy' (in Greek; good summary in English), in A. Joannes-Theofanes and A. Papademetriou (eds.), *Acta: First Panhellenic and International Conference on Ancient Greek Literature* (Athens: Elliniki Anthropistiki Etaireia, 1997), pp. 351–71; W. M. Tyrrell and L. J. Bennett, *Recapturing Sophocles' Antigone* (Lanham, MD: Rowman & Littlefield, 1998), chapter 6; L. McNeil, 'Bridal cloths, cover-ups, and χάρις: the "carpet scene" in Aeschylus' *Agamemnon*', *G&R* 52 (2005), 1–17; R. Mitchell-Boyask, 'The marriage of Cassandra and the *Oresteia*: text, image, performance', *TAPA* 136 (2006), 269–97; P. Debnar, 'The sexual status of Aeschylus' Cassandra', *CP* 105 (2010), 129–45; L. A. Swift, *The Hidden Chorus: Echoes of Genre in Tragic Lyric* (Oxford: Oxford University Press, 2010), chapter 6. On wedding imagery comparing the bride to plants and animals see D. Feeney, 'Catullus 61: epithalamium and comparison', *CCJ* 59 (2013), 70–97.

CHAPTER 14

The Structural Problems of Marriage in Euripides

I

> But fight at the ships together. And whoever of you is struck and meets death and his fate, let him die. For it is not unseemly for a man to die fighting for his country; but his wife is safe and his children after him, and his household and his portion of land unharmed, if the Akhaians go away with their ships to their dear fatherland.

This is Hektor encouraging his troops in the *Iliad* (15.494–9). Death in battle is made acceptable by the thought of the continuity of the household (*oikos*). As an ancestor a man remains in a relation with his progeny, a relation concretely manifested in the cult of the dead.[1] Hence the peculiar horror of the oaths and curses that refer to the destruction not only of the man but also of his offspring and household. Hektor in fact loses the continuity of his household as well as his life. As is predicted in the *Iliad*, and enacted in Euripides' *Trojan Women*, his son is killed and his wife sold into slavery. His *oikos* is annihilated by violence.

Violence was not the only threat to the continuity of the *oikos*. The danger of disappearance through lack of a male heir is a familiar worry in the city-state, which legislated in various ways to prevent it.[2] But there is yet another danger, and this will be the main concern of this chapter: the threat presented to the continuity of the *oikos* by the fact that it is not normally self-reproducing. The means of the continuity of the household is marriage, which, as patrilocal, generally requires the introduction of a woman from another household. Almost every marriage is therefore a conjunction of two households, and as [152] such contains the possibility of competing claims. The wife may be in an ambiguous position, between her family of origin and her family by marriage. It is an ambiguity which the

1 Lacey 1968: 147–9. By a man's *oikos* (household) I mean his property and his offspring as inheritors of his property (excluding his married daughters and their offspring).

2 Lacey 1968: 22–3, 73, 77, 89–90, 141, 146; Dem. 43.57.

ritual of the wedding seems designed to prevent, with its elaborately symbolic removal of the bride from her parental home in a cart to the home of her husband. In Boeotia, for example, the axle of the cart was burnt, 'signifying', as Plutarch puts it, 'that the bride must remain, since her means of departure has been destroyed'.[3] The rites of incorporation of the bride into her new home seem to have centred on the hearth. In taking up a position at the hearth she is envisaged as a suppliant, entirely dependent on her new master.[4] At a later stage of what is in a sense the same process her child will, a few days after birth, be attached to its father's hearth in the ritual at the hearth called Amphidromia. The bride changes not only household but also domestic cult.[5] It is perhaps in the light of this separation of the woman from her family of origin that we should see the distinction in the second book of Thucydides between the exhortation to soldiers (2.11.2) 'not to appear worse than your fathers' and the exhortation to widows (2.45.2) 'not to be worse than your natures'.[6] The woman is systematically denied the past continuity of her household of origin.

Although the wife may, of course, in fact retain links with her natal family, symbolically she is, in the wedding ritual, irreversibly transferred from her family of origin to the household of her husband, with whom she is united 'for the ploughing of legitimate children' (as the formula has it), in the hope of sons who will succeed their father in the *oikos*. I will look at various ways in which, in the plays of Euripides, this model of transferral, monogamy and continuity may be imagined as threatened. Section 2 concerns cases in which marriage or sexual union represents a danger to the girl's family of origin. Section 3 concerns cases in which the wife puts her husband above her family of origin. Section 4 concerns cases in which the wife puts her family of origin above her family by marriage. In all these cases the problem is in one way or another the failure of transferral: the woman remains implicated in two different lineages, a contradiction which may endanger the continuity of one or the other of them. In the remaining cases continuity is threatened by the failure of the other important element of the model, monogamy: the problems arise from the

[3] *Mor.* 271d. Pausanias (3.20.10–11) tells a story that suggests the bridal veil may have had a similar significance. Penelope has to choose between her father and her bridegroom and veils herself to indicate preference for her bridegroom.

[4] Gould 1973: 97–8.

[5] Including perhaps the cult of the dead, as is maintained by de Coulanges 1874: 47; presumably he is thinking of Rome (I know of no such evidence for Greece).

[6] Noticed, but not explained, by Dover 1974: 98.

man's relationship [153] with another woman (Section 5) or the woman's relationship with another man (Section 6).

These problems are neither invented nor discovered by Euripides. They inhere in his mythical material, versions of which must predate even the city-state. But the development of the city-state is, as we shall see in the next section, not without its effect on marriage and the household. It may be, therefore, that Euripides' selection and treatment of myths, and in particular the frequency in his work of the themes discussed in this chapter, reflect to some extent the social changes accompanying the development of the city-state. This suggestion might receive support from a study of the various deviations from the monogamic model in Greek mythology as a whole on the one hand and specifically in the mythical products of the city-state on the other. Here, though, I am concerned with Euripides (but will occasionally refer, mainly in the notes, to other tragedians, as well as to Menander). Plays mentioned without author are by Euripides.

2

The sexual union of a girl may endanger her natal family in various ways. She may assist a male intruder against her natal family, as in the story of Ariadne assisting Theseus dramatised in the *Theseus*, or of Jason and Medea dramatised in Sophocles' *Kolchides*. Another kind of danger is presented by a daughter who has no brothers. In the *Danae*, Danae's father, Akrisios, has no sons. It is presumably he who says (fr. 318) 'A woman, leaving her paternal home, belongs not to her parents but to her husband. But the *male* kind remains permanently in the house as a defender of paternal gods and tombs.' According to Apollodorus (*Bibl.* 2.4.1), Akrisios, being without sons, enquired of the oracle how to get them, and the god replied that his daughter would give birth to a son who would kill him. This is presumably the oracle referred to in fr. 330a of Euripides' play. The household with female but no male offspring has no successors, or rather the successors come from another household, the house of the daughter's husband. And so the daughter's son may, to the extent that he belongs to an alien household, be imagined as representing a threat to the family of origin. This is, I think, the problem expressed, in the extremist [154] logic of myth, by the oracular response to Akrisios. How can it be solved?

Apart from the unsatisfactory method employed by Akrisios, who locked his daughter up, there are three main solutions, which I will exemplify from Homer. One is to produce a son from another woman. Helen produced only a daughter (Hermione) for Menelaos, and so he had a son

(Megapenthes) by a slave-girl (*Od.* 4.11–14). Another solution is to marry the daughter to a man who does not belong to another kinship group. Such a man will fall into one of two categories. Either he belongs to the same extended family as the girl, or he is an outsider whose links have been cut off from his own family.[7] To the former category belongs Iphidamas, who was brought up in the house of his maternal grandfather Kisseus (*Il.* 11.221–6). We do not hear of any sons of Kisseus, only of two daughters, of whom one is Iphidamas' mother and the other is offered in marriage to her nephew Iphidamas: with this offer Kisseus sought to keep Iphidamas in his household. The very same phrase, 'he tried to detain him there', is used elsewhere in the *Iliad* (6.192) of the King of Lykia detaining the valiant exile Bellerophon with an offer of his daughter and land. Bellerophon falls into our second category, the man isolated from his own *oikos*, like, for example, Odysseus in Phaiakia offered the hand of Nausikaa by her father King Alkinoos.[8] An isolated man can be made part of the girl's natal family. He is in effect adopted. And if he is valiant, like Bellerophon or Odysseus, this will have the advantage of increasing the household's strength. Indeed, the practice of bringing husbands into the bride's natal family for military reasons is found even where the bride undoubtedly has brothers. The best example is the house of Priam, which contains both sons and sons-in-law (*Il.* 6.245–50). Othryoneus was promised Kassandra by Priam in return for military service (*Il.* 13.364–9). And Hektor even boasts that he will hold the city merely with the aid of his brothers and his sisters' husbands (*Il.* 5.473–4).

By the time of Euripides, however, the military self-sufficiency of the family was a thing of the past. The military function of the kinship group, together with, for example, its role in vengeance for murder, had passed to the polis, the city-state. The consolidation of the city-state also produces a change in the function of marriage. 'One can speak', according to Vernant, *[155]*

[7] See Vernant 1982b: 45–70. It should be added that the former practice does not *ipso facto* preserve the household of the girl's father. For that the bridegroom must be adopted by the bride's father, or the children of the marriage must remain in the household of their maternal grandfather (see Schaps 1979: 32); but these arrangements may have been facilitated by a pre-existing kinship bond between father and bridegroom (as seems to have been the case with Kisseus and Iphidamas); and failing that, a man's daughter's children would at least, if their parents were, say, cousins, preserve (entire) the *oikos* of his *father* (rather than contributing their maternal inheritance to the *oikos* of a complete outsider).

[8] *Od.* 7.311–15; see also *Il.* 14.119–22 (cf. 5.410–15); *Od.* 7.65–6. Cf. the story of Penelope's father wanting Odysseus to remain with him in Lakedaimon (n. 3 above).

> of a break between archaic marriage and marriage as it became established within the framework of a democratic city in Athens, at the end of the sixth century. In the Athens of the period after Kleisthenes matrimonial unions no longer have as their object the establishment of relationships of power or mutual service between great autonomous families; rather, their purpose is to perpetuate the households, that is to say the domestic hearths which constitute the city, in other words to ensure, through strict rules governing marriage, the permanence of the city itself through constant reproduction. It is agreed that the measures which established the supremacy of the type of 'legitimate' marriage should be dated to the period of Solon or just after.[9]

The polis limits the autonomy of the household in respect of its sexual relations in various ways, and does so in the interests of *defining* the body of citizens (by the legitimacy of their parents' marriage) and of *maintaining* the citizen body (by legislation to ensure the legitimate continuity of the citizen households). The opposition between the legitimate wife and the concubine becomes more marked than it is in Homer. It was not a simple matter for a citizen without a son and heir from his wife to produce one, as Menelaos did, from a slave-girl, for such a son would be a full member neither of the *oikos* nor of the polis.[10] But the other two solutions we found in Homer were also available in the city-state. Citizens might be adopted from one family into another. But then the law required that 'the separation of an adopted son from his original family was total'.[11] And presumably males already isolated from their kin were less numerous, and less attractive as adoptees, in the city-state than in the world imagined or described by Homer. The exiled Perseus, who would to a militarily autonomous family be welcome as a heroic son-in-law, was in the *Andromeda* apparently rejected by Andromeda's father (anachronistically) as a pauper and a bastard (frr. 141, 142). As for the third of the solutions we described, marriage within the kinship group, this was very common in the Athenian polis;[12] and the brotherless girl, on whom her father's *oikos* would devolve, could by law be claimed in marriage by her next of kin on the male side, the so-called law of the *epikleros*. [*156*]

On the whole, as suggested in the previous section, we will find that the selection and treatment of myth by Euripides reflects to some extent these

[9] Vernant 1982b: 50.

[10] It has been suggested that bastards (*nothoi*), though disadvantaged in inheritance and excluded from the phratries, may nevertheless after the reforms of Kleisthenes have been eligible for citizenship: see, for example, most recently MacDowell 1976. But cf. Humphreys 1974; Rhodes 1978 and 1981: 496; Hansen 1986: 73–6. See also Erdmann 1934: 369, 375 ff.; Vernant 1982b: 50.

[11] Lacey 1968: 147.

[12] Erdmann 1934: 185; Thompson 1967; Lacey 1968: 106.

social changes. Let us start, though, with a theme that seems anachronistic in the polis. The *Temenos* may have concerned the murder of Temenos by his sons as a result of their fear that Temenos would make his son-in-law Deiphontes his successor, a fear based perhaps on Temenos' choice of Deiphontes as his chief military officer.[13] And in the *Arkhelaos* the Thracian king Kisseus promises the exiled Arkhelaos his daughter and his kingdom in return for military service, but is then persuaded by his 'friends' to go back on his promise. ('Friends' in Hyginus is *amici*, deriving probably from the Greek *philoi*, which could include his kin.) Eventually Arkhelaos kills Kisseus. These plays[14] are about the disaster to the girl's natal family that results from the claim established by her husband's military service. In Homer we find the practice of military service by the son-in-law, but not any resulting conflict. This distinction is in keeping with the general tendency of the *Iliad* and the *Odyssey* to avoid conflict within the *oikos* and the contrasting tendency of tragedy to focus on it. But the danger to the *oikos* dramatised in *Temenos* and *Arkhelaos* was unlikely to arise in Athens of the fifth century, where the *oikos* had, of course, no need of military aid, and so a father with existing sons was presumably unlikely to adopt his son-in-law. We do not, so far as I know, find the problem anywhere else in Euripides. The closest case is from the *Suppliants* (132–44, 219–25): the Argive Adrastos, having married his daughters to aliens (*xenoi*), the Aetolian Tydeus and the Theban Polyneikes, feels obliged to lend *them* military service in what turns out to be a disaster, the famous attack on Thebes. More successful was the Argive military support of Peisistratos, led by his son by his Argive wife, which helped him to the tyranny of Athens ([Arist.] *Ath. Pol.* 17.4).

Although the military dimension of the problem was an anachronism in the time of Euripides, this does not mean that the relation with the son-in-law was necessarily felt to be without its dangers. The audience of the *Suppliants* may well have felt the force of the general terms in which Adrastos is censured by Theseus (221–5):

> you gave your daughters to *xenoi* … and mixing your bright house with a muddy one you have wounded your [157] house. No wise man should mix unjust bodies with just ones, but should obtain as *philoi* for his house people of good fortune.

[13] Or this may have been the theme of the *Temenidai*: see Harder 1991.

[14] In the *Erechtheus*, Xouthos may have appeared as an adopted son of Erekhtheus, who dies in battle: Webster 1967: 128–9; van Looy 1970: 112. See also Pacuvius, *Hermione* (esp. frr. 184–6 Warmington); Hyg. *Fab.* 100 (from Soph. *Mysoi*?).

And Adrastos himself seems to regret that he did not marry his daughters to kin (οὐκ ἐγγενὴς κηδεία). In the *Phoenician Women* the attack on Thebes is imagined, from the perspective of the Thebans, with the metaphor of Polyneikes bringing in a *foreign* bride (343 γάμων ἔπακτον ἄταν, cf. 349).

The importance of marriage within the kinship group is central to Herodotus' (5.92) account of the Bakchiadai, the endogamous ruling clan of Korinth. It is through a girl of the family, Labda, who because lame is married outside the clan, the *genos*, that it is overthrown – by her son Kypselos. This story illustrates the importance of endogamy to the well-being of a *genos*, but also – because it is still an autonomous *genos* within a state, the *ruling genos* – the potential importance of endogamy to political power. So too Adrastos should have married his daughters within the *genos*, i.e. to an Argive: the Argives are, it seems, envisaged as kin, a *genos*, just as the citizens of Athens suppose themselves to be Erekhtheidai, the descendants of Erekhtheus. The exclusivity of endogamy has a role even in the democratic state. The developing city-state of Athens tends to marginalise marriages and sexual unions with non-Athenians, a tendency which culminates[15] in the Attic citizenship law of 451 which required that both a man's parents be citizens for him to be a citizen, and which, whatever its motives, struck a blow at the interstate marriages that we find not only in myth but also among the tyrants and such families as the Athenian Alkmaionidai.[16] This point brings us to the *Ion*.

Erekhtheus, although given sons in the later tradition, is in Euripides imagined as without a son and heir. His daughter Kreousa has been given as wife to a *xenos*, Xouthos from Akhaia, in return for military service. Xouthos has inherited the house of Erekhtheus, but the marriage has produced no children. Xouthos is led by the oracle at Delphi to believe that Ion, a temple servant there, is his son, and supposes him to be the result of a drunken sexual encounter. Xouthos' desire to make Ion his successor is desperately resisted by Kreousa. But in the end Ion turns out to be the offspring of a premarital sexual *[158]* encounter not of Xouthos but of Kreousa – with Apollo in Athens. Ion can then take his place as the rightful successor to the house of Erekhtheus.

The alien origins of Xouthos are constantly stressed. He is οὐκ ἐγγενής (63) – not of the kin, the *genos*; he is ἐξ ἄλλης χθονός (290), brought in from another land. 'How', it is asked, 'could a *xenos* marry a woman who was *engenēs*?' (293): i.e. why did she not marry someone of her own *genos*?

[15] Vernant 1982b: 57.

[16] Erdmann 1934: 168–7; Lacey 1968: 67–8.

(The answer is that the Athenians needed military help.) And so on (813–16, 1070, 1296–9). The marriage is tolerable for the house of Erekhtheus (the adoption of a valiant outsider as son-in-law was after all one of the solutions we found in Homer to the lack of a male heir), provided that it produces a successor. But it has not done so. And then events at Delphi threaten to produce the worst possible outcome. The old servant of the royal household complains that Xouthos 'has as a *xenos* married you and come to Athens and taken over your house and inheritance, and is now proved to have produced children secretly from another woman' (813–16). The house of Erekhtheus is, it seems, about to disappear entirely, its inheritance to pass to a man of alien blood. But finally, although Ion will indeed be Xouthos' heir, the situation turns, in a manner that prefigures Menander (*Epitrepontes*, etc.), into its opposite. Ion turns out to be the son of Kreousa by Apollo, and the anxious desire of the chorus, 'may nobody rule the city other than the well-born offspring of Erekhtheus' (1058–60), is in the end fulfilled. For Ion is, as Athena says, 'the offspring of Erekhtheus, and so entitled to rule my land' (1573–4). And Kreousa can proclaim, 'No longer are we childless. The house has a hearth, the land has a ruler. Erekhtheus is young again, and the earth-born house no longer looks on darkness' (1464–7). The continuity of the house of Erekhtheus triumphs in the end over the spectre of its annihilation.

More than once in the play the house of Erekhtheus is described as 'earth-born' (γηγενέτας) or 'sprung from the land itself' (αὐτόχθων). This cannot fail to be associated with the 'autochthonous' nature of the Athenians as a whole, which is also stressed in the play. 'They say', declares Ion, 'that Athens is autochthonous, not a race brought in from outside (590 οὐκ ἐπείσακτον γένος; cf. 29). In the *Erechtheus* (fr. 360.7–8) the Athenian people are called 'not brought in (ἔπακτος) from [159] elsewhere, but autochthonous'. But in the *Ion*, Xouthos is twice called ἔπακτος, brought in from outside (290, 592). The conclusion to the play represents, therefore, a vindication of the Athenians' proud claim to autochthony against the danger that seemed about to annihilate it. The four Attic tribes, Athena announces at the end (1575–81), will be named after Ion's sons, and the Ionians after Ion himself.[17] In earlier versions ([Hes.] *Cat.*, Hdt.) Ion was the natural son of Xouthos. Whether or not Euripides was the first to make him the son of Apollo,[18] the play seems to express the incompatibility between marriage with foreigners and the identity of the Athenians

[17] So too Hdt. 5.66.2; see Parker 1987: 206–7. For autochthony in the play see Saxonhouse 1986.

[18] Parker 1987: 207.

as Erekhtheidai, 'offspring of Erekhtheus'. The same incompatibility is expressed in the Athenian citizenship law of 451. The aristocratic, inter-state marriage of Xouthos and Kreousa, based on military service, has in the city-state become not only anachronistic but even undesirable.

The advantage of having a god (Apollo) as Ion's father is not only in his superior status. It is also that he does not belong to another human household, and in this respect resembles the noble exile adopted as son-in-law, who, we saw, represented one solution in Homer to the problem of the brotherless daughter. Homer also provides cases of the union of a god with a mortal girl producing offspring. Hermes, for example, falls in love with Polymele, daughter of Phylas. The result is Eudoros. Polymele then marries a mortal, but Eudoros stays in the home of his mother's father: 'old Phylas brought up Eudoros, loving him as if he had been his own son' (*Il.* 16.191–2). This seems a highly satisfactory arrangement, and the other Homeric examples are no more problematic.[19] In a number of Euripidean plays, on the other hand, *Alope*, *Antiope*, *Auge*, *Danae* and *Melanippe Sophe*, a girl having offspring by a god creates conflict within her natal family.[20] It is, for example, presumably Kerkyon, after discovering his daughter's unmarried motherhood, who says (*Alope* fr. 111; cf. fr. 320) 'What is the point of guarding women? The best-brought-up ones destroy households more than those whom nobody bothers about.'

This distinction between Homer and tragedy is in keeping with the tendency of tragedy to focus on family conflict, which Homer tends to avoid. It may also reflect the changed nature of marriage in the city-state. The military advantages of marriage in the Homeric world (alliance and offspring) are replaced in [*160*] the city-state by new ones: the dowry (the bride's share of the inheritance) and the legitimacy required to produce children who will be full members of *oikos* and polis.[21] In contrast to the more autonomous family of the Homeric texts, the continuity of the later family is limited by the polis to the offspring of a legitimated, monogamous union. This is one reason perhaps for the preoccupation of the Attic polis with the chastity of its women.[22] In a well-known passage of Lysias (1.33) it is claimed that the adulterer is punished by death because, getting what he wants by persuasion, he corrupts the woman's mind as well as

[19] *Il.* 2.514–15, 6.198, 16.174–8. See further Erdmann 1934: 373 ff.

[20] Other tragedians: Soph. *Akrisios, Danae, Tyro*; Astydamas, *Tyro*; Carcinus II, *Alope*; Aphareus, *Auge*.

[21] This is not to say that there was no interest in the quality of in-laws in the polis (see, for example, Erdmann 1934: 147 ff.), although marriage does not seem to have been a widespread way of creating political alliances: see Humphreys 1983: 24–6.

[22] Lacey 1968: 113; one might add perhaps the greater opportunities for adultery provided by urban life.

her body, and casts doubt on her children's parentage. Certainly the all-important matter of the legitimate continuity of the *oikos* can be attained only by ruling out the mere possibility of adultery. The wife is a means not so much of an alliance between households as of this continuity. It is an imperative which would no doubt have affected the choice as well as the treatment of a wife. There is evidence to suppose that an Athenian girl who had been seduced would not find a husband, and might even by a law of Solon be sold into slavery. Sanctions or restrictions on non-marital coitus are in general more severe in 'inchoate incorporative states', a category to which the Attic polis in the classical period certainly belongs, than in other forms of society.[23]

A fragment of the *Melanippe Sophe*[24] (fr. 497) appears to be spoken by someone urging punishment of Melanippe for her unmarried motherhood: 'Punish her. For this is why women go wrong. Men who have taken a bad wife do not destroy her, either in hope of children or because of her kin. And then this vice affects many women and spreads.' If Melanippe is not put to death, she may be married off, and the vice will spread. In the *Cretan Women* Aerope, seduced by a servant, was handed over by her father to Nauplios with instructions to throw her into the sea, but he instead engaged her to Pleisthenes. She was then inherited by Atreus and seduced by his brother Thyestes. A *male*'s promiscuity, on the other hand, does not endanger the continuity of his *oikos*; and this distinction would undermine, at least from the male perspective, the kind of argument used by Phaidra (in the first *Hippolytus*) when she defends her extramarital passion by reference to the transgressions of Theseus (Plut. *Quomodo adul.* 28a).

Along with the disgrace of the girl there is the problem of the [161] destiny of the child. In *Alope, Antiope, Auge, Danae, Ion* and *Melanippe Sophe* the god's male offspring is rejected and exposed either by its mother in fear of disgrace (e.g. *Ion* 898, 1497), or as punishment by her father, or, in at least one case (*Danae*), by her father in fear of his new grandson. It may have been characteristic of this kind of play that the girl's claim that her lover was a god is disbelieved (*Bacch.* 27–31; *Ion* 1523–7; *Danae* frr. 322, 342–8; cf. Pherecydes *FGrH* 3 F10), so that the truth may have

[23] Athenian girl: Lacey 1968: 115. Comparative anthropology: Cohen 1969, who argues *inter alia* that the marital tie when strengthened contributes to the weakening of local and kin groups, but does not constitute a challenge to state authority. An 'inchoate incorporative state' is the centrally ruling body of a society that has 'been united by groups who are geographically contiguous and who are at approximately the same level of cultural development', but that 'has not yet completely subverted local sources of solidarity, allegiance and authority'.

[24] It has also been attributed to the *Melanippe Desmotis*: see Webster 1967: 147–9.

to be revealed or confirmed by a deity. Certainly it does seem that all these plays (except *Auge*) ended with a divine demand or prophecy that the exposed offspring will succeed to the kingdom of his maternal grandfather.[25] (Similarly, in Herodotus' account of the endogamous Bakchiadai, oracles predict that Kypselos, son of the lame Labda by an outsider, will replace his mother's family as rulers of Korinth. And one of the oracles compares Kypselos to a lion conceived *in the wild*.) This succession from the outside to the kingdom may resolve a conflict within the family (*Ion*, *Melanippe Sophe*) or it may on the other hand involve violence within the family (*Antiope*, *Danae*, *Alope*?). With the first type we should compare Menander's *Epitrepontes*, in which, in the relatively realistic world of New Comedy, an unambiguously happy ending is created by the revelation of the father of the exposed child not as a god but as the girl's husband, who had without realising the girl's identity raped her before marrying her. With the second type we should compare the *Bacchae*, in which the son of Semele and Zeus is rejected by his kin (26–31), returns to Thebes, destroys his kin and installs his cult.

The theme of exposure in the wild and return is not of course confined to the myths we have been considering. The theme seems to derive from the initiatory practice of departure to the margins of civilisation as a preparation for return to a new status as an adult.[26] In the wild the young person is outside the household, but will return, the male to his own household (Jason, Paris, etc.), the female to a new one (her husband's: e.g. the Proitids). The ambiguity of this location in the wild, in which the young person is outside the household but will succeed to it, is the necessary element of 'liminality' in the transition from childhood to adulthood. But in the myths we have been considering it has been deployed to express another kind of ambiguity, the ambiguous position of the daughter and her son, *[162]* who on the one hand should move out of her natal household but on the other hand may exercise a claim to it (particularly if she has no brothers). An ambiguity of ritual origin has been deployed to express an ambiguity in the social structure. The deployment is facilitated by the

25 *Danae*: cf. Apollod. *Bibl.* 2.4.4; *Antiope*: Hyg. *Fab.* 7; *Mel. Soph.*: Ennius fr. 119 (Jocelyn) (and Webster 1967: 149); *Alope*: Hyg. *Fab.* 187 (Poseidon appeared at the end, it seems); *Ion*: 1571–5; even Telephos, the son of Auge, was said in one version of the myth (Alcidamas, *Odysseus* 14–16) to have returned to his birthplace: Hyg. *Fab.* 100 (from Soph. *Mysoi*?); *Anth. Pal.* 3.2. See in general Webster 1967.

26 On the theme generally see Binder 1964. For a recent treatment of our theme ('the girl's tragedy') see Bremmer and Horsfall 1987: 27–30.

presence of conflict even in those myths in which a son returns to his own household (Oidipous, Paris, Theseus, etc.).

As an example of the type we have been discussing, let us look more closely at the *Antiope*. The myth of Antiope of Thebes was as follows. Made pregnant by Zeus in a cave, she escapes from the wrath of her father Nykteus to the mountainside, from where she is taken as wife by an outsider, Epaphos of Sikyon. After the consequent suicide of her father, she is recaptured and imprisoned by her uncle Lykos. But on the way back to Thebes she gives birth to the twin sons of Zeus, Zethos and Amphion, who are brought up by a shepherd. Antiope eventually escapes again to the mountainside, and with the help of the young men, revealed as her sons, turns the tables on Lykos' wife, Dirke, who had come to kill her. Zethos and Amphion are then prevented from killing Lykos himself by Hermes, who tells Lykos to yield the kingdom to Amphion.[27]

We do not know all the details of Euripides' lost play.[28] Zethos and Amphion are already grown up, and the earlier part of the story was presumably narrated. The play is set on the mountainside, where Antiope had been sexually united with Zeus and then later abducted by Epaphos. The story centres on the polarity between the seclusion of the girl in the home by her natal family and the dangerous loss of control of the girl on the mountainside. It is a polarity which seems to express, in the extremist logic of myth, the dilemma of the family with a daughter (particularly a brotherless one, as Antiope seems to be) between the two undesirable alternatives, on the one hand of retaining her within the household,[29] and on the other hand of releasing her, the heiress of the household, into the control of an outsider.

The polarity between the woman confined and the woman or her offspring in the wild recurs in Euripides. Pasiphae, in the *Cretans*, is imprisoned after being sexually united, presumably in the pastures, with a bull. In both *Alope* and *Melanippe Sophe*, apparently, it is proposed that the unmarried mother be confined and left to die (like Antigone in Sophocles), her offspring [163] exposed in the limitless wild, to be brought up as it turns out by shepherds (like Zethos and Amphion in *Antiope*). In the *Melanippe Desmotis* Melanippe is a prisoner, but the action turns

[27] See esp. Hyg. *Fab.* 7 and 8; Apollod. *Bibl.* 3.5.5; schol. Ap. Rhod. 4.1090; *Anth. Pal.* 3.7; Prop. 3.15.11–42.

[28] See Kambitsis 1972.

[29] With the mythical theme of imprisonment one might compare the small and probably dark interior of urban houses, and Klytaimestra's reference to her daughters (*IA* 738) as 'guarded well in the secure maiden quarters'.

on the victory in the wild of her sons over their enemies. In *Danae* the daughter is first imprisoned, to preserve her virginity, and then, when this fails, she is enclosed in a chest with her baby son and sent out into the limitless sea.[30] In *Auge* too the girl is submerged by her father with her son in a chest in the sea.[31]

One way in which women, married and unmarried, may pass from the male-dominated enclosure of the home to the dangerous freedom of the mountainside is in the worship of Dionysos. Maenadism represents in an extreme form the loss of control by the male of the female, and was indeed imagined as involving the danger of illicit sex.[32] In *Ino*, when Ino goes to the mountain as a maenad her husband, Athamas, thinks she is dead and marries again. Discovering the truth, he has her brought back and conceals her; his second wife, on discovering her, takes her to be a captive. The story of *Antiope* is closely associated with Dionysos. Zeus takes the form of a satyr, one of Dionysos' mythical followers, to make love to her. According to Pausanias (9.17.6) she roamed all over Greece in a frenzy inflicted by Dionysos. Her miraculous escape from imprisonment to the mountainside is described by Apollodorus (*Bibl.* 3.5.5) in a manner strongly reminiscent of the miraculous escape to the mountainside of the maenads imprisoned by Pentheus in the *Bacchae* (445–6). From the fragments of Euripides we can detect that the play was set before a cave sacred to Dionysos and that Dirke arrives there with a chorus of maenads.[33]

Another girl associated in tragedy with maenadism is Antigone. In Sophocles her burial of her brother represents loyalty to her natal family at the expense of her marriage to Haimon. About to be confined in a ghastly 'bridal chamber', she looks forward to her welcome from her natal family in Hades, and even says, in words wrongly deleted by some editors, that she would not have done what she did for a husband or children (i.e. for a family by marriage). The chorus compare her fate with Danae's and then, after Kreon's panicked order for Antigone's release, sing a prayer for Dionysos to come down from the mountain to purify the city (1115–54, esp. 1144). In the *Phoenician Women*, as in Sophocles' *Antigone* (73), Antigone expresses her devotion to her dead brother in almost erotic terms,

[30] Danae was imprisoned, according to Euripides' contemporary Pherecydes (*FGrH* 3 F10), in a bronze underground chamber (*thalamos*) in the courtyard of the house, according to Euripides himself in a bronze bridal chamber (*Archelaos* fr. 228a.7), and according to Hyginus (*Fab.* 63) within a stone wall. She is *enclosed* in the chest in Pherecydes, and in Euripides: Johannes Malalas, *Chronographia*, p. 25.27–30 Thurn.

[31] Strabo 13.1.69.

[32] Aesch. frr. 382, 448; Eur. *Bacch.* 223, 233–8, 260–2, 353–4, 487, 957–8; Daraki 1985: 101–3.

[33] Webster 1967: 205–11; Kambitsis 1972.

simultaneously rejecting marriage *[164]* with Haimon.[34] And she is in this play closely associated with her father. They are both confined within the house, Antigone as a maiden (194), her incestuous father enclosed by his sons in the 'dark inner chamber' (64, 1541). Antigone emerges as a 'maenad of the dead' (1489–90), and is at the end of the play told by Oidipous to go to the mountain shrine of Dionysos, where she has in the past been a maenad (1751–70). In Euripides' lost *Antigone* the external, Dionysiac pole of the confinement/independence polarity is of still more importance. Antigone escapes the death penalty (presumably death by seclusion, as in Sophocles) and goes to the mountainside. It seems that she was recaptured, and appeared on stage as a maenad, and that Dionysos himself appeared *ex machina*.[35] The assimilation of the story to the type represented by Antiope seems to have extended still further: Antigone is married to Haimon and has a son, whose eventual entry into Thebes may have been predicted by Dionysos.[36]

One of the solutions we noted to the dilemma of keeping a daughter unmarried at home or losing her to an outsider is endogamy. Accordingly, we find that in some versions of the myth Antiope is sexually united with her uncle (and captor) Lykos, and that in some versions Danae, while in confinement, is sexually united with her uncle Proitos.[37] Whether these events formed part of the Euripidean versions we do not know. We have already emphasised the quasi-erotic passion of Antigone for her brother in the *Phoenician Women*. A Euripidean play which may well have concerned the erotic love of father for daughter is the *Oinomaos*: almost all we know about this play is that it was presumably about the famous chariot race in which Pelops won Hippodameia from her father, Oinomaos, who was unwilling to give her in marriage – either because of an oracle that he would be killed by her husband or (and this is what the scholiast on Euripides' *Orestes* 990 affirms) because of his incestuous passion for her. Certainly Euripides dealt directly with the theme of marriage within the family in the *Aiolos*. Makareus and his sister Kanake have secretly produced a child. Makareus persuades his father, Aiolos, to marry off his daughter to their brothers, using the argument that this will retain the wealth within the family.[38] But a happy outcome is prevented, apparently by the drawing of

[34] Eur. *Phoen.* 1659 (cf. Aesch. *Ag.* 1446, *Cho.* 906, 894–5 (and Garvie 1986: *ad locc.*), 1671–5).
[35] Hyg. *Fab.* 72; cf. Eur. fr. 177; Scodel 1982.
[36] Hyg. *Fab.* 72; compare Hypoth. 'Aristophanis' to Soph. *Ant.*; cf. n. 35.
[37] Antiope: Apollod. *Bibl.* 3.5.5; schol. Ap. Rhod. 4.1090; Hyg. *Fab.* 7; Prop. 3.15.12. Danae: Pind. fr. 284 (at fr. 70d *app. crit.*, p. 79); Apollod. *Bibl.* 2.4.1.
[38] Frr. 20 and 22; [Dion. Hal.] *Rhet.* 9.11; Jäkel 1979. On this theme in Aeschylus' *Suppliants* see Seaford 1987c[13]: 117–18; for the phenomenon generally see, for example, Rosenfeld 1957; cf. Barth 1954.

lots, which fail to assign Makareus to Kanake, and by Aiolos' discovery of Kanake's child, which causes him to send her a [165] sword with which to kill herself. Makareus then succeeds in reconciling Aiolos, but too late to prevent Kanake's suicide, and he too probably kills himself. A favourable outcome would have been the one that occurs in *Ion*, *Melanippe Sophe* and Menander's *Epitrepontes*: the family conflict created by an illegitimate child is eliminated by recognition of the child as the successor to the household; and indeed Kanake's son Triopas had a glorious future.[39] But in fact, as in the myths of Oidipous and Iokaste, and of Lykourgos, incest ends in self-destruction.

3

In some plays a woman puts loyalty to her husband above loyalty to her natal kin. The *Temenidai* may have continued the story of *Temenos* (described in §2 above).[40] Temenos has been murdered by his sons because they feared he might make his son-in-law Deiphontes his successor. They then try to persuade their sister Hyrnetho to leave her husband, Deiphontes, and return to Argos. Failing in this, they take her by force, and in the ensuing battle with Deiphontes Hyrnetho and her brothers are killed. The unsuccessful attempt by a father to detach his daughter from her husband is a theme of New Comedy.[41] In other plays the loyalty of the wife is the more remarkable for being to a *lost* husband. In *Suppliants* Euadne defies her natal family (her father) by throwing herself on to the funeral pyre of her husband. In the *Protesilaos* Laodameia comes into conflict with her father, Akastos, as a result of her devotion to a statue of her dead husband. Akastos orders the statue to be burnt, and so Laodameia throws herself onto the blaze.[42] The story of *Alkmaion in Psophis* is told in Apollodorus (*Bibl.* 3.7.5–6): Alkmaion, as an exile, first marries Arsinoe and then, exiled by famine, he marries Kallirhoe. When he regains by trickery the wedding present he had given to Arsinoe, so as to give it to Kallirhoe, and the trickery is discovered, Arsinoe's brothers kill him. When Arsinoe complains at this, her brothers enclose her in a chest and

39 Webster 1967: 159.

40 Though not according to Harder 1991.

41 Menander, *Adelphoi* A (or *Philadelphoi*), *Epitrepontes*, *Daktylios* (?). Cf. Aeschylus' *Niobe*. For real life see Dem. 41.4.

42 It seems that Akastos wanted her to remarry: see Oranje 1980 (on fr. 653). Cf. *Od.* 19.158–9 (Penelope's natal family pressing her to remarry).

send her off to Tegea to be a slave.[43] Most remarkable of all perhaps is Euripides' version of the Oidipous myth, in which it appears that, after the discovery of Oidipous' killing of Laios, Iokaste expressed a loyalty to Oidipous which brought her into conflict with her brother Kreon. Mention might also be made here of *Alcestis* and *Antigone*, in which the husband is alienated *[166]* from his natal family, in the *Alcestis* with the irony that the continuity of the *oikos* for which Alkestis dies is combined with total estrangement within the male line of descent.

4

We turn now to those plays in which a wife's residual loyalty to her natal family damages her family by marriage (the reverse of §3 above). Despite Hippolytos' regret that children have to be engendered rather than bought (*Hipp.* 616–24), and despite Apollo's argument in Aeschylus' *Eumenides* that the parent of the child is the male, a woman – generally from another household, an outsider[44] – is required for the continuity of a man's household. The child, as we have already seen (§1 above) is attached to its father's hearth in the ritual called Amphidromia. This association between child and hearth is expressed in the story of Meleager. Seven days after his birth (i.e. at the time the Amphidromia was normally celebrated) the Fates declared that he would die when a brand burning on the hearth burnt out. His mother, Althaia, took the brand and kept it safe in a chest. After the hunt of the Kalydonian boar, Althaia's brothers, in dispute with Atalanta for the skin, were killed by Meleager, who was in love with Atalanta. As a result, Althaia killed her own son by returning the brand to the fire. There is here a poignant combination of opposites: the symbol of Meleager's belonging to the hearth and the household of his father, the brand, is used by his mother in such a way as to put her loyalty to her natal family, her brothers, above her loyalty to her family by marriage, her son. Meleager, on the other hand, rates the sexual tie above kinship. In *Iliad* book 9 mention is made of Meleager killing his mother's brother and of her consequent prayers for his death: this is one of the rare exceptions to the rule that Homer excludes conflict within the *oikos*, though even here the death of

[43] We do not, of course, know all the details of Euripides' play. Other tragedies on this story may have been Soph. *Alkmaion*, and plays called *Alphesiboia* (see Paus. 8.24.8) by Achaeus, Chairemon and Timotheus.

[44] Cf. *Alc.* 532–3, 778 with schol., 805, 810–14, 828, 1117; Visser 1986: 161 n. 14.

Meleager was not described. But the death was certainly important in Euripides' version (*Meleager*), and so was Althaia's consequent suicide.

Meleager hunts with his maternal uncles. We are reminded of Odysseus, 'as soon as he reaches manhood' (*Od.* 19.410), visiting his maternal grandfather, Autolykos, and joining his maternal uncles in the hunt in which he received his famous scar. The importance of hunting in initiation into adulthood is well [*167*] known.[45] In order to return to his household and community as an adult, the young man must leave it to spend some time in the wild (§2 above). The temporary reversal of norms characteristic of initiation may include a spell of association with his maternal kin. Fosterage by maternal kin is a theme of Indo-European myth.[46] Greek examples include Hippolytos, Theseus, Pyrrhos and the sons of Periander.[47] In the case of Meleager the temporary association, in the wild, with his mother's natal family serves to realise the potential contradiction with her family by marriage, and the consequent catastrophe is irreversible.

In the *Melanippe Desmotis* the situation is comparable.[48] Two young men, Aiolos and Boiotos, are believed to be the children of Metapontos and Siris but are in fact the children of Melanippe by Poseidon. It seems that they had been exposed, and then introduced by Siris secretly into the household as her own. But then Siris gave birth to children of her own. While out hunting Aiolos and Boiotos are attacked by Siris' brothers, i.e. by the men they take to be their maternal uncles, whom they kill. What has happened, it appears, is that Siris has conspired with her brothers to kill them so as to ensure the succession for her own children. Again the hunt, in which a woman's family by marriage (her sons) should be associated with her family of origin (her brothers), is in fact the scene of their conflict, except that here Aiolos and Boiotos (unlike Meleager) turn out not to be her own sons. The theme is combined with the theme of the wicked stepmother (§5 below) and with the type represented by *Antiope* (§2 above): once again, the ambiguity of the location of the young outside the household in the wild (and, in this case, the association there with maternal kin) has been deployed to express ambiguity and conflict over succession to the household. Another example of the association with maternal kin occasioning family conflict is the story told in Herodotus (3.50–3) of the sons of Periander: they were taken in by their maternal

45 See, for example, Lonis 1979: 202.

46 Bremmer 1976 and 1983b; Bremmer and Horsfall 1987: 53–6; cf., for example, Goody 1959; Keesing 1975: 46–7.

47 Apollod. *Bibl.* 3.13.8, *Epit.* 5.11; Plut. *Thes.* 4; Paus. 1.22.2; Hdt. 3.50–3.

48 For this play see van Looy 1964; Webster 1967: 150 ff.

grandfather, who, by hinting at the truth that their father had murdered their mother, succeeded in alienating one of them from his father.

In *Andromache* the Spartan Hermione is married to Neoptolemos, the son of Akhilleus, but is barren. He has offspring only by his Trojan concubine, Andromakhe. In the consequent attack on Andromakhe and her sons which forms the theme of the play, Hermione is assisted by her father, Menelaos. *[168]* We will return to this play in §5 below. Suffice it here to note Hermione's stunning first entry, dressed in Spartan style (*Andr.* 147–53): 'This golden headdress', she begins, 'and this lavish robe do not belong to the house of Akhilleus or Peleus. They are from Sparta. My father Menelaos gave them to me along with many gifts, so that I have freedom of speech.' A divorced woman would take her dowry with her back to her kin.[49] Plato wanted to abolish the dowry, so that wives would be less insolent and men less servile.[50] And the undesirability for a man to marry above himself is a recurrent piece of wisdom in Euripides (*El.* 936–7, frr. 213, 502, 775, [*Rhes.*] 168).

In *Medea*, Medea destroys her family by marriage and then escapes in a chariot which, she says (1321–2), has been given her for the purpose by her grandfather, the Sun. It is also worth mentioning the prologue of *Alcmene*, in which it seems that Alkmene is described as saying that she will marry nobody other than the avenger of her brothers.[51] Plays by other authors in this category include several about Meleager (e.g. Sophocles' *Meleager* and perhaps Phrynichus' *Pleuroniai*), perhaps also Xenocles' *Likymnios*, in which it appears that Alkmene lamented her brother Likymnios killed by her grandson Tlepolemos, and Moschion's *Pheraioi*, which probably concerned the murder of Alexander of Pherai by his wife assisted by her brothers.[52] The theme occurs also in New Comedy: in Menander's *Misoumenos* Krateia rejects Thrasonides as a husband because she believes him to have killed her brother, and when the belief is found to be mistaken they marry.

5

This section and the next concern plays in which the mutual loyalty of monogamy and the unequivocality of succession to the household are

[49] Lacey 1968: 108–9; cf. n. 41 above.

[50] *Leg.* 6.774c; cf. Gluckman 1953 (and Leach 1953); Goody and Tambiah 1973.

[51] Fr. *87b.

[52] For Moschion, and the minor tragedians generally, see *TGrF* I.

threatened not by the contradiction between households connected by marriage but by a second sexual union, whether the man's with another woman (§5) or the woman's with another man (§6 below). This theme is sometimes combined with the earlier one, as in *Andromache*.

We noted (§2 above) that one of the solutions to the problem of a barren wife was to produce offspring by another woman. There are two Homeric passages known to me which imply a wife's resentment at the infidelity of her husband.[53] But I know [*169*] of no examples in Homer of a triangular situation producing conflict over *offspring* – indeed children produced outside the marriage may live without disadvantage in the parental home. I gave earlier (§2 above) the example of Megapenthes, son of Menelaos. Another is Pedaios, son of Antenor, a bastard 'brought up by Theano equally with her own children, to gratify her husband' (*Il.* 5.70). And there are others.[54] However, again in keeping with our distinction between the genres and with the development of the polis (§2 above), Euripides focuses on conflict over succession. I cannot resist inserting here the (unreliable, of course) tradition recorded by Aulus Gellius (*NA* 15.20) that Euripides himself once had two wives simultaneously.

In *Andromache* Neoptolemos lives with two women, his barren wife Hermione and his concubine Andromakhe, who has produced for him a son. Hermione believes that Andromakhe has made her barren by sorcery and that she wishes to replace her as Neoptolemos' wife (32–5, 156–8). Neoptolemos' paternal grandfather, Peleus, defends Andromakhe against the aggression of Hermione and Menelaos, arguing that if Hermione 'has the misfortune to produce no children, does that mean that *we* must remain without children?' (713–14). But of course at the time the play was produced Attic law did not allow legitimacy to children produced by a concubine. Hence perhaps Hermione's fear of being replaced as *wife* by Andromakhe, despite the power of her Spartan natal family and the powerlessness of Andromakhe (155–6, 196–7), whereas in Homer there is no suggestion that, for example, Helen feared replacement by the mother of Menelaos' only son (§2 above), for in Homer such replacement would be unnecessary. But there is an extra complication. The Attic law of 451 (§2 above) required that for a man to be a citizen both his parents must be citizens. Transposed intact to heroic Phthia, such a law would marginalise even the marriage of Neoptolemos with the Spartan Hermione. But much

[53] *Od.* 1.432 (Laertes and Eurykleia), *Il.* 9.450–1 (the parents of Phoinix); cf. also *Od.* 11.421–3 (Agamemnon and Klytaimestra).

[54] *Il.* 8.283–4, 14.202–4.

more obviously against the spirit of the legislation would be marriage with Andromakhe, who is not even Greek. 'Will Phthia endure my offspring, if you are barren?' she asks (201–2), trying to persuade Hermione that she is no threat. And later in the play Hermione herself, with good reason now to regret her plot against Andromakhe, recognises that Andromakhe's children would have been, as 'half slave and illegitimate' (942), [*170*] no threat. The inconsistency of this with her earlier position has its dramatic advantages, but may also to some extent reflect the historical shifts in attitudes to marriage during the transmission of the myth, in the period in which the city-state was formed.

Alkmaion in Korinth also concerned a wife's fear of being replaced. According to Apollodorus (*Bibl.* 3.7.7), Alkmaion left his two children, Amphilokhos and Tisiphone, in Korinth in the care of Kreon. But Kreon's wife sold Tisiphone into slavery, in fear that Kreon would marry her. Alkmaion then happened to buy Tisiphone without recognising her as his daughter, and finally returned to Korinth, where he also recovered his son. The play seems to have contained a struggle between Alkmaion and Kreon for the children. The role of Kreon's wife would presumably have been to make the identities of Alkmaion and his two children known to each other, so as to be rid of them and thereby of the threat to her position. If Webster is right to suppose that fr. 76 – 'See the tyrant. He goes into exile, a childless old man' – refers to Kreon, then his wife was barren, and this perhaps explains her fear of being replaced by Tisiphone. In *Medea*, on the other hand, the replaced wife, Medea, does indeed have children by her husband. But she is foreign, abandoned by Jason for a local princess. The pathos of this should be seen in the context of the citizenship law of 451, which, twenty years before the play was first produced, marginalised marriages with non-Athenians.

It cannot have been uncommon in the city-state for one of the marriage partners to have offspring from a previous marriage.[55] The potential conflict in such a situation is obvious, and we hear of protective and preventive legislation.[56] In Homer no man remarries. But in *Aegeus* and in his second *Phrixus*[57] Euripides dramatised the scheming of the stepmother against her husband's children. In a fragment (fr. 338) of *Dictys* somebody, presumably urging Polydektes not to marry Danae, says 'you already have

[55] Erdmann 1934: 403–8; Thompson 1972; Lacey 1968: 108.
[56] Erdmann 1934: 404–5.
[57] For Ino as Athamas' second wife in this play (in the papyrus hypothesis in *POxy.* 2455 = *TGrF* V.2 p. 861f.) see Luppe 1984.

offspring, but want to beget new children in the house and thereby create very great hostility to your children'. Alkestis' last request to Admetos is that he should not inflict a stepmother on their children (*Alc.* 303–10; cf. *Hipp.* 858–9). In *Ino* the situation is complicated by the reappearance of Athamas' first wife, Ino, who had been presumed dead. His second wife, Themisto, plans to kill Ino's children, but is tricked by Ino into killing her own children by mistake instead. The [171] *Melanippe Desmotis* (§4 above) also contains the wicked stepmother motif (Siris), and so does the *Ion* (§2 above) – although here Kreousa's murder plot against Ion turns out to be based on an error and the step-parent turns out to be Xouthos.[58] This brings us to our final category.

6

Given the frequency of death in battle, and the fact that women married much younger than men, it was perhaps more often women than men who brought to a new marriage the offspring of a previous one.[59] Young widows, even with children, were expected to remarry.[60] W. E. Thompson finds fifty-three people in Athens of the fifth and fourth centuries who remarried, of whom thirty are women and twenty-three men.[61]

In *Phaethon*, Phaithon is believed to be the son of Merops and Klymene. But Klymene has revealed to him that in fact his father is Helios. Phaithon resists the marriage arranged for him by Merops, but we do not know whether this conflict also set Klymene against her husband. In *Cresphontes*, Polyphontes has killed his own brother Kresphontes and married his widow, Merope. He has also killed two of Kresphontes' sons; the third, also called Kresphontes, escaped, but has returned unrecognised to the palace and eventually, with the help of Merope, kills Polyphontes during a sacrifice to mark Merope's feigned reconciliation with Polyphontes. If this reconciliation contained any reference to Polyphontes' desire to have children by Merope,[62] that would

[58] Other plays in this category include *Tennes* (probably Euripidean), Soph. *Euryalos*, *Tyro* and *Phineus*, and perhaps also the plays (by various authors) called *Athamas* and *Phrixos*.

[59] On the other hand it appears from skeletal remains that women tended to die younger than men (see, for example, Pomeroy 1975: 68).

[60] Lacey 1968: 108; Thompson 1972: 222–3.

[61] Thompson 1972.

[62] This is apparently the theme of a fragment of Ennius' *Kresphontes* (fr. 54 Jocelyn (see Jocelyn 1967: *ad loc.*). For a full recent discussion of *Kresphontes* see Harder 1985.

be an extra element of irony in the brutal assertion, by the son of her earlier marriage, of his right to succession.

As the extruded child who eventually returns and inherits the kingdom, Kresphontes resembles Perseus, Ion, Hippothoon (in *Alope*), Aiolos and Boiotos, Zethos and Amphion. But the closest parallel is with Orestes, whose return, like Kresphontes', ends with the killing of the usurping king, his mother's new husband, at a sacrifice. But between Kresphontes and Elektra there is one crucial difference. Klytaimestra, unlike Merope, supports her living husband rather than her dead one. This means that the close link between mother and son that we have seen in so many plays is broken. The matricide is the more horrible for reversing the typology. And one reversal gives rise to another. Orestes, like Oidipous, fails to remain as king in succession to his father. [172] As a matricide (*El.* 1250–1) he has to leave Argos, never to return. And so does Elektra. In the type to which *Electra* half belongs, and which is represented by *Aegeus*, *Alope*, *Antiope*, *Danae*, *Ion*, *Cresphontes*, *Melanippe Sophe*, *Melanippe Desmotis* and other plays, the family conflict surrounding an extruded male child (or children) is ended, with or without violence, by the prophesied or actual inheritance of the household by the child. Internal contradiction is resolved in the final continuity of the household. But to *Electra* there is no such positive conclusion. It is the contradiction that prevails. The type is reversed. The house of Atreus is destroyed utterly, not, like the house of Hektor, by its external enemies, but by its own internal contradictions.[63]

POSTSCRIPT

Further relevant work includes N. S. Rabinowitz, *Anxiety Veiled: Euripides and the Traffic in Women* (Ithaca, NY: Cornell University Press, 1993); C. Patterson, *The Family in Greek History* (Cambridge, MA: Harvard University Press, 1993); V. Wohl, *Intimate Commerce* (Austin: University of Texas Press, 1998); Cox 1998; K. Ormand, *Exchange and the Maiden: Marriage in Sophoclean Tragedy* (Austin: University of Texas Press, 1999); H. Foley, *Female Acts in Greek Tragedy* (Princeton: Princeton University Press, 2001), Part II ('The contradictions of tragic marriage'); J. Redfield, *The Locrian Maidens: Love and Death in Greek Italy* (Princeton: Princeton University

[63] I am grateful to the editor of this volume [A. Powell (ed.), *Euripides, Women, and Sexuality* (London: Routledge, 1990)], and to Jan Bremmer, Helene Foley and David Harvey for their improvement of an earlier draft of this chapter.

Press, 2003), chapter 2; K. Ormand, 'Marriage, identity, and the tale of Mestra in the Hesiodic Catalogue of Women', *AJP* 125 (2004), 303–38; M. Griffith, 'Extended families, marriage, and inter-city relations in (later) Athenian tragedy: dynasts II', in D. M. Carter (ed.) *Why Athens? A Reappraisal of Tragic Politics* (Oxford: Oxford University Press, 2011), pp. 175–208; D. Lyons, *Dangerous Gifts: Gender and Exchange in Ancient Greece* (Austin: University of Texas Press, 2012).

PART V

New Testament

CHAPTER 15

1 Corinthians 13.12: 'Through a Glass Darkly'

Concerning Paul's use of the term *mysterion* A. E. Harvey has recently argued cogently that 'even if all the instances of *mysterion* can be "explained" in terms of [the Semitic] *raz*, it does not follow that the writer did not intend, and the reader did not pick up, some echo of the Greek mystery-metaphor'.[1] He gives as the clearest examples three passages from 1 Corinthians (4.1, 13.2, 14.2), adding that it is perhaps significant that they were intended for Korinth, 'where Paul's hearers and readers may have been particularly well placed to pick up allusions to pagan institutions'.

At 1 Cor. 13.12, βλέπομεν γὰρ ἄρτι δι᾽ ἐσόπτρου ἐν αἰνίγματι, τότε δὲ πρόσωπον πρὸς πρόσωπον ('for we see now through a mirror, in a riddle, but then we will see face to face'), the author was clearly influenced by Num. 12.8 στόμα κατὰ στόμα λαλήσω αὐτῷ, ἐν εἴδει καὶ οὐ δι᾽ αἰνιγμάτων ('I will speak with him face to face, openly and not through riddles'), which however certainly does not 'explain' his usage.[2] Various hypotheses concerning the phrase δι᾽ ἐσόπτρου ἐν αἰνίγματι have been exhaustively reviewed and dismissed by Hugedé.[3] For example, neither catoptromancy (Achelis)[4] nor the magical mirror of Hellenistic mysticism (Reitzsenstein)[5] is consistent with the *negative* function of the mirror here, quite apart from the other difficulties in these theories.[6] The metaphor of the negative function of the mirror, based on the indirectness of the mirror-image, is in fact found in popular Stoicism.[7] The metaphor is combined with *ainigma* by Plutarch (*Is.* 382a), who says that if celebrated philosophers have seen an αἴνιγμα τοῦ θείου ('riddle of divinity') even

1 Harvey 1980.
2 See Hugedé 1957: 38–44; Conzelmann 1975: 227.
3 Hugedé 1957: *passim.*
4 Achelis 1918; Hugedé 1957: 89–94.
5 Reitzenstein 1927: 252–4; Hugedé 1957: 45–75.
6 Hugedé 1957: 45–94.
7 Hugedé 1957: 127–37.

in inanimate objects, we should the more love natures that have soul and perception, using them as clearer mirrors (ἐναργεστέρων *[118]* ἐσόπτρων) through which to honour τὸ θεῖον. For Hugedé this is sufficient to explain Paul's usage: the combination of mirror-image and *ainigma* is natural in Greek, because both are indirect (not necessarily obscure) representations of reality.[8]

It seems to me, however, that Hugedé, and the subsequent commentators, leave much unexplained. The eschatological transition to complete knowledge is expressed in two images: in the transition from childhood to adulthood (v. 11), and in the transition from seeing indirectly to seeing face to face. And the second image elaborates (γάρ) the first. What remains to be explained is how the second image illustrates a transition, and how it illustrates these particular transitions.

The mysteries of course concerned a transition, from the uninitiated to the initiated state. It has been argued that this transition may sometimes have been expressed in terms of the transition from childhood to adulthood.[9] It was sometimes imagined as a passage through death to a state of unending felicity,[10] and usually involved a transition from ignorance to knowledge.[11] The end-point of the transition was the τέλος or τέλειον of the mysteries[12] (cf. 13.10 ὅταν δὲ ἔλθῃ τὸ τέλειον). And so, if the second image derives from the mysteries, it is well suited to the transitions that it illustrates. Furthermore, it has been recognised that the style of the passage is one associated with the mysteries.[13]

But if the phrase δι' ἐσόπτρου ἐν αἰνίγματι is a mystery-metaphor, from what element of the mysteries does it derive? Demetrius in his essay *On Style*[14] points out that any hinting expression (ὑπονοούμενον) is disturbing (φοβερώτερον), and will be variously interpreted, whereas what is stated clearly and obviously is likely to be despised. *[119]* He continues: 'for that

[8] Hugedé 1957: 145–8.

[9] References in Hugedé 1957: 177.

[10] See e.g. Nock 1972: 101; Merkelbach 1962: *passim*; the process is well described by Burkert 1985: 276–304.

[11] Hence the well-known use by philosophers of the stages of mystic initiation to express progress towards the relatively inaccessible in philosophy (refs. in Burkert 1983b: 250 n. 11), from which indeed Harvey 1980: 332 believes that ἐὰν ... εἰδῶ τὰ μυστήρια πάντα in 13.2 derives overtones.

[12] See e.g. Pl. *Sym.* 209e–10a: 'In these erotic matters you too could be initiated; but in the final initiation and revelation (τὰ τέλεα καὶ ἐποπτικά), for which these are a preliminary ..., I do not know whether you could'; Greg. Naz. *Or.* 7 (*PG.* 35.776c, quoted below); Clem. Al. *Paed.* 1.6; Hugedé 1957: 177 n. 1.

[13] Thomson 1953; Conzelmann 1975: 229 n. 108.

[14] Demetr. *Eloc.* 100–2; written at some time between 275 BCE and the end of the first century CE: Russell and Winterbottom 1972: 172.

reason allegory is also used in the language of mystery cult, to provoke disorientation and anxiety, just like darkness and night. For allegory is similar to darkness and night.' He then proceeds to warn against excess in this 'that our language might not be reduced to riddles' (ὥς μὴ αἴνιγμα ὁ λόγος ἡμῖν γένηται). From this neglected passage, and others like it,[15] it seems that riddling expressions might be used in the mysteries to confuse the initiand.[16] And in the course of the ritual the ignorance and fear would eventually be dispelled.[17]

Demetrius compares the intellectual effect of *allegoria* with the visual effect of darkness. What then of the mirror? Ancient mirrors could of course be obscure. And the association of *ainigma* in the passage of Plutarch adduced by Hugedé is in fact with the obscurer kind of mirror. The use of the mirror in the mysteries of Dionysos is noted by Hugedé, and explained as recalling the story of the death of Dionysos at the hands of the Titans.[18] But of course the mirror in the myth derives from its use in the ritual. What was this use? Not, I think, catoptromancy, which has no apparent function in mystic initiation. In the Dionysiac initiation depicted in the Pompeian Villa Item, it has been argued that the function of the bowl held by Silenos, into which the young satyr looks intensely, is to present a (no doubt confusing) reflection of the Silenos-mask held up behind him.[19] Rather than repeating this argument here, I will merely add to it two points. First, the only known function in ritual of the Silenos-mask (by itself) is as an object of revelation.[20] Second, if the argument is correct, then the scene corresponds thematically as well as formally with the scene on the other side of the central divine couple, which shows the partial revelation of the Dionysiac sacra. Presumably the satyr will eventually come face to face with the mask.[21]

To conclude, it is insufficient to agree with Hugedé that the conjunction of mirror and *ainigma* is 'natural' in Greek. It seems to derive, remotely perhaps, from their analogous function in mystic *[120]* initiation, the function of confusing and stimulating the initiand as a prelude to the

[15] Casel 1919: 36, 60, 63, 79, 92–3, 120–1, 122; Iambl. *VP* 103–4, 227; Porph. *Plot.* 15, *Vit. Pyth.* 41; Plotinus, *Enn.* 5.1.7 (cf. 3.6.19, 1.6.6); Merkelbach 1962: 161, 168, 334; cf. Zuntz 1971: 343; Burkert 1977: 439.

[16] This underlies, perhaps, Pl. *Phd.* 69c, Plut. *Mor.* 389a.

[17] Just as in the ritual darkness would be dispelled by a great light: e.g. Plut., fr. 178.

[18] Hugedé 1957: 83 n. 1. The mirror was used to entice the child (Firm. Mat. *Err. prof. rel.* 6.2); he is killed while looking in it (Nonnus, *Dion.* 6.173; *Orph. fr.* 209K = 274.ii etc. B).

[19] See e.g. Herbig 1958: 28 ff. On bowls used as mirrors see e.g. Plin. *HN.* 33.129.

[20] See e.g. Lehmann 1962: 64, fig. 2.

[21] Cf. Merkelbach 1962: 22. Isis is reflected in mirrors in the mystic procession at Apul. *Met.* 11.9.

final revelation. This does not mean that Paul had direct knowledge of the mysteries.[22] Plutarch, of course, did have this direct knowledge,[23] and was fond of metaphors derived from the mysteries, notably from the *transition* contained in mystic ritual.[24] Finally, it can hardly be a coincidence that of the three remaining occurrences of the conjunction of mirror and riddle, two are clearly in a context of initiation:[25] (1) [Dionys. Areop.] *Eccl.* 2.4.1: the τελετή (initiation: the initiands are called τελούμενοι) of baptism is described as having 'riddles of a vision worthy of god, which are modelled after actual mirrors used by people' (ἀξιοθέου θεωρίας[26] αἰνίγματα φυσικοῖς καὶ ἀνθρωποπρεπέσιν ἐσόπτροις εἰκονιζόμενα). (2) Greg. Naz. *Or.* 7 (*PG* 35.776c):

> May we receive from there no mere rivulet, such that it manifests itself in mirrors and riddles (ὅσον ἐν ἐσόπτροις φαντάζεσθαι καὶ αἰνίγμασιν), but rather may we come upon the very source of beauty, with pure mind beholding (ἐποπτεύοντες)[26] the pure truth, and in return for the devoted toil we have expended here for the sake of beauty may we find this as our reward: the more perfect (τελεωτέραν) participation in and vision (θεωρίαν) of beauty there. For this is what sacred books and inspired souls proclaim as the culmination of our mystic initiation (ὅπερ δὴ τῆς ἡμετέρας τέλος μυσταγωγίας βίβλοι τε καὶ ψυχαὶ θεολόγοι θεσπίζουσιν).

POSTSCRIPT

For recent work on Dionysiac mystery cult and early Christianity see in this volume the postscript to 'Thunder, lightning, and earthquake in the *Bacchae* and Acts of the Apostles' (chapter 16), especially the recent book by Friesen.

See also e.g. M. Bockmuehl, *Revelation and Mystery in Ancient Judaism and Pauline Christianity*, Wissenschaftliche Untersuchungen zum Neuen Testament 2.36 (Tübingen: Mohr, 1990); H.-J. Klauck, *Religion und Gesellschaft im frühen Christentum. Neutestamentliche Studien*,

[22] See the remarks by Harvey 1980: 320–1.
[23] See e.g. *Mor.* 611d.
[24] E.g. *Mor.* 47a, 81e, 943c; perhaps also from the use of mirrors (717c 'concerning the mysteries, in which it is possible to receive the greatest reflections and apparitions of the truth about the gods ...'; 354c '... have a share in philosophy, though this is for the most part hidden by words and stories which contain obscure reflections and apparitions of the truth') and of riddles (see above, n. 16).
[25] The third is Tert. *Adv. Prax.* 16.6; cf. also *Acta Andreae* 15, 'I count as blessed (μακαρίους) those who have become obedient to the hidden words and through them see, as in a mirror (ὀπτριζομένους), the mysteries concerning their own nature.'
[26] And in the mysteries: see e.g. Theo. Sm. *Math.* 15.1–3 Hiller; Pl. *Phdr.* 250b; Thomson 1935: 23–7; Procl. *In R.* 372 (1.85.8 Kroll).

Wissenschaftliche Untersuchungen zum Neuen Testament 152 (Tübingen: Mohr Siebeck, 2003), pp. 171–93 ('Die antiken Mysterienkulte und das Urchristentum: Anknüpfung und Widerspruch'); J. Bremmer, *Initiation into the Mysteries of the Ancient World* (Berlin and New York: de Gruyter, 2014), chapter 6 ('Did the mysteries influence early Christianity?'). For the mystic mirror see Seaford (1996a) 223 on Eur. *Bacch.* 918–19.

CHAPTER 16

Thunder, Lightning and Earthquake in the Bacchae *and the Acts of the Apostles*

In Section 1 I discuss a remarkable set of similarities between three famous passages, one from Athenian tragedy, the others from the New Testament. In Section 2 I will argue that one of the common elements (thunder, lightning, earthquake) was a feature of mystic initiation, and that the similarities derive from the effect of the pattern of this ritual on all three passages. In Section 3 I will explore further the function, in the ritual, of thunder, lightning and earthquake. The investigation suggests the importance of the rite of passage as a factor in the imagining of divine power.

1

In the famous 'earthquake scene' of Euripides' *Bacchae* the god Dionysos is imprisoned in darkness in the house of King Pentheus. The chorus of his followers then sing a hymn, which is interrupted by the voice of the god (576, etc.) and then by an earthquake (causing the collapse of the house: 585, 595, 602–3, 633), thunder and lightning (594–5, cf. 598–9), and fire on the tomb of Semele (596–7, 623–4). The chorus throw themselves to the ground (600–1). Dionysos appears, and tells them to rise up, take courage and stop trembling. He relates how he escaped from imprisonment, telling of how meanwhile, within the house, Pentheus performed a series of frantic and fruitless actions that culminated in a physical attack on a miraculous light[1] (as if it was his prisoner) created by the god.

I want to compare this passage to two famous passages in the Acts of the Apostles. The first is the Conversion of Saul (9.3–7):[2]

> Now as he was going along and approaching Damascus, suddenly a light from heaven flashed around him (περιήστραψεν). He fell to the ground

[1] The mss. reading φῶς in 630 is certainly correct.

[2] The translations are from the New Revised Standard Version, with correction 'light' for 'lights' at 16.29.

> and heard a voice saying to him, 'Saul, Saul, why do you persecute me?' He asked, 'Who are you, Lord?' The reply came, 'I am Jesus, whom you [140] are persecuting. But get up and enter the city, and you will be told what you are to do.' The men who were travelling with him stood speechless because they heard the voice but saw no one.

The same event is narrated (put into the mouth of Paul himself) twice elsewhere in Acts (22.6–11 and 26.12–18), with a few variations, some of which will be mentioned below.

The second passage of Acts that I want to compare with our scene from the *Bacchae* is the miraculous release of Paul and Silas from prison at Philippi (16.25–30):

> About midnight Paul and Silas were praying and singing hymns to God, and the prisoners were listening to them. Suddenly there was an earthquake, so violent that the foundations of the prison were shaken; and immediately all the doors were opened and everyone's chains were unfastened. When the jailer woke up and saw the prison doors wide open, he drew his sword and was about to kill himself, since he supposed that the prisoners had escaped. But Paul shouted in a loud voice, 'Do not harm yourself, for we are all here.' The jailer called for light, and, rushing in, he fell down trembling before Paul and Silas. Then he brought them outside and said, 'Sirs, what must I do to be saved?'

Commentators on these two passages of Acts have compared (a) the Conversion of Saul with another passage of the *Bacchae*, which in fact resembles it far less than does the earthquake scene, namely 1078–83, in which the voice of Dionysos is heard from above and 'a light of holy fire towered between heaven and earth';[3] (b) the phrase 'Why are you persecuting me?' (spoken by Saul) with the assumption at *Bacchae* 784–95 that the god is persecuted if his followers are persecuted; (c) Acts 26.14, 'It is hard to kick against the pricks (πρὸς κέντρα λακτίζειν)' (spoken by Saul), with Dionysos urging Pentheus not to kick against the pricks (*Bacch.* 795); (d) the miraculous opening of the door and unfastening of the chains in Acts 16.26 with the same combination in the earlier brief narration of the liberation of the maenads at *Bacch.* 447–8. None of these parallels have been taken to indicate any detailed or significant relation between the passages of the *Bacchae* and Acts. After all, (c) and (d) are *topoi* that are also found in other texts. The closest I have found to an awareness that there might be a structural similarity involved is in a brief remark in a footnote by Friedrich Brenk that 'the "palace miracle" in *Bacchae* 616–41 has several

[3] Nestle 1900; Brenk 1994: 421.

affinities with Acts 16.25–34'.[4] It is a symptom of the intellectual division of labour that in his recent detailed commentary (1994) on the first half of Acts C. K. Barrett adduces various stories, mostly from the Bible, as similar to the Conversion of Saul, but not the most similar of all, the earthquake scene in the *Bacchae*. [141]

I now list the elements of the *Bacchae* scene, each one of which is paralleled by an element from one or other, or both, of the Acts narratives.

1. **The Persecutor**. Pentheus, Saul, the jailer. Pentheus and Saul both represent uncompromising authority, embody animated hostility to the new cult, and threaten to kill its adherents (*Bacch.* 240–1, 356–7, 796–7; Acts 9.1 'breathing threats and murder against the disciples of the Lord').
2. **Imprisonment**. Dionysos, and Paul and Silas, are imprisoned.
3. **Darkness**. Dionysos is imprisoned in darkness (*Bacch.* 510, 549, 611). The liberation of Paul and Silas takes place at midnight (so that the jailer brings in light – see below).
4. **Hymn**. The followers of Dionysos are, like Paul and Silas, singing a hymn to their god as the epiphany occurs.
5. **Suddenness**. At *Bacch.* 576 the voice of Dionysos breaks in unexpectedly on the choral song. In Acts the suddenness of divine manifestation is in both cases made explicit (9.3 ἐξαίφνης, 16.26 ἄφνω).
6. **Invisible Voice**. The group hears the voice of the god but does not see him, at *Bacch.* 576–95 and Acts 9.7.[5] It is the individual (Pentheus, Saul) who sees the god (as light – see 13 below).
7. **Lightning**. Thunder and lightning appear in the *Bacchae* (594–5, cf. 598–9). At Acts 9.3 the light from heaven περιήστραψεν, literally 'lightninged around' (ἀστραπή is lightning). The same (rare) verb is used at 22.6.[6] We will return to this theme below.
8. **Earthquake**. In the *Bacchae* and at Acts 16.26 the house is shaken by an earthquake, creating the possibility of escape for the imprisoned.
9. **Drawing the Sword**. Both Pentheus (628) and the jailer prepare to use a sword.
10. **Rushing into the House**. Both Pentheus and the jailer rush (*Bacch.* 628 ἵεται, Acts 16.29 εἰσεπήδησεν) into the dark interior, Pentheus to

[4] Brenk 1994: 421 n. 23.

[5] In the *Bacchae* the god does subsequently appear to the group. In the version at Acts 22.9 the group sees the light but does not hear the voice.

[6] Though not at 26.13, where however the light is called brighter than the sun. Cf. Luke 17.24.

attack the miraculous light (mistaken for the prisoner) with his sword, the jailer having called for light.

11. **Falling Trembling to the Ground**. The jailer falls down trembling. Pentheus eventually 'collapses' (635). The followers of Dionysos fall down trembling (600–7). In two versions of the Conversion it is only Saul who falls to the ground, but in the third (26.14) the group does as well.
12. **The Command to Rise Up** is given by Dionysos to his followers (606) and by the Lord to Paul.
13. **Light as God**. Dionysos is greeted as 'greatest light' by his [142] followers (608). Similarly Pentheus takes the miraculous light for Dionysos, but attacks it. The jailer calls for light and rushes inside. Each version of the Conversion implies or states that Saul saw the Lord (9.7 the others 'saw no one'; 22.14 Saul saw 'the Just One'; 26.16 'I have been seen by you'). And so, according to Haenchen in his commentary (1971), 'Presumably … Luke imagined the occurrence in such a way that Saul's companions saw only a formless glare where he himself saw in it the figure of Jesus.'
14. **Acceptance of God**. Both the jailer and Saul are converted by the epiphany. Similarly the followers of Dionysos undergo a complete reversal, being transformed from trembling, isolation, desolation and despair to joy by the miraculous appearance of their god, their 'greatest light' (604–10). In stark contrast, Pentheus violently rejects the light that he takes to be his prisoner, and who is in fact the god Dionysos.
15. **Escape Unnecessary**. Dionysos emerges from the place of his imprisonment, but assures Pentheus that he will not run away (659). So too Paul reassures the jailer that the prisoners have not run away (16.28). As noted above, the miraculous opening of doors and loosening of chains at Philippi is paralleled in the *Bacchae* in the earlier report of the freeing of the maenads that Pentheus had imprisoned (447–8).

2

Of these fifteen elements all appear in the *Bacchae*, eight on the road to Damascus and twelve at Philippi. The accumulation of similarities is too detailed to be a coincidence. How do we explain it? Scholars are divided over whether the author of Acts was anywhere influenced by the *Bacchae*,[7]

[7] Vögeli 1953: 427 summarises views up to 1953. Hackett 1956 argues against influence.

with the evidence including the occurrence in both texts of 'to kick against the pricks' (as noted above) and of the root θεομαχ- (fighting against deity).[8] Whatever the truth of that, it seems to me impossible that the detailed structural similarity that I have described can be wholly explained by such influence. What we have is rather a pattern of action whose powerful effect on the imagination was persistent enough to make itself felt in these two texts separated by five centuries. I suggest that the power and persistence of the pattern may derive, at least in part, from its relation with the powerful and persistent ritual of mystic initiation.

I have elsewhere argued in detail that a large number of the actions and experiences of Pentheus in the *Bacchae* reflect (or rather refract) mystic initiation.[9] Given the general conservatism of ritual and the [*143*] observable continuity of the mysteries, the argument may, with caution, take some of its evidence for the mysteries from a period much later than the *Bacchae*. For example, Pentheus' strangely agitated actions and experiences (as narrated by Dionysos) in the earthquake scene correspond in a remarkable way to those described four centuries later by Plutarch (fr. 178) as the sufferings that occur in mystic initiation (an account influenced by, but certainly not wholly dependent on, Plato). Whereas Pentheus persists in this anxiety, even attacking the light, the chorus' reaction to the 'greatest light' reflects the mystic transition from despair to joy. And so the 'earthquake scene' contains both the mystic transition (the chorus) and its rejection (Pentheus). Rather than repeating the argument here, I want to extend it to the elements common to our three passages.

Most of the elements do in fact seem to be reflections (or rather refractions) of mystic ritual: the animosity of the persecutor,[10] the hymn,[11] trembling, rushing vainly into the dark house,[12] liberation from imprisonment, the command to rise from the ground, the light in the darkness, god as light,[13] as well as the central element, which is my main concern here: thunder, lightning and earthquake.

[8] Acts 5.39; *Bacch.* 45, 325, 1255, cf. 635–6.

[9] Seaford 1981a, 1987a, 1996a: 42.

[10] The negative emotions of the initiand combine, in their projection onto the mythical figure of Pentheus, with the theme (characteristic of aetiological myth) of resistance to the cult, perhaps also even with a distant historical memory of actual resistance: Seaford 1996a: 43, 188 (on 480), 201 (on 616–37).

[11] See n. 23 below.

[12] Plut. fr. 178 'at first wandering and tiring runnings around and certain frightening journeys through the darkness that lead nowhere, then before the completion itself all the terrible things, terror and trembling and sweat and amazement etc.'

[13] Seaford 1996a: 190 (on 496–7), 200 (on 606–9 and 608), 201–2 (on 628). On impressions of great light ('photisms') during recorded accounts of the experience of conversion see James 1902: 251–3. Cf. also the 'being of light' seen in near-death experiences (induced perhaps in the mysteries).

A fragment of a dithyramb by Pindar describes a ritual of Dionysos (fr. 70b.6 Βρομίου [τελε]τάν) on Olympos, in which the ecstatic celebrations include the 'all-mastering thunderbolt breathing fire' as well as '*rhomboi* of drums' (fr. 70b.9, 15–16). *Rhombos* here seems to mean 'whirling', but its basic meaning is the bull-roarer, an instrument whirled round to produce a roar, used in the Dionysiac mysteries.[14] In Euripides' *Helen* a list of accoutrements of the Dionysiac thiasos includes 'the whirling circular earthquake-in-the-air (ἔνοσις αἰθερία) of the *rhombos*' (1362–3). A function of this instrument in the mysteries may have been, as it was in native Australian initiations,[15] to frighten the initiands[16] with a sound of unseen source. The following fragment (fr. 57) of Aeschylus' *Edonians*, a play similar in plot and in detail to the *Bacchae*, is probably from the entry-hymn of the Dionysiac chorus: 'Twanging shrieks out, and bull-voiced mimes bellow in answer from some unseen place, and the image of the drum,[17] as of thunder under the earth, is carried along, deeply terrifying.' Here the 'thunder under the earth' suggests the terrifying roar that accompanies an earthquake (and indeed seems to be the converse of the 'earthquake-in-the-air' in the *Helen* passage).[18] The combination of thunder and earthquake, the confusion of man and bull, the voice from an unseen source, all these are also found in the earthquake scene of the *Bacchae*. These and various other passages when taken *[144]* together suggest that the Dionysiac thiasos used drums and torches in their ritual to evoke earthquake, thunder and lightning. In Sophocles' *Antigone* Dionysos is as 'earth-shaker' (ἐλελίχθων) closely associated with dancing at Thebes (152–4). A third-century CE graffito from Dura-Europas records an invocation of Dionysos in which it seems that he has the title 'Earthquake', apparently so as to shake his followers.[19] In the *Bacchae* Earthquake (Ἔννοσις) is invoked (probably by Dionysos) to shake the earth (585) on which Dionysos' followers are standing. Earlier in the play the drums, which the chorus are instructed to beat around the house of Pentheus (60–1),

[14] West 1983: 155, 157, 171; Kannicht 1969: 357.

[15] This was first pointed out over a century ago by Andrew Lang (1884: 39, 41).

[16] On frightening the mystic initiands see e.g. Schol. Ar. *Vesp.* 1363b.

[17] τυπάνου δ' εἰκών, a generally accepted emendation of the mss. τυμπάνου εἰκών. It is translated 'semblance' or 'echo', but may, I argue elsewhere (1998a), be related to the practice of using the tympanon as a mirror.

[18] With this confusion cf. the confusion of sounds implied in the Pindar fragment, and the confusion of heaven with earth in Polyphemos' Dionysiac mystic vision at Eur. *Cyc.* 578–80 (see Seaford 1984b: *ad loc.*). Cf. also Ar. *Lys.* 772–3 and Hor. *Carm.* 1.34.12–14 quoted below.

[19] καὶ σὺ μόλε πᾶν τὸ μέδω[ν] κάλεσον Βρόμιε [σ]ῶν προπόλων Εἴνοσι … (of the last three letters only the bottom half is preserved). If Εἴνοσι goes with προπόλων cf. γῆς ἔνοσις at *Orph. fr.* 285.24K = 778.24B. Porter 1948: 29, 35–6 (in fact Εἴνοσις always means earthquake, literally or metaphorically).

are described in the subsequent dithyrambic entry-hymn as βαρύβρομος (156), a word used elsewhere by Euripides of thunder.[20] A fragment from Aeschylus' (Dionysiac) *Bassarai* (fr. 23a) contains the words 'the pine-wood flash of the lightning' (i.e. the torch).

Why did the Dionysiac thiasos evoke earthquake, thunder and lightning? The birth of their god was effected by Zeus' thunderbolt, which destroyed the baby's mother, Semele. This violent birth of Dionysos was a central theme of the dithyramb,[21] as was also accordingly the thunderbolt.[22] Indeed in the *Bacchae* they are themes (along with his second birth from the thigh of Zeus) both of the dithyrambic entry-hymn of the chorus and of their hymn that is interrupted by the earthquake scene, in which the tomb of Semele, which is still smouldering with the fire of the thunderbolt by which she was killed (8), flares up with the flame 'which once Zeus' thunderbolt-hurled thunder left' (597–9). This element of the scene signifies both the death of Semele and the birth of the god.

The evocation of the thunderbolt by the Dionysiac group is clearly connected with the myth of the thunderbolt at the god's birth that was narrated especially in the dithyramb. But the myth is not by itself enough to explain the ritual, of which it may to some extent be the projection. We need also to seek an explanation in the nature and function of the ritual. Choral song and dance seem to have been features of mystic initiation,[23] and the dithyramb, which exhibits signs of association with mystic initiation,[24] may once have been this kind of song. Among these mystic features of the dithyramb is the theme of the (double) birth of Dionysos. It therefore remains to demonstrate, again by a combination of passages, that there is a connection between the thunderbolt and the process of mystic initiation.

The first passage is from the aetiological myth of the Eleusinian mysteries, narrated in the *Homeric Hymn to Demeter*, in which various details of the ritual are prefigured. Demeter gives instructions for the [*145*] building of the Eleusinian temple, says that she will prescribe the rituals (ὄργια) to be performed and is then transformed from her disguise as an old women into a beautiful goddess. 'Light shone far out from the goddess's immortal skin, and her fair hair flowed over her shoulders, and the well-built house was filled with radiance like lightning' (278–80), with the result that Metaneira

20 *Phoen.* 182; cf. *Hipp.* 1201–2. Cf. Dionysos' title Bromios ('roaring').
21 Pl. *Leg.* 3.700b; Seaford 1994b: 268 n. 148; Mendelsohn 1992: 115–16.
22 Archil. fr. 120; Pind. fr. 70b.15–16 (quoted above); Mendelsohn 1992.
23 Ar. *Ran.* 382–7; Lucian, *Salt.* 15; Plut. fr. 178; Aristid. Quint. 3.25 [Chapter 8 above].
24 Seaford 1981a: 268.

is left amazed and voiceless. Riedweg points out that this radiance goes beyond that normally found in an epiphany, and compares a passage of what he shows to be sustained mystic imagery in Plato's *Phaedrus*, which contains the same concentration of words for radiance as do the lines of the hymn just quoted (φέγγος, λαμπρόν, αὐγῇ, ἔλαμπεν in 250b3–d1) and culminates, as does the hymn passage, in lightning – the ἀστράπτουσαν (flashing as lightning, 254b5) sight of the beloved.[25]

Just before this epiphany Demeter's attempt to immortalise the infant Demophon by hiding him 'in much fire' had been fatally interrupted by Metaneira. This episode has been related to an event in the ritual of the Eleusinian mysteries, the nocturnal announcement, accompanied by much fire (ὑπὸ πολλῷ πυρί), of the birth of a child to the goddess.[26] Further, because this child was sometimes identified with Dionysos, and because the thunderbolt was in antiquity regularly envisioned as fire, it has been suggested that this fire (expressed presumably as torchlight in the darkness) was associated with the thunderbolt by which Dionysos was born.[27] This thunderbolt was meant to *immortalise* Dionysos (and Semele),[28] and the precinct where she was blasted was called 'the island of the blessed'.[29] In a myth that clearly reflects mystic initiation[30] the Titans kill the infant Dionysos and are then struck by a thunderbolt. In the inscribed funerary 'gold leaves', that almost certainly contain formulae of mystic initiation,[31] occurs the claim to be of the race of the gods, but to have been stuck down by thunder and lightning. I have argued (1986a[9]) that the initiand is in fact claiming to be one of the Titans once consigned by the thunderbolt of Zeus to Tartaros (as described in Hesiod's *Theogony*), and that the thunderbolt and earthquake with which Prometheus is consigned to Tartaros at the end of *Prometheus Bound* belong to a mystic pattern. Others have taken the thunderbolt on the gold leaves to be the one that punished the Titans for killing the child Dionysos.[31a] Finally,[32] it is of interest that the word ἠχεῖον

[25] Riedweg 1987: 51, 63.
[26] Hippol. *Haer.* 5.8.40; Richardson 1974: 26–7, 233.
[27] Mendelsohn 1992: 119.
[28] Diod. Sic. 5.52.2.
[29] *Suda* and Photius s.v. Μακάρων νῆσος; Tzetzes *ad* Lycoph. 1194, 1204 (11.340.30–341.5, 347.1–10 Scheer). μάκαρ is a word associated with the permanent happiness achieved by mystic initiation. 'Elysion' seems to derive from ἐνηλύσιον ('struck by lightning'): Burkert 1960.
[30] West 1983: 140–75.
[31] Seaford 1996a: 41.
[31a] [E.g. Guthrie 1935: 174.]
[32] I omit various other passages that may reflect the association of the thunderbolt with fictive death or rebirth in initiation: Eur. *Phoen.* 1039–43, fr. 472.11 (ms. βροντὰς); Ar. *Nub.* 265; Hdt. 4.79.2; Pl. *Resp.* 10.621b, *Phdr.* 254b; Diog. Laert. 1.5; Porph. *Plot.* 17.

('gong') was used both in the theatre, where it was also called βροντεῖον (as imitating thunder),[33] and in mystic initiation.[34]

I infer that, in the enactment of mystic initiations, the Dionysiac thiasos created (with drums and bull-roarers) the impression of a [146] thunderbolt and perhaps also of the roar of an earthquake. In myth the thunderbolt was associated with the birth of Dionysos, and in the ritual may well have served to terrify the initiands. The thunder, lightning and earthquake in the *Bacchae* belong to a series of experiences and actions that reflect a rite of passage, mystic initiation. These experiences and actions are those of, on the one hand, the chorus, whose transition from despair to joy reflects the same transition in the ritual, and, on the other hand, Pentheus, whose anxious, hostile resistance does not give way, as it does in the ritual, to joy at the light that embodies the god, but rather persists as a physical attack on this light. In both passages of Acts, on the other hand, the transition is made to acceptance of the god. Once this is understood, we have an explanation of the similarity between the passages of Acts and of the *Bacchae*: the pattern common to all three of them derives from a rite of passage, mystic initiation.

A. D. Nock distinguished between on the one hand *adhesion*, 'an acceptance of new worships as useful supplements and not as substitutes', with no new way of life to replace the old, and on the other hand *conversion*, which is a reorientation of the soul, 'a turning which implies a consciousness that a great change is involved, that the old was wrong and the new is right'.[35] Despite the emotional claims of much Dionysiac cult, initiation into it is largely a matter of adhesion rather than conversion. Our pattern originates as an expression of *adhesion* but is nevertheless, given the contradictory emotions of mystic initiation, also able to express *conversion*.

3

In this section I will concentrate on the question of why thunder, lightning and earthquake should occur in mystic initiation. Section 2 contained more about thunderbolt than earthquake, but in fact the two often go together in the Greek imagination. In some cases this combination consists in the notion of subterranean thunder, a notion influenced no doubt by the roar that accompanies earthquakes. In particular, there are four passages

[33] Schol. Ar. *Nub.* 292; Poll. 4.130.
[34] Apollod. *FGrH* 244 F110.
[35] Nock 1933: 7.

of tragedy, apart from the *Bacchae*, in which it seems to mark a significant transition. One is the ending of the *Prometheus Bound*, mentioned above. Another is from the ending of *Oedipus at Colonus*, where it seems to announce the imminent death of Oidipous (1606). A third heralds the emergence from the sea of the bull that destroys Hippolytos (Eur. *Hipp.* 1201–2). And so when the chorus of Euripides' *Electra*, at the crisis of the action, compare the distant shouting, which means either death or salvation, to 'the [*147*] subterranean thunder of Zeus' (748), it is a comparison with awesome associations.

Apart from their similarity of sound, earthquake and thunderbolt are perhaps the most dramatic manifestation of the helplessness of humankind before the power of nature or of deity. The thunderbolt, 'all-mastering' in the Pindaric dithyramb quoted above, according to Heraclitus 'steers everything'.[36] As for earthquakes, I can testify from my own experience of one, in Kalamata in 1986, to a sense (easily imagined as life-changing) of something uncanny, a unique helplessness, an irresistible impression of there being someone shaking the earth. For Christianity earthquakes have been generally taken to be divine punishment for sin, as for example the great Lisbon earthquake of 1755. At the centre of ancient Greek religion, on the other hand, is ambivalence of various kinds. An earthquake might be thought to be punishment for sacrilege (against Poseidon),[37] or divine discouragement for a military expedition, but also divine *encouragement* for a military expedition (Xen. *Hell.* 4.7.4). Earthquake and thunderbolt, with their dramatic destructiveness, are enacted in the ritual, and so are brought from the realm of uncontrolled nature into the realm of culture, where their terror is manageable: it has a function in the ritual.

What was this function? It belongs, primarily, to the negative aspect of the rite of passage. The initial stage of a rite of passage must detach the initiands from their previous identity and prepare them for their new one. Walter Burkert uses a significant metaphor (but without any thought of the connection we have established between initiation and earthquake): 'the unsettling experience has the effect of shaking the foundations of the personality and making it ready to accept new identities'.[38] Detachment from the previous identity may require divine force; and indeed the need for this force, to enable the rites of passage to perform their vital roles, was one source of the Greek conception of the power of deity. For instance,

[36] DK 22 B 64 (cf. 66): for the place of this in the mystic pattern of his thought see Seaford 1986a[9]: 18.
[37] Diod. Sic. 15.49; Paus. 7.24.5.
[38] Burkert 1987: 102.

because the Greek girl was imagined to resist the transition to marriage,[39] she is in myth imagined as forced from her parental home by deity – e.g. the Proitids by 'all-mastering' Hera,[40] or Io by Zeus on pain of her whole family being destroyed by his thunderbolt.[41] So too, in the *Bacchae*, Dionysos forces the women of Thebes in frenzy from their homes, to be initiated into his thiasos (32, 36), and Dionysos is imagined to be present[42] to 'compel' initiation (469–70).[43] Thunderbolt and earthquake may have played a role in this process of disorientation and detachment (though *[148]* they did not succeed with Pentheus), thereby contributing to the fear and suffering that we know (from evidence of various kinds from various periods) to have been imposed on the initiand in the initial stages of mystic ritual.[44]

This is not to say that the thunderbolt and earthquake were simply one of various ways of terrifying the initiand. In the earliest mention of the dithyramb Archilochus (fr. 120) says that 'I know how to lead the dithyramb, the fine song of Dionysos, when my mind is thunderbolted with wine' (οἴνῳ συγκεραυνωθεὶς φρένας). The thunderbolt at the birth of Dionysos was, we have seen, a central theme of the dithyramb. Here the singer envisages his own inebriated inspiration as a kind of participation in the blast. Experience of the thunderbolt turns out to have a positive aspect. The invocation at Dura-Europas seems to ask Dionysos to come as 'Earthquake', apparently to shake up the group making the invocation. My experience at Kalamata was of a kind of exhilaration mixed up with fear. In the *Bacchae*[45] and in Aeschylus' *Edonians* (fr. 58) the shaking of the house of Dionysos' enemy Pentheus is envisaged in terms of Bacchic frenzy.[46] This suggests two further functions of the earthquake. First, it is assimilated to the frenzy of the worshipper: in both cases, earthquake and frenzied dance, the god inspires an irresistible shaking that through disorientation detaches you from your previous identity. Second, this power is stronger than the power people have over you. The potential of

[39] Seaford 1987c[13]: 106–7.

[40] παγκρατής (Bacchyl. 11.43–6), like the thunderbolt in the Pindaric dithyramb (2.15 = fr. 70b); Seaford 1988.

[41] [Aesch.] *PV* 667–72.

[42] On the presence of deity in the mysteries see Riedweg 1987: 24–5, 142–7.

[43] Cf. Livy 39.18.8 *necessarium* of Dionysiac initiation. Somewhat different is the resolution by the goddess Isis (in a vision) of the fears of Lucius about being initiated into her mysteries: Apul. *Met.* 11.19, 22; cf. 5, 28, 29.

[44] E.g. Burkert 1987: 92–3, 104, 114; Riedweg 1987: 63–7. See also nn. 12 and 16 above.

[45] Seaford 1996a: 199 (on 587 and 592).

[46] As is also the destruction of the house in Euripides' *Heracles* (896–7, 905, 1142, etc.) and *Erechtheus* (fr. 370.46–54), and in Plautus' *Amphitryo* (1094–6).

cults such as the Dionysiac to attract political repression,[47] and the need to ensure continued performance of the cult by telling of initial resistance that caused catastrophe, combine to create myth in which the deity who shakes is able to invade not only the souls of those whom he makes his adherents but also the space enclosed by rulers, space that expresses the exclusivity of their authority as well as their power to enclose by imprisonment the adherents of the god. The thunderbolt can even be a reminder of the instability of cosmic (and political) structure: 'Zeus who thunders on high will put the above beneath' (Ar. *Lys.* 772–3). Horace, claiming to have been converted to religious belief by thunder from a clear sky, muses 'god has the power to exchange the lowest with the highest, and diminishes the famous, advancing the obscure' (*Carm.* 1.34.12–14). Another factor, conceivably, in the ambivalence of the thunderbolt is that despite its violence it might be the herald of fertilising rain. More importantly, lightning can kill, but is also not dissimilar – as bright, unpredictable, divinely created light – to the light that brings salvation in the mysteries.[48]*

POSTSCRIPT

Investigation of the relationship between *Bacchae* and the Acts of the Apostles has burgeoned. See J. Moles, 'Jesus and Dionysus in the Acts of the Apostles and early Christianity', *Hermathena* 180 (2006), 65–104.; D. Dormeyer, 'Bakchos in der Apostelgeschichte', in R. von Haehling (ed.), *Griechische Mythologie und frühes Christentum* (Darmstadt: Wissenschaftlichen Buchgesellschaft, 2005), pp. 153–72; D. Ziegler, *Dionysos in der Apostelgeschichte. Eine intertextuelle Lektüre*, Religion und Biographie 18 (Münster: Lit, 2008); J. Schäfer, 'Zur Funktion der Dionysosmysterien in der Apostelgeschichte: eine intertextuelle Betrachtung der Berufungs- und Befreiungserzählungen in der Apostelgeschichte und der *Bakchen* des Euripides', *ThZ* 66 (2010), 199–222.

See also J. R. C. Cousland, 'Dionysus Theomachos? Echoes of the *Bacchae* in 3 Maccabees', *Biblica* 82 (2001), 539–48; P. Wick, 'Jesus gegen Dionysos? Ein Beitrag zur Kontextualisierung des Johannesevangeliums', *Biblica* 85 (2004), 179–98; F. Massa, *Tra la vigna e la croce. Dioniso nei discorsi letterari e figurativi cristiani (II–IV secolo)*, Potsdamer

[47] The classic case is narrated by Livy, 39.8–19.

[48] Note the emphasis on beholding the fire of the thunderbolt at *Bacch.* 596 (cf. e.g. also in mystic imagery at 2 Cor. 4.3–4).

* My thanks go to David Catchpole for his comments on this paper.

Altertumswissenschaftliche Beiträge, Bd 47 (Stuttgart: Franz Steiner Verlag, 2014).

We now have a comprehensive and detailed treatment of the ancient reception of *Bacchae*: C. Friesen, *Reading Dionysus: Euripides'* Bacchae *and the Cultural Contestations of Greeks, Jews, Romans, and Christians* (Tübingen: Mohr Siebeck, 2015).

A brief overview of Dionysos in early Christianity is contained in Seaford 2006a: chapter 9.

PART VI

The Inner Self

CHAPTER 17

Monetisation and the Genesis of the Western Subject

The western conception of the person as a bounded, unique, more or less integrated motivational and cognitive universe; a dynamic centre of awareness, emotion, judgement and action organised into a distinctive whole and set contrastively against other such wholes and against a social and natural background is, however incorrigible it may seem to us, a rather peculiar idea within the context of the world's cultures.

Clifford Geertz, '"From the native's point of view": on the nature of anthropological understanding[1]

Hail the world's soul, and mine!

Ben Jonson's Volpone addressing his gold (1.i.3)

Sohn-Rethel and the Transcendental Subject

The idea of the universe as an intelligible system subject to the uniformity of impersonal power first occurred in the Ionian polis of the early sixth century. *[79]* In my *Money and the Early Greek Mind* I related this radical development to the fact that Ionia in exactly this period was also the first society in history to be pervasively monetised, through the invention and rapid spread of coinage.[2] The first 'philosophy', produced in the leading commercial polis of Ionia (Miletos), imagines that the universe consists in – and is controlled by – a single semi-abstract substance that is transformed (like money) from and into everything else. Money is semi-abstract substance in that it is the material embodiment of economic (abstract) value. The universe is no longer imagined as controlled by a monarch but by what may seem to be an all-powerful, all-pervasive impersonal substance,[3]

[1] Geertz 1984: 59.
[2] Seaford 2004c. The only comparable attempt is Thomson 1961.
[3] What seems to be the universal social power of money is projected as cosmic power. The Greeks were well aware of money's universal social power (Seaford 2004c: 162–5), and even joked that Zeus rules the gods because he has the most money (Ar. *Plut.* 131).

and the first and only such substance in history is money. In this chapter I take the argument further by discussing a sample of the texts that bear on the relationship between monetisation and the Greek conception of the subject.

This will involve engagement with the attempt by Alfred Sohn-Rethel to fill a gap left by Marx and Engels: they 'have not left us with a blueprint for the staircase that should lead us from the base to the superstructure'. The result was his Marxist critique of epistemology, and in particular his theory of the historical origin of the (in Kantian terms) transcendental unity of the self-consciousness.[4]

I begin by summarising the theory. In order to be exchanged, commodities have to be separated (abstracted) from use. This is 'real abstraction', not in mind but in fact. In their separation from use-value for the purpose of exchange, commodities are as if unchanging and their (numerical) exchange-value is abstracted from their sensual qualities. It is 'real abstraction operating in exchange that engenders the ideal abstraction basic to Greek philosophy and to modern science'.[5] The formal elements of commodity exchange are identical with the formal constituents of cognition, namely the Kantian categories *a priori*, which are not spontaneously generated within the mind but implicit in the social process of commodity exchange. The Kantian division of knowledge according to principles of *a priori* and *a posteriori* 'meant the singling out of a part of our being which is underivable from our physical and sensorial nature'.[6] *[80]* We take for granted this duality of the sources of knowledge, but the point is to uncover its historical origin.

In this way the form of abstract thought preceded abstract thought itself.[7] But how did the former engender the latter? Commodity exchange may occur without engendering abstract thought. What makes the difference is money. 'The real abstraction inherent in exchange becomes discernible only in coined money.'[8] As we shall soon see, commodity exchange may occur without money in the full sense. As the material substance embodying real abstraction, money makes possible the idea of abstract substance.

Two different currencies in the same place will quickly be brought together, through an exchange rate, as different embodiments of the

4 Sohn-Rethel 1978.
5 Sohn-Rethel 1978: 28.
6 Sohn-Rethel 1978: 36.
7 By 'abstract thought' I mean thought about processes or entities that are abstracted from (and so devoid of) sense-reality and admit only of quantitative differentiation.
8 Sohn-Rethel 1978: 69.

same monetary value. The essential *unity* of money (there can in principle be only one money) depends on the form of exchangeability of all commodities: they are all exchangeable for the same thing. Sohn-Rethel claims that

> a closer analysis would reveal that the transcendental unity of the self-consciousness, to use the Kantian expression for the phenomenon here involved, is itself an intellectual reflection of one of the elements of the exchange abstraction, the most fundamental one of all, the form of the exchangeability of the commodities underlying the unity of money and of the social synthesis. I define the Kantian 'transcendental subject' as a fetish concept of the capital function of money.[9]

The significance of this account is described by Adorno thus:

> Sohn-Rethel was the first to point out that hidden in this [transcendental] principle, in the general and necessary activity of the mind, lies work of an inalienably social nature. The aporetical concept of the transcendental subject – a nonentity which is nonetheless to act, a universal that is nonetheless to have particular experiences – would be a soap bubble, never obtainable from the autarkic immanent context of consciousness, which is necessarily individual. Compared with consciousness, however, the concept represents not only something more abstract; by virtue of its coining power it also represents something more real ... abstraction itself is the principle whereby the subject comes to be a subject at all. Abstraction is the subject's essence. That is why going back to what it is not must impress the subject as external and violent.[10]

The phenomenon for which Sohn-Rethel uses the Kantian expression 'transcendental unity of self-consciousness' originates, he maintains, in Greece. However, his definition of the 'Kantian transcendental subject' as 'a fetish *[81]* concept of the capital function of money' raises a problem that he does not confront, namely that the capital function of money was much less developed in the sixth century BCE than it was in the time of Kant.[11] And indeed there are, accordingly, significant differences between the Kantian transcendental subject and the subject as conceived by Greek philosophy. Nevertheless, I will demonstrate that it is possible to relate the genesis of the ancient Greek idea of a unitary and transcendent

[9] Sohn-Rethel 1978: 77.

[10] Adorno 1973: 177–81.

[11] For antiquity Marx denied the existence of the capitalist mode of production (Marx 1981: 449–50) or even of 'capital' (Marx 1973: 512–13; 1981: 953), but allowed nevertheless that there was 'money-capital' (Marx 1976: 247–8; 1978: 554) or 'commercial capital' (Marx 1981: 449–50). See further n. 12 below, and the *mise au point*, with further references to Marx, by de Ste Croix 1981: 504–5.

self-consciousness to the historical process of *monetisation*.[12] This account has an origin independent of Sohn-Rethel, but converges with his theory of the genesis of the consciousness of self.

Sohn-Rethel was not aware of the confirmatory evidence from literary and philosophical texts that I will adduce. And his knowledge of the history of the period was also rather limited. And so I must begin by briefly supplementing and correcting his historical account. First, commodity exchange was in fact, long before the invention of coinage, practised in the ancient Near East, without obtaining the central position that it did in the Greek polis. For Marx, commodity exchange involves money. But this principle requires historical qualification. In surveying what we now know about the economies of the ancient Near East before the Greek adoption of coinage, we can find much that we would call commodity exchange (rather than barter) that does not involve what we can confidently call money. In ancient Egypt, for instance, commodities might be exchanged according to a measure of value but without the transfer of money: for example, the exchange of a bed for wine might be based on their each being worth the same weight of silver, but without any actual silver being involved and without silver being a *general* measure of value. Silver here performs only a single money function (as a measure of value), although not even generally, and so without being money in the full sense. In Mesopotamia commodities were often exchanged for specific amounts of silver or grain, which nevertheless lacked most of what we regard as the features of money: they were neither a general means of payment or exchange, nor a general *[82]*
measure of value, nor issued by the state. The first society in which all these features were combined into a single entity (coined money), producing the first ever words for and thought about *money*, is the Greek polis of the sixth century. Coined money is something new: the single, ubiquitous and *visible* embodiment of universal exchange-value. Were we nevertheless to retain the absolute connection between 'money' (or money functions) and commodity exchange, that would not diminish this crucial distinction between the Greeks and their predecessors.

12 The monetisation of the Greek polis was limited (from the standpoint of contemporary capitalism) in the sense that money was not widely used for certain purposes: it was barely used for investment in production and the purchase of land; wage-labour and instruments of credit were relatively undeveloped; and so on. Nevertheless, in the ancient polis money functioned as what Marx called 'money-capital' or 'commercial capital' (see n. 11 above), as well as being pervasive in the sense of being a universal means of payment and exchange, and a universal measure and store of value (as well as being issued by the state). For my argument here this is all that is required.

True, it has often been assumed – and occasionally even argued – that money (mainly uncoined silver) was used in the ancient Near East centuries before it was used by the Greeks. However – and this is my second historical point – I have reviewed the evidence advanced for this claim and argued that (on any usefully narrow definition of money) this is not so.[13] The link between money and abstract thought can therefore be retained.

Third, the link is reinforced by the down-dating of the invention of coinage. Sohn-Rethel reported a date of circa 680 BCE, but opinion has now shifted to a date towards the end of the seventh century, shortly before 'philosophy' began at Miletos.[14]

A final preliminary is necessary. My argument may seem economically deterministic or reductive. It has been put to me by a reader of this paper that 'a materialistic understanding and explanation of such rarefied things as "consciousness" and "subjectivity" … should take into account the whole complexity of the conditions of life and production in which human beings find themselves'. Well, of course it should.[15] But a materialist understanding of the development of the ancient Greek subject is in its infancy. If we restrict ourselves to setting out 'the whole complexity' all at once, we will never get started. What I set out here is a strand that will eventually, I hope, be woven into a rich tapestry.

The Homeric *Psyche*

The earliest Western literature, the Homeric epics, acquired their definitive form through being written down in the sixth century after a long period of largely oral transmission. The society they represent belongs, at least to
[83] some extent, to the eighth century. It is an anthropologically consistent society, in which the state is weak and the reciprocal exchange of gifts and favours is socially central. It is a pre-monetary society that shows signs of being about to produce money.

It was long ago pointed out that in Homer there is no word for the whole of consciousness, corresponding to our 'mind' or 'subject', combining thought, emotion and the origination of movement.[16] There are instead various organs, each with a separate mental function.

13 Prehistoric Mesopotamia and some of the surrounding areas are rich in economic data, mainly in the form of clay tablets recording economic transactions. Hence the modern attempts to reconstruct Mesopotamian economies, which I have critiqued in Seaford 2004c: 318–37.

14 See, for example, Bammer and Muss 1996: 89; Seaford 2004c: 129–31.

15 I have gone some way along the road of integrating politics, religion, material conditions, economics, philosophy and literature in Seaford 2004c.

16 Snell 1953: 1–22.

True, there is a word for 'soul' (*psyche*), but it has no relationship to the body other than to leave it at loss of consciousness (fainting or death). It is this separability of the *psyche* from the body, as a second self within the body, that much later qualified it to be – most influentially in Plato – something like our 'subject' (in a pre-Cartesian state), the comprehensive centre of the person, the site or organ of unitary consciousness that originates decision and action. Alas, classical scholars have been more inclined to view this development as lexical than as historical.

Inasmuch as the Homeric *psyche* is what departs from the body at death (and is then a shade in Hades), it may be valued as what keeps a person alive, as when Hektor runs – and Akhilleus pursues him – 'for the *psyche* of Hektor'.[17] Now there is one passage in which this value of the *psyche* is described in a way whose significance for the later development of the notion has been ignored. Akhilleus is refusing to fight because of the dishonour done him by Agamemnon, who then attempts to persuade him back to the battle by numerous gifts. In refusing the gifts, Akhilleus claims that even vast wealth is not equivalent in value (ἀντάξιος) to his *psyche*, not even all the wealth of Troy or of the temple of Apollo at Delphi. The gifts are 'hateful' to him.[18] We can easily make sense of this. It would be foolish to exchange life for wealth. But the passage is unique in Homer in explicitly conferring value on the *psyche*.

What is this value? 'Not *antaxios*' implies that the *psyche* is more valuable than (and so comparable to) a mass of material goods. On the other hand, because the *psyche* is invisible as well as fundamental, a different kind of thing from material goods, 'not *antaxios*' implies that its value is incommensurable – beyond equivalence – with material goods as such. This combination of the *psyche* being both more valuable than all goods and beyond them implies that it transcends them. (By 'transcendent' I mean possessing power or value that is separate (from beyond) but comprehensive). [*84*]

What has produced this, the earliest focus on the desirability of the *psyche*? It is the isolation of Akhilleus arising from the breakdown of economic relations. More specifically, Akhilleus' refusal of the gifts belongs to a *breakdown of reciprocity*. Voluntary requital (reciprocity) forms a dominant code of social relations in the society described or implied by Homeric epic. Akhilleus states that the distribution of rewards (in return for fighting) has been unfair, that no amount of gifts will be effective, and

[17] *Il.* 22.161.
[18] *Il.* 9.401–5, 378.

even that he does not *need* the honour of gifts – because he is honoured by the distribution of *Zeus*.

In many pre-monetary societies the gift may continue to be associated with its donor, and thereby embody interpersonal connections – of honour, loyalty, gratitude, friendship, subservience and alliance of various kinds. This phenomenon is found in Homer.[19] But Akhilleus isolates himself from such interpersonal connections and from their material embodiment. His identity is now shaped not at all by the relations (of honour etc.) embodied in gifts from mortals, but rather by the unspecified honour provided by Zeus. This transcendent abstract honour seals his social isolation, in which his invisible *psyche* is imagined both in terms of economic value and yet as transcending it.

But why is his *psyche* so valuable? The reason he gives is that 'cattle and sheep may be seized, and tripods and horses obtained, whereas the *psyche* of a man cannot be seized or taken so as to come back once it will pass the barrier of his teeth'.[20] The word translated 'pass' here is in fact ἀμείψεται, 'exchange'. The inevitable implication, in this context, is that the *psyche* is lost by an exchange-*transaction*. Whereas animals and tripods may be lost and gained, the *psyche* is lost by an 'exchange' in which nothing ever returns. The *psyche* here is not the real person, as for instance in the later ideas of it being imprisoned or entombed in the body, for instance in Plato. It is rather a *possession*. As such it belongs entirely to a single owner, from whom – in contrast to gifts and plunder – it is separable irreversibly.

In the heroic world, goods circulate by plunder and by gift-giving, which elicit reciprocity (negative and positive): the persistent association of goods (plundered or given) with their original owner demands a reciprocal act (of plunder, of a favour or of a gift). But this is the system of reciprocity that has, in the *Iliad*, broken down: Akhilleus fought, but was not given his rightful share of the plunder. And to accept the gifts now would be to subordinate himself to their donor. He therefore isolates himself altogether from the power of goods, and accordingly reaches towards a conception of his own *psyche* as a possession [85] that is isolated from – and contrasts with – the kind of goods that in the heroic world circulate as plunder and as gifts. He rejects reciprocity in favour of a possession of a different kind – of transcendent value, entirely his own and entirely separable from him.

Such absolute separation does not happen to the gift, in which the identity of the donor persists: object and subject seem to interpenetrate. Money,

[19] E.g. *Od.* 21.11–41.
[20] *Il.* 9.406–9.

by contrast, can function only by being absolutely transferable, and so must be imaginable as absolutely separate from all people and all goods. It is as a result of this practical imperative of absolute separation that the sphere of monetised exchange, once it has become all-pervasive, seems to constitute a second nature. Purchase seems governed by objective necessity, impersonal equivalence of value, with the result that the separation of the transactors from commodities and money – and therefore from each other – is absolute. There is polarisation: to the absolute (isolated) objectivity of commodities and money corresponds the absolute (isolated) subjectivity of the transactors.

The historical importance of what Akhilleus says is that – though still in the pre-monetary world – he prefigures this polarisation. At one pole, in rejecting the interpersonal reciprocity in which reward does not correspond to contribution, he thereby implicitly favours the impersonal equivalence of value. At the other pole, in isolating himself from the social connectivity of gifts, he values instead his own *psyche*, which consequently seems more like an inner self than it does anywhere else in Homer. From the breakdown of the reciprocal economy emerges the isolated self-identical unitary individual.[21] In putting himself beyond the influence of gift exchange, Akhilleus implies the idea of an autonomous inner *psyche*, which contrasts with – and is isolated from – gift exchange (true though it is that it cannot be beyond *all* interaction: its only form of 'exchange' is irrecoverable loss).

Akhilleus' *psyche* is imagined as a possession that is subject to absolute loss, and that is greater in value than a mass of goods, which it moreover transcends. The earliest known approximation to an inner self or subject is obtained by imagining it in terms of transcendent exchange-value that is absolutely alienable. As such, it is analogous to the abstract value of *money*. Although he does not of course express any preference for commerce over reciprocity, and indeed rejects the influence of *all* goods, Akhilleus' isolation does nevertheless prefigure the isolation of the subject of monetised exchange. But how, given that there is no money in the *Iliad*, is such prefiguration possible? Because the [*86*] *Iliad* reached its final form in the sixth century (albeit containing much material from much earlier), but in its nostalgia for the heroic age, excluded – or rather declined to include – *explicit* mention of a number of contemporary developments such as

[21] Compare Marx's observation in the *Grundrisse* on the 'Robinsonades': 'In this society of free competition, the individual appears detached from the natural bonds etc. which in earlier historical periods make him the accessory of a definite and limited human conglomerate' (Marx 1973: 84).

money, writing and many functions of the polis. But this does not mean that it excluded issues accompanying these developments.[22]

What do I mean here by isolation? Whereas gifts tend to leave donor connected to recipient, a monetised transaction concerns only the equivalence of money with goods, and *qua* monetised transaction leaves the transactors unrelated to each other.[23] Each transactor is completely separated both from what the other transactor has received and from the transactor him- or herself. The monetised transactor is *individualised.* What is more, the ease with which coined money is stored, preserved, concealed, transported and exchanged makes it highly suitable for possession and use by the autonomous individual. The gift, like, for example, kinship or the communal possession of land, unites individuals, whereas money tends to make them autonomous.

Sohn-Rethel analyses commodity exchange as the reciprocal exclusion of ownership, which he calls 'practical solipsism'. With this analysis of the *form* of commodity exchange my account of the isolating *practice* of monetised commodity exchange converges.

Money and *Psyche*

The first extant mention of the human *psyche* in philosophical cosmology is by the Milesian Anaximenes, active in about the middle of the sixth century. He maintained that the single substrate of the cosmos is air, and that 'as the *psyche* being air holds us together, so does *pneuma* [wind or breath] enclose the whole cosmos'.[24] But very little survives of Milesian philosophical cosmology. The earliest extant descriptive focus on the *psyche* as a unitary site of consciousness is in the 120 or so short fragments from the lost book of Heraclitus of Ephesus, active about a generation after Anaximenes. [87]

For Heraclitus the cosmos is 'an ever-living fire' (DK 22 B 30).[25] 'All things are an exchange for fire and fire for all things, like gold for goods

[22] For issues in Homer accompanying the development of the polis see Seaford 1994b.

[23] Compare the opening words of Georg Simmel's essay on prostitution: 'Only transactions for money have that character of a purely momentary relationship which leaves no traces, as is the case with prostitution. With the giving of money, one completely withdraws from the relationship; one has settled matters more completely than by giving an object, which, by its contents, its selection, and its use maintains a wisp of the personality of the giver' (Simmel 1971: 121).

[24] DK 13 B 2. There is scholarly disagreement about the precise words used by Anaximenes, but the general sense is almost certainly his.

[25] The references are to the fragments as ordered by DK.

and goods for gold.' (B 90).[26] This exchange is elsewhere specified as a cycle, in which the elements are transformed into each other (B 31a). The *psyche* is composed of fire, and is accordingly subject to the same cycle of transformation: 'for *psychai* [souls] it is death to become water, for water death to become earth, water becomes from earth, and *psyche* from water' (B 36).

B 90 is not the only fragment in which the transformation is envisaged as *commercial* exchange: 'it is difficult to fight *thumos* (anger or strong desire), for what it wants it buys at the price of *psyche*' (B 85). It is difficult to fight *thumos* because it is driven by the fieriness of the *psyche*, the loss (extinguishing, transformation) of which is envisaged as *expenditure*.

These transformations, and indeed everything that happens in the cosmos, happen according to the *logos* (B 1). *Logos* could mean 'word', but also – as here – a measure or formula that ensures balanced order (B 31b). In the fifth century it is found meaning a monetary account, and probably had this meaning already in the sixth.[27] Projected onto the cosmos is the *logos*, the ubiquitous monetised abstraction (for example, one vase is worth six drachmas) that somehow ensures the peaceful transformation of goods into and from money and so seems to regulate the entire economic cycle. But how does the *logos* exercise its power? Just as money, which underlies all goods and embodies numerical abstraction, drives the unceasing economic cycle, so fire, which underlies all things and embodies the *logos*, drives the unceasing cosmological cycle.

The *psyche*, being composed of fire, partakes of the agency and the *logos* that are embodied in fire. Accordingly, 'the dry *psyche* is wisest and best' (B 118), and 'the limits of the *psyche* you would not find, even by travelling along every path: so deep a *logos* does it have' (B 45). The *psyche* here occupies an unlimited space. Hence perhaps 'I sought for myself' (B 101). Why unlimited? Another unsolved puzzle is 'of the *psyche* there is a *logos* increasing itself' (B 115). Why the self-increase? When the six drachmas received for the vase are used to make or buy two such vases for resale, and so on, then the economic process seems to have no limit. In general the Greeks are, from Solon in the sixth century to Aristotle in the fourth, struck by the *unlimitedness* of the desire for, and accumulation of, money, which seems itself unlimited.[28] Further, the cycle of [*88*] commercial

[26] This was not in fact true of gold. There was no Greek word meaning precisely 'money', and 'gold' was one of the words used for it.

[27] Seaford 2004c: 231.

[28] Seaford 2004c: 165–9. In a passage quoted at length by Marx (1976: 253) to illustrate that 'the movement of capital is limitless', Aristotle distinguishes economics from chrematistics. The former

exchange may seem to have neither temporal nor spatial limit, especially when vigorously promoted – as in the lifetime of Heraclitus – by the recent invention of coinage. These dynamic functions belong to money in its role of what Marx called 'money-capital' or 'commercial capital'.[29] They seem to be regulated and caused by the *logos*, which accordingly seems to be both unlimited and self-increasing.

This unlimited, self-increasing *logos* seems to regulate the *cosmic* transformation, but is located by Heraclitus also in the *psyche*, which participates in cosmic transformation. The *logos* (in each *psyche*) is not limited (to each *psyche*). 'Although the *logos* is communal, the many live as if having private understanding' (B 2). 'The waking share one common world, whereas the sleeping turn away each into the private' (B 89). Thinking is communal to all, and all things happen according to the *logos*, according to which all things are one (B 1, 50, 113, 114).[30]

Each individual *psyche* is a unitary substance with depth and intelligence. And yet Heraclitus emphatically privileges the communal aspect of cognition over its private aspect. It may seem paradoxical that the first extant account of the individual inner substance insists on its communality in the context of the impersonal unity of all things. But it is through the *communal* abstraction of *logos* that each *psyche* is a unity. This reflects a historical fact: it was the unprecedented unification of (almost) all goods by an impersonal abstract substrate (money) that was in the lifetime of Heraclitus promoting unprecedented autonomy for the individual.[31] Individual subjectivity is shaped by the new communal abstract measure of the objective. The relation of money to goods is external and comprehensively controlling, and so may be described as transcendent. Just as in the surviving fragment of Anaximenes, *psyche* and *cosmos* are each held together by the invisible substrate of all else (air), so in Heraclitus *psyche* and *cosmos* are each unified by the *logos* embodied in the fire of which they consist. In neither case is this (as scholars sometimes maintain) simply because they are imagined in terms of each other: it is rather *[89]* because both are imagined in terms of the new all-unifying abstract transcendence of money.

is limited to procuring true wealth, i.e. use-values, 'for the amount of property that is needed for procuring a good life is not unlimited'. But the making of money (chrematistics) is unlimited (Arist. *Pol.* 1.8–9). This corresponds to Marx's distinction between C-M-C and M-C-M^1.

[29] See nn. 11 and 12 above.

[30] Money creates a communal sphere irrespective of such fundamental divisions as that between citizen and slave. Moreover, as Aristotle points out (*Eth. Nic.* 1133a17–21), commodity exchange requires the parties to it to be equalised.

[31] Compare the similar complementarity set out by Hegel in *Philosophy of Right* (1952: §182).

Once exchanges become generally monetised, the vital necessity for money to be absolutely separable from its possessors creates a sphere that seems both autonomous and impersonal. But this sphere or 'second nature' also seems all-pervasive, and so may seem to constitute an impersonal *cosmos*, entirely reified and devoid of subjectivity. And yet of course subjectivity itself may, paradoxically, seem all-pervasive and potent, especially now that money bestows a sense of autonomy on an individual universalising subject. In Heraclitus this contradiction is resolved by both cosmos and *psyche* being composed of fire, in which *logos* is embodied. With the death of the individual, whose self-sufficiency is an illusion, the fire of his or her *psyche* re-enters the mass of fire undergoing the cosmic cycle. Fundamentally the *psyche* is impersonal (composed of fire) and subject to the impersonal *logos*.

I could give numerous further instances of death as an economic transaction, and generally of the association of *psyche* with money. But I will confine myself to a remarkable papyrus discovered in 1962 but only fully published recently (the 'Derveni Papyrus'). It contains a fourth-century allegorising commentary on an 'Orphic' mythological poem. Here is the comment on the mythological detail that all things were once absorbed into Zeus.

> In saying this he makes clear that mind [*nous*] itself being alone is worth everything, just as if everything else were nothing. For it would not be possible for them to exist, if the things were without the mind. And in the verse following this he said that mind is worth everything: 'And (now) he is king of all and will be afterwards.' It is clear that mind and king of all is the same thing.[32]

The unification of all diversity is here equated in our three spheres of cosmos, mind and value.

The impersonal and seemingly autonomous power of money actually belongs to its owner, and so there may – from the perspective of interpersonal relations – seem to be little difference between money and its owner. The new subject – detached by monetisation from (in principle) all goods and persons – becomes constituted instead by the invisible (abstract) unification of diversity that permits her practical autonomy. For it is through an abstraction, the abstract unity of the diversity of goods, that money bestows power on the autonomous individual. The unifying power of money to control diversity depends on the active desire of its individual owner for the

[32] Laks and Most 1997: 16–17. [= *PDerveni* XVI.8–15 = §§50–51K]

diverse goods, but seems to belong to the money itself: it constitutes both money and subject. We [90] would accordingly expect mind and money to be imagined in terms of each other. And that is what we find: money is imagined to act, and the *psyche* or mind is imagined as money. Philo of Alexandria, for instance, calls the *psyche* 'currency', its mark the eternal *logos* impressed by the seal of God.[33] The coin and its owner (i.e. its owner's body) each embodies an invisible essence (value, *psyche*) that is present in others but may be imagined as self-identical within each individual – i.e. as separate from the social process by which it is formed.

To conclude, the *psyche* is imagined as an autonomous ('self-moving')[34] transcendent abstraction that controls and unifies diversity, may be irrevocably expended and is in a sense impersonal. In all this it resembles money, whose practical transcendent abstraction it is that shapes the ideas of cosmos and of inner self. The new unified autonomy of the individual mind is imagined in a form shaped by what made it possible.

Reincarnation

In a fifth-century version of the view advanced by Akhilleus, 'this is for mortals the only expenditure that once expended cannot be recovered, the mortal *psyche*, whereas there are means of acquiring money',[35] the words for 'expend' here (ἀνάλωμα, ἀναλίσκειν) are regularly used both for expending money and for killing. The expenditure of the *psyche* (death) and of money (purchase) are imagined as analogous because both involve absolute separation from the possessor. But the soul, unlike money, cannot be recovered. In this respect my analogy between the soul of Akhilleus and money also contains a significant difference. From the old perspective of gift exchange, in which Akhilleus is still partly situated, the idea that two different pieces of precious metal are in fact the same thing (money) would be incomprehensible. What informs the words of Akhilleus is the breakdown of reciprocity that results in the isolation of the individual for whom – in this case because his fighting was dishonoured rather than being rewarded – value is withdrawn into himself rather than being dispersed among gifts that embody the identities of himself and of others. With the breakdown of reciprocity, for Akhilleus

[33] Seaford 2004c: 297–8.
[34] The initiation of movement (of itself and of other things) is, according to Aristotle (*De An.* 403b29ff., 404b30, 405b11–12, 31ff.), the primary feature of some early accounts of the *psyche*.
[35] Eur. *Supp.* 775–7.

death in battle would be the absolute and unreciprocated loss of his soul, i.e. of all value. [91]

But the breakdown of reciprocity involved also (in the Greek polis at least) the post-Homeric growth of money, which confirmed the isolation of the individual by enabling absolute ownership of – and so absolute separation from – his or her goods. This isolation and absolute separation were prefigured by the withdrawal of transcendent value into the individual soul of Akhilleus, which is therefore analogous to money. But post-Homeric awareness of the circulation of money produced awareness also of its (socially unifying) sameness in different pieces of metal, and hence of the difference between expenditure of soul and of money. This did not mean, however, that the conceptualisation of the soul and of money lose contact with each other. The *circulation* of money influences the idea of the passage of the *disembodied* soul, as we shall now see.

The origin of knowledge *a priori* was of as much concern to Plato as to Kant and Sohn-Rethel. In his *Meno* Plato questions an uneducated young slave about geometrical figures, and thereby shows that the boy possesses mathematical knowledge that he did not learn in this life and so must have known in a previous life. What for Sohn-Rethel originates in the necessary exclusion of all empirical content by real abstraction is for Plato to be explained by the doctrine of reincarnation, as taught – he states – by priests, priestesses and poets. These priests and priestesses are those of mystery cult, a rite of passage that – centring around a rehearsal of death – imparted the doctrine of reincarnation, and in various ways profoundly influenced both Heraclitus and Plato. The *psyche* subject to reincarnation is separable from the body though not necessarily incorporeal. That is to say, the explicitly incorporeal (abstract) *psyche* in Plato does not spring from the idea of reincarnation alone.

It is not coincidental that the earliest extant reference to reincarnation is also the earliest text in which the *psyche* seems to constitute the person him- or herself (rather than merely, as with Akhilleus, the valuable *possession* of a person). Xenophanes (an older contemporary of Heraclitus) refers to Pythagoras recognising the *psyche* of a friend in the cry of a dog being beaten (B 7). Heraclitus' cycle of cosmological transformation was influenced by the circulation of money, but also by reincarnation. His imagination merges the observable cycle of cosmological transformation with both the traditional cycle of reincarnation and the relatively new cycle of monetisation.

The reincarnated *psyche* is not self-identical. It may have from its previous identity memories that may be re-awakened – Plato emphasises – by recollection. In some cultures belief in reincarnation produces the idea of more than one soul within the same body, and may be used to explain psychic depth. For Heraclitus, too, the individual consciousness is not self-identical. Fire is [92] transformed into the cosmological elements without losing its identity as fire (embodying *logos*), and the 'death' of the fiery *psyche* is in fact no more than a transition, a stage in its participation in this cyclical transformation. The Greek doctrine of reincarnation itself sometimes took the form of the cyclical transition of the *psyche* through the cosmological elements. This resembles the Heraclitean (B 36) cyclical transformation of the fiery *psyche* into the other cosmological elements (while in a sense continuing to be fire). But there is a difference. In reincarnation the same individual *psyche* occupies various bodies, or passes through various elements. But the Heraclitean *psyche* is subject to *transformation* into the various elements, and is at all times linked to other *psychai* – and indeed to the whole cosmos – by the communal *logos* embodied in the fire of which it is composed: in this respect individual identity and individual thought are for Heraclitus limited or even perhaps illusory. This difference from the normal idea of reincarnation expresses the transformation (from the transactors' perspective) of goods and money into each other. But it also corresponds to another feature of the mystic rite of passage, the transition from anxious individual isolation to belonging to a joyful group. The Dionysiac mystic initiate 'joins his *psyche* to the thiasos' (the initiated group).[36] Just as the communal basis of money is concealed from the individualised possessor of money, so the communal destination of the mystic transition is deliberately concealed – in the preliminary phase of mystic initiation – from the fearful and isolated initiand.

The result is an ambivalence. In Heraclitus the fire of which *psyche* is composed undergoes the cycle of transformations back into fire, but does this mean that the same *psyche* is reconstituted? In Plato the individual *psyche* is in general treated as self-identical, but in his *Timaeus* the *psyche* 'of the all' is mixed and divided into individual *psychai*.[37] The same ambivalence obtains in the monetary cycle. The separation of the purchaser from his or her money is (in contrast to gift-giving) absolute: purchase is self-contained. But inasmuch as all money is the same abstract thing, money expended is in a sense recoverable in the cycle of exchange.

This brief discussion of reincarnation suggests the need for an interdisciplinary research programme, of which I can here only provide a tentative

[36] Eur. *Bacch*. 75.
[37] Pl. *Ti*. 41d.

sketch. The belief in reincarnation has been widespread in various parts of the world. But in only two cultures has reincarnation been *ethicised*, in Greece and – at about the same time – in northern India: variations in well-being are explained by the ethical quality of previous lives. Even in the surviving [93] fragments of Heraclitus it seems that certain kinds of conduct determine the post-mortem condition of *psychai* (B 25, 63, 136).

There has been much speculation about whether Greek and Indian ideas of reincarnation influenced each other. But the crucial issue is rather this: reincarnation has generally been imagined as *within the lineage* (a soul passes from grandfather to grandson, for instance), but in both the ethicised cases the reincarnation occurs outside the lineage (extending even to animals) – what I dub *indiscriminate incarnation* as opposed to lineage reincarnation. Ethicisation and indiscriminate reincarnation are both exceptional, and go together. Moreover, in both Greece and India there is desire for *escape* from the cycle of reincarnation, whereas lineage reincarnation is generally regarded as positive. Why did this distinctive form of reincarnation occur only in Greece and northern India?

Where the unit of well-being or misery is the lineage, as a result of shared activity or shared property, the idea of reincarnation within the lineage is unproblematic. The passage of the (not incorporeal) soul is imagined as occurring within – or in close association with, or even as an expression of – the manifest physical bond between members of the lineage. But when different members of the lineage vary greatly in well-being, notably in wealth or status because pursuing different activities, then it becomes less easy to believe that the same soul or souls are being transmitted within the lineage. The diversity of well-being requires an explanation. The explanation may be provided in part by ethicisation, which may however by itself be insufficient: given the solidarity of the kinship group, any perceived ethical variety of previous lives within it may not be sufficient to explain the diversity of well-being in current lives. But if the soul may have come from anywhere outside the lineage, then there is no difficulty in imagining the delinquency or virtue needed to explain what may be considerable diversity of individual well-being within the lineage. It is the break-up of the solidarity of the lineage, with wealth and status coming to be possessed by the individual rather than by the lineage, that promotes the idea of ethicised indiscriminate reincarnation.

A study by Obeyesekere has much advanced the comparative understanding of reincarnation in Greece and northern India.[38] He is averse

[38] Obeyesekere 2002.

to any materialist explanation of the parallels. But a factor in the break-up of lineage solidarity was surely the rapid development of commerce from about the sixth century, accompanied or followed by monetisation, in the Greek polis and the Ganges valley. We have already emphasised the individualising effect of monetisation. The individual becomes isolated from his or her kinship group by *[94]* his or her possession of money and by the unitary consciousness that goes with it. In Greece this isolation is expressed above all in tragedy, the genre whose astonishing genesis and cultural pre-eminence occurred shortly after the introduction and rapid spread of coinage in Attica. Money is a frequent theme of tragedy, and the extreme isolation of the tragic individual from both kin and deity has no precedent in literature. Having discussed this elsewhere,[39] here I add merely the words of a father in Euripides who refuses to die to save his son: 'we should live with one *psyche*, not two'.[40]

The monetised individual is isolated, but depends on interaction. How is this paradoxical interaction of the isolated individual to be envisaged? His unitary consciousness is shaped by the abstract unification of diversity that is effective (as money) only by virtue of its persistence as (self-identical) abstract value through the cycle of transformations (exchange). Through this persistence it acquires universal power, and so is projected onto the cosmos. And so the interaction of the individual unitary consciousness with the cosmos is imagined as participation in the persistence of abstraction through the cosmic cycle of transformations. Hence the analogy between indiscriminate reincarnation and the monetised cycle of exchange: in both cases what is abstracted is projected onto a cosmic cycle in which it may be indiscriminately transformed. The departure of the soul (death) may be imagined as a monetary transaction. And in various Greek texts the reincarnated soul is said be *paying a penalty*. Whereas lineage reincarnation occurs within a specific lineage, the social universality of unlimited monetary circulation is projected as the cosmic cyclicality of indiscriminate reincarnation.

The resemblance of a child to his or her parent or grandparent, and his or her physical origin in them, may confirm the association of reincarnation (including any sense of having a multiple soul) with the physical continuity of the lineage. But indiscriminate reincarnation is unlikely to be imagined as bringing to its new life any of its old body or any memory of its past life. More suitable therefore is the idea of the soul as *unitary abstract*

[39] Seaford 2004c: 305–15.
[40] Eur. *Alc.* 712.

substance. Monetisation promotes indiscriminate reincarnation not only by dissolving the solidarity of lineage but also by providing the idea of the soul as unitary abstract substance.

To conclude, the advantage of envisaging monetisation as a precondition for indiscriminate reincarnation is that it provides for it both a cause (individualisation) and a model (the all-pervasive cycle of abstract substance). But all this requires systematic investigation, to include a comparison of the [95] Greek cycle of monetised reincarnation with the role of *karman* ('karma') in fuelling the cycle of reincarnation in India.

Parmenides and Plato

The Heraclitean circulation of fire as substrate through the constant exchange or transformation of elements regulated by the abstract *logos* is a projection of the constant circulation of money as substrate through the exchange or transformation of goods regulated by the abstract *logos*. For his younger contemporary Parmenides, by contrast, all that exists is 'One', invariant in time and space (eternal, unchanging, unmoving, homogeneous), abstract, self-sufficient, limited, to be perceived by the mind not by the senses.

Money is valuable only in payment and exchange. As Marx observed of money, 'if I want to cling to it, it evaporates in my hand to become a mere phantom of real wealth'. And so, because it is also possessed only by being *withheld* from payment and exchange, money is a 'contradiction'.[41] It is money both by virtue of being changed into all goods and by virtue of permanently maintaining its unitary abstract identity. Both these opposed features of money seem essential to it. Heraclitean cosmology is a projection of the former, of the unlimited cycle of monetised exchange regulated by abstraction (*logos*). But Parmenidean being, the 'One', is a projection of the latter, of monetary substance abstracted completely from exchange, and is therefore limited,[42] unitary, abstract, and temporally and spatially invariant. Greek *ousia*, 'substance' or 'being', can also mean 'property'. This summarises an argument that I have set out elsewhere.[43] My concern here is to develop the argument with respect to the relation between subject and cosmos.

[41] Marx 1973: 233–4.

[42] This opposition between Parmenides and Heraclitus corresponds to the 'antagonism between the quantitative limits of money and its qualitative boundlessness' described in Marx 1976: 227–32.

[43] Seaford 2004c: 231–65.

Parmenides' extant fragments have been rightly hailed as containing the first known chain of deductive reasoning to demonstrate what exists (as opposed to dogmatic pronouncements). How is it that the same thinker produced both the deductive innovation and the odd idea of the 'One'? How were these innovations possible historically? What and whence were the preconceptions that by supplying the premises of the deduction shaped its odd conclusion? Modern scholarship generally ignores these vital questions, [96] focusing instead on the impressive chain of reasoning. Aristotle on the other hand notes, about Parmenides and his followers, that the conclusions seem to follow from the arguments but that to believe them is 'close to insanity'.[44]

For Sohn-Rethel, Parmenides is important as the first 'pure thinker', whose abstract thought expresses the social postulates of the exchange abstraction (especially that no physical change occurs in the commodities) divorced from all empirical reality. The concepts of the abstract intellect, separated though they are from all traces of their empirical origin, originate in the physical act of commodity exchange (involving real abstraction), and so 'constitute an all-encompassing pattern or framework of nature in the abstract'. Further, as a result of this separation the abstract intellect 'emerges with a peculiar normative sense all its own, serving as its "logic"'. This emergence involves both 'self-alienation' and 'self-direction'.[45]

It was his analysis of the form of commodity exchange that brought Sohn-Rethel to Parmenides. The detail of Parmenides' argument, which Sohn-Rethel did not examine, does in fact help to confirm and develop his insight. Parmenides gives the appearance of starting from premises that are self-evident. What is must *be*, it cannot also *not* be.[46] But in asserting what seems to be a truth of logic he is in fact attacking the Ionian cosmologies exemplified by Anaximenes, for whom air may be air that is *not* air (for example, air condensed as earth), and by Heraclitus, for whom the *kosmos* is an ever-living *logos*-embodying fire that is nevertheless constantly being transformed from and into other elements. Such cosmologies are projections of the universal semi-abstract substance (money) embedded in circulation. When Parmenides rejects them, and insists instead that 'it must be completely or not at all' (DK 28 B 8.11), and so (because the latter is impossible) that 'all is full of being' (B 8.24), this is a projection

[44] Arist. *Gen. corr.* 325a18–20.
[45] Sohn-Rethel 1978: 65–70.
[46] DK 28 B 6.4–9; B 7.1–5; B 8.15–16.

of universal abstract (monetary) value abstracted even from its material embodiment in circulating money.

Why does Parmenides take abstraction to this extreme? We must here introduce the Greek privileging of *self-sufficiency*. This is prominent across the range of economics, politics, ethics, metaphysics and theology. We find, for instance in Aristotle, the principle that 'it is the mark of an *eleutheros* [free man, gentleman] not to live for the benefit of another', the general assumption that 'self-sufficiency is an end and what is best', and the implication that the individual household should be as self-sufficient as possible.[47] [*97*]

In contrast to the ideology of capitalism, self-sufficiency was a central tenet of a static propertied class whose main form of property was land (generally inherited). The land has monetary value and yields money, but is not a capital investment producing profit through the purchase of free labour. The monetary abstraction promotes freedom from preoccupation with its static material origin. Hence the combination – characteristic of Greek philosophy – of abstraction with self-sufficiency.

Parmenides was said to have been 'of illustrious family and wealth'. His vision is intensely individualist: he describes how he was carried *alone* in a chariot to the house of the goddess who revealed to him the truth (B 1). But he is not an eccentric mystic. His mode of thought is frequently manifest in the no less aristocratic Plato, in whose *Timaeus*, for instance, the (personal) universe is constructed according to the principles that the homogeneous is better than the unlike and that self-sufficiency is better than lack.[48]

Economic self-sufficiency was an ideal already in the pre-monetary world of Hesiod. Subsequent monetary abstraction increased the possibility of individual autonomy. Further, for money to be freely transferable it must seem self-identical, independent of any internal connection with people or goods, and this may seem to enhance the desired self-sufficiency of its possessor.[49] This sense is of course illusory, because in fact money is valuable only in exchange. But the illusion is reinforced by yet another factor, the ideological desirability of distance from the vulgarity and insecurity of commerce. The abstraction that originates in commodity exchange turns its back on empirical reality for ideological as well

47 Arist. *Rh.* 1367a32; *Pol.* 1252b35, 1256a4–58b56.
48 Pl. *Ti.* 33d.
49 Seaford 2004c: 246–9.

as practical reasons, and the ideology is in turn sustained by the seemingly self-sufficient abstraction.

Parmenides' 'One' is, accordingly, self-sufficient. It remains fixed within limits, and 'is not lacking – if it were, it would lack everything' (B 8.26–33). It is money *in circulation* that by contrast has no limits and 'lacks everything'. This self-sufficiency seems to belong to the fullness of its being that was established earlier. But how – in the deductive chain – was this fullness of being established? Partly – we saw – by what seemed logically self-evident (what is *is*). And partly by *introspection.*

There are, we are told, only two paths of enquiry, one that *it is*, the other that *it is not*. The latter path is indiscernible, because 'you could not know what is not – that cannot be done – nor express it' (B 2.7–8), 'for the same thing is to think (to be thought of) and to be' (B 3). Similarly, 'what is there to say and think must needs be; for it is here for being, but nothing is not' (B 6.1–2). And [98] 'what is for thought is the same as why there is thought; for you will not find thinking without what is, in which thinking is expressed' (B 8.34–6).

Whatever the precise meaning of these passages, Parmenides is here finding *in the working of the mind* the fullness of being that – we maintain – expresses the ideologically overdetermined abstraction of monetary substance from exchange. The impossibility of non-being (i.e. the fullness of being) is discovered by introspection as a datum from which is deduced the nature of the One. But in fact what introspection discovers in the individual mind is the ideologically preconceived self-sufficiency of abstract being.

Parmenides' most detailed appeal to introspection is as follows: 'Look equally at absent things that are firmly present to the mind. For you will not cut off for yourself what *is* from holding to what *is*, neither scattering everywhere in every way in order nor drawing together' (B 4). This is directed against Heraclitus, whose orderly cycle of universal transformation is to be rejected as a result of introspection. The mind (*nous*) sees absent things, and so is clearly distinguished from perception. What exists is seen by imaginative introspection to be not only full but *unitary and continuous*, just as subsequently what exists is said to be 'one, continuous' (B 8.6).

We may object that in fact the mind may easily imagine plurality, diversity, change, scattering and drawing together. What is 'present' to it is unitary and continuous only by virtue of abstraction. Here again what introspection discovers is what the mind is predisposed to imagine. The preconceived unity of the mind is the premise from which the fullness and invariance of being can be deduced.

We argued above that the self-contained unity of both cosmos and individual consciousness is generated by the transcendent power of money that unites all goods and constitutes the individual. Now we see Parmenides deriving the abstract unity of being from the imagined unity of the contents of the individual mind. This suggests that the force giving rise to the first ever chain of deductive reasoning derives not just from the intellectual abstraction arising from commodity exchange, in the somewhat mysterious emergence of 'self-direction' indicated by Sohn-Rethel. It is not just that deduction is a natural path from one abstraction to another. Rather, here too we detect the ideology of economic self-sufficiency. The sameness of inner self and cosmos (both unified by monetary abstraction) allows the individual, made self-sufficient by money, to imagine within himself the abstract oneness of all that exists. The choice of deductive abstract reasoning expresses a sense of an overall unity, between the abstract unity of the subject (premise) and the abstract unity of its object – what exists (conclusion).

Our basic elements of the *psyche* – unification of diversity, assimilation to its abstract object, and assimilation to money – reappear in the lengthy and *[99]* sophisticated discussion of the *psyche* in Plato's *Phaedo*. On the one hand, when the *psyche* inquires through the senses, the result is confusing diversity: it may be 'dragged by the body into things that are always changing, and itself wanders about and is agitated'. But, on the other hand, it is invisible and separable from the body, and succeeds in being 'by itself' by gathering itself from all parts of the body.[50] It is assigned to the category of true being (invisible, uniform, grasped by reason, self-sufficient, changeless), to which it is also *assimilated*. For when it inquires 'by itself', it consorts with purity and unchanging being, to which it is 'akin', and through contact with them it becomes like them, and acquires *phronesis* ('wisdom'), which is the 'only right *nomisma* ('currency'), for which all those things [pleasures, pains, fears] must be exchanged'. Such a *psyche* will on death 'go away into what is like itself, invisible, divine, immortal and wise', and 'as the mystic initiates say, lives truly for the rest of time with the gods'.[51] It thereby obtains freedom from the cycle of reincarnation.[52]

[50] Pl. *Phd.* 67c, 80e, 83a. Cf. *Phdr.* 249b. Elsewhere I have discussed the neo-Platonic development of this idea from the perspective of psychic fragmentation in the Lacanian mirror-stage of infantile development (Seaford: 1998a).

[51] Pl. *Phd.* 79d, 69a, 81a. Plato also maintains that the guardians of his ideal state should have divine money in their souls: *Resp.* 3.416e.

[52] Pl. *Phd.* 81d–82a, 84ab, 114bc, *Phdr.* 249a.

Heraclitus, Parmenides and Plato each construct the subject out of traditional mystic doctrine influenced by monetisation, but each from a different ideological position. From Heraclitus' communal perspective, individual self-sufficiency is an illusion, and there is a kind of immortality in the engagement of the *psyche* in a cosmic cycle that consists of a synthesis of monetary circulation with mystic doctrine (reincarnation, merging of individual *psyche* in the group). But Parmenides from his individualist perspective assimilates subjectivity and being to each other: the unchanging self-sufficient abstract unity of being is deduced from the contents of the individual mind. In his prologue, Parmenides relates how he journeyed alone into the next world: it was there that the whole deductive argument was revealed to him, as to a lone mystic initiate, by a goddess.[53] In general the mystic initiand might be assimilated to what was revealed to him.[54] In such a context the abstract self-sufficient unity of the individual mind is at one with the abstract self-sufficient unity of being and seems to partake of its immortality.

The position of Plato falls between these two extremes. In some respects he resembles Heraclitus: there is in the *Timaeus* a *psyche* 'of the all', death is for the *[100]* *psyche* a transition, and for most *psychai* the transition is entry into a cosmic cycle (reincarnation). On the other hand, Plato maintains that in the transition the individual *psyche* retains its identity. And some *psychai* – those made pure by philosophy – are eternally freed from the cycle of reincarnation. This purification of the *psyche* takes the form – we noted – of the unification of diversity in which it is assimilated to abstract being. This brings Plato closer to Parmenides. Whereas for Parmenides the unity of being can be deduced from the unity of the individual mind, for Plato the mind is unified by contemplation of the abstract unity of being. Moreover, this wonderful mental unity transcends the passage between life and death: it may – like mathematical knowledge – derive from a previous life. The 'comprehension of what is said universally, arising from many sensations and being collected into one by reasoning', is due to recollection of an antenatal mystic initiation, in which we were 'ourselves whole' and saw 'whole visions'.[55] In Plato's *Symposium* the mystic vision of abstract self-sufficient unity culminates in the achievement of immortality.[56]

[53] Burkert 1969.
[54] Seaford 2004c: 227 n. 49.
[55] Pl. *Phdr.* 249b–250c.
[56] Pl. *Symp.* 212a.

Heraclitus represents, from a communal perspective, the necessity for money to circulate. Parmenides represents, from an individualist perspective, the need to imagine value as self-sufficient. It is left to Plato to imagine the ascent of the philosopher from the multiplicity of sense-perception to contemplation of self-sufficient abstract unity, by which his soul is assured escape from the cycle of exchange both in this life and the next. For Plato as for Heraclitus, *logos* orders both the (virtuous) soul and the cosmos.[57] But whereas in Heraclitus *logos* is translated as 'measure' or 'formula', in Parmenides and Plato it is translated as 'reason'. In Heraclitus, *logos* is the cosmic projection of (and so detachment from) the formula or measure governing monetised exchange. By acquiring the more general meaning 'reason', *logos* is further detached from the specificity of monetised exchange, and for Plato this allows a refuge for the virtuous soul in a cosmos that is ordered by *logos* but entirely detached from the cycle of exchange.

We have come a long way from the basic insights of Sohn-Rethel. His starting point was Marx on the commodity, from which he went on to perceive the importance of the real abstraction for Kantian epistemology, for Greek philosophy and even for modern science as a whole. My work on Greek *[101]* philosophy started independently of Sohn-Rethel, with the attempt to provide a historical account of its genesis, but has provided abundant new confirmation of his basic insights, and I hope helps to stimulate further consideration of these insights not only in the study of ancient Greece.[58]

POSTSCRIPT

See subsequently T. Noutsopolos, 'The role of money in Plato's *Republic*, book I: a materialistic approach', *Historical Materialism* 23.2 (2015), 131–56; A. Toscano, 'The detour of abstraction', *Diacritics* 43.2 (2015), 68–90. My work on money, notably Seaford 2004c, is discussed largely outside the sphere of Classics, in the blogosphere and across a range illustrated by Graeber 2011; R. Bellah, *Religion in Human Evolution* (Cambridge, MA: Belknap Press of Harvard University Press, 2011); D. Black, *The Philosophical Roots of Anti-Capitalism: Essays on History, Culture, and*

[57] Charles Taylor (1989: 124) argues that for Plato this excluded the development of the modern sense of the *inwardness* (internalisation) of the self, in which the order involved in the paramountcy of reason is *made*, not found, and of which the representative figure is Descartes.

[58] My thanks go to Chris Gill, Margherita Pascucci and the anonymous readers for valuable comments.

Dialectical Thought (Lanham, MD: Lexington Books, 2013); U. Duchrow, *Gieriges Geld: Auswege aus der Kapitalismusfalle – Befreiungstheologische Perspektiven* (Munich: Kösel, 2013); L. Murrey, *Nietzsche: The Meaning of Earth* (Bethlehem, PA: Lehigh University Press, 2015); G. Wagenfuhr, *Plundering Egypt: A Subversive Christian Ethic of Economy* (Eugene, OR: Cascade, 2016).

CHAPTER 18

The Fluttering Soul

I will argue, on the basis of passages of different kinds, that the idea of the dying soul as a fluttering bird (fearfully desiring to fly) was present in the rehearsal of death in mystic initiation. This will I hope in turn shed light on some of the passages. It is a small tribute to the large contribution made by Fritz Graf to our understanding of – *inter alia* – mystic initiation.

1. In a famous section of the *Phaedrus* Plato imagines the soul as winged. The wing naturally soars upwards (246c1, 248c1, etc.), and the soul that loses its wings or has them broken falls to earth (246c2, 248b3–c9). It then enters a series of incarnations, in which the soul of the philosopher can become winged and remember its closeness to god, 'undergoing a continuous initiation into perfect mysteries' (249c7–8). More specifically, he sees beauty on earth (a reminder of true beauty), becomes winged and is described as 'fluttering eagerly to fly upwards,[1] but unable to, looking upwards like a bird, and neglecting things on the ground' (249d6–9; cf. 255c7–d2). Thus some may attain to a dim memory of our initiation into 'the most blessed of initiations' (250b9). The first reaction of the 'recently initiated' (ἀρτιτελής), when he sees a beautiful face or body, is to shudder (ἔφριξε), along with some negative reactions (fear, sweat, fever), and then his soul re-grows its wings (251). Finally, philosophers when they die 'become winged and light' (256b4).

The idea that the soul leaves the body as a bird is implied by some Attic visual representations of the dead or dying.[2] Sophocles compares departing souls to birds (*OT* 174). And death himself is winged. In *Phaedrus* the idea takes a more complex form: the winged soul is initiated into divine mysteries, but may lose its wings, fall to earth, enter the body, re-grow

[1] ἀναπτερούμενος προθυμούμενος ἀναπτέσθαι.
[2] Vermeule 1979: 18–19.

its wings, remember its initiation, and on death fly with wings from the body. [407]

2. In *Phaedo* (108a–b) Plato maintains that the road to Hades has many forks and windings. This he infers 'from the rituals (ὅσια) and ceremonies (νόμιμα) practised here (on earth)', by which he surely means mystery cult.[3] He then distinguishes between on the one hand the orderly and wise soul, which follows its guide and understands its circumstances, and on the other the soul that is in a state of desire for the body. This latter kind of soul flutters (ἐπτοημένη) around the body for a long time, and after much resistance and suffering is led away by its appointed *daimon* and – on arriving at the place where the other souls are – is avoided by everybody and wanders around alone, whereas the pure soul finds gods as companions and guides.

In both the Platonic passages the fluttering of the soul derives from *tension*, albeit of opposite kinds: in *Phaedrus* the soul desires to fly from the body, but cannot, whereas in *Phaedo* it desires to stay with the body but cannot. Now the anxiety and suffering in the transition to the next world was rehearsed in mystic initiation.[4] The importance of mystic initiation in both our passages[5] suggests the possibility that the idea of the fluttering soul was present in mystic initiation. The possibility is strengthened by the following passages.

3. In Aristophanes' *Clouds*, which represents the initiation of Strepsiades into Socrates' school as mystic initiation,[6] Strepsiades says that his soul is fluttering.[7]

4. Fluttering (πτόησις) is, according to Plutarch, an ingredient in the emotions suffered by mystic initiands:[8] he describes good souls after death as suffering, in the meadows of Hades, a period of purification of pollutions contracted from the body, and then, as if returning home after exile, experiencing joy like that of mystic initiands (τελούμενοι, those being

[3] Mystic initiation expounded the nature of the next world and gave instructions on the route to be taken by the dead: e.g. with Plato's 'many forks and windings' cf. the route instructions (e.g. 'journey on the right-hand road') in the mystic formulae (of the classical period) on the funerary gold leaves: Graf and Johnston 2013: 99–100, 110–11.

[4] E.g. Plut. fr. 178; Demetr. *Eloc.* 101; the passages cited below in n. 32.

[5] For *Phaedrus* see Riedweg 1987: 30–69.

[6] See e.g. Byl 1988.

[7] Ar. *Nub.* 319. The verb here is ποτάομαι (the frequentative of πέτομαι), translated by LSJ as 'flutter', as is also πτοεῖσθαι.

[8] *Mor.* 943c. It also occurs to characterise an undesirable effect of bodily desires at Pl. *Phd.* 68c9, *Resp.* 4.439d7, *Leg.* 6.783d1; Arist. *Eth. Eud.* 1231a.

initiated), joy mixed with commotion and πτόησις and accompanied by pleasant hope. [408]

5. The musical theorist Aristides Quintilianus reports that in Bacchic initiations there is cleansing of the πτόησις of the more ignorant people, through music and dance.[9]

6. In Euripides' *Bacchae*, as Pentheus first appears, he is described by the words 'what a flutter he is in' (214 ὡς ἐπτόηται), and soon thereafter is told 'you are mad (μαίνῃ) in the most painful way' (326), 'you are flying' (πέτῃ) (332) and 'you are now mad, after earlier leaving your mind' (359). All this cannot be explained as merely a natural reaction to what has happened. And indeed the mental state of Pentheus will become even more odd. Every detail of it, and much else in the play, can be explained by (and only by) the hypothesis that it reflects the ritual of initiation into the Dionysiac mysteries.[10] That Pentheus' πτόησις is Dionysiac is confirmed by Kadmos asking Agaue, as he brings her out of her maenadic frenzy, whether there is still fluttering (τὸ πτοηθέν) in her soul (1268).

7. The sixth column of the fragmentary Derveni Papyrus is as follows:[11]

> prayers and sacrifices appease the souls, and the incantation of the magi is able to transform the *daimones* when they impede. Impeding *daimones* are avenging souls.[12] This is why the magi perform the sacrifice, as if paying a penalty. On the offerings they pour water and milk, from which they make the libations also. They sacrifice innumerable and many-knobbed cakes, because the souls also are innumerable. Initiands (μύσται) make preliminary sacrifice to the Eumenides in the same way (κ[ατὰ τὰ] ạὐτὰ) as magi do. For the Eumenides are souls. Because of these, he who is about to sacrifice to the gods, first ọ[ρ]ν̣ί̣θ̣[ε]ιον ... [409]

After this point very little can be gleaned from this column of the papyrus. Betegh (2004: 77) notes that ὀρνίθειον can mean 'of a bird', 'belonging to

[9] Aristid. Quint. 3.25. He says at the beginning of the chapter that this πτόησις 'of the more ignorant people' is a result of the fall of the soul into body and world (a neo-Platonic idea). Characteristic of the 'purification' inherent in mystic ritual would be to intensify the πτόησις in order to expel it. So too in neo-Platonism the return of the soul from the body to itself produces a 'bacchic revel' (ἀναβακχεύεσθε, Plotinus, *Enn.* 1.6.5; cf. Olymp. *in Phd.* p. 111 Norvin, 4–190) and is envisaged in terms of mystic ritual (Plotinus, *Enn.* 6.9.9).

[10] Seaford 1996a: esp. 42 n. 70.

[11] *PDerveni* VI.1–11 = §17–18K (with φ[ο]ρ̣τ̣ίον instead of ọ[ρ]ν̣ί̣θ̣[ε]ιον).

[12] This sentence of the translation depends on the supplement ψ[υχαὶ τιμω]ροί rather than ψ[υχαῖς ἐχθ]ροί. But the previous sentence anyway strongly implies that the *daimones* are indeed souls. See Betegh 2004: 88 and – on angry dead souls – Johnston 1999: 127–60. Souls prevent a soul from entering Hades at *Il.* 23.71–4. Note also that in mystic initiation fellow initiates may push aside or trample on each other but subsequently form the happy company of the blessed: e.g. Plut. fr. 178.

a bird' or 'birdlike'. He rejects the view of Tsantsanoglou that it refers to the sacrifice of birds, arguing instead that it refers to the birdlike nature of the Eumenides or the souls. I suggest that it is the birdlike nature of the Eumenides/souls that gives point to bird sacrifice. The initiands sacrifice 'in the same way as' the magi not (or not only) because they are both sacrificing to souls, but because in both cases *what is sacrificed resembles the recipients.* Just as the magi make 'innumerable' sacrifices 'because the souls too are innumerable', so the initiands sacrifice birds for the Eumenides (identified as souls) who are imagined as winged, i.e. as souls like birds.[13] Indeed, the creatures called Eumenides or Erinyes are often represented with wings.[14]

The point of these rituals is to overcome the 'terrors of Hades' (v. 6 = §14K), to ease passage into the next world, almost certainly in mystic initiation, which was a rehearsal for death, or conceivably at the funeral of a fellow initiate. Terrifying *daimones* who impede the passage to the underworld are known from other texts, and are sometimes said to be present in mystic initiations.[15] The painful resistance to dying, such as we find in the fluttering soul in *Phaedo*, is given objective form in the impeding *daimones*. Given the tendency to imagine animal sacrifice as somehow embodying or standing for human death, not least in mystic initiation,[16] the temporary fluttering[17] of a bird being sacrificed is apt precisely as a 'preliminary sacrifice' in the ordered appeasement of the *daimones*, embodying the fluttering of the human soul that precedes benign acceptance into the underworld. Their appeasement is described here as transformation,[18] i.e. perhaps into the Eumenides mentioned six lines later.[19] There is at any rate in the papyrus much overlap between the four categories of beings in the underworld ('souls', *daimones*, Erinyes and Eumenides).

The Erinyes are in the papyrus seemingly identified with righteous souls,[20] and elsewhere are often associated or identified with maenads.[21] And [*410*] conversely maenads are sometimes associated with Hades,[22] and in

[13] Further, ὀρ̣ν̣ί̣θ̣ε̣ιόν τι is generally read at II.7, in the traces immediately after ἑκάστο[ι]ς ('for each dead soul?').
[14] Eur. *Or.* 275–6 (and Willink 1986: *ad loc.*), 317, *IT* 289; Prag 1985: pls. 50–2.
[15] Johnston 1999: 130–9.
[16] Seaford 1994b: 281–301.
[17] If it is the fluttering that matters, this would explain the (otherwise surprisingly indiscriminate) 'something birdlike (ὀρνίθειόν τι)', if the right reading at II.7.
[18] μεθιστάναι (VI.3), which might conceivably mean removal; but see Tsantsanoglou 1997: 111–12.
[19] So Johnston 1999: 278: 'After this transformation, the initiates might safely approach these entities on their own behalf and offer sacrifices to them as well.'
[20] Tsantsanoglou 1997: 100–1, 106–9.
[21] Seaford 1994b: 348.
[22] Seaford 1994b: 323.

vase painting sometimes seem to be imitating birds.[23] Both these features of maenads occur in the fragments of Naevius' *Lycurgus*.

8. In Naevius, *Lycurgus* fr. 40 *TrRF* (= fr. 39W),

> *palliis patagiis crocotis malacis mortualibus*
>
> with gowns, edgings, soft saffron dresses, clothes of death,

the plural suggests that these robes belong to the chorus of maenads. *Mortualia* ('clothes of death') has not been explained. Compare the description of Pentheus' maenadic disguise in *Bacchae* as 'the adornment in which he will go off to Hades' (857). Inasmuch as mystic initiation is an entry into the underworld, funerary dress is apt for the initiand.

9. Naevius, *Lycurgus* fr. 18 *TrRF* (= fr. 30–32W)

> *Alis sublime in altos saltus*
> *inlicite, ubi bipedes volucres lino lumina linquant.*
>
> With wings high upwards into lofty glades lure them, where let biped birds in linen [nets] leave the light.[24]

This seems to be a command by Lykourgos, perhaps in response to a messenger's comparison of the maenads to birds (as in *Bacchae*: see passage 12 below). The 'birds' are called 'biped' because they are in fact human (maenads), but also because, caught in lime, they are unable to fly. This would be the cruelly sarcastic perversion of a mystic symbol. Very similar in this respect is dying 'in linen'. The maenadic-funerary costume donned by Pentheus is of linen (Eur. *Bacch.* 821). According to Herodotus (2.81) the Egyptians buried their dead not in wool but in linen, and 'in this they agree with those who are called Orphics and Bacchics, but are Egyptians and Pythagoreans'. Centuries later, Lucius in Apuleius' *Golden Ass* puts on a linen robe for his mystic visit to Hades.[25]

The sarcasm derives in all likelihood from the Aeschylean version (*Lykourgeia*), which no doubt influenced (directly or indirectly) Naevius' version, just as it did Euripides' *Bacchae*.[26] In *Bacchae* Pentheus' linen maenadic-funerary costume reaches to the feet (833 πέπλοι ποδήρεις), and

[23] Beazley 1958.
[24] I translate Bücheler's emendation; *sublimen alios* mss. But the textual problem does not affect my point.
[25] Apul. *Met.* 11.14–15, 23. Linen grave garments have been found at Eleusis, and with one of the mystic gold leaves: Seaford 1996a: 222.
[26] Dodds 1960: 31–3.

the very same [411] adjective is used of Dionysiac costume in Aeschylus' *Lykourgeia* (fr. 59). Reaching to the feet was an aspect of the funerary robe, and this was the basis for the irony – again in Aeschylus – of Agamemnon being trapped in a funerary robe of which is said 'you would call it a net and robes that cover (or bind) the feet (ποδιστῆρας πέπλους)'.[27] If Naevius' maenads were to be trapped in their garments, then the linen of passage 9 was the same as the *mortualia* (*lethal* funerary garments) of passage 8.

The death of fluttering birds unable to fly off, like the dying fluttering soul in Plato's *Phaedo*, seems to evoke (and pervert) a mystic doctrine of dying. The fluttering may even have become a *topos*, for all three of the Euripidean dramas that contain most evocations of mystic initiation (*Cyclops*, *Ion*, *Bacchae*)[28] have thiasos members imagined as fluttering or trapped birds (or vice versa).

10. *Cyclops*. Silenos, at his first drink of wine after long abstention, is described thus: 'held by the cup as if in lime he flaps with his wings (πτέρυγας ἀλύει)' (433–4).

11. In the messenger speech in *Ion* a bird drinks poisoned wine and immediately 'shook its well-feathered body and went into a bacchic frenzy (εὔπτερον δέμας ἔσεισε κἀβάκχευσεν)', gasps for breath and dies (1203–7).

12. *Bacchae*. Pentheus imagines the maenads 'in the thickets, like birds, held in the most pleasant nets of sex' (957–8). But he is wrong (685–8). By contrast, it is in their extraordinary cohesion as a group that the maenads are compared by an eye-witness to a group of soaring birds (748 ἀρθεῖσαι).

Indeed, soaring upwards is a joy. It is only *impediment* to flight that causes fluttering and its underlying anxiety. Mystic ritual provides *release*,[29] and typically consists of a transition from isolated anxiety to joyful belonging to the group.[30] The idea of the fluttering soul would belong to the initial stage. In *Phaedrus* the wings of the soul naturally soar upwards to the divine, but the sight of a beautiful face or body causes the 'recently initiated' (ἀρτιτελής) to shudder (ἔφριξε) and fear before growing the wings of his soul (251a). Given that this is a discussion of sublimated erotic desire (ἔρως), we should compare the following two passages, for they are the only other extant instances of the verb φρίσσειν used of ἔρως, both of them – remarkably – in the form ἔφριξ' ἔρωτι. [412]

[27] *Cho.* 1000 with Garvie 1986: *ad loc.*; cf. *Ag.* 1115 etc.; Seaford 1984c[11].
[28] For *Bacchae* and *Cyclops* see Seaford 1981a; for *Ion* see Zeitlin 1989.
[29] E.g. Graf and Johnston 2013: 132.
[30] E.g. Plut. fr. 178: Seaford 2004c: 299.

13. Aeschylus, fr. 387:

> ἔφριξ' ἔρωτι (ἔρως δὲ L) τοῦδε μυστικοῦ τέλους.
>
> I shuddered with strong desire for this mystic completion/ritual.

14. Sophocles, *Ajax* 693:

> ἔφριξ' ἔρωτι· περιχαρὴς δ' ἀνεπτάμαν.
>
> I shuddered with strong desire, and flew up with joy.

This is the chorus' first reaction to the 'deception speech' in Sophocles' *Ajax*, a passage marked by a pattern of evocations of mystic ritual.[31] And so the only three instances of the combination of φρίσσειν and ἔρως all occur in a mystic context, and two of them (passages 1 and 14) follow initial φρίσσειν with *flying upwards*. φρίσσειν, its noun φρίκη and ἔρως all occur frequently to describe the emotion of the mystic initiand.[32] But none of them ever refers to joy, and so the way in which passage 14 is generally translated – 'I thrilled with joy' vel sim. – is wrong. The unusual combination of φρίσσειν and ἔρως in all three passages (1, 13 and 14) is precisely the combination of *fear* and *strong desire* that we would expect in the death-like transition to mystic bliss. Similar is the mystic combination of commotion and πτόησις with joy and pleasant hope in passage 4. And indeed the combination of hope with distress and fear is a regular feature of descriptions of the emotions of the mystic initiand.[33] What is more, φρίσσειν – besides meaning an emotion – also means the bristling of an animal mane, or of the feathers on a bird.[34] This combination of the subjective with the objective is essential to the mystic idea of the soul as a bird.

What might be the significance of post-mortem flying upwards? The astonishingly detailed similarities between Greek mystic initiation and the cross-cultural phenomenon of the near-death experience make it most unlikely that the former was uninfluenced by the latter.[35] And so we may here note that a common feature of the latter is the experience of looking down from a height on to one's own body.[36] However, 'looking down on' in mystic initiation is looking down on *other* (struggling) initiands

[31] Seaford 1994c[10].
[32] Plut. fr. 178, *Ages*. 24.7; Demetr. *Eloc*. 101; Aristid. *Or*. 22.2. *Eros*: Eur. *Bacch*. 813; Max. Tyr. 31.3.
[33] E.g. Aristid. *Or*. 48.28; Artem. 2.39; Plut. *Mor*. 47a.
[34] See LSJ. A fine example of φρίσσειν of feathers is Pind. *Pyth*. 4.183; of birds also at e.g. Arist. *Hist. an*. 560b8; Plut. *De soll. an*. 980f.; Opp. *Hal*. 1.628, *Cyn*. 3.123.
[35] The similarity was noted already in Plut. fr. 178. Cf. Seaford 2005b.
[36] Blackmore 1993: 165–82.

(notably ἐφορῶν in Plutarch fr. 178), never – so far as I know – on one's own body. [413]

In general mystic initiands are imagined as obtaining happiness in the *underworld*, a destination that does not generally require wings. This seems to contradict Plato's vision of mystic initiation as a *celestial* vision that requires the soul to soar upwards on wings. Even the meadow, common as a place for mystic happiness in the underworld, seems in *Phaedrus* to be somewhere in the sky (248c1). We have argued that the idea of fluttering was present in mystic initiation to express the anxiety of dying. But the mystic transition to happiness is not associated with flying – with one exception, a fourth-century gold leaf from Thurii (GJ 5.5–6).

> Κύκλου δ' ἐξέπταν βαρυπενθέος ἀργαλέοιο,
> ἱμερτοῦ δ' ἐπέβαν στεφανοῦ ποσὶ καρπαλίμοισι.

> I have flown out of the painful circle of heavy grief,
> I have reached with swift feet the lovely crown.

This 'circle' is generally taken to be the cycle of reincarnation.[37] Here then, in a mystic formula, we find something similar to the Platonic idea of the soul growing wings to fly out of the cycle of reincarnation. 'Swift feet' then puts beyond doubt the human identity of the initiate.

POSTSCRIPT

For more on the subjective experience of mystic initiation see Seaford 2010b; another perspective on the *psyche* is provided in Seaford 2017d.

[37] Graf and Johnston 2013: 127.

PART VII

India and Greece

CHAPTER 19

Why Did the Greeks Not Have Karma?

I will argue that a basic similarity and a basic difference between early Greek and early Indian metaphysics should be understood in the historical context of the monetisation of both societies. The similarity is the advent of an impersonal universal power-entity and of the subjection of the individual to a cosmic cycle. The difference is the absence from Greece of an individually owned metaphysical power-entity (in India karma).

1. Presocratic Thought and Monetisation

In early sixth-century Ionia it began to be believed, first in the city of Miletos, that the cosmos is an intelligible order subject to the uniformity of impersonal power. In my *Money and the Early Greek Mind* (2004c) I argued that an important factor in this intellectual revolution was the advent of the all-pervasive, impersonal, semi-abstract power of money. I will begin by briefly summarising the three separate considerations on which this conclusion was based.

First, central instruments of social integration tend, at least in pre-modern societies, to be unconsciously projected onto the cosmos. The unknown can be envisaged only in terms of what is known. The trans-individual comprehensiveness of social power is reified as transcendent. This is obvious with e.g. the power of Zeus imagined as patriarchal monarchy,

Abbreviations

AN	*Aṅguttara Nikāya*
AV	*Atharvaveda*
BU	*Bṛhadāraṇyaka Upaniṣad*
CU	*Chāndogya Upaniṣad*
JB	*Jāiminīya Brāhmaṇa*
RV	*Ṛgveda*
SB	*Śatapatha Brāhmaṇa*
TB	*Taittirīya Brāhmaṇa*
TU	*Taittirīya Upaniṣad*

and it did not suddenly cease with the advent of money, the new instrument of social integration, impersonal but seemingly all-powerful, that pervaded the polis from the early sixth century.

Second, the earliest clearly visible pervasive monetisation in history was the rapid spread of coined money from about 600 BCE in Ionia, of which the commercial centre was Miletos. And so the Presocratic revolution in thought occurred at exactly the same time and in exactly the same place as the earliest pervasive monetisation that we know of. By money I mean a distinct entity whose only or main functions are to be a general means of payment and exchange and a general measure and store of value. This narrow definition of money is not the only possible one, but it is especially useful for our purpose.

Third, the Presocratic cosmos is astonishingly similar in various respects to money, for instance in the idea that the cosmos is a single (semi-abstract) entity that is transformed from and into everything else. This does not, of course, mean that it *is* money or is *reducible* to money. Moreover, in its projection onto the cosmos numerous other factors may be involved.[1]

Of my further conclusions in *Money and the Early Greek Mind* I confine myself here to summarising a single one. Money works by being imagined to have *value* that is (ideally) unchanging and ubiquitous. The other precondition or essence of money is its *circulation*: a society in which no money circulates is in effect moneyless. Money has therefore two essences, both of which are required for it to be money: value and circulation. But of course these two essences interact. Although money must be imagined as containing power and value entirely within itself, nevertheless in fact it has power and value only by circulating. To the extent that it is imagined in absolute separation from circulation it will seem to be a (universal, invisible, unchanging) *entity*. As such it is projected (sublimated) as the Being (or One) of Parmenides,[2] ruthlessly separated – not least by the ideology of aristocratic individual self-sufficiency – from (communal) circulation. The constantly circulating fire (embodying the abstract *logos*) of Heraclitus, on the other hand, is a projection of this (communal) circulation.

A common reaction to this argument has been to suggest that abstract thought may have preceded and influenced the adoption of coined money (rather than vice versa). However, in my book I gave a historical account of the genesis of coinage that does not require abstract thought as a precondition, whereas I know of no money-excluding explanation of why

[1] Seaford 2004c: 11–12 (esp. n. 40).

[2] Parmenides DK 28 B 8.13–14, 26–31, 36–7, 48; Seaford 2004c: 246–9.

and how the ontology of abstraction, and Presocratic cosmology generally, developed when and where they did, or indeed why they developed at all. The abstraction originates not as an (inexplicable) merely intellectual phenomenon but from the practical necessity inherent in the (explicable) convenience of monetised exchange. I would also appeal to our own experience in imagining abstract value as a universal entity embodied in all commodities (while ignoring the various sources of the value).

2. The Metaphysical Revolution in India and Greece

However, the case I made in 2004 was incomplete. There appeared in India a new set of fundamental ideas about the universe, and the place of the self in it, that is strikingly similar to the new set of ideas that appeared at about the same time among the Greeks (and nowhere else). Furthermore, it is more than a shared set of ideas. What is strikingly similar between the two cultures is the *transition* from one shared set of ideas to another. I will briefly illustrate this in three areas: the universe, the inner self and the hereafter.

(1) Both the *Ṛgveda* and Homer imply a conception of the universe that I call polytheist reciprocity. The universe is controlled largely by a variety of personal deities for whom humans provide offerings, sustenance, prayer and praise in order to elicit in return various forms of well-being. In the early Upanishads and Presocratics, by contrast, personal deities have been marginalised by the idea that everything is in fact a single entity (monism). In both cultures monism takes various forms, including what I call abstract monism, in which the single entity is abstract.

(2) In the world imagined by the *Ṛgveda*, as in Homer, there are various organs of consciousness but no comprehensive, unitary organ of consciousness containing thought, sensation, emotion, intention, etc. And there is no incorporeality (not to be confused with invisibility). But in the early Upanishads and Presocratics (and then in Plato) the comprehensive unitary inner self (*ātman*, *psyche*) acquires central importance, shares identity, substance or form with the universe, and is eventually explicitly incorporeal.

(3) In the *Ṛgveda* and Homer the passage to the hereafter is linear and irreversible. But in the early Upanishads we see the beginning of a different conception, in which death is followed by return to earth, creating a cycle that contrasts with linear transition to permanent

well-being. This eventually becomes what I call ethicised indiscriminate reincarnation (EIR), indiscriminate in the sense that the rebirth may be into any creature (depending on the ethical quality of the previous life), producing a miserable cycle (*saṃsāra*) from which escape (*mokṣa*) is desirable. EIR continues to be a fundamental belief in religions created in India, and occurred in some ancient Greek texts, but nowhere else.

It must be emphasised that there are, of course, numerous differences in the forms taken by these developments and ideas between the two cultures (and even within the same culture). And we should never forget that what we know of ancient thought is confined to the socially limited range of the surviving texts. I submit nevertheless that the similarity between the fundamental transitions I have selected is sufficient to require explanation. In fact the similarity is so great that any explanation that has been applied to the one but is impossible for the other (such as the advent of literacy[3]) is thereby seriously disadvantaged.

Two explanations of the similarity of transition would avoid this disadvantage: (a) the shared Indo-European origin of the two cultures and (b) influence (in one direction or the other). But neither of these explanations works.[4]

(a) The transition from the earlier to the later set of ideas occurs after the *Ṛgveda* and Homer, i.e. well after the divergence of the Indo-Europeans to India and Europe. The shared Indo-European inheritance may at most contain shared practices and linguistic features conducive to the development of shared ideas: it cannot by itself explain the development (or why nothing like it occurred endogenously in other Indo-European societies).[5]

(b) The striking similarities between Indian and Greek metaphysics, including those discussed in this chapter, all developed (probably in the two or three centuries) before Alexander crossed the Indus in 326 BCE. But in this period, which I will call 'our period', the chance of the influence of metaphysical ideas in either direction is close to

[3] Literacy was emphasised as a factor in the genesis of Greek philosophy by Eric Havelock in various works, but there is no evidence for it in the vast Gangetic area before the mid-third century BCE, well after the intellectual revolution.

[4] I also exclude as explanatory a miraculous advent of 'reason', which is a human universal, and rare in the early Upanishads as in the Presocratic fragments; and, in any case, its supposed advent would *require* explanation.

[5] Note, however, the sophisticated comparison by Pinchard 2009 of the dynamics of Greek and Indian wisdom traditions.

zero. The widespread appeal of influence as an explanation is that it seems to solve the problem very simply, and is in accord with our own experience of the ease with which metaphysical or religious ideas are transmitted across cultures. But before 326 there is evidence neither of Greeks visiting India nor of Indians visiting Greece (apart from a contingent of Indians in Xerxes' army).[6] If there was any influence, it was most likely to occur at the Achaemenid court, where there were Indians and Greeks, including – in the late fifth century – Ctesias, who wrote about India. But the Upanishads were produced in a part of India far beyond the Achaemenid empire. And in Greek texts before 326 (including Plato and Aristotle) there is no trace of the reception of any *idea* from India, which is throughout envisaged as a land of marvels. Ctesias (*FGrH* 688 F45 (12)) even makes the absurd claim that the sun appears ten times larger in India than in any other land. Although travellers have always acquired language needed for their purposes (notably trade),[7] there is no evidence of any Greek author before 326 knowing any foreign language at all (let alone Sanskrit or Prakrit). As for the Indian texts that are certainly or almost certainly pre-326, Greece and Greeks are entirely absent.

Moreover, the latter set of ideas shared between Greece and India is found nowhere else. It has for instance left no trace in the beliefs known from the vast area – the Achaemenid empire – between Greece and India. This counts against the hypotheses of influence and of the metaphysical similarities deriving from a third culture.

There is not even evidence before 326 for transmission between the two cultures of what is transmitted relatively easily: discoveries, narratives, artefacts, things of practical value. Metaphysical ideas, by contrast, are likely to be transmitted only as part of a dominant culture. How were anti-empirical but fundamental ideas – such as that all things that are real are in fact a single abstract entity – adopted by an exclusive, introverted and self-confident elite, the Brahminical authors of the Upanishads (or by Parmenides in furthest Elea), from a remote culture that they never mention?

Any explanatory factor will be advantaged if it is able to explain not just the similarity of ideas between India and Greece but also the *shape* of the

[6] Hdt. 8.113.2.

[7] Known examples of Persian acquired by Greeks in the Classical period (for practical purposes) are Histiaios (Hdt. 6.29.2), Themistokles (Thuc. 1.138.1), perhaps Alkibiades (Ath. 12.535e) and Laomedon (Arr. *Anab.* 3.6.6). There were no doubt many others (e.g. translators).

similar ideas, how they all *cohere*, the similarity of *transition* and why it occurred in only these two cultures. And it will be further advantaged if it is also able to explain the conceptual *differences*. I propose that monetisation is the only factor that has anything approaching these advantages. But in order to allay suspicion that I have exaggerated the conceptual similarities, or selected for discussion only those that fit my explanation, my main focus in this chapter will be on what I regard as a substantial conceptual *difference*, the absence from Greek thought of the impersonal power-entity karma (Sanskrit *karman*, Pali *kamma*). It will also illustrate the point that any explanation must ignore neither the important factor of monetisation nor other potential factors.

We will see that something like the well-known and long-lasting doctrine of karma first appeared in the earliest Upanishads. This belongs to the transition we described above in the *hereafter* (3). I will leave discussion of other aspects of the transition, such as *monism* (1) and the centrality of the *inner self* (2), to my planned monograph, in which I will also provide most of the detail that underlies the broad argument of this chapter.

3. Monetisation in India

The earliest Greek coins were produced probably towards the end of the seventh century in western Asia Minor, and in the course of the next decades spread in very large numbers across the Greek world.[8] The Greek polis of the sixth century is the earliest society of whose pervasive monetisation we can be certain. And it remained for at least two centuries the only pervasively monetised society, apart from India and China.[9] A cause and effect of monetisation is the development of individual property. The Greek evidence for these developments is copious and well known, and I have no space for it here.

The archaeology of northern India tells us that there was rapid and considerable urbanisation in the sixth and fifth centuries. Of the six cities selected by Buddhist tradition as fit to receive the remains of the Buddha – Campa, Kasi, Sravasti, Kausambi, Rajagriha and Saketa – the first five are also the earliest urban centres known from archaeology (along with Ujjain). The cities clearly stated by their excavators to have been fortified by 550 are Rajagriha, Campa, Kasi and Ujjain.[10] These early cities extend throughout

[8] Seaford 2004c: 129–31, with bibliography.
[9] Seaford 2004c: 128–9.
[10] Erdosy 1995: 109–10, 115.

a vast area, with Kasi and Campa on the river Ganges, Kausambi on the river Yamuna, Sravasti to the north in Kosala, Rajagriha to the south-east in Magadha, and Ujjain to the south-west in Avanti. As for the period 550–400, Erdosy describes, in the Allahabad district, an exceptionally high increase in the size of the sites, producing *inter alia* 'towns providing a full complement of manufacturing activities' but dwarfed by the capital Kausambi.[11]

Large urban settlements are not necessarily pervaded by commerce, because they may be the sites of centralised redistribution, as were the prehistoric riverine cities of ancient Egypt, Mesopotamia and (almost certainly) the Indus valley.[12] But in those areas the economic centralisation is reflected in the archaeological record, whereas by contrast in the towns and cities of the Ganges area – where there seems to have been continuity of layout from the beginning[13] – there are market places,[14] 'a striking absence of monumental public buildings'[15] and 'little evidence for a citadel or acropolis distinct from the residential area ... the absence of large-scale warehouses or granaries in these towns again suggests that political authority was still relatively decentralised'.[16] This is precisely the kind of context – large but relatively decentralised towns – in which we would expect monetisation, which would have promoted and been promoted by the discernible development of individual property.[17] If (as is likely) money took the form of gold and silver, it was too valuable to be left for archaeology to discover.

The monetisation of northern Indian cities eventually took the form of coinage. Early coins of the Ganges area were silver punch-marked coins sufficiently small and numerous to suggest that they were used for everyday transactions.[18] The rapid advent of large numbers may derive from their

[11] Erdosy 1995: 107.

[12] The absence of decipherable texts from the Indus valley civilisation makes certainty impossible, but archaeology reveals river-dependent agriculture (as in Mesopotamia and Egypt), evidence for centralised (as well as for independent) production, no evidence for anything indicating money (but numerous seals, as in Mesopotamia and Egypt), and cities with large non-residential buildings (often taken to be granaries) and public works requiring centralised planning: e.g. Wright 2010: 33, 117–27, 183–5, 236–7, 240–2, 271. In 2014 a large building claimed to be a granary was discovered at Rakhigarhi.

[13] Erdosy 1995: 111.

[14] Thapar 1984: 99.

[15] Thapar 1984: 91.

[16] Thapar 1984: 99.

[17] On the development of individual property in India see Kosambi 1951: 186; Rau 1957: 50; Kosambi 1965: 100–1; Ghosh 1973: 37; Thapar 1984: 36, 76, 78, 88–9; Chakravarti 1987: 91–2, 177; Erdosy 1988: 93–4; Erdosy 1995: 114.

[18] E.g. Gupta and Hardaker 2014: 19.

adoption by the state, for instance to pay soldiers. The *idea* of coinage may have derived ultimately from Greece. Indeed, if there was influence between Greece and India in this period, it was much more likely to be the indirect influence of trading practices (from which metaphysical ideas may be indirectly influenced) than of metaphysical ideas themselves. Even with coinage, however, there was the difference that, whereas Greek coins were stamped, Indian coins were punched (often several times).

Cribb (2005) argues that the attempts to push the dating of the earliest Gangetic coins much further back than the mid-fourth century (archaeological context, varieties and phases of the coins, weight loss through use, correlation of historical events) are all fatally flawed. On the other hand, an earlier date certainly cannot be excluded. According to Erdosy the radiocarbon dating of Northern Black Polished ware suggests that 'the introduction of coinage into the subcontinent could be dated to 400 BCE at the earliest'.[19] Hardaker in a detailed numismatic study published in 2014 argues that the earliest coinage in Maghada 'is unlikely to have originated later than about 430 BCE, but this date could be somewhat earlier'.[20] We should note that monetisation in all likelihood preceded coinage, perhaps by a considerable period.

What are we told by the surviving texts? The world of the *Ṛgveda* is semi-nomadic, and has no towns. Like Homer, it has no money and only a few slight indications of commerce.[21] Subsequent Vedic literature contains almost no mention of towns but some mentions of commerce.[22] In the earliest Upanishads, the *Bṛhadāraṇyaka Upaniṣad* and *Chāndogya Upaniṣad* (henceforth 'BU' and 'CU'), which may be reasonably placed anywhere from the seventh century to the fourth,[23] specified numbers of cows (generally a thousand) are given in exchange (or reward) for wisdom.[24] In other texts of about the same period, notably the *Śatapatha Brāhmaṇa* (henceforth 'SB'), gold given to the priests might be specified as of a certain weight,[25] and it might be given in pieces, or pieces of a

[19] Erdosy 1995: 105, cf. 113.

[20] In Gupta and Hardaker 2014: 44–8.

[21] RV 1.112.11; 4.24.9; 5.45.6.

[22] Collected by Rau 1957: 28–9, to which add esp. AV 3.15.

[23] Olivelle 1996: xxxvi first states that 'the seventh to sixth century BCE may be reasonable, give or take a century or so' (i.e. from eighth to fifth), but adds that – given the downdating of the death of the Buddha to 375–355, which he favours – 'then the dates of the early Upaniṣads should be pushed forward a century or so' (the early Upanishads show no Buddhist influence).

[24] BU 2.1.1; 4.1.2–7; 4.3.14–16, 33; 4.4.7; CU 4.2.1–4.

[25] E.g. SB 12.7.2.13; 13.2.3.2; 13.4.1.6–7; 13.4.2.10; 13.4.2.13; TB 1.8.9.1; 1.7.8.2; *Taittirīya Saṃhitā* 2.3.11.6; *Maitrāyaṇī Saṃhitā* 1.6.4; 2.2.2.

certain weight.[26] In BU King Janaka declares to the assembled Brahmins that the most learned man of them should drive away a thousand cows, to the horns of each of which are attached ten pieces of gold (3.1.1). Silver, a comparative newcomer, had negative associations (e.g. AV 8.13.7), which for Falk 'explains why the Brahmins did not usually accept silver as gift at sacrifices'.[27] There are in these texts hardly any indications of the *functions* of money as general means of payment and exchange, measure of value or store of value.[28] And there are no indications of coinage. The references to coins in early Indian texts are undatable.[29] The earliest date is from a Roman text: according to Curtius Rufus[30] tribute of marked silver (*argentum signatum*) was paid by the king of Taxila (in the north-west) to Alexander, i.e. circa 325.

The earliest Buddhist texts refer to inter-city trade, individual property, rich merchants, market towns, shops and the use of money, including coinage and money-lending,[31] and some of this may go back to the fourth century.[32] The contrast with the early Upanishads may be due to the Buddhist texts being later and from a different milieu, but also to the well-documented Brahminical rejection of urban life.[33] Further, money tends to dissolve distinctions between groups separated by status, as indicated in an early Buddhist text,[34] and so was likely to be ignored or rejected by Brahmins.[35] The Brahmins subsequently also rejected another radical innovation, writing, insisting instead on the exact oral transmission of their wisdom.

In the early history of money there is not necessarily a specific word for it. There was no such Greek word until long after the Greek polis was monetised. It is possible to reject money while being profoundly (if only unconsciously) influenced by it.[36] Plato recommends secluding the

[26] SB 5.4.3.26; 5.5.5.16; *Pañcaviṃśa Brāhmaṇa* 18.3.2.

[27] Falk 1991: 111.

[28] The mention of a buried treasure of gold at CU 8.3.2 may suggest that gold was used, at least sometimes, as a store of value.

[29] The earliest mention seems to be in the north-west, by Panini (*rūpya*: Falk 1991: 115), but is not certainly earlier than 326. Words in (possibly) earlier texts that have been claimed to mean coins may in fact refer to ornaments (e.g. *niṣka*) or weights (*śatamāna*): Prasad 1966. They may anyway have been for *thesaurisation*, stored for prestige not exchange.

[30] Curt. 8.12.42.

[31] E.g. Thapar 1984: 90–104; Bailey and Mabbet 2003: 15–18, 24, 56–76.

[32] Gombrich 2009: 95–110.

[33] Thapar 1984: 93; Gombrich 2006: 56; Bronkhorst 2007: 251–5.

[34] The courtesan episode in *The Questions of Milinda*, quoted below in §8.

[35] Perhaps even as polluting (as Plato does at *Resp.* 3.416e6–8).

[36] How religion and morality may borrow commercial concepts to protest against commerce is a theme of Graeber 2011: e.g. 89, 186.

guardians of his ideal polis from the polluting money of commerce, but requires them to be told that they have divine gold and silver money (χρυσίον καὶ ἀργύριον) in their souls (*Resp.* 3.416e4–6). In the Upanishads there is barely any awareness of what lies outside their tradition, be it urbanisation, monetisation or the new religious movements. But it would be difficult for the Brahmins to lead lives entirely isolated from the rapidly self-replicating convenience of money. They received gifts or payment from the non-Brahmin wealthy (Kṣatriyas and others), and sacrifice itself required provisions. And in fact the necessity for the Brahmins to engage in (undesirable) monetised commerce is, I suggest, beautifully expressed in a ritual enactment described in the SB (3.3.3.1–7), a text closely connected – and roughly contemporary – with the BU.

A priest (Brahmin) purchases a vital ingredient of the sacrifice, soma. He bargains with the soma-seller, 'therefore any and everything is vendible here'.[37] That is to say, the bargaining is imagined to be the origin of universal commerce. The priest's first offer is of one-sixteenth of a cow, which, however, he agrees is insufficient: 'Yes, King Soma is worth more than that; but great, surely, is the greatness of the cow.' He then lists the various good things that come from the cow. That is to say, after first accepting commercial *quantification* (one-sixteenth of a cow), he then praises the greatness of the cow and the variety of its products, even though they cannot alter his admission that his *quantitative* offer is insufficient. And so the priest then offers instead a hoof, and finally the whole cow. This the soma-seller accepts, saying 'name the kinds!', to which the priest responds by offering a variety of goods: gold, a cloth, a goat and various cows. This is explained as the origin of bargaining: 'And because they first bargain and afterwards come to terms, therefore about any and everything that is for sale here, people first bargain and afterwards come to terms.' Moreover 'the reason why only the priest enumerates the virtues of the cow, and not the soma-seller those of the soma, is that soma is already glorified, since soma is a god'. The soma transcends – and is exempted from – the new, universal, unprecedented, *explicitly self-interested* process of bargaining.

All this is to prepare for the sacrifice. 'The priest then makes [the sacrificer] say on the gold "You, the pure, I buy with the pure", for he indeed buys the pure with the pure, when [he buys] soma with gold', and similarly (in place of 'pure') 'brilliant' and 'immortal'. This reflects the importance of gold as a means of exchange. But here the gold is personalised, and praised not for its monetary value but as itself having the purity, brilliance and

[37] I use Eggeling's translation.

immortality of the soma for which it is exchanged. The equivalence of gold and soma is here not *quantitative* (exchange-value) but endowed with the *qualities* (use-value) with which gold is used in Brahminical ritual.[38] In this context, all this is a reaction against the vulgar (mere) quantification that defines monetised commerce. The inevitability of the commercial act is acknowledged, but assimilated to ritual.[39] The metal offered is accordingly gold, which had long been valued in ritual, rather than silver, which besides being inauspicious was (or subsequently became) the main metal of the earliest Indian coins.

The priest then transfers the cow from soma-seller to sacrificer, by offering gold as compensation, but then 'draws [the gold] back to the sacrificer, and throws it down, with, "Ours be thy gold!", whereby he [the sacrificer] takes unto himself the vital energy, and the soma-seller gets only the body'. The priest here reasserts his control of the transaction, on behalf of the sacrificer, who receives not only the cow but also the (abstract) vital energy of the gold, the quality it bestows on ritual, whereas the soma-seller is left with nothing but its (merely corporeal) body. This ritualised absorption by the sacrificer of the incorporeal power (vital energy) separated from the body of the gold illustrates a phenomenon that will be important for our overall argument: the convergence of the abstract (invisible) power of money with the invisible power of ritual.

To summarise: the enactment (a) identifies Vedic ritual as the authoritative origin of the universality of (self-interested) commercial practice; (b) nevertheless expresses the Brahmins' sense of superiority to monetised commerce – despite their need to engage in it – by absorbing it (including the abstract value of money) into their ritual; (c) expresses the tension between quantification and pre-monetary value.

To conclude this section, it seems very likely that the cities of the Ganges region were in the course of the fifth century, if not earlier, being pervasively monetised, and that this could easily have been the period also in which SB and the earliest Upanishads were produced. Elsewhere in this period, pervasive monetisation occurs only in the Greek polis and (almost certainly) in China.[40] These are also the only three societies which,

[38] *Kaṭha Upaniṣad* 2.3 is based on the acceptability of gold used in ritual as opposed to gold desired as wealth.

[39] Such assimilation is facilitated by the fact that Vedic sacrifice itself involved exchange.

[40] Our understanding of monetisation and the early development of coinage in China have recently been much advanced by archaeology and by the systematic studies of Emura 2011 and Kakinuma 2011, both in Japanese but sympathetically reviewed (in English) in detail by von Falkenhausen 2013 and 2014.

in about the same period, produced 'philosophy': to be more precise, in them all it begins to be imagined that there is a universally powerful, all-pervasive impersonal entity[41] that has a special relationship to the individual inner self.

4. Cosmic Cycle and Metaphysical Merit

The transition to the next world in Homer is linear and irreversible. So it is also for the most part in the *Ṛgveda*: the dead individual is generally imagined as joining a community (of fathers or gods); well-being in the hereafter and immortality may be requested directly[42] or acquired in return for gifts.[43]

In later Vedic texts this conception changes. In the Brahmanas repeated death (*punarmṛtyu*) in the afterlife is feared,[44] and at SB 10.4.3.10 is distinguished from being born after death for immortality. When *punarmṛtyu* in the afterlife is followed by rebirth in this world, we are on the way to the idea of a repeated cyclical passage between this world and the next, from which escape is desirable. Bodewitz notes that

> the concept of redeath lost its significance as soon as the concepts of rebirth and release had become accepted. The limited period in which *punarmṛtyu* played a role indicates that it belonged to a period of transition to new ideas.[45]

Another change is in the power of the offering. An offering has the power to obtain good will from the recipient, from which may result benefit to the donor: the donor acquires benefit indirectly (reciprocally). But to the extent that this power comes to be imagined separately from the recipient, the offering will seem to obtain well-being automatically; and there may develop the idea of offerings that are – separately from any recipient – *stored* in the next world for the well-being of the donor. In

[41] In India *brahman*, in Greece the Presocratic ἀρχή (e.g. air for Anaximenes, fire for Heraclitus). As in Greece and India, there is in China a rejection of the practise of ritual along with an 'inward turn', which 'took a giant step forward in the fourth century BCE with the emergence of the new cosmology of *qi*. According to this new theory, the *qi* permeates the entire cosmos. It is in constant movement and, when differentiated and individuated, all things in the world are formed. … only by turning inward to nourish the most refined *qi* in the heart can one hope to attain oneness with the cosmos': Yü 2003: 72, citing Mencius 2A: 2.

[42] E.g. RV 9.113.7–8; 10.15.4.

[43] RV 1.125.6; 10.107.2; cf. 10.14.8; 10.15.4; 10.16.4.

[44] E.g. SB 2.3.3.9; 10.1.4.14; 11.5.6.9; TB 3.10.11.2; 3.11.8.5–6; *Kausītaki Brāhmaṇa* 25.1; Deussen 1906: 326–7; Keith 1925: 573; Collins 1982: 46–7; Smith 1989: 118 n. 196.

[45] Bodewitz 1996: 34.

Vedic texts we can detect this development. There is in the *Ṛgveda* only one mention of what is accumulated in the next world by action in this one – in one of the two late passages that have been claimed to refer to rebirth, in the afterlife, on earth.[46] The word used for it is *iṣṭāpūrta*, which is etymologically connected with sacrifice, and could refer to the result of sacrifice, but eventually could mean material wealth in this world or the totality of merit accumulated in a life (not only by sacrifice).[47] It 'appears to be a synonym for *nidhi* (treasure), deposit in heaven, consisting of religious merit, something on a man's credit side in the invisible world or in the life hereafter'.[48] Similarly, *karman*, which in its earliest occurrences refers to ritually correct action,[49] comes to refer to (among other things) the metaphysical results of action in general.

Gonda discusses texts in which 'there is a more or less fixed relation between the ritual acts and the merits gained by them on the one hand and the *loka* (desirable place or 'world') resulting from them on the other'.[50] A single offering may obtain a variety of valuable things (AV 9.5.22–36). The good and evil done by the dead are quantified in heaven (JB 1.18), where there is a pair of scales (SB 11.2.7.33). And just as the store or result of offerings may accumulate in the afterlife, so too it may also decrease or be exhausted. But there are solutions. The alternation of day and night destroys *sukṛta* (merit in the next world accumulated by sacrifice in this one),[51] which can however be 'freed' from death by the right ritual.[52] And the *sukṛta* and *loka* obtained by some sacrifices are imperishable.[53]

Why did these developments – repeated death (*punarmṛtyu*) and an exhaustible store of merit in the next world – occur when they did? Bodewitz argues convincingly against all the explanations previously offered for the advent of *punarmṛtyu*, before advancing his own. The problem of *punarmṛtyu* always turns up together with its solution (often through ritual) and 'is especially connected with the topic of the transitoriness of the (mostly ritual) merits'. And so

[46] RV 10.14.8; Jurewicz 2010: 292–320 (esp. 316–17); see also Jurewicz 2016: 577–644.
[47] Keith 1925: 250, 409, 478; Biardeau and Malamoud 1976: 165; Krishan 1997: 4–5, 33; Halbfass 2000: 59.
[48] Krishan 1997: 5.
[49] E.g. Gombrich 1996: 31, 2006: 46.
[50] Gonda 1966: 137; AV 3.29.3; 9.5.22.
[51] Gonda 1966: 125–30.
[52] SB 2.3.3.10–11.
[53] SB 1.6.4.16; 2.3.3.11; 2.3.6.1; Gonda 1966: 125–30.

> the problem of *punarmṛtyu*, introduced together with its solution and with emphasis on this solution, reflects the reaction of the ritualists to attempts made by non-ritualists to devalue the ritualistic claims. The ritualists probably tried to refute the opinion of other circles that ultimately the merits become exhausted in heaven.[54]

But the 'refutations' claimed non-ritual as well as ritual ways of overcoming repeated death, and so it is misleading to ascribe them to 'the ritualists' alone. Moreover, we should ask why criticism of ritual selects the exhaustibility of sacrificial merit: there are many other, more obvious ways of indicating the inefficacy of ritual. Why did the concept of merit, the problem of its decrease and the opposition to ritual occur no earlier than they did?

Blutzenberger identifies various eschatological conceptions in Vedic texts that, he argues, came together to form the doctrine of reincarnation.[55] The argument is – so far as it goes – correct (the evidence-free assumption that reincarnation must derive from external influence is a symptom of ignoring the relation between changes in metaphysics and in socio-economic formation). But he sees the development and merging of these conceptions for the most part as a purely intellectual process. A crucial step towards the idea of transmigration he describes as follows: 'In considering and evaluating the effect of a ritual act, some *Brāhmaṇas* made the disturbing discovery that the individual amount of *karman*, once achieved, was not imperishable, but liable to diminution, and to wearing away (*kṣaya*, e.g. JB 2.53f.).'[56] It is odd to describe an imagined feature of an imaginary construct as the object of a disturbing discovery. The question should be: why did they imagine *karman*, and imagine that it was liable to diminution? If the 'discovery' of its perishability was so 'disturbing', why not imagine it as imperishable? The questions cannot be answered without reference to the factor of monetisation that we have independent reasons for believing was occurring in this period.

Gifts establish or maintain interpersonal relationships by embodying in the recipient some personal *reciprocal* relation (memory, gratitude, obligation) to the donor. Generosity creates a subjective, unquantified claim on its recipient. The *Ṛgveda* proclaims that 'the wealth of one who gives does not become exhausted, and the non-giver finds no one to show mercy … he who eats alone has only evil', before proceeding to deny the correlation

[54] Bodewitz 1996: 36.
[55] Blutzenberger 1996, 1998.
[56] Blutzenberger 1996: 107.

of quantity with power.[57] This is from the late tenth book, and may contain lines late enough to be a reaction against incipient monetisation.[58] The payment of money is merely an agreement to exchange quantified impersonal power (embodied in the money) for goods or services, and can occur without benevolence. The historical advance of commercial exchange and monetisation, at the expense of gift exchange and reciprocity, leaves the transactors isolated from each other. The monetised individual needs (in principle, albeit not necessarily in reality) nothing but his money.

Money is a quantity that is accumulated by action, stored and exhaustible – like the metaphysical merit that appears in texts later than the *Ṛgveda*. True, metaphysical merit is not always necessarily a projection of *money*; it may in some cases be a projection of a store of wealth such as food. But I submit that the development of (for instance) *iṣṭāpūrta* and *karman* into the all-important, durable, abstract – and never edible – consequence of all actions (not just sacrificial actions) is influenced by monetisation.

At BU 4.4.6 it is said that

> A man who's attached goes with his action (*karman*),
> to that very place to which
> his mind and character cling.
> Reaching the end of his action,
> of whatever he has done in this world –
> From that world he returns
> back to this world,
> back to action.
>
> That is the course of a man who desires. Now a man who does not desire, who is without desires, who is freed from desires, whose desires are fulfilled, whose only desire is the self – his vital functions (*prāṇa*) do not depart. *Brahman* he is, and to *brahman* he goes.[59]

Karman here is already not just ritual action but action in general in this world. Inasmuch as a human accompanies it (presumably to the next world), it is to some extent reified. And so 'reaching the end' of it (and so returning to this world) implies exhausting it,[60] whereas the one who is free

57 RV 10.117. Verse 8, according to Jamison and Brereton 2014: III.1586, 'suggests that sheer quantity isn't the measure of power and effectiveness: the more "feet"an entity has, the less its autonomy and power'.

58 Cf. Jamison and Brereton 2014: 1.17. RV 10.95 was known at the time of SB to have had fewer verses than at present: Bronkhorst 2007: 340.

59 For the Upanishads I use the translation of Olivelle 1996.

60 Olivelle emails me that '"exhausting" is clearly correct, although I would not use it in a translation'.

from desire 'becomes immortal, and attains *brahman* in this world', for 'this incorporeal (*aśarīra*) and immortal lifebreath (*prāṇa*) is nothing but *brahman*'. For the incorporeal lifebreath permanent escape (into *brahman*) from the *karman*-driven cycle is acquired not by reified action, which can be exhausted, but by freedom from desire (except for desire for the self). I will return to this passage in §10.

The idea of a decrease in metaphysical substance resulting in re-entry into the cycle of rebirth is indicated in the so-called two-path doctrine that occurs (in different versions) at BU 6.2 and CU 5.10. Both versions start with the so-called five-fire doctrine, which consists in the transformation into each other of five fundamental entities through the intermediary of fire, ending with man, who is cremated. There follows the two-path doctrine, in which the first phase consists of passing into the flame (*devayāna*, path of the gods) or the smoke (*pitṛyāna*, path of the fathers). The *devayāna* leads ultimately to *brahman* (CU 5.10.2) or – for some 'exalted people' – 'the worlds of *brahman*', from which 'they do not return' (BU 6.2.15), whereas the *pitṛyāna* leads in both versions eventually to the moon, where they remain 'as long as there is a residue' (CU 5.10.5), then in both versions return to earth and are reborn, and – the BU version adds – 'rising up again to the heavenly worlds, they circle round in the same way' (6.2.16). The *devayāna* is followed by 'those who know this (the five-fire doctrine) and those there in the wilderness who venerate truth as faith (*śraddhā*)',[61] whereas the *pitṛyāna* is followed by 'those who win heavenly worlds by offering sacrifices, by giving gifts, and by performing austerities' (BU 6.2.16), or 'the people here in the villages who venerate thus: gift-giving is *iṣṭāpūrta*' (CU 5.10.3).

Six observations need to be made about this innovative narrative.

(a) The two-path doctrine describes the repeated cosmic cyclicality of the hereafter, from which escape is possible. The newness of this conception emerges from Killingley's examination of several passages (in the Brahmaṇas and Upanishads) that are similar to the five-fire and two-path doctrines.[62] He shows that they were used by a redactor to produce BU 6.2 and CU 5.10, and concludes that in all these texts (those similar to the five-fire doctrine) we are presented with a linear series, not a cycle. They were worked into a cycle by our redactor, who clearly did not get all his ideas ready-made from some hypothetical

[61] BU 6.2.15; similarly CU 5.10.1.
[62] SB 11.2.2.1; 11.6.2; JB 1.45–6; *Muṇḍaka Upaniṣad* 2.1.5; TU 2.1; CU 6.2–5; cf. JB 1.1–2.

non-Aryan circle, but operated with material derived from the Vedic tradition of ritual and cosmological thought.[63]

He also notes that the Five Fires and the Two Paths occur together only at BU 6.2 and CU 5.10. The redactor's principal innovations, he concludes, were to bring together the two groups of material pertaining to these two doctrines, and to 'transform each of them from a linear series into a cycle'.[64]

(b) In the BU version those who take the *pitṛyāna* are, when they reach the moon, eaten by the gods, and return to earth to be reborn. In the CU version they (described as giving offerings as *iṣṭāpūrta*) go to the moon, which the gods eat, and remain there as long as there is a *saṃpāta* (residue of sacrifice) before returning to earth for rebirth. The exhaustibility of what is produced by sacrifice (*iṣṭāpūrta*, *saṃpāta*) is what condemns them to rebirth.[65] After all, sacrifices, offerings, and the performance of austerities all 'come to naught' (BU 3.8.10), and 'in the hereafter a world won by merit (*puṇyajīta*) comes to an end' (CU 8.1.6). Those on the other hand who take the *devayāna* and so escape the cycle do so not by sacrificial offerings or merit but by knowledge.

(c) Both versions of the five-fire and two-path doctrines are expounded to a Brahmin (Uddālaka) by a king (Pravahāna Jaivali), who begins by saying that 'this knowledge has never before been in the possession of a Brahmin'.[66] This is not the only passage in the early Upanishads (and SB) in which innovative metaphysics is expounded by kings (members of the Kṣatriya class).[67] Whether such doctrines actually originated among the Kṣatriyas, or were Brahminical doctrines attributed to Kṣatriyas so as to advertise their value to Kṣatriyas, it is significant that metaphysical shifts shaped (in part) by money are expounded by Kṣatriyas, on whose wealth – drawn at least in part from the new urban (probably monetised) milieu – the Brahmins depended.

63 Killingley 1997: 13.

64 Killingley 1997: 17.

65 Not (as in the BU version) being eaten by the gods (in CU it is the moon that the gods eat). Olivelle notes that *saṃpāta* generally refers to the residue of sacrifice, but takes it here to mean the residue of the moon being eaten. But this would imply the total disappearance of the moon, which is unlikely (and cf. 'Decrease! Increase!' in BU 6.2.16). And there is no reason why *saṃpāta* cannot mean what it normally does: it is giving offerings as *iṣṭāpūrta* that distinguishes these people from those who escape the cycle.

66 BU 6.2.8; CU 5.3.7, which adds 'As a result in all the worlds government has belonged exclusively to royalty.'

67 Black 2007: 101–31.

(d) Some exalted people escape permanently to *brahman*. In the *Ṛgveda*, *brahman* referred to invisible power, generally created in ritual (especially by ritual utterance),[68] and only later – notably in the early Upanishads – becomes clearly detached from ritual, and means an entity that is fundamental to all else, universal and eternal.[69] With these changes the invisibility of *brahman* tends to become abstraction, and the questions arise of what *brahman* is and how it is to be accessed.[70] The advent of the fundamentality and universality of *brahman* belongs to the advent of monism, in which the complex system of connections between resembling phenomena, the web of *bhandus* integral to vedic ritualism, and hierarchical distinctions are collapsed in monistic thought into the ultimate connection: the equation of self and cosmos (without the ritual intermediary) formulated as the identity and full equality of *ātman* and *brahman*.[71]

(e) For Tull the distinction between the *pitṛyāna* and the *devayāna* is 'between a traditional path of worship, one that maintains the relationship between gods, priests and sacrificers, and a path that concentrates on the individual to the point of actually "interiorising" the sacrifice.'[72]

The focus on the individual sacrificer as himself beneficiary of the sacrifice is taken further in other texts. SB 11.2.6.13–14 distinguishes between the sacrificer for the gods (*devayājin*, 'god-offerer') and the sacrificer for the self (*ātmayājin*, 'self-offerer'). The *devayājin* 'is as the inferior who brings tribute to the superior, or like a man of the people who brings tribute to the king: indeed, he does not win such a place (in heaven) as the other'. Whereas the *devayājin* attains the benefit of the sacrifice through the intercession of the gods, the *ātmayājin* attains it directly. If the *devayājin* is like the inferior who brings tribute to the superior, the implication is that the *ātmayajin* is like the economically autonomous individual.

At SB 9.5.2.12–13 performing rites for another has many negative consequences, with the result that 'he becomes poorer daily who

[68] Gonda 1950: 13–14, 40–42, 58; Cohen 2008: 46–8.

[69] E.g. BU 1.4.10; 2.5.1–4; 4.1.7; 4.4.7, 17, 18; Deussen 1915: 240–70; Smith 1989: 72.

[70] Brereton 1990: 118 calls *brahman* in the Upanishads 'an open concept', 'the designation given to whatever principle or power a sage believes to be behind the world and to make the world explicable'.

[71] Smith 1989: 194.

[72] Tull 1989: 34, also 39: 'the traditional sacrificial format and a form of sacrifice that emphasises the individual to the point of excluding the priests and perhaps even the gods'; Heesterman 1993: 82, 216.

performs these rites for another', whereas 'he who does not perform these rites for another becomes more prosperous daily. Indeed this rite is his divine, undying *ātman*'. This suggests a commercial world in which reciprocity (voluntary requital) has broken down: gifts do not necessarily elicit corresponding benefits in return, and so may impoverish the giver,[73] whereas prosperity is attained through the individual autonomy bestowed by the possession of money, an autonomy that marginalises even the gods. Intermediate between reciprocity and commerce are compulsory gifts, *tribute*, identified negatively above with gifts to the gods.

At BU 1.4.10 one man knows 'I am *brahman*', and becomes 'this whole world', and 'not even the gods are able to prevent it'. He is contrasted with one who worships another deity, thinking 'he is one and I am another'. The latter does not understand, and relates to the gods as livestock do to men, and so 'it is not pleasing to the gods when men know this'. Like those who pay tribute to their superiors, animals serve the economic interests of men, and some sacrificers benefit gods. On the other hand 'if someone venerates himself alone as his world, that rite of his will never fade away, because from his very self he will produce whatever he desires' (1.4.15). Metaphysical autonomy is economic autonomy, in the sense of being independent of others for the fulfilment of desire.

(f) The new configuration prefigures – and probably does not pre-date by much, if at all – the Indian form of EIR: there is a metaphysical store (corresponding to karma) and a repeated cosmic cycle of life and death (corresponding to *saṃsāra*) from which escape into a permanent state (corresponding to *mokṣa*) is possible and desirable. The relationship between store and cycle is undeveloped, and not yet thoroughly ethicised as is EIR, although the passage of CU continues (in what may be a later addition) thus:

> people here whose behaviour is pleasant can expect to enter a pleasant womb, like that of a woman of one of the Brahmin, the Kṣatriya, or the Vaiṣya class. But people of foul behaviour can expect to enter a foul womb, like that of a dog, a pig, or an outcaste woman. (5.10.7)

I suggest that in these and similar texts the value of money as substance and its circulation (what I described in §1 as the two essences of money) are projected as metaphysical merit and cosmic cycle. Just as diminution

[73] Cf. Heesterman 1993: 210.

of money-substance forces the individual into the monetised cycle of exchange, so diminution of metaphysical merit forces the individual into the cosmic cycle of rebirth. This hypothesis is speculative, but is supported by the idea – found in both India and Greece – of cosmic debt.

5. Cosmic Debt

The main focus of the Vedic sacrifice is on the individual sacrificer:[74] in a cosmic rite of passage he is reborn, and taken up to the sky, whence he must return to earth in a victory over death, after entering and obtaining a *loka* to which he will go when he dies.[75] The sacrificial cycle is also the payment of a debt: 'Indeed, even in being born, man, by his own self, is born as a debt to death. And in that he sacrifices, he thereby redeems himself from death.'[76] Malamoud writes of 'the general economy of debt and ransom which, in Brahminism, governs not only the individual life of men but also the whole organisation of the world, and notably the sacrifice'.[77] In the 'whole organisation of the world' another necessary cosmic cycle, in which the sacrifice participates, is the cycle of fertility. Sacrifice nourishes the gods, who send the rain that nourishes plants, and thereby animals, humans and (through sacrifice again) the gods.[78] Nature, the cosmic rite of passage, and debt – each forming a cycle driven by necessity – influence and inform each other, are imagined in terms of each other. We use 'debt' here in the broad sense of *reified obligation to compensate* (whether by providing something or by suffering), of which commercial debt is only one manifestation.

In Greece the cosmic rite of passage, giving temporary access to the next world as a way of ensuring eventual permanent happiness there, is mystic initiation, which is in this respect the equivalent of the Vedic sacrifice.[79] Mystic initiation (sometimes) propounded the cycle of reincarnation,[80] wherein transitions involved *payment*. Plato, in a passage (*Meno* 81a–c) in which he attributes the doctrine of reincarnation to priests and priestesses (probably of mystery cult), also quotes a statement of Pindar (fr. 133) that Persephone will return to the sun above, in the ninth year, the souls of

[74] Biardeau and Malamoud 1976: 157–8.
[75] Lévi 1898: 87–90, 103–6, 130–1; Gonda 1966; Biardeau and Malamoud 1976: 190–5; Collins 1982: 47–8; Tull 1989: 106, 113–15.
[76] SB 3.6.2.16; cf. SB 1.7.2.1–2; 2.2.2.6; 1.9.3.1.
[77] Biardeau and Malamoud 1976: 194 (my translation from the French).
[78] Biardeau and Malamoud 1976: 24; Heesterman 1993: 12, citing SB 5.3.5.17; 7.4.2.22.
[79] Pinchard 2009.
[80] Pl. *Leg.* 10.870e, *Meno* 81a–b, *Crat.* 400c (with *Phd.* 62d); Pind. *Ol.* 2.68–73.

those from whom she will receive ποινὰν (penalty or payment) παλαιοῦ πένθεος (for[81] ancient grief). Whatever the identity of the 'ancient grief', the ποινά may be the same as the 'ποινά for unrighteous deeds' that – in a mystic formula inscribed on gold leaves of the fourth century[82] – the dead initiate claims to have paid as he supplicates Persephone to send him to the seats of the pure. On another leaf of the same period is written 'enter the holy meadow, for the initiate is without ποινά (ἄποινος)'.[83] In the mystic doctrine of reincarnation in Pindar's second Olympian the 'helpless spirits of those who die pay ποινάς here immediately' (i.e. by dying), before then being sentenced beneath the earth.[84] In early Greek texts the idea is common that loss of *psyche* (death) is a payment.[85] In mystic initiation the payment is sometimes of cosmic debt incurred by transgression. To return to the two paths: 'May we be debtless in this, debtless in the other, debtless in the third world! What paths there are trodden by the gods and trodden by the fathers – may we abide debtless on all [those] paths!' (TB 3.7.9.8).[86]

6. Heraclitus

In the five-fire doctrine, fundamental entities are transformed into each other through the intermediary of fire, ending with a man whose cremation then introduces the two-path doctrine: those who have knowledge (of the five-fire doctrine) take the path to permanent residence in the worlds of *brahman*, whereas those who perform ritual (sacrifice) and make offerings rejoin the cosmic cycle. Similarly, for Heraclitus the cosmos is an ever-living fire, kindling in measures and going out in measures (DK 22 B 30), in a cycle of transformations (of the elements) to which the (fiery) soul is subject. Everything happens according to the *logos*, of which it is important to have knowledge,[87] whereas ritual as actually practised – including mystic initiation – is rejected.[88] At the same time Heraclitus presents his doctrine in the form in which cosmological wisdom is traditionally imparted,

[81] Or (much less likely) 'consisting of'.

[82] GJ 6 and 7. Another (GJ 4: fourth century) contains – along with obscure mentions of cosmological elements – the word for 'exchange' (ἀνταμοιβή) used by Heraclitus in DK 22 B 90 (see below).

[83] GJ 27, from Pherai.

[84] Pind. *Ol.* 2.56–8. For this interpretation of the passage (and against others) see Edmunds 2009: 667–9.

[85] Seaford 2017d: 16–19.

[86] Similarly AV 6.117.3.

[87] B 1, 2, 17, 34, 40, 50, 72, etc.

[88] B 5, 14, 15.

mystic initiation,[89] and may therefore be said to interiorise (or introject) the cosmic rite of passage, a phenomenon widespread in Vedic texts of our period, and found also in Parmenides and Plato.[90]

Fire, with its universal power of constant transformation into and from itself, is the ideal vehicle for the cosmic projection of the monetised cycle. As Heraclitus himself puts it, 'all things are an exchange (ἀνταμοιβή) for fire and fire for all things, like goods for gold and gold for goods' (B 90). The cosmic fire embodies (as does money) abstract *logos*,[91] and so does each soul (B 45, 115), which – being composed of part of the cosmic fire – is subject to the cosmic–monetised cycle: it is accordingly expended by the spirit (*thumos*) that 'buys what it wants at the price of soul (ὃ γὰρ ἂν θέλῃ ψυχῆς ὠνεῖται)' (B 85).[92] In interiorising the cosmic rite of passage Heraclitus both projects money onto the cosmos and introjects (interiorises) it into the inner self.

There are similarities here not only with the five-fire and two-path doctrines, but also with another Vedic text. I have noted that the problem of repeated death could be resolved non-ritually as well as by ritual (§4). In the *Taittirīya Brāhmaṇa* (3.11.8) Naciketas is told to build the fire altar so as to obtain the indestructability of sacrifice and *iṣṭāpūrta* and to keep off repeated death. This is a ritual solution. But there follows immediately an action that expresses the inadequacy of the ritual. Prajapati throws gold three times into the sacrificial fire, which is however not pleased by the gold, and so he throws the gold 'into himself, into his heart, into the omnipresent fire.[93] This is why gold is the dearest of all valued objects, and the smallest' (this refers to the high value of a small amount). The gold is then identified with the *dakṣiṇa* (gift or payment to the priests), which Prajapati keeps for himself (not having found anybody to give it to), thereby making himself 'able' (a secondary meaning of *dakṣiṇa*).

[89] Seaford 1986a[9]. What we do not, however, find in the surviving fragments of Heraclitus is escape from the cycle.

[90] Seaford 2016a. There are also significant differences: (1) Vedic sacrifice was a context of *exchange*, producing individual possession or control, but the conclusion of mystic ritual (as of Greek sacrifice) was generally *communal*, the incorporation of the individual into the group; (2) Vedic metaphysics emerged from the interiorisation of the cosmic rite of passage (sacrifice) under the influence of monetisation, whereas in Greece access to the cosmology produced by the projection (by citizens) of money was sometimes represented in a traditional form of cosmological instruction (mystic initiation).

[91] Seaford 2004c: 233 n. 12.

[92] See further Seaford 2017d.

[93] At AV 10.2.29 the *ātman* is in a golden treasure chest in a citadel. At TU 1.6.1 the immortal person (within the heart) that consists of mind is golden.

The tension between the traditional power of performed ritual (involving gifts for the priests) and the new interiorised power of money is expressed in the actions of Prajapati, who becomes 'able' by keeping the gift, in the form of interiorised gold, for himself (instead of giving gifts to the priests and performing sacrifice), with the result that gold is – though rejected by ritual (the sacrificial fire) – the most valued and most valuable thing. The passage expresses the historical transition from reciprocity and performance of the ritual to its monetised individualisation and interiorisation,[94] as in Heraclitus. The association of individualisation with metaphysical merit is much later made explicit, in the *Laws of Manu* (9.111): brothers may live together, 'or they may live separately if they wish for religious merit; for religious merit increases in separation, and so separate rituals are conducive to religious merit'.[95]

Even non-monetary individual property has a close relation to the inner self. At BU 1.5.15 a man is said to consist, like Prajapati, of sixteen parts. 'His fifteen parts consist merely of his wealth, while his sixteenth part is his *ātman*. He is like a wheel, with his *ātman* as hub and his wealth as rim [or plate].' In Plato τὰ ἑαυτοῦ ('the things of oneself') is juxtaposed with ἑαυτός ('oneself').[96] Even closer to the inner self is money. Its invisible power depends for its activation entirely on – and directly enacts – his individual will, and so occupies the boundary between internal and external space. For Greece I have elsewhere demonstrated that the earliest conception of the invisible, controlling, unitary inner self is constructed by introjection of the abstract power-substance of money by which the plurality of possessions (and goods generally) is pervaded and controlled.[97] For Plato, for instance, thinking (*phronesis*) is 'the only right currency (νόμισμα), for which all those [pleasures, pains, fears] must be exchanged' (*Phd.* 69a).

The configuration of ideas shared by Heraclitus with the Prajapati and five-fire/two-path narratives – fire's universal transformative power into and from itself, our subjection to a repeated cosmic cycle, the privileging of knowledge over the performance of ritual, the introjection (interiorisation) of ritual and of money, the inner self as universal fire – is in both cultures *new*, even revolutionary. How do we explain its advent? The idea of a repeated cosmic cycle owes something to cyclical phenomena in nature (day and night, the seasons), as well as to such phenomena as the rise of

94 For the detail of this transition (but with no mention of money) see Heesterman 1985: 26–44; Tull 1989; Heesterman 1993.

95 Trans. in Doniger and Smith 1991: 210.

96 *Resp.* 4.443c–d; *Ti.* 72a5, 77b–c.

97 Seaford 2004c: 297–8, 2017d.

smoke and fall of rain: but there is nothing new about such phenomena in our period, and so they cannot explain the advent of our configuration.

What seems to have occurred in both cultures is the synthesis of three cycles: of nature, of the cosmic rite of passage and of monetised exchange. The idea of the cosmic cycle is influenced by debt, which in the sixth and fifth centuries becomes monetised and so an objective necessity (rather than a moral requirement to reciprocate). The new impersonal omnipotence of money transcends debt, seems more powerful even than the cosmic rite of passage, and traps and absorbs the mass of humankind in an impersonal cycle of activity driven by the alternating need to acquire and expend money (monetised debt). The cycle is projected as a miserable cycle of rebirth, in which the individual – unable to accept (or even imagine) the self-identical isolation imposed on him or her by monetisation – finds other identities, as well as legitimation of the present and hope for the future. In the pre-monetary world of Homer and the *Ṛgveda*, by contrast, there is no cycle of reincarnation and no desire to escape from life.

7. Ethicised Indiscriminate Reincarnation (EIR)

In both Indian and Greek metaphysics of our period there is a strikingly similar development – of EIR – that may be considered a more advanced stage of the developments that we have already described.

In EIR we are trapped in a repeated cycle of reincarnation in which the ethical quality of a life affects the well-being or status of the next life. Credit goes to Gananath Obeyesekere for showing that EIR has never been autonomously generated other than in archaic Greece and archaic India, whereas (unethicised) reincarnation within the kinship group (what I call lineage reincarnation) has been a belief of numerous societies. For India he suggests that lineage reincarnation was transformed into EIR by 'ethicisation', which was itself a result of the concern of new religions 'for the salvation of the ordinary person … Buddhists and Jainas established connections with the lay community in a systematic manner'.[98] True, this new kind of outreach may indeed be connected with the development of EIR, but by itself cannot explain its form or motivation, and is anyway itself in need of explanation. And there is no evidence for such an explanation in Greece.

By contrast, endogenous monetisation as a factor has all four advantages: it is itself explicable (ultimately through practical convenience),

[98] Obeyesekere 2002: 111–12.

explains both the form of EIR and the motivation for adopting it, and applies equally to India and Greece and almost nowhere else.[99]

We have mentioned the development of individual property in India and Greece, as well as the tendency of money to isolate, to make the individual self-sufficient. These developments, together with the indiscriminate engagement of the individual in economic transactions outside his or her lineage, would tend to dissolve the solidarity of the lineage,[100] and to increase differences in the prosperity of individuals, even within the same lineage. Commerce is more easily conducted by the individual than is agriculture, and much more easily than is the semi-nomadic pastoralism of the *Ṛgveda*.

Moreover, money is in principle indifferent to status: in monetised transactions the transactors are – *qua* transactors – equal. Its universal power combines people of different wealth and status into a universal system, and so is easily projected onto the universe as karma, which simultaneously reproduces the form of the monetised cycle (the commercial cycle is driven by the universal power-substance money, the cosmic one by the power-substance karma) and – as ethicised – also provides the perfect universal antidote to the injustice or arbitrariness of its outcome. Its universality transcends lineage, and explains and justifies the inequality of individuals (be it of status, wealth or well-being) both generally and within the lineage (souls are reincarnated from outside the lineage).

In Greece reincarnation was propounded by Empedocles, Pherecydes, Pythagoras, Pythagoreans and probably also in Orphic theogony.[101] As for its ethicised form (EIR), we have already seen clear evidence for it in Pindar and in mystic initiation (§5), and it is also propounded by Plato.[102]

In both India and Greece the cycle of reincarnation is miserable, and it can be escaped through the cosmic rite of passage and through knowledge. One of the fourth-century funerary gold leaves from Thurii (GJ 5.5–6) contains the mystic formula 'I have flown out of the painful circle (κύκλος) of heavy grief. I have approached the longed-for crown with swift feet.' The

[99] The exception is China, which seems in the same period to have been endogenously monetised but did not endogenously develop EIR: a countervailing factor may have been the exceptional strength of the lineage, especially in the form of ancestor cult.

[100] On a number of gold leaves the mystic initiate says 'I am child of earth and the starry sky' (GJ 1.10, 2.6, 8.12, 10.3, 11.3, 12.3, 13.3, 14.3, 16.3, 25.8, 29.3; cf. 18.3).

[101] Empedocles: DK 31 B 115, 118, 119, 120, 122, 124, 126, 127, 146–7; Pherecydes: West 1971: 25; Pythagoras: Xenophanes DK 21 B 7 and 21, and Dicaearchus *ap*. Porph. *VP* 19; Pythagoreans: Arist. *De An*. 407b20; Orphic: West 1983: index s.v. 'metempsychosis'.

[102] *Phd*. 70c, 72a, 81e–82b, 83d, 113a; *Resp*. 10.614–21; *Phdr*. 248c–249d; *Leg*. 9.870d–e, 872e, 10.903d–904e; *Meno* 81b; *Ti*. 42b–c, 91–2. Much later there is Plotinus, *Enn*. 3.2.13.

painful circle here is generally regarded as the cycle of reincarnations.[103] For Plato the escape of some individual souls from the miserable cosmic cycle of reincarnation into a permanent state of well-being is achieved through fundamental knowledge (philosophy) and freedom from corporeal desire.[104]

On the Indian cycle of reincarnation (*saṃsāra*) Gombrich acutely observes that

> society with its web of obligations becomes an analogue for the entire cycle of *saṃsāra*, and on the other hand the homeless life with no social ties becomes an analogue for that release from rebirth for which it is conceived to be literally a preparation.[105]

This requires two modifications. First, the implication that the social is based on the metaphysical ('Society ... becomes an analogue') should be reversed: metaphysics of this kind is constructed (in part) out of socio-economic formation. Second, what is analogous to *saṃsāra* is the cycle of *economic* obligations: cyclical in the sense that goods or services are exchanged for money, which is then exchanged for goods or services. This indiscriminate cycle seems driven by the power-substance money, just as the indiscriminate cycle of reincarnation is driven by karma. The monetised inner self, invisible and isolated, is trapped in both cycles. And if imagining this inner self involved introjection of the abstract power-entity (money),[106] then denial of its existence (by the Buddhist doctrine of *anatta*) would go naturally with the aspiration to escape from the cycles. Buddhism is one of the forms taken by the intellectual transformation with which we are concerned, representing a rupture with Vedic beliefs but also substantial continuity.[107]

Finally, if (as Obeyesekere proposes) lineage reincarnation had survived,[108] then it may have been a factor – along with the cycles of nature, ritual and commerce – in the emergence of the cosmic cycle of indiscriminate reincarnation. The corporeal solidarity of lineage is dissolved into the indiscriminate reincarnation of the isolated incorporeal self.

[103] Graf and Johnston 2013: 127; Zuntz 1971: 321. For Pythagoras the *psyche* was reincarnated in a 'circle of necessity' (κύκλος ἀνάγκης) according to Diog. Laert. 8.14 (probably from Aristoxenos). See also *Orph. fr.* 229K = 348B; Pl. *Phd.* 72b1.

[104] *Phd.* 82b–84b; *Phdr.* 249a–c.

[105] Gombrich 2006: 48.

[106] For this phenomenon in Greece see n. 97 above, and for India my forthcoming monograph.

[107] E.g. Gombrich 2009.

[108] Some evidence for it in the RV has been claimed by Jurewicz: see n. 46 above.

8. Karma

It is impossible to give a comprehensive account of karma, given its variations in time, in space and in different religions and schools of thought. It has nevertheless a core meaning, as a universally ordering power-entity, impersonal and invisible, that is accumulated by individuals and will affect their future well-being. The persistent and widespread appeal of this idea requires explanation. Given the impossibility of comprehensiveness, I will focus on the early Buddhist idea of karma, on the grounds that it is likely to be earlier than most, and is the theme of a detailed study (by McDermott).

Karma is (besides being action, power, entity) a flow or process[109] whose uniform operation has produced the idea that it represents a general principle.[110] It is 'the principle of continuity not just from one life to the next, but from one moment to the next throughout our lives'.[111] In words attributed to the Buddha,

> I am the owner of my karma. I inherit my karma. I am born of my karma. I am related to my karma. I live supported by my karma. Whatever karma I create, whether good or evil, that shall I inherit.[112]

Besides resembling karma in all these respects, money moves – like karma[113] – between subjective and objective, and between abstract and concrete. The invisible power of money is really the power it bestows on its owner, on whose intention it depends (and may seem to merge with).[114] It imposes universal order, and yet as individuals we use it as we choose. Similarly karma is conditioned, and yet – because it is identified with intention[115] – not strictly determined.[116]

Karma projects money beyond this world. A man when he dies takes with him not his property but what he does.[117] 'Even a heavenly being exhausts his stock of good *karman*.'[118] Money combines numerous actions into a causally related sequence, and karma 'inserts a being into a cosmic

109 E.g. McDermott 1984: 111–12; Obeyesekere 2002: 2.
110 E.g. McDermott 1984: 70.
111 Gombrich 2009: 73.
112 *Upajjhathana Sutta* = AN 5.57.
113 Gombrich 1996: 50–1.
114 Just as the (ubiquitous) power of money is on the boundary between internal and external space (§6), so for the Jains (ubiquitous) karma, composed of atoms, is (as a result of action) absorbed into the soul from the outer world: Halbfass 2000: 75; Krishan 1997: 54–5.
115 E.g. AN 3.415.
116 Gombrich 2009: vii, 13.
117 *Saṃyutta Nikāya* 3.20 (also 3.4).
118 Gombrich 2006: 48.

continuity existing outside him'[119] and yet attached to him and experienced by him, and 'fuels the rebirth cycle'.[120]

Ancient and modern descriptions of karma use the terminology of money, wealth and debt.[121] The early Buddhist *Questions of Milinda* contains a simile in which, just as in a shop various goods can be bought, so 'in the Blessed one's bazaar all manner of merchandise advantages are to be bought for karma'.[122] On another passage of the same work, in which a courtesan says that she has always given service for cash whatever the status of the payer, Gombrich comments that

> in economic life, cash is the common denominator, the great universalizer. The Buddha's concept of *kamma* is the precise equivalent in the ethical sphere: no matter who you say you are, you're as good as the quality of your *kamma*.[123]

Good karma may create material wealth.[124] The Buddha compared certain mendicants' speculations on their fate in the next world to the speculation of traders on their various future acquisitions,[125] and maintained that the outcome of trade depends on the trader's offerings to mendicants in a previous life.[126] There is a compatibility between material wealth and spiritual merit that is not confined to Buddhism.[127]

A remarkable characteristic of karma as a *religious* concept is that its power is impersonal, not (usually) dependent on deity. I can accumulate my own money and my own karma, both of which may influence my future without the intervention of any other agent human or divine. With both money and karma there is a causal law[128] or sequence in which actions indirectly affect subsequent actions or states – through creating a store (of money, of karma) that constitutes deferral of the consequences of action.

But money is the same whether obtained by good or bad action, and whether the action it enables is good or bad, whereas karma may be itself

[119] McDermott 1984: 13.

[120] Obeyesekere 2002: 1–2, 82, 126.

[121] E.g. payment: Obeyesekere 2002: 134; inheritance, possession: McDermott 1984: 2, 9, 21; treasure: McDermott 1984: 35–6, 38, 57–8; price: McDermott 1984: 119–20. 'Just like a written contract imperishable karma is like a debt': Nagarjuna (fl. second/third century CE), *Mūlamadhyamakakārikā*, 17.14.

[122] 5.21 (341) (Rhys Davids 1894: 229–30).

[123] Gombrich 2006: 83; Obeyesekere 2002: 184–6; McDermott 1984: 7.

[124] McDermott 1984: 12–13.

[125] *Majjhima Nikāya* 2.132; Wagle 1966: 145. This way of thinking was not confined to Buddhism: see e.g. Malamoud 1983: 39; *Nārada Smṛti* 4.5.

[126] AN 2.81–2; Wagle 1966: 145–6.

[127] Malamoud 1983: 39; *Nārada Smṛti* 4.5.

[128] Karma and the law of causation: Krishan 1997: 195–204.

either good or bad, according to the moral quality of the action. Karma as *ethical* substance uses the deferral inherent in money to connect virtue with reward (and immorality with punishment). Rather as the just ruler of the cosmos (*cakravartin*) is an ethicised cosmic projection of the universal power of monarchy, so karma is an ethicised cosmic projection of the universal power of money. And yet karma is profoundly ambivalent.[129] On the one hand, as ethicised money, it upholds morality and social cohesion. On the other hand it seems to be bondage, because it retains the universal compulsion inherent in money.

The relation between money and karma is not just one of analogy. Nor should we call it metaphor, which might imply the conscious comparison or merging of two known realities. Rather, money was an element with which the imaginary power-entity of karma was constructed. There were, of course, other such elements, notably the ethical and the agricultural.[130] Despite the various respects in which my account is selective, I claim to have provided the only possible way of explaining simultaneously the core meaning of karma, the time and place of its genesis, and its widespread and persistent popularity.

We have in the course of this chapter noted several Indian developments: of exhaustible metaphysical merit, of the cycle of reincarnation, of *karman* and of *brahman* beyond the ritual sphere to mean invisible universal power-entities, of self-directed individualism, of the transformation of numerous ritual correspondences into a single equivalent for all things (monism), and of the automatisation and interiorisation of ritual – resulting in the marginalisation of deity and of reciprocity. I suggest that these seemingly disparate developments are seen to cohere once we accept that an important factor (albeit not the only factor) was the historically explicable development of an impersonal power-entity, universal and abstract, that transcended ritual.

9. Fundamental Differences

The emergence from the clan, through monetisation, of the increasingly autonomous individual was likely to lead to unjustifiable or seemingly arbitrary differences in the flourishing of individuals, which in turn surely contributed to the widespread belief in compensatory metaphysics. Both cultures adopted EIR, but Greek belief in EIR was far less widespread and

[129] E.g. Krishan 1997: 17, 26.
[130] E.g. Gombrich 1996: 50–1; Collins 1982: 218–23.

persistent than it has been in Indian religions, and it always lacked anything corresponding to karma.

This and other differences between Indian and Greek metaphysics can be related to two fundamental differences: (1) the greater individualism of the Indian rite of passage, and (2) the emergence of Indian metaphysics from within the sacrificial tradition.

(1) Greek sacrifices are frequently communally organised, typically end with a communal meal (sometimes on a vast scale), and might be performed e.g. 'on behalf of the Athenians'.[131] The polis may be called a sacrificial community.[132] The Greek cosmic rite of passage, mystic initiation, typically concludes by merging the individual initiand into the group of initiates, and – like sacrifice – could extend to dramatising and reinforcing the solidarity of the polis.[133] By contrast, neither the organisation nor the beneficiary of the Vedic sacrifice is communal,[134] and there is no communal meal.[135] It is the achievement of an individual (the *yajamāna*, sacrificer) for himself,[136] assisted by Brahmin priests. In Vedic ritual and metaphysics the state played no part.[137]

(2) Hesiod and others narrate how, when men and gods feasted together, Prometheus divided the meat into two portions, the best meat wrapped in skin and paunch, and the bones covered with fat. Zeus chose the latter, which became forever after the portion given to the gods in the sacrifice, while mortals eat the best meat.[138] Prometheus was punished, after bringing to mortals not only fire from heaven but also – in a later version of the myth – 'all their techniques'.[139] The myth is aetiological of the communal sacrificial feast for mortals, and of their separation from the gods into a permanently autonomous sphere. The Vedic aetiological myth of sacrifice, by contrast, contains no such autonomy: men and gods once ate together but were separated, and sacrifice is an attempt to restore their

[131] Parker 2005: 95–7.
[132] Seaford 2004c: 41, 49.
[133] Animal sacrifice: Seaford 2004c: 41, 49; mystic initiation: Seaford 2012a: 44–6, 275; the Eleusinian mysteries in particular: Parker 2005: 343.
[134] Apart from some temporary groups that disband after the sacrifice: Keith 1925: 258; Heesterman 1993: 35.
[135] Malamoud 1996: 171; Keith 1925: 273–4.
[136] Biardeau and Malamoud 1976: 157–8. But it may have had political significance, as the site of exchange between priests and a powerful individual.
[137] Even the royal consecration (*rājasūya*) 'is not concerned with society or polity but exclusively with the metaphysical fate of the single sacrificer as a private individual': Heesterman 1993: 69.
[138] Hes. *Theog.* 535–60.
[139] [Aesch.] *PV* 506.

togetherness.[140] The Greek sacrifice is performed at a greater distance from the gods than is the Vedic. The next episode narrated by Hesiod is the conflict of the new order of Olympians with the older disordering gods (Titans). In the corresponding Indian conflict between the new order of gods (devas) and the older disordering asuras, the conflict occurs – in significant contrast to the Greek version – by means of, and for control of, the sacrifice.[141] The priests performing the Greek animal sacrifice were not members of a priestly caste but citizens.

As a result of (1) and (2) combined, there emerged from the Greek communal sacrificial meal (in contrast to the impregnable individualism of the Vedic sacrifice) a sacrificial community (without a priestly caste), the polis controlled by the community of citizens, and ultimately a separate human sphere.[142] The Greek communal distribution of meat used iron spits, which were durable, of standard size and easily portable and storable, as well as enjoying divine sanction and communal confidence. As such, they were able to be a stage on the way to coinage, giving their name (*obelos*) to obol coins.[143] Coinage – made possible (like the polis itself) by sacrificial community – was produced and controlled by the polis, whose emblem it bore, and quickly lost all association with sacrifice. The Presocratic thinkers who imagined the universe in terms of the communal power of coined money did so not as priests but as citizens.[144]

Vedic sacrifice was a site of substantial debt-driven payment, but lacked communal distribution – and so could not contribute to the development of coinage or of polis. But it retained a central role in the transformation of cosmology, under the influence of (externally derived) monetisation, within the impregnable priestly (Brahminical) tradition.

10. *Brahman* and *Karman*

Among metaphysical entities *brahman* and *karman* are exceptionally universal, and become exceptionally important. They both originate in the sphere of ritual performed on behalf of the individual, but extend their

140 SB 2.3.4.4; 3.6.2.26.

141 Lévi 1898: 36–61; BU 1.3.1–7; CU 1.2.1–7; SB 2.1.2.13–17.

142 Cf. Halbfass 1991: 266: 'there is no tradition of explicit and thematic thought about man as man in India, no tradition of trying to define his essence and to distinguish it from other forms of life', in contrast to western anthropocentrism.

143 Detail in Seaford 2004c: 102–15.

144 E.g. for Heraclitus and the polis see DK 22 B 2, 44, 114; for Parmenides and the polis see Speusippus *ap*. Diog. Laert. 9.23; Plut. *Adv. Col.* 1126a; Strabo 6.1.1 (C 252).

meanings beyond the ritual sphere, and from power/action to include entity/substance. Despite this extension, driven in part by monetisation, *brahman* and *karman* both retain their connection with individual access to metaphysical salvation.

But there is polarisation between *brahman* and *karman*. *Brahman*, referring originally to ritual *power*, came to express *unchanging universal value*, from the perspective of individual *ownership* (separated from circulation, like Parmenidean Being). The exalted people who attain *brahman* have separated themselves permanently from cosmic circulation (§4). This is analogous to separation from monetised circulation by accumulating or owning sufficient abstract value. However, the exalted people have attained *brahman* not by accumulating metaphysical merit, which decreases, but rather by *knowledge* (I will explain below how this is possible).

By contrast karma, which referred originally to the *correct practice* of ritual, came accordingly to *ethicise* money from the perspective of individual *practice*: the individual accumulation of money benefits its owner within the exchange cycle, of karma within the reincarnation cycle. In contrast to *brahman*, which is comprehensive, indivisible and unchanging, karma (*karman*) is accumulated by individuals for their future well-being and (like money driving the cycle of exchange) drives the cycle of reincarnation.

This returns us again to the two essences of money (§1). What corresponds to unchanging ubiquitous value is Parmenidean Being and *brahman*, whereas what corresponds to value-in-circulation and Heraclitean fire is karma. There are, however, substantial differences between the Greek and the Indian concepts.

Parmenidean Being and *brahman* are unchanging, universal, invisible and ontologically privileged: they are each, in part, a projection of the universal but invisible value of money from the perspective of individual ownership. But it is as an economically self-sufficient citizen that Parmenides imagined the ruthless separation of Being from circulation, whereas it is as purveyors of metaphysical salvation to wealthy individuals that the Brahmins imagined a universal principle (*brahman*) that originated as the power of ritual, takes various forms and could be related or identified with various entities.[145] *Brahman* is a synthesis of two kinds

[145] For *brahman* in the Upanishads as an 'open concept' see n. 70 above.

of invisible, transcendent power, each fuelled by wealth and directed by the individual to his or her own benefit: the power of sacrifice and of money. In this synthesis the ritual is interiorised, the worlds that it obtains are absorbed into the subject. The resulting relation between subject and object is expressed in the idea that the individual subject (*ātman*) contains everything, or obtains (or is identified with) *brahman*.[146] The attainment of the 'worlds of *brahman*' is – in the two-path doctrine – for some 'exalted people' a permanent escape from the cycle of reincarnation (§4). The individual subject, the agent and beneficiary of sacrificial ritual, remains – with the monetised interiorisation of the ritual – irreducibly at the heart of the resulting metaphysics, for which he or she may still depend on Brahminical knowledge. Parmenidean Being, expressing the ideology of absolute separation of value from circulation, is all that there is, whereas the Brahminical ideological imperative is the access of the individual subject through Brahminical knowledge to a metaphysical power or principle that is universal but specific.

It is from the same perspective that we should see the similarities and differences between karma and the *logos*-embodying Heraclitean fire. They share characteristics shaped by money: as universal principles that order the cosmic cycle (including the cyclical passage of the soul) and combine objective with subjective.[147] But it is as a citizen that Heraclitus sublimates (projects) monetary circulation, from the communal perspective: fire is constantly transformed into all else, the individual soul is not identified (as is *ātman*) with the universe, but participates in it (as a fragment of the universal circulating fire), and any ethical imperative centres on the communality of the all-directing *logos*.[148] By contrast karma – as owned and accumulated in order to benefit its owner by exercising ethicised power within the cycle – sublimates money from the perspective of individual practice.

11. Plato

Especially illuminating of the absence of karma in Greece is the Greek proponent *par excellence* of EIR, namely Plato. In the *Republic* (3.416e) Plato

146 E.g. BU 1.4.10; 3.4.1–2; 4.4.5–7; CU 3.14; 8.14.

147 I defer to my monograph the most striking resemblances between Heraclitean and Indian fire (in Buddhism).

148 DK 22 B 2, 44, 89, 113, 114, 102: 'for god all things are fine and good and just, but men have supposed some things unjust and some just'.

stipulates that his guardians are to be told that they have divine, unpolluted gold and silver money in their souls and have no need of human money, for 'many impious things have been done in connection with the coin of the multitude, whereas theirs is unpolluted'. Here, as well as less obviously elsewhere, monetary value is abstracted from circulation and interiorised (introjected) as self-sufficient invisible being. But it is not only from the circulation of *money* that the philosopher is separated by his interiorisation of self-sufficient abstract *ousia* (property or Being); it is also from the cycle of *rebirth*: philosophical absorption in abstract Being separates him from the attachment to corporeality that causes rebirth.[149] Reality turns out to have at its heart a metaphysical projection of the unchanging abstract *ousia* from which Plato and other privileged citizens derive their economic self-sufficiency.

Heraclitus sublimates all-pervasive monetary circulation as all-pervasive fire (embodying the abstract *logos*), whereas Parmenides sublimates all-pervasive abstract *ousia* imagined in isolation from circulation. Plato partially adopts both positions. On the one hand he privileges unchanging abstract Being, which is accordingly – like Parmenidean abstract Being[150] (and karma) – strongly (albeit differently) *ethicised*, as 'the form of the good'.[151] But on the other he also describes the cosmic projection of the miserable monetised cycle (EIR), from which permanent escape is possible by virtuous and wise adherence to abstract Being. And in the same vein he attempts in various ways (not entirely successfully) to relate and subordinate concrete multiplicity (simply denied in the Parmenidean 'way of truth') to abstract Being.

With the freedom from corporeal desire enjoined by Plato as conducive to escape from the cycle of reincarnation we should compare the similar idea in BU 4.4.6 (quoted in §4). But for Plato the escape is achieved by philosophical absorption in unchanging abstract reality, which is impeded by corporeal desire. He recommends (sublimated) desire,[152] and has no objection to action as such, whereas in the BU passage identification with unchanging *brahman* is – it is implied – impeded by (reified, exhaustible) action (*karman*), which derives from desire. This doctrine, propounded by

[149] *Phd.* 80d–84b; *Phdr.* 248c–249d. Plato, calling the good (from which the objects of knowledge receive knowability and *ousia*) 'beyond *ousia*' (*Resp.* 6.509b), expresses the self-sufficiency of value (given that for him *ousia* (Being) is not entirely separated from circulation).

[150] DK 28 B 8.14–15, 30–32, 37–8, 48.

[151] See esp. *Resp.* 6.505a, 508a–e, 7.532b1; *Leg.* 12.965b–966b.

[152] See e.g. *Symp.* 210a1, 212b; *Phdr.* 244a–257b.

the sage Yajnavalkya, prefigures the doctrine of renunciation, and indeed he becomes a renouncer (4.4.6–5.1).

Monetisation creates in this world a miserable cycle, from which there are two ways to withdraw. One is from above (ownership of sufficient money), the other from below (renunciation, homelessness). Paradoxically, the Indian renouncer's withdrawal from below is (as metaphysically powerful) one way of attaining a universal but invisible entity (*brahman*) that is shaped in part by individual ownership of the universal but invisible entity money. We saw that in BU certain exalted people escape the reincarnation cycle, and attain *brahman*, by knowledge. It is immediately after expounding the self-knowledge required to attain *brahman* that Yajnavalkya becomes a renouncer.

The withdrawal recommended by Plato involves attainment of an entity (abstract Being) comparable to *brahman*, but is limited to *inner* withdrawal – from the disturbance created by certain emotions and sensations and by corporeal desire. The aristocratic Plato was said to have left no debts and considerable wealth.[153] The guardians of his ideal republic, although they own no private property and are forbidden from polluting the divine money in their souls by mixing it with monetary circulation, are nevertheless *citizens*, provided with an income (μισθός) by other citizens.[154]

The withdrawal of the Indian renouncer, by contrast, could be extreme. Inasmuch as actions (even eating) require money, i.e. create debt, which necessitates further action (work), the pure form of renunciatory escape from the monetary cycle is the *rejection* of action (even eating), as recommended by the Jains and the Ajivikas. They reject all money, whether metaphysical (karma) or worldly, both of which are created by action, which accordingly they also reject.[155]

The logic that might drive even a wealthy sage such as Yajnavalkya[156] to become a renouncer is, I suggest, illustrated in CU 7. We start with a long chain of dependences: speech depends on mind, which depends on intention, and so on. Towards the end of the chain, action depends on (22) *sukha* (happiness, well-being), which is (23) identified with plenitude (*bhūman*), which is identified with prosperity. Then we are told that 'where

[153] Diog. Laert. 3.41–3: two country estates, four household servants and a certain amount of gold and silver. I (merely) note here the importance of slavery for Plato's metaphysics.

[154] *Resp*. 3.416d–e.

[155] Another way of avoiding being bound to karma is *niṣkāmakarma*, action done without desire for the fruits of karma, propounded especially in the *Bhagavad Gītā*.

[156] Black 2007: 95.

a man sees, hears, or discerns no other thing, that is *bhūman*', which is immortal (24). Similarly, Parmenides finds in the content of the mind the plenitude of Being[157] that – we maintain – introjects monetary Being abstracted from exchange.

'On what is *bhūman* based?' The answer is 'on one's own greatness. Or perhaps not on greatness.' For what people here call greatness is cattle and horses, elephants and gold, slaves and wives, farms and houses. 'But I don't consider them that way; no I don't, for they are all based on each other.'[158] Rather (25) *bhūman* extends over the whole world. 'Next, the substitution of the word "I"', and of *ātman*, both of which extend over the whole world. Someone who sees, thinks and perceives it thus takes pleasure in the self, mates with the self, etc., becomes his or her own master and obtains freedom to move in all the worlds, and (26) the whole world springs from his or her *ātman*, whereas those who perceive it otherwise are ruled over by others and obtain perishable worlds.

To regard individual possessions and prosperity as *bhūman* – i.e. fundamental in the chain of dependence and identified with well-being – makes practical sense. But alternatively *bhūman* is where someone perceives no other thing, i.e. the extreme self-sufficiency of the subject that is united with all else. *Bhūman* and *ātman* are co-extensive with the universe. The self-sufficient freedom brought by *bhūman* (normally individual property) is redefined as the devotion to *ātman* that means not being ruled by others. *Bhūman*, fundamental and immortal, is both *introjected* as *ātman* and *projected* as the universe (as is *ātman*), thus assimilating object to subject, universe to inner self. So too in early Greek metaphysics money is both projected and introjected, also with the immortalising assimilation of object to subject.[159] Individual possessions are rejected because 'they are all based on each other', whereas true *bhūman* is universal: once there is a universal measure of value, the value of each possession is determined by the value of others, and it is only (abstracted) monetary value that is universal, transcendent and fundamental. It is the introjection (and projection) of this true *bhūman* (rather than escape from above through wealth) that brings self-sufficient freedom.

[157] DK 28 B 8.22–5, B 4.

[158] This is Olivelle's translation of *anyo hy anyasmin pratiṣṭhita iti*, literally 'for another is based/founded on another', a single syntactic unit referring to the things listed in the previous sentence.

[159] E.g. Seaford 2004c: 229, 251–2.

Monetisation both created a new problem (individuals isolated in unjustifiably different states) and was itself projected as the solution in the form of the metaphysical scheme of karma, *saṃsāra* and escape. Karma retained the role it had in the ritual sphere of providing individual access to metaphysical salvation, while acquiring a new role as the ethicised projection of individually owned value from the perspective of individual practice.

The popular appeal of such a perspective may have been the basis of the establishment – noted by Obeyesekere – of enduring lay communities, especially by the Buddhists. Buddhism early banned its monks from handling money,[160] but (in contrast to the Jains and Ajivikans) did not idealise complete inaction. For Buddhism there may be good and bad karma, just as money may be earned or owed. It arose in a commercial milieu, and there is evidence for Buddhist monks early associating with merchants.[161] Accordingly the rise of Buddhism has been interpreted by some as legitimating, and by others as rejecting, the commercial values of the new society. On this controversy Gombrich correctly observes that 'having it both ways is precisely what religions excel at': satisfying very different needs may promote success.[162] We may add, more specifically, that (in the practice of monks) Buddhism idealised moneylessness while ethicising money in the universe as karma.

For the millions trapped in the monetised cycle, as well as for renouncers, there was – in Buddhism and Hinduism alike – enduring appeal in the combination provided by karma: legitimation, hope and the transcendent ethicising of the everyday oppressive omnipotence of money from the perspective of individual practice. This had no counterpart in Greece. Parmenides and Plato were wealthy aristocratic citizens.[163] Their ethicised projection of unchanging abstract value from the perspective of individual ownership (separate from practice) expressed an aristocratic ideology of monetised debtlessness, of withdrawal from the cycle from above, that could have little popular appeal. At the other extreme, the projection of circulation from the austerely communal perspective of Heraclitus was unlikely to engage the monetised individual, whether rich or poor. Greek philosophy was produced by (often wealthy) citizens. The Brahmins and Buddhists of our period were by contrast primarily not self-sufficient

[160] Gombrich 2006: 104–5.
[161] See §3 above; Gombrich 2009: 27, 95–110; *Vinaya* 1.152; 2.158–9; Gombrich 2006: 52–6, esp. 54.
[162] Gombrich 2006: xii, 14.
[163] For Parmenides see Sotion *ap.* Diog. Laert. 9.21: 'of illustrious family and wealth'. For Plato see n. 153 above.

controllers of abstract value but purveyors of the knowledge required for metaphysical well-being. In Greece the state had greater stability, power and loyalty than it did in India, and so the popular need for ultimate justice was more likely to be met by a cosmic tribunal than by ethicised money. This fundamental difference between India and the west is still with us.[164]

164 My thanks for valuable comments on this chapter go to Greg Bailey, Robert Bostock, Mik Burley, Matylda Obryk, Alexis Pinchard, Chiara Robbiano and Paolo Visigalli. I am also grateful to the Arts and Humanities Research Council for funding the research from which this chapter is drawn.

PART VIII

Money and Modernity

CHAPTER 20

Form and Money in Wagner's Ring *and Aeschylean Tragedy*

The evidence for the influence of Greek tragedy on Wagner includes numerous statements by Wagner about Greek tragedy and numerous specific thematic similarities between Greek tragedy and his operas. This evidence has been repeatedly discussed,[1] and I do not have space here even to summarise it. Nor do I have space for any kind of overall interpretation, or to consider the musical dimension. I focus rather on suggesting a specific similarity between the *Ring* as a whole and the Aeschylean trilogy. In doing so I will suggest some influences on Wagner (or at least striking similarities) that – except where I acknowledge it – I have not found in any of the scholarship.

I must start by stating three things that *are* already well known. First, there is the similarity of form between Aeschylus and the *Ring*. Wagner achieves Aeschylean coherence and economy by combining episodes that in his Nordic and Germanic sources were quite separate from each other, but also by eliminating numerous events and characters, so as to produce a single coherent narrative, marked by a sense of inexorability over three successive generations, in a trilogy[2] consisting of a few decisive actions in a sequence of (often agonistic) scenes, in many of which there are only two or three characters.

Second, the unity of the *Ring* depends largely on the ring itself: made by Alberich from gold stolen from the Rhine, the ring is then stolen from Alberich by Wotan, cursed by Alberich, paid by Wotan to the giants for building Valhalla, guarded by Fafner, coveted by Alberich and Mime, taken by Siegfried after slaying Fafner, given by Siegfried to Brünnhilde, still coveted by Alberich and by Hagen, snatched from Brünnhilde by Siegfried, and finally returned to the Rhine. The ring is contested almost throughout

[1] Most notably by Schadewaldt 1970: 341–405 and Ewans 1982, and recently by Foster 2010.

[2] The Wagnerian trilogy is preceded by a 'Vorabend' (*Rheingold*); the Aeschylean is followed by a satyr play.

the *Ring*, desired by dwarves, gods and giants, mediating their interactions, and possessed in succession by a dwarf, a god, a giant, a dragon, a hero, an ex-Valkyrie, the hero again and finally the Rhinedaughters.

Third, the ring – it is frequently emphasised by various characters – bestows great wealth, and power over the whole world. With it Alberich forces the Nibelungs to amass for himself by their labour wealth that 'will increase in the future'. The desirability and cursed power of the ring expresses the ambivalence of *money*. None of this is new.[3] My own suggestion begins with a simple observation about the relationship between form and theme.

It is the potential omnipotence of money, and its consequent near-universal desirability, that unifies the disparate mythical material combined by Wagner. The result is coherence not only of form but also of form with theme, for it is precisely the power of money that – in the *Ring* as in reality – brings together heterogeneous agents and mediates relations between them. Gold, says Alberich, is desired by 'all that lives', and he would rather Wotan take his life than the ring.[4]

Formal unity is created not just by the universal desirability of money but also by the temporal continuity inherent in the movement of money. At the end of *Rheingold*, as the gods triumphantly proceed to Valhalla, there appear the Rhinedaughters demanding their gold back, and then in *Die Walküre* Wotan, fearing that Alberich will regain the ring, declares that he must wrest it back from the giant to whom he paid it. At the end of *Agamemnon* the triumphant Aigisthos' plan to use Agamemnon's money to rule the citizens (1638–9) is met by a prediction of the coming of Orestes, already foreseen by Kassandra. Throughout both *Ring* and *Oresteia* each success necessitates disaster. The principle that causes a metaphorical net to fall over Troy to punish its excess (*Ag.* 355–84, 461–70, etc.) seems to trap its conqueror in a net (1382–3, etc.). Likewise, Wotan laments that 'these are the bonds that bind me; I, lord of contracts, am now a slave to the contracts', and that 'in my own fetters I caught myself'.

Oresteia

In a famous passage of his autobiography Wagner describes the powerful impact on him (in 1847) of reading Aeschylus in the translation by Droysen, in particular the *Oresteia*. Distinct (albeit loosely connected)

[3] E.g. on form see Ewans 1982: 63–6; on money see Shaw 1923.

[4] The strange preference for money over life occurs at Soph. *Ant.* 322, and is implied at Aesch. *Sept.* 697 (if correctly interpreted).

epic narratives – the murders of Agamemnon and Klytaimestra – were combined by Aeschylus[5] with previous and subsequent events into a single narrative. What holds this new narrative together is conflict, over three generations, for the power and wealth of the royal household, which is disputed by the brothers Atreus and Thyestes, then taken from Atreus' son Agamemnon by Thyestes' son Aigisthos, from whom it is taken by Agamemnon's son Orestes. The violence of the successive struggles is frequently represented as for economic benefit, or at least in terms of economic exchange.[6] It also frequently seems impelled by unseen forces, in particular the curse and its agents.[7] Droysen sometimes even introduces the curse where it is not in the Greek, with the result that 'his *Oresteia* is the saga of a curse-ridden house'.[8] Similarly, Wagner in the *Ring* created coherence around curse-driven conflict for the emblem of money.

The Aeschylean and Wagnerian patterns are each obtained by condensing and reshaping a combination of traditional narratives. But the Germanic and Nordic narratives out of which Wagner created the *Ring* are so diverse[9] that he had to be more eclectic than Aeschylus in creating the 'unitarian (*einheitvolle*) form' that for the Greek tragic poet 'lay mapped out for him in the framework of the myth'.[10] A ring occurs in various of Wagner's sources, but without ever having the potential to confer mastery over the world.[11] He innovates by giving the ring not only universal power but also a structuring role from beginning to end of the narrative – by providing it with the Rhine as origin and final destination.[12] As for the curse on the ring, it did occur in the Prose Edda: the dwarf Andvari, robbed of treasure and ring by the gods, 'said that the ring should cost everyone who possessed it his life'.[13] But Alberich's curse on the ring is much more elaborate, bringing to its possessors not just death but unhappiness ('as long as he lives let him die yearning to die, lord of the ring as slave of the ring'), and, to those who do not possess it, ravaging envy. The curse proves effective.

[5] This is uncertain, because so much earlier Greek literature has been lost.

[6] *Ag.* 1331–42, 1560–2, 1638–9; *Cho.* 135–6, 301, 306–13, 372, 518–21, 801, 943; *Eum.* 319–20, 757–8; Seaford 2012a: 196–205.

[7] *Ag.* 1086–93, 1477, 1481–2, 1501–3, 1565, 1583–1602; *Cho.* 692, 924, 1075–6; *Eum.* 417.

[8] Shown by Ewans 1982: 30.

[9] Detailed account in Cooke 1979.

[10] Wagner, *Opera and Drama*, at Wagner 1900: 156. In tragedy, which took mythical compression to an extreme (155), myth expresses itself as a single decisive action in which a great idea reveals itself (156).

[11] For the closest to an exception see Cooke 1979: 138.

[12] In Wagner's sources the treasure (not the ring) is hidden or thrown into the Rhine, but not to conclude a narrative: Cooke 1979: 135.

[13] Cooke 1979: 223–4.

Thebes

The sources of Aeschylus' Theban trilogy were also diverse. One lost Theban epic (*Oidipodeia*) told the story of Oidipous, including his curse on his sons Eteokles and Polyneikes; another (*Thebais*) narrated the unsuccessful siege of Thebes by Polyneikes supported by six external warriors; and a third (*Epigoni*) related the eventual successful capture of Thebes by the sons of the slain seven. Droysen describes how Aeschylus concentrated these events into two trilogies, his mode being 'to increase affliction through affliction and *Schuld* [guilt, debt] through *Schuld*'.[14] The only surviving play, the *Septem*, frequently refers to invisible forces operating over generations, in particular to Oidipous' curse to the effect that his sons will divide their property by the sword.[15] Here too, as in the *Oresteia* and the *Ring*, diverse narratives have been combined around conflict for power and wealth. Scholars have detected numerous specific Aeschylean influences on Wagner without recognising this fundamental similarity, and they have neglected the Theban trilogy.

In his *Opera and Drama* (1851) Wagner discusses the Theban myth. The incest of Oidipous and Iokaste was not contrary to nature, but rather an offence against custom (*Gewohnheit*). When subsequently Eteokles refused to abide by his oath to share the kingship with his brother Polyneikes, the citizens sided with Eteokles, and in doing so

> showed a practical instinct for the nature of property (*Eigenthum*), which everybody wanted to enjoy alone, not to share with another. Every citizen who recognised in property the guarantee of customary (*gewohnte*) quiet was thereby an accomplice of the unbrotherly deed of Eteokles, the supreme proprietor (*Eigenthümer*). The power of self-serving *Gewohnheit* thus supported Eteokles. (Wagner 1900: 185)

Gewohnheit (custom) 'had already become their virtual lawgiver'. And in the subsequent rule of Kreon, who deprived Polyneikes of burial, the state (*Staat*) came to represent nothing but abstract *Gewohnheit*, only to be overthrown in the overthrow of Kreon (the *Staat* personified) by the pure human love (*reine Menschenliebe*) embodied in Antigone. 'The

[14] 2.153. All translations are my own (except for the letter to Liszt), but for Wagner's prose I give page references to the unsatisfactory translation by Ashton Ellis.

[15] *Sept.* 819, 832, 840–1, 886, 894, 898, 945–6, 954, 977–88; and mentioned earlier at 70, 655, 695–701, 709, 720–3, 766–7. Note also 801–2, 842, 742–5 'a transgression born long ago, quickly punished but remaining to the third generation'.

love-curse (*Liebesfluch*) of Antigone annihilated the *Staat*.' The kernel of the concrete *Staat*

> appears to us in the Oidipous saga: as the seed of all crimes we recognise the sovereignty of Laios, who for the sake of its undiminished possession became an unnatural father. From this possession become ownership (*Eigenthum*), which amazingly is regarded as the basis of all good order, flows all the wickedness of myth and history. (Wagner 1900: 192).

But the downfall of the *Staat* is inevitable. In the Oidipous myth 'we win an intelligible picture of the whole history of humankind from the beginnings of society to the necessary downfall (*Untergang*) of the *Staat*' (Wagner 1900: 191). The 'whole history of humankind' moves from nature to the *Staat* based on self-serving *Gewohnheit* and *Eigenthum*, and from there to the final destruction of the *Staat* by human love.

Opera and Drama was published in November 1851, in a period in which the *Ring* was taking shape in Wagner's mind. The relevance of its discussion of the Theban myth to the *Ring* was finally recognised in 1982 by Borchmeyer,[16] but even he did not describe the full significance for the *Ring* of Droysen's account of the Theban trilogy. As well as reading Aeschylus in Droysen's translation, Wagner praised the *comments* of Droysen,[17] who describes as follows what he calls the main content (*Hauptinhalt*) of the trilogy to which *Septem* belonged:

> The most terrible paternal curse, the power of blind, inexhaustible wildness, rages on and on against the particular lineage, until the last branch withers, until the last memory of its unhappy existence is extinguished, and a new, milder *Geschlecht* [family, race] rules more happily in the palace of the Kadmea.[18]

Oidipous' curse is familiar from the *Septem*. But whence the 'new, milder *Geschlecht*'?

Droysen describes the trilogy as reconstructed by Welcker, but also proposes a reconstruction of his own, in which the sequence of plays is *Nemeans*, *Septem*, *Epigoni*. He assumes that in the lost *Epigoni* the sons of the seven slain besiegers of Thebes succeeded in destroying the city rather than just capturing it. The only surviving fragment of the play

[16] Translated in Borchmeyer 1991: 306–7.

[17] Droysen 1832. It is important to be aware that Wagner in Dresden in 1847 possessed the 1832 edition, for Droysen's comments 'in the later versions appear substantially changed or abbreviated': von Westernhagen 1966: 39, 84.

[18] Droysen 1832: II.109.

mentioned marriage, from which Droysen infers that this was the marriage of Antigone to a son of Kreon. Fate was finally fulfilled in the downfall (*untergehen*) of the royal family, and of the city itself, at the hands of a new and milder *Geschlecht*, and the marriage of Antigone (to a relative, we note) formed a joyful contrast to the destruction (*Vernichtung*) of the city. Elsewhere Droysen characterises Aeschylean tragedy as a whole as moving from initial 'dark, silent doom (*Verhängnis*)' to the advent of 'a new, happier *Geschlecht*' (Droysen 1832: 11.283). In the *Ring*, Wotan fathers a new race, the Wälsungs, a *Wunschgeschlecht*, that – in the context of the imminent downfall of the gods – he hopes will free him from guilt and conflict, and that in fact will embody the antithesis presented by heterosexual love (even if incestuous) to power. This idea is not found in Wagner's northern source, the *Volsunga saga*.[19]

As for the annihilated royal family, Laios became an unnatural father – Wagner tells us – for the sake of his undiminished possession of rulership, which grew into *Eigenthum* (ownership), the source of all crimes. Sovereign power is here united with wealth in *Eigenthum*, the persistent source and object of the conflict, from Laios exposing his son to Eteokles being cursed to fight his own brother for *Eigenthum*. The *Septem* is a powerful dramatisation of curse-driven conflict for *Eigenthum*, especially in the departure of Eteokles, impelled by the curse to divide his inheritance with the sword.[20] In both Aeschylean trilogies, as in the *Ring*, the curse is uttered by a victim in the persistent conflict for *Eigenthum* (Thyestes, Oidipous, Alberich). And most of the curse-driven conflict for the ring is, as in *Septem*, between brothers (Alberich–Mime, Fafner–Fasolt, Hagen–Gunther).

Prometheia

Numerous similarities have been observed between the *Prometheia* and the *Ring*. Here again, Wagner was influenced by Droysen's *comments*. Only one play of the trilogy survives (*Prometheus Bound*),[21] in which Zeus is the cosmic projection of the typical *tyrannos*. As a god, he does not express concern with money, but is frequently called *tyrannos*, and has the isolation and the absolute power bestowed on the human *tyrannos* by money,[22] as

[19] Cooke 1979: 282–307.
[20] *Sept.* 695, 700, 709, 720–33.
[21] In the lifetime of Wagner it was assumed to be by Aeschylus.
[22] *PV* 186–7, 224–5, 304–6, etc.; Seaford 2003d[5].

well as his *insecurity*: Zeus is no less anxious than Wotan to ensure a permanent future.

According to Droysen, the victory of Zeus was the victory of the human spirit (*Menschengeist*) embodied in his ally Prometheus. But subsequently the *Menschengeist* 'succumbed to the individual life (*Einzelleben*), the finiteness of creaturely existence', the *Gattung* (species, type) breaks up into individuals, innocence succumbs to wilfulness, and 'the blind selflessness of natural life comes to an end in the intense centralisation of selfishness and of consciousness'.[23] As a result, Zeus wants to destroy the human race, but Prometheus saves it and gives it the power to win back the world it has lost. Droysen had also explained (1832: II.160) that Zeus wanted to create a new, more obedient *Geschlecht*. But Zeus is under the curse of his displaced father, Kronos,

> for the ethical world which he rules is based on the overthrow of the previously ruling world order, and every age of the world that perishes, every declining epoch of history, leaves the same curse as inheritance for its successor in the domination of the world.

From this paternal curse Zeus can be freed only by a hero born of – in a fragment from the play – 'a mortal woman from earth-born seed' (fr. 369). The influence of this liberating mortal hero (Herakles) on Wagner, and of much else in the *Prometheia*, has been recognised.[24] But there is more. A morally serious combination – of a persistent curse, an order (political or cosmic) based on selfish individualism, the destruction of the order, and a new *Geschlecht* – occurs not only in Droysen's account of the *Prometheia* but also in his account of the Theban trilogy, in Wagner's account of the Theban myth and in the *Ring*. The selfish individualism of tragic *Eigenthum* is in Wagner embodied in the cursed ring.

Isolation

It was in the latter half of the sixth century BCE, probably during the rule of the *tyrannos* Peisistratos, that coinage was introduced into Athens, in a period of significant and rapid cultural development that included the creation of the spectacular and entirely new genre of tragedy. Whether or not this development was facilitated by monetisation, tragedy develops in – and reflects – a world that had recently been rapidly and pervasively

[23] Droysen 1832: II.210.
[24] Ewans 1982: 256–60 downplays this influence.

monetised by the arrival of coinage.[25] This is an important and generally unrecognised fact about Athenian tragedy.

The unprecedented[26] *isolation* of the individual of Athenian tragedy, in conflict with those closest to him (Agamemnon, Orestes, Oidipous, Kreon, Eteokles and Zeus, among many others), owes something, I believe, to the isolating potential of the new all-pervasive phenomenon of money. In the Theban tragedies of Sophocles, for instance, Oidipous and Kreon are each preoccupied by money, described as *tyrannos*[27] and alienated from their closest kin, a combination found also in the *tyrannoi* described in historiography and philosophy:[28] for instance, the *tyrannos* Polykrates murdered one of his brothers and exiled the other, and eventually fell through trying to amass enough money to rule the whole of Greece.[29] In the *Oresteia* and the Theban trilogy, within the family one individual struggles with another for its *Eigenthum*, which provides both content and form: the universal motivation it provides in the real world (as money) holds together the trilogic narrative. Similarly, in the *Ring* several of the leading individuals are isolated, each in conflict with his closest kin (Wotan with Fricka and Brünnhilde, Alberich with Mime, Fafner with Fasolt, Hagen with Gunther), and all these male characters are drawn into conflict for the ring, which gives coherence to the *Ring*. The isolating effect of money is expressed not only in the scenes of conflict over the ring but also, exquisitely, in Wotan's rejection of the pleas of the other gods, his kin, to give the ring to the giants (in return for Freia), until instructed to do so by Erda.

Props

In the *Ring*, in contrast to Aeschylus, the curse is embodied in a single object: money takes the form of a talismanic artefact, which in (pre-monetary) myth has magical power but seems to an audience in a monetised society to be also a *symbol* (of money). The same revealing combination of opposites – of money with pre-monetary (talismanic or magical) object – occurs in the ring that bestowed invisibility and thereby sovereign power on Gyges.[30] Similarly, the *tyrannos* Polykrates threw his seal-ring – as an

[25] Seaford 2012a.

[26] In Homer even the otherwise isolated Odysseus has the firm support of Athena and of his family.

[27] Soph. *OT* 124–5, 380–9, 541–4, 873–4, etc.; *Ant.* 293–301, 322, 326, 1036–9, 1056, 1062–3, etc.

[28] Seaford 2003d[5].

[29] Hdt. 3.39, 122–5.

[30] Pl. *Resp.* 2.359d–360b, 10.612b (ring and helmet of invisibility). On Wagner's devotion to Plato see von Westernhagen 1966: 50–1.

emblem of his monetised prosperity – into the sea to avoid the resentment of the gods.[31] The ring in Wagner, finally thrown into the Rhine, is an emblem of the *universal* power of money, while the *invisibility* of monetary power is embodied in another magical object (the *Tarnhelm*), and its *substantiality* in the treasure of gold. The invisible ubiquity of monetary power is dramatically embodied in Alberich, made invisible by the *Tarnhelm* ('I am everywhere'), using the ring to force the Nibelungs to produce wealth 'for him alone'. But gold partially reverts to being mere object when it covers Freia's body as ransom for her, rather as in Aeschylus' lost *Phrygians* it is weighed against Hektor's body as ransom for it.

Some other objects visible in the *Ring* also embody power. Donner's hammer, embodying the power of nature, yields to Wotan's contract-guarding spear, which also overcomes the sword Nothung (emblem of heroism and sexuality) wielded by Siegmund, but is eventually overcome by Nothung wielded by Siegfried. Props in the *Ring* are limited in number but significant, as in Greek tragedy, in which they are sometimes magical and often ambivalent.[32] 'The gifts of enemies are no gifts', says Ajax before killing himself with the sword given him by Hektor.[33] Siegmund proposes to kill Sieglinde and himself with 'this sword, which a deceiver gave to a true man, which betrays me to my enemy'. No less ambivalent is the ring, promising to its possessor unlimited power and wealth but also unhappiness and death, created through the renunciation of love but becoming the embodiment of the love between Siegfried and Brünnhilde.

As an example of an ambivalent stage property in the *Oresteia*, consider the textile 'bought with silver' (*Ag.* 949) on which Agamemnon walks into the house (to his death). Agamemnon hesitates to damage what he calls the wealth of the house, but Klytaimestra responds that the sea is inexhaustible in 'nourishing a wholly renewable gush, equal to silver, of much purple dye' (from a shellfish), and that 'the house does not know to be poor'. The natural source of this artefact is, as of the ring, a vast mass of water. But the natural inexhaustibility of sea and dye here matters only if there is inexhaustible silver to buy it, and this implies the *unlimitedness* which the Greeks saw as a dangerous characteristic of money, and which repeatedly marks the power and wealth bestowed by the ring.[34] The

[31] It is narrated by Herodotus (3.41), a copy of whose work Wagner possessed at Dresden: von Westernhagen 1966: 94.

[32] E.g. the magically destructive garments as gifts in Sophocles' *Trachiniae* and Euripides' *Medea*, or the libations in Aeschylus' *Choephori*.

[33] Soph. *Aj.* 665.

[34] Wellgunde in *Rheingold* 1 ('Masslose Macht'), Wotan in *Rheingold* 2 ('Macht und Schätze … ohne Mass'), Alberich in *Rheingold* 4 ('Macht ohne Mass'), Wotan in *Die Wälkurie* 2 ('masslose Macht').

textile is closely associated[35] with the textile that Klytaimestra uses both to trap Agamemnon and as a shroud, describing it as 'a covering without limit (ἄπειρον) … a bad wealth of cloth' (1382–3). The ambivalent textile is associated with the shocking unlimitedness of the money by which it is bought – one instance among many of Athenian tragedy using (pre-monetary) myth to represent the disruptive effect of money. At the end of the *Choephori* Orestes addresses this same shroud as a physical link with the father he never met (as does Siegfried addressing Nothung), while he descends into frenzy (*Cho.* 997–1025).

Nature and Love Against Money and Power?

We return to the relation of content to unitary form. According to Wagner the Germanic sagas were originally all variations of a definite type of event, a type that derived from one simple religious notion, taken from the beholding of nature. But subsequently Christianity 'annulled the religious faith, the fundamental view (*Grundanschaung*) of nature's essence' (Wagner 1900: 162), with the result that the unity of the myth dispersed itself 'into a thousandfold plurality; the kernel of action into a vast quantity of actions'. Our natural inference that Wagner envisaged the unitarian form of the *Ring* as restoring the primeval unity of Germanic Mythos is confirmed by the fact that it is from the narrative of Siegfried that he derives his conception of the religious beholding of *nature* as underlying Germanic myth: 'In one saga – that of Siegfried – we may now look with some clarity into its original kernel, which teaches us not a little about the essence of myth in general' (Wagner 1900: 161). Set against the *single* abstract (invisible) power of money is the *single* notion that Wagner found at the root of authentic Germanic myth, *nature* embodied in the heroic individual (Siegfried).

Wagner invented the forging of the ring from gold stolen from the Rhine, and so as transgressive against nature. But its creation also transgressed against love. Wagner also invented Alberich's renunciation – of the power and delight of heterosexual love – that is a precondition for the forging of the ring. This then resonates in Fafner's – and Wotan's – preference for the ring over Freia, and in the paradoxical transformation of the ring into an embodiment of love. Siegfried states that for love he would gladly forgo the world obtained by the ring.

35 Taplin 1978: 79–82.

This is not the place to enter the debate on the meaning of the ending of the *Ring* (in its various versions). Suffice it to say that it contains, not least in the music, an element of redemption – whether in the return of the ring to nature (the Rhine) or in the love of Brünnhilde for Siegfried – that has seemed at odds with Greek tragedy. For instance, 'in the *Ring* in general we find something profoundly alien to the spirit of an ancient tragedy ... Wagner, believing in the essential goodness of human feelings, is not a true tragedian'.[36] Greek tragedy does not on the whole set nature or love against money.[37] But the *Oresteia*, the Theban trilogy,[38] the *Prometheia* and the *Ring* each combine older narratives to conclude with a permanent end (in polis or cosmos) to the cycle of conflict driven by individual self-interest. The essential goodness of human feelings was the issue neither for Wagner nor for Aeschylus. What mattered for them both was (among much else) the hope inherent in the spectacular musical dramatisation of communal myth by which monetised individualism is permanently transcended.

Conclusion

The 'closeness and affinity' of Wagner with Aeschylus[39] is paradoxical, given the vast gap in time and their many obvious differences. It derives, I suggest, from a specific similarity between their *historical* position. Fruitful influence across centuries and between different kinds of society is especially favoured by there being a specific similarity between the influencing and influenced works in respect of the historical conditions governing their main preoccupations. It is not just that Wagner admired Aeschylus and so was – as has often been noted – influenced by him in various details. Despite the enormous and unbridgeable differences between fifth-century Athens and mid-nineteenth-century Germany, historical developments led both men to dramatise – each in his different way – the transcendence, by pre-monetary myth, of the universal power of monetised wealth that unifies both the content and the form of the myth.

[36] Lloyd-Jones 1982: 140; note also George Steiner's ill-informed antithesis between Greek tragedy and the optimism of *Götterdämmerung* (1961: 127).

[37] Although the omnipotence of money is equated with *erōs* at e.g. Euripides fr. 324 and *fr. trag. adesp.* 129. And those *Naturwesen* the satyrs are not infrequently ignorant or contemptuous of money in the remains of satyric drama.

[38] Not only in Droysen's reconstructions. The original version of *Septem* (third play in the Theban trilogy) ended with the saving of the polis (793–6, 820) and by prefiguring the polis hero cult of the fratricides (1002–4 were the final lines: cf. Pausanias 9.18.3). In general the Aeschylean transition from the age of heroes to the present is not unlike the 'Feuerbachian' transition some have detected in the *Ring* from gods to humanity.

[39] Nietzsche, *Richard Wagner in Bayreuth* at Nietzsche 1983: 208.

Aeschylean tragedy was created in a society that on the one hand still accorded a central place to myth but on the other hand had been recently monetised. The *Ring* was created in a society that had long been monetised, but in which the power of money, its tendency as capital to dissolve all other relations, was advancing in the way memorably described in the *Communist Manifesto* the year after Wagner, soon to be a revolutionary in Dresden, first read the *Oresteia*: 'All fixed, rusted relations with their following of ancient and venerable ideas and opinions are dissolved, all new-formed ones age before they can ossify. Everything established and standing evaporates, everything holy is profaned ....' In a society becoming ever more pervaded by money, be it Athens or Dresden, the power of pre-monetary myth provides an effective way of relativising the power of money.

What the form and content of the Aeschylean trilogy owed to the recent advent of a single omnipotent object of universal desire contributed to the possibility of its profound and fruitful influence on the mythical dramatisation of the power of money in the nineteenth century. But it was, of course, not by Aeschylus that Wagner was impelled to dramatise the omnipotence of money. In his letters and autobiography he sometimes alternates between absorption in the creative power of myth and disgust at having to be preoccupied with money. 'It is not my business to "earn money"', he wrote to Liszt, 'but it is the business of my admirers to give me as much money as I want, to do my work in a cheerful mood' (3 October 1855). In 1881 he wrote:

> Clever though be the many thoughts expressed by mouth or pen about the invention of money and its enormous value as a civiliser, against such praise of it we should consider the curse to which it has always been exposed in saga and poetry. If *gold* here appears as the demon strangling the innocence of humanity, our greatest poet shews at last the invention of paper money as devil's mischief. The doom-laden ring of the Nibelungs might as a stock-exchange portfolio (*Börsenportefeuille*) bring to completion the gruesome picture of the ghostly master of the world.[40]

We cannot end without acknowledging the darker side of this vision. Just as the tragic Kreon projected the corrupting all-pervasiveness of money onto barbarian orientals, so Wagner associated it with the Jew, who 'rules, and will rule, so long as money remains the power before which all our doing and our activity lose their vigour'.[41]

[40] *Know Thyself* at Wagner 1897: 268.
[41] Soph. *Ant.* 1037–9; Wagner, *Judaism in Music* at Wagner 1907: 81.

CHAPTER 21

World Without Limits

What makes the ancient Greeks worth studying is that they are sufficiently like us to be comprehensible but sufficiently unlike us to be worth making the effort to understand. It may be a common theme among the enthusiastic modern supporters of the Classics that the Greeks and Romans were very much like us (and that they therefore legitimate the present). Most academics, on the other hand, prefer to emphasise how different and simultaneously how similar they were. The culture of – say – Pharaonic Egypt is, despite its fascination, beyond the grasp of all but a few specialists, whereas ancient Greece and Rome are both inside and outside our ken.

Let me explore just one example. A crucial factor in this pattern of 'similarity and difference', and one with tremendous resonance in the early twenty-first century, is money. As I argued some years ago in *Money and the Early Greek Mind* (Seaford 2004c), the pivotal position of the Greeks in world culture stems largely from the fact that the sixth-century polis was the first society in history (with the conceivable exception of China) to be pervaded by money. Coinage was invented towards the end of the seventh century, and spread rapidly in the Greek city-states from the beginning of the sixth. Did not the Babylonians, for instance, use silver as money well before that? On any sensibly narrow definition of money, no – they did not.

This new and revolutionary phenomenon of money itself underpinned and stimulated two great inventions of the Greek polis of the sixth century, 'philosophy' and tragedy. 'Philosophy' (or rather the idea of the cosmos as an impersonal system) was first produced in the very first monetised society, early sixth-century Ionia, and – even more specifically – in its commercial centre, Miletos. The tendency of pre-modern society to project social power onto cosmology (for example, 'King Zeus rules the world') applies to the new social power of money. And the following description applies equally to money and to much of the cosmology of the early philosophers: universal power resides not in a person but in an impersonal, all-underlying, semi-abstract substance.

But the relationship of money and tragedy is no less striking. Tragedy was created shortly after the introduction into Athens of coinage. This – though it has no place in the voluminous literature on the subject – seems to me one of the most important facts about tragedy. Greek myth is, of course, largely pre-monetary, but in tragedy it is shaped by the new all-pervasive power of money. It is not only the obsession with money of some tragic tyrants (Oidipous, for example) that I have in mind. An entirely new feature of money is that its possession renders unnecessary *in principle* all pre-monetary forms of social relationship: reciprocity, redistribution, kinship, ritual, and so on. Money allows you to fulfil all your needs. It provides the power to increase itself. And it tends to promote predatory isolation. Hence the focus of much Athenian tragedy on the extreme isolation of the individual – from the gods and even (through killing) from his or her closest kin. I know of no precedent for this in literature, certainly not in the pre-monetary society depicted in Homer. This horrifying possibility is embodied in the figure of the tyrant (*tyrannos*), who in historiographic, philosophical and tragic texts characteristically kills his own kin, violates the sacred and is much concerned with money as a means of power. The word 'hero', the preoccupation of so much critical literature on the subject, barely occurs in Athenian tragedy, but *tyrannos* (or some form of that word) occurs over 170 times.

Money is so desirable and powerful that some people will do anything for it. Moreover, there is no limit to its accumulation or to the desire to accumulate it. All this is familiar to us, but it was new to the Greeks, who can therefore help us to look afresh at the singularity of money. The unlimitedness of money is described disapprovingly by the sixth-century sage Solon and later by Aristotle, and it is brought to life in Aristophanes' *Wealth*. This wonderful comedy is (almost certainly) the earliest surviving text on economics, a subject that thereafter has become less entertaining. It describes the homogenising effect of money (everything happens for its sake) and its omnipotence; and a rapid dialogue reveals that – whereas one can have enough sex, or loaves, or music, or dessert, or honour, or cakes, or manliness, and so on – money is different: if someone has thirteen talents (a lot of money) he is eager for sixteen, and if he obtains sixteen he swears that his life is unbearable unless he obtains forty. What, we may add, would have been the point in Homeric society of accumulating a million of those prestige items that embody wealth, such as tripods? Money is different. It isolates the individual, and it is unlimited.

But it is not only in tragedy that myth was influenced by money. The most obvious instance of a myth about the (disastrous) unlimited homogenising power of money is Midas transforming everything by his touch into gold. Consider also the myth of Erysichthon, a full version of which can be put together from a few sources (notably Callimachus and Ovid). Erysichthon cuts down a sacred grove to make himself a banqueting hall and is punished by being made insatiable. No food is enough – whether from land, sea or air – to satisfy him. He is driven to sell his daughter in marriage, from which she returns to him, and the process is constantly repeated. In the end he eats himself. The myth contains a unique combination of unusual features: the transformation of nature into product, selling to obtain food, and eating the self. The constant return of the daughter from marriage excludes progeny (the future). The Greeks had a myth for many of our central concerns, and here is one for global warming: exploitation of nature produces pathological insatiability, the unlimited need for a source of income that sacrifices the future, and self-destruction.

The Greeks had money but not capitalism, in which constant innovation is a precondition for survival, and in which accordingly – as Marx and Engels famously put it 'all that is solid melts into the air, all that is holy is profaned', producing an age of 'everlasting uncertainty and agitation'. Here constant intense desire for novelty means that new fashions and ideas 'become antiquated before they can ossify into custom'. Even this we now simply take as part of nature. In Greco-Roman antiquity, by contrast, investment, and techniques of production and marketing, remained crude and relatively static, and a poetic genre, for instance epic, could remain fundamentally the same for a thousand years.

And yet, after two and a half millennia, money remains isolating, unlimited and homogenising. The Greeks were struck and sometimes horrified by this. Aristotle maintained that using money to make money is – in contrast to other forms of economic activity – unlimited and unnatural. And so he would be equipped to understand the novelty contained in the following typical observation, from a recent textbook of economics: 'International financial flows hold out the promise of liberating a country's rate of investment from the limitation imposed by its savings.'

This liberation is just one element in a universal deregulation or 'unlimitedness' that has in the last generation changed the world. This has involved the destruction of limits of all kinds: limits on the movement of capital (once controlled by nation-states); limits articulating cultural space, with the result that a Holiday Inn in Minneapolis is now exactly the same as a Holiday Inn in Mombasa (money homogenises); limits on the salaries-cum-bonuses that the money-controllers pay themselves; limits on the gap between rich and poor (an unlimitedness that makes common purpose impossible). It has also destroyed the limit of speculative price by any internal relation to its financial or artistic product (investing in junk bonds is essentially the same as investing in junk art, and done by some of the same people).

Aristotle might also recognise the concomitant deregulation of the subject, the liberation of signs from the limits imposed by reality. The myth of Midas marked the replacement of money as a means of exchange by money as the primary but strangely unreal object of aspiration. Aristotle cites the myth to illustrate the nonsensicality of money, the arbitrariness of the monetary sign; and so he would be equipped to understand the claim that money has now been joined (or even replaced) in the unlimited realm of hyper-reality by the images purveyed by media and advertising.

Greeks of the classical period were anxious about the potentially unlimited scope and power of money, and this anxiety contributed to their explicit privileging of limit over the unlimited, especially but not only in metaphysics and ethics. For instance, Plato in the *Philebus* states that limit should control the unlimited, and that the introduction of limit brings safety in countless spheres, notably in health and music. Aristotle says in the *Nicomachean Ethics* that 'bad is of the unlimited, as the Pythagoreans surmised, and good is of the limited'. This persists into Pythagorean and Platonic philosophies that remained popular throughout antiquity.

But these Greek ideas are not confined to philosophical texts. If I were forced to characterise the outcome of Aeschylus' *Oresteia* in a single abstract formula, I would call it the victory of limit over the unlimited, in various respects that include the limitation of the potentially unlimited cycle of revenge and of the potentially unlimited accumulation of wealth. Among the ancient Greeks there is what I call a culture of limit. By contrast, our culture is characterised by hostility to closure (limit) in various spheres: economic, metaphysical, conceptual, narrative and others.

This opposition is related to an opposition in basic forms of life. For the Greeks, the realm of freedom (economic and ethical) was stable self-sufficiency and this determined the manner in which they (or at least those whose voices have survived) reacted to the unlimitedness of money. But we react to it in a manner determined by the fact that for us the realm of freedom is constant exchange. 'Metaphysical categories', wrote Adorno, 'are not merely an ideology concealing the social system; at the same time they express its nature, the truth about it, and in their changes are precipitated those in its most central experiences.'[1] The same is true of the modern theoretical *hostility* to metaphysics, the postmodern fetishisation of fragmentation, depthlessness and indeterminacy, and its sublimation of the universe of free-floating images.

The postmodern devotion to abolishing 'Western' (that is Greek) metaphysics would be illuminated by considering the economic conditions of its genesis. Just as our politico-economic discourse assumes the maximisation of earning and expenditure (even of borrowing) by groups and individuals alike, so our theoretical discourse is hostile to all forms of closure. But let us turn again to global warming, which our own culture of the unlimited makes it so difficult for us to confront. The myth of Erysikhthon lacked a central element of our own contemporary predicament, that is our knowledge that our actions will cause our self-destruction. For this we look to tragedy, Aeschylus' *Seven Against Thebes*. During the siege of Thebes, the chorus implore King Eteokles not to go out to fight his own brother. But he is compelled to do so by his father Oidipous' curse, which doomed the brothers to divide up their inheritance with the sword. He rejects the possibility that he can be saved by ritual or helped by the gods, and rushes out for the mutual fratricide. As he does so, he claims that the curse is telling him to put *kerdos* (selfish gain) first, death afterwards (*kerdos proteron husterou morou*).

This implies that *kerdos*, in this case the inheritance, is worth dying for. *Kerdos* has replaced honour as the one thing more powerful even than the desire for life. Here is the typical tragic individual, completely alienated from the gods and from his closest kin. A mysterious and terrifying power of pre-monetary myth, the curse, has been adapted to express a new and mysterious terrifying power, the unlimited isolating passion for individual gain, more powerful even than the instinct for self-preservation. With global warming the unlimitedness and conscious self-destructiveness of money reaches a logical conclusion. We are still, now as a species, under the curse of Oidipous.

What did the Greeks have with which to combat this horror? The original ending of the play is, it seems, lost, but its last extant authentic words indicate – in contrast to Eteokles' rejection of ritual – the founding of a ritual for the whole polis. The polis had communal ritual to save it from unlimited individual greed, but we do not. Such (fragmented) rituals as we do have tend, like ancient Greek ritual, to sustain existing myths and patterns of belief. But they may also, in contrast to their ancient function,

[1] Adorno 1974: 231.

serve the agenda of the unlimited. Our contexts of powerful decision-making tend to be ritualised – by reassuring familiarity of dress, seating arrangements, syntax, tone of voice, body language, and so on. And ritualisation tends to foster the unconscious formation of 'group-think'. How can politicians continue to assume the desirability of unlimited economic growth that is patently inconsistent with preventing global warming? One small but unremarked factor is the power of ritualisation, now and in the past, to efface inconsistency of belief. A meeting on economic policy or to plan the expansion of aviation is ritualised, and ritualisation generates and confirms its appropriate beliefs and decisions. On the *Titanic* as we are, we should be ridiculing not the rearrangement of the deckchairs but the formal dress and reassuring protocols of the captain's table.

In the final year of the First World War, the presidential address to the Classical Association was given by Gilbert Murray, then Professor of Greek at the University of Oxford. He was, unsurprisingly, gloomy. The 'horizon looks dark' for classical studies, he said. And he ended with an attack on 'the enemy', he

> who has forgotten that there is such a thing as truth, and measures the world by advertisement or by money ..., whose innermost religion is the worship of the Lie in his soul ... From him and his influence we find escape by means of the Grammata into that calm world [of the Greeks], where stridency and clamour are forgotten in the ancient stillness.

Some thirty-five years later, after the Second World War, Murray gave a radio broadcast in which that view of Ancient Greece as a refuge from the present had been transformed into Ancient Greece as inspiration for the future. 'The old Hellenistic world had three great aspirations', he observed. 'It aimed at a Hellenising or humanising of the brutal world; it longed and strove for Homonoia, Concord, between community and community, between man and man; lastly, it proclaimed a conception of the world as One Great City ...'. And he urged support for what he called 'the same aspirations ... at work in the modern world', especially through the work of the United Nations. American readers may be pleasantly surprised to learn that, despite his pessimism about Europe, 'there is waiting across the Atlantic a greater Rome which may at best establish a true world peace, and will at worst maintain in an ocean of Barbarism a large and enduring island of true Hellenic life'.

This was broadcast in 1953, the year in which British and American secret services – well below Murray's radar – replaced the democratically elected government of Iran by a dictatorship that, though savage, was favourable to the British and American oil interest, thereby initiating a new world order. This was called 'Operation Ajax', a name not alas symptomatic of true Hellenic life but inspired by the household cleaning liquid.

The politics of Gilbert Murray now seem as loftily unrealistic as does his political and cultural ambition for Hellenism, and not only because of his tendency to overlook the shortcomings of ancient Greek society. But he was the last prominent proponent of the idea that Hellenism has implications for every sphere of life, including politics. And this I cannot help admiring. Did not Perikles say, in the supreme expression of the culture of ancient democracy, the funeral speech reported by Thucydides, that the Athenians 'regard the person who does not participate in politics as useless'? Can the understanding of the ancient past still contribute, as it did for Murray, to an active engagement with the present?

We cannot use the systematic Greek respect for limit to subvert the systematic unlimitedness of our own self-destructive culture. But the Greek culture of the limit provides a place that allows us to see the oddness, the historical contingency of the lethally limiting unlimitedness in our economy, social practices and theory. Hellenism is one of a number of precious resources – a way of being, understanding and perceiving – that can help to liberate us from the homogenised sensibility of our hyper-monetised, atomised and self-destructive culture of the unlimited.

References

RICHARD SEAFORD: PUBLICATIONS (EXCLUDING REVIEWS)

(1975). Some notes on Euripides' *Cyclops*. *CQ* **25**: 193–208.
(1976a). Euripides' *Cyclops* 393–402. *CQ* **26**: 315–16.
(1976b). On the origins of satyric drama. *Maia* **28**: 209–21.
(1977–8). The 'hyporchema' of Pratinas. *Maia* **29**: 81–94. [= Chapter 7]
(1978). *Pompeii*, London: Constable.
(1980). Black Zeus in Sophocles' *Inachos*. *CQ* **30**: 23–9.
(1981a). Dionysiac drama and the Dionysiac mysteries. *CQ* **31**: 252–75.
(1981b). The Dionysiac mysteries at Pompeii. In H. W. Stubbs, ed. *Pegasus: Classical Essays from the University of Exeter*. Exeter: University of Exeter Press, pp. 52–68.
(1981c). What was a satyr-play? *Omnibus* **2**: 26–8.
(1982). The date of Euripides' *Cyclops*. *JHS* **102**: 161–72.
(1984a). 1 Corinthians 13.12. *JTS* **35**: 117–20. [= Chapter 15]
(1984b). *Euripides: Cyclops*, Oxford: Clarendon Press.
(1984c). The last bath of Agamemnon. *CQ* **34**: 247–54. [= Chapter 11]
(1984–5). L'ultima Canzone Corale delle *Supplici* di Eschilo. *Dioniso* **55**: 221–9.
(1985). The destruction of limits in Sophokles' *Elektra*. *CQ* **35**: 315–23. [= Chapter 12]
(1986a). Immortality, salvation and the elements. *HSCP* **90**: 1–26. [= Chapter 9]
(1986b). Wedding ritual and textual criticism in Sophocles' *Women of Trachis*. *Hermes* **114**: 50–9.
(1987a). Pentheus' vision: *Bacchae* 918–22. *CQ* **37**: 76–8.
(1987b). Silenus erectus: Euripides *Cyclops* 227. *LCM* **12**(9): 142–3.
(1987c). The tragic wedding. *JHS* **107**: 106–30. [= Chapter 13]
(1988). The eleventh ode of Bacchylides: Hera, Artemis and the absence of Dionysos. *JHS* **108**: 118–36.
(1989a). The attribution of Aeschylus, *Choephori* 691–9. *CQ* **39**: 302–6.
(1989b). Homeric and tragic sacrifice. *TAPA* **119**: 87–95. [= Chapter 1]
(1990a). The imprisonment of women in Greek tragedy. *JHS* **110**: 76–90.
(1990b). The structural problems of marriage in Euripides. In A. Powell, ed., *Euripides, Women, and Sexuality*. London: Routledge, pp. 151–76. [= Chapter 14]

(1991). Il dramma satiresco in Euripide. *Dioniso* **61**: 75–89.
(1993). Dionysos as destroyer of the household: Homer, tragedy, and the city-state. In Carpenter and Faraone 1993: 115–46. [= Chapter 2]
(1994a). How to be happy in the next world. *Omnibus* **27**: 14–16.
(1994b). *Reciprocity and Ritual*, Oxford: Clarendon Press.
(1994c). Sophokles and the mysteries. *Hermes* **122**: 275–88. [= Chapter 10]
(1995). Historicising tragic ambivalence: the vote of Athena. In B. Goff, ed., *History, Tragedy, Theory*. Austin: University of Texas Press, pp. 202–21.
(1996a). *Euripides: Bacchae*, Warminster: Aris and Phillips.
(1996b). Something to do with Dionysos: tragedy and the Dionysiac. In Silk 1996: 284–94.
(1996c). Fourteen articles in *OCD*[3]: *Arion, Dionysia, Epigenes, Hippolytus, Kyklopes, Lenaia, Masks, Phallus, Pratinas, Procession, Python, Satyric drama, Thespis, Tragedy – Greek (part).*
(1997a). George Thomson and Ancient Greece. *Classics Ireland* **4**: 121–33.
(1997b). Thunder, lightning and earthquake in the *Bacchae* and the Acts of the Apostles. In A. B. Lloyd, ed., *What is a God?* London: Duckworth, pp. 139–51. [= Chapter 16]
(1998a). In the mirror of Dionysos. In S. Blundell and M. Williamson, Eds., *The Sacred and the Feminine in Ancient Greece*. London: Routledge, pp. 128–48.
(1998b). Introduction. In *Reciprocity in Ancient Greece*, in Gill, Postlethwaite and Seaford 1998: 1–11.
(1998c). Tragic money. *JHS* **108**: 119–39. [= Chapter 4]
(2000a). Aristotelian economics and Athenian tragedy. *New Literary History* **31**: 269–76.
(2000b). The Dionysiac don responds to Don Quixote: Rainer Friedrich on the new ritualism. *Arion* **8**: 74–98.
(2000c). Reply to a critic. *Mnemosyne* **53**: 83–7.
(2000d). The social function of Attic drama: a reply to Jasper Griffin. *CQ* **50**: 30–44.
(2002a). Ancient Greek drama in the twentieth century. In C. Chambers, ed., *Continuum Companion to Twentieth Century Theatre*. London: Continuum, pp. 24–6.
(2002b). *Bacchae*, ritual, and tragedy: concluding remarks. *Arion* **9**(3): 166–8.
(2002c). Money makes the world go round. *Omnibus* **43**: 18–19.
(2002d). Reading money: Leslie Kurke on the politics of meaning in archaic Greece. *Arion* **9**(3): 145–65.
(2003a). Aeschylus and the unity of opposites. *JHS* **123**: 141–63. [= Chapter 6]
(2003b). Dionysos, money, and drama. *Arion* **11**: 1–19. [= Chapter 3]
(2003c). Monetisation and the genesis of philosophy. *Ordia Prima* 2: 87–117.
(2003d). Tragic tyranny. In Morgan 2003: 95–115. [= Chapter 5]
(2004a). Introduction. In G. Thomson, trans., *Aeschylus: The Oresteia*. New York: Knopf, pp. ix–xxxvii.
(2004b). Monetisation, ritual, and the genesis of tragedy. In D. Yatromanolakis and P. Raillos, eds., *Greek Ritual Poetics*. Washington, DC: Center for Hellenic Studies, pp. 71–93.

(2004c). *Money and the Early Greek Mind*, Cambridge: Cambridge University Press.
(2005a). Death and wedding in Aeschylus' *Niobe*. In F. McHardy, J. Robson and D. Harvey, eds., *Lost Dramas of Classical Athens*. Exeter: Exeter University Press, pp. 113–27.
(2005b). Mystic light in Aeschylus' *Bassarai*. *CQ* **55**: 602–6.
(2005c). Tragedy and Dionysus. In R. Bushnell, ed., *A Companion to Tragedy*. Malden, MA: Blackwell, pp. 25–38.
(2006a). *Dionysos*, London: Routledge.
(2006b). Ritual and money in Aeschylus' *Agamemnon*. *Omnibus* **52**: 30–1.
(2006c). An unedited text and the beginnings of philosophy: the Derveni Papyrus. *Critical Quarterly* **48**(2): 101–6.
(2007a). From ritual to drama: a concluding statement. In Csapo and Miller 2007: 379–401.
(2007b). Money and the confusion of generations in Sophocles' *Oedipus Tyrannus*. In T. Baier, ed., *Generationskonflikte auf der Bühne*. Tübingen: Narr, pp. 23–8.
(2007c). Karl Kerényi's interpretation of Dionysos. In R. Schlesier and R. Sanchino Martinez, eds., *Neuhumanismus und Anthropologie des griechischen Mythos. Karl Kerényi im europäischen Kontext des 20. Jahrhunderts*. Locarno: Rezzonico, pp. 95–106.
(2008a). Money and tragedy. In W. V. Harris, ed., *The Monetary Systems of the Greeks and Romans*. Oxford: Oxford University Press, pp. 49–65.
(2008b). Why does Hippolytus reject sex? In A. Beale, ed., *Euripides Talks*. London: Bristol Classical Press, pp. 69–77.
(2009a). Aitiologies of cult in Euripides: a response to Scott Scullion. In J. Cousland and J. Hume, eds., *The Play of Texts and Fragments: Essays in Honour of Martin Cropp*. Leiden and Boston: Brill, pp. 221–34.
(2009b). *Ancient Greece and Global Warming*. Classical Association Presidential Address. London: Classical Association.
(2009c). The fluttering soul. In Dill and Walde 2009: 406–14. [= Chapter 18]
(2009d) Origins of Greek tragedy. In V. Liapos, ed., *The Literary Encyclopedia*, www.litencyc.com/php/stopics.php?rec=true&UID=5811 (accessed 19 February 2018).
(2009e). World without limits. *Times Literary Supplement*, 19 June (French translation in *Commentaire* **128** (2009–10): 871–5). [= Chapter 21]
(2010a). Beyond tragedy: Thucydides and the Sicilian expedition. *Omnibus* **60**: 22–3.
(2010b). Mystic light and near-death experience. In M. Christopoulos, E. D. Karakantza and O. Levaniouk, eds., *Light and Darkness in Ancient Greek Religion*. Lanham, MD: Lexington, pp. 201–6.
(2010c). Zeus in Aeschylus: the factor of monetisation. In J. N. Bremmer and A. Erskine, eds., *The Gods of Ancient Greece: Identities and Transformations*. Edinburgh: Edinburgh University Press, pp. 178–92.
(2011a). The Greek invention of money. In H. Ganssmann, ed., *New Approaches to Monetary Theory: Interdisciplinary Perspectives*. London and New York: Routledge, pp. 37–45.

(2011b). Response to Anne Duncan. In D. Carter, ed., *Why Athens? A Reappraisal of Tragic Politics*. Oxford: Oxford University Press, pp. 85–91.

(2011c). Articles on Exchange, Hekatomb, Libation, Maenads and Sacrifice. In M. Finkelberg, ed., *The Homeric Encyclopedia*. Chichester: Blackwell.

(2012a). *Cosmology and the Polis*, Cambridge: Cambridge University Press.

(2012b). Monetisation and the genesis of the Western subject. *Historical Materialism* **20**(1): 78–102. [= Chapter 17]

(2013a). Aeschylus, Herakleitos, and Pythagoreanism. In Cairns 2013: 17–38.

(2013b). The politics of the mystic chorus. In J. Billings , F. Budelmann and F. Macintosh, eds., *Choruses, Ancient and Modern*. Oxford: Oxford University Press, pp. 261–79. [= Chapter 8]

(2013c). Articles on Mystery cult and Wedding ritual. In H. Roisman, ed., *The Encyclopedia of Greek Tragedy*. Chichester and Malden, MA: Wiley-Blackwell.

(2014). Geld und das Griechische Wunder. *Neue Rundschau* **125**(4): 58–69.

(2015). On the ideology of imagining that 'each age gets the thought it needs'. In I. Morris, *Foragers, Farmers, and Fossil Fuels: How Human Values Evolve*. Tanner Lectures in Human Values. Princeton: Princeton University Press, pp. 172–9.

(2016a). The interiorisation of ritual in India and Greece. In R. Seaford, ed., *Universe and Inner Self in Early Indian and Early Greek Thought*. Edinburgh: Edinburgh University Press, pp. 204–19.

(2016b). Money and the construction of the inner self in Ancient Greece. In K.-H. Brodbeck and S. Graupe, eds., *Geld! Welches Geld? Geld als Denkform*. Marburg: Metropolis, pp. 103–20.

(2016c). Mysteries and Politics in *Bacchae*. In D. Stuttard, ed., *Looking at Bacchae*. London: Bloomsbury, pp. 83–90.

(2016d). Articles on Bacchai, Bacchantes, Dionysos and Thiasos. In E. M. Orlin, L. S. Fried, J. Wright Knust, M. L. Satlow and M. E. Pregill, eds., *The Routledge Encyclopedia of Ancient Mediterranean Religions*. New York and Oxford: Routledge.

(2017a). Form and money in Wagner's *Ring* and Aeschylean tragedy. In R. Kennedy, ed., *Brill's Companion to the Reception of Aeschylus*. Leiden and Boston: Brill, pp. 348–61. [= Chapter 20]

(2017b). Laughter and tears in early Greek literature. In M. Alexiou and D. Cairns, eds., *Greek Laughter and Tears: Antiquity and After*. Edinburgh: Edinburgh University Press, pp. 27–35.

(2017c). On Vedic sacrifice, and its differences from Greek sacrifice. In K. Bielawski, ed., *Animal Sacrifice in Ancient Greece: Proceedings of the First International Workshops in Kraków (12–14.11.2015)*. Warsaw: Wydawnictwo Naukowe Sub Lupa, pp. 87–106.

(2017d). The *psuchē* from Homer to Plato: a historical sketch. In R. Seaford, J. Wilkins and M. Wright, eds. *Selfhood and the Soul: Essays on Ancient Thought and Literature in Honour of Christopher Gill*. Oxford: Oxford University Press, pp. 11–31.

(2017e). Sacrifice in drama: the flow of liquids. In S. Hitch and I. Rutherford, eds., *Animal Sacrifice in the Ancient Greek World.* Cambridge: Cambridge University Press, pp. 223–35.

(2018a). Monetised psyche and Dionysiac ecstasy. In P. Bishop and L. Gardner, eds., *The Ecstatic and the Archaic: An Analytical Psychological Inquiry.* London: Routledge, pp. 117–26.

(2018b). Mystic initiation and the near-death experience. In J. Lauwers, J. Opsomer and H. Schwall, eds., *Psychology and the Classics: A Dialogue of Disciplines.* Berlin and Boston: de Gruyter, pp. 271–7.

GENERAL REFERENCES

Achelis, H. (1918). Katoptromantie bei Paulus. In H. Achelis et al., eds., *Theologische Festschrift für G. N. Bonwetsch*, Leipzig: Deichert, pp. 56–63.

Adorno, T. W. (1973). *Negative Dialectics*, trans. E. B. Ashton, New York: Seabury Press.

(1974). *Minima Moralia*, trans. E. F. N. Jephcott, London: New Left Books.

Alexiou, M. (1974). *The Ritual Lament in Greek Tradition*, Cambridge: Cambridge University Press.

Alexiou, M. & Dronke, P. (1971). The lament of Jephtha's daughter: themes, traditions, originality. *Studi Medievali* **12**(2): 819–63.

Arias, E., Hirmer, M. & Shefton, B. (1962). *A History of Greek Vase Painting*, London: Thames and Hudson.

Armstrong, D. & Ratchford, E. (1985). Iphigenia's veil: Aeschylus, *Agamemnon* 228–48. *BICS* **32**: 1–12.

Arnott, P. (1962). *Greek Scenic Conventions in the Fifth Century* B.C., Oxford: Clarendon Press.

Arthur, M. (1981). The divided world of *Iliad* VI. In H. Foley, ed., *Reflections of Women in Antiquity*, New York: Gordon and Breach Science Publishers, pp. 19–44.

Babut, D. (1975). Héraclite et la religion populaire. *REA* **77**: 27–62.

Bailey, G. & Mabbett, I. (2003). *The Sociology of Early Buddhism*, Cambridge: Cambridge University Press.

Bammer, A. & Muss, U. (1996). *Das Artemision von Ephesos*, Mainz am Rhein: von Zabern.

Barceló, P. (1993). *Basileia, Monarchia, Tyrannis. Untersuchungen zu Entwicklung und Beurteilung von Alleinherrschaft im vorhellenistischen Griechenland*, Stuttgart: Steiner.

Barrett, C. K. (1994). *A Critical and Exegetical Commentary on the Acts of the Apostles*, vol. 1, Edinburgh: T. & T. Clark.

Barrett, W. S. (1964). *Euripides: Hippolytos*, Oxford: Clarendon Press.

Barth, F. (1954). Father's brother's daughter marriage in Kurdistan. *Southwestern Journal of Anthropology* **10**: 164–71.

Battegazzore, A. M. (1979). *Gestualità e oracolarità in Eraclito*, Genoa: Istituto di filologia classica e medievale.

Beazley, J. D. (1958). A hydria by the Kleophrades painter. *AK* **1**: 6–8.

Becker, J. (1912). *De Pratina*. Ph.D. thesis. University of Münster.

Bekker, I. (1814). *Lexica Segueriana*, vol. 1 of *Anekdota Graeca*. Berlin: Nauck.

Belfiore, E. (2000). *Murder among Friends*, New York: Oxford University Press.

Bergson, L. (1982). Nochmals Artemis und Agamemnon. *Hermes* **90**: 137–45.

Betegh, G. (2004). *The Derveni Papyrus*, Cambridge: Cambridge University Press.

Bethe, E. (1929). *Odyssee, Kyklos, Zeitbestimmung*, vol. II.2 of *Homer. Dichtung und Sage*, 2nd edn. Leipzig and Berlin: B. G. Teubner.

Biardeau, M. & Malamoud, C. (1976). *Le Sacrifice dans l'Inde ancienne*, Paris: Presses Universitaires de France.

Binder, G. (1964). *Die Aussetzung des Königskindes: Kyros und Romulus*, Meisenheim am Glan: Hain.

Black, B. (2007). *The Character of the Self in Ancient India*, Albany: SUNY Press.

Blackmore, S. (1993). *Dying to Live: Near-Death Experiences*, London: Grafton.

Blech, M. (1982). *Studien zum Kranz bei den Griechen*, Berlin and New York: de Gruyter.

Bloch, M. (1989). The symbolism of money in Imerina. In Parry and Bloch 1989: 165–90.

Blutzenberger, K. (1996). Ancient Indian conceptions on man's destiny after death: the beginnings and the early development of the doctrine of transmigration I. *Berliner Indologische Studien* **9–10**: 55–118.

(1998). Ancient Indian conceptions on man's destiny after death: the beginnings and the early development of the doctrine of transmigration II. *Berliner Indologische Studien* **11–12**: 1–84.

Boardman, J. (1955). Painted funerary plaques and some remarks on prothesis. *ABSA* **50**: 51–66.

(1972). Herakles, Peisistratos and sons. *RA*: 57–72.

(1975). Herakles, Peisistratos and Eleusis. *JHS* **95**: 1–12.

Bodewitz, H. (1996). Redeath and its relation to rebirth and release. *Studien zur Indologie und Iranistik* **20**: 27–46.

Bohringer, F. (1980). Mégare: traditions mythiques, espace sacré et naissance de la cité. *AC* **49**: 5–22.

Bond, G. W. (1981). *Euripides: Heracles*, Oxford: Clarendon Press.

Borchmeyer, D. (1991). *Richard Wagner: Theory and Theatre*, trans. S. Spencer, Oxford: Clarendon Press.

Bowersock, G. W., Burkert, W. & Putnam, M. C. J., eds. (1979). *Arktouros: Hellenic Studies Presented to Bernard M. W. Knox on the Occasion of His 65th Birthday*, Berlin and New York: de Gruyter.

Boyancé, P. (1960–1). L'antre dans les mystères de Dionysos. *RPAA* **33**: 107–27.

Brelich, A. (1958). *Gli eroi greci. Un problema storico-religioso*, Rome: Adelphi.

(1969). *Paides e Parthenoi*, Rome: Ateneo.

(1970). La corona di Prometheus. In *Hommages à Marie Delcourt*. Coll. Latomus 114. Brussels: Latomus, pp. 234–42.

Bremmer, J. N. (1976). Avunculate and fosterage. *JIES* **4**: 65–78.

(1983a). *The Early Greek Concept of the Soul*. Princeton: Princeton University Press.

(1983b). The importance of the maternal uncle and grandfather in archaic and classical Greece and early Byzantium. *ZPE* **50**: 173–86.

Bremmer, J. N. & Horsfall, N. M. (1987). *Roman Myth and Mythography. BICS* suppl. 52.

Brenk, F. J. (1994). Greek epiphanies and Paul on the road to Damascus. In U. Bianchi, ed., *The Notion of 'Religion' in Comparative Research*. Rome: L'Erma di Bretschneider, pp. 415–24.

Brereton, J. (1990). The Upaniṣads. In W. T. de Bary and I. Bloom, eds., *Eastern Canons: Approaches to the Asian Classics*. New York: Columbia University Press, pp. 115–35.

Bronkhorst, J. (2007). *Greater Maghada: Studies in the Culture of Early India*, Leiden and Boston: Brill.

Brown, A. L. (1987). *Sophocles: Antigone*, Warminster: Aris & Phillips.

Buchholtz, H. (1871). *Die Tanzkunst des Euripides*, Leipzig: Teubner.

Burkert, W. (1960). Elysion. *Glotta* **39**: 208–13 (= Burkert (2001–11): IV.129–34).

(1966). Greek tragedy and sacrificial ritual. *GRBS* **7**: 87–121 (= Burkert (2001–11): VII.1–36).

(1969). Das Proömium des Parmenides und die Katabasis des Pythagoras. *Phronesis* **14**: 1–30 (= Burkert (2001–11): VIII.1–27).

(1972). *Lore and Science in Ancient Pythagoreanism*, trans. E. Minar, Cambridge, MA: Harvard University Press.

(1975). Le laminette auree: da Orfeo a Lampone. In *Orfismo in Magna Grecia. Atti del XIV Convegno di Studi sulla Magna Grecia*. Naples: Arte Tipographica, pp. 81–104 (= Burkert (2001–11): III.21–36).

(1977). *Griechische Religion der Archaischen und Klassischen Epoche*, Stuttgart: Kohlhammer.

(1983a). Eraclito nel papiro di Derveni: due nuove testimonianze. In L. Rosetti, ed., *Atti del Symposium Heracliteum 1981*. Rome: Ateneo, pp. 37–42.

(1983b). *Homo Necans*, trans. P. Bing, Berkeley: University of California Press.

(1985). *Greek Religion*, trans. J. Raffan, Cambridge, MA: Harvard University Press.

(1987). *Ancient Mystery Cults*, Cambridge, MA: Harvard University Press.

(1996). *The Creation of the Sacred*, Cambridge, MA: Harvard University Press.

(2001–11). *Kleine Schriften*, 8 vols., Göttingen: Vandenhoeck & Ruprecht.

Burnett, A. P. (1983). *Three Archaic Poets: Archilochus, Alcaeus, Sappho*, London: Duckworth.

(1985). *The Art of Bacchylides*, Cambridge, MA: Harvard University Press.

Buxton, R. G. A. (1980). Blindness and limits: Sophokles and the logic of myth. *JHS* **100**: 22–37.

(1982). *Persuasion in Greek Tragedy*, Cambridge: Cambridge University Press.

Byl, S. (1988). Encore une dizaine d'allusions éleusiennes dans les *Nués* d'Aristophane. *RBPh* **66**: 113–38.

Cairns, D., ed. (2013). *Tragedy and Archaic Thought*, Swansea: Classical Press of Wales.

Cairns, F. (1972). *Generic Composition in Greek and Roman Poetry*, Edinburgh: Edinburgh University Press.
Caldwell, R. S. (1974). The psychology of Aeschylus' *Supplices*. *Arethusa* **7**: 45–70.
Campbell, J. K. (1964). *Honour, Family and Patronage*, Oxford: Clarendon Press.
Cannatà Fera, M. (1980). Peani, ditirambi, treni in Pind. fr. 128c S-M. *GIF* **11**: 181–8.
Carden, R. (1974). *The Papyrus Fragments of Sophocles*, Berlin and New York: de Gruyter.
Carpenter, T. H. (1993). On the beardless Dionysus. In Carpenter and Faraone 1993: 185–206.
Carpenter, T. H. & Faraone, C. A. (1993). *Masks of Dionysus*, Ithaca: Cornell University Press.
Carson, A. (1982). Wedding at noon in Pindar's *Ninth Pythian*. *GRBS* **23**: 121–8.
Casel, O. (1919). *De philosophorum Graecorum silentio mystico*, Giessen: Töpelmann.
Ceccarelli, P. (1998). *La pirrica nell'antichità greco-romana*, Pisa and Rome: Istituti Editoriali e Poligrafici Internazionali.
Cerri, G. (1982). Antigone, Creonte, e l'idea della tirannide nell'Atene del V secolo (alcuni tesi di V. di Benedetto). *QUCC* **39**: 137–55.
Chakravarti, U. (1987). *The Social Dimensions of Early Buddhism*, New Delhi: Oxford University Press.
Chantraine, P. (1968–80). *Dictionnaire étymologique de la langue grecque*, Paris: Klincksieck.
Cohen, J. A. (1969). Ends and means in political control: state organization and the punishment of adultery, incest, and violation of celibacy. *American Anthropologist* **71**: 658–87.
Cohen, S. (2008). *Text and Authority in the Older Upaniṣads*, Leiden and Boston: Brill.
Cole, S. G. (1984). *Theoi Megaloi: The Cult of the Great Gods of Samothrace*, Leiden: Brill.
Collard, C. (1975). *Euripides: Supplices*, 2 vols., Groningen: Bouma's Boekhuis.
Collins, S. (1982). *Selfless Persons: Imagery and Thought in Theravāda Buddhism*, Cambridge: Cambridge University Press.
Connor, W. R. (1985). The razing of the house in Greek society. *TAPA* **115**: 79–102.
(1987). Tribes, festivals and processions: civic ceremonial and political manipulation in archaic Greece. *JHS* **107**: 40–50.
(1989). City Dionysia and Athenian democracy. *C&M* **40**: 7–32.
Conzelmann, H. (1975). *1 Corinthians: A Commentary on the First Epistle to the Corinthians*, trans. J. W. Leitch, Philadelphia: Fortress Press.
Cooke, D. (1979). *I Saw the World End: A Study of Wagner's Ring*, Oxford: Oxford University Press.
Cornford, F. M. (1952). *Principium Sapientiae*, Cambridge: Cambridge University Press.
(1968). *The Origin of Attic Comedy*, 3rd edn, Gloucester, MA: Smith.

Cox, C. A. (1998). *Household Interests: Property, Marriage Strategies, and Family Dynamics in Ancient Athens*, Princeton: Princeton University Press.

Cramer, J. (1839). *Anecdota Graeca e codd. manuscriptis bibliothecae regiae parisiensis*, vol. 1, Oxford: Clarendon Press.

Crane, G. (1990). Ajax, the unexpected, and the deception speech. *CP* **85**: 89–101.

Cribb, J. (2005). *The Indian Coinage Tradition: Origins, Continuity and Change*, Nashik: IIRNS Publications.

Cropp, M. (1988). *Euripides: Electra*, Warminster: Aris & Phillips.

Csapo, E. (2008). Star choruses: Eleusis, Orphism and New Musical imagery and dance. In Revermann and Wilson 2008: 262–90.

Csapo, E. & Miller, M., eds. (2007). *The Origins of Theater in Ancient Greece and Beyond*, Cambridge: Cambridge University Press

Cunningham, M. L. (1984). Aeschylus, *Agamemnon* 231–247. *BICS* **31**: 9–12.

D'Alessio, G. B. (2004). Past future and present past: temporal deixis in Greek archaic lyric. *Arethusa* **37**: 267–94.

D'Angour, A. (1997). How the dithyramb got its shape. *CQ* **47**: 331–51.

Dale, A. M. (1950). Stasimon and Hyporcheme. *Eranos* **48**: 14–20 (= *Collected Papers* (Cambridge: Cambridge University Press, 1969), pp. 34–40).

(1968). *The Lyrics Metres of Greek Drama*, 2nd edn, Cambridge: Cambridge University Press.

Danforth, L. M. (1982). *The Death Rituals of Rural Greece*, Princeton: Princeton University Press.

Daraki, M. (1985). *Dionysus*, Paris: Arthaud.

Daremberg, C. & Saglio, E. (1877–1919). *Dictionnaire des Antiquités grecques et romaines d'après les textes et les monuments*, Paris: Hachette.

Davies, M. (2004). Aristotle, fr. 44 Rose: Midas and Silenus. *Mnemosyne* **57**: 682–97.

Davison, J. A. (1955). Peisistratus and Homer. *TAPA* **86**: 1–21.

Dawe, R. D. (1982). *Sophocles: Oedipus Rex*, Cambridge: Cambridge University Press.

(2006). *Sophocles: Oedipus Rex*, revised edn, Cambridge: Cambridge University Press.

de Coulanges, F. (1874). *The Ancient City*, trans. W. Small, Boston: Lee & Shepard.

de Heer, D. (1969). *Makar – Eudaimōn – Olbios – Eutukhes*, Amsterdam: Hakkert.

de Martino E. (1958). *Morte e pianto rituale nel mondo antico*, Turin: Einaudi.

de Polignac, F. (1995). *Cults, Territory, and the Origins of the City-State*, trans. J. Lloyd, Chicago: University of Chicago Press.

de Romilly, J. (1969). Il pensiero di Euripide sulla tirannia. *Dioniso* **43**: 175–87.

de Ste Croix, G. E. M. (1981). *The Class Struggle in the Ancient Greek World*, London: Duckworth.

Denniston J. D. (1954). *The Greek Particles*, 2nd edn, Oxford: Clarendon Press.

Denniston, J. D. & Page, D. L. (1957). *Aeschylus: Agamemnon*, Oxford: Clarendon Press.

Detienne, M. (1977). *The Gardens of Adonis: Spices in Greek Mythology*, trans. J. Lloyd, London: Harvester Press.

(1979). *Dionysos Slain*, trans. M. and L. Muellner, Baltimore: Johns Hopkins University Press.

Deussen, P. (1906). *The Philosophy of the Upaniṣads*, trans. A. S. Geden, Edindurgh: T & T Clark.

(1915). *Allgemeine Geschichte der Philosophie. Mit besonderer Berücksichtigung der Religionen*, vol. I.I: *Allgemeine Einleitung und Philosophie des Veda bis auf die Upanishads*, Leipzig: Brockhaus.

Devereux, G. (1973). The self-blinding of Oidipous in Sophokles: *Oidipous Tyrannos*. *JHS* **93**: 36–49.

(1976). *Dreams in Greek Tragedy: An Ethno-Psycho-Analytical Study*, Berkeley: University of California Press.

Dewald, C. (2003). Form and content: the question of tyranny in Herodotus. In Morgan 2003: 25–58.

Dill, U. & Walde, C., eds. (2009). *Antike Mythen. Medien, Transformationen und Konstruktionen*, Berlin and New York: de Gruyter.

Dodds, E. R. (1960). *Euripides: Bacchae*, 2nd edn, Oxford: Clarendon Press.

Doniger, W. & Smith, K. (1991). *The Laws of Manu*, Harmondsworth: Penguin.

Donlan, W. (1998). Political reciprocity in dark age Greece: Odysseus and his *hetairoi*. In Gill, Postlethwaite and Seaford 1998: 51–71.

Douglas, M. (1966). *Purity and Danger*, London: Routledge.

Dover, K. J. (1968). *Aristophanes: Clouds*, Oxford: Clarendon Press.

(1973). Some neglected aspects of Agamemnon's dilemma. *JHS* **93**: 58–69.

(1974). *Greek Popular Morality in the Time of Plato and Aristotle*, Oxford: Blackwell.

Droysen, J. G. (1832). *Des Aischylos Werke. Uebersetzt von J.G. Droysen*, 2 vols., Berlin: Finke.

du Boulay, J. (1982). The Greek vampire: a study of cyclic symbolism in marriage and death. *Man* **17**: 219–38.

Duke, T. (1954). Murder in the bath: reflections on the death of Agamemnon. *CJ* **49**: 325–30.

Dunbar, N. (1995). *Aristophanes: Birds*, Oxford: Clarendon Press.

Easterling, P. E. (1982). *Sophocles: Trachiniae*, Cambridge: Cambridge University Press.

(1984). The tragic Homer. *BICS* **31**: 1–8.

(1985). Anachronism in Greek tragedy. *JHS* **105**: 1–10.

(2013). Sophocles and the wisdom of Silenos: a reading of *Oedipus at Colonus* 1211–48. In Cairns 2013: 193–204.

Edmonds, R. G. III (2013). *Redefining Ancient Orphism: A Study in Greek Religion*, Cambridge: Cambridge University Press.

Edmunds, L. (2009). A hermeneutic commentary on the eschatological passage in Pindar, *Olympian* 2. In Dill and Walde 2009: 662–77.

Einarson, B. & de Lacy, P. H. (1967). *Plutarch: Moralia*, vol. XIV, Cambridge MA: Harvard University Press.

Eisler, R. (1910). *Weltenmantel und Himmelszelt*, Munich: Beck.

(1925) *Orphisch–Dionysische Mysteriengedanken in der christlichen Antike*, Leipzig: Teubner.

Eitrem, S. (1926). Die vier Elemente in der Mysterienweihe I. *SO* **4**: 39–59.

(1927). Die vier Elemente in der Mysterienweihe II. *SO* **5**: 39–59.

Emura, H. (2011). *Shunjū Sengoku jidai seidō kahei no seisei to tenkai*. Kyūko sōsho 96. Tokyo: Kyūko Shoin.

Erdmann, W. (1934). *Die Ehe im Alten Griechenland*, Munich: Beck.

Erdosy, G. (1988). *Urbanisation in Early Historic India*, Oxford: BAR International.

(1995). City states of north India and Pakistan at the time of the Buddha. In R. Allchin, ed., *The Archaeology of Early Historic South Asia*, Cambridge: Cambridge University Press, pp. 99–122.

Ewans, M. (1982). *Wagner and Aeschylus: The Ring and the Oresteia*, London: Faber and Faber.

Falk, H. (1991). Silver, lead and zinc in early Indian literature. *South Asian Studies* **7**: 111–17.

Farnell, L. R. (1909). *The Cults of the Greek States*, vol. v, Oxford: Clarendon Press.

Fauth, W. (1959). *Hippolytus und Phaidra. Bemerkungen zum religiösen Hintergrund eines tragischen Konflikts*, Wiesbaden: Verlag der Akademie der Wissenschaften und der Literatur in Mainz.

Fehling, D. (1969). *Die Wiederholungsfiguren und ihr Gebrauch bei den Griechen vor Gorgias*, Berlin: de Gruyter.

Ferguson, W. S. (1938). The Salaminian Heptaphylai and Sounion. *Hesperia* **7**: 1–76.

Ferrari, G. (2008). *Alcman and the Cosmos of Sparta*, Chicago: University of Chicago Press.

Festa, V. (1918). Sikinnis. *Memorie della Reale Accademia di Archeologia* **3**: 37–74.

Festugière, A. J. (1972). *Études de religion grecque et hellenistique*, Paris: Vrin.

Feyerabend, B. (1984). Zur Wegmetaphorik beim Goldblättchen aus Hipponion und dem Proömium des Parmenides. *RhM* **127**: 1–22.

Finley, M. I. (1952). *Studies in Land and Credit in Ancient Athens, 500–200 BC: The Horos-Inscriptions*, New Brunswick: Rutgers University Press.

Fischer, U. (1965). *Der Telosgedanke in den Dramen des Aischylos*, Hildesheim: Olms.

Foley, H. P. (1982). Marriage and sacrifice in Euripides' *Iphigeneia in Aulis*. *Arethusa* **15**: 159–80.

(1985). *Ritual Irony: Poetry and Sacrifice in Euripides*, Ithaca: Cornell University Press.

Foster, D. H. (2010). *Wagner's Ring Cycle and the Greeks*, Cambridge: Cambridge University Press.

Fraenkel, E. (1950). *Aeschylus: Agamemnon*, 3 vols., Oxford: Clarendon Press.

Frazer, J. (1907–13). *The Golden Bough*, 8 vols., 3rd edn, London: Macmillan.

Freud, S. (1935). *The Interpretation of Dreams*, London: Allen & Unwin.

Fridh-Haneson, B. (1987). Votive terracottas from Italy. In T. Linders and G. Nordquist, eds., *Gifts to the Gods*. Uppsala: Academiae Upsaliensis, pp. 67–75.

Friedrich, R. (1996). Everything to do with Dionysus? Ritualism, the Dionysiac, and the tragic. In Silk 1996: 257–83.
Friis Johansen, H. & Whittle, E. W. (1980). *Aeschylus: The Suppliants*, 3 vols., Copenhagen: Gyldendal.
Friis Johansen, K. (1967). *The Iliad in Early Greek Art*, Copenhagen: Munksgaard.
Fritz, K. von (1934). Haimons Liebe zu Antigone. *Philologus* **89**: 19–33 (repr. in *Antike und moderne Tragödie* (Berlin: de Gruyter, 1962), pp. 227–40).
Funke, H. (1966). ΚΡΕΩΝ ΑΠΟΛΙΣ. *Antike und Abendland* **12**: 29–50.
Furley, W. D. (1986). Motivation in the parodos of Aeschylus' *Agamemnon*. *CP* **81**: 109–21.
Gagarin, M. (1976). *Aeschylean Drama*, Berkeley: University of California Press.
Galavotti, C. (1935). Novi Laurentiani Codicis Analecta. *Studi Bizantini e Neoellenici* **4**: 205–36.
Gallistl, B. (1979). *Teiresias in den Bakchen des Euripides*. Thesis. University of Zürich.
Gantz, T. N. (1977). The fires of the *Oresteia*. *JHS* **97**: 28–38.
Garland, R. (1985). *The Greek Way of Death*, London: Duckworth.
Garner, R. (1992). Mules, mysteries, and song in Pindar's *Olympian* 6. *ClAnt* **11**: 45–67.
Garrod, H. W. (1920). The Hyporcheme of Pratinas. *CR* **34**: 129–36.
Garvie, A. F. (1969). *Aeschylus' Supplices: Play and Trilogy*, Cambridge: Cambridge University Press.
(1986). *Aeschylus: Choephori*, Oxford: Clarendon Press.
Geertz, C. (1984). 'From the native's point of view': on the nature of anthropological understanding. In *Local Knowledge: Further Essays in Interpretive Anthropology*. New York: Basic Books, pp. 55–70.
Gernet, L. (1981). *The Anthropology of Ancient Greece*, trans. J. Hamilton and B. Nagy, Baltimore: Johns Hopkins University Press.
Gernet, L. & Boulanger, A. (1970). *Le génie grec dans la religion*, 2nd edn, Paris: Albin Michel.
Ghosh, A (1973). *The City in Early Historical India*, Simla: Indian Institute of Advanced Study.
Gill, C., Postlethwaite, N. & Seaford, R., eds. (1998). *Reciprocity in Ancient Greece*, Oxford: Clarendon Press.
Ginouvès, R. (1962). *Balaneutike. Recherches sur le bain dans l'antiquité grecque*, Paris: de Boccard.
Giorgini, G. (1993). *La città e il tiranno*, Milan: Giuffrè.
Girard, R. (1977). *Violence and the Sacred*, trans. P. Gregory, Baltimore: Johns Hopkins University Press.
Gluckman, M. (1953). Bridewealth and the stability of marriage. *Man* **53**: 141–3.
Goldhill, S. (1984). *Language, Sexuality, Narrative: The Oresteia*, Cambridge: Cambridge University Press.
(1986). *Reading Greek Tragedy*, Cambridge: Cambridge University Press.
(2000). Civic ideology and the problem of difference: the politics of Athenian tragedy once again. *JHS* **120**: 34–56.

Gombrich, R. (1996). *How Buddhism Began*, London and Atlantic Highlands, NJ: Athlone.
(2006). *Theravada Buddhism*, 2nd edn, London and New York: Routledge.
(2009). *What the Buddha Thought,* Sheffield: Equinox (rev. edn 2013).
Gonda, J. (1950). *Notes on Brahman*, Utrecht: Beyers.
(1966). *Loka: World and Heaven in the Veda.* Verhandelingen der Koninklijke Nederlandse Akademie van Wetenschappen, Afd. Letterkunde, n.s. 73.1. Amsterdam: Uitgevers.
Goody, J. R. (1959). The mother's brother and the sister's son in West Africa. *Journal of the Royal Anthropological Institute of Great Britain and Ireland* **89**: 61–88.
Goody, J. R. & Tambiah, S. N. (1973). *Bridewealth and Dowry*, Cambridge: Cambridge University Press.
Gould, J. (1973). Hiketeia. *JHS* **93**: 74–103.
Goux, J.-J. (1993). *Oedipus Philosopher*. Stanford: Stanford University Press.
Gow, A. S. F. (1965). *Theocritus*, vol. II: *Commentary*. Cambridge: Cambridge University Press.
Graeber, D. (2011). *Debt: The First 5000 Years*, New York: Melville.
Graf, F. (1974). *Eleusis und die orphische Dichtung Athens in vorhellenistischer Zeit*, Berlin and New York: de Gruyter.
(1996). *Pompai* in Greece: some considerations about space and ritual in the Greek polis. In R. Hägg, ed., *The Role of Religion in the Early Greek Polis.* Stockholm: Swedish Institute at Athens, pp. 55–6.
Graf, F. & Johnston, S. I. (2013). *Ritual Texts for the Afterlife*, 2nd edn, London: Routledge.
Griffin, J. (1977). The epic cycle and the uniqueness of Homer. *JHS* **97**: 39–53.
Griffith, M. (1978). Aeschylus, Sicily, and Prometheus. In R. D. Dawe, J. Diggle and P. E. Easterling, eds., *Dionysiaca: Nine Studies in Greek Poetry by Former Pupils: Presented to Denys Page on His Seventieth Birthday*. Cambridge: The Editors, pp. 105–39.
(1983). *Aeschylus: Prometheus Bound*, Cambridge: Cambridge University Press.
Griffiths, J. G. (1975). *Apuleius of Madauros: The Isis-Book (Metamorphoses, Book XI)*, Leiden: Brill.
Guépin, J.-P. (1968). *The Tragic Paradox*, Amsterdam: Hakkert.
Guggisberg, P. (1947). *Das Satyrspiel.* Ph.D. thesis. University of Zurich.
Gupta, P. L. & Hardaker, T. (2014). *Punchmarked Coins of the Indian Subcontinent: Maghada-Mauryan Series*, Mumbai: IIRNS Publications.
Guthrie, W. K. C. (1935). *Orpheus and Greek Religion*, London: Methuen.
(1962). *A History of Greek Philosophy*, vol. I, Cambridge: Cambridge University Press.
(1965). *A History of Greek Philosophy*, vol. II, Cambridge: Cambridge University Press.
Hackett, J. (1956). Echoes of Euripides in the Acts of the Apostles? *Irish Theololgical Quarterly* **23**: 218–27, 350–66.

Haenchen, E. (1971). *The Acts of the Apostles: A Commentary*, trans. B. Noble and G. Shinn, Philadelphia: Westminster Press.
Halbfass, W. (1991). *Tradition and Reflection: Explorations in Indian Thought*, Albany: SUNY Press.
(2000). *Karma und Wiedergeburt im Indischen Denken*, Munich: Diederichs.
Hall, E. (1996). Is there a *polis* in Aristotle's *Poetics*? In Silk 1996: 295–309.
Hansen, M. H. (1986). *Demography and Democracy*, Herning: Systime.
Harder, A. (1985). *Euripides' Kresphontes and Archelaos*, Leiden: Brill.
(1991). Euripides' *Temenos* and *Temenidai*. In H. Hofmann and A. Harder, eds., *Fragmenta Dramatica. Beiträge zur Interpretation der greichischen Tragikerfragmente und ihrer Wirkungsgeschichte*. Göttingen: Vandenhoeck & Ruprecht, pp. 117–35.
Hardie, A. (2000). Pindar's 'Theban' cosmogony (the First Hymn). *BICS* **44**: 19–40.
(2004). Muses and mysteries. In Murray and Wilson 2004: 11–38.
Harrison, A. R. W. (1968). *The Law of Athens: The Family and Property*, Oxford: Clarendon Press.
(1971). *The Law of Athens: Procedure*, Oxford: Clarendon Press.
Harrison, J. (1927). *Themis*, 2nd edn, Cambridge: Cambridge University Press.
Harvey, A. E. (1955). The classification of Greek lyric poetry. *CQ* **5**: 157–75.
(1980). The use of mystery language in the Bible. *JTS* **31**: 320–36.
Heesterman, J. (1985). *The Inner Conflict of Tradition: Essays in Indian Ritual, Kinship, and Society*, Chicago: University of Chicago Press.
(1993). *The Broken World of Sacrifice. An Essay in Ancient Indian Ritual*, Chicago: University of Chicago Press.
Hegel, G. W. F. (1952). *Hegel's Philosophy of Right*, trans. T. M. Knox, Oxford: Clarendon Press.
Heinze, R. (1892). *Xenocrates*, Leipzig: Teubner.
Hemberg, B. (1950). *Die Kabiren*, Uppsala: Almqvist & Wiksell.
Henderson, J. (2003). Demos, demagogue, tyrant in Attic Old Comedy. In Morgan 2003: 155–79.
Henrichs, A. (1990). Between country and city: cultic dimensions of Dionysos in Athens and Attica. In M. Griffith and D. J. Mastronarde, eds., *Cabinet of the Muses: Essays on Classical and Comparative Literature in Honor of Thomas G. Rosenmeyer*. Atlanta: Scholars Press, pp. 257–77.
(2013). Dionysos: one or many? In A. Bernabé, M. Herrero de Jáuregui, A. I. Jiménez San Cristóbal and R. Martín Hernández, eds., *Redefining Dionysos*. Berlin and New York: de Gruyter, pp. 554–82.
Herbig, R. (1958). *Neue Beobachtungen am Fries der Mysterienvilla in Pompeii*, Baden-Baden: B. Grimm.
Herington, C. J. (1963). A study in the *Prometheia*: part I. The elements in the trilogy. *Phoenix* **17**: 180–97.
(1985). *Poetry into Drama: Early Tragedy and the Greek Poetic Tradition*, Berkeley: University of California Press.

Hertz, R. (1960). *Death and the Right Hand*, trans. R. and C. Needham, London: Routledge.
Howgego, C. (1995). *Ancient History from Coins*, London: Routledge.
Huffman, C. A. (1993). *Philolaos of Croton*, Cambridge: Cambridge University Press.
Hugedé, N. (1957). *La Métaphore du miroir dans les epîtres de saint Paul aux Corinthiens*, Neuchatel: Delachaux et Niestlé.
Humphreys, S. C. (1974). The *nothoi* of Kynosarges. *JHS* **94**: 88–95.
(1983). *The Family, Women and Death*, London: Routledge.
Huntingdon, R. & Metcalf, P. (1979). *Celebrations of Death*, Cambridge: Cambridge University Press.
Hutchinson, G. O. (1985). *Aeschylus: Seven Against Thebes*, Oxford: Clarendon Press.
Jaccottet, A. F. (2003). *Choisir Dionysos: Les Associations dionysiaques ou la face cachée du dionysisme*, vol. 1, Zurich: Akanthus.
Jäkel, S. (1979). The *Aiolos* of Euripides. *GB* **8**: 101–18.
James, W. (1902). *The Varieties of Religious Experience*, London: Longmans.
Jameson, M. (1993). The asexuality of Dionysus. In Carpenter and Faraone 1993: 44–64.
Jamison, S. & Brereton, J. (2014). *The Rigveda*, 3 vols., New York: Oxford University Press.
Jebb, R. C. (1891). *Sophocles: The Plays and Fragments. Part III: The Antigone*, 2nd edn, Cambridge: Cambridge University Press.
(1894). *Sophocles: The Plays and Fragments. Part VI: The Electra*, Cambridge: Cambridge University Press.
Jenkins, I. (1983). Is there a life after marriage? A study of the abduction motif in vase paintings of the Athenian wedding ceremony. *BICS* **30**: 137–45.
Jocelyn, H. D. (1967). *The Tragedies of Ennius*, Cambridge: Cambridge University Press.
Johnston, S. I. (1999). *Restless Dead*, Berkeley: University of California Press.
Jones, J. (1962). *On Aristotle and Greek Tragedy*, New York: Oxford University Press.
Jones, J. R. M. (1993). *Testimonia Numaria: Greek and Latin Texts Concerning Ancient Greek Coinage*, vol. 1: *Texts and Translations*, London: Spink.
Jurewicz, J. (2010). *Fire and Cognition in the Ṛgveda*, Warsaw: Dom Wydawniczy Elipsa.
(2016). *Fire, Death and Philosophy: A History of Ancient Indian Thinking*, Warsaw: Dom Wydawniczy Elipsa.
Kakinuma, Y. (2011). *Chūgoku kodai kahei keizaishi kenkyū*. Kyūko sōsho 92. Tokyo: Kyūko Shoin.
Kallet, L. (2003). *Dēmos tyrannos*: wealth, power, and economic patronage. In Morgan 2003: 117–53.
Kambitsis, J. (1972). *L'Antiope d'Euripide*, Athens: Hourzamanis.
Kannicht, R. (1969). *Euripides, Helena*, vol. 11, Heidelberg: Winter.
Kavoulaki, A. (1999). Processional performance and the democratic polis. In S. Goldhill and R. Osborne, eds., *Performance Culture and Athenian Democracy*. Cambridge: Cambridge University Press, pp. 293–320.

Keesing, R. M. (1975). *Kin Groups and Social Structure*, New York: Holt, Rinehart and Winston.

Keil, H. (1857). *Grammatici Latini*, vol. VI.I, Leipzig: Teubner.

Keith, A. B. (1925). *The Religion and Philosophy of the Veda and the Upaniṣads*, 2 vols., Cambridge, MA: Harvard University Press.

Kells, J. H. (1973). *Sophocles: Electra*, Cambridge: Cambridge University Press.

Killingley, D. (1997). The paths of the dead and the five fires. In P. Connolly and S. Hamilton, eds., *Indian Insights: Buddhism, Brahmanism and Bhakti: Papers from the Annual Spalding Symposium on Indian Religions*. London: Luzac Oriental, pp. 1–20.

King, H. (1983). Bound to bleed: Artemis and Greek women. In A. Cameron and A. Kuhrt, eds., *Images of Women in Antiquity*. London and Canberra: Croom Helm, pp. 109–27.

Kingsley, P. (1995). *Ancient Philosophy, Mystery, and Magic: Empedocles and the Pythagorean Tradition*, Oxford: Clarendon Press.

Kirk, G. S. (1981). Some methodological pitfalls in the study of Ancient Greek sacrifice (in particular). In J. Rudhardt and O. Reverdin, eds., *Le Sacrifice dans l'Antiquité*. Entretiens de la Fondation Hardt 27. Geneva: Fondation Hardt, pp. 41–90.

Kirk, G. S., Raven, J. E. & Schofield, M. (1983). *The Presocratic Philosophers*, Cambridge: Cambridge University Press.

Kiso, A. (1984). *The Lost Sophocles*, New York: Vantage Press.

Knox, B. (1957). *Oedipus at Thebes*, New Haven: Yale University Press.

(1961). The *Ajax* of Sophocles. *HSCP* **65**: 1–37.

(1964). *The Heroic Temper: Studies in Sophoclean Tragedy*, Berkeley: University of California Press.

Koerte, A. (1915). Zu den eleusinischen Mysterien. *ARW* **18**: 116–26.

Kolb, F. (1981). *Agora und Theater: Volks- und Festversammlung*, Berlin: Mann.

Koller, V. H. (1954). *Die Mimesis in der Antike*, Bern: Francke.

Kosambi, D. (1951). Ancient Kosala and Maghada. *Journal of the Bombay Branch of the Royal Asiatic Society* **27**: 180–213.

(1965). *The Culture and Civilisation of Ancient India in Historical Outline*, London: Routledge.

Kossatz-Deissmann, A. (1978). *Dramen des Aischylos auf Westgriechischen Vasen*, Mainz am Rhein: von Zabern.

Kotwick, M. E. (2017). *Der Papyrus von Derveni*. Sammlung Tusculum. Berlin and New York: de Gruyter.

Koukoules, P. (1951). *Βυζαντινῶν Βίος καὶ Πολιτισμός*, vol. IV, Athens: Ekdoseis Papazese.

Kouremenos, T., Parassoglou, G. & Tsantsanoglou, K. (2006). *The Derveni Papyrus*, Florence: Olschki.

Kovacs, D. (1985). Castor in Euripides' *Electra* (*El.* 307–13 and 1292–1307). *CQ* **35**: 306–14.

Kowalzig, B. (2004). Changing choral worlds: song-dance and society in Athens and beyond. In Murray and Wilson 2004: 39–65.

(2007a). 'And now all the world shall dance' (Eur. *Bacch.* 114): Dionysus' *choroi* between drama and ritual. In Csapo and Miller 2007: 221–51.

(2007b). *Singing for the Gods: Performances of Myth and Ritual in Archaic and Classical Greece*, Oxford: Oxford University Press.

Kowalzig, B. & Wilson, P., eds. (2013). *Dithyramb in Context*, Oxford: Oxford University Press.

Kraay, C. (1976). *Archaic and Classical Greek Coins*, London: Methuen.

Kranz, W. (1919). Die Urform der attischen Tragödie und Komödie. *Neue Jahrbücher* **43**: 145–68.

Kraus, C., Goldhill, S., Foley, H. P. & Elsner, J., eds. (2007). *Visualizing the Tragic: Drama, Myth, and Ritual in Greek Art and Literature*, Oxford: Oxford University Press.

Krishan, Y. (1997). *The Doctrine of Karma*, New Delhi: Motilal Banarsidass.

Kurke, L. (1991). *The Traffic in Praise: Pindar and the Poetics of Social Economy*, Ithaca: Cornell University Press.

(1999). *Coins, Bodies, Games, and Gold: The Politics of Meaning in Archaic Greece*, Princeton: Princeton University Press.

(2007). Visualizing the choral: epichoric poetry, ritual, and elite negotiation in fifth-century Thebes. In Kraus, Goldhill, Foley and Elsner 2007: 63–101.

Kurtz, D. & Boardman, J. (1971). *Greek Burial Customs*, London: Thames and Hudson.

Lacey, W. K. (1968). *The Family in Classical Greece*, London: Thames & Hudson.

Lada-Richards, I. (1999). *Initiating Dionysos: Ritual and Theatre in Aristophanes' Frogs*, Oxford: Clarendon Press.

Laks, A. & Most, G. W., eds. (1997). *Studies in the Derveni Papyrus*, Oxford: Clarendon Press.

Lambin, G. (1986). Trois refrains nuptiaux et le fragment 124 Mette d'Eschyle. *AC* **55**: 66–85.

Lammers, J. (1931). *Die Doppel- und Halbchöre in der antiken Tragodie*, Paderborn: Schöningh.

Lang, A. (1884). *Custom and Myth*, London: Longmans.

Lanza, D. (1977). *Il tiranno e il suo pubblico*, Turin: Einaudi.

Laplanche, J. & Portalis, J. B. (1988). *The Language of Psychoanalysis*, trans. D. Nicholson-Smith, London: Karnac (orig. publ. Hogarth Press, 1973).

Lavecchia, S. (2000). *Pindari Dithyramborum Fragmenta*, Rome and Pisa: Ateneo.

Lawrence, S. E. (1976). Artemis in the *Agamemnon*. *AJP* **97**: 97–110.

Leach, E. R. (1953). Bridewealth and the stability of marriage. *Man* **53**: 179–80.

Lebeck, A. (1971). *The Oresteia: A Study in Language and Structure*, Washington, DC: Centre for Hellenic Studies.

Lee, K. H. (1973). Observations on ΕΡΕΣΣΕΙΝ, ΜΑΣΤΟΣ and Eur. *Tro.* 570–571. *Philologus* **117**: 264–6.

Lehmann, K. (1962). Ignorance and search in the Villa of the Mysteries. *JRS* **52**: 62–8.

Lesky, A. (1966). Decision and responsibility in the tragedy of Aeschylus. *JHS* **86**: 78–85.

Lévi, S. (1898). *La Doctrine du sacrifice dans les Brahmaṇas*, Paris: Leroux.
Lévi-Strauss, C. (1972). *The Savage Mind*, London: Weidenfeld and Nicolson.
Linforth, I. M. (1941). *The Arts of Orpheus*, Berkeley: University of California Press.
Lloyd-Jones, H. (1952). The robes of Iphigeneia. *CR* **2**: 135–8.
(1953). Aeschylus, *Agamemnon* 146f. *CQ* **3**: 96.
(1966). Problems in early Greek tragedy: Pratinas and Phrynichus. In H. Lloyd-Jones et al., eds., *Estudios sobre la tragedia griega*. Madrid: Consejo Superior de Investigaciones Cientificas, pp. 11–33.
(1971). *The Justice of Zeus*, Berkeley: University of California Press (rev. edn 1983).
(1982). *Blood for the Ghosts*, London: Duckworth.
(1983). Artemis and Iphigeneia. *JHS* **103**: 87–102.
Long, H. S. (1948). *A study of the doctrine of metempsychosis in Greece from Pythagoras to Plato*. Ph.D. thesis. Princeton University.
Lonis, R. (1979). *Guerre et religion en Grèce à l'époque classique*, Paris: Les Belles Lettres.
Lonnoy, M.-G. (1985). Arès et Dionysos dans la tragédie grecque: le rapprochement des contraires. *REG* **98**: 65–71.
Loraux, N. (1985). *Façons tragiques de tuer une femme*, Paris: Hachette.
Lorimer, H. L. (1950). *Homer and the Monuments*, London: Macmillan.
Lucas, D. W. (1969). Ἐπισπένδειν νεκρῶι, *Agamemnon* 1393–98. *PCPS* **15**: 60–8.
Luck, G. (1969). König Midas und die orphischen Mysterien. In J. Bibauw, ed., *Hommages à Marcel Renard*, vol. II: *Histoire, histoire des religions, épigraphie*. Coll. Latomus 102. Brussels: Latomus, pp. 470–7.
Luppe, W. (1984). Die Hypothesis zum 'Phrixos Deuteros' des Euripides. *APF* **30**: 31–7.
Maas, P. (1951). Aeschylus, *Agam*. 231ff., illustrated. *CQ* **1**: 94.
Macchioro, V. (1922). *Eraclito. Nuovi studi sull' Orfismo*, Bari: Laterza.
Macdonald, G. (1905). *Coin Types: Their Origin and Development*, Glasgow: Maclehose.
MacDowell, D. M. (1976). Bastards as Athenian citizens. *CQ* **26**: 88–91.
MacKinnon, J. K. (1978). The reason for the Danaids' flight. *CQ* **28**: 74–82.
Macleod, C. W. (1975). Clothing in the *Oresteia*. *Maia* **27**: 201–3.
(1982). *Homer: Iliad XXIV*, Cambridge: Cambridge University Press.
Magnien, V. (1936). Le mariage chez les grecs anciens: l'initiation nuptiale. *AC* **5**: 115–38.
Malamoud, C. (1983). The theology of debt in Brahmanism. In C. Malamoud, ed., *Debts and Debtors*. New Delhi: Vikas, pp. 21–40.
(1996). *Cooking the World: Ritual and Thought in Ancient India*, Oxford: Oxford University Press.
Mannhardt, W. (1905). *Wald- und Feldkulte*, vol. II: *Antike Wald- und Feldkulte*, Berlin: Gebr. Borntrager.
March, J. R. (1989). Euripides' *Bakchai*: a reconsideration in light of vase paintings. *BICS* **36**: 33–66.
Marcovich, M. (1967). *Heraclitus*, Merida, Venezuela: Los Andes University Press.

Martin, R. (2007). Outer limits, choral space. In Kraus, Goldhill, Foley and Elsner 2007: 35–62.

Marx, K. (1973). *Grundrisse: Foundations of the Critique of Political Economy (Rough Draft)*, trans. M. Nicolaus, Harmondsworth: Penguin.

(1976). *Capital.* vol. I, trans. B. Fowkes, Harmondsworth: Penguin.

(1978). *Capital.* vol. II, trans. D. Fernbach, Harmondsworth: Penguin.

(1981). *Capital.* vol. III, trans. D. Fernbach, Harmondsworth: Penguin.

McDermott, J. P. (1984). *Development in the Early Buddhist Concept of kamma/karma*, New Delhi: Munshiram Manoharlal.

McGlew, J. (1993). *Tyranny and Political Culture in Ancient Greece*, Ithaca: Cornell University Press.

Mendelsohn, D. (1992). Συγκεραυνόω: dithyrambic language and Dionysiac cult. *CJ* **87**: 105–24.

Merkelbach, R. (1962). *Roman und Mysterium in der Antike*, Munich: Beck.

Miles, L. K., Nind, L. K. & Macrae, C. N. (2009). The rhythm of rapport: interpersonal synchrony and social perception. *Cognition* **190**: 585–9.

Millett, P. (1991). *Lending and Borrowing in Ancient Athens*, Cambridge: Cambridge University Press.

Moles, J. M. (1979). A neglected aspect of *Agamemnon* 1389–92. *LCM* **4**(9): 179–89.

Moreau, A. (1985). *Eschyle. La violence et le chaos*, Paris: Les Belles Lettres.

Morgan, K., ed. (2003). *Popular Tyranny: Sovereignty and its Discontents in Ancient Greece*, Austin: University of Texas Press.

Most, G. (1997). The fire next time: cosmology, allegoresis, and salvation in the Derveni Papyrus. *JHS* **107**: 117–35.

Murnaghan, S. (1986). *Antigone* 904–920 and the institution of marriage. *AJP* **107**: 192–207.

Murray, G. (1933). *Aristophanes: A Study*, Oxford: Clarendon Press.

(1934). *The Rise of the Greek Epic*, 4th edn, Oxford: Clarendon Press.

Murray, P. & Wilson, P., eds. (2004). *Music and the Muses: The Culture of Mousike in the Classical Athenian City*, Oxford: Oxford University Press.

Murray, R. D. (1958). *The Motif of Io in Aeschylus' Suppliants*. Princeton: Princeton University Press.

Mylonas, G. E. (1961). *Eleusis and the Eleusinian Mysteries*. Princeton: Princeton University Press.

Nagler, M. (1974) *Spontaneity and Tradition: A Study in the Oral Art of Homer*. Berkeley: University of California Press.

Nagy, G. (1990). *Pindar's Homer: The Lyric Possession of an Epic Past*, Baltimore: Johns Hopkins University Press.

Naiden, F. S. (2007). The fallacy of the willing victim. *JHS* **127**: 61–73.

Neitzel, H. (1979). Artemis und Agamemnon in der Parodos des aischyleischen *Agamemnon*. *Hermes* **107**: 10–32.

Nestle, W. (1900). Anklänge an Euripides in der Apostelgeschichte. *Philologus* **59**: 46–57.

(1905). Heraklit und die Orphiker. *Philologus* **64**: 367–84 (repr. in *Griechische Studien* (Stuttgart: H.F.C. Hannsmann, 1948), pp. 133–50).
Nietzsche, F. (1983). *Untimely Meditations*, trans. R. Hollingdale, Cambridge: Cambridge University Press.
Nilsson, M. P. (1967). *Geschichte der griechischen Religion*, vol. 1, 3rd edn, Munich: Beck.
Nisbet, R. G. M. & Hubbard, M. (1970). *A Commentary on Horace: Odes, Book 1*, Oxford: Clarendon Press.
Nock, A. D. (1933). *Conversion*, Oxford: Clarendon Press.
(1972). *Essays on Religion and the Ancient World*, ed. Z. Stewart, Cambridge, MA: Harvard University Press.
Norden, E. (1913). *Agnostos Theos. Untersuchungen zur Formengeschichte Religiöser Rede*, Leipzig and Berlin: Teubner (repr. 1923).
(1915). *Die Antike Kunstprosa*, 3rd edn, Leipzig and Berlin: Teubner.
Nussbaum, M. (1986). *The Fragility of Goodness*, Cambridge: Cambridge University Press.
O'Brien, D. (1959). *Empedocles' Cosmic Cycle*, Cambridge: Cambridge University Press.
O'Daly, G. J. P. (1985). Clytemnestra and the elders: dramatic technique in Aeschylus, *Agamemnon* 1372–1576. *MH* **42**: 1–19.
Oakley, J. H. (1982). The anakalypteria. *AA* **97**: 113–18.
Obbink, D. (1997). Cosmology as initiation vs. the critique of Orphic mysteries. In Laks and Most 1997: 39–54.
Obeyesekere, G. (2002). *Imagining Karma*, Berkeley: University of California Press.
Ogden, D. (1997). *The Crooked Kings of Ancient Greece*, London: Routledge.
Olivelle, P. (1996). *Upaniṣads*. Oxford World Classics. Oxford: Oxford University Press.
Olson, S. D. (2011). *Athenaeus: The Learned Banqueters*, vol. VII, Cambridge, MA: Harvard University Press.
Oranje, H. (1980). Euripides' *Protesilaus*: *P. Oxy.* 3214, 10–14. *ZPE* **37**: 169–72.
Oudemans, T. & Lardinois, A. (1987). *Tragic Ambiguity: Anthropology, Philosophy and Sophocles' Antigone*. Leiden: Brill.
Page, D. L. (1934). *Actors' Interpolations in Greek Tragedy*, Oxford: Clarendon Press.
(1938). *Euripides: Medea*, Oxford: Clarendon Press.
Parker, R. (1983). *Miasma: Pollution and Purification in Early Greek Religion*, Oxford: Clarendon Press.
(1987). Myths of Early Athens. In J. Bremmer, ed., *Interpretations of Greek Mythology*. London: Routledge, pp. 187–214.
(1996). *Athenian Religion: A History*, Oxford: Clarendon Press.
(1998). Pleasing thighs: reciprocity in Greek religion. In Gill, Postlethwaite and Seaford 1998: 105–25.
(2005). *Polytheism and Society in Athens*, Oxford: Oxford University Press.
Parker, V. (1998). Τύραννος: the semantics of a political concept from Archilochus to Aristotle. *Hermes* **126**: 145–72.

Parry, J. & Bloch, M. (1989). Introduction: money and the morality of exchange. In Parry and Bloch 1989: 1–32.
Parry, J. & Bloch, M., eds. (1989). *Money and the Morality of Exchange*, Cambridge: Cambridge University Press.
Parsons, E. C. (1916). Holding back in crisis ceremonialism. *American Anthropologist* **18**: 41–52.
Parsons, M. (1988). Self-knowledge refused and accepted: a psychoanalytic perspective on the *Bacchae* and the *Oedipus at Colonus*. *BICS* **35**: 1–14.
Pearson, A. C. (1917). *The Fragments of Sophocles*, 3 vols., Cambridge: Cambridge University Press.
Peek, W. (1955). *Griechische Vers-Inschriften*, vol. I: *Grab-Epigramme*, Berlin: Akademie-Verlag.
Peradotto, J. J. (1964). Some patterns of nature imagery. *AJP* **85**: 378–93.
(1969). The omen of the eagles and the ἦθος of Agamemnon. *Phoenix* **23**: 237–63.
Petropoulou, A. (1987). The sacrifice of Eumaeus reconsidered. *GRBS* **28**: 135–49.
Pfeiffer, R. (1968). *A History of Classical Scholarship from the Beginnings to the End of the Hellenistic Age*, Oxford: Clarendon Press.
Pfleiderer, E. (1886). *Die Philosophie des Heraklit von Ephesus im Lichte der Mysterienidee*, Berlin: Reimer.
Pickard-Cambridge, A. (1946). *The Theatre of Dionysus at Athens*, Oxford: Clarendon Press.
(1962). *Dithyramb, Tragedy and Comedy*, 2nd edn, Oxford: Clarendon Press.
(1968). *The Dramatic Festivals of Athens*, 2nd edn, rev. J. Gould and D. M. Lewis, Oxford: Clarendon Press.
Pinchard, A. (2009). *Les Langues de sagesse dans la Grèce et l'Inde anciennes*, Geneva: Droz.
Pohlenz, M. (1954). *Die griechische Tragödie*, vol. II: *Erläuterungen*, 2nd edn, Göttingen: Vandenhoeck & Ruprecht.
Polanyi, K. (1977). *The Livelihood of Man*, New York: Academic Press.
Politis, N. (1931). *Λαογραφικὰ Σύμμεικτα*, vol. III, Athens: Leone.
Pomeroy, S. B. (1975). *Goddesses, Whores, Wives, and Slaves*, New York: Schocken.
Porter, H. N. (1948). A Bacchic graffito from the Dolicheneum. *AJP* **69**: 27–41.
Prag, A. (1985). *The Oresteia: Iconographic and Narrative Tradition*, Warminster: Aris & Phillips.
Prasad, M. (1966). Literary evidence on the chronology of punch marked coins. In A. Narain and L. Gopal, eds., *Seminar Papers on the Chronology of Punch Marked Coins*. Varanasi: Banaras Hindu University, pp. 161–70.
Pritchett, W. K. (1974). *The Greek State at War*, vol. II, Berkeley: University of California Press.
Privitera, G. A. (1965). *Laso di Ermione*, Rome: Ateneo.
(1970). *Dioniso in Omero e nella poesia greca arcaica*, Rome: Ateneo.
Prott, J. von & Ziehen, L. (1906). *Leges Graecorum sacrae e titulis collectae*, vol. II.1, Leipzig: Teubner.
Raaflaub, K. A. (2003). Stick and glue: the function of tyranny in fifth-century Athenian democracy. In Morgan 2003: 59–93.

Radcliffe-Brown, A. R. (1922). *The Andaman Islanders: A Study in Social Anthropology*, Cambridge: Cambridge University Press.
Rappaport, R. (1999). *Ritual and Religion in the Making of Humanity*, Cambridge: Cambridge University Press.
Rash, J. N. (1981). *Meter and Language in the Lyrics of the Suppliants of Aeschylus*, New York: Arno Press.
Rau, W. (1957). *Staat und Gesellschaft im Alten Indien nach den Brāhmaṇen-Texten dargestellt*, Wiesbaden: Harrassowitz.
Redfield, J. M. (1975). *Nature and Culture in the Iliad*, Chicago: University of Chicago Press.
(1982). Notes on the Greek wedding. *Arethusa* **15**: 181–201.
Reitzenstein, R. (1900). Die Hochzeit des Peleus und der Thetis. *Hermes* **35**: 73–105.
(1927). *Die hellenistischen Mysterienreligionen. Ihre Grundgedanken und Wirkungen*, 3rd edn, Leipzig: Teubner.
Revermann, M. & Wilson, P., eds. (2008). *Performance, Iconography, Reception: Studies in Honour of Oliver Taplin*, Oxford: Oxford University Press.
Rhodes, P. J. (1978). Bastards as Athenian citizens. *CQ* **28**: 89–92.
(1981). *A Commentary on the Aristotelian Athenaion Politeia*, Oxford: Clarendon Press.
Rhys Davids, T. W. (1894). *The Questions of King Milinda*, vol. II, Oxford: Clarendon Press.
Richardson, N. J. (1974). *The Homeric Hymn to Demeter*, Oxford: Clarendon Press.
Riedweg, C. (1987). *Mysterienterminologie bei Platon, Philon und Klemens von Alexandrien*, Berlin and New York: de Gruyter.
Robertson, D. S. (1924). The end of the *Supplices* trilogy of Aeschylus. *CR* **38**: 51–3.
Rohde, E. (1925). *Psyche: The Cult of Souls and Belief in Immortality among the Greeks*, 8th edn, trans. W. B. Hillis, London: Kegan Paul.
Roller, L. (1984). The Greek view of Anatolia. In H. Brijder, ed., *Ancient Greek and Related Pottery: Proceedings of the International Vase Symposium in Amsterdam*. Amsterdam: Allard Pierson Museum, pp. 260–3.
Roos, E. (1951). *Die tragische Orchestik im Zerrbild der altattischen Komödie*, Lund: Gleerup.
Roscher, W. H. (1884–1937). *Ausführliches Lexikon der griechischen und römischen Mythologie*, 7 vols., Leipzig: Teubner.
Rose, H. J. (1947). The grief of Persephone. *HThR* **36**: 247–50.
(1963) *Hyginus: Fabulae*, 2nd edn, Leiden: Sijthoff.
Rosenfeld, H. (1957). An analysis of marriage and marriage statistics for a Muslim and Christian Arab village. *International Archives of Ethnography* **48**: 32–62.
Rösler, W. (1970). *Reflexe vorsokratischen Denkens bei Aischylos*, Meisenheim am Glan: Hain.
Russell, D. & Winterbottom, M. (1972). *Ancient Literary Criticism*, Oxford: Clarendon Press.
Rusten, J. S. (1985). Interim notes on the papyrus from Derveni. *HSCP* **89**: 121–40.
Rutherford, I. (1994–5). Apollo in ivy: the tragic paean. *Arion* **3**(1): 112–35.
(2001). *Pindar's Paeans*, Oxford: Oxford University Press.

(2003). The prosodion: approaches to a lyric genre. In F. Benedetti and S. Grandolini, eds., *Studi di filologia e tradizione greca in memoria di Aristide Colonna*. Naples and Perugia: Edizioni Scientifiche Italiane, pp. 713–26.

Rutherford, R. (1982). Tragic form and feeling in the *Iliad*. *JHS* **102**: 145–60.

Rycroft, C. (1968). *A Critical Dictionary of Psychoanalysis*, London: Nelson.

Saïd, S. (1985). *Sophiste et Tyran*, Paris: Klincksieck.

Sale, W. M. (1987). The formularity of the place-phrases in the *Iliad*. *TAPA* **117**: 21–50.

Salviat, F. (1964). Les théogamies attiques, Zeus Téleios et l'*Agamemnon* d'Eschyle. *BCH* **88**: 647–54.

Saxonhouse, A. (1986). Autochthony and the beginning of cities in Euripides' *Ion*. In J. P. Euben, ed., *Greek Tragedy and Political Theory*. Berkeley: University of California Press, pp. 253–73.

Schadewaldt, W. (1970). *Hellas und Hesperien*, vol. II, Zürich and Stuttgart: Artemis.

Schaps, D. M. (1979). *The Economic Rights of Women in Ancient Greece*, Edinburgh University Press.

Schefer, C. (2000). 'Nur für Eingeweihte!': Heraklit und die Mysterien. *AA* **46**: 46–75.

Schlesier, R. (1988). Die Bakchen des Hades: Dionysische Aspekte von Euripides' *Hekabe*. *Mètis* **3**: 111–35.

(1993). Mixtures of masks: Maenads as tragic models. In Carpenter and Faraone 1993: 89–114.

(1995). Lust durch Leid: Aristoteles' Tragödientheorie und die Mysterien. In W. Eder, ed., *Die Athenische Demokratie im 4. Jahrhundert v. Chr.* Stuttgart: Steiner, pp. 389–415.

Schönewolf, H. (1938). *Der jungattische Dithyrambos*. Thesis. University of Giessen.

Schultz, W. (1912). *Rätsel aus dem Hellenischen Kulturkreise*, vol. II, Leipzig: Hinrichs.

Scodel, R. (1982). *P. Oxy.* 3317: Euripides' *Antigone*. *ZPE* **46**: 37–42.

Scott, K. (1928). The deification of Demetrius Poliorketes part II. *AJP* **49**: 217–39.

Séchan, L. (1911). La légende d'Hippolyte dans l'antiquité. *REG* **24**: 105–51.

Segal, C. (1971). Andromache's *anagnorisis*: formulaic artistry in *Iliad* 22.437–76. *HSCP* **75**: 33–58.

(1997). *Dionysiac Poetics and Euripides' Bacchae*, Princeton: Princeton University Press.

Seidensticker, B. (1979). Sacrificial Ritual in the *Bacchae*. In Bowersock, Burkert and Putnam 1979: 181–90.

Shaw, B. (1923). *The Perfect Wagnerite: A Commentary on the Niblung's Ring*, 4th edn, London: Constable.

Shell, M. (1978). *The Economy of Literature*, Baltimore: Johns Hopkins University Press.

Shipp, G. P. (1972). *Studies in the Language of Homer*, 2nd edn, Cambridge: Cambridge University Press.

Sifakis, G. M. (1971). *Parabasis and Animal Choruses*, London: Athlone Press.

Silk, M. S. (1974). *Interaction in Poetic Imagery*, Cambridge: Cambridge University Press.

Silk, M. S., ed., (1996). *Tragedy and the Tragic*, Oxford: Clarendon Press.
Simmel, G. (1971). Prostitution. In D. Levine, ed., *Georg Simmel on Individuality and Social Forms*. Chicago: University of Chicago Press, pp. 121–6.
(1978). *The Philosophy of Money*, trans. T. Bottomore and D. Frisby, London: Routledge.
Smith, B. (1989). *Reflections on Resemblance, Ritual and Religion*, New York: Oxford University Press.
Snell, B. (1953). *The Discovery of the Mind*, trans. T. Rosenmeyer, Cambridge, MA: Harvard University Press.
Sohn-Rethel, A. (1978). *Intellectual and Manual Labour: A Critique of Epistemology*, London: Macmillan.
Sokolowski, F. (1955). *Lois sacrées de l'Asie Mineure*, Paris: de Boccard.
(1969). *Lois sacrées des cités grecques*, Paris: de Boccard.
Sommerstein, A. H. (1980). Artemis in the *Agamemnon*: a postscript. *AJP* **101**: 165–9.
(1989). *Aeschylus: Eumenides*, Cambridge: Cambridge University Press.
(2002). Comic elements in tragic language. In A. Willi, ed., *The Language of Greek Comedy*. Oxford: Oxford University Press, pp. 151–68.
Sourvinou-Inwood, C. (1971). Aristophanes, *Lysistrata*, 641–647. *CQ* **21**: 339–42.
(1987). A series of erotic pursuits: images and meanings. *JHS* **107**: 131–53.
(1997). Reconstructing change: ideology and the Eleusinian mysteries. In M. Golden and P. Toohey, eds., *Inventing Ancient Culture*. London: Routledge, pp. 132–64.
Stanford, W. B. (1939). *Ambiguity in Greek Literature*, Oxford: Blackwell.
Steiner, D. (1994). *The Tyrant's Writ: Myths and Images of Writing in Ancient Greece*, Princeton: Princeton University Press.
Steiner, G. (1961). *The Death of Tragedy*, London: Faber and Faber.
Stengel, P. (1920). *Die griechischen Kultusaltertümer*, 3rd edn, Munich: Beck.
Stevens, P. T. (1971). *Euripides: Andromache*, Oxford: Clarendon Press.
(1986). Ajax in the Trugrede. *CQ* **36**: 327–36.
Stinton, T. C. W. (1975). *Agamemnon* 1127 and the limits of hyperbaton. *PCPS* **21**: 82–93.
Stirrat, R. L. (1989). Money, men and women. In Parry and Bloch 1989: 94–116.
Stroud, R. S. (1974). An Athenian law on silver coinage. *Hesperia* **43**: 157–88.
Sutton, D. F. (1975a). A series of vases illustrating the madness of Lycurgus. *Rivista di Studi Classici* **23**: 356–64.
(1975b). The staging of *Anodos* scenes. *Rivista di Studi Classici* **23**: 347–55.
Sutton, R. F. (1981). *The interaction between men and women portrayed on Attic red-figure pottery*. Ph.D. thesis. University of North Carolina.
Szegedy-Maszak, A. (1981). *The Nomoi of Theophrastus*, New York: Arno Press.
Taplin, O. (1977). *The Stagecraft of Aeschylus*, Oxford: Clarendon Press.
(1978). *Greek Tragedy in Action*, London: Routledge.
(1979). Yielding to forethought: Sophocles' *Ajax*. In Bowersock, Burkert and Putnam 1979: 122–9.
Tarrant, R. J. (1976). *Seneca: Agamemnon*, Cambridge: Cambridge University Press.

Taylor, C. (1989). *Sources of the Self: The Making of the Modern Identity*, Cambridge: Cambridge University Press.

Thapar, R. (1984). *From Lineage to State*, Bombay: Oxford University Press.

Thompson, W. E. (1967). The marriage of first cousins in Athenian society. *Phoenix* **21**: 273–82.

(1972). Athenian marriage patterns: remarriage. *CSCA* **5**: 211–25.

Thomson, G. (1932). *Aeschylus: The Prometheus Bound*, Cambridge: Cambridge University Press.

(1935). Mystical allusions in the *Oresteia*. *JHS* **55**: 20–34.

(1946). *Aeschylus and Athens*, 2nd edn, London: Lawrence & Wishart.

(1949). *Studies in Ancient Greek Society*, vol. I: *The Prehistoric Aegean*, London: Lawrence & Wishart.

(1953). From religion to philosophy. *JHS* **73**: 77–83.

(1961). *Studies in Ancient Greek Society*, vol. II: *The First Philosophers*, 2nd edn, London: Lawrence & Wishart.

(1966). *The Oresteia of Aeschylus*, 2nd edn, Amsterdam: Hakkert.

(1971). The *Suppliants* of Aeschylus. *Eirene* **9**: 25–30.

Toutain, J. (1940). Le rite nuptial de l'*anakaluptērion*. *REA* **42**: 345–53.

Traglia, A. (1952). *Studi sulla lingua di Empedocle*. Bari: Adriatica.

Tsantsanoglou, K. (1997). The first columns of the Derveni Papyrus and their religious significance. In Laks and Most 1997: 93–128.

Tsantsanoglou, K. & Parássoglou, G. M. (1987). Two gold lamellae from Thessaly. *Hellenica* **38**: 3–16.

Tull, H. W. (1989). *The Vedic Origins of Karma*, Albany: SUNY Press.

Turner, V. (1967). *The Forest of Symbols*, Ithaca: Cornell University Press.

Usher, M. D., (2002). Satyr play in Plato's *Symposium*. *AJP* **123**: 205–28.

Valdesolo, P. & DeSteno, D. (2011). Synchrony and the social tuning of compassion. *Emotion* **11**: 262–6.

van Gennep, A. (1960). *The Rites of Passage*, trans. M. B. Vizedom and G. L. Caffee, London: Routledge.

van Looy, H. (1964). *Zes verloren Tragedies van Euripides*, Brussels: Paleis der Academiën.

(1970). L'*Erechthée* d'Euripide. In *Hommages à Marie Delcourt*. Coll. Latomus 114. Brussels: Latomus, pp. 115–22.

Vermeule, E. (1966). The Boston Oresteia krater. *AJA* **70**: 1–22.

(1979). *Aspects of Death in Early Greek Art and Poetry*, Berkeley: University of California Press.

Vernant, J.-P. (1982a). From Oedipus to Periander: lameness, tyranny, incest in legend and history. *Arethusa* **15**: 19–38.

(1982b). *Myth and Society in Ancient Greece*, trans. J. Lloyd, London: Routledge.

(1983). *Myth and Thought among the Greeks*, trans. J. Lloyd, London: Routledge.

Vernant, J.-P. & Vidal-Naquet, P. (1988). *Myth and Tragedy in Ancient Greece*, trans. J. Lloyd, 2nd edn, New York: Zone Books.

Vidal-Naquet, P. (1988). Hunting and sacrifice in Aeschylus' *Oresteia*. In Vernant and Vidal-Naquet 1988: 141–59.

Visser, M. (1986). Medea: daughter, sister, wife and mother – natal family *versus* conjugal family in Greek and Roman myths about women. In M. Cropp, E. Fantham and S. E. Scully, eds., *Greek Tragedy and Its Legacy: Essays Presented to D. J. Conacher*. Calgary: University of Calgary Press, p. 149–65.

Vlastos, G. (1970). Equality and justice in early Greek cosmologies. In D. J. Furley and R. E. Allen, eds., *Studies in Presocratic Philosophy*, vol. 1. London: Routledge, pp. 56–91.

Vögeli, A. (1953). Lukas und Euripides. *ThZ* **9**: 415–38.

Vollgraf, W. (1924). Le péan Delphique à Dionysos. *BCH* **48**: 97–208.

von Falkenhausen, L. (2013). Review of Emura 2011. *Tōyōshi kenkyū* **72**(2): 139–48 (English version posted on Academia.edu).

(2014). Review of Kakinuma 2011. *Zhejiang University Journal of Art and Archaeology* **1**: 278–92.

von Reden, S. (1995). *Exchange in Ancient Greece*, London: Duckworth.

von Westernhagen, C. (1966). *Richard Wagner's Dresdener Bibliothek 1842–1849*, Wiesbaden: Brockhaus.

Wagle, N. K. (1966). *Society at the Time of the Buddha*, Bombay: Popular Prakashan.

Wagner, R. (1897). *Richard Wagner's Prose Works*, vol. VI: *Religion and Art*, trans. W. A. Ellis, London: Kegan Paul.

(1900). *Richard Wagner's Prose Works*, vol. II: *Opera and Drama*, trans. W. A. Ellis, London: Kegan Paul.

(1907). *Richard Wagner's Prose Works*, vol. III: *The Theatre*, trans. W. A. Ellis, London: Kegan Paul.

Webster, T. B. L. (1967). *The Tragedies of Euripides*, London: Methuen.

Welcker, F. G. (1824). *Die Aeschylische Trilogie Prometheus*, Darmstadt: Leske.

Wellesz, E. (1957). *New Oxford History of Music*, vol. 1, London: Oxford University Press.

West, M. L. (1966). *Hesiod: Theogony*, Oxford: Clarendon Press.

(1971). *Early Greek Philosophy and the Orient*, Oxford: Clarendon Press.

(1978). *Hesiod: Works and Days*, Oxford: Clarendon Press.

(1979). The Prometheus trilogy. *JHS* **99**: 130–48.

(1981). Tragica V. *BICS* **28**: 61–78.

(1982). The Orphics of Olbia. *ZPE* **45**: 17–29.

(1983). *The Orphic Poems*, Oxford: Clarendon Press.

(1990). *Studies in Aeschylus*, Stuttgart: Teubner.

Whallon, W. (1961). Why is Artemis angry? *AJP* **82**: 78–88.

(1964). Maenadism in the *Oresteia*. *HSCP* **68**: 317–27.

Wilamowitz-Moellendorff, T. von (1917). *Die dramatische Technik des Sophokles*, Berlin: Weidmann.

Wilamowitz-Moellendorff, U. von (1883). Die beiden Elektren. *Hermes* **18**: 214–63.

(1891). *Euripides. Hippolytos. Griechisch und Deutsch*, Berlin: Weidmann.

(1913). *Sappho und Simonides*, Berlin: Weidmann.

Williams, D. J. R. (1984). Close shaves. In H. A. J. Brijder, ed., *Ancient Greek and Related Pottery*. Amsterdam: Allard Pierson Museum, pp. 275–81.

Willink, C. W. (1986). *Euripides: Orestes*, Oxford: Clarendon Press.

Wilson, P. (2000). *The Athenian Institution of the Khoregia*, Cambridge: Cambridge University Press.

(2003). The politics of dance: dithyrambic contest and social order in Ancient Greece. In D. J. Phillips and D. Pritchard, eds., *Sport and Festival in the Ancient Greek World*. Swansea: Classical Press of Wales, pp. 163–96.

Wiltermuth, S. S. & Heath, C. (2009). Synchrony and cooperation. *Psychological Science* **20**: 1–5.

Winnington-Ingram, R. P. (1980). *Sophocles: An Interpretation*, Cambridge: Cambridge University Press.

Wissowa, G. (1902). Monatliche Geburtstagsfeier. *Hermes* **37**: 157–9.

Wright, R. (2010). *The Ancient Indus*, Cambridge: Cambridge University Press.

Young, D. (1964). Gentler medicines in the *Agamemnon*. *CQ* **14**: 1–23.

Yü, Y.-S. (2003). Between the heavenly and the human. In W. Tu and M. E. Tucker, eds., *Confucian Spirituality*, vol. 1. New York: Crossroad, pp. 62–80.

Zakhos, E. (1966). *Poésie populaire des Grecs*, Paris: Maspéro.

Zeitlin, F. (1965). The motif of the corrupted sacrifice in Aeschylus' *Oresteia*. *TAPA* **96**: 463–508.

(1989). Mysteries of identity and designs of the self in Euripides' *Ion*. *PCPS* **35**: 144–97.

(1990). Thebes: theater of self and society in Athenian drama. In J. Winkler and F. Zeitlin, eds., *Nothing to Do with Dionysus*. Princeton: Princeton University Press, pp. 130–67.

Ziebarth, E. (1892). *De Iureiurando in Iure Graeco Quaestiones*, Göttingen: Kaestner.

Zielinski, T. (1885). *Gliederung der altattischen Komödie*, Leipzig: Teubner.

Zuntz, G. (1965). *An Inquiry into the Transmission of the Plays of Euripides*, Cambridge: Cambridge University Press.

(1971). *Persephone*, Oxford: Clarendon Press.

Index Locorum

Indian Texts

General Index